INTRODUCTION TO
OLD
TESTAMENT
THEOLOGY

A CANONICAL APPROACH

OTHER BOOKS BY JOHN H. SAILHAMER

The NIV Compact Bible Commentary

The Pentateuch as Narrative: A Biblical-Theological Commentary

INTRODUCTION TO
OLD TESTAMENT THEOLOGY

A CANONICAL APPROACH

John H. Sailhamer

ZondervanPublishingHouse
Grand Rapids, Michigan

A Division of HarperCollinsPublishers

Introduction to Old Testament Theology
Copyright © 1995 by John H. Sailhamer

Requests for information should be addressed to:
Zondervan Publishing House
Grand Rapids, Michigan 49530

Library of Congress Cataloging-in-Publication Data

Sailhamer, John.
    An introduction to Old Testament theology : a canonical approach / John H. Sailhamer
        p.   cm.
    Includes bibliographical references and index.
    ISBN 0-310-23202-3
    1. Bible. O.T.–Theology. I.Title.
BS1192.5.S23   1995
230'.04–dc20
                                        94-42823
                                          CIP

Interior design by Susan A. Koppenol
Edited by Elizabeth Yoder

Printed in the United States of America

95 96 97 98 99 00 /❖ DH/ 10 9 8 7 6 5 4 3 2 1

This edition is printed on acid-free paper and meets the American National Standards Institute Z39.48 standard.

CONTENTS

Preface 5

Abbreviations 7

PART 1
INTRODUCTION

ONE: Introduction 11

PART 2
THE METHODOLOGY OF OLD TESTAMENT THEOLOGY

TWO: Methodology 29

THREE: Text or Event 36

FOUR: Criticism or Canon 86

FIVE: Descriptive or Confessional 115

SIX: Diachronic or Synchronic 184

PART 3
A CANONICAL THEOLOGY OF THE OLD TESTAMENT

SEVEN: A Proposal for a Canonical Theology 197

APPENDICES

APPENDIX A: The Mosaic Law and the Theology of the Pentateuch 253

APPENDIX B: Compositional Strategies in the Pentateuch 272

APPENDIX C: The Narrative World of Genesis 290

APPENDIX D: 1 Chronicles 21:1—A Study in Inter-Biblical Interpretation 298

Author Index 313

Subject Index 319

To my friend and mentor
Dr. Bruce K. Waltke

PREFACE

Though it attempts to do many things, the present work is primarily an introduction to the study of OT theology; it attempts to provide a student-oriented, comprehensive overview of this discipline. Students need to learn both how others before them have mined the OT for its theological treasures and how they themselves can begin that same task. This book also seeks to clear new ground in defining the task of OT theology. It is a truism to say that biblical theology, and particularly OT theology, has been largely defined as a historical discipline. It is a discipline that seeks merely to describe Israel's faith as it is expressed in the OT Scriptures. While not denying the legitimacy of such an aim, it has become increasingly clear to many biblical theologians that there is more to OT theology. Just what that "more" consists of is still uncertain. Therefore, part of our aim is to cast some light on what that "more" can consist of, both by interacting with the contemporary discussion and by attempting to contribute to it. It is with that purpose in mind that the present work concludes with a "proposal" for doing OT theology.

A word should be said about the guidelines we have followed in this work when quoting from original sources. The reader will note that much of the material in the footnotes is quoted in its original form (e.g., German, Latin, Hebrew, and Greek). There is also much material that has been translated. When, in our judgment, the material in the footnotes is necessary for the student to follow, we have provided a translation and omitted the original. When, however, the material is primarily supplementary, we have left the quotations as written, since much of the material is in inaccessible sources and should be evaluated in its original form. It goes without saying that we do not intend students to interact at that level; they can safely ignore that material.

A third need that this work attempts to address is related to a particular audience—contemporary evangelical OT scholarship. Evangelicalism has traditionally defined itself as a text-oriented faith. The Scriptures are held to be the Word of God. In my opinion, evangelical OT theologians and exegetes have not always appreciated the full range of implications their view of Scripture has for biblical theology, nor have they fully appreciated the strains that commonly held views about the task of OT theology have put on their view of Scripture. The present work raises some of these issues within the context of evangelical theology and provides at least one response to them. We are not suggesting that our response is the only possible one. Rather, we have attempted to provide a framework within which several distinct evangelical responses can be seen as valid and appropriate.

I want to express my appreciation to some who have helped in the writing of this book. The dedication page notes my personal gratitude to my friend and former seminary professor, Dr. Bruce Waltke. It was in his classes that the importance of God's Word and the necessity of the study of OT theology were fully articulated. To have studied with this scholar is a rare privilege. I would also like to thank my friend and colleague Dr. Walter C. Kaiser Jr. Both in his writings and in personal conversation, Dr. Kaiser has taught me much about the theology of the OT. Though I would like to mention others by name, I will simply say that I owe most of my gratitude to my students at Bethel Theological Seminary and Trinity Evangelical Divinity School, whom I would like to thank for their patience in letting me learn along with them. Finally, I am grateful to the editors at ZondervanPublishingHouse—Stan Gundry, Ed van der Maas, James Ruark, and Verlyn Verbrugge—for their constant willingness to help.

ABBREVIATIONS

APOT	R. H. Charles (ed.), *Apocrypha and Pseudepigrapha of the Old Testament*
BDB	Brown, Driver, Briggs, *Hebrew and English Lexicon of the Old Testament*
BHS	*Biblia Hebraica Stuttgartensia*
BKAT	Biblischer Kommentar: Altes Testament
BSac	*Bibliotheca Sacra*
BZAW	Beihefte zur *ZAW*
DBSup	*Dictionnaire de la Bible, Supplément*
EBC	*Expositor's Bible Commentary*
EvT	*Evangelische Theologie*
HAT	Handbuch zum Alten Testament
ICC	International Critical Commentary
IDB	*Interpreter's Dictionary of the Bible*
IDBS	*Interpreter's Dictionary of the Bible Supplement*
JBL	*Journal of Biblical Literature*
JETS	*Journal of the Evangelical Theological Society*
JSOT	*Journal for the Study of the Old Testament*
JSOTS	*Journal for the Study of the Old Testament* Supplements
KB	L. Kohler and W. Baumgartner, *Lexicon in Veteris Testamenti libro*s
KEK	Kritisch-exegetischer Kommentar über das Neue Testament
MT	Masoretic Text
NICOT	New International Commentary on the Old Testament
RB	*Revue biblique*
RGG	*Religion in Geschichte und Gegenwart*
SBLSP	*Society of Biblical Literature Seminar Papers*
SJT	*Scottish Journal of Theology*
Str-B	H. Strack and P. Billerbeck, *Kommentar zum Neuen Testament*
SVT	*Studia in Veteris Testamenti*
TRE	*Theologische Realenzyklopädie*
TrinJ	*Trinity Journal*
TWNT	*Theologisches Wörterbuch zum Neuen Testament*
TynBul	*Tyndale Bulletin*
VT	*Vetus Testamentum*
VTSupp.	*Vetus Testamentum*, Supplements
WBC	Word Biblical Commentaries
ZAW	*Zeitschrift für die alttestamentliche Wissenschaft*
ZDMG	*Zeitschrift der deutschen morgenländisches Gesellschaft*
ZThK	*Zeitschrift für Theologie und Kirche*

Abbreviations

PART I

INTRODUCTION

ONE

INTRODUCTION

1.1. WHAT IS OLD TESTAMENT THEOLOGY?

Since not everyone is agreed on what Old Testament theology is or should be, we begin this work with an attempt to clarify for the reader our own understanding of its nature. The purpose of these introductory remarks, then, is to give a preliminary description of the task of OT theology. We do not mean to imply that our description is valid for all, but merely to set forth clearly the approach we will take.

As is clear from the name, OT theology is a certain kind of theology. It is the study of theology that has the Old Testament as its primary subject matter. It would seem that little else need be said since it is common knowledge what the Old Testament is and every reader of the Bible knows what theology is. But there are several questions that arise as soon as we begin to look more closely, even concerning the nature of theology itself.

There is diversity of opinion about how one's understanding of the term *theology* is affected when it is applied to the Old Testament. Is it correct to say that "Old Testament theology" is merely that branch of theology that has the Old Testament as its subject matter? Does not the label "Old" have some effect on the sense of the term *theology?* Does not the idea of an *Old* Testament theology also suggest that there is a distinction between it and a *New* Testament theology? If so, then the sense of the term *theology* will not be the same in both cases.

For the sake of clarity in understanding the nature of OT theology, it is important to come to some agreement on the meaning of the term *theology*. Only then can we speak with confidence about the nature of OT theology. What, then, is theology?

In discussions of OT theology, the term theology has generally been associated with two quite different concepts: divine revelation[1] and religion. In one sense these two concepts, revelation and religion, may seem close in meaning. However, as the

---

[1]We are using the term revelation in the limited sense of the Scriptures as God's special revelation.

11

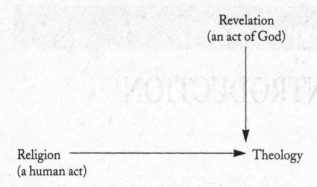

Figure 1.1

words have been used in discussions of OT theology, they have each taken on a particular sense and have grown poles apart in meaning. We will have to examine each of these concepts more closely to see what is meant by each term and how each affects our understanding of the nature of theology.

The word "revelation" is usually taken as a term which describes an act of God.[2] God, we say, has revealed himself in the Bible. On the other hand, "religion" is a term which describes an act of man.[3] The relationship between the two terms can be demonstrated by saying humanity accepts God's revelation and acts in accordance with it and that is called religion.[4] The chart in Figure 1.1 shows how each of these concepts is related to the nature and task of theology.

When our understanding of the nature and purpose of theology is related to either of these two terms, it takes on a particular and distinct meaning. Since this meaning will carry over to our understanding of OT theology, we should look more closely at the two senses of theology which are related to these two terms.

1.1.1. Theology and Revelation

The German poet, Rainer Maria Rilke, has aptly expressed what the notion of theology means when it is linked to the concept of divine revelation:

> Catch only what you've thrown yourself, all is mere skill and little gain; but when you're suddenly the catcher of a ball thrown by an eternal partner . . . catching then becomes a power—not yours, a world's.[5]

---

[2]C. M. Edsman, "Offenbarung, I. Religionsgeschichtlich," *Die Religion in Geschichte und Gegenwart,* 3rd ed. (Tübingen: J. C. B. Mohr [Paul Siebeck], 1957ff), 4:1597–1599.

[3]The origin of religion has been variously explained either by means of "illusion" (e.g. Hume; Feuerbach) or natural knowledge (e.g., Baier, "*lex illa Dei . . . in ipsa creatione animae hominis implantata.*" Friedrich Aug. Berth. Nitzsch, *Lehrbuch der Evangelischen Dogmatik* (Freiburg: J. C. B. Mohr [Paul Siebeck], 1892), 46–58.

[4]C. H. Ratschow, "Religion IV B. Theologisch," *RGG,* 5:976–984.

[5]Quoted in Hans-Georg Gadamer, *Wahrheit und Methode* (Tübingen: J. C. B. Mohr [Paul Siebeck], 1975), v.

When one understands theology in relation to the concept of divine revelation, it is the study of what God has revealed about himself or about the world. It is, in Rilke's words, a catching of "a ball thrown by an eternal partner." As such it is a power not one's own, but "a world's." It is in this sense that the task of theology has been classically understood. The late orthodox theologian David Hollaz, for example, defined theology as "God given" (*habitus Theosdotos divinitus datus*) because for him it was a "revealed theology" (*theologia revelata*): "With respect to its principle, revealed theology is called a God-given way of thinking (*habitus*); not as though it is immediately infused into one's mind, but because its fundamental basis (*principium*) is not human reason but rather divine revelation. Therefore revealed theology is called *wisdom coming from on high*."[6] Conceived in this way, theology, being to some extent also a science, is an attempt to formulate God's revelation into themes and propositions. It is the scientific explication of revelation. It works on the premise that God has revealed himself in ways that can be observed and restated in more or less precise language. The task of theology in this sense is the restatement of God's self-revelation. To quote Rilke again, it is a "catching [that] then becomes a power."

In connecting theology with revelation, it is important to note that theology, in this sense, is put in a direct relation to a special process that has been initiated by God.[7] God has spoken and acted. God has revealed himself in observable and communicable ways. Theology's task is to pick up the trail and pursue the line of discourse, taking its clues from God's acts and words and translating their meaning to particular audiences and times.

It is easy to see that within such an understanding of the term, theology is given a high place among the sciences. Indeed, for many it is the "queen of the sciences." Theology's standing at one end of a process begun by God gives it not only a special rank, but also a unique authority. Theology can dare attempt to say, "Thus saith the Lord." What other field of study would make such a claim? Theology cannot claim to speak with divine authority nor can it be *equated* with divine authority, but it can and must claim to speak *on behalf of* God's revelation and hence expects its word to carry more than its own weight. Insofar as theology can rightly grasp God's revelation and accurately translate it into a particular setting, theology can lay claim to be normative. It can expect to be taken as a standard by which to measure oneself against the Word of God.

When such an understanding of the term *theology* is given to the phrase *Old Testament theology*, it raises several questions. How, for example, can an *Old* Testament theology claim to be normative? Does not the notion of the term *Old* suggest that the

---

[6]"Respectu cujus principii Theologia revelata dicitur habitus θεόσδοτος divinitus datus, non quasi sit immediate infusus, sed quia principium ejus non est humana ratio, verum divina revelatio. Idcirco Theologia revelata vocatur *sapientia superne veniens*" (David Hollaz, *Examen Theologicum Acroamaticum Universam Theologiam Thetico-Polemicam* [J. N. Ernesti, 1707], 11).

[7]"Requirimus ut Deus ejus specialis sit autor, quia ad scripturam talem non sufficit concursus communis. . . . Necessarius ergo est impulsus peculiaris, qui autoribus omnibus sacris praesto fuit, quotiescumque Deus eorum calamo usus est" (Andreas Rivetus, *Isagoge, seu Introductio generalis, ad Scripturam Sacram Veteris et Novi Testamenti* [Lugdunus, 1627], 8).

value of this theology has passed and that it has been replaced by the *New?* Is it not a serious problem to label one Testament "Old" and the other "New" and then to hold them both as normative? How can both continue to be a standard of one's understanding of God? If they are both the standard, in other words, why do we call the one "Old" and the other "New"? The problem we are raising here is not a new one, nor is it insoluble. It is, however, one that lies at the heart of every Christian's attempt to understand OT theology.

An understanding of the term *theology* that sees its task as the restatement of God's revelation and hence as normative, has far-reaching implications for one's understanding and approach to OT theology. It will influence much of what is proposed for OT theology in this book. Not everyone, however, agrees that this is the nature and purpose of theology. For many today the notion of theology is tied not to the concept of revelation, an act of God, but to religion, a purely human act. We should thus also take a close look at the sense of the term *theology* when it is linked to the concept of religion.

1.1.2. Theology and Religion

For some, the essence of the biblical faith is religion, not revelation, thus the task of theology is the explication of religious beliefs. The historian Emanuel Hirsch has argued that this view of theology owes its origin and development to the influential eighteenth-century theologian Sigmund Jacob Baumgarten. For Baumgarten revelation was separated from Scripture, and Scripture was turned into a human expression (*religio*) of divine revelation. As Baumgarten used the term, *revelation* was the "manifestation of things previously unknown."[8] On the other hand, for Baumgarten, the term *inspiration* was understood as "the means by which direct revelation was communicated and recorded in books."[9] Thus for Baumgarten, divine revelation was not identified with Scripture, but rather, Scripture was identified as the recording of that which had been communicated directly to the mind of the biblical writers. This is, admittedly, a subtle distinction, but it is one that had far-reaching consequences. Hirsch states that "German Protestant theology reached a decisive stage with Baumgarten. It went from being a faith based on the Bible to being one based on revelation—a revelation for which the Bible was in reality nothing more than a record once given." For Baumgarten and those that followed him the Bible was not divine revelation, but a response to a divine revelation. As such the Bible was a religious artifact,

---

[8]"rerum ignotarum manifestatio" (Sigmund Jacob Baumgarten, *diss. de discrimine revelationis et inspirationis* [Halle, 1745], 6). Quoted in Emanuel Hirsch, *Geschichte der Neuern Evangelischen Theologie* (Gütersloh: C. Bertelsmann, 1951), 2:378.

[9]"medium, quo revelatio immediata mediata facta inque libros relata est," ibid.

[10]In Baumgarten, revelation was separated from Scripture and Scripture was turned into a human expression (religio) of divine revelation. "Alles in allem darf man wohl sagen: die deutsche evangelische Theologie is mit Baumgarten in das entscheidende Stadium des übergangs vom Bibelglauben zu einem Offerbarungsglauben getreten, dem die Bibel im Wesentlichen nichts ist als die nun einmal gegebne Urkunde der Offenbarung," ibid.

not itself a divine revelation.[10] Within such a view of the Bible and revelation, theology becomes the statement of the religious opinions and beliefs of those with whom and among whom God has acted.

It is important to note that this understanding of theology differs from that of the previous understanding in one basic respect: as an explication of religion rather than revelation, theology does not stand at the end of a special process initiated by God, but rather of one initiated by man. Religion, as it is thus understood, is a human act. God may have acted in history and in the affairs of his people revealing himself in many ways. All this is still possible within this understanding of theology. But the important distinction is that theology's task is seen as the explication of the religious consequences of God's acts or of God's work, not a reckoning of God's revelation itself.

The net effect of such a distinction is to remove the normative status from the concept of theology. Theology is understood as a restatement of man's beliefs about God and humanity. It does not venture to recount God's will as such. How, then, does this view of theology affect one's understanding of OT theology? In this sense, OT theology has the task of merely recounting what the biblical writers believed or held to be true about God. Theology, then, should not say, "Thus says the Lord"; it can only say, "This they believed."

It is not hard to see that such a view of theology, like the former, gives rise to several interesting questions. By removing from it any claim to be normative, this understanding of theology has cut itself off from the community of faith, the church. The church, which must have a norm or a standard by which to measure its own life and action, cannot look to theology, at least not biblical theology. The trail pursued by theology leads back to a human initiative in establishing a religion rather than to God's act of revelation. The theologian ultimately finds one like himself at the other end of his quest. The Scriptures were a product of divine revelation, not a source of that revelation. The church, likewise, finds only itself as a community on either end of the line running from human beliefs about God (religion), to human expression of those beliefs (theology). There is no basis for a claim to authority. The church cannot hear the Word of God if it only hears human words when it reads the Old Testament. If the OT theologian hears only human words, how does the church know when they are hearing the Word of God?

1.1.3. Summary

There are, then, at least two distinct ways to understand the task and nature of theology. The point of departure between the two ideas is the question of whether the Bible is a record of God's revelation or of human religion. The consequence of the distinction in meaning is the question of authority. Does theology have a right to make claims about the normativity of its statements? Does theology stand at one end of a special process begun by God, or is it a purely human enterprise? Can the theologian ever hope to say to the church, "Thus saith the Lord"?

1.1.4. Should Theology Claim to Be Normative?

In the last analysis, the question that must be addressed by anyone wishing to understand OT theology is whether such a theology is to be understood as normative for the Christian today. Is one's theology to be taken as binding because it is a restatement of what God himself has revealed? Or is theology merely the description of human beliefs about God? In short: has God spoken? Is the Bible a record of what God has said? Can we claim, or dare, to speak God's word as it has come to us in the OT?

Although much of this book is an attempt at addressing these questions, certain points are assumed from the start and should be set forth clearly here at the beginning of our discussion. These are not to be understood as presuppositions that are beyond defense or argument. They are rather part of a theological prolegomena that lies outside the scope of this book. They are given here, not as a basis for proceeding with the description of OT theology, but as a basis for understanding the author's own theological commitment. They will affect the nature of the author's own proposal for doing OT theology, however, as will become evident throughout the book.

In the first place, I take it that the Bible is the Word of God and that in the Bible God has spoken. The Bible is not merely a record of what God said in the past; it is, in fact, a record of what God is saying today. By means of the words of the Scriptures, God has spoken and speaks to us today.

If God has spoken in the Bible, then the task of theology is made considerably more clear. The task of theology is to state God's Word to the church in a clear and precise manner. What else can be expected of theology than an understandable restatement of the Word of God?

Such is the understanding of the term *theology* in the mind of the author of this book. Theology is the restatement and explication of God's revelation, the Bible. It intends to state what should be heard as normative for the faith and practice of the Christian believer.

In light of what has been said here about the task of theology, we should remember that theology, like all other fields of study, is a human endeavor. As such it is subject to all the limitations of human fallibility. No statement of the Bible's theological message can claim to speak with the same authority as the Bible itself. Only the Bible is infallible, not our theological systems.

1.2. DEFINITION OF OLD TESTAMENT THEOLOGY

Having gained some understanding of the goal of theology, we can now look more closely at the nature of OT theology. No single definition of a field so diverse can hope to please everyone or claim to be comprehensive. We should also keep in mind that this definition is largely determined by the set of assumptions about Scripture and revelation discussed in the previous section. A definition will be helpful as long as it is understood not to be exclusive but to be only an aid to further understanding and clarification. In other words we should not think of a definition as a way of ruling out different approaches. It should rather be seen merely as a way of setting our objectives more clearly in sight. The following definition is offered with that end in view: *Old Testament theology is the study and presentation of what is revealed in the Old Testament.*

Although this is a simple definition, it raises at least four important issues about which there is much debate.

1.2.1. The Study of the Old Testament

The first feature of OT theology reflected in the definition is the idea that an important dimension is the *study* of the OT. Whether study rightly deserves a place in the description might be disputed. Is not OT theology the end product of the study of the OT? Does it not come as the capstone of much labor in the text? While it is correct to say that OT theology comes at the end of the exegetical process, there is a sense in which it should not be thought of merely as the last stage. There is much theology at work even in the initial stages of biblical studies. All of the stages that lead to an OT theology do themselves involve theological reflection. At no point along the way are we free from having to make theological decisions. Since that is the case, we are justified in including the study of the text itself as one of the principle features of OT theology.

There are at least four major areas of biblical study that involve theological reflection in the initial stages of the work of OT theology.

(1) **Hermeneutics**: The study of biblical or OT hermeneutics is a subject that lies at the base of an OT theology. Since hermeneutics deals with the science or art of interpreting texts, it is easy to see that decisions made in this area will affect a theology based on the biblical text. Many of the issues dealt with in this book are hermeneutical. It is important to see that far from being the mere starting point, or presupposition of an OT theology, hermeneutics and hermeneutical decisions are the material out of which it is made. So interrelated are hermeneutics and theology that many have called for a "special hermeneutic" that treats the biblical text as a unique use of interpretation. Gerhard Maier, for example, has suggested that the very uniqueness of the Bible within the context of world literature calls for a "special biblical hermeneutic."[11]

(2) **Language and Translation**: Since the Old Testament is a book of words written in a language quite different from English, the task of reading or translating the text is one that must be resolved before any progress can be made in theology. At the same time it must be recognized that the task of translating the Bible is itself a theological one. Before any text can be translated, it must be understood and interpreted. No matter how distasteful the idea may be to us, the process of understanding a text or a passage and then translating it is latent with theological decisions. It is not an exaggeration to say that a translation is already a rudimentary biblical theology. Translations range from very literal to extreme paraphrases, but in every case they are a reflection both of the original and the theological decisions of the translators. This is something with which every

---

[11] Cf. Gerhard Maier, *Biblische Hermeneutik* (Wuppertal: R. Brockhaus, 1990), 12: "Für eine spezielle biblische Hermeneutik spricht zunächst die Beobachtung, dass die Bibel—wenn sie auch nur ein wenig recht hat—der seltsamste und einzigartigste, ja ein unvergleichlicher Gegenstand ist. Nirgendwo in der Weltliteratur gibt es ein Buch wie dieses."

student of OT theology must reckon.[12] Ancient, as well as modern translations of the Old Testament are fertile soil for the growth of theology.[13]

(3) **Exegesis:** The theology of the Old Testament is the sum of the theology of its various parts. Exegesis is the task of interpreting and understanding the meaning of specific biblical texts. Each part of the Old Testament must be understood before the whole can be arranged into a complete theology of the Old Testament. Before one can understand the parts, however, there must be a sense of where the whole is leading. There is a circle of understanding that is basic to OT theology. The whole of the Old Testament must be understood in order to shed light on its parts. At the same time, the understanding of the whole must come through an understanding of the parts. Exegesis (understanding the parts), then, is an integral part of the task of OT theology (understanding the whole), and OT theology is basic to exegesis. Exegesis is the path that leads to an OT theology, but OT theology is the light that guides the way.

(4) **Old Testament Introduction:** The study of OT theology is based also on introductory questions such as the authorship and date of the various biblical books and the resolution of special problems relating to each book. In recent years the question of the canon of the Old Testament has again been raised and shown to be crucial to a theological understanding of the Bible. Not only is the origin and date of the collection of Old Testament books an important question, but also the theological reflections behind the canonical order and arrangement has become an object of interest for OT theology and cannot be ignored.

The development of an OT theology cannot be done in isolation from a serious study of the Old Testament itself. In fact, the study of the Old Testament proceeds along lines that are clearly theological. The question is not whether OT theology is related to the other disciplines of biblical study, but only whether it is to be related to them consciously or unconsciously.

---

[12]This raises the question of the theological influence of the early versions of the OT, e.g., Septuagint, on the writers of the New Testament. See Klaus Haacker and Heinzpeter Hempelmann, *Hebraica Veritas, Die hebräische Grundlage der biblischen Theologie als exegetische und systematische Grandlage* (Wuppertal: R. Brockhaus Verlag, 1989).

[13]See John H. Sailhamer, *The Translational Technique of the Greek Septuagint for the Hebrew Verbs and Participles in Psalms 3–41* (New York: Peter Lang, 1991); Abraham Geiger, *Urschrift und Uebersetzungen der Bibel in ihrer Abhängigkeit von der innern Entwickelung des Judenthums* (Breslau: Julius Hainauer, 1857); Armin Schmitt, "Interpretation der Genesis aus hellenistischem Geist," *ZAW*, 86, (1974), 137–63. "The presence of interpretation in the Septuagint of Genesis can be demonstrated from several different angles. In the realm of language Hebrew and Semitic idioms are adapted to the structure of the Greek language and to its feeling for style. The attempt is made to render the breadth of meaning of Hebrew nouns by a variety of translations. The presence of modifications and aids to understanding point to the concern for interpretation. It is frequently possible to demonstrate the Egyptian and Alexandrian background from within which the interpretation is made. Particular instances of Greek and Hellenistic interpretation are found in the primeval history and in the realm of anthropology. Interpretation can also be seen in a concern to exclude possible misunderstandings. In isolated instances specific religious terms from the Greek and Hellenistic world are introduced into the Septuagint. Finally the outlook of this world is manifested in the way the divine name is rendered" (163).

1.2.2. The Presentation

One of the most debated topics in OT theology is the proper mode of presentation. Early biblical theologians used to speak of the skill of understanding the Bible and the skill of explaining the Bible.[14] It is one thing to have a good understanding of what the biblical writers were saying and of their theology. It is altogether another matter to communicate one's understanding of that theology. There are a number of ways in which the material can be presented. The debated question is which is the most appropriate.

It could be argued that the Old Testament is already a theology, that the biblical writers were themselves theologians and their writings are their theologies. If such be the case, then the Old Testament already has a mode of presentation. It is the one chosen by the writers themselves, and is quite different than modern conceptions of what a theology should look like. But, even if this is the case, as it probably is, there may still be sufficient reason for seeking a different arrangement or plan of presentation. As a theological undertaking, OT theology must seek to make the message of the Old Testament as clear and precise to a given audience as it possibly can. It must present itself as an integrated whole. It must show how the parts fit into the whole. In other words, it must be able to present the inherent structure of the biblical message in its entirety, and thus it is faced with the problem of how to arrange its parts meaningfully.

The structures of presentation chosen by OT theologians can be grouped into four types.

(1) **Systematic:** It has been customary in systematic theology to arrange theological systems under three major headings—God, humanity, salvation. First the topic of God is discussed and all those matters dealing with his being and attributes are treated. This is followed by a discussion of humanity and after that the subject of salvation. Taking this lead, many OT theologies have chosen to arrange the material in the same threefold scheme.[15] This approach to presentation has been criticized by some as being too artificial. The biblical texts, they argue, do not fit neatly into such schemes. By superimposing our own categories on the text, we fail to see the true picture of the message of the biblical writers.

Though there is some truth to these criticisms of the method, in recent years it has been noted that a theoretical model, which is what the scheme God-Humanity-Salvation really amounts to, can be a valuable way to sift through complicated systems. As long as the model is not mistaken for the biblical systems themselves, a systematic approach has much merit. It is thus a common method of presenting OT theology.

---

[14]Cf. Johan Iacob Rambach, *Institutiones Hermeneuticae Sacrae* (Jena: Hartungian, 1725), 272: "Exposuimus libris superioribus subsidia et adminicula hermeneutica. . . . Superest denique, ut ostendamus, qua ratione sensus, istis subsidiis inuentus ac detectus, cum aliis etiam *communicari*, solide *demonstrari*, et salutariter *adplicari* debeat."

[15]E.g., Ludwig Köhler, *Theologie des Alten Testaments* (Tübingen: J. C. B. Mohr [Paul Siebeck], 1966), 260: Erster Teil: von Gott; Zweiter Teil: vom Menschen; Dritter Teil: von Gericht und Heil.

(2) **Historical:** The OT is made up of many historical narratives that tell of a history ranging from Creation to the last centuries before Christ. In many OT theologies, this line of history is taken to be the central organizing principle holding the theology of the OT intact.[16] In the last century and continuing to the present, the historical approach dominated the field of OT theology. There was a time, in fact, when OT theology even ceased to be called theology and was simply called "the study of the history of Israel's religion."[17]

With new discoveries in biblical archaeology and further refinements in method, our knowledge of Israel's history has been greatly enhanced. As we learn more about what happened in Israel during the biblical period, the historical approach would seem to be all the more important. Our increasing understanding of the events in Israel's history, however, has also led others to become more wary of a historical approach to presenting OT theology. As we learn more about biblical history it is all the more possible to lose sight of the role of the Bible itself and its view of Israel's history. OT theology is to be a theology of the OT. That is, what we are after is not the general quest of "that which happened to Israel," but rather the specific goal of understanding the Old Testament. The Old Testament is the Word of God; it is the revelation of the will of God. Certainly it is history, but it is also more than history. It is an inspired interpretation of history. No amount of further light from archaeology or historical studies can alter the importance of listening to the inspired authors' retelling of that history.

The most serious critique of the historical approach has come from those who stress the importance of seeing the OT as a text, a document, not only historical in nature but with definite literary traits as well. The fact that the Bible is historical, they say, should not detract from the fact that it is also literature. The biblical narratives have plots and central characters, which the writers of the OT were careful to develop just like any other author would do. They gave their narratives a setting and were careful to mark the sequence of events so that their accounts are as akin to stories as they are to history. Thus, by insisting on a purely historical approach to the presentation of an OT theology, it might be argued that other features of the biblical texts, such as their sense of story, can too easily be overlooked.

(3) **Central Theme:** Many attempts have been made to arrange OT theology around a single integrating theme. Is there a single theme running through all the Old Testament? Does its message hold together? If so, what is this central theme and how should it be expressed? Do we state it in categories derived from the OT itself? Or should we put it in categories more like those of the NT or systematic theology?

There has been little agreement on these questions. Some have suggested that the central theme of the OT is the notion of a *covenant*, that is, a formal agreement or

---

[16]E.g., Wilhelm Möller, *Biblische Theologie des Alten Testaments in heilsgeschichtlicher Entwicklung* (Zwickau: Johannes Herrmann, ca. 1935), 527.

[17]Gustav Hölscher, *Geschichte der israelitischen und Jüdischen Religion* (Giessen: Töpelmann, 1922), 267; Rudolf Kittel, *Die Religion des Volkes Israel* (Leipzig: Quelle & Meyer, 1921), 210; Eduard König, *Geschichte der Alttestamentlichen Religion* (Gütersloh: C. Bertelsmann, 1912), 606; Ernst Sellin, *Israelitisch-Jüdische Religionsgeschichte* (Leipzig: Quelle & Meyer 1933), 152.

arrangement between God and Israel.[18] It is this notion of an ongoing relationship between God and his people, they say, that forms the theological center of the OT. Others have agreed with the notion that a relationship between God and Israel lies at the center of the OT, but they argue that the concept of a covenant is too narrow to include all that is presented in the OT. They have suggested the use of more general terms such as God's love, or the knowledge of God.[19] Some have suggested that since an OT theology must eventually reckon with the New Testament, the concept of the *kingdom of God*, which plays an important role in the NT theology, is the most appropriate single, integrating concept.[20]

In recent years the suggestion has been made that a single theme is too limiting to the variety of OT expressions about God. The only way to organize an OT theology around a central theme, it is argued, is to see that theme as a cluster of major themes woven throughout Scripture.[21] Although this suggestion falls short of the goal of finding a single theme, it goes a long way toward unifying the theological message of the OT and at the same time of easing the pressure of having to fit all of the OT around a single theme.

(4) Some OT theologians have advocated abandoning altogether the attempt to rearrange the existing order of the Old Testament's message. Any attempt to superimpose a structure on the Old Testament's own way of presentation, they say, will of necessity distort the theological picture of the OT, if not the theology itself.[22]

In this last approach, if taken to an extreme, OT theology would consist of little more than the mere rereading of the text itself. In the last analysis, such an approach may offer the best solution. It should at least be recognized, however, that any attempt to go beyond a single rereading of the text will involve some decision on how the restatement is to be organized and presented. It seems that if we are to say anything about the theology of the OT, we will have to settle on a plan of presentation, however minimal that may be.

1.2.3. Divine Revelation

The definition of OT theology offered above assumes that the term *theology* finds its meaning in relation to the concept of revelation. Old Testament theology is concerned with that revelation of God's will given in the OT. It expects to find in its study of the OT that which comes from God.

To speak of the OT as revelation is not to speak in the past tense. If God has spoken in the text of Scripture, then there is no reason to limit that Word to the past.

---

[18]Walther Eichrodt, *Theology of the Old Testament* (Philadelphia: Westminster Press, 1961).

[19]Th. C. Vriezen, *An Outline of Old Testament Theology* (Newton: Charles T. Branford, 1970).

[20]Hans-Joachim Kraus, *Systematische Theologie im Kontext biblischer Geschichte und Eschatologie* (Neukirchen-Vluyn: Neukirchener, 1983).

[21]Gerhard Hasel, "The Problem of the Center in the OT Theology Debate," *ZAW*, 86 (1974), 65–82.

[22]Gerhard von Rad, *Old Testament Theology* (New York: Harper & Row, 1962).

If he has spoken, it does not matter when he spoke. If God has spoken, his voice is still to be heard today. The OT, then, *is* the revelation of God's will; and a theology of the OT must seek to be a presentation, or restatement, of God's Word.

In other words, the task of OT theology implied in the definition given above is a normative one. It has taken up the idea of revelation. It seeks to say "Thus says the Lord." It seeks to be a theology like any other. The only limitation on an OT theology is that it has confined itself to the books of the OT.

1.2.4. The Old Testament

We often overlook how much is implied in the title "Old Testament." Embedded in this label are several important assumptions and distinctions. These can be seen by giving emphasis to each of the two parts of the title.

1.2.4.1. The **Old** *Testament*

An important assumption lying at the heart of the use of the name *Old Testament* is the notion of a New Testament. To speak of an *Old* Testament is to confess the existence and legitimacy of the *New* Testament.[23] Otherwise, what would be the sense of calling the Testament *Old?* It is *Old* in relation to the *New*.

One of the unique features of OT theology is that its foundation, the Hebrew text of Scripture, is shared by at least one other religion, Judaism, which makes of it something quite different. The Christian (that is, New Testament) orientation of OT theology can be clearly seen from the fact that the Bible would not be called the *Old* Testament in Judaism. There would be no *Old* Testament theology in Judaism, because such terminology acknowledges the *New* Testament as a legitimate extension of the *Old*. In comparison with Judaism, then, OT theology can be more clearly seen to be a strictly Christian endeavor. OT theology, then, has intentionally opened one of its

---

[23]"And yet there is this *second aspect*, looking on towards the New Testament. Anyone who studies the historical development of the OT finds that throughout there is a powerful and purposive movement which forces itself on his attention. . . . This movement does not come to rest until the manifestation of Christ, in whom the noblest powers of the OT find their fulfillment. . . . The affinity with the NT is not, however, exhausted by a bare historical connection, such as might afford material for the historian's examination but no more. It rather confronts us with an essential characteristic, which must be taken into account if the OT is to be understood. . . . Hence to our general aim of obtaining a comprehensive picture of the realm of OT belief we must add a second and closely related purpose—to see that this comprehensive picture does justice to the essential relationship with the NT and does not merely ignore it. . . . In expounding the realm of OT thought and belief we must never lose sight of the fact that the OT religion, ineffaceably individual though it may be, can yet be grasped in this essential uniqueness only when it is seen as completed in Christ" (Walther Eichrodt, *Theology*, 26–27).

[24]"Ist Christus der Mittelpunkt der Theologie, so scheint das Alte Testament ausserhalb einer geschichtstheologischen Betrachtung zu liegen. Denn in Geschichte und Glauben Israels liegt eine vorchristliche Geisteswelt vor, die höchstens in Jesus Christus ihren Schlusspunkt findet. Der Neue Bund tritt dem Alten gegenüber und hebt hin auf. Indessen schon als Schlussgestalt des Alten Testaments lässt sich Jesus aus der Betrachtung nicht ausschalten, und so unzerreissbar er mit dem Alten Testamente zusammenhängt, so unablöslich ist es von him. Seine geschichtliche Gestalt, in der er fassbar für uns ist, hat es

boundaries to the New Testament. This was not and is not accidental. It is basic to the nature of OT theology and has several important implications.

(1) The first implication is that the study of OT theology is not complete in itself. By acknowledging its place alongside a New Testament, OT theology confesses that its scope is not narrowly circumscribed around its own canonical borders. Its line of sight extends beyond itself to something more—the New Testament.[24] OT theology anticipates the study of NT theology and there is no possibility of working without this anticipation.[25] To fail to see this is to run the risk of being blind to our most basic assumptions. OT theology can only be complete as the first part of a *biblical* theology, one that includes both an Old and a New Testament theology in a final integrated whole.[26]

(2) There is a second implication to the fact that an OT theology acknowledges its allegiance to the New Testament. If we can speak of an *Old* Testament over against a *New* Testament, then it must also be the case that the Old Testament has its own identity. As a whole, it has a shape and fits together. It makes sense. We don't need to suppose that something must be added to it before it can be understood.

Very often when the Old Testament is seen in relation to the New, it is not given its due consideration as a work that stands on its own and has its own meaning. The idea of an *Old* Testament theology, however, is opposed to such a view. What is it that we are calling *Old*? We must have something in mind that we are labeling *Old*. Implicit in the opposition that we have set up in the labels *Old* and *New* is the notion that the *Old* can stand on its own alongside the *New*.

To acknowledge the loyalty between the Old and the New Testaments, then, is not to do so at the expense of the wholeness and meaningfulness of the Old Testament in its own right. It is the burden of OT theology to find the answer to the theological meaning of the Old Testament and its relation to that of the New Testament. It is the responsibility of NT theology to wait on this answer. There is a true distinction between the Old and the New Testaments and each can be considered in its own right, though neither would retain its identity alone. The Old Testament not only stands on its own, but the New Testament stands on its shoulders.

---

zum Hintergrunde. . . . Durch die Gestalt Christi ist demnach das Alte Testament mit dem Neuen in unlösliche Verbindung gebracht." Otto Procksch, *Theologie des Alten Testaments* (Gütersloh: C. Bertelsmann, 1950), 7–11.

[25]"In this book we start from the view that both as to its object and its method Old Testament theology is and must be a Christian theological science." Th. C. Vriezen, *Outline* 147.

[26]Hans-Joachim Kraus, *Die Biblische Theologie, Ihre Geschichte und Problematik* (Neukirchen-Vluyn: Neukirchener Verlag, 1970).

[27]"Nam hoc est, quod Vetus Testamentum appellatur passim. Vetus, quum aliud ei successisset Novum: Prius, quatenus secundum aliquod est, quod posterius executionem habet. Quae distinctio divini Testamenti non significat mutationem divini propositi, sed duas partes unius consilii de filiis Abrahami" (Johannes Coccejus, *Summa Doctrinae de Foedere et Testamento Dei, Opera Omnia* [1701], 7:282). "There exists, however, within the basic unity of the testamental relationship a real historical development. The primary gradation lies between the older and the newer testaments, as is marked by the very division of the Bible into 'Old Testament' and 'New Testament'" (J. Barton Payne, *The Theology of the Older Testament*

(3) The third implication of the designation *Old* and *New* is the question of value that is assumed in the use of the two terms. To many readers of the Bible, the designation *Old* and *New* implies that the former stands in a subordinate relationship with the latter. In opposition to *new*, the adjective *old* takes on the sense of outmoded or no longer valid. Most Old Testament theologians and Christians do not intend to imply that the Old Testament is outmoded or no longer valid, but often that is the result of the use of the terms Old and New.[27]

It is the task of OT theology to sort out the inherent difficulties in the notion that OT theology is both *theology* and *Old*. Old Testament theology claims to be both normative (theology) and, by implication, also subordinate to the New Testament. Thus, a central task of OT theology is the question of the unity of the Bible, as Old and New Testaments.

1.2.4.2. The Old Testament

Another important assumption lies behind the use of the term Old *Testament*. To speak of a testament, or covenant, is to point to that which is most distinct about the Old Testament in the context of ancient Near Eastern religions.[28] The Testament (Covenant) bears witness to the fact that among all the religions of the world, the Old *Testament* claims to witness to a unique relationship between God and man. To speak of an Old *Testament* theology is to mark it off from the theologies and the religious texts that abound in the setting of the ancient Near East. An important aspect of OT theology, then, is the investigation of the lines of communication that lie between the OT and its cultural heritage.

A twofold relationship exists between the OT and its ancient setting, that of assimilation and polemic. It is not difficult to point to lines of assimilation that draw the OT together with its environment. The most obvious is also the most basic, its language. The OT was written in the language of the people of Canaan. In assimilating its message to such a basic cultural structure, the OT also embodied many of its most exalted concepts in the dress of everyday Near Eastern ways of thought. Most notably in the use of poetic imagery and in the apparent use of legal formulas, the biblical writers felt free to use existing conventions familiar to everyone in that setting.

At the same time that they were aggressively exploiting the conceptual treasure house of the ancient Near East, the biblical writers were also actively engaged in a rigorous polemic with the same cultural heritage. Not content merely to adapt to the thought forms of the ancient religions, the writers of the OT filled those forms with radically new meaning and with constant vigilance guarded against any confusion

---

[Grand Rapids: Zondervan, 1962], 74). In a footnote, Payne explains his use of the term "older testament" as follows: "So throughout this study 'older' will be used for God's former saving arrangement, both to emphasize its essential unity with the 'newer' and also to distinguish it from the 'Old,' capitalized, the first 39 inspired books of the canon" (74).

[28]We are using the term *Testament* (בְּרִית) in its lexical sense and not in the sense it has come to have from the Greek διαθήκη, "last will and testament," nor that of covenant theology, "Est enim *Dei Foedus* nihil aliud, quam divina declaratio de ratione percipiendi amoris Dei, et unione ac communione ipsius potiendi" (Johannes Coccejus, *Summa Doctrinae*, 45).

between the form of expression and the content of the religious ideas. In fundamental points, such as their monotheism, prohibition of images, and morality, the biblical writers held a line of absolute intolerance of any encroachment into their theology from the religious ideas of the ancient Near East.

It is the task of OT theology to lay bare the lines of assimilation and polemic that run between the Bible and the ancient Near East in order to show clearly the essential distinctions of the Old Testament against its environment.

1.2.5. Summary

It should now be clear that the study of OT theology has many dimensions and includes various tasks. It is both the final goal of the study of the OT and the basis upon which most of the other branches of OT study rest. No one who hopes to understand the OT and live under its authority can dispense with the need to study OT theology.

PART II

THE METHODOLOGY OF OLD TESTAMENT THEOLOGY

TWO

METHODOLOGY

2.1. METHODOLOGY

In the previous chapter a general description of the nature of OT theology was given. We attempted to answer the question, What is OT theology? Here our interest is in method. How do we *do* OT theology? What is the best approach to understanding the theological message of the OT?

Whether consciously or not, anyone who attempts to understand the OT follows a method or plan of approach. Often the problem is how to follow a consistent method. The key word here is "consistent." It is all too easy to be unaware of conflicting assumptions in one's methodology. Without a conscious effort to uncover and reflect on one's own approach, the Bible student or theologian runs the risk of an inconsistent and sometimes confused understanding of Scripture.

The goal of this chapter is to provide a set of categories or tools for evaluating approaches to OT theology. The various methodological questions and approaches will be presented in their simplest form.

2.1.1. Analytical Procedure

There are many and various ways of going about the task of OT theology. Gerhard Hasel has helpfully summarized most of the approaches taken by recent OT theologians and has sorted them into at least ten distinct groups.[1] In most cases, the approaches noted by Hasel are quite complex and involve numerous underlying assumptions. It is often the case that although we may find some features of one theologian's approach appealing, we may find other features of that approach quite unacceptable. In developing one's own approach to OT theology, one is often forced to "pick and choose" various aspects of an OT theology and combine them with aspects

---

[1]Gerhard Hasel, *Old Testament Theology: Basic Issues in the Current Debate*, 4th ed. (Grand Rapids: Eerdmans, 1991), 28–114.

of another. While such an approach has some merit, if not done carefully and thoughtfully, it can, at best, lead to eclecticism in methodology, and, at worst, result in an inconsistent and contradictory approach. Fortunately, it is possible to simplify the various contemporary approaches to OT theology by breaking them down into smaller components. In the present chapter we will attempt to do just that. Rather than focusing our discussion on specific OT theologians and the approaches they have followed, our discussion of method will attempt to uncover the varying assumptions that have gone into their treatment of the OT.

In our explanation and discussion of their methodological assumptions, we will use an analytic procedure borrowed from the field of linguistics called *feature analysis* or *componential analysis*.[2] When linguists analyze the meaning of words, they recognize that words are able to generate specific meanings because each word, like a cake recipe, is made up of particular combinations of meaning, or semantic components.

Let us illustrate the approach with an example from linguistics. The English words *hill*, *mountain*, and *peak*, for example, are similar in meaning because they each contain the same semantic components, such as geographical location, dry land, and elevation. The word *lake*, however, is dissimilar to these three words because it does not share all of the same components.

The chart in Figure 2.1 shows the effect of a feature analysis of these English words. At a glance one can see what features each of the words have in common and which features each uniquely contains.

	Hill	Mountain	Peak	Lake
1. Geographical location	+	+	+	+
2. Land	+	+	+	-
3. Elevation	+	+	+	-
4. Water	-	-	-	+
5. High	-	+	+	0

Figure 2.1

A feature analysis of these words can, moreover, help us appreciate the distinct meanings of each word. Note that each of the three words, *hill*, *mountain*, and *peak*, also contains certain ingredients that the others do not. The word *hill*, for example, contains a semantic ingredient that qualifies the "elevated" ingredient as "not high" (- high). The word *mountain* contains the opposite qualifier (+ high). The word *lake*, however, does not contain the ingredient "high" in either form. Thus the word *hill* is

---

[2]J. Lyons, *Introduction to Theoretical Linguistics* (Cambridge: Cambridge University Press, 1968), 470–80; Benjamin Kedar, *Biblische Semantik, Eine Einführung* (Stuttgart: W. Kohlhammer, 1981), 187–90.

composed of the semantic combination "geographical location" + "elevated" + "not high." Whereas, the word *mountain* is composed of the semantic combination "geographical location" + "elevated" + "high." Each word has a distinct meaning because it contains its own particular combination of ingredients. Often in feature analysis, the various ingredients are represented as sets in *binary opposition*. Binary opposition means that a particular component is marked either positively or negatively. The feature *high*, for example, can be represented as +/- high (which should be read as "plus or minus the concept *high*"). Such a notation means that a word which contains this particular ingredient can be marked either as "high" (+ high), e.g., mountain, or "not high" (- high), e.g., hill. Thus, according to the procedure of feature analysis, the meaning of a particular word depends on what specific ingredients (features) it has and how those features are marked (binary opposition). The procedure can be particularly helpful in analyzing the precise range of meaning in words that are close in meaning. Often the meaning of a word can be reduced to the presence or absence of just one or two features. Thus feature analysis can be a way of mapping the specific semantic components in the meaning of a word. It helps make explicit the meaning of a word that we already know as native speakers of the language.

2.1.2. Options in Feature Analysis

To use the procedure of feature analysis in addressing the question of method in OT theology, we will look at the various approaches to OT theology as specific configurations of central components. We will show that each component consists of distinct steps or options that one may take in the process of doing OT theology. For the sake of clarity, we will present and discuss each option in terms of a choice between two opposite positions; that is, we will express it in terms of a "binary opposition." Depending on what choices one makes between the various components of method, the end result will be a distinctly unique combination of assumptions or objectives. In the following sections we will discuss each of these components in detail.

The first choice or set of options we will discuss is that between an OT theology which focuses on the text of Scripture as the locus of revelation, and that which looks beyond the text to the events in the history of Israel or to the ideals embodied in the text as the locus of revelation. We will call this option *Text or Event*. The second option is the choice between an approach to OT theology that is based on a critical understanding of the OT and one based on the OT as we have it in the OT canon. This option will be called *Critical or Canon*. The third option is that between an OT theology that treats the OT as one would any other book and one which approaches it with a special hermeneutic or method of interpretation—*Descriptive or Confessional*. The fourth option is that between viewing the OT in terms of its parts, that is, diachronically, and viewing it as a whole, synchronically—*Diachronic or Synchronic*.

The chart in Figure 2.2 shows how four basic approaches to OT theology can be compared using feature analysis.

	Approach A	Approach B	Approach C	Approach D
1. Text or Event	+	−	+	+
2. Criticism or Canon	+	−	−	+
3. Descriptive or Confessional	+	+	+	−
4. Diachronic or Synchronic	−	−	−	+

Figure 2.2

A summary interpretation of the chart above shows:

APPROACH A

1. Text or Event	+	1. An OT theology based on the text of the OT rather than the event;
2. Criticism or Canon	+	2. It views the text of the OT critically and thus is not based on the text just as we have it in the OT canon;
3. Descriptive or Confessional	+	3. It treats the OT as any other book, without a special hermeneutic;
4. Diachronic or Synchronic	−	4. It attempts to view the whole of the OT as a unit, rather than looking only at the parts.

Figure 2.3

APPROACH B

1. Text or Event	−	1. An OT theology based on the historical events in Israel's past, rather than looking specifically at the text of Scripture;
2. Criticism or Canon	−	2. It views those events just as they are portrayed in the OT narratives as we now have them in the canon;
3. Descriptive or Confessional	+	3. It treats the OT just as it would any other book;
4. Diachronic or Synchronic	−	4. It attempts to view the whole of the OT as a unit, rather than in each of its parts.

Figure 2.4

APPROACH C

1. Text or Event	+	1. An OT theology based on the text of the OT rather than the event;
2. Criticism or Canon	−	2. It views the text of the OT just as we have it in the OT canon;
3. Descriptive or Confessional	+	3. It treats the OT just as it would any other book;
4. Diachronic or Synchronic	−	4. It attempts to view the whole of the OT as a unit, rather than in each of its parts.

Figure 2.5

APPROACH D

1. Text or Event	+	1. An OT theology based on the text of the OT rather than the event;
2. Criticism or Canon	−	2. It views the text of the OT as we have it in the OT canon;
3. Descriptive or Confessional	−	3. It treats the OT with a special hermeneutic;
4. Diachronic or Synchronic	+	4. It approaches the OT in terms of each of its parts rather than attempting to view it as a whole.

Figure 2.6

The value of a componential analysis approach to developing an OT theology is that it enables us to isolate the various components that go into an OT theology and treat them as individual, interchangeable elements of a complete methodology. In modern parlance, the approach is modular. We can individually shape an approach by variously combining these elements. It thus becomes a useful tool not only in analyzing approaches to OT theology but also in shaping one's own approach.

The objective of the remainder of this section will be to define and develop these essential components of OT theology mentioned above and to show how they can be combined to form the basis of a methodology. Since the essential methodological components of OT theology can be configured in many equally valid ways, we should recognize at the start that there will always be varieties of OT theologies. Not every approach, however, will be equally valid to all concerned. Often the criteria of validity will lie outside the sphere of OT theology itself. Since such is the case with the present work, we wish here to turn briefly to one of its central underlying assumptions.

As will be clear in the present work, the determining factor in our approach to OT theology and that assumption which determines its choice of method is the belief that the Scriptures are the inspired Word of God. We will say more about this below, but it should be acknowledged early on that the particular methodological configuration recommended in the present work rests on the view that the OT Scriptures, along with the NT, are God's revelation. Having said this, we should also point out that the aim of this book is not merely to provide a rationale or defense for a particular approach, but also to present the various components of OT theology in such a way that the reader is able to settle on his or her own approach.

One last word before turning to our discussion of methodological components. Because our underlying assumption is that the Scriptures are inspired, our OT theology is open to much earlier work in the area of biblical studies and theology not normally considered in introductions to OT theology.

The study of OT theology is relatively new in the history of theology. Only in the last two centuries have the unique problems posed by the theology of the OT been the subject of specialized study. The inaugural address of Johann Philipp Gabler in 1787, "Concerning the proper distinction between biblical theology and dogmatics and rightly determining their own distinct purpose" (De justo discrimine theologiae biblicae et dogmaticae regundisque recte utriusque finibus), is generally taken to be the "first systematic formulation of the basic issues involved in the pursuit of biblical theology."[3] Before that time the Old Testament was treated along with the whole of the Bible as a unity.[4] Though we do not dispute this long-accepted understanding of OT theology, we wish to emphasize also that there was much worthwhile reflection during the earlier periods on the unique problems of the OT.[5] Much of such discussions centered on the question of typology and "spiritual" or "mystical" interpretation.[6] In our opinion, though we should read these earlier works from our own contemporary perspective, much still remains of value in them.[7] In light of the fact that many spe-

---

[3]John H. Hayes and Frederick C. Prussner, *Old Testament Theology, Its History and Development* (Atlanta: John Knox Press, 1985), 2. Both Hayes (4–5) and Kraus trace the origins of biblical theology back to the Protestant principle *sola scriptura*. "Begriff und Vorstellung einer 'Biblischen Theologie' konnten nur unter dem reformatorischen Prinzip 'sola scriptura' entstehen. Doch zugleich bricht das angezeigte methodologische Problem auf: Wie verhalten sich bibel-Theologie und Lehrsystem zueinander? Wie und wo kann der Primat der Exegese zur Geltung kommen, ohne dass die Schriftaussagen den Gestaltungskategorien der doctrina verfallen?" (Hans-Joachim Kraus, *Die Biblische Theologie: Ihre Geschichte und Problematik* [Neukirchen-Vluyn:Neukirchener Verlag, 1970], 17–18).

[4]"Man behauptete den höchsten denkbaren Grad der Heiligkeit für die ganze Schrift, ohne Unterscheidung der Testamente" (Ludwig Diestel, *Geschichte des Alten Testamentes in der christlichen Kirche* [Jena: Mauke's Verlag, 1869], 475).

[5]Ibid., 474–534.

[6]"Kein Wunder, wenn daher hier die Bezüge zwischen dem Alten und Neuen Bunde lebhaft und vielseitig erörtert wurden, wenn die Typik vorzugsweise blühte. Sie war die Form, in welcher die ganze Zeit, in ihrer eigenthümlichen Neigung fürs Emblematische (die durch viele Gebiete hindurchgeht), den spröden Stoff des A.T. mit christlicher Wahrheit zu durchdringen suchte . . ." (ibid., 480).

[7]The reflections of the orthodox biblical and theological scholars on the unique problems of the OT was, of course, not carried out within the context of what later was to be known as historical criticism and thus, as Diestel's comment illustrates, has by and large not been appreciated by subsequent biblical schol-

cialized questions dealing with OT theology still remain unresolved, there is a growing appreciation among biblical scholars for the contribution of earlier theologians to
the special problems facing an OT theology today. From our point of view, one chief
value in these earlier works is that they were written in a considerably different theological environment than today. Their basic assumptions about the Bible were, in fact,
very similar to those of the present work, that is, among other things, that Scripture is
God's Word.

During the time that modern OT theology was in its early stages of development, the late eighteenth century, the process of developing and shaping the historical-critical method was well underway. In most cases, consequently, the formation of
theological method was indistinguishable from that of historical criticism.[8] The question of the inspiration of Scripture is a case in point. For most biblical theologians by
the end of the eighteenth century, it was considered impossible to approach the Bible
critically and still retain the notion that the text itself was inspired.[9] This was true even
of many otherwise conservative biblical scholars and theologians.[10] Consequently, the
contribution of earlier biblical scholars who had held to the belief that the Scriptures
were inspired often either went unnoticed or became a foil for the development of new
historical methodology.[11] In the present work we will devote our attention not only to
the theologies of the last two centuries, but also to the earlier theologians who
addressed the problem of the theology of the OT within the context of a commitment
to inspired Scripture.

---

arship, ". . . das Ganze ein Beleg für die bizarre Combinationsgabe und den ungeschichtlichen Sinn der
Orthodoxie, atheistis larga ridendi occasio, meinte Thomasius" (ibid., 477).

[8]"Dass der Durchbruch zum historisch-kritischen Schriftverständnis ein Ereignis von tief ein-
schneidender Bedeutung gewesen ist, hinter das eine wissenschaftlich arbeitende Theologie nicht mehr
zurückkann, wird heutzutage in der Regel anerkannt" (Gottfried Hornig, *Die Anfänge der historisch-kritischen Theologie* [Göttingen: Vandenhoeck & Ruprecht, 1961], 37).

[9]"Der Ring des orthodoxen Schriftprinzips, der in der 'Critica sacra' und in der gesamten Spä-
torthodoxie bis zum äussersten Grad der Dehnbarkeit geweitet worden war, konnte die Erkenntnisse der
'Critica profana' nicht mehr umschliessen; er wurde zersprengt. Zwar versuchen es bis zur Mitte des 18.
Jahrhunderts einige Gelehrte, unter ihnen vor allem Johann David Michaelis, den zerberstenden Ring des
Inspirationsdogmas zu flicken und zu erhalten, aber es gelingt ihnen nicht. Johann Salomo Semler vollen-
det die Zerstörung des geltenden Schriftdogmas und sucht neue Grundlagen einer protestantischen
Bibeltheologie" (Kraus, *Geschichte*, 93).

[10]Stephan Holthaus, *Fundamentalismus in Deutschland, Der Kampf um die Bibel im Protestantismus
des 19. und 20. Jahrhunderts* (Bonn: Verlag für Kultur und Wissenschaft, 1993), 140–44.

[11]"Semlers Kritik war gegen die Fundamente der gesamten orthodoxen Theologie gerichtet, und
Semler hat sie an einem zentralen Punkt der orthodoxen Dogmatik bis ins einzelne durchgeführt, nämlich
an der Schriftlehre" (Hornig, *Die Anfänge*), 59.

THREE

TEXT OR EVENT

2.2. TEXT OR EVENT (+/- TEXT)

The methodological question we turn to first is that of defining the immediate object or focus of the study of OT theology. Simply put, the question is: Does an OT theology focus its attention on the scriptural text of the OT itself, or is the text primarily a witness to the act of God's self-revelation in the events recorded by Scripture? This is the component we will call *Text or Event*.

Such a choice represents an increasingly important option in OT theology today and has been an important part of biblical theology in the past.[1] When we approach the OT, do we understand it, as a text, to be God's revelation to us today? Or are the OT Scriptures more appropriately understood as a witness to God's acts of revelation in the historical events recorded in the OT? This latter view was ably represented by the OT theologian George E. Wright: "Biblical theology is *the confessional recital of the redemptive acts of God* in a particular history, because history is the chief medium of revelation. . . . The Bible thus is not primarily the Word of God, but the record of the Acts of God, together with the human response thereto."[2]

Hans W. Frei has been particularly helpful in uncovering the importance of this component. Frei has argued that the history of biblical interpretation can be understood by classifying scholars into at least three groups: those who have focused on the text of Scripture as the locus of meaning in biblical narrative (pre-critical); those who focus on external historical events as the locus of meaning (empirical); and those who focus on the "ideas" embodied by and referenced in the biblical text (idealistic). In Frei's terms, a "pre-critical" understanding of Scripture characterized the older Protestant reading that saw in the biblical narratives a coherent world in its own right that had a reality of its own and into which the biblical interpreters had to fit their own lives.[3] According to Frei, such a way of reading biblical narratives largely passed from the

---

[1]Hans W. Frei, *The Eclipse of Biblical Narrative* (New Haven: Yale University Press, 1974), is a thorough treatment of this subject.

[2]George E. Wright, *God Who Acts, Biblical Theology as Recital* (London: SCM Press, 1962), 13 (italics added) and 107.

[3]Frei, *The Eclipse*, 90.

scene with the rise of historical criticism. It was replaced by the empiricists' and idealists' positions. Thus the meaning of Scripture came to be identified with either the historical events referred to by the biblical narratives (empiricism) or the concepts to which those narratives referred (idealism).[4]

The chart in Figure 3.1 shows the three realms of meaning that have been commonly identified in biblical narrative.

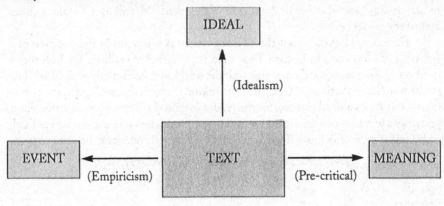

Figure 3.1

Frei's categories are helpful if we allow for the continuing validity of the pre-critical understanding of narrative. The pre-critical view is, in fact, virtually the same as that of modern evangelicalism. The OT narratives record real historical events that provide the framework for the early history of the world and of humanity, and it is precisely that history that envelops the history of the New Testament, the church, and the modern world. Moreover, it is that history that will culminate in the return of Christ. In this sense, real history is that history recorded in the text of Scripture and that text is the focal point of divine revelation.

The importance of making this point in the present study lies in the fact that, as we will see, evangelical OT theologians have not always been clear on the issue raised by this set of questions. We will maintain in the following discussion that while professing to be text-centered in their approach, evangelical biblical theologians sometimes treat the text of Scripture as a means of getting at what they perceive to be the *real* locus of God's revelation—the events in the history of Israel or the religious ideals that lie behind the text. In doing so they fail to appreciate the implications of their own orthodox view of Scripture as divine revelation.

---

[4]The idealist Christian Wolff "had in effect equated meaning with the transconceptual essence or possible reality to which a concept and word refer. . . . To understand anything is to know its possible reality or essence; the sense of a statement is its reference. Locke and his followers had similarly held a theory of meaning-as-reference. But to the extent that for Locke ideas were those of sensation (rather than reflection, the only other 'idea' one can have), they refer to substances or space-time occurrences and not to 'real essences' and whatever stood behind them. His theory was one of ostensive reference. Wolff's theory of meaning-as-reference, on the other hand, is ideal. The reality to which a concept or a word refers is the ideality or possibility underlying either an actual thing or a general truth" (Frei, *The Eclipse*, 101).

The charts in Figures 3.2 and 3.3 show the differences between an OT theology that takes its point of origin from the biblical events (Fig. 3.2) and one that is based on the biblical text (Fig. 3.3).

Where does God's special revelation lie for us today? Is it the text of Scripture or the events referred to in the text? If we look at the OT Scriptures themselves for the answer, we find that they are ambivalent. They present evidence to us that suggests revelation was located either in the text or in the event. We will have to take a closer look at the evidence.

For example, throughout the OT, the reader is often put in the position of a spectator of God's acts in history. That is, in the very act of reading, one becomes a third-party observer of God's dealings with the world, and particularly with Israel. The reader watches the actions of God and humankind through the medium of the narrative text. It is possible, therefore, for the reader to gain the impression that the text is primarily a window into the sacred events he or she reads about in the text where God, on his initiative, reveals himself to humanity. One can easily overlook the obvious point

Where is the locus of revelation for OT theology today?

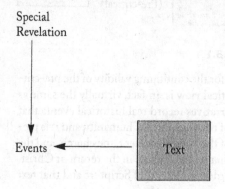

Special Revelation

a. The text is revelation insofar as it gives an accurate access to the event.

b. The text is a *witness* to revelation in the event.

c. The text is a *window* into revelation in the event.

Figure 3.2

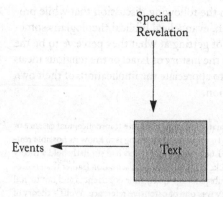

Special Revelation

a. The text is the *source* of divine revelation.

b. The text is a *depiction* of the event, not the event itself.

Figure 3.3

that in reading one is, in fact, looking at words on a page. One is not actually present on the scene of the real-life events. As Iser puts it, "It is in this way that the reader experiences the text as a living event. . . . The experience of the text as an event is an essential correlative of the text. . . ."[5] Consequently, the OT can be read as if it were merely the means of knowing about God's sacred acts, and the events themselves were the real arena of divine revelation.

What we are really saying is that the Bible does its job of recounting events so well that the chain of historical events it depicts in its narratives, rather than their depiction, becomes the proper object of study in OT theology. In reading, the text as such is not the focus of the reader's attention. The reader focuses on the events recorded as if they were the real thing right before one's eyes. One is thus led to focus on a holy history (*Heilsgeschichte*) behind the text in place of a holy history within Scripture itself.

On further reflection into the nature of the OT narratives, however, we find that the impression that the text is no more than a window into the event is incorrect, or at least inadequate. The reader's apparent position as a third-party spectator of God's acts can be compared to that of an audience in a theater. Though the audience may look like a mere spectator, its relationship to a play or film is really quite different. In actual fact, the play or film in the theater is directed precisely and only at the audience. It is not produced for the sake of the actors, but for the audience. The play or film addresses the audience by putting the events before their eyes. In the same way, biblical narrative texts address their readers by means of the events they depict. They narrate events for the reader. The events depicted in the narratives are part of the fabric of the text which has its own specific message to present to the readers. The recounting of events in the narrative is not intended to direct the readers' attention outside the text but rather within the text and to the narrative world depicted there. The reader, as audience, is to understand the meaning of the events through the author's development of the plot structure and characterization of the narrative. Thus divine revelation may be thought of as lying within the narrative text of Scripture as a function of the meaning of the events in their depiction.

While biblical theologians have generally faced this question with a clear awareness of the issue, evangelicals as a rule have not always appreciated the nature of the problem.[6] The unique feature of evangelical theology lies in its view of Scripture as the inspired Word of God, a belief not held by modern biblical theology. Thus when the issue of revelation in history and in Scripture is cast in terms general enough to

---

[5]". . .it arises out of the manner in which the strategies disrupt consistency-building, and by thus opening the potential range and interaction of *gestalten*, it enables the reader to dwell in the living world into which he has transmuted the text. . . . What this really means, though, is that as we read, we react to what we ourselves have produced and it is this mode of reaction that, in fact, enables us to experience the text as an actual event. We do not grasp it like an empirical object; nor do we comprehend it like a predicative fact; it owes its presence in our minds to our own reactions, and it is these that make us animate the meaning of the text as a reality" (Wolfgang Iser, *The Act of Reading* [Baltimore: Johns Hopkins University Press, 1978], 128–29).

[6]For a discussion of this issue as it relates to evangelical theology, see John H. Sailhamer, *The Pentateuch as Narrative* (Grand Rapids: Zondervan, 1992), 7–22.

include Bultmann, von Rad, and Pannenberg, as is usually the case in evangelical discussions of this issue, it is easy to overlook the specific problem it poses for the evangelical's belief in an inspired text. Recognizing the importance of the inspired text of Scripture, evangelicals want to affirm that a theology of the OT should look to the text itself as its source. However, wanting also to affirm the importance of history and God's actions in real events, they, for good reason, do not want to relinquish the importance of actual historical events.[7] Consequently, the inclination of evangelical theologians has been to attempt to retain both options. They want a theology based both on revelation in the events themselves and revelation in Scripture. We will attempt to show that this has led to considerable confusion in evangelical approaches to OT theology.

By way of illustration we may point to the example of Colin Brown, who has argued for just such an approach to revelation in history in his essay "History and the Believer." In his opening remarks, Brown makes it clear that he belongs to that group of evangelical theologians "who believe that a Christian view of revelation must embrace revelation in history (both biblical and universal history), revelation through the Word of God and revelation in ongoing human experience."[8] He argues, for example, that "it would be equally wrong to treat history and language as mutually exclusive media of revelation. One of the great theological needs today is for a coherent account of revelation as it occurs in the Word, history, nature and experience."[9] Moreover, Brown says, "There is a second and kindred danger to which Christians are prone in speaking of Scripture as the Word of God. That is to confine revelation merely to the verbatim pronouncements of the text."[10]

---

[7]"Heilsgeschichtliches Denken bewahrt vor geschichtsloser Bibelbetrachtung und gottloser Geschichtsbetrachtung" (Helge Stadelmann, *Grundlinien eines bibeltreuen Schriftverständnisses* [Wuppertal: R. Brockhaus Verlag, 1985], 123). The central concern of Stadelmann for the question of the historicity of the biblical texts is apparent in his foreword to papers presented at the 4th Theologischen Studienkonferenz des Arbeitskreises für Evangelikale Theologie (AfeT), at Albrecht-Bengel-Haus, Tübingen: "Die Frage nach dem rechten Verständnis von Glaube und Geschichte ist eine Schicksalsfrage der Theologie in unserem Jahrhundert. Hat Gott konkret in der Geschichte gehandelt? Kann die Theologie glaubwürdig von 'den grossen Taten Gottes' reden—oder hat sie es vielmehr mit Gemeindetheologien, Wortgeschehen und geschichtslosem Kerygma zu tun? ... Geht es bei der biblischen Rede von Gottes Offenbarung in Raum und Zeit um historische Realitäten—oder nur den Entwurf einer Glaubens-'Geschichte'?" (*Glaube und Geschichte, Heilsgeschichte als Thema der Theologie*, ed. Helge Stadelmann [Wuppertal: R. Brockhaus Verlag, 1986], vii).

[8]Colin Brown, "History and the Believer," *History, Criticism & Faith* (Downers Grove: InterVarsity, 1976), 185. As this statement suggests, Brown is dependent on both Pannenberg and Barth in his formulation of the question. Brown has embraced Pannenberg's notion of revelation in biblical history (*Heilsgeschichte*) and universal history (*Weltgeschichte*). From Barth, Brown has taken the concept of the Word of God, complete with the notion of the Living Word (Jesus), Written Word (Scripture), and the Preached Word (Christian proclamation). Brown is also quite clear throughout the essay that his concept of revelation includes Kierkegaard's *incognito Dei*, ". . .not all such situations [in history and individual experience] are revelatory at the time. . . . There is in life a kind of divine incognito which may cease to be incognito only in retrospect. In making this point we are brought back to the point made early on in the discussion of Kierkegaard, that from one point of view historical events can be described in secular terms, but from another point of view the same events can be seen in relation to God" (ibid., 195).

[9]Ibid., 193.

[10]Ibid., 194.

One can see in Brown's statements a counteroffensive to Karl Barth's denial of natural revelation. Nevertheless, in making his case for natural revelation, Brown goes far beyond that to build a case that the Bible encourages the Christian to look for divine revelation not only in God's handiwork in nature (Ps 19; Ro 1; Ac 14 and 17) but also in human experience. "There is a sense in which for [the biblical writers] the whole of life and reality is sacramental. Natural events and human actions, while still remaining natural events and human actions, point beyond themselves and have a significance that is wider than the dimensions of time and space. In so doing, they bring God right into the midst of life."[11] Brown thus links a biblically sanctioned natural revelation with revelation in universal history, something which the Bible does not speak to.

> My contention is that all experience (and with it, of course, history) is in principle capable of being revelatory. This is not to say that we see the significance of it at the time or even that we shall necessarily come to see the revelatory significance of any particular event. Rather, it is to say that events are in principle capable of being understood at the three levels of significance just noted: at the levels of nature, of man and of God. It is on this last level that revelation, in the Christian sense, takes place. When we see the significance of an event as disclosing something about our relationship with God, and with each other in relation to God, revelation takes place.[12]

In the subsequent and final section of the essay, Brown argues persuasively for the apologetic importance of history to the believer and, in my judgment, rightly contends that the truth of the Christian religion rests on the historical veracity of the Christian stories. "If an event such as the exodus is seen as a paradigm of God's care for his people, the comfort and hope that the believer is exhorted to draw from it are surely ill-founded if there is no corresponding historical base. Similarly, the Christian hope for the future and his view of the shape of history are grounded in the historicity of the resurrection of Jesus."[13] We are not contending with this aspect of Brown's focus on history and revelation. We are suggesting, however, that this emphasis of Brown on the apologetic importance of history as the basis of divine revelation is quite a different matter than his earlier emphasis on history as the *source* of divine revelation.

In attempting to hold to a theology based both on revelation in historical events and revelation in Scripture, evangelicals like Brown have sometimes failed to appreciate the nature of a more subtle problem. As important as the question of the historicity of God's redemptive acts is, there is no reason why it should cause us to adopt an event-oriented understanding of revelation. While it is true that modern theologians such as Bultmann and von Rad have rejected the idea of revelation in history in favor of a revelation in the confessional statements of Scripture, it is also true that these theologians do not hold to a belief

---

[11]Ibid., 195. Brown finds biblical support for divine revelation in human actions from Matthew 25:40, the judgment of the nations by the Son of Man: "Truly, I say to you, as you did it to one of the least of these my brethren, you did it to me." He goes on to argue that "this last passage suggests that not all such situations are revelatory at the time. For the righteous may well be unaware of what they were doing. And similarly the unrighteous protests that they never saw the Son of man in these situations" (ibid.).

[12]Ibid., 196.

[13]Ibid., 198.

in the inspiration of Scripture. The problem with the modern biblical theologians' emphasis on the "Word of God" as the source of revelation over against historical events is that they do not identify the "Word" with Scripture and they do not take Scripture to be historically true. Thus the choice, for the evangelical, is not between revelation in Scripture and an historically-based faith. Evangelicals should and do affirm the absolute importance of both. Neither is the question, for the evangelical, whether God has acted in history or whether the Bible is historically true. The evangelical view of Scripture also affirms both of these points. The historical basis of biblical faith is of fundamental importance and will be discussed in the next section. The issue we are attempting to raise here is simply that of our commitment to an inspired *written* Word of God as the locus of God's special revelation. For the Christian today we must again raise the question: Where does the locus of God's special revelation lie? Does it lie in the meaning of historical events provided by the Scriptures or does it lie in the meaning we ourselves attach to the events of Israel's history? We will argue that both Scripture itself and the classical formulations of the doctrine of Scripture in the church lay the stress on the *written Word of God* as the locus of special revelation.

In 2 Timothy 3:16 Paul writes, "All scripture is inspired by God." In calling Scripture "inspired," Paul gives it the highest claim to authority. It is specifically "Scripture" that Paul points to as the locus of God's revelation. We should add that it was the OT that Paul was primarily referring to in this passage as Scripture. Moreover, in 2 Peter 1:20–21, Peter says, "First of all you must understand this, that no prophecy of scripture is a matter of one's own interpretation, because no prophecy ever came by the impulse of man, but men moved by the Holy Spirit spoke from God." Passages such as these in the NT have been primarily responsible for the classical identification of Scripture (*sacra scriptura*) and God's Word (*verbum dei*) in Protestant theology.[14]

Although such an understanding of the nature of Scripture cannot claim universal acceptance among modern theologians,[15] it remains the hallmark of those theologians who call themselves evangelical.[16]

---

[14]"Zu den Grundsätzen der orthodoxen Schriftlehre gehört seit der Frühorthodoxie die Identitätsthese, welche die Schriftwerdung des Wortes Gottes in dem Sinne bestimmt, dass Wort Gottes und Heilige Schrift identisch sind" (Hornig, *Die Anfänge*, 45). "Unicum Theologiae principium est Verbum Dei in Scripturis sacris propositum" (Johann Gerhard, *De Scriptura sacra* [Geneva, 1639], 1); "Scriptura S. est verbum Dei immediato Spiritus S. afflatu per Prophetas in Veteri, Evangelistas et Apostolos in N. Testam. literarum monumentis consignatum ad aeternam hominum salutem" (Calov, *Systema locorum theologicorum*, I:448), "God, taking pity on the human race, was pleased to commit his word to writing (*Deus generis humani misertus, Verbum suum literis mandari voluit*)" (Benedict Pictet, *Theologia Christiana Ex puris S. S. Literarum Fontibus hausta* [Langerak, 1723], 16–17).

[15]"An keinem Punkt der Dogmatik hat Semler und die ihm folgende historisch-kritische Aufklärungstheologie des 18. Jahrhunderts so radikal mit den orthodoxen Traditionen gebrochen wie hinsichtlich der Schriftlehre. . . . In übereinstimmung mit der reformatorischen Auffassung bekennen sie sich zur Heiligen Schrift als der alleinigen Offenbarungsquelle" (Hornig, *Die Anfänge*, 40–41).

[16]"Durch die Lehre von der Verbalinspirationslehre, die man durch den Hinweis auf 2 Tim. 3, 16 und andere Schriftstellen zu begründen sucht, wird behauptet, dass sowohl die alttestamentlichen wie die neutestamentlichen Schriften in ihrem Wortlaut göttlich inspiriert seien und deshalb als unfehlbar betrachtet werden müssten. Der Begriff der Inspiration oder Theopneustie hat im Rahmen der orthodoxen Schriftlehre eine ganz bestimmte Bedeutung. Er bezeichnet den besonderen Akt, durch welchen Gott, als der Autor der Heiligen Schrift, sein Wort den Propheten und Aposteln mitteilte und sie gleichzeitig dazu antrieb, dasselbe niederzuschreiben. Diese Offenbarung Gottes, welche auf dem Wege der Inspiration

2.2.1. The Old Testament Is a Text

To say, with Paul, that the Old Testament is Scripture, is to acknowledge that it is written. It is a book or, rather, a collection of books. From a linguistic perspective we can say that the Old Testament is a text.[17] As a text the Old Testament has certain properties that distinguish it from non-texts. For example, texts are made of words, phrases, clauses, sentences, paragraphs, and the like; that is, texts are composed of language. They are structured utterances. They represent the work of an author.

A commitment to an understanding of the Old Testament as Scripture, then, implies an exegetical method and biblical theology that is a direct function of the meaning of a text. It means that exegesis and theology must ask: How does a text have meaning? One must seek to discover the way in which the authors of Scripture have construed their words, phrases, clauses, and the like, into whole texts. With the same effort and care with which we pore over the smallest archaeological artifact because of its importance for history, we must pore over every word and letter in the OT because of its importance for theology.

Over the years those who have held most faithfully to the orthodox identification of Scripture and God's Word have not always appreciated the nature of the narrative texts they identified as divine revelation. In terms of modern linguistics, we could say they had no clear "text theory."[18] Before going any further, therefore, it is important to have clearly in mind what a narrative text is. We often take it for granted that we know what a text is, and for the most part, we do. We have had enough experience with various kinds of texts to recognize one when we see it. It is helpful, however, to review some of the basic features that make up a text, if for no other reason than that it may help us take them more seriously in the process of reading the Bible.

By its very nature a narrative text is something that does not project itself on us as such. When reading a text we are not constantly reminded of the fact that we are looking at words on a page, just as in watching a movie we are rarely conscious of looking at light on a screen. The function of a narrative text is to be a vehicle for telling a historical story. As such, biblical narrative texts rarely self-consciously reflect back on themselves. Even when a text ostensibly does, as in Deuteronomy 31:24 (author's translation), "And it came about when Moses finished writing the words of this law upon a book, completely," it serves only to conceal the fact that we are reading the very text that Moses has just finished writing. The statement that Moses

---

erfolgt, geschieht nach orthodoxer Auffassung in der Absicht, das Wort Gottes in seiner ursprünglichen und authentischen Gestalt unverfälscht und unverändert an kommende Generationen weiterzugeben" (Hornig, *Die Anfänge*, 41).

[17]According to Dressler and de Beaugrande, a text is "a COMMUNICATIVE OCCURRENCE which meets seven standards of TEXTUALITY," that is, (1) cohesion, (2) coherence, (3) intentionality, (4) acceptability, (5) informativity, (6) situationality, and (7) intertextuality (Robert-Alain de Beaugrande and Wolfgang Ulrich Dressler, *Introduction to Text Linguistics* [London: Longman, 1981], 3).

[18]"Eine Texttheorie wird nach diesen Erläuterungen gesehen als die umfassende Rahmentheorie für die Bestimmung von Text-Kontext-Relationen in kommunikativen Handlungsspielen . . ." (Siegfried J. Schmidt, *Texttheorie, Probleme einer Linguistik der sprachlichen Kommunikation*, 2nd ed. [München: Wilhelm Fink Verlag, 1976], iv).

finished writing the book "completely," shows that the author of the Pentateuch wants us to understand this as a reference to the completion of the entire Pentateuch, *including verses 24ff.* Thus, within the Pentateuch itself, we are allowed to read about the completion of the Pentateuch. It will not do to argue that the book which Moses has just finished is an earlier edition of the Pentateuch. We can see that from 31:22, where the text says, "In that day, Moses wrote this song." Since the "song" referred to in this verse can only be that found later, in Deuteronomy 32:1–43, it is apparent that the author already has the whole of the Pentateuch in mind. An important part of becoming a sensitive reader is developing an awareness of the biblical narratives as texts. No matter how self-evident the following characteristics may seem, it is not uncommon to find one or more of them overlooked in the process of reading and interpreting biblical narrative.

2.2.1.1. The Old Testament Text Is a Written Document

Though it is possible to understand the nature of a text in terms larger than merely a written document,[19] our primary interest is in Scripture, the written Word, and thus we can safely stay within such a limited definition.[20]

The first requirement of a text is that it be written and that it can be read. That is, a text is composed of a written language, biblical Hebrew in our case. Meir Sternberg has put it well when he speaks of a text as a "web of words."[21]

Two important implications of this basic feature of a text should be noted. First, since it is composed of language, a text must follow the rules of the language in which it is written. The author of a text is not free to do or say what he or she pleases when composing a text. One cannot invent new rules of grammar and add new words to the lexicon. If it is to be understood, the biblical text must be composed within the constraints of Hebrew vocabulary, grammar, and syntax. Such things are the "given" part of the text. They are the "raw material" with which the author must work. They form the common ground between the author of a text and the readers, thus ensuring the possibility of the text's being understood.

By the same token, a reader is not free to do or say whatever he or she pleases about the meaning of a text. The reader must understand the text in terms dictated by

---

[19]The science of semiology is the study of all forms of texts, written and unwritten sign systems. Cf. Roland Barthes, *Elements of Semiology*, trans. Annette Lavers and Colin Smith (New York: Hill and Wang, 1967 [orig. 1964]): "Semiology therefore aims to take in any system of signs, whatever their substance and limits; images, gestures, musical sounds, objects, and the complex associations of all these, which form the content of ritual, convention or public entertainment: these constitute, if not language, at least systems of signification" (9). Ferdinand de Saussure's *Course in General Linguistics*, trans. Wade Baskin (New York: Philosophical Library, 1959 [orig. 1915]), was the first to propose the study of sign systems within human culture (16).

[20]Much insight can be gained from the study of "non-written" texts and sign-systems in general. As a guide to understanding biblical texts, however, it seems best to limit the range of our terms to that which corresponds directly to biblical texts, namely, *written* texts.

[21]Meir Sternberg, *The Poetics of Biblical Narrative, Ideological Literature and the Drama of Reading* (Bloomington: Indiana University Press, 1985).

the grammatical and syntactical constraints of the language in which it is written. The same is to be said for translations of the Bible. The importance of this point is not difficult to appreciate. The reader of biblical narrative texts cannot dispense with the necessity to pay close attention to the grammar, syntax, and lexicography of Hebrew (or English, in the case of a translation). While it is true that reading a biblical text is more than merely a grammatical, syntactical, and lexical study of the Hebrew Bible or translation, it is certainly not anything less than that.

The second implication of the statement that a text is a written document, though not as immediately self-evident as the first, is nevertheless just as important. It has to do with the fact that biblical narrative texts consistently render a realistic depiction of the world. As far as the reader is concerned, the world of historical events (*res gestae*)[22] in the Bible comes mediated through the "textual world" (*verba*).[23] The biblical text gives the reader an account of those historical events. The reader, as a reader, stands always before the text (*textus*). Thus the world that one stands before *as a reader* is never more than a *representation* of the "real world." In the case of the Bible, the text is a true representation and an accurate representation.[24] However, no matter how true or how accurate the text is, the accuracy of the Scriptures should not be allowed to obscure the fact that the text is, in fact, a representation of those actual events.

A photograph of a tree is a good example of the distinction between a text and the event depicted in it. A photograph is a representation of a tree. It represents the tree accurately and realistically, yet it does not have bark and leaves, nor is the sky behind the tree in the photograph a real sky. Nevertheless the actual bark and leaves of the real tree are represented in the photograph and so is the real sky. We can readily understand the fact that the whole of the photograph is a representation of its subject matter, which in this case is a real tree.

To say that a photograph only represents the tree but is not actually the tree, does not mean that the tree never existed or that the photograph is inaccurate because it only shows one side of the tree. The same can be said of the biblical narrative texts. To

---

[22]Though he does not develop the historical question of the status of the *res*, Augustine (354–430) defined the central terms of Christian biblical hermeneutics. The "things" (*res*) are those bits of *realia* that are in themselves without meaning. "Words" (*verba*), however, are bits of *realia* that always signify and hence are always meaningful. For Augustine, some "things" could also signify (*De Doctrina Christiana*, Book I: *Things* [Turnholt, Brepols, 1962], 7). Thomas Aquinas based his hermeneutics on Augustine's notion of *res* and *verba*, "Auctor sacrae scripturae est deus, in cujus potestate est, ut non solum voces ad significandum accommodet, quod etiam homo facere potest, sed etiam res ipsas" (Summa Theol. I.10).

[23]M. Sekine, "Vom Verstehen der Heilsgeschichte Das Grundproblem der alttestamentlichen Theologie," *ZAW,* 75 (1963): 145–54.

[24]An important corollary of the orthodox, hence evangelical, view of inspiration is the understanding that the biblical narratives render a true and accurate picture of reality: "Die orthodoxe Verbalinspirations-lehre zwingt dazu, die Schriftautorität als einen objektiven und rein formalen Tatbestand zu behaupten, weil vorausgesetzt wird, dass alle Schriftaussagen—und zwar ganz unabhängig von ihrem Inhalt und ihrer Beziehung zum Heilswerk Jesu Christi—als göttlich inspiriert und unfehlbar zu betrachten sind. Demgemäss ist es nicht nur zulässig, sondern erforderlich, die Bibel in dem Sinne als eine Quelle zu betrachten, dass alle ihre geschichtlichen Aussagen, wie z.B. die Schöpfungsberichte, mit der historischen Wirklichkeit übereinstimmen" (Hornig, *Die Anfänge*, 44–45).

say that they represent real events but are not those events themselves, merely recognizes a very obvious fact about historical texts.[25] As readers of these texts we stand before them as their authors have construed them and we look to the texts themselves for our understanding of the "world" they depict.

The history of art offers an interesting example of the distinction between the representation of reality and the real world itself. In the early part of this century, there was a well-known still life painting of a man's pipe. Just under the pipe the artist had painted the words, "This is a pipe." The painting was so well done that it could easily have been mistaken for a photograph. This very fact, however, created a strong reaction to the painting among the artist community, particularly the Dadaists and Surrealists, who had long struggled with the question of the purpose of art. The task of the artist, they felt, was the expression of reality and the statement of truth. Yet, did a work of art such as the painting of a pipe mean that art needed only to reproduce an image of the real world? If so, then the painting of the pipe could just as well have been a photograph. Since a simple camera could produce a near perfect image and anyone could use a camera, the invention of the camera threatened to replace not only art but also the artist.

In response to the painting of the pipe, the surrealist painter Rene Magritte painted an exact replica of the painting of the pipe. The only difference between Magritte's painting and the original painting was that on his painting Magritte wrote the words "This is *not* a pipe." He had made his point. A painting of a pipe, however realistic its representation, was *not* a pipe. Magritte had shown that the artist still had a role in the expression of truth that the camera could never replace. When later asked about the painting, Magritte said, "The famous pipe. How people reproached me for it! And yet, could you smoke my pipe? No, it's just a representation, is it not? So if I had written on my picture 'This is a pipe,' I would have been lying!"[26]

2.2.1.2. The Old Testament Text Represents an Author's Intention

Thus far our description of a text has focused on elements of the written document itself. But it is also necessary to look beyond the document to its author to get a complete picture of what a text is. Texts do not originate out of thin air. Texts have authors—real persons who write with a sense in mind of what the text is about. Biblical texts are no exception, whatever one's view is of inspiration and revelation.[27] A text

---

[25]The question raised here is not that of the accuracy of the depiction in the "textual world." That question should rather be raised in the context of the relationship between the reader and the real world. Though the importance of that question cannot be overlooked, it is a question of the *historical accuracy* of the biblical narratives and as such belongs to the task of apologetics. That question should not be allowed to cloud the issue at hand, which is that the biblical narratives present themselves to their readers as *representations* of the real world.

[26]Harry Torczyner, *Magritte: The True Art of Painting* (New York: Harry N. Abrams, Inc., 1979), 85.

[27]There was considerable variation in the understanding of the role of the human authors of Scripture among early Protestant scholars. **Johann Gottlob Carpzov:** "Quare nec iis accedimus, qui ex traditione πατροπαραδότωι ea, quorum ipse pars non fuit, hausisse Mosen et in literas redegisse credunt. Quamvis enim nonnulla de his, quae tradidit in Genesi, habare potuerit ab Amramo patre suo, qui proavo Jacobo per tempus aliquod coaevus eundem, uti Jacobus Abrahamum, et hujus pater Thara Noam audire potuit, cujus pater Lamech LVI. annos cum Adamo transegit, quibus *Patribus Deus mandaverat, opera sua nota facere fil-*

is thus an embodiment of an author's intention, that is a strategy designed to carry out that intention.[28]

2.2.1.3. The Old Testament Text Has a Communication Situation

One of the developments of recent text theory is the emergence of the idea that a text is a system of signs that can be understood as an act of communication and thus implies a communication situation.[29] A typical communication situation consists of a speaker who transmits information[30] to a hearer via a shared mode of communication or sign system:

Speaker   ------->   Sign System   ------->   Hearer

Seen within such a context, a text can be understood as the sign system bearing the information in an act of communication. Thus, if we replace the general notion of information in the diagram above with the specific idea of a text and put the author and reader in the place of speaker and hearer, we can construct the following diagram to show the role of a text within a communication situation:

Author   ------->   Text   ------->   Reader

iis; ut cognoscat generatio altera, Ps. LXXVIII, 5. Gen. XVIII, 19. rectius tamen soli θεοπνευστίαι omnia tribuimus, absque qua fuisset, tot temporum, locorum personarum, nominum praesertim et genaealogiarum circumstantias, nulla hominum memoria complecti facile, aut absque lapsus et erroris periculo suppeditare potuisset" (*Introductio ad Libros Canonicos Bibliorum Veteris Testamenti Omnes* [Leipzig: Lanckisian, 1757 [orig. 1714–21]), 62–63); **Johann Henrich Heidegger**: "non ex mera utique traditione (quanquam ex traditione Majorum, utpote quartus a Jacobo, neque adeo remotus ab iis temporibus, quibus Adamus ipse superstes fuit, plurima haurire potuit) sed ex Divina praecipue inspiratione, absque qua fuisset, tot temporum, locorum, personarum, circumstantias, genealogiarum differentias, aliaquie ejusmodi non cognovisset. Fuit igitur, sicut et reliqui Scriptores Sacri, παρηκολουθηκὼς ἄνωθεν πᾶσιν ἀκριβῶς, assectus omnia coelitus accurate. Luc. I. 3." (Enchiridion Biblicum Iermnhmonikon [Jena: Bielckium, 1723], 18); **Campegius Vitringa**: "Mosem collegisse, digessisse, ornasse et ubi deficiebant, complesse et ex iis priorem librorum suorum confecisse" (Observationum Sacrarum Libri VI, 1683–1708).

[28]Closely akin to the notion of intentionality in texts is that which de Beaugrande and Dressler call "acceptability," that is, the notion that the reader's own cooperation in receiving a text as a cohesive and coherent unit plays a major role in textuality. "People can and do use texts which, for various motives, do not seem fully cohesive and coherent. We should therefore include the attitudes of text users among the standards of textuality. A language configuration must be **intended** to be a text and **accepted** as such in order to be utilized in communicative interaction. These attitudes involve some tolerance toward disturbances of cohesion or coherence, as long as the purposeful nature of the communication is upheld" (Robert-Alain de Beaugrande and Wolfgang Ulrich Dressler, *Introduction to Text Linguistics* [London: Longman, 1981], 113). Already in the first work on Protestant hermeneutics there is the recognition of the need for acceptability in overcoming the *causae difficultatis sacrarum literarum*, "Saepissume enim sit, ut vel verba, vel constructio, seu forma orationis, vel denique etiam sententiae aut res, si ad Latinum morem examinentur, parum respondeant praecedentibus: aut plane non adsint; sed tantum intelligi debeant" (*Clavis Scripturae seu de Sermone Sacrarum Literarum* [Leipzig, 1695 (orig. 1567)], 3).

[29]Schmidt, *Texttheorie*.

[30]The term *information* is used here in a very general sense. It stands for any "message" which the speaker intends to transmit to the hearer. The use of the term does not mean to suggest that only "information" in a quantitative sense is transmitted in texts.

On the basis of the diagram above, it is possible to formulate a view of a text as a written linguistic communication between an author and a reader.[31]

Viewing a text within such a model of communication acts enables us to understand various features of a text in terms familiar from other acts of communication in everyday life. In other words, the features of a text, which are primarily linguistic, can be related to familiar functions in ordinary conversations. For example, in an ordinary conversation a speaker often has to adjust his or her words to what he or she perceives to be the level of understanding and comprehension of the hearer. One gains clues from the hearer's immediate response (feedback) to what one has said. The hearer may interrupt the speaker to ask a question of clarification or may simply have a puzzled look. In any case, the speaker can pick up such feedback and adjust the information accordingly. The message is, then, constantly being adjusted to suit the new level of "information awareness" of the hearer.

In a text, however, the author does not have access to such immediate responses of the actual readers. Rather, the author must *anticipate* the reader's questions and construct the text in such a way that responses which a reader is likely to have will be satisfied as the text is read or reread.

An example of a textual device for interacting with a reader is *repetition*. In a conversation, a speaker is often asked to repeat or restate what he or she has said. This serves not only the purpose of memory, but also it helps to clarify ideas and correlate them with other ideas developed within a speech act. In a text, such repetitions often become an essential part of an author's strategy. In reading the biblical text, repetitions are helpful guides to the purpose and intention of the author.

2.2.1.4. The Old Testament Text Has a Literary Form

It is not difficult to see a difference between the kind of literature that makes up the biblical narratives and that which is found, for example, in the book of Psalms. Whatever terms we may use to distinguish the two types of texts, the important point is that there is a recognizable difference between them. Compare, for example, the "literary types" represented in the selections below from Genesis 1 and Psalms 33.

> *Genesis 1:1–3* In the beginning God created the heavens and the earth. Now the earth was formless and empty, darkness was over the surface of the deep, and the Spirit of God was hovering over the waters. And God said, "Let there be light," and there was light. (NIV)

> *Psalm 33:6* By the word of the LORD were the heavens made, their starry host by the breath of his mouth. (NIV)

The two texts clearly differ. The differences are not in the subject matter, since both texts speak of God's creation of the universe, but rather in the *way* the two texts present their subject matter. Genesis 1 sets out to tell a story, a history of Israel's beginnings. The author recounts events from the past in a straightforward, realistic manner

---

[31]More technically, we can say that through a text, a deficiency of information between the two communication partners, the author and the reader, is overcome. See Robert Oberforcher, *Die Flutprologe als kompositions-schlüssel der biblischen Urgeschichte* (Tyrolia, 1981).

as they happened in the real world. Such a literary type is akin to that used in everyday language, in newspapers, books, and conversation.

In the psalm, on the other hand, we can recognize a different literary type. One does not need to be an expert in poetic analysis to recognize that Psalm 33:6 is different from the narrative of Genesis 1 and that it is a kind of poetry. We recognize it as such because, like most poetry we are familiar with, it is written in distinguishable lines, having a sense of proportion and rhythm. Our understanding may stop there, but nearly everyone can sense a difference between the two literary types at this level. Our ability to distinguish these two types is part of what makes us literate readers. Certainly not everyone has the same degree of literary sensitivity, but one would not get very far in understanding texts without at least a rudimentary ability to distinguish between these two basic types.

One of the assumptions of the present study is that along with the ability to distinguish basic literary types, readers as a rule also possess the ability to respond appropriately to the various types. When a reader recognizes a text as a narrative or story, he or she is able to draw on a reservoir of expectations that has been acquired through reading other stories. These expectations give one a sense of what to look for in a story and what a story may be setting out to do. To a great extent one's enjoyment and appreciation of a story stem from the expectations brought to the story in the process of reading it. The same is true of poetry. Such expectations are by and large acquired through reading and hearing stories or poems, and thus they vary greatly among individuals. Those who are well-read have a greater, more refined reservoir of expectations. Knowing what to expect, they often come away from a story with a greater understanding and appreciation than one who has little idea of what stories are about.

Historical narrative is a convenient label for a general category or type of literature found in the Hebrew Bible. It is the literary type representative of the large stretches of texts that range from the book of Genesis through the book of Kings. There are also smaller narrative works such as the books of Ruth, Esther, and Jonah, as well as the *framework* for many other books of the Bible, for example, the prologue and epilogue to the book of Job.[32] The nearly equivalent term in English is *prose*, though the usual connotations of that term do not do full justice to this type of biblical literature. In order to maintain the similarity between historical narrative in biblical texts and the notion of prose in English, we can propose a preliminary definition of historical narrative as "a prose-like literature that seeks to render a *realistic* picture of the world."

Such a preliminary definition focuses on one of the most characteristic features of narrative, namely its attempt to mimic the real world, that is, to reproduce the real world in linguistic terms. In the study of narrative texts, it is easy to overlook this essential characteristic of historical narrative by simply taking it for granted. In going about the task of exegesis, however, it is helpful to pay particularly close attention to this feature of narra-

---

[32]In Job the historical narrative texts are a kind of "shelving" on which is laid the poetic discourses that make up the body of the work. The same is true for many of the prophetic books. The poetic discourses of the prophets are arranged within the framework of an historical narrative. This same procedure can be found within the Pentateuch, where the large blocks of "legal" discourses are set within the very thinly-built narratives of the "wilderness wanderings."

tive. The biblical writers did not necessarily want their narrative depictions of reality to be noticed as such. They were aiming at our reading their narratives as versions of the events themselves and to a great extent they succeeded. Nevertheless, it is important to keep an eye on the text and its own particular way of representing the great acts of God in history.

A biblical narrative text takes the raw material of language and shapes it into a version of the world of empirical reality. Its essentially *linguistic* structures[33] are adapted to conform to events in real life.[34] The constraints that shape real life (e.g., the limitations of time, space, and perspective) are the constraints that historical narrative texts must strive to conform to in their imitation of real life. The more conformity a text shows to such real-life constraints, the more realistic the historical narrative will prove to be. Events and characters are put before the reader as happening just as they happen in real life. The reader looks at the events in the narrative in much the same way as he or she would look on events in real life. They happen in the text before one's eyes. As Benveniste put it, "The events are chronologically recorded as they appear on the horizon of the story. . . . The events seem to tell themselves."[35]

The chart in Figure 3.4 illustrates the relationships at play in historical narrative texts.

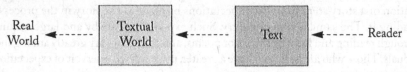

Figure 3.4

As the diagram in Figure 3.4 shows, in historical narrative, the text bears an important relationship to the real world that it depicts. It must conform to the requirements of that real world. If, for example, in the real world depicted in the text, birds fly and fish swim, so also in the narrative, birds will fly and fish will swim. In such an historical narrative, however, a fish would not fly. That would not conform to the way things are in the real world.

The diagram in Figure 3.4 also shows that as a narrative, the text bears an important relationship to the reader. It must be written in a language that is known to the reader

---

[33]What is meant here is the simple fact that languages have their own sets of rules by which they operate. In learning to use a language, one must master such rules in the form of a grammar and syntax. There may be some general rules that all or most languages follow, but for the most part each specific language has its own unique set. Historical narrative texts written in classical Hebrew, then, must follow the rules of grammar and syntax that govern that language.

[34]"Since biblical narrative is a *reproduction* of the real world, its 'narrative world' is a *facsimile* of that world and thus follows the rules of the real world. Consequently, elements that assure 'breaks' or segmentation in the 'narrative world' are the same as those that exist in real life" (John H. Sailhamer, "A Database Approach to the Analysis of Hebrew Narrative," *MAARAV*, 5–6 [Spring, 1990]: 328). Examples of such linguistic features in Hebrew are forms such as WAYYIQTOL ckauses, that provide the effect of sequence in time, and φ + X + QATAL clauses that break into time.

[35]Emile Benveniste, quoted by Hayden White, "The Value of Narrativity in the Representation of Reality," *Critical Inquiry* (1980): 7.

and follow the normal rules of that language. Moreover, if the author expects the text to be understood by the general reader, the author will represent the text as the central focus of the reader—that is, the author will not assume that the reader will be looking elsewhere for the information it intends to transmit. While it is possible for authors to do this sort of thing and virtually abandon their readers, narrative texts are known for their steady supply of information to the reader regarding the events they are depicting. Biblical narratives, in particular, are noticeably reader conscious. One rarely has the impression in reading them of being left alone. The authors have their way of guiding the reader along, even though in most cases the reader is unaware of their presence. An example of a reader-conscious remark in the narrative is Genesis 26:1, "Now there was a famine in the land—besides the earlier famine of Abraham's time—and Isaac went to Abimelech king of the Philistines. . . ." To avoid an apparent misreading of the narrative, the explanation is given the reader that this was not the same famine as in the earlier chapter of Genesis.

Still another important relationship exists within a historical narrative that is shown in the diagram in Figure 3.5

Though the reader approaches the real world through a text, if it is an historical narrative, the real world also exists independently of the text as its subject matter. In other words, historical narratives make "ostensive reference"[36] to the real world outside the text itself. As important as the text is for our purposes here, we should not overlook the fact that it is only one of the several avenues through which the reader may gain information about the real world that lies outside the text. In making this point, however, it should be clear that other avenues through which information can be rightly gained about the real world events beyond the text (e.g. history, archaeology, sociology, and sociolinguistics) are, in fact, not a part of the text and are not controlled by the author of the text. Whatever may be said about the world behind the narratives, it should not be identified with that which is depicted in the text itself. The text is a version of the events it depicts. It should not be taken as their replacement.[37]

We have briefly discussed the essential nature of narrative texts and have distinguished them from their subject matter, historical events in time and space. We will now attempt to describe more carefully the nature of those historical events themselves. Our primary purpose will be to clarify the point made earlier in this chapter, that events are quite different kinds of things than texts.

2.2.2. The Old Testament Is About Events

Put simply, an event is something that happens in time and space. It is an occurrence. A history is an accumulation of connected events. The word *history*, however, is ambiguous. We will see in the next section that the term *history* can be used to denote

---

[36]"Ostensive reference" is "the spatiotemporal occurrence or state of affairs to which it (the text) refers" (Frei, *Eclipse*, 79).

[37]". . .the passion which may excite us in reading a novel is not that of a 'vision' (in actual fact, we do not 'see' anything). Rather it is that of meaning, that of a higher order of relation which also has its emotions, its hopes, its dangers, its triumphs" (Roland Barthes, *Image Music Text*, trans. Stephen Heath [New York: Hill and Wang, 1977], 124).

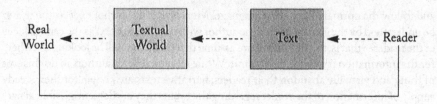

Figure 3.5

not only a flow of events in time and space, but also the written record of the flow of events. Thus the term *event* is a more precise way of speaking about history when we want to distinguish it from a written record (text) about history.

The study of historical events is as old as the earliest human civilizations. In most early attempts to uncover the past, historians relied heavily on tradition, accounts handed down from earlier ages. Modern historiography not only relies on tradition but has also developed more sophisticated tools for reconstructing the way things were. Its primary procedure is to reconstruct past events by means of three basic principles: causality, correlation, and analogy.[38]

The principles of causality and correlation start with the assumption that every historical event is best understood as the result (causality) of a series (correlation) of earlier events. The historian can understand an event from the past by attempting to describe what caused an event or the series of events in which it occurred. Various factors or causes have been suggested for the general flow of historical events. Some have suggested that human events are determined by invariable laws, such as economic determinism.[39] The specifically Christian view of historical events is that they are determined ultimately by God's providence.[40] This is not the place to discuss the mer-

---

[38]"Kraft des Analogieprinzips urteilt er über wahrscheinlich oder unwahrscheinlich. Kraft de Prinzips der Korrelation ordnet er die geschichtlichen Begebenheiten in den Zusammenhang alles geschichtlichen Geschehens ein, 'wo keine Veränderung an einem Punkte eintreten kann ohne vorausgegangene und folgende Aenderung an einem anderen, so dass alles Geschehen in einem beständigen korrelativen Zusammenhange steht und notwendig einen Fluss bilden muss, in dem Alles und Jedes zusammenhängt und jeder Vorgang in Relation zu anderen steht' (a.a.)., 108/109" (Peter Stuhlmacher, *Vom Verstehen des Neuen Testaments, Eine Hermeneutik* [Göttingen: Vandenhoeck & Ruprecht, 1979], 22–24); *Historical Criticism and Theological Interpretation of Scripture*, trans. Roy A. Harrisville [Philadelphia: Fortress Press, 1977]; Ernst Troeltsch, *Ueber historische und dogmatische Methode in der Theologie, Gesammelte Schriften* (Aalen, 1962), 2:729–53; Gerhard Maier, *Biblische Hermeneutik* (Wuppertal: R. Brockhaus, 1990), 24.

[39]E.g., Karl Marx, *Das Kapital*, "in which all history is absorbed into an economic process moving toward a final world revolution and world renovation" (Karl Löwith, *Meaning in History* [Chicago: University of Chicago Press, 1949], 33).

[40]"Mundum non creavit Deus, ut per se ac sua ipsius virtute, manu Dei subducta, subsisteret: quod somniavit Taurellus. sed eum perpetuo fert" (Johann Coccejus, *De Providentia Dei, etiam circa mala, Summa Theologiae ex Scripturis repetita, Opera Omnia* [Amsterdam 1701], 2:217); "Respondeo dicendum, quod auctor sacrae Scripturae est Deus, in cujus potestate est, ut non solum voces ad significandum accommodet (quod etiam homo facere potest) sed etiam res ipsas" (Thomas Aquinas, *Summa Theologica* [Rome: Forzan, 1894], 25).

its of one view of history over another. Whatever one's particular view, it is agreed that human events are interrelated and that they can be understood best by describing the nature of their causal inter-dependence.

The principle of analogy, on the other hand, is the code by which the historian draws up a description of a past event. According to this principle, the set of causes used to describe past events must be similar to or analogous to causes of events in the present. We should not expect human affairs to have been any different in the past than they are in the present.

In relationship to biblical studies, Peter Stuhlmacher has objected to the exclusive use of the principles of causality, correlation, and analogy on the grounds that they automatically rule out our appreciation for a unique event in history and narrow our focus to only those aspects of history that fit our schemata.[41] These principles were used by biblical critics, for example, to rule out the miraculous events recorded in the Bible. They argued that since the category of miracle is not used in writing modern history, it should not be used in describing events from the past. The resolution of this problem goes far beyond our purposes here.[42] However the question is decided for exegesis, the fact remains that these principles are indispensable for the historian as a tool for reconstructing the past.[43]

This brings us to the events recorded in the OT. If we are to understand these events we will certainly need to employ the tools of causality and analogy. An evangelical approach to the events recorded in the OT almost surely would employ not only the notion of God's providence in explaining the causes of the biblical events, but also knowledge of the events gained from ancient records and archaeology. In doing so we would simply be following the lead of the biblical writers whose purpose was to show the hand of God in all the affairs of humanity. Secondly, an evangelical approach, as in classical orthodoxy, would not hesitate to use the principle of analogy. To be sure, one would not rule out the possibility of miracles, for the past or the present; nevertheless, there is no reason why we would not also seek an explanation for biblical events in the reconstructions of modern archaeologists and historians who used analogy in their reconstructions.

Enough has been said to show the nature of historical events and the procedures for understanding them. What should by now be clear is that events (*res gestae*)[44] are

---

[41]"Wir gewinnen kraft des zusätzlichen Prinzips des Vernehmens die Möglichkeit zurück, Neues und Analogieloses in der Geschichte zu entdecken, neben den grossen religiösen Einzelnen auch wieder die geschichtliche Bedeutung von sozialen Gemeinschaften zu würdigen und die uns zur Gewohnheit gewordenen kausalen Korrelationsschemata durch neue Erkenntnisse aufzuweiten und zu korrigieren" (Peter Stuhlmacher, *Vom Verstehen*, 220).

[42]Cf. Gerhard Maier, *Biblische Hermeneutik* (Wuppertal: R. Brockhaus, 1990), 432?–347: "Da eine biblisch-historische Auslegung von ihrer Wurzel her die Analogielosigkeit der Begegnung mit dem lebendigen Gott betont, kann sie die Analogie nicht mehr als Wahrheitskriterium gebrauchen" (345). Colin Brown, *History, Criticism & Faith* (Downers Grove: InterVarsity, 1976): (173). "So then we must look for analogies between our present understanding of history and the data we are examining. But we must be careful not to overpress them and reject that which does not fit."

[43]"To comprehend history, we need to make use of whatever techniques are appropriate for the historian; but history itself and the reality it contains must determine our techniques and modify our presuppositions" (Brown, *History, Criticism & Faith*, 177).

[44]"One science differs from another in that it finds out things of a different kind. What kind of things does history find out? I answer, *res gestae*: actions of human beings that have been done in the past. Although

quite different kinds of things than texts. We have seen this from the side of texts, which are written documents (a "web of words") *about* events as well as from the side of events, which are single acts or series of actions in a "web of causes and effects." As Troeltsch has put it, "All events stand in a continuous network of correlations and thus necessarily make up a sort of stream in which each and everything is interrelated and each process stands in some relationship to others."[45]

2.2.3. Revelation in Scripture (Text) and in History (Event)

How has God revealed himself in the Bible? Has God revealed himself only in Scripture, or has he also revealed himself in history? The texts of the OT are historical narratives, and hence are about events in the real world.[46] In speaking of historical narrative, important distinctions have to be maintained in the use of the term *history*. It is not enough to say with Hans Frei that the biblical narratives are only "history-like" and to relegate them to the level of "realistic narrative."[47] Although much has yet to be investigated regarding the categories of history and fictionality,[48] it can be said with reasonable certainty that the authors of the biblical narratives intended to write history and not fiction.[49] Their aim, they imply throughout, is to record what actually happened in human history. Gunkel's description of the purpose behind the creation narrative in Genesis 1 gives a helpful insight into the historical interest of the author of the final version of the Pentateuch:

> He is not a poet who attempts to comprehend the material in a living way and to describe it visually, but rather he is a scientific person who desires to penetrate to the very nature of the thing itself and who wants to divide the whole of the data into classes and reflect on the various characteristics of the classes. Even though these classes may appear to us quite simple, nevertheless they reflect the work of a real scientific spirit—one could even say a kind of rationalistic spirit.[50]

---

this answer raises all kinds of further questions many of which are controversial, still, however they may be answered, the answers do not discredit the proposition that history is the science of *res gestae*, the attempt to answer questions about human actions done in the past" (R. G. Collingwood, *The Idea of History* [London: Oxford University Press, 1946], 9).

[45]"So dass alles Geschehen in einem beständigen korrelativen Zusammenhange steht und notwendig einen Fluss bilden muss, in dem Alles und Jedes zusammenhängt und jeder Vorgang in Relation zu anderen steht'" (Ernst Troeltsch, *Ueber historische*, quoted by Peter Stuhlmacher, *Vom Verstehen des Neuen Testaments*, 23).

[46]See John Sailhamer, "Exegetical Notes, Genesis 1:1–2:4a," *Trin J* (1984): 73–82.

[47]Hans W. Frei, *The Eclipse of Biblical Narrative: A Study in Eighteenth and Nineteenth Century Hermeneutics* (New Haven: Yale University Press, 1974), 10.

[48]Manfred Oeming, "Bedeutung und Funktionen von 'Fiktionen' in der alttestamentlichen Geschichtsschreibung," *EvT* (1984): 254–66; Siegfried J. Schmidt, "Towards a Pragmatic Interpretation of Fictionality," in *Pragmatics of Language and Literature*, T. A. van Dijk (1976), 161–78; Sternberg, *Poetics*, 23–35; Hayden White, "The Value of Narrativity in the Representation of Reality," *Critical Inquiry*, 7 (1980): 5–27.

[49]"Hence the Bible's determination to sanctify and compel literal belief in the past. It claims not just the status of history but, as Erich Auerbach rightly maintains, of *the* history—the one and only truth that, like God himself, brooks no rival." Meir Sternberg, *The Poetics of Biblical Narrative* (Bloomington: Indiana University Press, 1985), 32.

[50]Hermann Gunkel, *Genesis übersetzt und erklärt* (Göttingen: Vandenhoeck & Ruprecht, 1977), 117.

It can also be said today with confidence that there is reasonable evidence that the biblical narratives recount reliable historical events. John Bright, for example, says,

> When the traditions are examined in the light of the evidence, the first assertion to be made is that already suggested, namely, that the stories of the patriarchs fit authentically in the milieu of the second millennium, specifically in that of the centuries sketched in the preceding chapter, far better than in that of any later period. The evidence is so massive and many-sided that we cannot begin to review it all. . . . Of course, nothing that has been said constitutes *proof* that the patriarchal narratives rest on traditions reaching back to the early second millennium. But the evidence, taken as a whole, certainly shows that they fit well in the circumstances of that age and fortifies our confidence that they preserve an old and tenacious historical memory.[51]

The point we are here attempting to raise is that in ordinary language the term *history* itself can have two very different meanings. On the one hand history can refer to the kind of text we suppose the biblical narratives to be, namely, nonfiction texts that intend to recount actual events from the past.[52] On the other hand, history can refer to the actual events from the past. In this sense the term refers to that which the biblical texts are about, that is, events in the real world (*res gestae*).[53] As Lonergan has said, "This word, history, is employed in two senses. There is history (1) that is written about, and there is history (2) that is written. History (2) aims at expressing knowledge of history (1)."[54]

This distinction is of some importance when attempting to develop an approach to the OT that is either text-oriented or event-oriented. We should recognize that in only one of the above senses does history actually refer to a text, that is, the recording of past events. In the other sense, history refers not to a text but to actual events (*res gestae*) in the real world. This distinction becomes important in using the expression "revelation in history." Which of the above senses is given to history in such formulas? Does one mean "revelation in history" as a revelation in a text or revelation in events (*res gestae*)?[55]

---

[51]John Bright, *A History of Israel*, 3d ed. (Philadelphia: Westminster, 1981), 77–83. Though more skeptical than Bright on the patriarchal material, Donner holds that "für die Geschichte Israels nach der Staatenbildung, also im 1. Jt. v. Chr., ist die Quellenlage günstig, auf manche Strecken sehr günstig" (Herbert Donner, *Geschichte des Volkes Israel und siner Nachbarn in Grundzügen* [Göttingen: Vandenhoeck & Ruprecht, 1984], 22). For an excellent treatment of the question of the historical value of the earliest biblical traditions see Kenneth A. Kitchen, *The Bible in its World* (Downers Grove: InterVarsity, 1978), 59–74.

[52]"Historians nowadays think that history should be (a) a science, or an answering of question; (b) concerned with human actions in the past; (c) pursued by interpretations of evidence; and (d) for the sake of human self-knowledge" (R. G. Collingwood, *The Idea of History* [London: Oxford University Press, 1946], 10–11).

[53]"What kind of things does history find out? I answer, *res gestae*: actions of human beings that have been done in the past" (ibid., 9).

[54]Bernard Lonergan, *Method in Theology* (New York: The Seabury Press, 1972), 175.

[55]As we have stressed earlier, the issue being raised here is not the question of whether a text is historically accurate. In both senses of the term *history* the accuracy of the text is without question. Fictionalized history or historical fiction, both legitimate literary categories, are not here in view. Both categories are anachronistic when applied to the biblical narratives. One cannot overemphasize the importance of the apologetic task of demonstrating the accuracy of Scripture, but that is no reason to push the hermeneutical

In the present work we are attempting to describe an approach to OT theology that is text-oriented. A text-oriented approach to the OT would insist that the locus of God's special revelation is in the Scriptures themselves, that is, in the text. Certainly there would be no reason to discount the fact that God has made known his will in other ways at other times. But, given the theological priority of an inspired text (2 Ti 3:16), one must see in the text of Scripture itself the locus of God's revelation today. The centrality of the written word in revelation has been forcefully stated by Packer:

> But what the claim that revelation is essentially verbal does imply is that no historical event, as such, can make God known to anyone unless God Himself discloses its meaning and place in His plan. . . . No event is self-interpreting at this level. The Exodus, for instance, was only one of many tribal migrations that history knows (cf. Amos 9:7); Calvary was only one of many Roman executions. Whoever could have guessed the unique saving significance of these events, had not God Himself spoken to tell us? All history is, in one sense, God's deed, but none of it reveals Him except in so far as He Himself talks to us about it. God's revelation is not through deeds without words (a dumb charade!) any more than it is through words without deeds; but it is through deeds which He speaks to interpret, or, putting it more biblically, through words which His deeds confirm and fulfill. The fact we must face is that if there is no verbal revelation, there is no revelation at all, not even in the life, death, and resurrection of Jesus of Nazareth.[56]

Thus, on the question of God's revelation in history, the sense of history in a text-oriented approach would be that of the record of past events. The history in which God makes known his will is the history which is recorded in the inspired text of Scripture. When formulated this way, evangelical biblical theology can be seen to be based on a revelation that consists of the meaning of a text with its focus on Scripture as a written document. Even the formula "revelation in history" is then a question of the meaning of a text.

Evangelical biblical scholars have not always been clear on this point. While they might hold to a view of Scripture as the locus of God's revelation, they have a tendency to interpret the formula "revelation in history" in such a way that the term *history* refers not to the text of Scripture but rather to the past events themselves. In other words, the locus of revelation is taken to lie not in the text of Scripture but in the events witnessed by the text. In such an approach the events lying behind the text of Scripture are read as a salvation history within which God makes known his will.

The distinction, though subtle, is a real one. The effect of overlooking the text of Scripture in favor of a focus on the events of Israel's history can often be a "biblical" theology that is little more than a philosophy of history, an exegetical method that is set on expounding the meaning of the events lying behind Scripture rather than those depicted in Scripture itself. Packer gives a helpful example of such an approach:

> Thus, for instance, George Every writes of Herbert Kelly: "In his own reflections on the Old Testament Father Kelly had a way of going directly to the event, without even notic-

---

question of the meaning of the text aside. Both questions are of utmost importance.

[56]J. I. Packer, *God Speaks to Man, Revelation and the Bible* (Philadelphia: Westminster, 1965), 51–52.

ing the interpretation given by the prophet or the prophetic historian" (H. Kelly, *The Gospel of God* [London, 1959 ed.], 34). In this Kelly was showing himself less a prophet to our time than a child of it. D. B. Knox comments: "It will be seen that if revelation is in the event rather than in the interpretation, revelation becomes like a nose of wax to be reshaped according to every man's whim" ("Propositional Revelation the Only Revelation," *Reformed Theological Review* 19 [February 1960]: 1:5).[57]

Meir Sternberg has aptly described such an approach:

> The theologian, qua theologian, dreams of piecing together a full picture of ancient Israelite religion, mutations and conflicts included. The historian wants to know what happened in Israelite history, the linguist what the language system (phonology, grammar, semantics) underlying the Bible was like. And the geneticist concentrates on the real-life processes that generated and shaped the biblical text.[58]

Even when one clearly has in view the goal to be biblical in the textual sense of the term, that is, to get at the meaning of the text of Scripture, it is all too easy to blur the boundaries between the text and the event and to handle the text as if one were in fact dealing with the event represented in the text. The effect of such a treatment of the text is to overlook its author's inspired interpretation of the event and to attempt to find one's own interpretation. Therein lies a fundamental threat among evangelicals to a genuine scripturally-based theology.[59]

According to the evangelical view of Scripture, the biblical message has been encoded in a text. Insofar as we say that this text is inspired and thus is the locus of God's revelation, then the meaning or content of that revelation is of the nature of the meaning of a text. To say that the text is an accurate portrayal of what actually happened is an important part of the evangelical view of Scripture, but it does not alter the fact that God's revelation has come to us through an inspired text, and thus no amount of delving into the history of Israel as an event apart from the text can take the place of the meaning of the text of Scripture. To quote Sternberg once more, our task is to understand

> the text itself as a pattern of meaning and effect. What does this piece of language— metaphor, epigram, dialogue, tale, cycle, book—signify in context? What are the rules governing the transaction between storyteller or poet and reader? . . . What image of a world does the narrative project? Why does it unfold the action in this particular order and from this particular viewpoint? What is the part played by the omission, redundan-

---

[57]Packer, *God Speaks to Man*, 53.

[58]Sternberg, *Poetics*, 15.

[59]The evangelical view of Scripture is in no way held by all Christians today. Many theologians today would reject the notion that the Bible is divine revelation. Emanuel Hirsch points to the influence of Sigmund Jakob Baumgarten at the University of Halle in the mid-eighteenth century as the decisive turning point from a view of Scripture as revelation to a view of Scripture as a record of a revelation in events, "All and all it may well be said that with Baumgarten German Protestant theology entered the decisive stage in its transition from a Bible-faith to that of a revelation-faith in which the Bible in reality is nothing more than a document of revelation given at a specific moment in time" (*Geschichte der Neuern Evangelischen Theologie im Zusammenhang mit den allgemeinen Bewegungen des europäischen Denkens* [Gütersloh: Bertelsmann, 1949], 2:378).

cies, ambiguities, alternations between scene and summary or elevated and colloquial language? How does the work hang together?[60]

It may be helpful to give an example of where it appears evangelical biblical scholarship has failed to see as clearly as it should this aspect of its commitment to an inspired text of Scripture and has looked beyond the text of Scripture in its exegesis to expound on the events behind the text. The most obvious example is that of the salvation-history school, an approach to biblical studies that was thoroughly evangelical in its origins[61] and continues to play an important role in evangelical theology. According to Helge Stadelmann,

> the Bible is the literary record of the revelation of God in salvation-history. It did not come into existence monolithically as a whole compendium of dogmatics. It, rather, documents for us the historical dealings of God with his people through the centuries and makes transparent for us the revelation-history of God through the ages from Creation to the last days. It is on the basis of this revelatory-history, that is, salvation-history that an appropriate exegesis is to be founded.[62]

It cannot be said that everyone taking a salvation-history approach to the OT necessarily overlooks the message of Scripture in favor of the meaning of events. From the beginning, however, that tendency can be seen within their writings.

Two prominent salvation-history (*Heilsgeschichte*) theologians in the nineteenth century were Richard Rothe[63] and J. Chr. K. von Hofmann.[64] Rothe's formulation of the problem of revelation and history laid the fundamental groundwork in the nineteenth century not only for biblical theology in general but also for evangelical theology in particular. Hofmann made the approach of Rothe more palatable for conservative theologians.

In Rothe's day the orthodox view of Scripture as God's divine Word had generally been replaced by the view that Scripture was both God's Word and man's word, that is, the human and divine Word of God. The evangelical version of this formula drew an analogy between Scripture and the two natures of Christ. Just as Christ, the living Word, was both human and divine, so also the Scriptures, the written Word,

---

[60]Sternberg, *Poetics*, 15.

[61]Hans-Joachim Kraus, *Die Biblische Theologie: Ihre Geschichte und Problematik* (Neukirchener, 1970), 240.

[62]"Die Bibel ist der literarische Niederschlag der Offenbarung Gottes in der Heilsgeschichte. Sie is nicht monolithisch in einem Nu als dogmatisches Kompendium entstanden, sondern dokumentiert uns das geschichtliche Handeln Gottes mit seinem Volk durch die Jahrhunderte und lässt uns die Offenbarungsgeschichte Gottes durch die Zeitalter von der Schöpfung bis zur Vollendung transparent werden. Auf diese offenbarungs- bzw. heilsgeschichtliche Dimension hat sich sachgemässes Exegese einzustellen" (Helge Stadelmann, *Grundlinien eines bibeltreue Schriftverständisses* [Wuppertal: R. Brockhaus Verlag, 1985], 122); *Epochen der Heilsgeschichte, Beiträge zur förderung heilsgeschichtlicher Theologie*, ed. Helge Stadelmann (Wuppertal: R. Brockhaus Verlag, 1984); *Glaube und Geschichte, Heilsgeschichte als Thema der Theologie*, ed. Helge Stadelmann (Giessen: Brunnen Verlag, 1986).

[63]Richard Rothe, *Zur Dogmatik* (Gotha, 1863).

[64]J. Chr. K. von Hofmann, *Weissagung und Erfüllung im alten und im neuen Testamente* (Nördlingen: C. H. Beck Buchhandlung, 1841).

were human and divine.[65] Rothe, however, felt obliged to reject this understanding of Scripture as essentially unhistorical and thus he rejected the classical notion of verbal inspiration:

> However attractive at first glance this formula might appear, I regret that I cannot accept it . . . because it prohibits us from viewing the Bible from a natural perspective and puts it in a totally unique category. . . . Such an exalted and privileged position in which one may desire to give it much acclaim in actual fact serves only to lessen its worth because it brings its reality into disrepute. I therefore will say quite openly and respectfully that I give up the thesis that the Bible is inspired. . . .[66]

On this reckoning, the Scriptures as divine revelation were reduced to being a record (*Urkunde*) about (*über*) divine revelation.[67] Rothe, in keeping with the mood of his day set by Schleiermacher, had put religious subjectivity at the center of the Christian's religious life—a place previously occupied by Scripture.[68] The difference in the approach of Rothe, however, was that for him there was a real,[69] historical act of God behind the religious subjectivity:

> Because, according to its primitive causality, the redemptive act of God could not be merely an act of natural humanity, it must be thought of as a *creative* act, thus as the absolute (i.e., *creative*) establishment of a new beginning of the human race—however as a creative establishment of a new beginning of the human race placed *within the old natural humanity*. If the new creative beginning was *not* established in the old natural humanity itself, we would have to reject the notion of any continuity in the historical development of humanity and forfeit the unity of this humanity.[70]

---

[65]"Unter denjenigen unserer heutigen Theologen, welche die Unmöglichkeit, jene alten Anschauungen [der Kirchenväter, Luthers usw.] aufrecht zu erhalten, empfinden, ist est ziemlich allgemein Sitte geworden, um den richtigen Gesichtspunkt für die Betrachtung der Heiligen Schrift zu bezeichnen, dieselbe ein gottmenschliches Werk zu nennen und zu fordern, dass man in ihr eine göttliche und eine menschliche Seite unterscheide . . ." (Richard Rothe, *Theol. studien und Kritiken* [Gotha, 1860], 262–79, quoted by Christiano Pesch, *De Inspiratione Sacrae Scripturae* [Freiburg: Herder, 1906], 233.

[66]"Ich bedaure, dass ich mir diese Formel, soviel Bestechendes sie auch auf den ersten Anblick hat, nicht anzueignen vermag. . . . Denn durch sie wird die Bibel für unsere Betrachtung aus dem natürlichen Gesichtspunkt herausgerückt und unter einen ganz singulären gestellt. . . . Eine solche eximierte und privilegierte Stellung, durch die man sie freilich ehren will, hat sie aber all Ursache zu depreciren; denn sie kann ihrer Wirksamkeit nur zum Nachteil gereichen. So verzichte ich denn auf alle Verhüllungen und gebe offen und ehrlich die These, dass die Bibel inspiriert sei, überhaupt auf . . ." (ibid., 234).

[67]"Das normative Ansehen der Bibel bleibt so völlig ungefährdet. . . . Dasselbe ist ja schon einfach in ihrer Eigenschaft als Urkunde über die göttliche Offenbarung begründet" (ibid., 234).

[68]"Ipse cum Schleiermacher religionis provinciam assignat sensum dependentiae a Deo, simul tamen inculcans se non pantheistam, sed theistam esse. Religio subiectiva supponit revelationem divinam" (ibid., 234).

[69]"Es kommt hiebei nur darauf an, dass uns die Offenbarung an sich selbst, abgesehen von der Bibel, wirklich etwas Reelles ist" (Rothe, *Zur Dogmatik*, 309).

[70]"Diese erlösende That Gottes, weil sie eben ihrer primitiven Causalität nach schlechterdings nicht die eigne That der natürlichen Menschheit sein kann, muss als eine *schöpferische* gedacht werden, also als die *absolute* (d.h. schöpferische) Setzung *eines neuer Anfange des menschlichen Geschlechts*. Aber als Schöpferische Setzung desselben bestimmt *in dem alten natürlichen Geschlecht*. Würde der neue schöferische Anfang *nicht* in der alten natürlichen Menschheit selbst gesetzt, so wäre jede Continuität der

According to Rothe, revelation (*Offenbarung*) was to be understood as God's self-disclosure in supernatural historical events (*die Manifestation Gottes*), "Revelation first and foremost consists in this: God himself entered into ordinary history as an active agent by means of an absolutely clear supernatural event and he presented himself to mankind in such proximity and closeness that it was evident even to those eyes of mankind which had been darkened by sin. This aspect of revelation we wish to call *Manifestation*."[71] Along with the express manifestation of God in real events, Rothe maintained that there was an inner divine enlightenment (*Erleuchtung*) which enabled one to correctly understand the revelation of God in the events. "Over against this manifestation, God must still introduce an inner enlightenment, that is a divine act which immediately gives understanding to the individual who sees the supernatural historical event so that he might correctly understand it. This is what we call *Inspiration*."[72] Revelation is thus the convergence of the manifestation of God's acts in salvation-history and the God-given inspiration to understand them.

According to Rothe, revelation was a gradual process that only reached its completion in Christ, the God-man.[73] In the OT period, the highest grade of divine inspiration is found in the Prophets. In the NT period, only Jesus was inspired, that is, enabled to understand the work of God in history. In Christ, revelation and inspiration converge. One finds absolute divine manifestation (revelation) in the objective acts of Christ and absolute divine inspiration in the subjective awareness of Christ.[74]

In Rothe's understanding of theology, the Scriptures are necessary as the means of preserving the revelatory history for later generations to experience. The Scriptures are not the actual revelation; they are rather the documents that preserve the revelatory history. They present the divine manifestation in the salvation history to the reader so that by divine inspiration the reader can understand it.

> The record of revelation must present to us latecomers the actual experience of the divine revelation and put us in such a position that also now still we are able to have an immediate personal experience of it.[75]

---

geschichtlichen Entwicklung der Menschheit abgerissen und die Einheit dieser letzteren schlechthin aufgehoben" (Rothe, *Zur Dogmatik*, 2.1.41, quoted by Kraus, *Die Biblischer Theologie*, 234).

[71]"Die Offenbarung wird zu allererst darin bestehen: Gott tritt mittels einer unzweideutig übernatürlichen Geschichte selbst als handelnde Person ein in die natürliche Geschichte und stellt sich damit dem Menschen in solche Nähe, dass er auch dem durch die Sünde verdunkelten Auge evident werden kann. Dieses Moment der Offenbarung wollen wir *Manifestation* nennen" (ibid., 235).

[72]"Zur Manifestation muss noch eine innere Erleuchtung durch Gott hinzutreten, eine unmittelbare Hervorbringung von Erkenntnissen im Menschen bei der Aufnahme der äusseren Kundgebung mittels übernatürlicher Geschichtsereignisse zum Behuf ihres richtigen Verständnisses, und sie nennen wir *Inspiration*" (ibid., 235).

[73]Quoted in Philippi, *Kirchliche Glaubenslehre*, vol. 1, 280.

[74]"Und eben deshalb schlägt in ihm die Offenbarung Gottes durch ihn in das reale Menschsein Gottes in ihm um" (*Theol. Stud. und Krit.* [1858], 47, quoted in Pesch, 234).

[75]"Die Offenbarungsurkunde muss uns Spätgebornen die eigene Erlebung der göttlichen Offenbarung vertreten und uns so in den Stand setzen, auch jetzt noch eine unmittelbare persönliche Erfahrung von derselben zu machen. Dies kann sie aber unfehlbar, wenn sie anders wirklich ist, was ihr Name besagt, Urkunde, d.h. eine solche Kunde, die selbst als integrierender Bestandteil der Tatsache mit angehört, welche sie kundmacht" (Kraus, 235; Pesch, 234).

Thus for Rothe the Scriptures are a means to an end—divine revelation—they are not that end itself. Moreover, for him the Scriptures are not inspired. Inspiration is a momentary enlightenment of individuals as they read the Scriptures.[76] The Scriptures are the witness of people who received inspiration as they experienced revelatory history; however, they are not the direct result of this inspiration. The traditional concept of an inspired Scripture, then, must be given up, not merely modified. "In reality," says Rothe, "the notion [of Inspiration] which I am here proposing is totally different than the church's classical doctrine of inspiration and in fact involves the actual renunciation of that doctrine."[77] Moreover, he continues, "I have said here nothing other than that which is the general conviction of our modern 'believing' German theologians, with the one exception that they prefer to express themselves as far as possible in terms of the classical doctrine of Scripture while I, on the other hand, would rather place myself in clear opposition to that doctrine. Moreover, I intentionally want to avoid the appearance of only modifying the classical doctrine of Scripture. . . ."[78]

Thus, for Rothe, the Bible is a merely human work that witnesses to the revelatory history. As such, the Bible is not without error and must be subjected to the discipline of historical criticism in order to extract from it that which is truly historical.

It is just at this point regarding the nature of Scripture that Hofmann's salvation-history approach takes its point of departure from Rothe. Like Rothe, Hofmann held that God had revealed himself in historical events and that Scripture is a witness to those events. Where Hofmann differed from Rothe, however, was the importance Hofmann attached to the idea of the inspiration of Scripture. For Hofmann, God's revelation is to be found both in historical events ("deed revelation," that is, *Tatoffenbarung*) and in Scripture ("word revelation," *Wortoffenbarung*). Scripture is our inspired witness to divine revelation in historical events. For Hofmann, however, inspiration is not limited to Scripture. Some historical events are also inspired:

> Traditionally, the notion of inspiration is taken to refer only to that word of the divine Spirit through which the books of the Holy Scripture came into being. Why, however, has a word with such a diverse meaning been so arbitrarily limited? The Scriptures themselves use the same word for describing the work of God with David when he wrote

---

[76]"Die Kraft der Erleuchtung und Bekehrung ist nicht in dem Worte eingeschlossen, der heilige Geist bleibt immer die letzte Causalität der Bekehrung, das agens principale, für welche das Wort das Organ oder Medium ist" (*Zur Dogmatik*, 295 quoted in Kraus, 235).

[77]"In Wahrheit ist die erörterte und soeben ausdrücklich gebilligte Ansicht etwas toto genere anderes als die kirchliche Inspirationslehre und involviert ganz bestimmt das Aufgeben dieser letzteren" (*Theol. Stud. und Krit.* [1860], 246, quoted by Pesch, 236).

[78]"Was ich gesagt, ist nichts weniger als neu und für die Leser dieser Zeitschrift kaum kontrovers. Ich habe ja hier im wesentlichen nichts anderes ausgesprochen, als was die allgemeine Ueberzeugung unserer modernen 'gläubigen' deutschen Theologen ist, mit dem alleinigen Unterschiede, dass diese es lieben, sich so viel als immer möglich an die alten kirchlich-dogmatischen Lehrbestimmungen und Ausdrucksweisen anzulehnen, während mein Absehen vielmehr grundsätzlich dahingeht, mich mit diesen möglichst klar und reinlich auseinanderzusetzen, und ich geflissentlich dem Schein ausweiche, als handle es sich für mich nur um eine modifizierende Fortbildung der traditionellen Lehrformeln unserer kirchlichen Theologie und nicht um wirklich neue Gestaltungen der theologischen Lehre, aber freilich einer durchaus, weil grundsätzlich undogmatischen" (ibid., 237).

prophetic psalms (Matt. 22:43) and when he carried out God's will in his royal office (1 Sam. 16:13). . . . The prophet reflected on something by means of the Spirit, and through the Spirit's work the prophet had a word of knowledge while through the Spirit's work the leaders performed their deeds. . . .[79]

There is, then, for Hofmann, a sort of continuum between inspired historical acts and inspired words recording those acts.[80] The task of biblical theology is the historical investigation and evaluation of both products of divine inspiration—the historical events and the written text. According to Kraus, "the task that now lay before the salvation-history theologians was to investigate and make sense of the historical situation of that which divine inspiration had produced."[81] Kraus points out that, like Rothe, Hofmann viewed Scripture as a kind of historical event embodied in words. One was not, however, thereby given a free hand to interpret the historical event, as was the case with Rothe, because the inspired shape given to the salvation history by the Scriptures worked as a control on the meaning which was drawn from the events.[82] In actual fact, however, Hofmann gave only secondary importance to the scriptural account. Oehler argues, for example, that "Hofmann . . . gives the written revelation little attention when compared with his overriding interest in historical events."[83] The salvation-historical approach, so prevalent in modern evangelicalism, is easily recognizable in Hofmann's biblical theology. One can see Hofmann's influence, for example, in Oehler's OT theology:

> The Old Testament revelation did not present itself simply in words and as a divine testimony concerning doctrine, but was made in a connected course of divine deeds and institutions, and on the basis of these produced a peculiarly shaped religious life. . . . Revelation, then, cannot possibly confine itself to the cognitive side of man. Biblical Theology must be a theology of divine *facts* . . . between the facts or the history of revelation on one side and the testimony of the divine word on the other, a *mutual correspondence* exists.[84]

---

[79]"Im Herkommen nennt man Inspiration nur diejenige Wirkung des göttlichen Geistes, durch welche die Bücher der heiligen Schrift entstanden sind. Wozu aber solche willkührliche Beschränkung eines Worts von weit umfassenderer Bedeutung? Die Schrift selber hat keine andere Bezeichnung für die Gotteswirkung in David, wenn er Psalmen der Weissagung schrieb (Matth. 22, 43), als für diejenige, vermöge welcher er in seinem königlichen Amte Gottes Willen für seine Zeit in Vollzug brachte (1 Sam. 16:13) (p. 26). . . . Durch des Geistes Trieb denkt der Prophet auf etwas, entschliesst sich der Held zu etwas, und durch des Geistes Wirkung gelingt jenem Erkenntniss und Wort, diesem die That . . ." (J. Chr. K. von Hofmann, *Weissagung und Erfüllung im alten und im neuen Testamente* [Nördlinger: C. H. Beck Buchhandlung, 1841], 28).

[80]"It still remained to exhibit the whole course of the Old Testament history of salvation in its organic continuity, and with due regard to the progressive mutual relation between the word of revelation and the events of history. This task was undertaken by J. Chr. K. von Hofmann" (Gustav Friedrich Oehler, *Theologie des Alten Testaments* [Stuttgart: J. F. Steinkopf, 1882]; *Theology of the Old Testament* [Funk & Wagnalls, 1883], 37).

[81]"Die heilsgeschichtliche Theologie hat nun die Aufgabe, die geschichtliche Stellung der Erzeugnisse der Inspiration zu erforschen und zu würdigen" (Kraus, *Die Biblische Theologie*, 250).

[82]Ibid., 250.

[83]Oehler, *Theology of the Old Testament*, 37.

[84]Ibid., 18; see also **Delitzsch:** "Der Herr ist im A.T. im Kommen, im Nahen, in Selbst-ankündigung seiner Erscheinung begriffen, und wir wollen uns in diese alttestamentliche Zeit versetzen und den

The influence of Hofmann's salvation history can also be seen in Kaiser's OT theology. For example, Kaiser argues that the prophets who received divine revelation were also participants "in the very events described in the the text." It was then necessary for them to correlate their revealed word with the events taking place around them and with earlier events in their own historical traditions.[85]

Already in the last century some evangelical theologians sensed the incipient threat that the view of Rothe and Hofmann posed to an evangelical view of Scripture. Benjamin Warfield, for example, raised the question of the meaning and use of the phrase *salvation history*.[86] Warfield argued that at times the notion of salvation history referred merely to the redemptive work of God in history, that is, specific acts of redemption by which God has brought about his promised salvation. Salvation history in this sense is the history of what God has done to effect human salvation and is not revelatory as such. Such a view of God's acts in history has been a common position among historical evangelicalism and was, in fact, the view of Warfield himself. It is in reference to this work of God in history that evangelicals have rightly stressed the importance of the historicity of biblical narratives. Carl F. H. Henry speaks for the evangelical generally when he says, ". . .without factual redemptive history evangelical faith would be null and void."[87] As we have seen,

---

Schritten des Kommenden nachgehen, die Spuren des Nahenden verfolgen, den Schatten, den er auf seinem alttestamentlichen Geschichtswege wirft, aufsuchen und besonders die Fingerzeige der Weissagung auf ihn zu verstehen suchen" (*Messianische Weissagungen in Geschichtlicher Folge* [Leipzig: Akademische Buchhandlung, 1890], 2–30); **Hävernick:** "Das A.T. mit seinem religiösen Inhalte will eine Offenbarung seyn. Es redet durchweg von Offenbarungen Gottes. Diese Offenbarungen sind aber nicht als einzelne oder als eine Summe durch göttliche Geistes-Mittheilung entstandener Lehren oder Befehle zu denken. . . . Es sind auch die Thaten Gottes, seine Wunder, Führungen des Volks mit herein zu nehmen. Es stellt uns ferner die subjektiven Wirkungen dieser Offenbarungen dar z.B. in den Psalmen, in den Thaten Einzelner, ja in der ganzen Existenz des Volkes in ihrer Eigenthümlichkeit. Nach beiden Seiten hin kommen wir also immer auf geschichtlich Thatsächliches zurück, woran sich die Lehre erst anschliesst. . . . Diese Thaten Gottes bilden also eine Einheit, verfolgen ein Ziel: sie bilden die Realisirung des göttlichen Rathschlusses, seines Heilsplans, der Verwirklichung der ganzen vollen Idee eines Reichs Gottes" (Heinr. Andr. Christ. Hävernick, *Vorlesungen über die Theologie des Alten Testaments* [Erlangen: Carl Heyder, 1848], 15–17).

[85]"This quest for a center, a unifying conceptuality, was at the very heart of the concern of the receivers of the divine Word and the original participants in the sequence of events in the OT . . . after all, in many instances they were the actual parties to or participants in these very events described in the text. Significance and correlation of these facts with what they had known or failed to apprehend of all antecedent events or meanings with which this new event might now be connected were much more important. . . . Should an inductive search of the OT record yield a constant pattern of progressive events, with meanings and teachings in which the recipients were made aware of each selected event's participation in a larger whole, then the path of the discipline's progress would have been set. . . . So there was real progress in revelation. . . . More often than not the growth was slow, delayed, or even dormant, only to burst forth after a long period in a new shoot off the main trunk. But such growth, as the writers of Scripture tell it, was always connected to the main trunk: an epigenetic growth, i.e., there was a growth of the record of events, meanings, and teachings as time went on around a fixed core that contributed life to the whole emerging mass" (Walter C. Kaiser, Jr., *Toward an Old Testament Theology* [Grand Rapids: Zondervan, 1978], 6–8).

[86]Benjamin B. Warfield, "The Idea of Revelation and Theories of Revelation," in *Revelation and Inspiration* (Oxford: Oxford University Press, 1927; Grand Rapids: Baker, 1981), 41–48.

[87]Carl F. H. Henry, *God, Revelation and Authority*, II (Waco: Word, 1976), 321; "Ohne ein vorangehendes Ereignis gibt es keinen Glauben" (Gerhard Maier, *Biblische Hermeneutik* [Wuppertal: R. Brockhaus, 1990], 182); "Seit jeher war heilsgeschichtliches Denken der Feind geschichtsloser theologischer Systeme" (Stadelmann, *Gundlinien*, 123).

however, in Warfield's day, and in our own, the notion of salvation history was increasingly understood in the broader context of the *revelation* of the will of God in history. God, through the concrete historical events of salvation history, had made known his will to humanity. This was the view of Richard Rothe, who wrote that

> Revelation consists fundamentally in the "manifestation" of God in the series of redemptive acts, by which God enters into natural history by means of an unambiguously supernatural and peculiarly divine history, and which man is enabled to understand and rightly to interpret by virtue of an inward work of the Divine Spirit.[88]

In this sense salvation-history is revelation history.[89] It is true that when God works in history he inevitably makes himself known, and thus revelation in history is a natural consequence of God's working in history. But God working in history is not the same as God revealing himself in history. In light of the need for further distinction, Warfield argued that the category of revelation alone is not sufficient to deal with the problems raised by the idea of salvation history. In order to show the limits of the revelation that comes from salvation history, Warfield argued, one must fall back on the classical formulation of the idea of inspiration. In the classical view of revelation, Scripture as a written text is more than a mere record of God's revelatory acts. It is itself divine revelation. To quote Warfield:

> Scripture records the direct revelations which God gave to men in days past, so far as those revelations were intended for permanent and universal use. But it is much more than a record of past revelations. It is itself the final revelation of God, completing the whole disclosure of his unfathomable love to lost sinners, the whole proclamation of his purposes of grace, and the whole exhibition of his gracious provisions for the salvation.[90]

Such a view of Scripture in Warfield's own day was regarded as sheer biblicism and continually faced the unjust charge of being merely a "repristination" of the outmoded dictation theory of inspiration.[91] Warfield was, of course, fully aware of the charge and in the face of it and in spite of it he offered his critique of the salvation-history theologians in his day, J. Chr. K. Hofmann, Richard Rothe, and A. B. Bruce. Warfield was not alone in his opposition to the views of Rothe and Hofmann, however. Several noted evangelical theologians had also entered the debate, for example,

---

[88]Richard Rothe, *Zur Dogmatik*, quoted in Warfield, "Idea," 43.

[89]A recent example is Stadelmann's identification of "salvation history" (Heilsgeschichte) and "revelation history" (Offenbarungsgeschichte) (*Grundlinien*, 122).

[90]Warfield, "Idea," 48.

[91]"In Deutschland waren charakteristische Vertreter der repristinatorischen Grundrichtung vor allem Hengstenberg und Philippi. . . . Denn seine [Hengstenberg] Arbeit stand unter der grossen Täuschung, dass er die historische Kritik des vergangenen Jahrhunderts auslöschen und wieder an die altprotestantische Wissenschaft anknüpfen könnte. Die Inspirationslehre war ihm die feste Grundlage aller Theologie. . . . Ja, er [Philippi] übernahm nicht einmal die altprotestantische Inspirationslehre restlos: ihre äusserlich-diktathafte 'Wörterinspiration' ersetzte er durch eine 'Wort-inspiration', in der göttlicher und menschlicher Geist sich allerdings so innig vermählten, dass keine Irrung and Trübung durch Menschliches möglich war; da die kanonischen Schriften zur bleibenden Norm aller Heils- und Wahrheits- erkenntnis bestimmt waren, mussten sie das reine Bild der Gottesoffenbarung darstellen" (Horst Stephan and Martin Schmidt, *Geschichte der evangelischen Theologie in Deutschland seit dem Idealismus*, 3d ed. [Berlin: Walter de Gruyter, 1973], 203–8).

F. A. Philippi,[92] W. Rohnert,[93] Ferdinand Walther, founder of the Lutheran Missouri Synod,[94] and Theodor Klieforth.[95] These theologians were united in their stand against the tendency to reduce Scripture to the role of witness to revelation, rather than the source of revelation. Their uniform position was the defense of the orthodox identification of revelation and Scripture. Rohnert, for example, argued that

> In the Holy Scripture, however, we possess not only the mere records of divine revelation, but also divine revelation itself. The Scripture wants not merely to be an historical monument, a book which renders authentic accounts of divine revelations in the past, but rather it wants to continue the divine revelation through all time right up to the present. It is the prophetic and apostolic proclamation of the divine word of revelation which continues through all time.[96]

Other representative evangelical theologians such as K. F. A. Kahnis, Friedrich A. G. Tholuck, and E. Ernst Luthardt[97] had moved significantly away from the orthodox notion that revelation rests in the written words of Scripture, largely under the influence of the prevailing interest in *Heilsgeschichte*. Kahnis, for example, argued that

> The old doctrine of inspiration has now hardly any representatives today. It has come to an end, and rightly so. . . . Inspiration is the assistance which the Holy Spirit gave to the witnesses of the Old and New Covenant in their work of rendering these covenants into written form. . . . Moses and the prophets, as well as Christ and the Apostles, spoke to those in their own time the eternal truth revealed to them in categories recognizable in those times. . . . The revelation of the Old and New Covenant developed historically so that each book, first of all, is to be understood from the stage of the salvation history to which it belonged. . . . The history of the salvation history, out of which flowed all the books and all the words in them can be comprehended, however, only by the one who has experienced in himself the Spirit who moves throughout the Holy Scripture.[98]

---

[92]Friedrich A. Philippi, *Kirchliche Glaubenslehre*, 5 vols. (C. Bertelsmann, 1883), 282ff.

[93]W. Rohnert, *Die Dogmatik der evangelisch-lutherischen Kirche* (Hellmuth Wollermann, 1902), 41ff.

[94]See W. Rohnert, *Die Dogmatik der evangelisch-lutherischen Kirche* (Hellmuth Wollermann, 1902), 105.

[95]Theodor Klieforth, "Der Schriftbeweis des Dr. J. Chr. K. v. Hofmann," *Kirchliche Zeitschrift*, 6 (1859), 129–80; 193–320; 493–657; 661–747; 748–800.

[96]"In der heiligen Schrift aber besitzen wir nicht bloss die Urkunde der göttlichen Offenbarung, sondern auch die Offenbarung selbst. Die Schrift will nicht bloss ein historisches Denkmal, eine aktenmässige Buchung der alten Gottesoffenbarungen sein, sondern will die Gottesoffenbarung durch alle Zeiten hindurch fortsetzen und bis zu den spätesten Geschlichtern weitertragen; sie ist die durch alle Zeiten fortzeugende prophetische und apostolische Verkündigung des göttlichen Offenbarungswortes an die Menschen" (W. Rohnert, *Die Dogmatik* 42); "vielmehr hat der Herr . . . die einfachste Form der schriftlichen Fixirung seiner Offenbarung gewält, denn auch auf diesem menschlich geschichtlichen Wege konnte sie treu bewahrt und unverfälscht erhalten werden" (F. A. Philippi, *Kirchliche Glaubenslehre*, 1:134).

[97]"Die Inspir. ist also zu begreifen als e. solche Wirkung des Geistes Gottes, durch welche diese Schrift u. ihre einzelnen Theile ihrem Zweck entsprechend wurden, der Kirche denjenigen Dienst zu leisten, den sie ihr leisten sollten. Dazu gehörte nicht bloss die psychol. Wirkung (so zwar, dass der psychol. Zustand der bibl. Schriftsteller als der der Einh. v. Receptiv. u. Spontan. zu denken ist), sondern auch die äusseren geschichtl. Fügungen in der Entstehung der Schriften und die literar. Gesch., welche etwa die einzelnen Schriften durchgemacht, um das zu werden, was sie werden sollten, näml. Bestandtheile des kanon. (norm.) Wortes Gottes" (Chr. Ernst Luthardt, *Kompendium der Dogmatik* [Leipzig: Dörffling & Franke, 1900], 339).

It is not difficult to see the influence of Rothe and Hofmann in this statement by Kahnis. Inspiration is not so much identified with the Scriptures themselves as with the process which produced the Scriptures. Instead of an inspired text, Kahnis has inspired authors of the text. There is a subtle but fundamental difference.

In Britain, the movement away from the orthodox identification of revelation and Scripture and its focus on historical events is represented with unusual clarity by William Temple:

> Most people who share our cultural tradition, if asked where Christians supposed that a particular revelation of God is to be found, would probably answer that it is in the Bible. At once the question arises whether the Bible is supposed to be itself the revelation, or to be the record of the revelation. Is the revelation in the book or in the events which the book records? . . .The traditional doctrine has rather been that the Book itself is the revelation than that it contains the record of it. . . .[99]

After rejecting the traditional identification of Scripture and revelation, Temple sets forth his own views on the matter. His views, as can be seen in the quotation below, are virtually identical with those of Rothe.

> The earlier and supposedly preparatory revelation . . . consisted primarily in historical events, and secondarily in the illumination of the minds of prophets to read those events as disclosing the judgments or the purpose of God. What we find in the Old Testament Scriptures is not mainly, if at all, authoritative declarations of theological doctrine, but living apprehension of a living process wherein those whose minds are enlightened by divine communion can discern in part the purposive activity of God. . . (p. 312). From all this it follows that there is no such thing as revealed truth. There are truths of revelation, that is to say, propositions which express the results of correct thinking concerning revelation; but they are not themselves directly revealed. On the other hand, this does not involve the result that there need be anything vague or indefinite about revelation itself. . . .The typical *locus* of revelation is not the mind of the seer but the historical event. And if the revelation is essentially an event or fact, then it can be perfectly definite, although it neither is nor can be exhaustively represented in propositions.[100]

For the sake of emphasis and clarity let us repeat Temple's last statement: ". . .the typical *locus* of revelation is not the mind of the seer but the historical event. And if the revelation is essentially an event or fact, then it can be perfectly definite, although it neither is nor can be exhaustively represented in propositions." Temple could not have

---

[98]"Die alte Inspirationslehre hat jetzt kaum noch einen Vertreter. Sie ist gefallen, un mit Recht (p. 288). . . . Inspiration ist der Beistand, welchen der heilige Geist den Zeugen alten und neuen Bundes bei der schriftlichen Darstellung desselben leistete (pp. 292–93). . . . Moses und die Propheten, Christus und die Apostel haben das Ewige, was ihnen geoffenbart war, in der Hülle der Zeit zu ihrer Zeit gesagt . . . die Offenbarung alten and neuen Bundes sich geschichtlich entwickelt habe, so dass jedes Buch zunächst aus dem Stadium der Heilsoffenbarung, dem es angehört, verstanden sein wolle. . . . Die Geschichte der Heilsoffenbarung, aus welcher alle Bücher, in den Büchern alle Worte geflossen sind, erschliesst sich aber nur dem, welcher den Geist, der die heilige Schrift durchwaltet, in sich selbst erfahren hat (2 Kor. 2, 14)" (Karl F. A. Kahnis, *Die lutherische Dogmatik historisch-genetisch dargestellt* [Dörffling and Franke, 1874], 299–91).

[99]William Temple, *Nature, Man and God* (London: Macmillan & Co., 1934), 307–8.

[100]Ibid., 312–18.

said it more clearly. Revelation for him lay in the meaning we as readers of Scripture derive from historical events. Temple's views of Scripture and revelation had a major impact on modern evangelicalism. His views, along with those of the salvation-history theologians from Germany, constitute a major part of the modern evangelical understanding of Scripture.

As a result of its mixed heritage, a confusion between reading the text as revelation and reading it as a witness to revelation exists today among evangelical OT theologies. The confusion exists primarily in the fact that the OT, which is clearly and simply a text, and as such gives only a representation of the events of God's work in history, is often treated as if it were the event itself (*res gestae*). Though earlier salvation-history theologians such as Rothe and Hofmann were aware of their looking past the text of Scripture to God's revelation in historical events, contemporary evangelicals often fail to give this feature of their method proper recognition. Both Rothe and Hofmann saw themselves as salvation-history theologians, whereas today's evangelicals, wanting to remain faithful to an orthodox view of Scripture as revelation, attempt to identify salvation history with the scriptural text itself. As Rothe said of the conservative theologians of his own day, who also held his view of revelation in historical events, "They prefer to express themselves as far as possible in terms of the classical doctrine of Scripture."[101] It is as if in looking at the biblical narratives they understand themselves to be looking at the actual events. Hence they treat these narrated events as they would the *res gestae* of actual history. They fail to distinguish what is "real history," that is, actual events, from "true history," that is, an accurate record of real history. In what can only be described as a collapse of the genre-category *text*, biblical revelation is made synonymous with "that which happened in the history of Israel" (*res gestae*), and revelation in Scripture is treated as if it were revelation in an event.

It is true, of course, that from a literary point of view, this is exactly what the biblical narratives set out to accomplish. Their purpose is to bring the events of history before the reader in a realistic way. The reader is supposed to view the events of the narrative as happening before his or her eyes. It is thus to the credit of the biblical narratives that they have often been naively identified with the actual events. Nevertheless, in the serious study of these narratives we should not lose our bearings and conclude that the narratives themselves, as written texts, are in fact the actual events. They certainly are accurate historical accounts of the events, but it is pure naiveté to treat them as the events themselves.

The "biblical theology" of Geerhardus Vos is a classical evangelical work that exhibits clearly the kind of mixture of text and event that characterizes many recent evangelical salvation-history approaches to the OT. For example, in his definition of biblical theology Vos defines its task as "to exhibit the organic growth or development of the truths of Special Revelation from the primitive preredemptive Special Revelation given in Eden to the close of the New Testament canon."[102] Inasmuch as this is his definition of biblical theology, what else can Vos mean than that it is possible to

---

[101]Richard Rothe, *Theol. Stud. und Krit.* (1860), 331f (quoted by Pesch, 237).
[102]G. Vos, *Biblical Theology: Old and New Testament* (Grand Rapids: Eerdmans, 1948), 5.

speak of a biblical theology already in the Garden of Eden? Can Vos's use of the word *biblical* be related to the sense of the word *biblical* as it is used of the Bible itself as Scripture? Does he think Adam and Eve had a Bible? Surely not.[103] However, when he speaks of a biblical theology in the days of Adam and Eve, Vos shows that he has not made a distinction between any kind of special revelation in history or the human heart and God's revelation of his will in the inspired Scriptures. Indeed Vos is clear that this is his understanding of the sense of biblical theology. It is any form of special revelation from the time before the Fall to the time of Christ.[104] The point here is not to criticize Vos's approach to biblical theology or his view of revelation. The point rather is to show how his salvation-historical approach has blurred the distinction between the Bible as a record of revelation and the Bible as that revelation itself. Just how nontextual Vos's understanding is can be seen in his further explanation that biblical theology is "the study of the actual self-disclosures of God in time and space which lie back of even the first committal to writing of any Biblical document, and which for a long time continued to run alongside of the inscripturation of revealed material."[105] For Vos, special revelation may go far beyond the scope of the text of Scripture. The category of *salvation history*, which he had apparently inherited from earlier theologians such as Hofmann, allowed him to see revelation in events quite apart from the text. At the same time his deep roots in Protestant orthodoxy kept him from severing completely his ties to the biblical text as revelation.

Thus both forms of revelation found their way into Vos's biblical theology but for two quite different reasons. The one form of biblical theology he called "biblical" because it focused on the revelation of God referred to (*res gestae*) in the Bible. The other form of biblical theology was "biblical" because it focused on the revelation of God that is the Bible itself (text). For example, in his biblical theology, Vos's discussion of the patriarchs is often not cast in categories derived solely from the text of the Pentateuch but rather from his own historical studies of ancient Israel. One clear indi-

---

[103]Earlier orthodox biblical scholars were much clearer on this point than Vos and other moderns. Coccejus, for example, states emphatically: "God, of course, did not instruct Adam regarding how he was to live, by giving him a book to read (*Sane Adamo Deus facienda non descripsit in libro*)" (*Summa Doctrinae de Foedere et Testamento Dei*, cap. II, para. 13).

[104]Behind Vos's notion of "the primitive preredemptive Special Revelation given in Eden," was no doubt the concept of "primeval revelation" (*Ur-Offenbarung*) found in early Protestant theology. Roman Catholics and Protestants were in agreement that God used oral tradition as a means of revelation before the writing of Scripture. Roman Catholics, however, concluded from this that since the church survived with only oral tradition as revelation during that time period, Scripture was not absolutely necessary. Protestants argued that oral tradition (ἄγραφον) during the time before the writing of Scripture did not essentially differ from the later written revelation (ἔγγραφον). Thus there was never a time when the church did not have *the* very divine revelation which is now recorded in Scripture. "Hinc orta distinctio *Verbi* in ἄγραφον et ἔγγραφον; quae non est divisio generis in species, ut Pontificii statuunt; quasi aliud esset Verbum non scriptum a scripto: sed est distinctio subjecti in sua accidentia, quia eidem Verbo accidit, ut fuerit non scriptum olim, et nunc sit scriptum: ἄγραφον ergo dicitur, non respectu temporis praesentis, sed praeteriti, quo visum est Deo Ecclesiam sola viva voce et non scripto edocere" (Franciscus Turrettini, *Institutio Theologiae Elencticae* [New York: Robert Carter, 1847], 55).

[105]Vos, *Biblical Theology*, 13.

cation of this is the title of the section, "Revelation in the Patriarchal Period." As can be seen from the title, Vos's focus in this section is not the author's depiction of Abraham in the text as such but the revelation made known to Abraham during the patriarchal period. Vos was interested in the religion that had been revealed to Abraham. Thus, when it is necessary to explain Abraham's role in God's revelation during this period, Vos is just as comfortable calling to his aid recent archaeological material to show that God brought Abraham to Canaan because "it was actually a land where the lines of intercourse crossed. In the fullness of time its strategic position proved of supreme importance for the spreading abroad of the Gospel unto the whole earth."[106] Although one may agree with Vos in his assessment of God's plan for Abraham and for Israel, it cannot be argued that such ideas can be derived from the narrative text of Genesis. The notion that the land of Canaan enjoyed a strategic position in the ancient Near East is not a point made in the text but must be derived from a knowledge of the geopolitical position of the land of Canaan in the ancient world. What is more, Vos appears fully aware of this. From his perspective it mattered little whether one's biblical theology was informed from Scripture alone or from both Scripture and archaeology, as long as the information was both historically accurate and not incompatible.

Vos's approach, which I take to be characteristic of many recent evangelical approaches to Scripture as well, was not one that had neglected Scripture in favor of a revelation in history. That is, it was not the extreme position of Rothe. Rather, it was an approach that can only be described as a curious lack of awareness of the way in which texts and events have meaning—for lack of a better term, a "text naiveté." At the same time that he could recall recent archaeological evidence as a means of explaining God's actions with Abraham at the end of the third millennium B.C., Vos could, in fact, appeal to the text of Genesis 15:6 to show the centrality of faith in the life of Abraham.[107] Genesis 15:6, however, was a text that Vos himself took to be written by Moses hundreds of years later than the time of Abraham. The only way such a treatment of the patriarchs can be held together is to say that Vos's idea of special revelation included but went far beyond what we now have as the text of Scripture.

To appreciate the naïveté of Vos's approach, we must recall the earlier discussion of biblical narrative and the distinction we attempted to make between the narrative world of Scripture and the real world of historicism (see p. 51). For Vos, the narrative world of Scripture has merged with the real world of history and archaeology. Thus what is true of the real world, he took to be true of the narrative world as well. We have to make continually clear that the issue we are attempting to raise here is not one of historical accuracy. Vos is not naive in taking the biblical narratives as accurate accounts of real events. The narratives are intended to be read as accounts of real events. Vos is naive, in my judgment, in simply identifying the world of the narratives with whatever we may come to know and understand about the historical events. The narrative world is a fixed reality. It is a function of the narration in the text. The real world is ever-changing and ever-increasing. When one identifies, or equates, the real world and the

---

[106]Ibid., 90.
[107]Ibid., 96.

narrative world as one and the same, the narrative world no longer remains constant. The narrative world changes as we gain more information about the real world. That is the unfortunate consequence of Vos's naïveté. The task of biblical theology is to allow the fixed reality of the narrative world to shape and inform our understanding of the real world, not the other way around.

Another interesting example of an evangelical OT theology that naively blurs the distinction between the text and the event is John Raven's *History of the Religion of Israel*.[108] Raven's work, which he intended as an OT theology,[109] "presents the religion of Israel in its origin and historical development."[110] It is clear that what Raven meant by this is both textual and historical in nature. He first argues, for example, that OT theology's method is "essentially historical," then suggests that its goal is to inquire into "the conceptions of the religion of the Bible at various stages of its development."[111] This, in turn, leads him to begin with a discussion of the "religion before Abraham"[112] that is little more than an explication of Genesis 1–11:

> This primitive religion—true as far as the imperfect knowledge of those remote ages would permit—was the religion of the ancestors of Abraham in the godly line of Seth and of Shem. . . . Their idea of God was very primitive and anthropomorphic. They believed that God formed man from the dust of the ground and breathed into his nostrils the breath of life in the most realistic fashion (Gen. 2:7). He planted a garden in Eden and put man there (Gen. 2:8, 15). He talked with man with audible voice (Gen. 2:16, 18; 8:8, 9–19; 4:6–7, 9–15; 6:3, 13–22; 7:1–5; 8:15–17; 9:1–17). He brought the animals to man to see what he would call them (Gen. 2:19). He formed woman from one of man's ribs (Gen. 2:21–22). He walked in the garden (Gen. 3:8). He spoke to the serpent (Gen. 3:14). He made coats of skins for Adam and Eve (Gen. 3:21). He drove them out of the garden (Gen. 3:24). . . . He came down to see the city and the tower which man built (Gen. 11:5). While we recognize that these statements, taken symbolically and figuratively, present very profound truth, it is not at all probable that primitive men so understood them.[113]

The last sentence in the above quotation makes clear what Raven has done in reconstructing the "religion before Abraham." He simply reads the narratives of Genesis 1–11 as if those who lived during that time had those very chapters somehow fixed in their heads as their own divine revelation. At the same time, however, Raven is clear that he understands these chapters to have been written by Moses many thousands of years later.[114] He thus appears to overlook completely the fact that Genesis 1–11, as such, is and has always been a written text, and that the theological message of those

---

[108]John Howard Raven, *The History of the Religion of Israel: An Old Testament Theology* (Grand Rapids: Baker, 1979 [orig. 1933]).

[109]"This subject was formerly treated under the title of Old Testament Theology" (Raven, *History*, 5).

[110]Ibid.

[111]Ibid.

[112]Ibid., 12.

[113]Ibid.

[114]Ibid., 8.

narratives is the product of that text. Again we have to repeat here that this is not a question of the historical accuracy of the early chapters of Genesis. Raven is not merely taking the description of these narratives at face value and using them as accurate historical records, which he has every narrative right to do. He is rather, as well, taking it for granted that the theological assumptions and statements of the author of the narrative texts are, in fact, those of the characters living during the time period described in the text.

It is one thing to say that Adam and Eve believed those truths about God and his will which are, in fact, revealed to them within the text, e.g., God's promise of a redeemer in Genesis 3:15, "I will put enmity between you and the woman, between your seed and her seed; and he will crush you on the head . . ." (author's own translation). It is another thing altogether, however, to say that Adam and Eve had a "primitive and anthropomorphic" idea of God because such an idea of God is found in the point of view of the narratives of Genesis 1–11.[115] There is no evidence in his discussion of this point that Raven appreciates the difference. He simply takes the narrative depiction of the events in Genesis 1–11 as the viewpoint of the biblical characters in those events, missing entirely the rather obvious fact that it reflects the point of view of the author of the Pentateuch. If he is going to argue that the narratives of Genesis 1–11 reflect a "very primitive and anthropomorphic" idea of God, then he should conclude that such was the viewpoint of the author of Genesis 1–11, not simply the characters in the narrative. We are not here concerned with whether Raven is right or wrong about assessing these narratives as "very primitive." Our point is rather that he mixes real events and narrative events. Raven rightly believes that the narrative events are real history. The narrative events are true and accurate. But Raven has not grasped the fact that real events and narrative events are different kinds of things. Raven, we believe, was naive because he failed to appreciate this feature of the biblical texts.

An obvious consequence of mixing the meaning of a text with that of an event concerns the question of perspective. It is characteristic of historical events that they stand open to multiple perspectives. As one recent philosopher of history has said, "Historical explanations are, in general, more tenuously constructed, more debatable, more subject to doubt than the explanations of natural scientists, and one of the reasons for this is the fact that they *are* often based on complex generalizations that apply to single instances while they are *not* supported by deduction from more fundamental truths."[116] The meaning or sense of an historical event lies in the ability of the viewer of that event to gather the appropriate data and evaluate it from a certain vantage point. Hofmann clearly recognized this feature of historical events and spoke of the need for a gauge (*Mass*) by which an event could be properly measured:

> In order to evaluate the historical position of that which divine inspiration has produced, one must first have found the gauge by which all historical phenomena are to be measured. This gauge, however, lies within those very events of history which intersect each

---

[115]Ibid., 12.

[116]Morton White, *Foundations of Historical Knowledge* (New York: Harper & Row, 1965), 29.

other in countless directions. The value and meaning of an individual historical fact lies in the relationship it has to the final shape of all history.[117]

Finding the meaning of historical events is quite different than finding the meaning of texts. In narrative texts the reader is given the privileged perspective of the author. "On this divine text, however, and in its best interests, the narrator superimposes his own [privileged perspective], designed for the reader's eyes only."[118] The reader has the advantage of the guidance of the author and his perspective on the event. Thus the world of the event "reaches us through the mediation of the words, selected and combined to form their own logic. . . More generally, the narrator's mediation offers the reader a preinterpreted image of reality," whereas those who attempt to interpret an event find only the "raw materials on their hands."[119] For the evangelical, the privileged perspective of the reader does not so much rest in the fact that one has only the perspective of the author to go on. That would be only making a virtue of necessity. Rather, it lies more importantly in the theological fact that the text, which gives the privileged perspective, is inspired. It is the Word of God.

What this amounts to is the simple fact that behind texts stand authors who have rendered their intentions in texts—inspired texts in the case of the Bible. It is this simple fact that makes a text-oriented approach to exegesis and biblical theology an important consideration for the evangelical. Our task is not that of explaining what happened to Israel in Old Testament times. Though worthy of our efforts, archaeology and history must not be confused with the task of exegesis and biblical theology. We must not lose sight of the fact that the authors of Scripture have already made it their task to tell us in their texts what happened to Israel. The task that remains for us as readers is that of explaining and proclaiming what they have written. The goal of a text-oriented approach is not revelation in history in the sense of events (*res gestae*) that must be rendered meaningful. Rather, the goal is a revelation in history in the sense of the meaning of a history recounted in the text of Scripture.

2.2.4. History of the Question of Text and Event

The most complete study of the history of the question of meaning in the text of Scripture and meaning in events is Hans Frei's book, *The Eclipse of Biblical Narrative*.[120] In this book, Frei traces what he takes to be a fundamental shift in Protestant biblical interpretation regarding the meaning of biblical narrative. The shift was, in fact, a move

---

[117]"Um die geschichtliche Stellung von Erzeugnissen der Inspiration würdigen zu können, muss man erst das Mass gefunden haben, mit welchem alle geschichtlichen Erscheinungen zu messen sind. Dieses Mass liegt aber im Ergebnisse der Geschichte, in welchem beschlossen ist, was zuvor in zahllosen Richtungen aus einander und durch einander gelaufen. In welchem Verhältnisse eine einzelne Thatsache zum Endergebnisse aller steht, das ist ihr Werth und ihre Bedeutung" (J. Chr. K. von Hofmann, *Weissagung und Erfüllung im alten und im neuen Testamente* [Nördlinger: C. H. Beck Buchhandlung, 1841], 1:33).

[118]Sternberg, *Poetics*, 162.

[119]Ibid.

[120]Hans W. Frei, *The Eclipse of Biblical Narrative: A Study in Eighteenth and Nineteenth Century Hermeneutics* (New Haven, Yale University Press, 1974).

away from finding the meaning of the Bible in the biblical narratives themselves and an accompanying attempt to find meaning in the actual historical events that are the subject matter of the Bible. Before the rise of historical criticism in the seventeenth and eighteenth centuries, Frei argues, the Bible was read literally and historically as a true and accurate account of God's acts in real historical events. It was assumed that the realism of the biblical narratives was in fact an indication that the biblical authors had described historical events[121] just as they had happened:

> Western Christian reading of the Bible in the days before the rise of historical criticism in the eighteenth century was usually strongly realistic, i.e. at once literal and historical, and not only doctrinal and edifying. The words and sentences meant what they said, and because they did so they accurately described real events and real truths that were rightly put only in those terms and no others.[122]

Moreover, according to the earlier understanding of the Bible, the real world was identified as the world actually described in the Bible, and one's own world was meaningful only insofar as it could be viewed as part of the world of the Bible. On this point, Frei acknowledges his dependence on Erich Auerbach's description of the real world in biblical narrative:

> The world of the Scripture stories is not satisfied with claiming to be a historically true reality—it insists that it is the only real world, it is destined for autocracy. All other scenes, issues, and ordinances have no right to appear independently of it, and it is promised that all of them, the history of all mankind, will be given their due place within its frame, will be subordinated to it. The Scripture stories do not, like Homer's, court our favor, they do not flatter us that they may please us and enchant us—they seek to subject us, and if we refuse to be subjected we are rebels.[123]

What this means is that in the early views of those who read these biblical narratives, the Bible had meaning because it described real and meaningful events. The concept of divine providence was the matting that held together the depiction of events in the biblical narratives and the occurrence of those events in history. God was the author of both. "With God postulated as double author, the biblical narrator can enjoy the privileges of art without renouncing his historical titles."[124] One can see this quite clearly in Thomas Aquinas' *Summa Theologica*: "The author of Scripture is God, in whose power it is not only to use words for making known his will (which any

---

[121]Frei suggests that these early theologians were mistaken in their understanding of the biblical narratives and that the narratives were intended only to be "history like," not real history. Sternberg, correctly we believe, takes issue with Frei on this important point. According to Sternberg, Frei has unduly limited the aim of biblical realism to a merely literary device. Frei "wishes to focus attention on the biblical text by cutting through the hopeless tangle that religious controversy has made of the issues of inspiration and history. But instead of suspending judgment on them as articles of faith. . . , he tries to neutralize them altogether" (Meir Sternberg, *The Poetics of Biblical Narrative* [Bloomington: Indiana University Press, 1985], 82).

[122]Frei, *The Eclipse*, 1.

[123]Erich Auerbach, *Mimesis, The Representation of Reality in Western Literature*, trans. Willard R. Trask (Princeton: Princeton University Press, 1953 [orig. 1946]).

[124]Sternberg, *Poetics*, 82.

human being is able to do), but also historical events in the real world."[125] For Thomas, the course of human events was a story written by God in the real world. History is "His story." This is precisely the biblical view described above by Auerbach. Frei calls such a reading of the biblical narratives a "precritical" understanding of Scripture. It is precritical in that it reflects an attitude of taking the Bible at face value and reading it as it had been originally intended.

It is Frei's argument that over the last two centuries the precritical understanding of Scripture, which looked to the narrative text for its clues to meaning, has been gradually replaced by a historical reading of the Bible, that is, one which looked for meaning beyond the narratives themselves to the events they recorded. As a result of this shift of focus from the text to the event, biblical theologians paid less and less attention to the text as such and devoted an increasing amount of attention to attempting to reconstruct historical events. Hence Frei speaks of an "eclipse" of the biblical narrative.

According to Frei, one can see the theologians' shift in attitude toward the biblical narratives most clearly[126] in the nature of their response to the challenge of English Deism in the eighteenth century.[127] On two important points Deism challenged the precritical attitude towards Scripture. First, Deism rejected outright the notion of divine providence, holding that the universe was guided by its own internal and universal laws and that the will of God was not a direct factor in its operation. Secondly, Deism rejected the idea of special revelation. God had not broken into the web of causes and effects to express his will directly to human beings.

As a result of the loss of the notion of divine providence, Frei argues, there was no longer any certainty that the course of God's acts in history were adequately reflected in the course those actions followed in Scripture. The link which Aquinas had seen between the things that happened in history and the description of them in the Bible could no longer be sustained. God was no longer the author of both Scripture and history. As Scholder has maintained,

> If the historical-critical theology is characterized by the fact that it has come to grips fundamentally and methodologically with the modern understanding of the world, then its

---

[125]"Respondeo dicendum, quod auctor sacrae Scripturae est Deus, in cujus potestate est, ut non solum voces ad significandum accommodet (quod etiam homo facere potest) sed etiam res ipsas" (Thomas Aquinas, *Summa Theologica* [Rome: Forzan, 1894], 25).

[126]Frei argues that the origin of the "eclipse" of biblical narrative had already begun to occur in the middle of the seventeenth century with the works of Johannes Coccejus. In his attempt to link biblical prophecy to events in his own day, Coccejus frequently identified the meaning of the prophetic message with contemporary historical events. The mourning spoken of in Isaiah 33:7, for example, is identified by Coccejus as a reference to the death of the Swedish king, Gustavus Adolphus: Haec optimè conveniunt in Gustavum Adolphum (*The Eclipse*, 46–50).

[127]Klaus Scholder has argued, and Frei agrees, that the breakdown of the link between the biblical world and the world view of modern man had begun to take hold much earlier, "In der Auseinandersetzung mit dem neuen Wirklichkeitsverständnis, das von den ersten Jahrzehnten des 17. Jahrhunderts an immer entschiedener auftritt, das immer deutlicher dem biblischen Welt und Menschenbild in seiner traditionellen Ueberlieferung widerspricht und diesen Widerspruch mit immer unwiderleglicheren Beweisen bekräftigt, entstehen die ersten Versuche der historischen Kritik, mit denen die historisch-kritische Theologie ihren Anfang nimmt" (*Ursprünge und Probleme der Bibelkritik im 17 Jahrhundert, Ein Beitrag zur Entstehung der historisch-kritischen Theologie* [München: Chr. Kaiser Verlag, 1966], 9).

origins must be linked with the rise of the new, modern world view. . . . From this very fact also is revealed the route whereby we may understand the origin of historical criticism. It must have begun just at the point where the modern view of reality reached its full form, that is, where the older unity of the Scriptures, the world view and faith became problematic—though admittedly this happened only in the case of certain key individuals. It was at that point where the Copernican system could no longer be overlooked and where the triumphant voice of the growing philosophical self-awareness could no longer be ignored.[128]

The loss of such a link meant that the task of describing the nature of the relationship between God's acts in history and the record of those acts in Scripture passed into the domain of historical science. Whereas previously one could turn to scriptural exegesis to learn about God's acts in history, now one must resort to a scientific reconstruction of the events.

2.2.4.1. The Precritical View of Biblical History

The chart in Figure 3.6 shows the correlation that existed in the precritical view between three fundamental spheres: (1) the biblical narratives, (2) the historical events depicted by them (ostensive reference), and (3) the world of the reader.

In the precritical view of Scripture, the course of the actual historical events, represented in the chart by A - > B - > C (Event A causes Event B which causes Event C) is precisely that which is depicted in the biblical narratives (A - > B - > C) and is understood as such by the reader (A - > B - > C). For example, in the precritical view of Israel's exodus from Egypt, the actual event consisted of the Israelites' sojourn into Egypt (A), which led to their bondage under the pharaoh (B), which in turn led to God's deliverance through the Red Sea (C). According to the precritical view, the event in real life happened just as it is recorded in the biblical narratives (Ge 46–Ex 15) and was to be understood as such by the precritical reader.

It can be seen quite clearly from this chart that for special revelation (the Bible) to be real history, there must be a providential link between the text (narrative) and the event (ostensive reference). With such a link, the biblical narratives provided an all-encompassing universal history which began at Creation. Christian theology, as Judaism before it, used this universal history embodied in the narratives to great apologetic advantage. When it came to the question of the truthfulness of pagan histories, for example, the personages and events of those histories were simply incorporated into the later framework of the biblical narratives. The reality of the ancient world was reinterpreted as part of the biblical reality. The framework of biblical history was governed by a chronological schema that accounted for the major world empires of the

---

[128]"Wenn die historisch-kritische Theologie dadurch charakterisiert ist, dass sie grundsätzlich und methodisch mit dem Wirklichkeitsverständnis der Moderne rechnet, so müssen ihre Anfänge mit dem Aufkommen des neuer, modernen Weltbildes verbunden sein. . . . Damit aber is zugleich der Frage nach der Entstehung der historischen Kritik der Weg gewiesen. Sie muss dort ansetzen, wo das moderne Wirklichkeitsverständnis Gestalt gewinnt, wo—wenn auch zunächst nur bei Einzelnen—die alte Einheit von Schrift, Weltbild und Glaube fragwürdig wird, wo das das kopernikanische System nicht mehr zu übersehen, wo die triumphierende Stimme des erwachenden philosophischen Selbstbewusstseins nicht mehr zu überhören ist" (Scholder, *Ursprünge und Probleme*, 9).

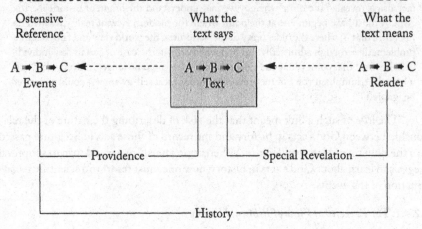

Figure 3.6

past, the events of the church, that is, the present, and an apocalyptic conclusion in the future. All history was thus brought into the sweep of the biblical story. There was no independent history or reality apart from it. For the most part, the chronological schema employed by the early Christian historians was biblically grounded in one of three ways: (1) the days of creation in Genesis 1 were interpreted as a foreshadowing of seven major epochs in world history; (2) the four kingdoms of Daniel were taken as a description of the totality of human history; or (3) the Trinitarian nature of the God-head served as a pattern for universal history.[129]

Two early works on "world history," Arias's *History of Humanity*[130] and Schedel's *Chronicles*,[131] illustrate the close association of the Bible and accounts of human history. A cursory reading of Arias's *History* shows that in giving his account of the early history of humanity, Arias merely paraphrased the narrative history of the Pentateuch and the rest of the biblical narratives, supplementing it with elements from later biblical texts such as Psalm 104 and Acts 7. Arias's understanding of the natural correlation between history and the biblical narratives is clearly sustained by his concept of divine providence. In writing of Israel's descent into Egypt, for example, Arias stated explicitly that Joseph's success with the pharaoh was due to God's unique and definitive care, "that singular providence of God."[132] In saying this Arias was only following the lead of the biblical text where Joseph tells his brothers, "You intended to harm me, but God intended it for good to accomplish what is now being done, the saving of

[129]*RGG*, 2:1482–83.

[130]Arias Montanus, *Liber Generationis et Regenerationis Adam sive De historia Generis humani* (Antwerp, 1593), 190–98.

[131]Hartmann Schedel, *Buch der Chroniken*, 1493. Reprinted as *The Nuremberg Chronicle, A Facsimile of Hartmann Schedel, Buch der Chroniken*, ed. Anton Koberger (New York: Landmark Press, 1979).

[132]"Singularis illa Dei prouidentia," Montanus, *Liber Generationis*, 191.

many lives" (Ge 50:20 NIV). Thus the narrative depiction was taken as synonymous with the real events of history.

Schedel's *Chronicles* is somewhat more complex, but nevertheless follows the framework of the biblical narratives closely. It extends the biblical history itself into a more expansive history of the world by also weaving various historical data from ancient pagan traditions into the biblical account. For example, after recording the success of Joseph in the house of Pharaoh, like Arias's following the biblical account verbatim, Schedel continues by giving what he takes to be a contemporary account of the founding of Greece:

> Here at this point arises the kingdom of the Greeks. There, in Greece, Ittachus, a son (as they say) of the ocean and the earth, in Isaac's 60th year, began to reign in Thessalia as the first king among the Greeks.[133]

One can see quite clearly that these two historians simply took the world of the biblical narratives as their "world history" and integrated all other known events into it. Other events of world history become meaningful as parts of the biblical world. There was a tremendous apologetic force to such conceptions of universal history. It meant, however, that the concept of divine providence was crucial to the Christian biblical self-understanding. It was not by accident that the rise of English Deism, which challenged the very concept of divine providence itself, posed such a threat to the truth of Christianity. The deistic view of the world, in fact, lay at the heart of modern historical criticism.

2.2.4.2. The Critical View of Biblical History

The critical view of biblical narrative is represented in the chart in Figure 3.7. One can see that there are fundamental differences between the critical and the precritical view of biblical narrative. In the critical view, the actual events in history (X - > Y - > Z) are not identical with the depiction of these events in the biblical narrative (A - > B - > C). Though the biblical text may recount a story of the Israelites' move into Egypt (A) and their becoming enslaved to the house of Pharaoh after the death of Joseph (B) and of their deliverance from Egypt under Moses (C), the actual course of events may be represented quite differently. According to a common modern reconstruction, for example, there were no Israelites before the Exodus (X). Those who came out of Egypt were only a small band of escaped slaves (Y) who found a sandbar at low tide and were able to bypass an Egyptian garrison by fleeing into the desert (Z). One can easily see that such an account does not mesh with what is recounted in the Bible.

What should be noted particularly in the chart above is the fact that in the critical view, the reader actually understands the meaning of the biblical account, not in its own terms (A -> B - > C), but in terms of its ostensive reference to "real" events (X - > Y - > Z). The narrative meaning (A - > B - > C) is replaced by the meaning of the actual events (X - > Y - > Z) as if that was really what the biblical narratives were about.

---

[133]"Hie entspringt das reich der kriechen. do yttachus ein sun (als sie sagen) des meers und der erden im. lx. iar von ysaacs gepurt bey den kriechen in thessalia erster koenig zeregirn angefangen hat . . ." (Schedel, *Chronicles*, 28).

CRITICAL UNDERSTANDING OF MEANING IN NARRATIVE

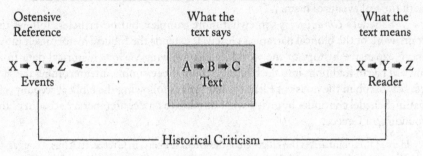

Figure 3.7

According to Frei, the chief issue raised by Deism, and hence historical criticism, was the question of miracles: Is it likely that divine revelation has actually happened in historical events? Such a question was tantamount to asking whether miracles were possible and whether the biblical accounts of them were credible. Frei argues that the course of historical criticism after the eighteenth century was shaped fundamentally in response to this question. Increasingly the task of investigating the truthfulness of the biblical narratives, and thus to many also their meaning, was taken over by the science of historical criticism. The new context of meaning for the events recorded in the biblical narratives became the critically-reconstructed history of the ancient world. The biblical events now became meaningful only as part of the modern historical accounts of the past. Rather than historical events finding their meaning in the context of biblical history, biblical history became meaningful as part of the general picture of ancient Near Eastern history.

This process can again be seen in the Exodus narratives. The major turning point in understanding the history of Israel during the time of the Exodus came with the decipherment of the Egyptian hieroglyphic script by Jean-Francois Champollion in 1822.[134] The availability of contemporary documents from Egypt meant biblical historians were no longer dependent solely on biblical and classical sources. One of the first Egyptologists to deal with the issue of the relationship between the biblical narratives and contemporary Egyptian records was Karl Richard Lepsius.[135] Lepsius's work with the Egyptian sources led him to the view that the biblical narratives should not be used as the framework of ancient Egyptian history. The Egyptologist, he maintained, must reconstruct the history of Egypt from the Egyptian sources alone. Rather than using the biblical narratives as the chronological framework of Egyptian history, one should use only the historical chronology of the Egyptian sources as the framework for understanding the biblical narratives.[136] That process has continued up to our

---

[134]Cf. W. R. Dawson and E. P. Uphill, *Who Was Who in Egyptology? A Biographical Index of Egyptologists; of Travellers, Explorers, and Excavators in Egypt*, 2nd rev. ed. (London: 1972), 58–60, quoted in Helmut Engel, *Die Vorfahren Israels in Aegypten* (Frankfurt am Main: Josef Knecht, 1979), 18.

[135]*Die Chronologie der Aegypter* (Berlin, 1849), quoted in Engel, 18.

[136]Ibid.

own day so that even among conservative biblical scholarship, the biblical narratives often derive their meaning from the historical context within which they are placed. How else could one explain the preoccupaton of conservative scholarship in this century with the question of the date of the Exodus? This was not an apologetic debate about the historicity of the Exodus, but rather an internecine struggle about the appropriate historical context for understanding the biblical narratives.

Furthermore, Frei argues that in responding to the questions raised by Deism, historical criticism found itself working with two crucial assumptions. The first was largely implicit: If the historical events recorded in the biblical narratives were true, that is, if they actually had happened, then the narratives could be said to be meaningful. The second assumption follows from the first: The meaning which the narratives themselves had was reduced to being merely the historical facticity of the events. In other words, the meaning of the narratives became whatever the historical critic could demonstrate had actually happened. In the case of Lepsius, the meaning of the events of the Exodus was simply that series of events which could be reconstructed from the Egyptian documents. Thus the meaning of Scripture came to be identified with the series of events it purported to recount, that is, its subject matter. Once thatassumption took hold, Frei argues, it precipitated a major shift in biblical hermeneutics. The source of the Bible's meaning was no longer the meaning of the narrative itself (text) but the meaning of the historical events (res gestae). Following the example above, the meaning of the account of the Exodus was not taken to be the sense gained from the text, namely, that God delivered Israel from bondage in Egypt (A - > B - > C). Its meaning was taken to be that which actually happened to Israel. To complicate matters more, the whole question of "What happened to Israel?" was variously reconstructed by means of historical criticism.[137]

It is not difficult to see this same process being played out today in the way in which the historically reconstructed events of the Exodus are used to form the basis of liberation theology. As we said earlier, if what actually happened in the Exodus was a popular uprising in which the people of Israel overthrew their oppressors in Egypt and were liberated in the Exodus, namely the X - > Y - > Z noted above, then the Exodus can be made into a paradigm of contemporary liberation movements. Ernst Bloch has, in fact, interpreted the Exodus narratives as a case for revolution and liberation.[138]

2.2.4.3. The Conservative Historical View of Biblical History

Though we have focused above on examples from the history of radical historical criticism, it is also possible to find among conservative scholarship examples of the replacement of the narrative meaning of a biblical text by a reconstructed historical version of its

---

[137]For an exhaustive discussion of the various approaches to the history of the Exodus see Helmut Engel, *Die Vorfahren Israels in Aegypten* (Frankfurt am Main: Josef Knecht, 1979).

[138]"Ein versklavtes Volk, das ist hier die Not, die beten lehrt. Und ein Stifter eben erscheint, der damit beginnt, dass er einen Fronvogt erschlägt. So stehen hier *Leid* und *Empörung* am Anfang, sie machen von vornherein den Glauben zu einem Weg ins Freie" (Ernst Bloch, *Das Prinzip Hoffnung* [1959], 1450ff, quoted in Hans-Joachim Kraus, *Biblisch-theologische Aufsätze* [Neukirchen-Vluyn: Neukirchener Verlag, 1972], 103).

event. The chart in Figure 3.8 represents a more subtle, but still important, replacement of narrative meaning by a conservatively-reconstructed historical meaning of the events. To distinguish it from a strictly critical approach, we will call it simply a "historical understanding of meaning." Note that in the chart below the only difference between the biblical narratives and the ostensive reference of those narratives is represented by the lowercase letter "b." Where the biblical narratives give one version of an event (B), the actual event, as it is understood by the historian, occurred in a slightly different manner (b).

HISTORICAL UNDERSTANDING OF MEANING IN NARRATIVE

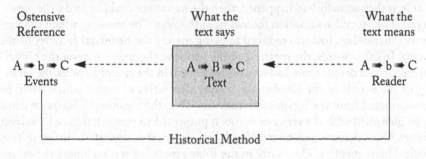

Figure 3.8

What the chart attempts to show is that the conservative historical understanding accepts the biblical account (A->B->C) as, in fact (though with slight modification), historical (A->b->C). Though by and large historically accurate, the actual event (b) referred to in the biblical text (B) is adjusted to what reasonable (uncritical) historical method suggests "actually happened." Since the text is read in terms of its ostensive reference, the reader's understanding of the meaning of the text is in fact that which he or she knows to have "actually happened" (b).

A specific example from the Exodus narratives can be found in the meaning commonly attached to the first plague: "Moses and Aaron did just as the LORD had commanded. He raised his staff in the presence of Pharaoh and his officials and struck the water of the Nile, and all the water was changed into blood. The fish in the Nile died, and the river smelled so bad that the Egyptians could not drink its water. Blood was everywhere in Egypt" (Ex 7:20 NIV). The intent of the narrative appears clear enough, that is, "all the water was changed into blood." Moses raised his staff (A) -> the water of the Nile became blood (B) -> the fish in the Nile died and the Egyptians could not drink the water (C). The earlier biblical commentators took this statement at face value and understood it to mean that the waters of the river actually became blood: the biblical narrative (A -> B -> C) was identical with the ostensive reference (A -> B -> C). Henry Ainsworth, for example, explains the text in the following manner: "as the Egyptians had shed the blood of the children of *Israel*, drowning them in the river, Exod. 1.22. so in this first plague, God rewardeth that, by turning their waters into blood . . . whereas the waters of *Egypt* served them for drinke, . . . God

turning them to stinking blood, and killing the fish: the plague was more grievous."[139]
The seriousness with which the earlier commentators read this narrative as real and
literal history can be seen in the remarks of Cornelius a Lapide:

> Wherein it should be noted that there was not merely one miracle here but many, or
> rather, one continuous conversion of the flowing waters of the Nile into blood which hap-
> pened for seven days. For the Nile in Ethiopia bore pure waters, but when they reached
> the borders of Egypt, the water immediately turned into blood persistently and contin-
> uously throughout the seven days. . . . The waters did not merely have the color of blood,
> but they also had the nature of blood and were, in fact, really blood.[140]

Later conservative, more "historically" oriented commentators, however, understood the sense of this passage quite differently. They retained the miraculous element,
but understood the meaning of the text in light of historical analogies. Keil, for example, says, "The changing of the water into blood is to be interpreted in the same sense
as in Joel iii. 4, where the moon is said to be turned into blood; that is to say, not as a
chemical change into real blood, but as a change in the colour, which caused it to
assume the appearance of blood (2 Kings iii. 22)."[141] Keil then gives the basis for his
interpretation of the narrative, using the principle of historical analogy:

> According to the statements of many travellers, the Nile water changes its colour when
> the water is lowest, assumes first of all a greenish hue and is almost undrinkable, and then,
> while it is rising, becomes as red as ochre, when it is more wholesome again. The causes
> of this change have not been sufficiently investigated. The reddening of the water is
> attributed by many to the red earth, which the river brings down from Sennaar . . . but
> Ehrenberg came to the conclusion, after microscopical examinations, that it was caused
> by cryptogamic plants and infusoria. This natural phenomenon was here intensified into
> a miracle, not only by the fact that the change took place immediately in all the branches
> of the river at Moses' word and through the smiting of the Nile, but even more by a chem-
> ical change in the water, which caused the fishes to die, the stream to stink, and, what
> seems to indicate putrefaction, the water to become undrinkable; whereas, according to
> the accounts of travellers, which certainly do not quite agree with one another, and are
> not entirely trustworthy, the Nile water becomes more drinkable as soon as the natural
> reddening begins.[142]

---

[139]Henry Ainsworth, *Annotations upon the Second Booke of Moses Called Exodus* (London: M. Parsons,
1639), 23.

[140]Cornelius a Lapide (d. 1637), "Ubi nota, non unum hic fuisse miraculum, sed multa, vel potius
unum continuatum, per continuam aquarum Nili affluentium in sanguinem conversionem, idque per septem
dies. Nam Nilus in AEthiopia puras ferebat aquas; ubi vero attingebat fines AEgypti, mox vertebatur in sanguinem, idque assidue et continuo per septem dies. . . . aquae non tantum colorem, sed et naturam habebant
sanguinis, erantque verus sanguis" (*Commentaria in Scripturam Sacram*).

[141]C. F. Keil, *Biblical Commentary on the Old Testament* (Grand Rapids: Eerdmans, 1971), 1:478.

[142]Ibid., 478–79. More recently, Kaiser has taken a similar position, "The sources of the Nile's inundation are the equatorial rains that fill the White Nile, which originates in east-central Africa (present-day Uganda)
and flows sluggishly through swamps in eastern Sudan; and the Blue Nile and the Atbara River, which both fill
with melting snow from the mountains and become raging torrents filled with tons of red soil from the basins
of both these rivers. The higher the inundation, the deeper the color of red waters. In addition to this discol-
oration, a type of algae, known as flagellates, comes from the Sudan swamps and Lake Tana along the White
Nile, which produces the stench and the deadly fluctuation in the oxygen level of the river that proves to be so

The point of this discussion is that in these historically conservative commentaries, the meaning of the biblical text ("the water became blood") is not taken as ostensively true but rather is identified with the meaning of the event as it has been reconstructed from similar events known from historical investigation ("the water became red *like* blood"). The miraculous element in the first plague is retained but it is nevertheless significantly reduced to that of an intensification of a natural phenomenon. However, the narrative link between the blood of the Hebrew children thrown into the Nile in Exodus 1 and the Nile becoming blood is lost in the process, and thus the text loses an important clue to its meaning.

It is not hard to see how such a shift in hermeneutics affected the task of OT theology. Once the meaning of revelation in the Bible became identified with what actually happened, the focus of biblical theology became the meaning of the historical event as such, apart from the sense of the narrative in the text. Hence, the goal of OT theology was to draw out the theological meaning of what actually happened in Israel's history, or at least what the historian was able to reconstruct as the event. The meaning of that event (ostensive reference) took the place of the meaning of the text.

In light of such a shift in focus it now becomes clear why the central concern of the nineteenth- and early twentieth-century evangelical OT theologians has increasingly been that of archaeology and salvation history. If the meaning of Scripture is reduced to its merely recounting what happened to Israel, then the goal of OT theology must become that of describing and retracing the history of God's saving acts.

In the diverse historical-critical approaches to OT theology, the consensus of what really happened varied considerably.[143] Moreover, between radical criticism and conservative criticism great diversity existed. On the one hand there was the literary-critical reconstructions of Israel's history of the Wellhausen school[144] and on the other there were the conservative views of such scholars as König[145] and Möller.[146] Each had its own reconstructed version of the biblical narratives in which they described "what actually happened" in Israel's history. In each case, however, it was in fact this reconstructed history which they then relied on as the historical basis for an OT theology.

The publication of the OT theology of Gerhard von Rad[147] marked a fundamental reversal of the historical focus of biblical theology by redirecting the biblical theologians' attention back to the narrative text or, at least, back in the direction of the text. Von Rad argued that because of the nature of the OT itself, it was impossible to

---

fatal to the fish. Such a process, at the command of God, seems to be the cause for this first plague rather than any chemical change of the water into red and white corpuscles . . ." (*EBC*, 2:350).

[143] An excellent account of the changing views of Israel's history within historical criticism is Rudolf Smend, *Das Mosebild von Heinrich Ewald bis Martin Noth* (Tübingen: J. C. B. Mohr [Paul Siebeck], 1959).

[144] E.g., B. Stade, *Biblische Theologie des Alten Testaments*, 1905; Gustav Hölscher, *Geschichte der israelitischen und jüdischen Religion* (Giessen: Alfred Töpelmann, 1922); Emil Kautzsch, *Biblische Theologie des Alten Testaments* (Tübingen: J. C. B. Mohr [Paul Siebeck], 1911); and Rudolf Kittel, *Die Religion des Volkes Israel* (Leipzig: Quelle & Meyer, 1921).

[145] Eduard König, *Geschichte der Alttestamentlichen Religion* (Gütersloh: C. Bertelsmann, 1912).

[146] Wilhelm Möller, *Biblische Theologie des Alten Testaments in heilsgeschichtlicher Entwicklung* (Zwickau [Sachsen]: Johannes Herrmann, n.d.).

[147] Gerhard von Rad, *Old Testament Theology*, trans. D. M. G. Stalker (New York: Harper & Row, 1962 [orig. 1957]).

speak of a historical event behind the biblical narratives. In von Rad's view, the OT, as a literary document, was a virtual anthology of early traditions with only a modicum of actual history behind them. This did not mean to von Rad, however, that we were without an historical event on which to base our OT theology. For von Rad the historical event that served as the historical foundation of Israel's faith was not the event *referred to* by the text but the actual *process of referring* by means of the text. The communication situation, namely, the very process (*Traditionsgeschichte*) through which the OT was formed, was in fact a real historical event. Someone, at some point in time, told the story of Israel's past and that act of telling or writing the story was itself an historical event. Moreover, von Rad argued, it was an event of the kind that could serve as the focus of an OT theology. Therefore, according to von Rad, OT theology should focus less on the attempt to reconstruct the events recorded in the Bible and more with the theological significance of the history of traditions lying behind the formation of the biblical texts. He thus set out to write a theology of the tradition history of the biblical text. This was a fundamental shift in historical focus and, in fact, had little effect on those whose interest lay in the events referred to in the Bible. Nevertheless, von Rad had cast some helpful light on a new area of study, and in that sense his studies in OT theology proved seminal for a new generation of biblical theologians.

More recently, building on von Rad's approach, Brevard Childs has argued that not only was the prehistory of the formation of the text an appropriate focus for OT theology, but also the formation of the biblical text as we now have it in the OT canon can serve as the focus of our theological study.

> The initial point to be made is that the canonical approach to Old Testament theology is unequivocal in asserting that the object of theological reflection is the canonical writing of the Old Testament, that is, the Hebrew scriptures which are the received traditions of Israel. The materials for theological reflection are not the events or experiences behind the text, or apart from the construal in scripture by a community of faith and practice.[148]

Hartmut Gese has moved beyond both von Rad and Childs by suggesting that not only the prehistory and canonical process but also the subsequent interpretive history of the OT text can and should serve as the focus of OT theology. For Gese, the whole of the history of the text of the OT before and after it reached its canonical form is a part of the salvation history in which we can discern divine revelation.[149]

2.2.5. Summary

We have been discussing the first of four components of an OT theology, that is, the question of whether to find divine revelation in the text of Scripture or in the events to which the Scriptures refer. Since in the present work we are proposing a text-

---

[148]Brevard S. Childs, *Old Testament Theology in a Canonical Context* (Philadelphia: Fortress Press, 1986), 6; Rolf Rendtorff, *Das Alte Testament, Eine Einführung* (Neukirchen-Vluyn: Keukirchener, 1983), 138, argues for an approach that includes both the prehistory and the final shape of the text.

[149]Hartmut Gese, "Erwägungen zur Einheit der biblischen Theologie," *ZThK* NF 67 (1970): 417–36; Hans-Joachim Kraus, "Theologie als Traditionsbildung?" *Biblische Theologie heute*, ed. Klaus Haacker (Neukirchen-Vluyn: Neukirchener Verlag, 1977), 61–73.

oriented approach to OT theology, it may be helpful to list what we think are the major consequences of this decision for OT theology. They are:

(1) The words of Scripture and the meaning of the biblical author are the first and primary goal. Our methodology and approach to OT theology should reflect this primary goal.

(2) Though there was inevitably revelation of some sort in God's actions in history, our only access to divine revelation now is through the interpretation of the inspired writers in the text of Scripture.

(3) There is an important distinction between the text of Scripture and the prehistory of that text. It is the written text as we have it in its final form that is inspired and useful for instruction. It is the message of this text that is the locus of revelation. Whatever prehistory we may be able to reconstruct for the text, it is not a source of revelation or inspired instruction.

(4) There is also an important distinction between the text of Scripture and its socio-religious context. The text means what the author intends it to mean. It means, in fact, what it says. The text may have played a specific role within the needs and events of its own day, but that role is not to be taken as the inspired meaning of the text. The socio-religious role of the Scriptures may be of historical or sociological interest, but it is not a part of the inspired meaning of the text.

(5) There is an important distinction between the text and the truths of reason and personal experience. The meaning of the text is what the text says (author's intent). This textual meaning should not be mixed or confused with what we may know from science or personal experience. This does not mean that the two sources of truth, revelation and reason, necessarily stand in opposition to each other. It only means that the two approaches should be allowed to operate on their own, within their own fields of knowledge. When rightly understood on their own terms, the two approaches can then be compared and, we believe, found to be compatible.

(6) There is an important distinction between the text and the subsequent interpretations of the text.[150] Every text of Scripture has its own history of interpretation. The meaning of the text remains that of the original author and not the interpretation of later generations. This is true even when the later interpretation happens to be within the Bible itself, that is, "inter-biblical." A text-oriented approach to OT theology would, then, reject the various attempts to impose later interpretation onto the original author's meaning. Examples of such attempts in the history of theology are:

(a) Scripture and tradition: the tradition becomes part of the inspired meaning of the text.

(b) Sensus plenior: the later interpretation of the NT is added to or replaces the meaning of the OT text.

(c) Typology: the later interpretation of the NT overshadows the meaning of the OT text.

(7) There is a distinction between the text and the literary-cultural universals of all texts. Every text has at least two possible levels of meaning: the author's intended

---

[150]Henning Graf Reventlow has stressed the importance of this hermeneutical dimension in OT theology, "Basic Problems in Old Testament Theology," *JSOT,* 11 (1979): 13.

meaning, that is, what he specifically intended to say in a particular text, and the archetypal meaning, that which all such texts say in essence. A text-oriented approach is based only on the former level of meaning, the author's intended meaning. It recognizes the value of the second level of meaning in texts, the archetypal meaning, but does not acknowledge its role in an OT theology.

The tree-diagram in Figure 3.9 shows the first set of options we have discussed. Old Testament theology can be focused on the text of Scripture or on the events. The proposal for an OT theology represented in this book will reflect the choice of the text as the locus of divine revelation. That choice is marked here with an arrow.

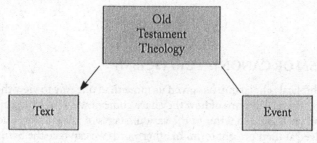

Figure 3.9

FOUR

CRITICISM OR CANON

2.3. CRITICISM OR CANON (+/- CRITICISM)

Modern biblical scholarship has given us more than one way to view the Scriptures. We can view them in terms of how they have come down to us by means of tradition, or we can view them in terms of the various stages of growth they underwent before they arrived at their present form. In other words we can take the Scriptures at face value as we now have them (canon), or we can apply the various methods of biblical criticism to attempt to "reconstruct" an earlier form of these texts (criticism). We are here speaking not only of textual criticism and the attempt to reconstruct the earliest form of the Hebrew text, but also of source criticism, form criticism, historical criticism, and any other kind of modern critical study of the text.

The question we are thus raising for OT theology is: Do we attempt to construct an OT theology on the basis of the text of the OT as we have it in its present canonical shape, or should we attempt to read the OT documents according to the form in which they were written at an earlier stage? This is the component we will call *Criticism or Canon* (or +/- Criticism). As will be the case throughout the remainder of the discussion below, the present question of Criticism or Canon must be discussed in terms of both a focus on the text of Scripture and a focus on the event, that is, in combination with the earlier choice between *Text or Event* (+/- Text). Figure 4.1 shows the various possible combinations of approaches to OT theology.

We will begin by viewing the question of *Criticism or Canon* as it relates to a text-oriented approach (+ Text) to OT theology, that is, approaches A and B in Figure 4.1. After that, we will view it from the perspective of an event-oriented OT theology (- Text), that is, approaches C and D.

Component	Approach A	Approach B	Approach C	Approach D
1. Text or Event	+ Text (Text)	+ Text (Text)	-Text (Event)	-Text (Event)
2. Criticism or Canon	+ Criticism (Criticism)	- Criticism (Canon)	+ Criticism (Criticism)	- Criticism (Canon)

Figure 4.1

2.3.1. Criticism or Canon and the Text (+ Text)

As the chart in Figure 4.2 shows, when viewed from the perspective of an OT theology that focuses on the text of Scripture (+ Text), the question of *Criticism or Canon* is simply whether an OT theology should be based on the methods and results of what we might call a *literature criticism* (Approach A), or, whether it should not apply a critical method to the text (- Criticism) and thus be based solely on the final shape of the text in the OT canon (Approach B).

Our primary object in this section will be to clarify the distinction between the various literature-critical approaches to the OT and those approaches that take as their starting point the form of the OT as we now have it in the canon. Maier expresses this difference in methodology by distinguishing between "hypothetical" reconstructions of the OT and the shape of the OT in the canon. The question is succinctly stated in his recent book on biblical hermeneutics.[1] According to Maier, critical scholarship is closely linked to the concept of science as the development of *hypotheses*. Revelation and faith, however, aim at *certitude*. Thus, Maier argues, in the use of critical hypotheses, exegesis puts itself at risk. Exegesis and theology are made to rest on literary hypotheses. Hypotheses, however, cannot provide a safe harbor for faith. Only the canonical text can do this.[2]

2.3.1.1. A Critical Approach to the Text (Approach A)

First, we must say a word about terminology. When we speak of a critical approach to the text of Scripture we cannot use terms such as text-critical or literary-critical because in biblical studies these terms have come to mean something quite specific and quite different than what we have in mind here. Thus we have chosen to use the neutral term *literature-criticism* to designate the concept we want to develop in this section. We are using this term as a translation of Wolfgang Richter's term *Literatur-wissenschaft*. Richter means by this term the scientific attempt to give an orderly descrip-

Component	Approach A	Approach B
1. Text or Event	+ Text (Text)	+ Text (Text)
2. Criticism or Canon	+ Criticism (Criticism)	- Criticism (Canon)

Figure 4.2

---

[1] Gerhard Maier, *Biblische Hermeneutik* (Wuppertal: R. Brockhaus Verlag, 1990).

[2] "Historische Arbeit bleibt verschwistert mit der Bildung von Hypothesen. Offenbarung und Glaube aber zielen auf Gewissheit. Die Exegese wagt sich also mit ihrer historischen Arbeit stets auf eine stürmische, immer wechselnde See. Um im Bild zu bleiben: Diese See ist allerdings nicht uferlos, sondern hat feste Ufer. Aber nicht die Hypothesen sind es, die diese Ufer bilden können, sondern nur der kanonische Text" (Maier, 344).

tion of the whole of the literary material of the OT according to its form and content.[3] As we will see below, literature-criticism is a broader term than the more technical term *literary criticism*, which already has a well-developed sense in OT studies.[4]

As we understand the term, literature-criticism includes such approaches to the OT as literary criticism (the critical analysis of the "coherency" of a text), source criticism (the attempt to reconstruct earlier sources used in a text), form criticism, tradition criticism, and structuralism. What each of these approaches has in common and what makes the term literature-criticism appropriate is the fact that they focus on some aspect of the text of Scripture apart from the final shape of the text. They apply a critical standard to the present shape of the text rather than accept it as it is.

What are the various kinds of literature-criticism and how do they affect one's approach to OT theology? To answer that question we must view each of these critical approaches individually and point briefly to its role in OT theology. We will attempt to illustrate the role of each of these critical methods by citing examples from standard studies in OT theology.

2.3.1.1.1. Literary Criticism

Literary criticism attempts to establish criteria of unity or disunity within a text in order to determine the "original" shape of a biblical text. As Richter has described it, the method proceeds primarily along two lines. First, one sets out to gather the criteria within a text that speak *against* its being a literary unity (criteria of disunity). Secondly, one makes an evaluation of the various parts of the text that have been isolated in order to determine "that which does not belong 'originally' to the text" (criteria of originality).[5] Literary criticism thus focuses on a hypothetical "early" stage of the text before it reached its present canonical shape.

In the Pentateuch, literary criticism is rarely practiced apart from source criticism. The various earlier and later parts of the Pentateuch are isolated and then combined with other parts to form hypothetical documents (e.g., the "Jahwist" or the "Priestly Document"). In other parts of the OT, however, literary criticism often stands alone and has been used as a basis for OT theology. This is particularly true of the prophetic literature. Hugo Gressmann's *Der Messias*,[6] for example, is based on his initial isolation of the various earlier portions of the prophetic books. Gressmann makes it quite clear that he does not approach the theological subject of the messianic hope

---

[3]"Its task is to describe and classify the whole of the literary material in the OT according to its formal and material shape" (Wolfgang Richter, *Exegese als Literaturwissenschaft, Entwurf einer alttestamentlichen Literaturtheorie und Methodologie* [Göttingen: Vandenhoeck & Ruprecht, 1970], 28).

[4]There is not yet a universal agreement on the specific sense of the term *Literature*-criticism (*Literaturwissenschaft*). Hardmeier, for example, uses the term in a broader sense than Richter, "As long as the exegesis of the Bible, or in our case the exegesis of the OT, limits itself to scientific methods and makes the claim to being scientific, that is, by recognizing its responsibility to the principle of an intersubjective verification of the results of its research, it can be designated as a science of literature (*Literaturwissenschaft*)" (Christof Hardmeier, *Texttheorie und biblische Exegese* [Chr. Kaiser, 1978], 28).

[5]Richter, *Exegese*, 49–50.

[6]Hugo Gressmann, *Der Messias* (Göttingen: Vandenhoeck & Ruprecht, 1929).

LITERARY CRITICISM

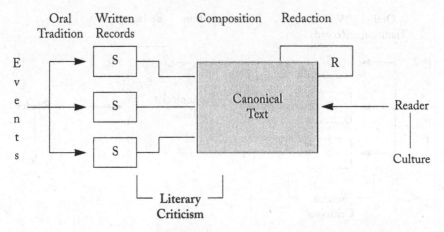

1. Criteria of unity or disunity of the text of Scripture
2. Determination of the "original" shape of the text of Scripture

Figure 4.3

in the OT by assuming the present prophetic books are literary units in their own right. These books are mere collections or anthologies of countless earlier prophetic sayings. Each of these earlier "pieces" of the text must first be isolated so that each part of the text can speak on its own. Gressmann argues that one should no more read the present text of the book of Isaiah as a literary unity than one would read the collected writings of Goethe as a single literary work. Both works have to be broken down into their original literary units before they can be properly understood. In the case of the prophetic books, however, there are no indications in the text where these earlier sayings begin and end. Hence a literary criticism of some type is necessary to isolate the smaller units.[7]

2.3.1.1.2. Source Criticism

Source criticism, which is based largely on the results of literary criticism, attempts to identify and reconstruct the various supposed literary documents that lie behind the present text: "Particularly in the Pentateuch, but also in the other books, it is customary to entrust to the method [of literary criticism] the further question of which texts are capable of being reconstructed into a single work."[8] The goal of source criticism is the reconstruction of a complete document from the various literary strands

---

[7]Gressmann, *Der Messias*, 68.

[8]Richter, *Exegese*, 50. Note the difference of terminology with Fohrer: "The so-called 'determination of the sources' is by and large viewed as the distinct task of literary criticism" (Georg Fohrer, *Introduction to the Old Testament*, trans. D. E. Green [Nashville: Abingdon, 1968], 48).

SOURCE CRITICISM

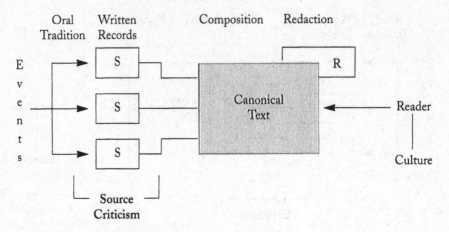

1. Based on results of Literary Criticism
2. Reconstructs earlier documents (S) from literary strands
   or fragments

Figure 4.4

or fragments in the present canonical text. Once isolated, these earlier documents become the focus of exegesis and theology.

There have been numerous attempts to write a biblical theology based on the hypothetical sources of the Pentateuch or on a reconstructed prophetic document such as Deutero-Isaiah. With the overwhelming success of the "documentary hypothesis" at the end of the nineteenth century, OT theology that relies on source criticism has dominated the field of biblical theology. In many cases, however, source criticism has merely provided the basis for an analysis of Israel's religion. That is, the focus has been on the religion that lies behind the sources rather than on the theology of the sources themselves.[9] As such, these approaches to OT theology belong under Approach C below.

Apart from this, the focus on the theology of the literary documents themselves has primarily been carried out in the interest of establishing criteria for identifying and dating specific sources. Holzinger, for example, devoted considerable attention to the "religious and ethical viewpoint" of the Jahwist,[10] the Elohist,[11] the Deuteronomist,[12] and the Priestly Source,[13] but his expressed purpose was to use the distinct theology of these various literary strands as the criteria for grouping them into a single document, not as a basis for OT theology as such.

---

[9]Rudolf Kittel, *Die Religion des Volkes Israel* (Leipzig: Quelle & Meyer, 1921), 36.
[10]H. Holzinger, *Einleitung in den Hexateuch* (Freiburg: J. C. B. Mohr [Paul Siebeck], 1893), 127–34.
[11]Ibid., 201–12.
[12]Ibid., 313–20.
[13]Ibid., 376–86.

During the early period of the study of source criticism, some biblical theologians focused more on the theology of the various literary documents. Emil Kautzsch is a notable example. In his *Biblical Theology of the Old Testament*[14] Kautzsch pays considerable attention to the theology of each of the supposed sources of the Pentateuch and of the various sources found lying behind the prophetic books. Kautzsch seems genuinely interested in the theology of each of the major documents for its own sake. Though his is a critically reconstructed text, he nevertheless focuses on the literary texts themselves and not on historical reconstructions of events. Nowhere is this quite so evident as in Kautzsch's exposition of the theology of the Priestly Source.[15]

In more recent times, much attention has been paid to the theology of each of the supposed literary sources in the OT. Entire books have been devoted to the "Theology of the Yahwist," and many articles and monographs have focused on various aspects of the theology of the other sources of the Pentateuch.

2.3.1.1.3. Form Criticism

Form criticism attempts to reconstruct the archetypical literary patterns that lie behind the present biblical texts.[16] The form critic studies the canonical text to discover evidence of literary patterns that point to historical and cultural practices in ancient Israel.

The form critic may, for example, discover a "praise psalm" or the remains of one, in a literary work and argue from it that a social practice once existed in Israel in which such a psalm would have functioned. If enough of these forms or parts of them can be discovered in the existing OT books, they can be used to reconstruct the social or cultural institutions themselves. These reconstructed institutions and the formal patterns they produced then become the focus of exegesis and biblical theology.

Kraus's recent biblical theology of the Psalms is an example of the dependence of an OT theology on the results of form criticism.[17] On the basis of the various psalm patterns (*Gattungen*), Kraus reconstructs an earlier form of the psalms in the context (*Sitz im Leben*) of Israel's worship. The theological message of the Psalms is then described in the light of that reconstructed context. The meaning of a "Jahweh-epithet," such as "king," for example, is derived from a reconstruction of Israel's preexilic worship, first in Shiloh and then in Jerusalem. Furthermore, Kraus associates other epithets, such as "Holy One" and "Most High," with the same *Sitz im Leben*, and thus is able to combine them with the meaning of the "king" epithet. The result is that, for Kraus, two of the central theological statements of the psalms can be reconstructed from the present book of Psalms, the ideas of "monarchical monotheism" and "cosmic universalism."[18]

---

[14]Emil Kautzsch, *Biblische Theologie des Alten Testaments* (Tübingen: J. C. B. Mohr [Paul Siebeck], 1911).

[15]Ibid., 328–53; see Kautzsch's article, "Religion of Israel" in James Hastings, *A Dictionary of the Bible* (Edinburgh: T & T Clark, 1904), 5:715–23.

[16]"Forms, that is, stereotyped combinations of words, which are found in several literary works, suggest a unity at a sociocultural level and thus also contexts which are prior to existing literary works" (Fohrer, 83).

[17]Hans-Joachim Kraus, *Theologie der Psalmen* (Neukirchen-Vluyn: Neukirchener Verlag, 1979), cf. 26–36.

FORM CRITICISM

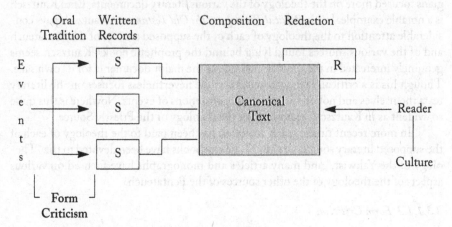

1. Discovers stereotyped patterns of words in Scripture
2. Reconstructs social or cultrual institutions in ancient Israel

Figure 4.5

Again it is important to note that the use of form criticism is not aimed at the meaning of the present OT text, but rather at the meaning of the social or cultural institutions in ancient Israel that produced the forms now found in the OT text.

2.3.1.1.4. Tradition Criticism

Tradition criticism attempts to describe the earlier oral and written stages of the material found in the biblical texts.[19] In most cases it assumes that traditions about Israel's experience of God's acts in concrete historical events were first transmitted orally within isolated tribal and family units. Using form criticism, it attempts to reconstruct the various settings in which these traditions were passed on from one generation to another and the settings in which they were later combined into larger complexes.

The theology of Gerhard von Rad is one of the clearest examples of an OT theology based on the approach of tradition criticism. For von Rad, the focus of an OT theology is not the text as we have it in the OT canon or the beliefs of Israel "as a world of religious concepts"[20] but rather the earlier traditions and the communities of faith which transmitted and transformed them to suit new situations. According to von Rad, tradition criticism has shown that "there were up and down the land many traditions which little by little combined into ever larger complexes of tradition," and that,

---

[18]Ibid., 34–35.

[19]"The aim [of Tradition Criticism] is the oral, or sometimes written, tradition which lies before the written literary works" (Richter, *Exegese*, 152).

[20]Gerhard von Rad, *Old Testament Theology, The Theology of Israel's Historical Traditions* (New York: Harper & Row, 1962), 112.

TRADITION CRITICISM

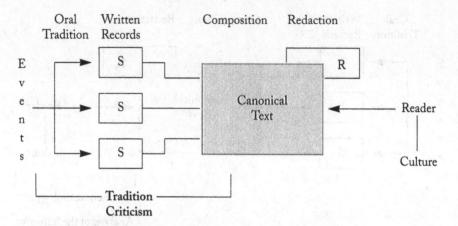

1. Reconstructs the oral and written stages of the tradition behind the present form of the scriptural text
2. Describes the interpretation and reinterpretation of the tradition in the stages before its use in the canonical text

Figure 4.6

"Theologically, these accumulations were in a state of constant flux."[21] At each moment in Israel's history, these traditions were applied anew to the lives of the people of God. The proper focus of OT theology, then, is the study of the faith of those who combined the smaller traditions into ever larger complexes. "If . . . we put Israel's picture of her history in the forefront of our theological consideration, we encounter what appropriately is the most essential subject of a theology of the Old Testament, the living word of Jahweh coming on and on to Israel for ever. . . ."[22]

2.3.1.1.5. Phenomenology

We are using the term *phenomenology* in a general way to describe any approach to the biblical text that attempts to distance it from the meaning it had in its original setting. The focus of such approaches is the "effective history" or subsequent interpretation of a canonical text.

Hans-Georg Gadamer[23] has argued that texts which are preserved by believing communities also make a lasting impression on those communities. There are, in effect, two horizons that meet in the process of reading a text such as the Bible. On the one hand, there is the sense of the biblical text itself, that is, what its original author

---

[21]Ibid.

[22]Ibid.

[23]Hans-Georg Gadamer, *Wahrheit und Methode, Grundzüge einer philosophischen Hermeneutik*, 4th ed. (Tübingen: J. C. B. Mohr [Paul Siebeck], 1975); also from the 2nd edition, *Truth and Method*, trans. Garrett Barden and John Cumming (New York: The Seabury Press, 1975).

PHENOMENOLOGY

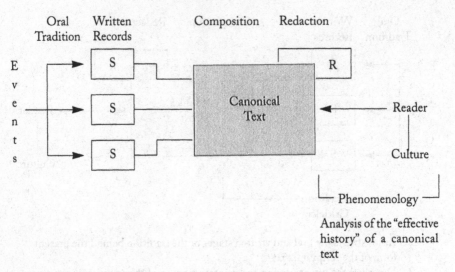

Figure 4.7

intended. On the other hand, there is the sense that the same text has for each new generation of readers, none of which have exactly the same cultural, intellectual, or religious outlook as the original author. If, however, the text is read in a believing community, one in which the text is held to be authoritative, the horizon of the readers has already been fundamentally shaped by the horizon of the text. If that be the case, then, although the two horizons are, by the nature of the case, quite different, the process of understanding a text such as the Bible is not necessarily hindered by the difference of horizons. It is, in fact, Gadamer argues, the ability of the text to occupy both horizons that makes understanding possible. Through the text the two horizons are merged into an act of understanding and sharing of horizons. The text can only be understood from the horizon of the reader, yet, in a believing community, the horizon of the reader has already been fundamentally shaped and prepared by the horizon of the text.

This category covers a wide range of approaches to the meaning of the OT. It is represented, for example, by numerous recent studies that focus on "inter-biblical" interpretation, that is, the study of how later biblical books read and understood earlier ones.[24]

There is a subtle, but important, distinction to be made between a phenomenological inter-biblical approach to the meaning of the OT and one that is based on the

---

[24]Rene Bloch, "Midrash," *DBSup* (1957), 5:1263–81; Michael Fishbane, *Biblical Interpretation in Ancient Israel* (Oxford: Clarendon Press, 1985); I. L. Seeligmann, "Voraussetzungen der Midrasch-Exegese," *Supplements to Vetus Testamentum*, Vol. 1 (Leiden: Brill, 1953); Geza Vermes, "Bible and Midrash: Early Old Testament Exegesis," *The Cambridge History of the Bible* (Cambridge: Cambridge University Press, 1970), 1:199–231; Thomas Willi, *Die Chronik als Auslegung* (Göttingen: Vandenhoeck & Ruprecht, 1972).

PHENOMENOLOGY: INTER-BIBLICAL

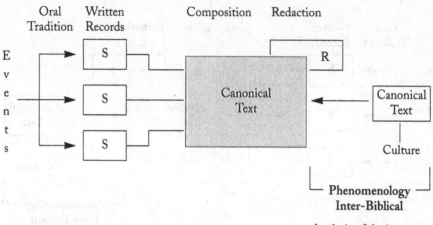

Figure 4.8

text-linguistic concept of inter-textuality. An inter-biblical approach to the meaning of an OT text focuses on how the meaning of the earlier text has *changed* in the understanding of the later community. An inter-textual approach, however, focuses on *how* the meaning of the earlier canonical text has *remained the same*. In an inter-biblical approach, the later canonical text is understood as a replacement of the earlier one. In an inter-textual approach, however, the later canonical text is understood as an explication or elaboration of the earlier text. In an inter-textual approach both the meaning of the earlier text and the meaning of the later text are kept intact. The meaning of an earlier text becomes an assumed part of that of the later text.

The phenomenological approach is represented in several recent approaches to OT studies. The various literary approaches to the OT, for example, fit in this category;[25] as do the approaches of Paul Ricoeur,[26] and various forms of structuralism, that is, those attempts to analyze the human and cultural universals embodied in the biblical text.[27] Henning Graf Reventlow has recently argued that it is only by means of a

---

[25]Robert Alter, *The Art of Biblical Narrative* (New York: Basic Books, 1981); Northrop Frye, *The Great Code, The Bible and Literature* (New York: Harcourt Brace Jovanovich, 1982); Meir Sternberg, *The Poetics of Biblical Narrative* (Bloomington: Indiana University Press, 1985).

[26]Paul Ricoeur, *Essays on Biblical Interpretation* (Philadelphia: Fortress Press, 1980): "Hence there is hermeneutics in the Christian order because the kerygma is the rereading of an ancient Scripture" (51).

[27]"What, then, are the distinctive properties of structuralism? In the first place it is presented as a method whose scope includes all human social phenomena, no matter what their form, thus embracing not only the social sciences proper but also the humanities and the fine arts. This is made possible by the belief that all manifestations of social activity, whether it be the clothes that are worn, the books that are written or the systems of kinship and marriage that are practiced in any society, constitute languages, in a formal

CONTRAST: INTER-BIBLICAL AND INTER-TEXTUAL APPROACHES

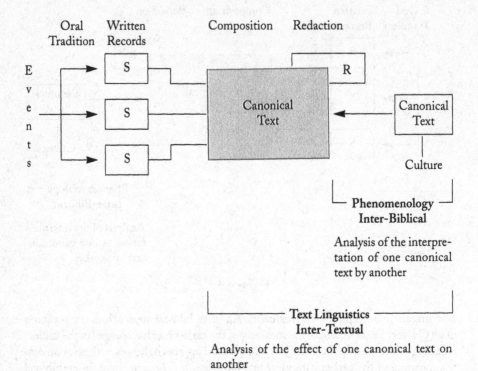

Figure 4.9

phenomenological approach to OT theology that the gap between faith and science can be narrowed.[28]

2.3.1.1.6. Summary

The chart in Figure 4.10 represents the various literature-critical approaches to the OT text and shows how each relates to the tasks of the others.

We recognize the legitimacy of these various literature-critical approaches to the study of the OT as well as the fact they can provide an appropriate basis for an OT theology. We also want to emphasize, however, that the goal of each of these approaches is not the explication of the text that lies before us in the canonical Scriptures. In each case they focus on a form of the text that has been reconstructed from the canonical text. Thus an OT theology that is based on one or more of these approaches would be textual in nature but its locus would be a text other than the present canonical one.

---

sense. Hence their regularities may be reduced to the same set of abstract rules that define and govern what we normally think of as language" (Michael Lane, ed., *Introduction to Structuralism* [New York: Basic Books 1970], 13–14).

[28]Henning Graf Reventlow, "Basic Problems in OT Theology," *JSOT*, 11 (1979): 2–22.

CRITICAL STAGES IN BIBLICAL NARRATIVE

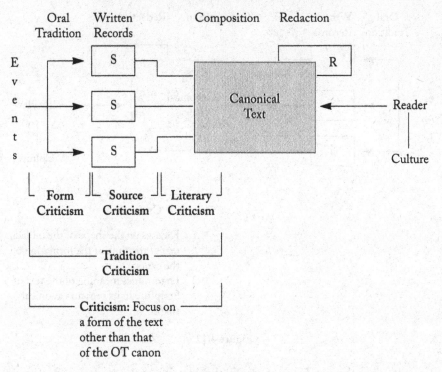

Figure 4.10

2.3.1.2. A Canonical Approach to the Text (Approach B)

Those approaches to the OT text that focus on its final canonical shape include canon criticism, composition criticism, redaction criticism, and text linguistics.

2.3.1.2.1. Canon Criticism

Canon criticism addresses the question of the meaning of the biblical texts in their present form in the OT canon. The major task of a canonical analysis of the Hebrew Bible is to understand the peculiar shape and special function of the books that comprise the Hebrew canon. Its focus is on the final form of the text itself.

We have a clear demonstration of the nature of an OT theology based on a canonical approach in the theology of Brevard Childs.[29] Childs states unequivocally that "the object of theological reflection is the canonical writing of the Old Testament, that is, the Hebrew scriptures which are the received traditions of Israel."[30] Childs is

---

[29]Brevard S. Childs, *Old Testament Theology in a Canonical Context* (Philadelphia: Fortress Press, 1986). See also Childs's *Biblical Theology of the Old and New Testaments* (Minneapolis: Fortress Press, 1992).
[30]Ibid., 6.

CANON CRITICISM

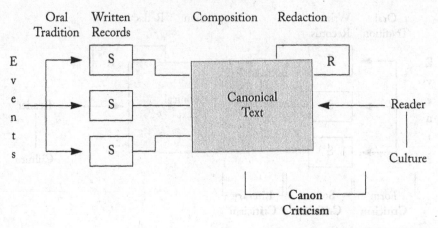

Figure 4.11

also quite clear that the focus of an OT theology is not the events or experiences behind the text, but the canonical text itself.[31]

2.3.1.2.2. Composition Criticism

Composition criticism attempts to describe the literary strategy of a biblical book. According to Fohrer, composition criticism seeks to explain the types and ways the biblical writers fashioned literary units into a complete literary whole. Moreover, it attempts to understand the theological characteristics of the smaller and larger compositions and the direction, goal, and tendency of the author of the whole work.[32]

The present work is an attempt to demonstrate the nature of an OT theology based on the approach of compositional criticism. We will attempt to show, for exam-

---

[31]Ibid. Childs also wants to emphasize that "the biblical text continually bears witness to events and reactions in the life of Israel," and hence "the literature cannot be isolated from its ostensive reference." Thus he concludes, "it is a basic misunderstanding to try to describe a canonical approach simply as a form of structuralism (*contra* Barton)" (6).

[32]Fohrer, p. 142; "Dabei liegt das Hauptgewicht auf dem Bemühen, Aufbau, Komposition und Absicht der Endgestalt der einzelnen Bücher zu erfassen. . . . Mit der Frage nach der Komposition der jetzigen Bücher tritt jedoch ein neuer Gesichtspunkt hinzu, der über die bisherigen Fragestellungen hinauszuführen versucht" (Rolf Rendtorff, *Das Alte Testament, Eine Einführung* [Neukirchen-Vluyn: Neukirchener, 1983], ix–x).

COMPOSITION CRITICISM

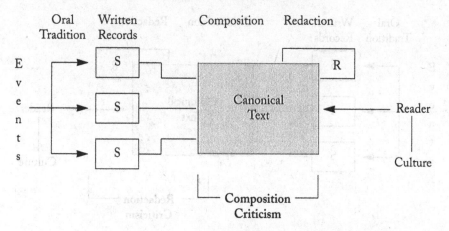

1. Approaches the OT text as a literary unit
2. Describes the literary strategy of the scriptural text

Figure 4.12

ple, that when viewed as a whole, the Pentateuch is a single literary unit composed of many smaller units of narrative, poetry, and law codes. In the interweaving of these parts into a whole, a discernible strategy can be traced throughout the entire work. Key poetic texts, for example, are deliberately placed after each large narrative segment in order to provide each segment with an eschatological and messianic interpretation. The various law codes within the Pentateuch are also deliberately placed within a larger narrative framework in order to show the continual failure of the law to produce obedience to God's will. The theological motivation or strategy of the work is twofold. The Pentateuch first intends to demonstrate the failure of the Sinai covenant and to engender a hope in the coming of a New Covenant. In this respect it is similar in meaning and intent to the rest of the books of the OT, particularly those of the prophetic literature. Secondly, the Pentateuch intends to look forward into the eschatological future to the coming of a savior-king who will defeat Israel's enemies and restore the blessing God originally intended for all humankind "in the last days."[33]

2.3.1.2.3. Redaction Criticism

Redaction criticism seeks to distinguish the various editions that a single text or a single composition may have experienced. Whereas composition criticism focuses on the final shape of a literary work, redaction criticism asks whether a work of liter-

---

[33]John H. Sailhamer, "The Canonical Approach to the OT: Its Effect on Understanding Prophecy," *JETS*, 30 (September 1987): 307ff; Sailhamer, "The Mosaic Law and the Theology of the Pentateuch," *Westminster Theological Journal*, 53 (1991): 241–61.

REDACTION CRITICISM

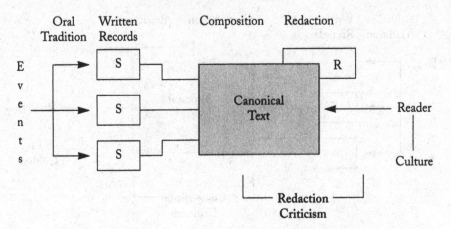

1. Determines the extent of reworking of an earlier text
2. Describes the meaning of the various stages of reworking

Figure 4.13

ature has been further edited or reworked and, if so, attempts to describe the extent and nature of that reworking.[34]

The present work will also seek to demonstrate the relevance of redaction criticism to a text-oriented approach to OT theology. It will do this by pointing to the various canon-conscious redactional seams that tie together the final pieces of the Hebrew Bible when viewed as a whole.

REDACTIONAL SEAMS IN THE OT CANON

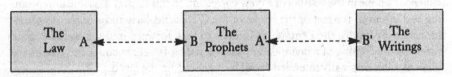

Figure 4.14

---

[34]". . .umfasst die Redaktion die literarische Bearbeitung im Anschluss an die Verschriftung von mündlich überliefertem Gut—sei sie vorläufig oder endgültig—oder an die sogleich erfolgte endgültige schriftliche Niederlegung. . . . Die Redaktionskritik soll das Ausmass und die Art und Weise der redaktionellen Bearbeitung erklären. Diese kann bei Aenderungen im Text von Einheiten im Hinzufügen von Rand-, Kontext- oder Interlinearglossen oder von grösseren Zusätzen (z.B. Hymenteile im Amosbuch), in bewussten Eingriffen in den Textbestand oder in Textumstellungen bestehen" (Fohrer, *Introduction*, 140–42).

TEXT LINGUISTICS

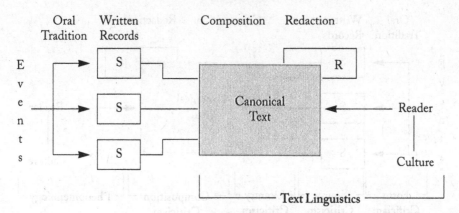

1. Establish criteria for the unity of a biblical text.
2. Describe linguistic features of the biblical text beyond the clause.
3. Formulate the "rules" that determine the semantic value of the biblical text

Figure 4.15

The last two chapters of the Pentateuch, Deuteronomy 33–34 (A in Figure 4.14), for example, are apparent additions to an earlier version of the Pentateuch[35] and serve to link it with Joshua 1:1–8 (B), and thus with the Former Prophets section of the Canon (Joshua-Kings). Moreover, the last section of Malachi, Malachi 4:4–6 (A'), appears to be a redactional addition to the book of Malachi which links it to the Writings section of the Canon, specifically to Psalm 1 (B'), the first textual unit of the Writings. Since the form and content of this material is strikingly similar (Deut. 34:1–5 = Mal. 4:4–6; Josh. 1:1–8 = Ps. 1), it appears to be the work of a single person. A text-oriented approach to OT theology would find such macro-structures to be of great importance for understanding the present shape of the OT.

2.3.1.2.4. *Text Linguistics*

Text linguistics attempts to describe the linguistic features that contribute to the meaning of a biblical book (see Fig. 4.15). While the study of the biblical languages is

---

[35]On virtually any reckoning of the authorship of the Pentateuch, these last two chapters must be considered as secondary additions. Critical scholarship, of course, has no difficulty viewing the chapters as secondary and late. It should also be clear, however, that even a very conservative approach to the Pentateuch that sees it as a final composition from the hand of Moses must view these last two chapters as additions. A conservative position would be that someone, after the death of Moses, added this mosaic blessing. Deuteronomy 33 is a poem written by Moses but attached to the Pentateuch "after his death." (Dt 33:1) Deuteronomy 34, of course, records the death of Moses (34:5–8) and is thus not only secondary to the Mosaic Pentateuch, but records the death of Moses presupposed in Dt 33.

CRITICAL AND CANONICAL STAGES IN BIBLICAL NARRATIVE

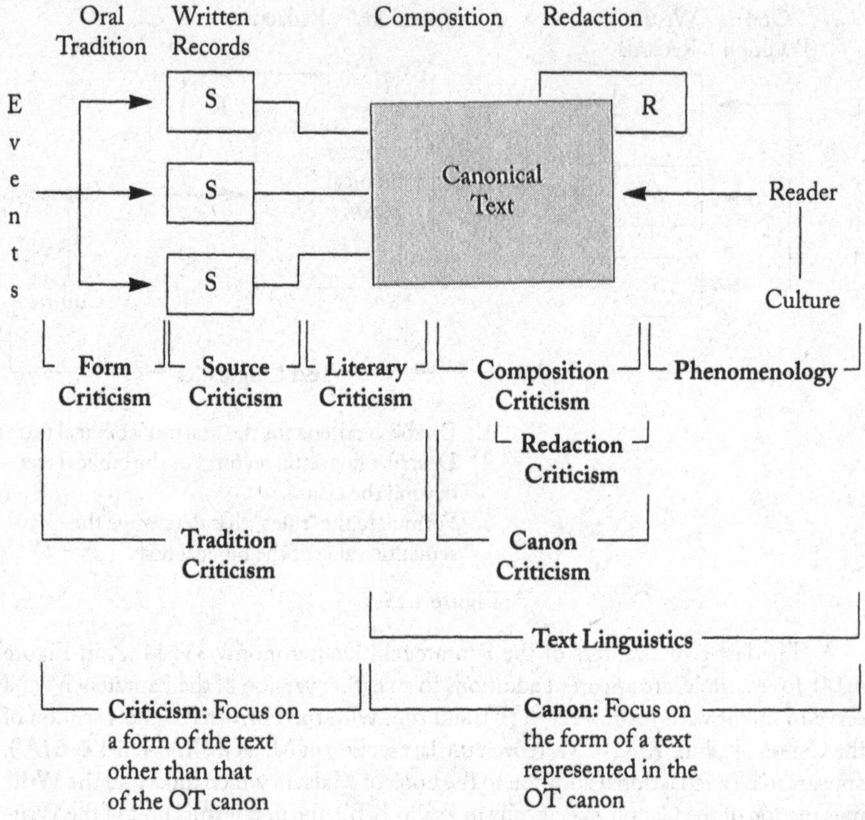

Figure 4.16

generally restricted to the level of words, clauses, and sentences, text linguistics starts from the awareness that the highest and most independent linguistic unit is not a clause, but a text.[36] It thus seeks to uncover the nature of the communication that happens in the biblical texts as such and to show the underlying order and structure of those texts.

In recent years, numerous text-linguistic approaches to the OT have been proposed.[37] The work of Hardmeier may be taken as a preliminary example of an attempt to base at least some aspects of OT theology on a text-linguistic approach.[38]

---

[36]Robert de Beaugrande and Wolfgang Dressler, *Introduction to Text Linguistics* (London: Longman, 1981).

[37]Franz Schicklberger, "Biblische Literarkritik und linguistische Texttheorie, Bemerkungen zu einer Textsyntax von hebräischen Erzähltexten," *Theologische Zeitschrift*, 34 (1978): 67–69; Christof Hardmeier, *Texttheorie und biblische Exegese* (Chr. Kaiser, 1978); Robert Oberforcher, *Die Flutprologe als kompositions-schlüssel der biblischen Urgeschichte* (Tyrolia, 1981); Heinrich F. Plett, *Textwissenschaft und Textanalyse* (Heidelberg: Quelle & Meyer, 1979); Gillian Brown and George Yule, *Discourse Analysis* (Cambridge: Cambridge University Press, 1983).

[38]Christof Hardmeier, *Texttheorie und biblische Exegese* (Chr. Kaiser, 1978).

Component	Approach C	Approach D
1. Text or Event	- Text (Event)	- Text (Event)
2. Criticism or Canon	+ Criticism (Criticism)	- Criticism (Canon)

Figure 4.17

2.3.1.3. Summary

The chart in Figure 4.16 summarizes the goal of each aspect of the study of the OT, and how each relates to the question of Criticism or Canon.

2.3.2. Criticism or Canon and the Event (- Text)

When viewed from the perspective of an OT theology that focuses on the historical events that are referred to in Scripture, the question raised by the choice of Criticism or Canon is whether an OT theology should be based on the historical event as it has been reconstructed by historical criticism,[39] or on the historical event as it is reflected and recounted in the OT canon.

We are not here raising the question of the problem of history, but rather that of the effect of critical methodology on one's understanding of particular historical events. Did the events of Israel's history happen as they are recorded in Scripture or must they be reconstructed and explained according to the criteria of modern historical method?

2.3.2.1. A Critical Approach to the Event (Approach C)

There are vast differences in the ways and the extent to which historical criticism is practiced in OT studies. At one end of the spectrum there are those biblical historians and theologians who discount considerable portions of the historical information in the OT. The basis of such a judgment is the view that, in their present form, the biblical sources are not eyewitness accounts. Though they contain much eyewitness material, the biblical histories, they argue, come to us by way of human tradition and as such cannot be used without critical assessment.

The recent history of Israel by Herbert Donner is an example of this type of use of critical methodology in reconstructing the events of Israel's history.[40] According to Donner, an historical critical investigation of the sources is demanded in the case of

---

[39]Hans-Joachim Kraus, *Geschichte der historisch-kritischen Erforschung des Alten Testaments* (Neukirchen-Vluyn: Neukirchener Verlag, 1969); Gottfried Hornig, *Die Anfänge der historisch-kritischen Theologie* (Göttingen: Vandenhoeck & Ruprecht, 1961); Klaus Scholder, *Ursprünge und Probleme der Bibelkritik im 17. Jahrhundert, Ein Beitrag zur Entstehung der historisch-kritischen Theologie* (München: Chr. Kaiser Verlag, 1966); Ludwig Diestel, *Geschichte des Alten Testamentes in der christlichen Kirche* (Jena: Mauke's Verlag, 1869); Gottlob Wilhelm Meyer, *Geschichte der Schrifterklärung seit der Wiederherstellung der Wissenschaften* (Göttingen: Johann Friedrich Röwer, 1802)

[40]Herbert Donner, *Geschichte des Volkes Israel und seiner Nachbarn in Grundzügen* (Göttingen: Vandenhoeck & Ruprecht, 1984).

RADICAL HISTORICAL CRITICAL UNDERSTANDING OF THE EVENT

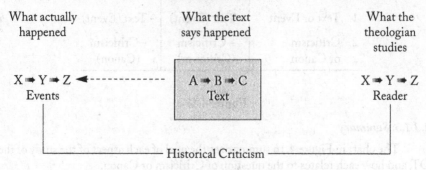

Figure 4.18

the history of Israel. The OT must be treated just as one would treat other ancient Near Eastern material. For the history of Israel after the time of the establishment of the kingship (the first millennium B.C.), Donner argues, the sources are quite good. The situation is different, however, for the time before the kingship (the second millennium B.C.). For this period, Donner suggests, there is less to go on from the records and it becomes even less so the farther back one goes into the past.[41]

At the other end of the spectrum there are biblical scholars who have argued that when applied to the OT texts, historical criticism can and should be used to demonstrate the essential *trustworthiness* of the biblical records. Hence, when they speak of the events referred to in the OT texts, they view those events in much the same way as they are recounted in Scripture. Though the textual version of the event is not taken for granted, the use of moderate historical criticism results in a version of the events that is essentially the same as that of Scripture.

Regarding the patriarchal history, for example, John Bright comes to a fundamentally different conclusion than that of Donner, quoted above. According to Bright, the patriarchal narratives are firmly anchored in history, that is, what we read in the patriarchal narratives is substantially the same as what actually happened.[42]

K. A. Kitchen also takes the view that the biblical narratives are founded on solid historical evidence. The patriarchal narratives are not "legendary" in form, but rather show clear signs of being grounded in actual history. The evidence is on the side of understanding the patriarchs as representing historical persons within historically-based traditions.[43]

We can see, then, that differences of opinion exist among biblical scholars about the extent to which historical criticism can confirm the essential historicity of the biblical narratives. For some, the actual events behind the biblical narratives have to be considerably

---

[41]Donner, 22–23.

[42]John Bright, *A History of Israel*, 3rd ed. (Philadelphia: Westminster Press, 1981), 77.

[43]K. A. Kitchen, *The Bible in Its World* (Downers Grove: InterVarsity Press, 1978), 65.

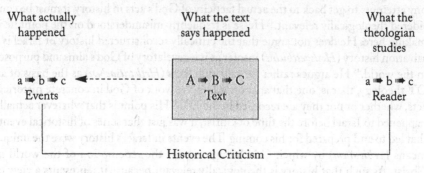

reconstructed before they can be taken as "real" history. To many others, however, the biblical narratives are remarkably accurate, even in the smallest detail. The point we are attempting to raise here is not which approach represents the more valid assessment of the biblical material. We want only to show that an event-oriented critical approach to OT theology seeks to build its theology on a critical reconstruction of the historical event rather than on the biblical narratives as face-value historical accounts of what actually happened.

2.3.2.1.1. A Radically Critical Approach to the Event: Franz Hesse

The theologian who has argued most distinctly for an event-oriented critical approach to OT theology is Franz Hesse.[44] Hesse accepts the radical critical reconstruction of OT history. According to Hesse there is little historical value in the present OT narratives. These narratives represent what Israel believed happened, not what actually happened. Though the OT may represent God's acts in the past as facts, the historical critic cannot accept them as such. He knows the "facts"[45] to be otherwise. It is just here, argues Hesse, that the major problem lies. A theology that claims to be based on scientifically verifiable facts of history must look somewhere other than the OT for the actual account of God's acts. For Hesse, it is the historical critical method that most accurately reproduces the facts of God's activities in history. Although such a critically reconstructed history of Israel is itself an interpretation ("Deutung")[46] of

---

[44]Franz Hesse, "Bewährt sich eine 'Theologie der Heilstatsachen' am Alten Testament?" *ZAW*, 81 (1969): 1–17.

[45]Hesse's focus is on the historical event, the "Ur-Faktum" or "*nudum, brutum factum,*" that lies behind any attempt at interpretation and meaning.

[46]Hasel's criticism of Hesse as falling prey to historical positivism seems to me to be unwarranted, as is his statement that Hesse "apparently does not recognize that the historical-critical version of Israel's history is also already interpreted history, namely, interpreted on the basis of historico-philosophical premises" (Gerhard Hasel, *Old Testament Theology: Basic Issues in the Current Debate* [Grand Rapids: Eerdmans, 1991], 119). Hesse is quite clear that the modern historical reconstructions of Israel's history are as determined by their presuppositions as those of the OT. "Auch die heutige historische Wissenschaft begnügt sich nicht mit der Aufspürung des nudum factum. . . . Solches zu konstatieren wäre uninteressant, ja

the facts, we may take it as a scientifically accurate reconstruction of God's acts because it attempts to follow modern historical methodology. Insofar as critical historiography attempts to get back to the actual facticity of God's acts in history, it must be considered theologically relevant.[47] Hesse is frequently misunderstood on the point he is making here. He does not argue that the critically reconstructed history of Israel is a salvation history (*Heilsgeschichte*) insofar as it is revelatory of God's aims and purposes in the world.[48] He argues rather for salvation facts (*Heilstatsachen*) as the basis of an OT theology, that is, one that acknowledges the work of God in concrete historical acts, whether or not they are recorded in the OT.[49] His point is that whatever actually happened to Israel before the time of Christ, it was just that series of historical events that led to and prepared for his coming. The events in Israel's history were the unique means (*vehiculum*) by which God brought about the redemption of the world in Christ. As such that history is theologically relevant because it represents a view of God at work in history, and whatever we can learn about it can contribute to our understanding of God's acts. From the vantage point of God's final act in Christ,[50] we know that God was at work in Israel's history, but because of the problematic nature of the factual content of the OT, we cannot always know what God actually did or, in fact, everything that he did. The historical critical method, because it can uncover such historical facts, can thus contribute to our understanding of God's work. It does not matter if the facts uncovered by the modern historical method give us a different picture of Israel's history than that presented in the OT. Oftentimes, Hesse argues, critical history will present us with facts not even represented in the biblical texts.

---

sinnlos. So sucht man nach einem komplexeren Faktum, das aussagekräftiger ist . . . was hier ein 'komplexes Faktum' genannt wurde, geht sicher schon in eine Deutung über . . ." (Hesse, "Bewährt sich," 14).

[47]"Gewiss kann die Theologie auf die weitergehende Frage, in welcher Weise und zu welchem Ziel Gott hier am Werke gewesen ist, nicht verzichten—dann jedenfalls nicht, wenn für sie die Geschichte das Feld des Handelns Gottes bleibt" (Hesse, "Bewährt sich," 15–16).

[48]The view of Hasel and others is that Hesse does, in fact, identify the critically reconstructed view of Israel's history with a salvation history: "Thus Hesse attempts to overcome the dichotomy of the two versions of Israel's history by closely identifying the historical-critical picture of Israel's history with salvation history" (Gerhard Hasel, *Old Testament Theology: Basic Issues in the Current Debate* [Grand Rapids: Eerdmans, 1991], 118). Such an understanding of Hesse's position is, in my opinion, incorrect.

[49]"Bewährt sich eine 'Theologie der Heilstatsachen' am Alten Testament? Bei der Beantwortung dieser Frage kommt es sehr darauf an, was man unter 'Heilstatsachen' versteht. Es geht jedenfalls nicht so, dass man von der Kette der Fakten, die die Geschichte Israels in politischer, militärischer, geistiger oder religiöser Hinsicht geprägt haben, behauptet, das seien die Heilstatschen, die auch unseren Glauben, sei es mittelbar, sei es unmittelbar, beträfen. Wieso können Fakten einer irdisch-menschlichen Geschichte, der Geschichte eines bestimmten Volkes—später einer Kultusgemeinde—Heilstatsachen, d.h. von Gott zum Heile der Welt gesetzte Fakten sein? Die Geschichte Israels ist genauso wenig Heilsgeschichte wie die Geschichte irgendeines anderen Volkes. Und doch hat sie eine einmalige Qualität: Sie ist das Instrument, mit dessen Hilfe Gott seine nur dem Glauben erkennbaren Heilstaten hin auf Christus durchführte" (Hesse, "Bewährt sich," 16).

[50]Hesse does not argue, as Hasel appears to suggest, that the historical critical view of Israel's history played "a historic role in NT times" (Hasel, 119). Hesse's point is rather that historical criticism can give the modern historian an understanding of the events in Israel's history that led up to the coming of Christ in the first century. To give an account of the historical forces operating at a particular point in time is not to assume that those present and active in those forces were aware of them as such.

Whether God's acts in history are correctly represented in the OT, misrepresented in the OT, or not represented in the OT at all, the historical method attempts to uncover God's actual work in history and in so doing is theologically relevant.[51]

2.3.2.1.2. Two Moderately Critical Approaches to the Event: Walther Eichrodt and Eduard König

The goal of an OT theology, according to Walther Eichrodt, is "to present the religion of which the records are to be found in the Old Testament."[52] Eichrodt's concern is not the theology of the text of the OT but rather the theology of the religion of Israel reflected in and by the OT. In other words, the object of his study and theological description is the historical entity that lies behind the present text of the OT. The OT is a witness to Israel's faith in that it is a product of that faith.

Eichrodt intends to present the religion of Israel in its "constant basic tendency and character"[53] despite the fact that as an historical entity their religion was cast in "ever-changing historical conditions." The starting point of Israel's faith and the central *datum* of that faith was the historical act of God in initiating a covenant relation-

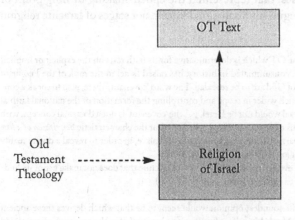

Figure 4.20

---

[51]"Deutungen, die die Bibel einem Ereignis, einem Vorgang gibt, können den Vorgang mehr verhüllen als erhellen: Wir kommen hier an das Faktum gar nicht heran, obwohl wir der Ueberzeugung sind, dass auch dieses so schwer erkennbare Faktum vehiculum der Heilstaten Gottes gewesen ist. In einem solchen Falle ist es eine legitime Aufgabe der Theologie, den Versuch zu machen, mit Hilfe der Methoden moderner historischer Wissenschaft sich dem Faktum selbst so weit wie möglich anzunähern und dieses Faktum u. U. auch auf eine Weise zu deuten, die im Gegensatz zu den Deutungen der Bibel steht. Auch Ereignisse und Vorgänge, die im Alten Testament nicht direkt bezeugt sind, die aber von der Forschung erschlossen werden können, haben durchaus für Glauben und Theologie ihre Bedeutung, weil auch sie Gott als Werkzeug für sein Heilshandeln mit dem Telos Christus gedient haben" (Hesse, "Bewährt sich. . .", 17).

[52]Walther Eichrodt, *Theology of the Old Testament*, trans. J. A. Baker (Philadelphia: Westminster, 1961), 1:11; ". . .die Religion, von der die Urkunden des Alten Testaments berichten darzustellen." *Theologie des Alten Testaments* (Leipzig: J. C. Hinrichs'schen Buchandlung, 1933), v.

[53]Eichrodt, *Theology*, 11.

ship with Israel.[54] In his understanding of this historical act of the formation of a covenant, Eichrodt relies on the conclusions and procedures of classical historical criticism,[55] as well as a kind of religious phenomenology that allows for treatment of the unique aspects of Israel's religion.[56] In substance, however, Eichrodt's view of Israel's early history, at least from the time of the Conquest, has more similarities to the biblical account than differences. In his discussion of the nature of Israel's covenant statutes, for example, Eichrodt accepts as essentially correct the biblical picture of Moses as the first law-giver.[57]

The OT theology of Eduard König[58] is similar in many respects to that of Eichrodt's. Like Eichrodt, König envisioned the task of OT theology as the historically-oriented description of the religious and ethical content of the OT rather than an explication of the OT text itself.[59] Moreover, König accepted the literary analysis of the current documentary hypothesis, though he held to a much earlier date for these documents than was typical.[60] The documents, he maintained, were not late inventions but reflected factual accounts of what actually happened during the time of the Conquest, the Exodus, and the Patriarchs.[61] Consequently, for König, it was the religion of Abraham, rather than Moses, that represented the epoch-making turning point of Israel's religion.[62] He thus begins his discussion of the major stages of Israelite religion

---

[54]". . .every expression of the OT which is determinative for its faith rests on the explicit or implicit assumption that a free act of God, consummated in history, has raised Israel to the rank of the People of God, in whom the nature and will of God are to be revealed. The word 'covenant,' there, is so to speak a convenient symbol for an assurance much wider in scope and controlling the formation of the national faith at its deepest level, without which Israel would not be Israel. . . . the 'covenant' is not a doctrinal concept, with the help of which a complete corpus of dogma can be worked out, but the characteristic *description of a living process*, which was begun at a particular time and at a particular place, in order to reveal a divine reality unique in the whole history of religion" (Eichrodt, *Theology*, 14, 18).

[55]Ibid., 28; "It is impossible even to conceive of a historical picture that does not make use of its findings, and to that extent not one of us can help being in its debt" (30).

[56]Ibid., 32.

[57]"Historically, therefore, the soundest opinion would seem to be that which derives these ancient collections of laws ultimately from Moses himself—always remembering that in the course of a long period of transmission they cannot have escaped a good deal of interference and alteration of one kind and another" (ibid., 72).

[58]Eduard König, *Theologie des Alten Testaments kritisch und vergleichend dargestellt* (Stuttgart: Chr. Belsersche Verlagsbuchhandlung, 1922).

[59]"Sie ist die biblische und daher geschichtlich orientierte Darstellung des religiös-sittlichen Gehaltes der alttestamentlichen Schriften" (König, *Theologie*, 1). König is not clear in this statement whether his focus is on the OT Scriptures or the historical events portrayed in Scripture. Elsewhere, however, he shows that the content of the OT which he has specifically in mind is the historical entity of Israel's religion which is reflected from the text, "des von der alttestamentlichen Religionsentwicklung zu zeichnenden Bildes" (7).

[60]Hans-Joachim Kraus, *Geschichte der historisch-kritischen Erforschung des Alten Testaments* (Neukirchen-Vluyn: Keukirchener Verlag, 1969), 375.

[61]König, *Theologie*, 9–16.

[62]"Also ist es das einhellige positive Urteil der israelitischen Geschichtsbücher, dass Abrahams Wegzug von seinen Verwandten eine neue Epoche in der Religionsgeschichte gebildet hat" (König, *Theologie*, 19).

with "the legitimate religion of Israel during the period of the patriarchs," describing its external forms as well as its internal characteristics.[63]

2.3.2.2. A Canonical Approach to the Event

An event-centered approach to OT theology that finds its starting point in the present shape of the OT canon is characterized by the fact that it accepts the historical events as they are reflected and recounted in the biblical narratives.

2.3.2.2.1. Gerhard Maier

Gerhard Maier has recently argued for such an approach. According to Maier, the biblical theologian must be open to the historical world presented in the canonical narratives. This openness is characterized by a willingness to have one's own views of history and the natural world corrected by the view found in the biblical narratives.[64] One must not make one's own worldview and experiences the measure of the biblical world and history. Maier thus calls for a replacement of the historical-critical approach by a "biblical-historical"[65] one. A biblical-historical approach first recognizes that, according to all indications in Scripture, Israel's community of faith never possessed another view of their history than that which lies before us in the Pentateuch or Hexateuch. An biblical-historical method should not contradict this view of Israel's history that is found in the Bible. According to Maier, this account of Israel's history is, in fact, established by the uniformity of the biblical accounts and thus we may rest on it as a point of departure for further discussion.[66]

CANONICAL UNDERSTANDING OF THE EVENT

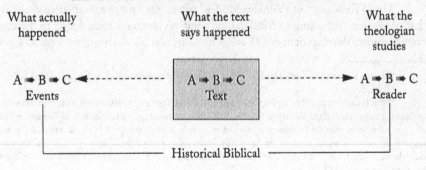

Figure 4.21

---

[63]Ibid., 91–93.

[64]Gerhard Maier, *Biblische Hermeneutik* (Wuppertal: R. Brockhaus, 1990), 349.

[65]Maier has chosen the term *biblical-historical* to replace his earlier use of the name *historical-biblical* to describe his approach because "Er wird m.E. der Besonderheit der Bibel eher gerecht, die eben eine bibelgemässe Auslegung fordert. Er bewahrt aber zugleich das ernsthafte historische Interesse, das nicht aufgegeben werden darf" (Maier, *Biblische Hermeneutik*, 349).

[66]Ibid.

2.3.2.2.2. Gustav Friedrich Oehler

The OT theology of Gustav Friedrich Oehler[67] represents an event-oriented approach that relies on the canonical version of the historical narratives. According to Oehler, OT theology is an historical science and, as such, has the task of "exhibiting the religion of the Bible, according to its progressive development and the variety of the forms in which it appears."[68] The history which is the focus of an OT theology, however, is not that which results from modern historians, but that "which the Holy Scriptures themselves give of the purpose of salvation which is carried out in Israel." Oehler is quite clear that although in some details the biblical view of Israel's history may not match that of the modern historians, the focus of OT theology is to be the view of the historical events that is found in the OT Scriptures.[69] Oehler, however, is just as clear that even when the biblical view of Israel's history may appear to be at odds with the modern view, he identifies himself with those who acknowledge "as facts what the Old Testament religion lays down as such, and are consequently convinced that the *thing believed* was also a thing which *took place*."[70] There is a further observation to be made regarding Oehler's sole dependence on the OT version of Israel's history. At the same time that he acknowledges his dependence on the OT, he also affirms the role of historical criticism. We can know more about the history of Israel and their religion by means of modern historical methods, but, says Oehler, what we learn from them is not theologically relevant.[71] In the chart in Figure 4.22, we have attempted to show Oehler's view that historical method concerns historical facts that both include (A -> B -> C) and go beyond (X -> Y -> Z) those that are the focus of OT theology.

2.3.2.2.3. Wilhelm Möller

The OT theology of Wilhelm Möller[72] represents a more conservative view than that of Oehler. According to Möller, God's self-revelation is to be found in the concrete historical development of OT religion.[73] The historical narratives in the OT give

---

[67]Gustav Friedrich Oehler, *Theology of the Old Testament* (Edinburgh: T & T Clark, 1873).

[68]Ibid., 5.

[69]"But because it ought to report what men in the Old Testament believed, in what faith they lived and died, it has to exhibit the history *as Israel believed it*. As it cannot be our task in an Old Testament Theology to harmonize the Old Testament history of creation and other things of this kind with the propositions of the newer physical sciences, we have only, in the exhibition of the history of revelation, to reproduce the view which Holy Scripture itself has. With ethnological and geographical research and the like we have nothing to do" (ibid., 9).

[70]Ibid., 10.

[71]"The history of Israel (*die israelitische Geschichte*), on the other hand, has not only to present all sides of the historical development of the people of Israel, even in its purely secular connections, thus necessitating the examination of chronological and such like questions, but to sift and vindicate, by historico-critical research, the real historical facts (*den geschichtlichen Thatbestand*) which the theology of the Old Testament reproduces as the contents of faith" (ibid., 7).

[72]Wilhelm Möller, *Biblische Theologie des Alten Testaments in heilsgeschichtlicher Entwicklung* (Zwickau [Sachsen]: Verlag Johannes Herrmann, n.d. [ca. 1935]).

[73]"denn die göttliche Offenbarung ist uns in heilsgeschichtlicher, d.h. aber eben in geschichtlicher Entwicklung gegeben" (Möller, *Biblische Theologie*, 6); "die ganze Heilsökonomie sich wirklich geschichtlich vollzogen hat. Geschichte und Theologie durchdringen sich in jedem Augenblick und vollkommen" (19).

OEHLER'S CANONICAL UNDERSTANDING OF THE EVENT

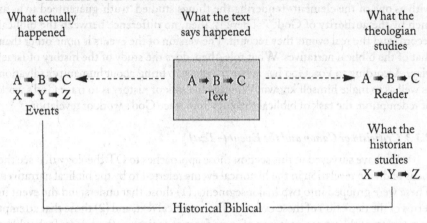

What actually happened	What the text says happened	What the theologian studies

Figure 4.22

us an accurate and complete picture of that development. Möller holds the OT narratives to be historically accurate not only for the time of the Conquest, the Exodus, and the period of the Patriarchs, but also for the earliest stages in human history. According to Möller, for example, the creation account in Genesis 1 describes what God did, just as it was done.[74] The historical accuracy as well as the historical information itself stems from the fact that the creation account was given to Adam by direct revelation and passed on to Moses either by word of mouth or in written form.[75] Möller is thus able to write an OT theology that begins with a primeval revelation to the first man and woman.

2.3.2.2.4. Geerhardus Vos

According to Geerhardus Vos, the task of a biblical theology is to write a history of special revelation.[76] Its principle of organizing the biblical material is historical, exhibiting the "organic growth or development of the truths of Special Revelation from the primitive preredemptive Special Revelation given in Eden to the close of the New Testament canon."[77] Furthermore, according to Vos, the starting point of a biblical theology, that is, God's special revelation, has been given to humanity in an "infallible" form by means of real communications "from God to man *ab extra*."[78] These commu-

---

[74]"In der Urgeschichte hat sich alles so zugetragen, wie es berichtet ist. . . . Hier liegt Geschichte vor im strengsten Sinne" (Möller, 30).

[75]Ibid., 41–42.

[76]Geerhardus Vos, *Biblical Theology, Old and New Testaments* (Grand Rapids: Eerdmans, 1948), 5; "Further, we have found that revelation is by no means confined to isolated verbal disclosures, but embraces facts. These facts moreover are not of a subordinate character: they constitute the central joints and ligaments of the entire body of redemptive revelation" (22).

[77]Vos, *Biblical Theology*, 5.

[78]"It is unfair to pass this off with a contemptuous reference to the 'dictation' view. There is nothing undignified in dictation, certainly not as between God and man. Besides, it is unscientific, for the statements

nications have also been recorded by divine inspiration which "needs to be reckoned with as one of the elements rendering the things studied 'truth' guaranteed to us as such by the authority of God."[79] There is, then, no difference between the biblical records and the real events they recount. The version of the events is none other than that of the biblical narratives. What role, then, does the study of the history of Israel play? According to Vos, God has acted in history to bring about humanity's salvation as well as to make himself known. Whereas the task of history is to trace God's work of redemption, the task of biblical theology is to trace God's work of revelation.[80]

2.3.3. Criticism or Canon and the Event (- Text)

We have surveyed in this section those approaches to OT theology that see the locus of divine revelation in the historical events referred to by the biblical narratives. These were grouped into two major segments, (1) those that understand the event in terms of the depiction of these events in the canonical text, and (2) those that attempt to reconstruct the events by means of some form of critical methodology. It should be noted that many of those we have discussed who focused on the event as the locus of divine revelation did not always understand themselves to be doing so, or at least understood themselves to be approaching the events only through the text. Many conservative biblical theologians were not very clear on the distinction between the text and events depicted in them and hence often looked beyond the text unintentionally or inadvertently. Our point here is only that, wittingly or unwittingly, many OT theologians have built their theologies upon the meaning of events, rather than texts.

2.3.4. Summary: Criticism or Canon (+/- Criticism)

It is possible to read the OT narratives as a straightforward depiction of historical events. Those who understand the Scriptures that way may, in fact, see the locus of divine revelation either in this straightforward narrative text (narrative meaning) or in the events referred to by such a text (ostensive reference). In either case, however, they approach the text *as it is*. Such an approach we have labeled "canonical" because it accepts the canonical text at face value.

We have not discussed the reasons why one might approach the text canonically; however, there may be several kinds of reasons. Some may argue that the text as it now

---

of the recipients of revelation show that such a process not seldom took place. Our position, however, does not imply that all revelation came after this objective fashion. . . . What we owe to the dignity of God is that we shall receive His speech at full-divine value" (Vos, *Biblical Theology*, 20–21).

[79]Ibid., 22. "Unless, therefore, the historicity of these facts is vouched for, and that in a more reliable sense than can be done by mere historical research, together with the facts the teaching content will become subject to a degree of uncertainty rendering the revelation value of the whole doubtful" (22).

[80]". . .in reclaiming the world from its state of sin God has to act along two lines of procedure, corresponding to the two spheres in which the destructive influence of sin asserts itself. These two spheres are the spheres of being and knowing. To set the world right in the former the procedure of redemption is employed, to set it right in the sphere of knowing the procedure of revelation is used. The one yields Biblical History, the other Biblical Theology" (ibid., 24).

stands represents the most accurate picture of Israel's history now available and should thus serve as the primary focus of our attention,[81] or simply that the OT is "inspired history" and thus must be taken at face value.[82] Others might argue that the community of faith in the church, accepted the canonical version of the scriptural text and events and thus we as Christians are committed to that decision;[83] moreover, they, as the earliest witnesses, have an inherent priority over any version of Israel's history which modern critical methods might provide.[84]

For those who are not convinced that the canonical version of the text or events should have priority, critical methodology is used to reconstruct an earlier version of the Scriptures. Such an earlier, reconstructed version—whether of the text or the event—then becomes the locus of divine revelation.

Once again we close this section with a tree-diagram (Fig. 4.23) illustrating the various options for OT theology discussed up to this point. As we noted at the close of the previous section, the choices reflected in the proposal at the conclusion of this book are marked with arrows.

---

[81]This has been the most common view of the OT's history throughout the history of the church, particularly in the "pre-critical" period, when it had virtually no rivals. Though not clearly articulated, many modern evangelical OT theologies appear to take this approach. According to Kaiser, for example, OT theology is grounded in the "historic progression" which is recorded in the biblical text and that account of Israel's history "is innocent until proven guilty by known data provided by sources whose truthfulness on those points can be demonstrated or which share the same general area of contemporaneity as the texts under investigation and whose performance record of producing reliable data has been good" (Walter C. Kaiser, Jr., *Toward Old Testament Theology* [Grand Rapids: Zondervan, 1978], 12, 28).

[82]Merrill, for example, states that his view of biblical history "approaches the task with the frank confession that the Old Testament is the revelation of God in written form. This confession, of course, presupposes its inspiration as the Word of God and asserts its inerrancy in every area, including history" (Eugene H. Merrill, *Kingdom of Priests, A History of Old Testament Israel* [Grand Rapids: Baker, 1987], 18).

[83]"Biblical Theology has as its proper context the canonical scriptures of the Christian church, not because only this literature influenced its history, but because of the peculiar reception of this corpus by a community of faith and practice. The Christian church responded to this literature as the authoritative word of God, and it remains existentially committed to an inquiry into its inner unity because of its confession of the one gospel of Jesus Christ which it proclaims to the world" (Brevard S. Childs, *Biblical Theology of the Old and New Testaments* [Minneapolis: Fortress, 1992], 8).

[84]"The role of the Bible is not being understood simply as a cultural expression of ancient peoples, but as a testimony pointing beyond itself to a divine reality to which it bears witness. . . . Such an approach to the Bible is obviously confessional. Yet the Enlightenment's alternative proposal which was to confine the Bible solely to the arena of human experience is just as much a philosophical commitment" (ibid., 9).

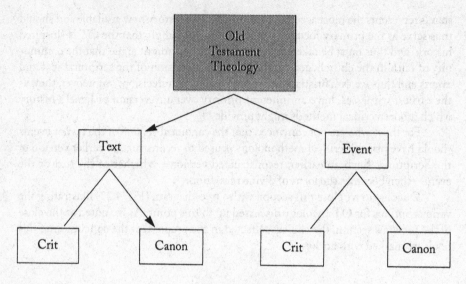

Figure 4.23

FIVE

DESCRIPTIVE OR CONFESSIONAL

2.4. DESCRIPTIVE OR CONFESSIONAL

The third component of OT theology is the question of one's faith commitment to Scripture. In going about the task of OT theology what role does our own personal faith play in shaping and in forming it? How should we approach the Bible? Is the OT like any other book from the past? Should the same principles of study be used for the OT as for other historical documents from the same period? Or does the fact that the OT is God's Word alter our approach? Does the notion of inspiration and revelation set the OT apart from other similar historical documents and make necessary a special approach to its interpretation? Because the OT is both a human and a divine book, can its depths be sounded with a method that looks only at its human side, the side it shares with all other books from antiquity?

As one might expect, there is a wide range of responses to these questions. Much depends on what is meant by the terms "inspiration" and "God's Word." Our understanding of how historical documents are to be interpreted will also play a determining role in how we respond. Underlying the diversity of responses, however, is the question of method: Should an OT theology rest on a purely historical basis or is there a need for a special theological method that involves our own personal faith?

For some, the only legitimate claims an OT theology can make are those that stand on equal footing with all other forms of human knowledge. In other words, OT theology can make no special use of its source. It must treat the OT fairly and within the limits of a recognized, scientific procedure. This means it must approach the OT merely as a historical document and rely on the scientifically accepted method for interpreting such documents.

Such a historical or descriptive approach to OT theology has largely defined the nature of biblical theology over the last two centuries. Much of the literature is driven by the assumption that this is the only valid approach. Since the present work is an attempt to broaden the concept of biblical theology beyond these specific limits, we will have to spend some time here showing how and why the scope was narrowed as

115

well as seeking to clear some new ground. We will do this by investigating the roots of biblical theology prior to the eighteenth century. It was in the eighteenth and nineteenth centuries that the notion of a strictly historical approach to OT theology became the dominant model.[1] In our opinion, however, there are legitimate antecedents to a variety of approaches to OT theology including, but not limited to, a historical approach, and it will be our task in this section to uncover them.

It is, of course, not true that those who approach the OT scientifically as a historical document necessarily deny that it is God's Word or that we cannot also use it in constructing a normative theology. The issue at stake is not one of ultimate goals but of method. Those who call for a historical approach do so most often because they are convinced it is the best method for accurately understanding the theology of the OT. It is, they argue, only by attempting to approach the theology of the OT from a purely objective, scientific point of view that we can be assured that our own beliefs and commitments will not influence the results. They maintain that our own beliefs can color and distort our reading of the OT. This is a point well taken, and it will have to be seriously considered by any approach that claims to be a fair and accurate reading of the OT. It must also be recognized, however, that some of those who argue for a strictly historical approach do so, in all honesty, because they are convinced that the OT is merely a document from the past which, to be properly understood, must be removed from the theological sphere and taken up strictly as a historical text. There are, in other words, various motives that lie behind one's choosing a historical (that is, descriptive) approach. We must look beyond these motives to evaluate the approach on its own merits.

There are others who insist that the OT is not like other human sources of knowledge. It is an ancient book, but, they maintain, it is a book or collection of books given to humanity by God. God's hand, as it were, was directly in the process. To limit the use of the OT by a strictly historical, scientific method would be to overlook this important feature. The fact that it is a God-given book, however, is the very feature of the OT that makes it unique among all other books. But, it is precisely this work of God which cannot be a part of a scientific method.

Let us look for a moment at the scientific method, a method that attempts to view the OT as a particular example of the application of a general set of principles. These principles are drawn from other historical documents and sources of historical knowledge (e.g., archaeology, sociology, anthropology). If the OT is viewed from a general scientific perspective, then those features that set it off from all other general phenomena must be discounted or treated as outside the realm of science. It is not hard to see that such a procedure eliminates from the start the element of the OT that makes it theologically important—the divine act of revelation. Some thus argue that for an OT theology to allow this erosion of its base would mean it would virtually cease to be a theology. At the very least, it could claim only to be a historical description of the theology of the OT.

---

[1] "Die eigentlichen entschiedenen Anfänge zu unserer Wissenschaft fallen erst in die Zeit, wo man sich in eine negirende Opposition zu dem Inhalte der kirchlichen Dogmatik selbst stellte" (Heinr. Andr. Christ. Hävernick, *Vorlesungen über die Theologie des Alten Testaments* [Erlangen: Carl Heyder, 1848], 6).

It is commonplace in the literature to view the historical (descriptive) and the theological (confessional) approaches in strict opposition. For many there is no possibility of bringing these two approaches into harmony. Over the last two centuries of the study of OT theology, and continuing today, one can find many examples of a rigid polarization between these two approaches. During the same period, however, there have been those who have understood historical and theological method in a more complementary relationship. They have on the one hand called for a rigorous use of the historical method, and at the same time for a clear recognition of the ultimate theological responsibility of the task. They have insisted that neither historical nor theological interests can rightly exist in isolation from the other. Both approaches are demanded by the human, yet divine, nature of Scripture. In biblical revelation, human beings stand before the Word of God; but also, in Scripture, the Word of God stands before us in a human form.

It is the purpose of the following discussion to attempt to put this issue into perspective. The approach we will propose is a confessional one. Anselm's dictum: *fides quaerens intellectum* (faith seeking understanding) is, in our view, the ultimate grounds for a biblical theology. We thus stand with those who view this issue in a polarized way. We readily recognize, however, the validity of other approaches and our evaluation of method will reflect that recognition.

2.4.1. Early History of Biblical Theology

Often our understanding of a theological task is determined, or at least shaped, by what we take to be its early history. This has especially been the case in OT theology. It is by now obligatory for introductions to OT theology to begin with an account of its origins. These accounts are largely determined by a prior understanding of what OT theology is. Thus there are several versions of the story of the origins of OT theology, and the question of origins has itself become a theological problem. In our attempt to deal with this problem below, our goal will be to take all of the current and past versions of the origin of biblical and OT theology into account. We are not, at least not intentionally, omitting any version of that history.

2.4.1.1. The Problem of the Origins of Biblical and Old Testament Theology

The early history of the use of a confessional or descriptive method in OT theology is tied to the larger question of the origin of biblical theology as a distinct branch of study. That, in turn, is often tied to a specific understanding of the nature and purpose of biblical theology itself. According to some, for example, OT theology had its origin, or at least its first full expression, in the so-called "proof text" theologies of the sixteenth and seventeenth centuries. These works, which were essentially separate treatments of the important biblical passages supporting the orthodox systems of doctrine, grew out of the Protestant Scholastics' view of the Bible as the inspired Word of God. Such a view of the Bible made it essential to demonstrate that church doctrine, that is, dogmatics, conformed to the teaching of the Bible in every detail. Since Christian doctrine had to be grounded in Scripture, it became necessary to prove that the various doctrinal propositions were "biblical," and thus one had to treat each doctrinal proof text within its own scriptural context. Eventually these treatments of OT and NT passages were published separately under the title of "biblical theology" and began to distance themselves considerably from their doctrinal roots. Not long after that, as the story goes, the OT and NT were treated separately as OT theology and NT theology. Thus within a relatively short period of about a century, what had begun as an "add on" support for Christian doctrine, became an independent theological rival of that very doctrinal system.

The problem with the above story of the origin and purpose of biblical theology is that it presupposes quite a narrow understanding of the nature of biblical or OT theology, one that is essentially descriptive, or historical in nature. It assumes an approach to biblical theology that has moved considerably away from its roots in classical orthodoxy. Thus, for such a view, the beginning stages of biblical or OT theology are naturally represented quite well by those theological works that show signs of separation and significant departure from classical dogmatics. If, however, we are seeking to find the origin, or at least the initial stages of a kind of biblical theology that includes both the confessional and descriptive approaches, it will be necessary to take a closer, and wider, look at the antecedents of biblical theology. We will, for example, need to look far beyond the "proof texts" of classical orthodoxy. Although early biblical theologians often claimed to be the heirs of those works known as *dicta probantia*, or "proof texts" of classical orthodoxy, the actual origin of what became known as biblical theology was far more complex and diverse.

2.4.1.2. Survey of the Histories of Biblical Theology

As we have been suggesting, not all accounts of the early history of OT theology are equally valid. In what follows we are not attempting to provide yet another history of its origins, but rather to broaden our understanding of the nature and task of OT theology by pointing to a variety of origins which have been noted at various times in the past. In an attempt to provide a comprehensive view of the origin and scope of OT theology, we thus offer here a selective survey of the various "histories" of biblical theology found in the theologies themselves or in articles and monographs. We will draw on histories not only from our own day, but from earlier works as well, keeping in mind that we can see some things more clearly with the historical distance we now have. Moreover, we will survey those histories that have proved definitive for the assessment of the nature of OT theology in their own time. From these accounts we will attempt to arrive at a composite picture of the origin of OT theology.

2.4.1.2.1. Hans-Joachim Kraus

Kraus's history of biblical theology[2] is today the most definitive version of the story. According to Kraus, the traditional view that biblical theology as such began as

---

[2]Hans-Joachim Kraus, *Die biblische Theologie, Ihre Geschichte und Problematik* (Neukirchener Verlag, 1970).

an offshoot of the orthodox concern for an exegetical defense of its proof texts is essentially correct but in need of more precision.[3] Moreover, Kraus argues, we must look for its origin also in places and at times before the actual use of the term biblical theology is found.

According to Kraus, it was the Reformer's call for *sola scriptura* that was the historical and theological basis on which the idea of a biblical theology was founded.[4] As early as Luther's Leipzig Disputation (1519) it was clear that the only principle upon which Protestant theology was founded was the teaching of Holy Scripture. "Not the tradition that originates from the Church fathers, not the Church Councils, not the Pope—the Holy Scriptures alone are the source and final judge in all questions of faith and doctrine. From that point on the notion of *sola scriptura* was operative because the Bible indeed represents itself as its own best interpreter. . . ."[5] In all questions of faith and doctrine, the Scripture alone was to be the basis and ultimate judge.[6] Kraus maintains that the origin of biblical theology lies, more precisely, in the fact that the Reformers were actually never able to work out the proper way in which a theology of faith and practice based on *sola scriptura* could be related to the doctrinal systems of the church.[7] This basic problem, according to Kraus, set the stage for the development of biblical theology and its corollaries OT and NT theology.

Early compendia, that is, collections of biblical doctrine, such as the *Syntagma* of Wigand and Judex,[8] and Matthias Flacius' *Clavis*,[9] though they were not called biblical theologies, nevertheless should be recognized as their early equivalents. They were attempts to come to terms with the Reformation concept of *sola scriptura* and the need for clarity of doctrine in a rapidly changing theological environment. Indeed, Melanchthon, Flacius, Wigand, and Judex were the leading forces contending for the

---

[3]Ibid., 18.

[4]This same view was also held by the evangelical OT scholar Heinrich A. C. Hävernick, "Man kann mit Recht den Anfang dieser Wissenschaft, welche jedenfalls der neueren Zeit recht eigentlich angehört, in das Zeitalter der Reformation zurück datiren" (*Vorlesungen über die Theologie des Alten Testaments* [Erlangen: Verlag von Carl Heyder, 1848], 4).

[5]"In der Leipziger Disputation von 1519 tritt das protestantische Schriftprinzip deutlich hervor: Nicht die von den Kirchenvätern ausgehende Tradition, nicht die Konzilien, nicht der Papst—allein die Heilige Schrift is *fons et judex* in allen Fragen des Glaubens und der Lehre. Fortan gilt es: *sola scriptura*. Denn die Bibel stellt sich selbst dar als 'ipse per sese certissima, facillima, apertissima, sui ipsius interpres, omnium omnia probans, judicans et illuminans.' (WA 7; 97, 23)" (Kraus, *Biblische Theologie*, 17).

[6]"Thus dogmatic theology in that time period, in opposition to medieval scholasticism, was indeed a simple biblical dogmatic. Thus, for example, Melanchthon's *Loci Communes rerum theologicarum* still had the primary form of a biblical theology. In the Reformed dogmatics as well, the older theologians displayed, procedurally, this type of biblical approach, e.g., Calvin's Institutes" (Hävernick, *Vorlesungen*, 4–5).

[7]"Doch alle unter dem Prinzip 'sola scriptura' vorgelegten theologischen Entwürfe der Reformatoren geben keine klare Antwort auf die methodologische Frage, welche Konsequenzen sich aus dem Primat der Schrift und mithin aus dem Primat der Exegese für die Ausbildung und Gestaltung christlicher Lehre ergeben" (Kraus, *Biblische Theologie*, 17). Kraus follows M. Kähler, RE3, 3:193, "ohne bestimmte Methodik in der Auswahl des biblischen Stoffes." Cf. Hävernick, *Vorlesungen*, 5.

[8]Joh. Wigandum and Matthaeus Judex, *Syntagma seu corpus doctrinae veri et omnipotentis Dei ex Veteri Testamento tantum, methodica ratione . . . dispositum*, 1563.

[9]Matthias Flacius (Illyricus), *Clavis Scripturae sacrae seu de sermone sacrarum literarum*, 1567.

shape and direction of Lutheran theology following the death of Luther.[10] (Kraus and others have concentrated their attention during this period on the development of Lutheran theology. We will later pick up the thread of Reformed theology during this same period and show that much was happening to the concept of *sola scriptura* on that side as well.)

There were, argues Kraus, three primary elements in the responses to the problem posed by *sola scriptura* which ultimately gave rise to the concept of biblical theology: (1) dogmatic biblicism, (2) ordo temporum, and (3) pietism.

(1) DOGMATIC BIBLICISM

As Kraus understands the term, *dogmatic biblicism* has a precise meaning. It is the belief that the basic theology of the divinely inspired Bible (biblicism) is one and the same with the central articles of faith expressed in the creeds of the church and Christian theologies (dogmatic). Dogmatic biblicism is more than the mere biblicism represented in the call for *sola scriptura*. Dogmatic biblicism works under the assumption that the Bible teaches precisely, and solely, that which is expressed in the dogmatic creeds of the church. It insists not only that the doctrines of the church are biblical, but also that the statements of the Bible are doctrinal.[11] Early on, Kraus argues, dogmatic biblicism necessarily mandated the justification of church doctrine by means of the independent exegesis of biblical proof texts.[12] These early works, originally incorporated into the doctrinal discussions themselves, quickly developed into full-scale *compendia* of doctrinal proof texts. These were often,[13] but not always,[14] called "biblical theology." However, because the actual term *biblical theology* had several distinct meanings during the period we need not worry about exact titles and terminology. These early biblical theologies, whatever they might have been called, were narrowly constrained by the systematic expression of orthodox theology. Nevertheless, in them one finds a precise and extensive exegetical treatment of the classical biblical passages used to support Christian doctrine.[15]

---

[10]*TRE*, 13, 512.

[11]"Die Orthodoxie unterschied oft zwischen proto- und deuterokanonischen Schriften des Neuen Testaments sowie zwischen dem Glauben, der der Schrift gebühre, und eigentlichen Glaubensartikeln. Man kann hier von einem 'dogmatischen Biblizismus' sprechen (H. E. Weber), aber nicht von einem allgemeinen; denn die Unmittelbarkeit zur ganzen Schrift wurde durch den praktischen Vorrang der Lehrsymbole, deren Biblizität vorausgesetzt wurde, und die Beschränkung auf biblische Beweisstellen gebrochen" (*TRE*, 6, 479).

[12]Thus Kraus also accepts the notion that biblical theology, in a strict sense, originated from the systems of *dicta probentia*. In this, Kraus follows Diestel: "Jener (Wigand) bildete mithin die erste Darstellung alttestamentlicher Theologie nach der älteren Weise, freilich völlig gebunden durch das Dogma und für eine richtigere Auffassung der alttest. Offenbarung ohne Ertrag" (*Geschichte des Alten Testamentes in der christlichen Kirche* [Jena: Mauke's Verlag, 1869], 290); also, Christiph Friedrich Ammon, *Biblische Theologie* (Erlangen, 1801), 1:4f; and Karl Gottlieb Bretschneider, *Systematische Entwickelung aller in der Dogmatik vorkommenden Begriffe* (Leipzig, 1825), 72–74. Cf. Hävernick, *Vorlesungen*, 5.

[13]Henricus A. Biest, *Theologia biblica*, 1643.

[14]Sebastian Schmidt, *Collegium Biblicum*, 1671.

[15]Kraus, *Biblische Theologie*, 20.

(2) ORDO TEMPORUM

According to Kraus, however, we must look beyond these specific exegetical works to get the whole picture. Crucial for the development of the concept of biblical theology were the early and often overlooked attempts to reformulate and express church doctrine within the context of "periods of time" (*oeconomia temporum*) rather than formal logical categories. Systematization and logical arrangement dominated theological discussion in the seventeenth century. While they were by no means in the majority, in the mid-seventeenth-century theologians such as Coccejus (1603–69) and Calixt (1586–1656) turned decidedly away from such traditional categories of logic and began to focus on God's acts in history (*oeconomia temporum*). Central for both Coccejus and Calixt was the belief that God's self-revelation could be understood best in terms of the period of time for which it was intended. The divine covenant of grace, for example, was to be understood in terms of three distinct time periods, or economies (*oeconomia*): (1) before the law (*oeconomia ante legem*), (2) under the law (*oeconomia sub lege*), and (3) after the law (*oeconomia post legem*). Calvin had earlier understood these same covenants in terms of their logical or systematic relationship to each other. According to Calvin, these covenants were the same "in substance and reality" but varied in "administration."[16] In the writings of Coccejus, however, there was the beginning of an approach to church doctrine that allowed for erstwhile logical distinctions to be based, instead, on "time periods." According to Kraus, the work of Calixt had little effect on the history of biblical theology, but that of Coccejus was foundational and can be seen most clearly in the role which the concepts of salvation history played in later works. Coccejus, of course, was on the Reformed side of the spectrum, but his historical approach made significant inroads into Lutheran theology.[17]

It should be noted here, however, that the "progressive order" (*ordo temporum*) of Coccejus's theology was not exactly, or always, the same as what we today might think of as the actual course of the historical events in themselves. Kraus also concedes that the "history" of the covenants found in Coccejus's system was in fact the diachronic schema of his own "federal theology." It was, in fact, a narrative history with which he worked, as opposed to an actual course of events knowable apart from Scripture. Coccejus was still far from approaching the Bible as a history book per se. The Bible remained for Coccejus, as for his orthodox colleagues, first and foremost a book of doctrine.[18] Coccejus was more interested in an "inner-biblical progression" than an actual historical process as such. Such a view of the Bible did, however, under the new conditions of the later eighteenth century, easily lead to a historical reading of the events recorded. Hans Frei argues that Coccejus's *ordo temporum* unwittingly played a key role in the development of a strictly historical interpretation of the Bible: "Cocce-

---

[16]"The covenant made with all the patriarchs is so much like ours in substance (*substantia*) and reality (*re ipsa*) that the two are actually one (*unum*) and the same (*idem*). Yet they differ (*variat*) in the mode of dispensation (*administratio*)" (Calvin, *Institutes*, 2.10).

[17]Gottlob Schrenk, *Gottesreich und Bund im Aelteren Protestantismus vornehmlich bei Johannes Coccejus* (Darmstadt: Wissenschaftliche Buchgesellschaft, 1967), 305–32.

[18]Kraus, *Biblische Theologie*, 21.

jus' contribution . . . lies in the unsteadiness of focus he has on the relation between history and depiction in his thoroughly conservative interpretation of scripture."[19] According to Kraus, Coccejus's concept of an "economy" (*oeconomia*) was all too easily later replaced by that of "history" (*historia*).[20] Coccejus thus had a profound effect on later developments in biblical theology, principally through the later writings of his students.[21]

(3) PIETISM

According to Kraus, the rise of Pietism also played an important role in the development of biblical theology. Pietism, a major force in Protestant theology in the early eighteenth century, was essentially a reaction to what was perceived to be the dead orthodoxy of seventeenth- and eighteenth-century Scholastic theology.[22] The pietistic reaction to dogmatic biblicism usually took the form of a rejection of formal statements of doctrine in favor of the simple and clear statements of Scripture.[23] In such a context biblical theology, which focused on the message of the Bible itself, was easily conceived to be a return to the pure teaching of the Bible, unencumbered by the academic and hairsplitting trivialities of traditional orthodox theologies. Though not necessarily a fair assessment of orthodoxy, Pietism managed to put its stamp on the developing form of biblical theology. Through Pietism's negative opposition to classical orthodoxy, biblical theology found a means to sever itself completely from the control of church doctrine and thus become a legitimate branch of theology in its own right.[24] It may be suggested that in this early stage, biblical theology as an independent discipline more or less used Pietism as a leverage to free itself from the constraints of dogmatic biblicism. Biblical theology became, or at least saw itself as, a kind of pure theological expression of the viewpoint of the biblical authors.

---

[19]Hans Frei, *The Eclipse of Biblical Narrative* (New Haven: Yale University Press, 1974), 47.

[20]Kraus, *Biblische Theologie*, 24.

[21]The most notable being (1) Johann Heinrich Majus (1653–1719), *Theologia prophetica*, (1709) and *Oeconomia temporum Veteris Testamenti, exhibens gubernationem Dei inde a mundo condito usque ad Messiae adventum per omnes antiqui hebr. codicis libros secundum seriem et similitudinem rerum* (4 Bd. 1706). "Majus hat recht eigentlich den Begriff der 'oeconomia temporum' in die biblische Theologie des 18. Jahrhunderts eingeführt. Stärker als Coccejus löste er sich von dem Lehraspekt, ohne ihn jedoch gänzlich preisgeben zu können" (Kraus, *Die Biblische Theologie*, 22); (2) Bengel; and (3) Vitringa: "Johann Albrecht Bengel (1687–1752), Repräsentant des Württembergischen Pietismus des 18. Jahrhunderts, hat die ideen des Johannes Coccejus durch Majus und den alttestamentlichen Exegeten Campegius Vitringa empfangen" (Kraus, *Die Biblische Theologie*, 23).

[22]That this was not an altogether fair assessment of Scholastic theology can easily be seen in the noted spirituality and emphasis on regeneration that characterized the opponents of Pietism such as David Hollaz, *Examen theologicum acroamaticum* (1707).

[23]A typical example of the Pietist's quest for the simple faith of the Scriptures was the widely ciculated work of Gottfried Büchner, *Biblische Real und Verbal Hand-Concordanz oder Exegetische-Homiletisches Lexicon* (1750). Büchner's aim was to treat the "articles of the Christian religion" as they are represented solely in the "nouns, verbs and adjectives" of Scripture.

[24]Kraus, *Biblische Theologie*, 25.

2.4.1.2.2. Gustav Friedrich Oehler[25]

We turn now to the account of the history of biblical theology according to Gustav Oehler. Oehler begins by recognizing that biblical theology and OT theology did not develop as modern sciences until the eighteenth century. He nevertheless asserts that there were, from the time of the early church on, many examples of "an earlier kind of Biblical Theology." Indeed, in Oehler's opinion, "the earliest treatment of the Old Testament, not simply practically, but theologically, is found in the New Testament."[26] Such an interest in the theology of the OT, Oehler argued, continues in the writings of Justin Martyr (*Dialogue with Trypho*), Tertullian (*Answer to the Jews*), Origen, and Augustine (*de Civitate Dei*, lib. xv.-xvii.). Regarding Augustine Oehler says, "We may regard these three books in Augustine's great work as in a certain sense the first treatment of the theology of the Old Testament."[27]

In the medieval period, Oehler finds few examples of OT theology among Christian biblical scholars, though he does note the value of rabbinical commentaries from that period.[28] Oehler is one of a very few to call attention to the contribution of Johannes Reuchlin to the study of OT theology. Reuchlin is usually noted for his epoch-making advances in the study of biblical Hebrew,[29] but he was himself more interested in the study of Jewish *kabbalah*, mystical treatises on the Hebrew Bible. Oehler plays down the contribution of Reuchlin's studies in *kabbalah* because, he notes, it had little effect on the Reformers. According to Oehler, "Reuchlin's immortal service consists in this, that he was the first to claim with the greatest emphasis that exegesis should be independent of the traditions of the Church."[30] We should note here, however, that kabbalistic studies continued to have a major effect on Christian theology, primarily through the Christian hebraists and the Coccejians.[31]

Oehler sees the major contribution of the Reformers to the study of OT theology to consist in their "recognition of the *difference between the law and the gospel* derived from Paul's epistles" which led to their finding "the simple way of salvation" in the Old Testament. Moreover, the Reformers "brought into a truer light the moral worth of the Old Testament law, and the corresponding educational aim of the Old Testament economy."[32] They did this by stressing the literal meaning of the OT, over against the medieval use of allegory and spiritualization.

---

[25]Gustav Friedrich Oehler, *Theologie des Alten Testaments* (Stuttgart: J. F. Steinkopf, 1882); *Theology of the Old Testament* (Funk & Wagnalls, 1883).

[26]Ibid., 23. Oehler has specifically in mind here the epistles of Romans, Galatians, and Hebrews.

[27]Ibid.

[28]"The Rabbins of the middle ages accomplished more, especially Moses Maimonides, who must often be consulted on Old Testament Theology, particularly on the ordinances and expositions of the Mosaic Law" (ibid., 24).

[29]Johannes Reuchlin, *De rudimentis linguae Hebraicae* (1506).

[30]Oehler, *Theology*, 25.

[31]Campegius Vitringa, the most notable of the Coccejians, devoted considerable attention to the study of *kabbalah* in his *Sacrarum Observationum Libri Quatuor*, 1700.

[32]Oehler, *Theology*, 24.

Where the Reformers fell short, however, argues Oehler, was in their lack of appreciation for the progression of thought and doctrine throughout the Scriptures. Both Luther and Calvin believed in a uniformity of doctrine from the earliest stages of God's dealings with human beings in the Garden of Eden down to the time of the New Testament. According to Oehler, "the unity of the Old and New Testaments was conceived of not as produced by a gradually advancing process of development, but as a harmony of doctrine." In order to justify such a view of the Old Testament, Oehler argues, "it was necessary to use a figurative exegesis."[33]

The later orthodox theologians, says Oehler, followed in the footsteps of the Reformers: "The contents of the Scriptures were set forth with strict regard to the systematic doctrines of the Church, and without respect to the historical manifoldness of the Scriptures themselves."[34] That position was maintained against both the Roman Catholic notion that the OT presented its doctrine in a rudimentary level (*doctrina inchoata*), the Socinians,[35] and syncretists, such as Calixt. The first shift in the orthodox view of the OT comes with the "system of periods" (*ordo temporum*) of Coccejus.[36]

Finally, Oehler arrives at the proof texts theologians of Protestant orthodoxy. Within the Lutheran church, from the end of the seventeenth century onward, the practice of publishing collections of proof texts of Christian doctrine became common. It is surprising how little Oehler valued the contribution of these works to the development of biblical theology. According to Oehler, "These lectures, which contained exegetico-dogmatical discussions of the most important prooftexts of the doctrines of the Church, gave some impulse to the study of biblical as distinguished from doctrinal theology, but cannot be regarded as of much consequence."[37]

Oehler's own historical understanding of the nature of OT theology led him to value the early histories of Israel more highly.[38] Pietism, argues Oehler, also contributed to the development of biblical theology by both stressing the importance of the Bible

---

[33]Ibid., 27.

[34]"The OT was used in all its parts, just like the New Testament, for proofs of doctrine. . . . it was taught on the side of the Protestants, that, in respect to fundamental doctrines, the Old Testament was in no way incomplete . . ." (ibid., 27). Gerhard: Quod ad rem ipsam sive mysteria fidei attinet, doctrina veteris testamenti *nequaquam est imperfecta*, siquidem *eosdem fundamentales fidei articulos* tradit, quos Christus et apostoli in novo testamento *repetunt*. Quod ad docendi modum attinet, fatemur, quaedam fidei mysteria clarius et dilucidius in novo testamento expressa esse, sed hoc perfectioni reali nihil quidquam derogat, cum ad perspicuitatem potius pertineat quam ad res ipsas cognoscendas (J. Gerhard, *Loci*, ed. Cott, vi. 138).

[35]"Socinus was not disposed to deny the divine origin of the Old Testament, but maintained that it was not essential for the establishment of Christian doctrine and possessed only a historical value. The connection of the two Testaments was made in a quite external way to consist chiefly in the fact that certain commands (viz., those of a moral nature) were common to both; but beyond this a considerable difference was held to exist between the perfect commands and perfect promises of God in the New Testament and the commands and promises found in the Old, and it was especially charged upon the Old Testament that it only taught temporal rewards and punishments and restricted forgiveness to mere sins of infirmity" (Oehler, *Theology*, 29).

[36]Ibid., 28.

[37]Ibid., 30.

[38]For example, F. Buddeus's *Historia ecclesiastica veteris testamenti*, 1726–29 (ibid., 30).

and depreciating that of the doctrinal scholasticism of the church.[39] Bengel's peri-odization of the OT history was of seminal value, for example, producing a view of biblical revelation both "organic and historical." Bengel's hermeneutical rule stating the basic premise of progressive revelation was at that time, says Oehler, "quite new."[40] The rule was: "God proceeded gradually in making known the mysteries of his king-dom, whether one has in view the details of the events themselves or merely the times. Initially that which was kept concealed was then understood openly. That which was given in whatever particular state, the saints were to understand, not taking more nor accepting less."[41] Though Bengel did not write on the OT, Oehler notes that his stu-dents continued to have an effect on the development of biblical theology,[42] but not in the mainstream.

Changes in the theological climate of the day, for example, the rise of English Deism and biblical criticism, resulted in little receptive ground for the ideas and approach of Bengel. Under the terms of the new theological climate, the ideas, beliefs, and institutions of the OT were explained not in terms of divine revelation, but in terms of the utilitarian (*Zweckmässigkeit*) value they had for Israelite society.[43] In Oehler's assessment of Semler, for example, he maintained that Semler "regards that which is serviceable for *moral improvement*, not that which edifies the Christian, as the one thing of importance, and as that by which, therefore, in the Holy Scriptures, the divine and the human, the material and the immaterial, must be distinguished."[44] Sem-ler held that "the Bible and Church doctrine contradict each other—a proposition which from his time onward was accepted equally by rationalists and supernaturalists." The only type of biblical theology that could survive in the new climate of criticism was one in which the teaching of the OT "became completely freed from the theol-ogy of the Church creeds."[45] Already in the work of G. T. Zachariae (*Biblische Theolo-gie*, 1772–75) biblical theology was turned critically against the dogmatic theology of the Church.[46]

A major transition point, according to Oehler, is marked by the academic lec-ture of Johann Philipp Gabler (*De justo discrimine theologiae biblicae et dogmaticae*).

---

[39]Ibid.

[40]Ibid.

[41]"*Gradatim* Deus in patefaciendis regni sui mysteriis progreditur, sive res ipsae spectentur, sive tem-pora. *Opertum* tenetur initio, quod deinde *apertum* cernitur. *Quod quavis aetate datur*, id sancti debent amplecti, non plus sumere, non minus accipere" (ibid., 30).

[42]Magnus Friederich Roos, *Fundamenta psychologiae ex sacra scriptura collecta*, and *Einleitung in die biblische Geschichte*, 1770; Phil. David Burk, *Lehre von der Rechtfertigung* (7 Theile, 1763–65), *Gnomon in XII Prophetas minores*, 1753, *Gnomon Psalmorum*, 1760; Phil. Heinr. Hiller, *System der Vorbilder des A.T.*, (2 Theile, 1758, 67); Oetinger; Christian August Crusius, *Hypomnemata ad theologiam propheticam*, 1764, 1771, 1778.

[43]"This system of referring the plan of the Old Testament revelation to prudential considerations of the most trifling character which J. Spencer in his learned work, *De legibus Hebraeorum ritualibus earumque rationibus*, 1686 . . . and Clericus had introduced, became quite predominant in Germany through the works of the learned orientalist of Göttingen, Joh. David Michaelis" (Oehler, *Theology*, 31).

[44]Ibid., 30.

[45]Ibid.

[46]Ibid., 32–33.

According to Oehler Gabler "is regarded as the first who distinctly spoke of Biblical Theology as a historical science."[47] Henceforth the task of a "rational"[48] biblical theology was to reconstruct "the religious ideas of Scripture as a *historical fact*, so as to distinguish the different times and subjects, and so also the different stages in the development of these ideas."[49] Much was lost from the OT in these theologies.[50] Ultimately the OT was reduced to the level of ancient myth and comparative religions.[51]

During this time, while rationalism was in its heyday, supernaturalists did little at first to contribute to the development of OT theology.[52] The contribution of the *rational supernaturalists* "was confined partly to the proof of the general doctrines of the Christian religion from passages of the OT, partly to the use of the OT prophecies for the defense of revelation."[53] Only Steudel's lectures can be considered "a complete exhibition of Old Testament Theology."[54]

According to Oehler, the publication of Hengstenberg's *Christology of the OT* in 1829–35 (2nd. ed. 1854–57) marked a new epoch in the theological study of the OT. Hengstenberg's *Christology* was "essentially that of the old Protestant theology . . . finding all the fundamental New Testament doctrines in the Old Testament, not in a process of growth, but ready made."[55] For Hengstenberg the OT Scriptures were divine revelation, in the same sense and to the same extent as the NT.[56] Hengstenberg's strong stance on Scripture sparked a reaction from Hofmann[57] who brought "to view the pro-

---

[47]Ibid., 32.

[48]In the late eighteenth and early nineteenth centuries, theologians were generally classed either as rationalists or supernaturalists. The rationalists, under the influence of Deism, did not allow for miracles or special revelation in the Bible. Supernaturalists allowed for such possibilities.

[49]Oehler, *Theology*, 33.

[50]Oehler maintained that the chief aim of these rationalistic theologies "was to eliminate everything which could be called temporary, such as form, orientalism and so forth, and thus to dilute the essential contents of the Bible and reduce them to a few very ordinary commonplaces" (ibid., 33).

[51]The religion of Israel is represented "not as exempt from the mythological process, but as working through it" (ibid., 34).

[52]"In only a few treatises is a living historical view of revelation to be found" e.g., (1) Johann Hess, *Von dem Reiche Gottes. Ein Versuch über den Plan der göttlichen Anstalten und Offenbarungen*, 2 Bde, 1781; (2) Gottfried Menken, *Versuch einer Anleitung zum eigenen Unterricht in der heil. Schrift*, 3. Aufl., 1833 (Oehler, *Theology* 36).

[53]Ibid.

[54]Steudel, *Vorlesungen über die Theol. des A.T.*, Berlin, 1940. "Although he [Steudel] acknowledges the necessity of studying the Old Testament word in its internal connection with the history of salvation, his book is confined to a systematic statement of the religious teachings of the Old Testament; and the progress of religious knowledge in the Old Testament is exhibited not as an organic development, but more from the outside as the gradual filling up of a *framework* given from the first" (Oehler, 36).

[55]Ibid., *Theology*, 36–37. Hengstenberg's most important student in the field of Old Testament theology was Hävernick. Heinrich A. C. Hävernick, *Vorlesungen über die Theologie des Alten Testaments* (Erlangen: Carl Heyder, 1848).

[56]In Germany Hengstenberg was the leading representative of the *Repristination* movement whose goal was the reestablishment of the orthodox doctrine in the life of the church. See Horst Stephan and Martin Schmidt, *Geschichte der evangelischen Theologie in Deutschland seit dem Idealismus* (Berlin: Walter de Gruyter, 1973), 203–7; and Stephan Holthaus, *Fundamentalismus in Deutschland* (Bonn: Verlag für Kultur und Wissenschaft, 1993).

[57]J. Chr. K. von Hofmann, *Weissagung und Erfüllung im Alten und Neuen Testament*, 1841–42.

gressive connection of prophecy with history" giving "the written revelation little attention when compared with his overriding interest in historical events."[58] For Hofmann the historical events as such were as revealing of divine truth as the words of Scripture.

2.4.1.2.3. Karl Immanuel Nitzsch[59]

It should be noted first that Nitzsch had a very complex view of the nature of biblical theology. In its most general sense it consisted of virtually any aspect of theology that involved the Bible. In a narrower sense it was the concern to articulate the actual theology contained in the Bible, as opposed to tradition and nature.

According to Nitzsch, biblical theology was characterized by both a negative and a positive component. Its negative component consisted of its use in keeping the doctrine of the church pure and aligned with Scripture by chipping away at the accretions of tradition and the attacks of heresy. Its positive component consisted of its ongoing discovery of new truth from Scripture. Thus for Nitzsch, whenever and wherever there has been an attempt to formulate Christian doctrine, there has also been the need to defend that doctrine by an appeal to Scripture and hence a need for biblical theology.

Nitzsch also held that biblical theology thus has its roots in the earliest debates of the church against heresies, as well as its dialogues with Judaism and paganism, and it has been an ongoing corrective to the excessive development of church tradition. Thus the origin of biblical theology is to be found in the origin of Christian theology itself. The earliest Alexandrian fathers, Clement and Origen, were biblical theologians "because they had to formulate the basic teaching of the apostolic message and lay the material foundation of Christendom, thereby striving to give it a thoroughgoing biblical defense as well as to articulate and organize all the material of divine revelation."[60] Irenaeus and Tertullian refuted the heresy of Gnosticism by means of carefully culled proof texts. They were thus biblical theologians, argues Nitzsch. An interesting example of such early lists of texts, says Nitzsch, is that of Cyprian's *de testimoniis*,[61] which treats thoroughly the relationship between the Old and New Testaments, prophecy and fulfillment, and provides answers to the questions raised in the debates with Judaism. In the last analysis, Cyprian insists on subordinating the doctrines of the church fathers to the Word of God and thus his work qualifies in a narrow sense as a biblical theology.[62] In the sixth century, at a time when the theological terminology had become excessively refined, Nitzsch points to the fact that Bishop Junilius made use of a "biblical theology of the Syrian school" that had come into his possession. He

---

[58]Oehler, *Theology*, 37.

[59]"Biblische Theologie," vol. 3, *Real Encyklopädie für protestantische Theologie und Kirche* (Stuttgart: Rudolf Besser, 1854).

[60]Ibid., 220.

[61]See *The Ante-Nicene Fathers*, eds. Alexander Roberts and James Donaldson (Grand Rapids: Eerdmans, 1957), 5:507–57.

[62]Nitzsch, "Biblische Theologie," 220.

used it to introduce into the theological discussion of his day a more biblical form of argumentation and terminology.[63]

The Middle Ages saw little advance in the development of biblical theology, according to Nitzsch. This was not surprising since the focus of theologians at that time was as much on the teachings of the church fathers and councils as it was on the genuine exegesis of Scripture.[64] There was, moreover, little use of the original languages in the Middle Ages. What genuine biblical theology there was during this time was found, ironically, among those who were persecuted by the official church for their faith. In their own defense, medieval mystics and "pre-Reformation" reformers turned to the study of the Bible with a growing interest in the use of the original languages which they had learned from the Jews and Greeks of their day. These early efforts paved the way for the Reformation. They reached their highest point in the work of Erasmus (*methodus ad veram theologiam perveniendi*, Basil, 1520) which, argues Nitzsch, had all the makings of a plan for a biblical theology.

Nitzsch holds that the early catechisms, confessions, and dogmatical works of the Reformers (e.g., Luther, Calvin) represented a return to the biblical texts in opposition to the traditions of the church. They were, as well, an attempt to formulate something new. In both senses, then, according to Nitzsch's criteria, they can be characterized as biblical theologies—though only in a kind of analogous way when compared to their fully developed form two centuries later.[65] Foreshadowings of biblical theology continue to be found in the post-Reformation period. Though it is true, argues Nitzsch, that much of what is found in the theologies of this period is a carryover from the theological and ecclesiastical traditions of the past, theologians of the day were firmly committed to the task of deriving their doctrine from Scripture alone.[66] To that extent they were representative of a growing interest in biblical theology. To the extent that these works were not organized critiques of traditional doctrine, however, they cannot be classified as full-fledged biblical theologies in Nitzsch's reckoning.

It was only after the dogmatic works of Protestant orthodoxy themselves began to take on the character of theological tradition equal in stature to that which the traditions of Rome once held, that we can begin to see the emergence of a countermovement of biblical theology in the true sense of the term. According to Nitzsch, Protestant Scholasticism had reached such a recalcitrant stage by the early and mid-eighteenth century, that it forced the full development of a mature biblical theology. There thus developed in the late eighteenth century a biblical theology that was both critical of the existing scholasticism and, as well, capable of making a positive contribution to the church's self-understanding. This fully developed biblical theology was represented in its elementary stages by the studies of proof texts, or *dicta*

---

[63]Junilius Africanus (c. 550) "wrote in 551 a treatise on biblical law, which was a sort of Introduction to the Bible which had been based on a Greek translation of an earlier Aramaic textbook written by a certain Persian named Paul." *RGG2*, III, 571.

[64]Nitzsch, "Biblische Theologie," 220.

[65]Ibid., 221.

[66]E.g., Matthew Vogel, *Thesauris theologicus e sola scriptura sacra depromtus* (Tübingen, 1607).

probantia, which accompanied scholastic theology[67] and in its mature stages by the "biblical theologies" of Hufnagel[68] and Ammon.[69] Even these "mature" biblical theologies, however, continued to follow the *loci* pattern of traditional dogmatics.

It was the seminal contribution of G.T. Zachariae[70] that was to set biblical theology on its own course in a completely new direction. In his biblical theology, Zachariae's aim was to develop the theology of the biblical writings on their own terms. Not wanting to be controlled by the issues and themes of classical dogmatics in his construction of a biblical theology, he set aside the *loci* structure and attempted to chart a new course, using as his guide the particular concerns and issues of the biblical texts themselves. This was to have a lasting effect on the structure of biblical theology.

2.4.1.2.4. Eduard König

König begins his discussion of the origin of biblical theology with his own definition: "It is the biblical, and therefore historically oriented, presentation of the religious and ethical content of the OT Scriptures."[71] It is therefore no surprise to find that for König there are no traces of biblical theology until the seventeenth and eighteenth centuries. In the early church, says König, there was not yet a systematic development of theology. In the middle ages church dogmatics was shaped by tradition. During this time one cannot find the slightest hint of a striving for a purely historically oriented presentation of the Christian religion—indeed, there is really no trace of even the preparation for such.[72] König apparently includes the Reformation itself in this verdict. For him nothing resembling biblical theology begins to take shape until after the sixteenth century.

Change began to occur, however, in the seventeenth and eighteenth centuries. There were, König argues, four essential factors that came together at that time which gave definitive shape to biblical theology.

(1) Anti-symbolism. Throughout much of its history the church has expressed its basic beliefs in official confessions of faith called "symbols." During the seventeenth and eighteenth centuries, says König, a growing aversion toward the dogmatic symbols of classical orthodoxy developed. This can be seen in the first instance in the writings of Coccejus (1603–69). In his influential work on the divine covenants, Coccejus developed a "symbol-free" dogmatic that was structured around the concept of a "revelatory history" (*Offenbarungsgeschichte*).[73]

---

[67]For example, Sebastian Schmidt, *Collegium biblicum*, 1689; and Heinr. Majus, *Theologia prophetica*, 1710 (Nitzsch, "Biblische Theologie," 221).

[68]Hufnagel, *Handbuch der biblische Theologie*, 1785.

[69]Christoph Friedrich Ammon, *Biblische Theologie* (Erlangen: Johann Jakob Palm, 1801).

[70]Gotthilf Traugott Zachariä, *Biblische Theologie oder Untersuchung des biblisches Grundes der vornehmsten theologischen Lehren*, 2 Aufl., 1775.

[71]Eduard König, *Theologie des Alten Testaments kritisch und vergleichend dargestellt* (Stuttgart: Chr. Belsersche Verlagsbuchhandlung, 1922), 1.

[72]Ibid., 1.

[73]J. Coccejus, *Summa doctrinae de foedere et testamentis Dei*, 1648.

(2) Desire for the simple words of Scripture. The rise of Pietism and the writings of J. Spener produced a widespread desire among Christians for an understanding of the Scriptures themselves, quite apart from the loci of Christian dogmatics. Works such as B. Büsching's *Theological Summary Drawn Solely From Sacred Scripture*,[74] and Majus's *Prophetic Theology*,[75] were a response to and an indication of such a desire for biblical simplicity in theology.

(3) Changing modern world view. There was, says König, a growing sense that the doctrinal formulations of the church were tied to earlier, outmoded ways of thinking about the world. As modern views of the world developed and hence increasingly demanded a response of some kind from theologians, it was felt that the simpler, truer, biblical conceptions were better suited for the task of expressing modern ideas. Since modern ideas at the time were essentially those of the Enlightenment, this meant that biblical theologians of the period became to some degree or another convinced that Enlightenment themes and ideas such as "freedom" and "autonomy" were, in fact, those of the biblical writers. Though naive in the extreme, there are a good many such biblical theologies.[76]

(4) Quest for an understanding of historical development. The seventeenth and eighteenth centuries were increasingly marked by an insatiable desire to know the historical development of ideas, including those of Christian theology. This led to the development of the study of the history of religions and, in particular, the history of biblical religion. The call for such an approach to Christian theology can be seen most clearly in Johann Philipp Gabler's lecture on the proper distinctions between biblical and dogmatic theology.[77] For Gabler, the study of biblical theology belongs in the domain of historical research, not dogmatics or Christian theology as such: "Biblical Theology, which is of the genre of historical writing, aims at presenting that which the sacred authors believed about divine things."[78] Two biblical theologies which represent Gabler's position most clearly are those of Ammon[79] and Bauer.[80]

According to König, a second wave of changes in the development of biblical theology came in the nineteenth century. These also amounted to four essential factors, but were too diverse to affect the development of biblical theology as a whole. They thus resulted in a parting of ways and fragmentation within the discipline itself.

---

[74]A. F. Büsching, *Epitome theologiae e solis literis sacris concinnatae, 1756.*

[75]Majus, *Theologia prophetica ex selectioribus V.T. oraculis,* 1710.

[76]E.g., Teller, *Topice Sacrae Scripturae* (1761); Karl Friedrich Bahrdt, *Versuch eines biblischen Systems der Dogmatik* (1769); Zachariä, *Biblischer Theologie oder Untersuchung des biblischen Grundes der vornehmsten theologischen Lehren* (1771); Hufnagel, *Handbuch der biblischen Theologie* (1785).

[77]Johann Philipp Gabler, *Oratio de iusto discrimine theologiae biblicae et dogmaticae regundisque recte utriusque finibus,* 1787.

[78]"Est theologia biblica e genere historico, tradens, quid scriptores sacri de rebus divinis senserint" (Gabler, *Oratio,* 1787).

[79]Christoph Friedrich Ammon, *Entwurf einer reinen biblischen Theologie* (Erlangen, 1792); *Biblische Theologie* (Erlangen: Johann Jakob Palm, 1801).

[80]Georg Lorenz Bauer, *Theologie des Alten Testaments,* 1796.

(1) The growing value of the practical. The new spirit of the age no longer wanted to ponder over detailed discussions of religious development. The desire was for summary and overview of the religious content of the Bible.[81]

(2) Interest in salvation history (*Heilsgeschichte*). The insistence of such theologians as Coccejus and Bengel on "an organic-historical presentation of biblical revelation with a close attention to its progressive development"[82] had a strong influence on later generations. Representing such an interest in a historical, progressive approach are the biblical theologies of Christian Augustus Crusius (Leipzig),[83] Johann Tobias Beck (Tübingen),[84] and J. Chr. Konrad von Hofmann.[85]

(3) The dominance of philosophy within biblical studies. In the post-Kantian era of the nineteenth century, biblical theologians were compelled to come to grips with the leading philosophical trends of the day. The rational empiricism of Kant and his follower, Jacob Friedrich Fries, is represented in the biblical theology of De Wette.[86] A strictly rationalist position was taken by von Cölln.[87] The philosophy of Hegel is represented by Vatke[88] and Bruno Bauer.[89] Though not strictly a philosophical system, the impact of Darwinian evolutionary theory was also felt in OT theology.[90] According to these works, the religion of Israel developed out of a particularly primitive form of religion and was furthered along by a spark of religious genius of the prophets.

(4) A thoroughly historical approach. According to König, modern approaches to OT theology are marked by a purely historical approach to the question of the nature and sources of Israelite religion. With regard to the methods of literary criticism, however, modern OT theologies fall into two distinct groups: those who accept the methods of source criticism and build their theology on its results,[91] and those who take a more traditional view of the scriptural sources.[92]

---

[81]The works of Julius A. L. Wegscheider (*Dicta probantia*, 1831) and Julius Müller (*Beweisstellen zur Dogmatik*, 1863) represent this factor.

[82]Johann Albrecht Bengel (d. 1752), says König, called for "an organic-historical understanding of revelation paying close attention to its progressive distinction."

[83]Christian Augustus Crusius, *Hypomnemata ad theologiam Propheticam*, 1764.

[84]Johann Tobias Beck, *Die christliche Lehrwissenschaft nach den biblischen Urkunden*, 1841.

[85]Johann Christian Konrad von Hofmann, *Der Schriftbeweis*, 1852–55; 2. Aufl. 1857.

[86]Wilhelm M. L. de Wette, *Biblischen Dogmatik*, 1813; 3. 1831.

[87]Daniel G. K. von Cölln, *Biblische Theologie*, 1836.

[88]Wilhelm Vatke, *Die biblische Theologie*, Bd. I: *Die Religion des A.T.*, 1835.

[89]Bruno Bauer, *Die Religion des A.T.*, 1838.

[90]Abraham Kuenen, *De godsdienst van Israel*, 1869; Duhm, *Die Theologie der Propheten*, 1875; Wellhausen, *Israelitischen und jüdischen Geschichte*, 1878; Smend, *Lehrbuch der alttestamentlichen Religionsgeschichte* (2. Aufl. 1899); Stade, *Biblische Theologie des A.T.*, 1. Bd. 1905, 2. A. Bertholet, 1911; Marti, *Geschichte der israelitischen Religion*, 5. Aufl. 1907; Budde, *Die Religion des Volkes Israel bis zur Verbannung*, 3. Aufl. 1912; Kautzsch, *Biblische Theologie des A.T.*, 1911; G. A. Barton, *The Religion of Israel*, 1918.

[91]H. Ewald, *Die lehre der Bibel von Gott* (4. Bde. 1871–76); Hitzig, *Vorlesungen über die biblische Theologie des A.T.* (1880); Herman Schultz, *Alttestamentliche Theologie* (4. Aufl. 1889; 5. verkürzte Ausgabe 1896); Riehm, *Altt. Theol.* (1889); Dillmann, *Handbuch der altt. Theol.* (1895); C. Knudson, *The Religious Teaching of the Old Testament* (1919); Rud. Kittel, *Die Religion des Volkes Israel* (1921).

[92]Baumgarten-Crusius, *Grundzüge der biblischen Theologie*, 1828; Steudel, *Vorlesungen über die Theologie des A.T.*, 1841; Hävernick, *Vorlesungen über die Theologie des A.T.*, 1848; Gustav F. Oehler, *Theologie des A.T.*, 1873,

2.4.1.2.5. Christian Hebraists

We noted earlier the contribution of Christian hebraists like Johannes Reuchlin to the development of biblical theology. Much more, however, needs to be said about this important aspect of the history of OT theology. The concept of Christian hebraism is a broad one.[93] Throughout most of the history of the church, especially before the time of the Renaissance and Reformation, Christian scholars devoted little attention to the study of the Bible in its original languages.[94] The final appeal of authority in matters of exegesis and theology was either ecclesiastical tradition or Jerome's Latin translation of the Bible, the Vulgate. Christian hebraism is the exception to that rule. The Christian hebraists were Christian scholars who had studied the Hebrew language, often directly from Jewish teachers, and were committed to the use of their knowledge of the language in the study of the Bible and theology.[95] Jerome himself was a Christian hebraist. There were several important hebraists during the medieval,[96] Renaissance,[97] and Reformation[98] periods—"hebraism had already had a long and colorful history before the Renaissance. It need not always necessarily have implied a knowledge of Hebrew; it was, in the long run, most closely tied to the study

---

2. Aufl. 1882, 3. Aufl. 1891; F. W. Schultz, Zöcklers *Handbuch der Theologischen Wissenschaften*, Bd. I (2. Aufl. 1884), 328–80; Schlottmann, *Kompendium der biblischen Theologie A. und N. Ts.*, 1889.

[93]Loewe, "Hebraists, Christian," *Encyclopaedia Judaica* (1971), 8:10–71; Aaron L. Katchen, *Christian Hebraists and Dutch Rabbis, Seventeenth Century Apologetics and the Study of Maimonides' Mishneh Torah* (Cambridge: Harvard University Press, 1984).

[94]"Notwithstanding the great reverence of the Fathers for the Old Testament, the Hebrew language was so little known in Christian antiquity that, excepting the authors of the Peshito translation, the only persons who distinguished themselves, and became famous for it, were *Origen*, whose knowledge of Hebrew was moderate, and *Jerome*, whose knowledge was considerable for that period" (R. Pick, "The Study of the Hebrew Language Among Jews and Christians," *BSac* [1884] 41:474).

[95]"It was the desired but not always attainable goal of many a humanist of the early sixteenth century to be *trium linguarum gnarus* (well acquainted with the three lanuages, Hebrew, Greek, and Latin)" (*The Cambridge History of the Bible* [Cambridge: The University Press, 1963], 3:40).

[96]"In the Middle Ages some knowledge of Hebrew was preserved in the church by converted Jews, as *Paulus Burgensis* (d. 1435), and even by Christian scholars, of whom the most notable were the Dominican controversialist, *Raymond Martini* (d. 1284), and the Fransiscan *Nicolaus de Lyra* (d. 1341), through whose popular commentaries the exegesis of Rashi was conveyed to Luther, and largely influenced his interpretation of Scripture" (Pick, *BSac.*, 475). Note also the English monk, Roger Bacon (1213–94) and Paul Christian (d. 1274) whose debate (1263) with Nahmanides had considerable effect on the interpretation of the Hebrew Bible.

[97]"But there was no continuous tradition of Hebrew study apart from the Jews; and in the fifteenth century, when the revival of independent scholarship kindled the desire to add a third learned language to Latin and Greek, only the most ardent zeal could conquer the obstacles that lay in the way. . . . Yet, in spite of all difficulties, there was a great thirst after the knowledge of Hebrew, and the cause of learning found its champion in John Reuchlin. . . . There were some hebraists before Reuchlin, as the two Tübingen professors, *Wilhelm Raymundi* and *Conrad Summerhart*, whose pupil *Conrad Pellicanus* (d. 1556), composed the first Hebrew grammar, "De modo legendi et intelligendi Hebraeum (Strassburg, 1504). . . . Besides these we must mention Sebastian Murrho, of Colmar, and a friend of Wimpheling and Reuchlin, John Wessel" (Pick, *Bib. Sac*, 476–77).

[98]Sebastian Münster (1489–1552); Santes Pagnini (1470–1536); Johannes Buxtorf the Elder (1564–1629); Franciscus Junius (1545–1602).

of Scripture and to a certain Biblicism that intensified toward the end of the sixteenth century."[99] For our purposes it is important to note that Christian hebraism experienced a profound growth and development in just those times and places where seminal studies in the Bible and theology were underway. The names of such hebraists as Johannes Reuchlin, Johannes Brenz, Johannes Oecolampadius, Paul Fagius, and Sebastian Münster may not be as familiar as those of Luther, Calvin, and Melanchthon, but it was these early hebraists that formed the exegetical and, in many points of detail, biblical theological basis for the work of the Reformers. Hebraism also made great strides in the Dutch Republic within the context of the struggles between Jacob Arminius (1560–1609) and Franciscus Gomarus (1561–1641) and the Synod of Dort (1618). "The foremost propagandists on either side were often Hebraists whose interest in and use of rabbinic literature stemmed as much from their internal squabbles as it did from any of the other purposes of Christian humanist scholarship."[100] Thus hebraism was having a direct effect on the formation and development of classical orthodoxy.[101]

There are many aspects to the contribution of the hebraists to biblical theology.[102] The most obvious lies in the editions of the Hebrew Bible, Hebrew grammars, lexicons, and commentaries that were produced by these scholars. In each of these areas the hebraists were largely dependent on medieval Jewish sources. Thus the variety of approaches to the Hebrew Bible found in medieval Judaism also made its way into the Christian study of biblical theology. Although medieval Jewish interpretation is usually divided into four distinct approaches to the text,[103] early on in their use of these sources, Protestant theologians were able to fit these four approaches into their own twofold schema of literal and spiritual senses: *sensus literalis et spiritualis (mysticus)*.[104] It was the medieval Jewish *peshat*, or "simple" meaning of the biblical text, that was identified by Christians as the "literal meaning" (*sensus literalis*).[105] This was the same

---

[99]Katchen, *Christian Hebraists*, 8.

[100]Ibid., 17.

[101]The impact on the English Bible of the technical Latin translations of Christian hebraists such as Sebastian Münster is well documented in Brooke Foss Westcott, *A General View of the History of the English Bible* (London: Macmillan, 1868).

[102]According to Kraus, one of the pressing needs of biblical scholarship is the further investigation of the influence and meaning of Jewish Bible exegesis on the development of Protestant biblical interpretation (Hans-Joachim Kraus, *Geschichte der historisch-kritischen Erforschung des Alten Testaments*, 2. Aufl. [Neukirchener Verlag, 1969], 13).

[103]Using the acronym *PRDS*, the four exegetical approaches within Judaism are (1) *Peshat* (simple), (2) *Remez* (typological), (3) *Derash* (allegorical), and (4) *Sod* (mystical).

[104]The two early and standard Protestant works on biblical interpretation in the seventeenth century were for Lutherans, Salomon Glassius, *Philologia Sacra* (Leipzig, 1623); and for Reformed, Andreas Rivetus, *Isagoge sive introductionem generalem ad Scripturam Sacram* (Batavia, 1627).

[105]The great Leiden (Reformed) hebraist, Peter Cunaeus, says of the sense of the Hebrew Scriptures "ejus est duplex significatio; una nuda, quae פשוט recte dicitur, altera obscura latensque, vel אגדתא vel דרש (= Kabbalah for Cunaeus) appellare licet, quia eruenda vestigandaque est" (*De Republica Hebraeorum*, 1617). The orthodox Lutheran view is stated clearly by Salomon Glassius in his monumental *Philologia Sacra*, which was the definitive work on biblical interpretation throughout the seventeenth and early eighteenth centuries:

as the "historical sense" (*sensus historicus*). The spiritual or mystical sense was equated most often with the Jewish notion of *kabbalah*.[106] That sense, however, was carefully distinguished from what today would be known as the "midrash" of typically rabbinical literature. Christian hebraists at the time of the Reformation saw very little value for exegesis and theology in the haggadic literature of early Judaism,[107] though their interest in Jewish *halakah* was often intense.[108] Many Christian Hebraists thus distinguished between a true *kabbalah* and a false one.[109] In the following discussion we will briefly outline the contribution of both the Jewish *peshat* and *kabbalah* methods of interpretation to the development of OT theology.

2.4.1.2.5.1. Jewish *Peshat* Interpretation and the Hebraists. The founder of the method of biblical interpretation known as *peshat* was the Jewish philosopher and biblical exegete, Saadia Gaon (882–941). Saadia's main objective in biblical interpretation was the refutation of the doctrines and allegories of the Karaites, that is, those Jews who rejected all tradition except Scripture.[110] To fulfill his objective, Saadia wrote in Arabic both commentaries and translations for the Pentateuch, Isaiah, Proverbs, and Job. According to Saadia, his translation was to be a "simple (*peshat*), explanatory translation of the text of the *Torah* written with the knowledge of reason and tradition."[111] In the Introduction to his translation of the Pentateuch Saadia says: "I wrote this book, a translation of the simple meaning (*peshat*) of the text of the Torah alone judged strictly on the bases of reason and tradition. Where it was possible to add a word or letter by means of which would be revealed the sense and purpose of those things which a mere suggestion would be sufficient in place of a word, I did so. May I be helped by God in all my efforts in matters of religion and the world." Saadia's "grammatical and lexicographical pioneering efforts laid the foundations for the many commentaries written in Spain, France and Germany."[112]

"Apud hebraeos literalis sensus vocatur מִשְׁמָע *aduitus* . . . in proprio et nativo literali sensu. Vocatur etiam הַפְּשָׁט . . . q.d. explicatio simplex, plana et clara, simplex et literalis sensus" (*Philologia Sacra*, [1623], 365).

[106]Cunaeus used the terms אגדתא and דרש synonymously with *kabbalah*: "Ego veram Cabalam appello mysticum intellectum earum rerum quae in Sacris libris latent" (3, VIII).

[107]In distinction from the *peshat* and *kabbalah*, which he favored, Cunaeus speaks of early rabbinical *haggadah* as "putida quaedam deliria et nugas plus quam aniles, easve expositiones quas ante Christi aevum et diu post illus Judaeorum Magistri quidem, febriculose mortales, ceu mysteria alii aliis tradidere" (3, VIII).

[108]See Katchen, *Christian Hebraists*.

[109]Coccejus, for example, taught that the New Testament doctrines taught in the Gospels had been handed down orally (*kabbalah*) from Moses and the prophets and were thus to be considered as true *kabbalah*: "Unde certi sumus, nos in Euangelio veram *Cabbalam* sive *Traditionem* habere" (*Consideratio Responsionais Judaicae, Omnia Opera*, 8:90).

[110]Esra Shereshevsky, *Rashi: The Man and His World* (New York: Sepher-Hermon Press, 1982), 63.

[111]Erwin I. J. Rosenthal, "Medieval Jewish Exegesis: Its Character and Significance," *Journal of Semitic Studies* 9, no. 2 (1964): 268.

[112]Rosenthal, 268: "Next to Karaism it was Muslim rationalist theology which caused Saadya to concentrate on peshat and to lay down precise conditions for allowing an inner, hidden meaning. If the literal sense runs counter to reason or established tradition or is in opposition to another biblical passage, then and then only is a figurative interpretation permissible and called for."

Saadia is followed by Rashi (ca. 1040–1105),[113] one of the most influential Jewish scholars of all time. Rashi, unlike Saadia, must be understood against the background of Jewish – Christian debate in the Middle Ages. According to Rosenthal, the central issue in Jewish – Christian relations in Rashi's day was "the claim of the church to represent the *verus [true] Israel* and to have in the New Testament the fulfillment of the Old which is interpreted in a christological sense." Rashi and Medieval Jewish exegesis "had a two-fold task: the affirmation of the faith of Judaism and the defense of the Jewish position against Christian attack and missionary activity—with special reference to the divine-human nature and Messiahship of Christ and the continuing validity of the Torah or its abrogation."[114]

The common ground in the debate was the desire of both sides to appeal to the true meaning of the Hebrew Bible. For Rashi, the primary weapon in such debate was the *peshat* interpretation, or simple meaning of the text. According to Rosenthal, "This weapon was primarily forged by Jews for Jews in the Middle Ages as the best means of safeguarding Judaism against Karaite and particularly against Christian attack. . . . We find that the medieval exegetes like Rashi and his successors, Qimchi, Abraham b. Ezra and others explicitly link the *peshat* with the 'answer' or rejoinder to the Christians. *This is clear evidence of the connection between literal interpretation and anti-Christian polemic*" (italics mine).[115] Rosenthal's thesis is that the *peshat*, or simple meaning of the text, as it was developed by Rashi and the medieval rabbis, was specifically designed as a counteroffensive to the Christian interpretation of the OT. This, we will see, had a far-reaching effect on later Protestant biblical interpretation and biblical theology which came to depend heavily on the "literal" meaning of the OT.

What was the nature of Rashi's rejoinder, the "answer" (*peshat*) in Christian polemics? Rashi's answer was quite straightforward: If a biblical text had been interpreted by Christians with reference to Jesus as the Messiah, Rashi would argue that its true reference was not messianic, but rather "historical." In most cases the "historical" sense amounted to showing that the passage in question had its simple historical reference to David, or one of the davidic kings in Judah. It did not matter to Rashi if longstanding Jewish tradition, as represented in the Targums, for example, referred the passage to the Messiah. Rashi was more willing to suffer a diminished messianic hope among Jews in his day than to concede the simple, plain meaning (*peshat*) of a passage to Christian interpretation. Thus in developing the *peshat* as a historical tool to explain the messianic texts, Rashi also had to be concerned with the fact that it was these very texts that sustained the faith and hope of medieval Jewry. "What is important is that in order to combat Christian interpretation he was prepared to depart from traditional exposition."[116]

---

[113]Rabi Solomon ben Isaac, see *Realencykopädie für protestantische Theologie und Kirche*, ed. Albert Hauck (Leipzig: J. C. Hinrichs'sche Buchhandlung, 1906).

[114]Rosenthal, 264–81.

[115]Ibid.

[116]Ibid., 272.

According to Rosenthal, "this kind of anti-Christian polemic is common to all Jewish medieval exegetes, notably to Qimchi. They were aware that it would not be enough simply to reject the christological interpretation. What was more important was a positive interpretation which asserted that a biblical historical person or event was meant and, especially, if this was linguistically and historically possible, that the passage in question contained a promise of the future redemption of Israel which all Jews then eagerly expected."[117]

The importance of Rosenthal's thesis lies in the fact that Christian hebraists, and Protestant theologians generally, identified the medieval Jewish "simple" (*peshat*) meaning with the "literal" meaning of the OT. Thus the "simple," literal meaning of the OT could no longer be linked to Christ. The literal meaning of the OT was identified with the historical events of Israel's past kingdoms. The OT was no longer read as a document about Christ and the church, but one about David and Jewish history. Christian hebraists followed the *peshat* interpretation of medieval Jewish scholars in two major areas affecting biblical theology: (1) their interpretation of the Mosaic Law and (2) their interpretation of prophecy, specifically, messianic prophecy.

2.4.1.2.5.1.1. Jewish Commentary and the Mosaic Law. Christian interpretation of the Mosaic Law before the time of the Reformation had generally followed the exegesis of the Law found in the NT.[118] The cultic laws of the tabernacle, priesthood, and sacrifices in the Pentateuch were understood as "a copy and shadow (*skia*) of what is in heaven" (Heb 8:5 NIV). The law was "only a shadow (*skia*) of the good things that are coming—not the realities themselves" (Heb 10:1 NIV).[119] Moreover, the religious festivals themselves were "a shadow (*skia*) of the things that were to come; the reality, however, is found in Christ" (Col 2:17 NIV).[120] Thus God's purpose in giving Israel the ceremonial law was to prefigure the coming of Christ.[121]

---

[117]Ibid.

[118]This was apparently anticipated in the Greek translation of the Pentateuch (LXX). By rendering virtually all forms of "law" and "statutes" by *nomos*, the translators showed their desire to read the Mosaic Law as legislation for the *polis*. The cultic ceremonies, by being subordinated to that viewpoint, were effectively nullified as such but rendered ethically relevant for the Diaspora. "So verwundert nicht, dass die Leser des griechischen Alten Testaments . . . den alttestamentlichen Kult allegorisch interpretieren" (Koch, *TRE*, 13, 50).

[119]See Pol (on Heb 10:1): Lex (ceremonialis scilicet, cum suis sacrificiis, et Sacerdotio; quatenus ab antitypo suo distinguitur, eique opponitur). . . . bonorum coelestis patriae, aeternorum; quae Patribus promissa sunt, in veteri Test. et futura, sive complenda, erant in novo Test. et suo tempore exhibita, per Christum et quidem iis temporibus quae Prophetae . . . nuncipabant. [Estius, Gerhardus, Jacobus Capellus, Menochius, Beza, Piscator] (*Critica Sacri*).

[120]"For the substance of those things which the ceremonies anciently prefigured is now presented before our eyes in Christ, inasmuch as he contains in himself everything that they marked out as future' (Calvin on Col. 2:17). Pol: scil. mysteriorum in Christo et per Christum completorum [Tirinus]: q.d. quae officia et beneficia Christi ac doctrinam Evangelicam obscure delineabant [Davenantius]" (*Critica Sacri*).

[121]"In short, the whole cultus of the law, taken literally and not as shadows and figures corresponding to the truth, will be utterly ridiculous. Therefore, with good reason, both in Stephen's speech [Acts 7:44]

Such a view of the Mosaic Law, though anticipated already in pre-Christian Judaism,[122] would hardly stand the test of medieval Jewish legal exegesis which was concerned with the application of the law to everyday life. In seeking to apply the law, it followed the simple (*peshat*) explanation of the text. Legal exegesis as such was not concerned with the mystical or spiritual meaning reflected in these laws. It was the law, as law, that occupied its attention.

One can easily see, then, that for the Christian hebraists who turned for guidance to these medieval Jewish commentaries on the law, there was potential for an appreciable loss of meaning in the OT. To be sure, that loss was well compensated for by the "nuts and bolts" approach to the law found in Jewish commentators such as Maimonides (1135–1204). One of the greatest scholars of medieval Judaism, Maimonides' contribution to the exegesis of biblical law is incalculable. He produced in c. 1180 his *Mishneh Torah*, a detailed treatise on the meaning and application of the 613 biblical laws.[123] Moreover, there was a real need in post-Reformation Europe for just such an approach to the Mosaic Law.[124] In the newly formed Protestant countries of Europe that need consisted of a biblical grounding for their new systems of law. Two nations played a central role in applying biblical law to European society, the Dutch Netherlands and Switzerland.

The Leiden University, a major center for seventeenth-century Christian hebraism, was itself established expressly for the purpose of being "a protestant university,. . . to fill the need for an intellectual and spiritual centre on which the budding [Dutch] nation could draw for its political leadership and religious autonomy."[125] The long-range goal of the conservative branch of Calvinists at the Synod of Dort was "to make their own Dutch Reformed Church the sole legitimate religious body in the Netherlands and to have that church established as a full-fledged partner in the affairs of state. Dutch Christian Hebraism drew some of its forcefulness from this strife. . . . The actual disputes within Calvinism played a central role in Dutch life. Politics often became tied up with obscure points of religious doctrine, debated heatedly."[126] When Calvinism replaced Roman Catholicism in the Netherlands, the United Provinces of the Netherlands was cast as the "true Israel" with the intent of applying God's law to human society. According to Katchen, "none bandied the idea about so vehemently as the orthodox Calvinists, however. They wielded it as a weapon and, with the appella-

---

and in The Letter to the Hebrews [Heb 8:5] very careful consideration is given to that passage where God orders Moses to make everything pertaining to the Tabernacle in accordance with the pattern shown to him on the mountain [Ex. 25:40]" (Calvin, *Inst.* 2.7.349).

[122]E.g. the Septuagint, Letter of Aristeas, Philo, and Josephus (cf. *TRE*, 13:50).

[123]Jewish tradition, even before Maimonides, had sought to identify and number each discreet law in the Scriptures. They counted 611 such laws in the Pentateuch, a number that is equivalent to the numerical value of the Hebrew word *Torah* (Law). It was customary also to add two others (Ex 20:1; Dt 6:4) to make a total of 613, the numerical value of the Hebrew expression "in the Torah."

[124]The Calvinist Beza, whose interest in the biblical laws was directly tied to his role in Geneva, was responsible for encouraging the first Protestant use of rabbinical sources for the study of biblical law (RGG2, I, 515–16).

[125]Katchen, *Christian Hebraists*, 16.

[126]Ibid., 17–19.

tion, claimed the prerogatives of the *ecclesia* in a theocracy, seeking to suppress any dissent from their dogmatic and ethical ideals. They sought, in other words, to convert the nation to their faith and their way of thinking; in the process, they sought to become transformed from a sect into the national church of a united state."[127]

Calvin's Geneva quickly became a testing ground for the application of biblical law to contemporary society. Both Calvin and his successors (e.g., Beza) were intent on building a human society that conformed in principle to the OT nation of Israel. The church did not control the state, nor was the state purely autonomous from the church. Both powers were divinely ordained and were to be obeyed by all citizens.[128] The state, as much as the church, was responsible for watching over and safeguarding both parts of God's commandments—those that call for the worship of God and those that govern the affairs of organized society.[129] Calvin, himself a lawyer, thus devoted much attention to biblical law and human society.[130] Theodor Beza followed Calvin in Geneva after the latter's death in 1564 and for the next forty-one years exerted considerable influence on both church and state.[131]

The Christian hebraists thus faced, in the post-Reformation period, a real dilemma in their treatment of the Mosaic Law. There was a pressing contemporary need in modern Europe for the kind of rigorous legal commentary on the Mosaic Law found in the Jewish sources. But they were also Christians and the NT clearly led them to look for and recognize Christ in the OT. Their theology, in fact, demanded it. However, in turning to Jewish commentaries for their explication and understanding of the OT laws (Maimonides' *Mishneh Torah*, for example), Christian hebraists were given a meaning for the law that was perfectly suited to their political needs, but one which was fundamentally non-messianic and, in fact, at cross-purposes with the NT. Thus in their growing dependence on medieval Jewish interpretation of the OT law, the Christian hebraists, and the theologians and biblical exegetes who were dependent on them, not only gradually and fundamentally altered the Christian interpretation of the OT law, but they did so in a way that made its simple meaning (*peshat*) no longer directly applicable to Christ.

The first Protestant[132] treatise on the Mosaic Law was that of Bonaventure Cornelius Bertram,[133] professor of Hebrew language in Geneva from 1566 to 1584. Bertram was encouraged by Theodore Beza, Calvin's successor in Geneva, to write a treatise on biblical law. The application of biblical law to European society was thus from the start a central concern of Bertram's work. Beginning his treatise with an account of the earliest human societies recorded in the Bible and discussing each successive stage, Bertram gives a detailed account of God's laws and human society. His thesis is that the laws of human societies have always been identical with those in the

---

[127]Ibid., 22–23.
[128]*TRE*, 7:586–87.
[129]*TRE*, 7:586–87.
[130]*TRE*, 7:587.
[131]*TRE*, 5:767.
[132]The first modern treatise was that of the Spanish Monk, Benedictus Aria Montanus, *De Actione*, 1571.
[133]*De Republica Ebraeorum*, 1574.

Mosaic documents. It is clear from the treatise itself, as well as from his own statements, that Bertram made use of rabbinical legal commentaries in his exposition of the meaning of the biblical laws.[134] It is also clear how little interest Bertram had for the nonlegal and cultic aspects of the Mosaic Law. This was a treatise on the Mosaic Law as law. In fact, he pays little or no attention to cultic laws, sacrifices, and rituals, the very laws which had traditionally been understood as prefiguring Christ, though he was clearly of a mind that such features of the law had their proper place.[135]

The study of Mosaic Law by Peter Cunaeus[136] also played a key role in the development of Protestant biblical theology. Cunaeus was a pioneer in the study of *Mishneh Torah*, Maimonides' great work on the Mosaic Law, a scholar of jurisprudence, and also a Christian hebraist of considerable standing.[137] The central purpose of his work was to present the Mosaic Law as "a guide for the magistrates of Holland and West Frisia to whom it was dedicated."[138] According to Cunaeus, not only was the OT commonwealth (Republica) the most holy of all others and rich in examples of good government, but also its very origin was not human but divine.[139] The immediate problem to which Cunaeus addressed his work was the political and theological schisms of the Dutch Republic at the time of the Synod of Dort. Cunaeus was convinced that the main problem of the disputes lay in detailed exegetical points of Scripture that in his opinion had been largely misunderstood by Christians in his day.[140] According to Katchen, the major contribution of Cunaeus's work "consists in its quarrying of the *Mishneh Torah* for the study of the ancient Jewish commonwealth" to address the problems facing his age.[141] In terms of the development of biblical theology and Protestant hermeneutics, however, Cunaeus played a decisive role in his introduction of Jewish legal exegesis into the study of biblical law, but, just as importantly, in his enthusiastic support of the use of the concept of Jewish *kabbalah* exegesis as well. In fact, it can be

---

[134]"Primogenitos solitos adhiberi ad Sacrificia apparet non solum ex Hebraeorum commentariis sed et ex eo quod in Lege. . ." *De Republica Judaica*, (cap. II). That Bertram's efforts were only the beginning of the process of interpreting biblical law by means of rabbinical commentary can be seen in the extensive additions from rabbinical sources to Bertram's work by L'Empereur (1641).

[135]"Denique hic locus postulare videretur ut aliquid de sacrificiorum Mosaicorum generibus et ritibus diceremus, sed quia illa non nisi pluribus pertractari possunt, ea in alium tractatum rejicimus" (*De Republica Judaica*, cap. VII).

[136]Peter Cunaeus, *De Republica Hebraeorum*, Libri III, 1617.

[137]Katchen, *Christian Hebraists*, 37. Of his study of rabbinical sources Cunaeus wrote, "We had repeated pleasure in thinking how much enjoyment our heart derived from Hebraism, when we would study the volumes of the Bible [with] the rabbinic commentaries and many other erudite works written by the Jews" (Katchen, 38). "Juvabat identidem cogitare quantopere animum nostrum delectavisset Hebraismus, cum Biblica volumina, Rabbinorum Commentarios, atque alia multa quae erudite a Judaeis scripta sunt, evolveremus" (P. Cunaeus, *Prolegomena in Lib. III*).

[138]Katchen, *Christian Hebraists*, 40.

[139]". . . offero Republicam, qua nulla unquam in terris sanctior, nec bonis exemplis ditior fuit. Hujus inita et incrementa perdidicisse omnino vestrum est, quoniam illa hercle non hominem quenquam mortali concretione satum sed ipsum Deum immortalem autorem fundatoremque habet . . ." (*Praefatio*).

[140]"Jam permulti cives vestri in partes nescio quas discessere, sententiisque contrariis inter sese pugnant, postquam orta inter eos inutilis dissensio est de religionum mysteriis, quae plerique non intelligunt" (*Praefatio*). It is remarkable how similar Cunaeus's remarks here are to those of Gabler's *Oratio*.

[141]Katchen, *Christian Hebraists*, 39.

seen in the work of Cunaeus that in the growing use of Jewish legal exegesis, which stressed the simple (*peshat*) interpretation of the Mosaic Law, the OT, as such, had begun to lose its straightforward sense of being about Christ. The *peshat* meaning of the text was not as transparently Christological as it had been to the earlier Reformers. There was now a need for an additional sense in which the Hebrew Bible could be related to Christ and the NT. For Cunaeus that additional sense was to be found in the Jewish concept of *kabbalah*. Hence, Cunaeus closes the third and final book of *De Republica Hebraeorum* with chapters on the mystical sense of Scripture (*kabbalah*)[142] and the Messiah.[143] In these two chapters Cunaeus maintained that the "spiritual," that is, "messianic" sense of the OT was preserved by means of an oral tradition (*kabbalah*) that accompanied the OT Scriptures from the time of Moses and the prophets up to the time of Jesus. We will discuss Cunaeus's view of *kabbalah* below.

Thus it was that the Christian hebraists, in their focus on the legal aspects of the law, virtually mandated for themselves the adoption of a mystical, or typological, reading of the Mosaic Law—one that did, in fact, point to Christ. Having taken the primary meaning of the OT to be essentially legal, they were in need of a method of exegesis that would allow them also to read it Christologically. Christian hebraists, like Cunaeus, who were primarily interested in a thoroughly legal exposition of the Mosaic Law, thus sought to justify the use of the concept of *kabbalah* in their mystical interpretations of Scripture. As we will see below, it is important to distinguish between the Christian hebraists' concept of *kabbalah*, that is, "an oral tradition of a mystical nature that accompanied the OT Scriptures," from the content of Jewish *kabbalah*, that is, Jewish mysticism. Though the mysticism of Jewish *kabbalah* fascinated many Christian scholars in the medieval period, Protestant biblical scholars largely repudiated it. In doing so, however, they still held on to the concept of a nonwritten, "true *kabbalah*," that had orally accompanied the Hebrew Bible.

2.4.1.2.5.1.2. Rabbinical Commentary.

2.4.1.2.5.1.2. Rabbinical Commentary. Quite apart from their concern for legal exposition of the OT, Christian hebraists were also responsible for the adoption of the medieval Jewish concept of *peshat* in their interpretation of the narrative texts of Scripture.[144] For the most part, this had already happened before the time of the Reformation.[145] As we have shown above, the aim of Jewish commentary in the development of the *peshat* was primarily polemical. Specifically, it was directed against the Christians' messianic claim that the Hebrew Scriptures pointed to Jesus. Thus a bewilderingly ironic shift with enormous consequences was introduced into the Christian interpretation of the OT. The polemical, anti-messianic, "simple" meaning

---

[142] *De Cabala, sive de lege quae scriptis mandata non est*, cap. VIII.

[143] *Quid de Messia perceptum cognitumve habuerint Hebrai in Veteri Ecclesia*, cap. IX.

[144] "Luther hat in den Werken des Nicolaus von Lyra studiert. Die reformierten Exegeten (vor allem Calvin, Bibliander, Pellicanus, Capito, Musculus und Vermigli) haben—über Nicolaus zurückgreifend—die exegetische Wissenschaft der jüdischen Gelehrten des Mittelalters in ihren Kommentaren rezipiert" (Hans-Joachim Kraus, *Geschichte der historische-kritischen Erforschung des Alten Testaments* [Neukirchener Verlag, 1969], 13).

[145] Beryl Smalley, *The Study of the Bible in the Middle Ages* (Notre Dame: University of Notre Dame Press, 1964 [1952]), 102–3.

of the Hebrew text, was identified by the Christian hebraists as the "literal sense" (*sensus literalis*), that is, "historical sense" of the Hebrew Scriptures. From the start, Protestant theologians thus found themselves in a quandary. They needed the literal sense of Scripture to argue against the Roman Catholic appeals to tradition.[146] But it was precisely that literal sense (*sensus literalis*) of Scripture that had been identified with the Jewish polemical response to Christianity's claim to the Hebrew Scriptures (*peshat*).

Calvin is an early and striking example of the impact of Jewish *peshat* interpretation on Protestant exegesis of the OT. Calvin, who drew heavily from medieval Jewish commentaries, was often hesitant to see Christ in key OT texts. In a traditionally messianic passage like Genesis 3:15, for example, Calvin follows medieval rabbinical exegesis closely in interpreting it "simply to mean that there should always be the hostile strife between the human race and serpents."[147] The true sense of the words is clear, Calvin argued, "I do not agree with others respecting their meaning; for others take the seed for Christ, without much close consideration; as if it were said, that some one would arise from the seed of the woman who would strike the head of the serpent."[148]

In his own day, and for some time after, Calvin was somewhat alone in his strict adherence to the *peshat* interpretation of texts of Scripture like these. Moreover, he did not always follow the logic of the *peshat*. In Genesis 49:10, for example, he makes a subtle and plausible attempt to find a reference to the Messiah in Jacob's blessing of Judah, even castigating the Jewish interpreters for not seeing it.[149]

While remaining true to the simple meaning of Scripture, other Christian hebraists in Calvin's day were by and large content also to find Christ in these passages by means of a figurative or mystical interpretation. Sebastian Münster, for example, who relied heavily on the Jewish *peshat* commentary, argued that the serpent was a real snake but one that had been possessed by Satan.[150] The sense of the passage thus looks far beyond the concerns of snakes and human fear of them. It looks to the saving work of Christ on the cross.[151]

---

[146]"Gegen diese Lehre vom mehrfachen Schriftsinn richtet sich die entschlossene Polemik Luthers, Melanchtons, Calvins und der anderen Reformatoren" (Kraus, *Geschichte*, 9).

[147]"Simpliciter interpretor, hostile semper fore dissidium humano generi cum serpentibus, quale hodie cernitur" (Calvin, *Comment. in Genesin*, 23). Rashi: "As you will have no height (not stand erect) you will be able to bite him only on the heel, but even at that spot you will kill him . . ." (M. Rosenbaum and A. M. Silbermann, *Pentateuch and Rashi's Commentary* [London: Shapiro, Vallentine & Co., 1929], 15).

[148]"In verbis quidem Mosis nulla est ambiguitas: de sensu vero mihi non convenit cum aliis. Nam semen pro Christo sine controversia accipiunt: acsi dictum foret, exoriturum ex mulieris semine aliquem qui serpentis caput vulneraret" (Calvin, *Comment. in Genesin*, 23). Note Luther: "Primum igitur hoc statuemus, serpentem esse verum serpentem, sed invasum et obsessum a Satana, qui per serpentem loquitur" (*Enarrationes in Genesin, Exegetica Opera Latina*, C. S. Th. Elsperger [Erlangen: Carl Heyder, 1829], 234–35).

[149]Calvin, *Commentary in Genesin*, ad loc.

[150]"Quando praeterea hic dicitur, serpentem locutum cum muliere, sciendum serpentem illum verum fuisse serpentem, sed obsessum a Satana, qui per serpentem loquebatur" (Sebastian Münster, *Annotata ad Genesis, Critical Sacra*, 1:111).

[151]"Additur ergo magna consolatio, nasciturum scilicet semen quod caput ejus conterat. Hominis calcaneus in periculo est, caput est salvum: Contra per semen mulieris, non cauda sed caput serpentis conculcandum dicitur. Hanc primam consolationem, tanquam fontem omnis misericordiae et omnium promis-

Early on, then, the Christian hebraists' dependence on medieval Jewish exegesis for the simple (*peshat*) meaning of the Scriptures, led them to adopt a mystical sense alongside that of the literal. Following the lead of medieval Jewish exegesis, and wanting to avoid any semblance of multiple meanings, many Christian hebraists looked to the concept of Jewish *kabbalah* exegesis as a way of expressing the hidden mystical component of the simple meaning.

2.4.1.2.5.2. Kabbalah. By the time of the Reformation, Christians had long been interested in the spiritual "mysteries" which the medieval Jewish writers had found hidden behind every letter of the Hebrew Scriptures. Christian hebraists like Johannes Reuchlin (1455–1522) and Pico della Mirandola (1463–94) devoted much of their Hebraic studies to the mining of this medieval Jewish mysticism. Though these works were not without effect on later developments in biblical theology, our interest here lies in the later use of *kabbalah* in Protestant biblical exegesis.

Protestant biblical scholarship largely repudiated the central core of Jewish *kabbalah* which had so fascinated earlier Christians. They had not rejected, however, the basic concept that a divinely intended "mystery" had accompanied the OT since its inception. This mystery, many Protestant scholars maintained, had accompanied the OT text as a form of tradition (*kabbalah*) which gave its spiritual sense alongside that of the literal meaning. It was in this spiritual meaning that theologians were often able to find references to Christ and the Gospel. Protestant biblical scholars viewed this christological, spiritual meaning as a form of "true *kabbalah*" (*Cabala vera*) that had been preserved by Jesus and the NT writers. The Jewish *kabbalah*, which had been studied and applied to Christian theology by earlier biblical scholars like Reuchlin, they viewed as a "false *kabbalah*" (*Cabala falsa*). True *kabbalah*, however, was understood to be an essential part of the meaning of the OT, and its interpretation played a key role in the development of Protestant biblical theology. To a great extent, this has been an untold story, but it is, nevertheless, an important chapter in the history of biblical theology.

The concept and development of a Christian kabbalistic OT interpretation within Protestant theology was principally the result of two well-known Reformed biblical scholars, Peter Cunaeus and Campegius Vitringa. These two hebraic scholars represent two quite different conceptualizations of the nature of *kabbalah*, however. For Cunaeus, the "mystery" of the true *kabbalah* was passed on orally alongside Scripture from the time of Moses and the prophets. It was recorded in writing only by the NT writers, and we now have it in their works. Vitringa, on the other hand, rejected Cunaeus' notion of *kabbalah* and argued instead that the "mystery" of the received tradition (*kabbalah*) lay hidden in the written OT itself. Jesus and the NT writers had searched the OT Scriptures and had discovered the true spiritual *kabbalah* intended

---

sionum scaturiginem, primi parentes et eorum posteri summa diligentia didicerunt. Non ergo agit hic Moses de serpente naturali, sed loquitur de diabolo, cujus caput sunt mors et peccatum, quae cum sint per Christum sublata, quid restat quam ut filii Dei salvemur?" (ibid.).

by Moses and the prophets. The mystery was in the text all along, needing only to be discovered. Both approaches to the OT text continued to have a major impact on the interpretation of Scripture in biblical theology for many years, indeed, for centuries.

Recent studies in the nature of the OT text have brought this issue to the forefront again. When one looks closely at the nature of inter-biblical interpretation, for example, it becomes clear that later OT writers often saw more in earlier OT texts than might meet the eye, at least at first glance. The nature of the composition of some biblical books, and the shaping and structure of the Canon, suggests that at a very early stage in its history the OT text was closely searched and read with a careful eye to the meaning of minute details. It has by now long been recognized that exegetical procedures and techniques used by later *kabbalists* were already operative in the composition of many of the OT books.[152]

We have seen above that Cunaeus played a central role in the development of the Reformed application of biblical law to contemporary European society. Having interpreted the Mosaic Law according to its simple (*peshat*) sense, the *sensus literalis*, and applied it to the everyday affairs of human society, Cunaeus turned to the Jewish concept of tradition (*kabbalah*) to justify his further messianic reading of these same OT texts. Cunaeus understood *kabbalah* as spiritual doctrine which, although given by God, was not transmitted in written texts. This doctrine was not written, Cunaeus maintained, because the ordinary Israelites, in the days of Moses and the prophets, were not able to comprehend or understand the deep mysteries they contained. Moses learned many of these mysteries on Mount Horeb when he spoke with God, but he did not write them down. Moses passed these unwritten traditions to other inspired men (*qui Spiritu Sacro agebantur*) who kept them intact for future generations. Cunaeus was quick to point out that this tradition was not to be identified with the Jewish traditions known to us from later rabbinical literature, for example the Talmud. The tradition (*kabbalah*) of which he speaks is that true *kabbalah* (*cabala vera*) that lies latent in the Scriptures themselves and that the ancient prophets knew to lie behind their own works. Such tradition accompanied the text but was kept secret from the common reader of Scripture.[153] It was not a tradition that was merely passed on from one generation to another by strictly human means, but was one that originated and was preserved through divine inspiration (*quam coelitus acceperunt viri sancti*) and ultimately is reflected in the New Testament's interpretation of the Old.[154]

---

[152]Abraham Geiger, *Urschrift und Übersetzungen der Bibel in ihrer Abhängigkeit von der innern Entwicklung des Judenthums* (Breslau: Verlag von Julius Hainauer, 1857); I. L. Seeligmann, "Voraussetzungen der Midrasch-Exegese, *SVT* (1953): 150–81; Michael Fishbane, *Biblical Interpretation in Ancient Israel* (Oxford: Clarendon Press, 1985); Jack M. Sasson, "Wordplay in the OT," *IDBS* (Nashville: Aingdon, 1976), 968–70.

[153]"Ego veram Cabalam appello mystericum intellectum earum quae in Sacris Libris latent. Is intellectus, cum antea penes Vates fuisset, sed non vulgandus mortalium seculis" (*Respublica*, cap. viii).

[154]"OT . . . tandem divino munere Apostolis et Euangeliorum concessus scriptoribus est, uti quod diu latuerat publica voce illorum proderetur universis" (*Respublica*, cap. viii).

The young Paul, sitting at the feet of his teacher Gamaliel, first learned a Jewish *kabbalah* (*Rabbinicam Cabalam*); but when he became an apostle, he learned the true *kabbalah* (*Cabalam veram*). Only then, says Cunaeus, did he understand that "the law was spiritual" (*Legem spiritualem esse*). As an example of this Christian *kabbalah*, Cunaeus turns to the narrative of Numbers 1–2. When these narratives speak of "leaders" and "potentates" among the people of God, they refer naturally to the historical leaders in Moses' day. That is their *peshat* meaning. According to Cunaeus, however, the apostle Paul understood a deeper sense in these texts (*sublimiore sensu*) and thus wrote publicly of the secret meaning latent in them. These leaders and authorities were part of a "mystery hidden for ages" (Eph 3:9–10) which Paul revealed in his letter to the Ephesian church. Moreover, Cunaeus argues, Moses did, in fact, write about the law in Deuteronomy 30, but Paul understood his words in a different sense altogether. Paul understood Moses to be speaking of Christ and the Gospel (Rom 10). Paul's understanding, says Cunaeus, comes from the "true *kabbalah*" which had long accompanied the Hebrew Bible and which Paul had received from God.

What is distinctive about Cunaeus' understanding of *kabbalah* is that while he believed the Christian "mystery" was latent in the words of Scripture, he also believed it could not be known apart from the accompanying oral tradition (*kabbalah*). It is just at this point where Vitringa will take issue with Cunaeus and introduce a new perspective on the concept of Christian *kabbalah*. Since Cunaeus was a major figure in the development of Reformed hermeneutics, as the frequent references to him in the contemporary literature attests,[155] his views on OT interpretation were taken seriously.

Vitringa defined *kabbalah* as a theological or philosophical doctrine transmitted orally which had to do with the most sublime objects of knowledge.[156] According to Vitringa, there was little value in the *kabbalah* which originated in Judaism only after or at the time of the first century. However, the early *kabbalah*, he maintained, concerns the secret doctrine of the ancient prophets and saints of antiquity, which was transmitted and propagated orally. "Our concern here is rather with a more ancient *kabbalah*, that is, secret doctrine, transmitted and propagated orally, which the prophets and saints of antiquity possessed."[157] This *kabbalah* was not a secret allegorical interpretation passed on to the NT apostles from Moses and the OT prophets, as Cunaeus had supposed. Rather, as Vitringa understood it, *kabbalah* was a "spiritual sense" which can be derived from the words of Scripture itself—a sense put there and understood

---

[155]The most important Lutheran work on hermeneutics of that period, Salomon Glassius's *Philologia Sacra* (1705), views Cunaeus as representative of Reformed (Calvinist) biblical interpretation (348–49).

[156]"Nos enim per *kabbalam* hic intelligimus *Doctrinam* non *Ritualem*, qualem Talmud complectitur, sed *Theologiam* sive *Philosophiam Dogmaticam*, *ore* traditam, quae agat de nobilissimis scientiae objectis" (Campegius Vitringa, *Dissertatio Secunda de Sephiroth Kabbalistarum*, 120). Vitringa follows Rivetus in his definition of *kabbalah*: "Ergo *Cabbala* est acceptio aut receptio, doctrina nempe, quam accipiunt posteri a majoribus ... usus tamen obtinuit, ut ... vocabula haec ad doctrinam non scriptam, sed ore traditam significandam, fuerint usurpata, et scripturis sive sacris literis opposita ..." (Andreas Rivetus, *Isagoge*), 36.

[157]"sed potius agimus de *antiquiore* aliqua *kabbala*, sive Doctrina arcana, *ore* tradita et propagata, quam habuerint Prophetae et Sancti antiquiorum temporum" (Vitringa, *Dissertatio*, 121).

by Moses and the prophets and discovered in those same OT texts by Jesus and the NT apostles: "I thus would rather think that Moses, the prophets, and the wise scholars of the Old Economy knew, in general, that certain mysteries lay concealed in the divine law. These mysteries, as much as they were able, the apostles searched out and discovered (in the OT text). . . ."[158] After the ascension of Christ, the apostles were led by the Spirit to understand the allegorical (spiritual) sense of the OT even to a greater extent than the OT prophets themselves, for they had seen the events to which the prophets referred and the Spirit had opened their minds to understand them in light of the OT Scriptures.[159]

For Vitringa, the *kabbalah* which the NT authors saw in the OT text was an "extraordinary Jewish doctrine of faith" (*ipsa Dogmata Fidei Judaica insigniora*) which the OT writers understood clearly but which was not understood at that time by the common Israelite. These dogmas included, according to Vitringa, the Trinity and the messianic hope. Such "mysteries" were concealed in the writings of the OT Scriptures, but they could be uncovered by careful scrutiny (exegesis) of the text.[160] It was necessary, then, for God to select faithful men throughout the ages who were to search the Scriptures diligently and understand them to be about Christ and his messianic office. These men were the OT prophets and priests to whom the interpretation of the law was entrusted. They were to study the Scriptures carefully and teach the people about the Christ who was to come. Thus a "hidden" (mystery) tradition accompanied the OT texts and was itself derived from those texts. The truths embodied in that tradition and discovered in the OT Scriptures, are the "true *kabbalah*."[161]

By means of such an appeal to a "true *kabbalah*," Vitringa laid the groundwork for the development of a distinct form of biblical theology. The simple (*peshat*) meaning of the text was retained against the Roman Catholic appeal to allegory. At the same time, however, the New Testament interpretation of the Old and hence the Christian understanding of the OT remained intact. While the *peshat* meaning of the OT was running its course into becoming the *sensus historicus*, and thus establishing itself as the sole means of interpreting the OT, the spiritual meaning of the OT continued to be the focus of an entire branch of OT theology that was soon to be relegated to the backwaters of the history of biblical theology—that established by Vitringa and continued by Bengel and his students. So different is this branch of biblical theology from the mainstream, that Diestel actually refuses to include them with the rest of the biblical

---

[158]"Ego igitur sic potius sentio, Mosen, Prophetas, et excellentiores Doctores Oeconomiae Veteris *in genere* scivisse, recondita esse quaedam in *Lege Divina* (quo nomine tum Scriptura disignabatur:) arcana: Illa arcana, quantam illa rerum constitutione ipsis licebat, rimatos et scrutos esse . . ." (ibid., 122).

[159]Ibid., 122–23.

[160]"Sed sentio, hanc *kabbalam* continuisse clariorem *exegesin* illarum sacrae Scripturae locorum, in quibus haec mysteria, licet obscurius, tradita sunt: ut adeo *Traditio* illa Oralis, etiamsi clarior fuerit Traditione Scripturaria, ad eam tamen conformata fuerit, et *ab ea dependerit*" (ibid., 123).

[161]Ibid., 126–27.

theologies, branding them with the pejorative label "Theosophists."[162] It is just this group, however, that we wish to examine more closely. Though they have received scant attention in the histories of biblical theology, they have produced an enormous posterity of biblical theologians who have flourished in the world of popular theology, if not in the academic world, for many generations. We have chosen to call this group of biblical theologians the school of Biblical realism or Eschatological realism.

2.4.1.2.6. Biblical Realism/Eschatological Realism

In the eighteenth and nineteenth centuries, a significantly new form of biblical theology developed out of covenant theology and German Pietism, principally through the influence of two conservative, orthodox theologians, Campegius Vitringa and J. A. Bengel.[163] Though often overlooked in tracing the history of modern biblical theologies, these *biblical realists* had a distinct view of the OT that made a fundamental contribution to the development of modern evangelical biblical theology. The primary contribution of Vitringa and Bengel lay in the central importance that these two biblical scholars had given to the role of biblical eschatology, particularly the books of Daniel and Revelation.

From the start, the classical orthodox view of Scripture contained elements that were subject to considerable variation and which over time, tended to shift in many conservative theologies. In the early nineteenth century, for example, the orthodox concept of an inspired, inerrant Scripture came to be understood by such conservative biblical theologians as Rothe and Hofmann primarily in terms of a historically accurate depiction of "inspired events" in Scripture. As a result of this shift, every detail of history became as important to the maintenance of doctrine as every detail of Scripture had been for the orthodox theologian. If, in fact, earlier orthodox biblical theologians can be called "dogmatic biblicists," then Hofmann can be called a "dogmatic historicist." While orthodox theologians had their *dicta probantia* (proof texts for doctrine), Hofmann had his *facta probantia* (proof facts for doctrine). For Hofmann, the truth of the Christian religion lay in the meaning of history.

There were, however, more marginal biblical theologians whose ideas about Scripture had not shifted in the same direction as Hofmann and other, more academic, theologians. Among those theologians, Vitringa's concept of the text as a repository of "hidden mysteries" had made a significant impression. For such conservative theologians, however, who had not abandoned the orthodox notion of an inspired written text, the locus of revelation not only remained the text itself, but was also extended in practice to every detail of the text. As Vitringa had argued, any and every detail of the written text may contain a "hidden mystery" waiting to be discovered by the discerning eye of the alert reader.

---

[162]Ludwig Diestel, *Geschichte des Alten Testamentes in der christlichen Kirche* (Jena: Mauke's Verlag, 1869), 698. Though the title is unfair and inaccurate, Diestel was correct in isolating the group from the other biblical theologies and treating it separately.

[163]This discussion follows closely that of Diestel, *Geschichte*, 698–708.

It should at this point be recalled that the view of Scripture in classical ortho-doxy had been dominated by what Weber called "dogmatic biblicism," in which the details of the written text were understood as an expression of the dogmatic creeds of the church. Thus the extent of divine revelation in Scripture, in the view of classical orthodoxy, had been controlled by the various "topics" (*loci*) of doctrine. This was a clear result of dogmatic biblicism. Insofar as the Scriptures touched on specific dog-matic topics, their every detail was of the utmost importance and was brought into the service of dogma by means of a special hermeneutic. Other details of the text, how-ever, were overlooked or considered of less importance.

With the diminishing hold that dogmatic theology had come to have on bib-lical theology, brought on largely in conservative circles through the influence of Pietism, the limitation placed on the theological importance of minor details of Scrip-ture was greatly reduced. In the absence of a doctrinal focus to help determine which parts of Scripture were important and which were not, each and every detail of Scrip-ture, no matter how seemingly insignificant, was raised to a level of importance equal to all others. Moreover, each and every detail may also contain a "hidden mystery" waiting to be revealed. Thus the orthodox identification of Scripture with the Word of God for these theologians now meant that every detail and section of the OT Scriptures contained divine revelation and was potentially meaningful for the life of the Christian in the contemporary world. Large sections of Scripture previously over-looked because they did not relate directly to the *loci* of the orthodox doctrinal sys-tems, were thus opened up for inclusion into a newly configured system of biblical theology. For Vitringa, Bengel, and others who followed them, this meant a new importance for the biblical apocalyptic literature which had been largely overlooked. Under the constraints of classical church dogmatics, books such as Daniel, Zechariah, and Revelation had received scant attention. When biblical theology was relieved of its task to represent only the doctrinal *loci*, a new, and largely untouched, array of bib-lical texts was opened up. It became, as it were, the "manifest destiny" of the biblical realists to explore and chart the new territory with all the exegetical and theological skills they could marshal. Those skills, incidentally, were impressive, even by modern standards.

The view that divine revelation was to be found even in the apparently insignif-icant and overlooked parts of Scripture was, furthermore, coupled with the orthodox view of the unity of the Bible (*unitas Sacrae Scripturae*). The biblical realists, who were also conservative "supernaturalists," thus began to read Scripture not merely in terms of a holistic meaning derived from credal statements or church doctrines as such, but in terms of a quite new consensus. That consensus was drawn from the holistic sense which each and every individual part of Scripture had when it was related to the total picture of God's work in history. Thus the search was on for a single, global meaning which could be assigned to Scripture and which could be derived from the sum of the individual texts of Scripture. A number of beliefs about the Bible became axiomatic for biblical realists, including (1) the complete unity of the text of Scripture, (2) its per-fect coherence, even in the most minute details, (3) the thorough symmetry of all the parts of Scripture and (4) the proper emphasis of each of its words.[164] Each of these beliefs about the Bible had been inherited by the biblical realists from classical orthodoxy, but they were now free to be applied without the constraints of the church creeds and dogmas.

The fundamental impact of Bengel and Vitringa in the development of this newly charted approach to Scripture is to be found in the central role these two scholars gave to the biblical apocalyptic books. Bengel not only devoted minute attention to the details of the NT Scriptures, even in often obscure textual-critical matters, but he also viewed these details within the context of the broad, all-encompassing, apocalyptic vision of the book of Revelation. While Bengel focused only on the NT, Vitringa viewed, in the same manner, the whole of the OT within the context of the visions of Daniel, Zechariah, and the book of Revelation. No detail of the written text of Scripture, however minor, fell outside the total eschatological picture of the future, particularly as it was to consummate in the return of Christ.[165] In the approach of these conservative scholars one finds, in addition, a reaction to both the growing "intellectualism" of late orthodoxy and the "idealism" of the Wolfian theology that had so dominated the modern theologies of their day.[166] That reaction can be seen in the emphasis these scholars seemed to put on reading the Scriptures "realistically."[167] To read the OT text accurately was to recognize, and give fair attention to, its earthly, and often coarse, subject matter. The focus of the OT, they argued, was not on mere ideas and philosophical concepts, but on the everyday affairs, the hopes and dreams of the people of Israel. Its focus, in other words, was on the physical world, not on the ethereal world of dogma and ethical ideas.[168] To miss this earthly dimension of Scripture was to miss its central focus—the earthly Kingdom of God. Millennialism and the return of the Jews to Palestine were thus central foci of these theologians.[169] For the most part, these and other concepts were viewed in highly realistic and holistic terms. What might appear to modern biblical scholars merely as images and literary devices of apocalyptic writings were understood by these biblical realists as depictions of actual events and places at specific times in human history. Bengel, for example, taking the symbolic

---

[164]"Die völlige Einheit der Schrift, ihr genauer Zusammenhang bis in Einzelnste, ihre durchgängige Symmetrie und Emphase sind die Moment jenes Axioms" (ibid., 700–701).

[165]Ibid., 701. Similar views are to be found in Oetinger and Crusius.

[166]Ibid.

[167]"Dieser Gegensatz erzeugte dasjenige theosophische Moment, welches die reine Geistigkeit verwirft und die 'Realitäten' der himmlischen Dinge, die 'groben, massive Anschauungen der Schrift' stark betont" (ibid., 701).

[168]Oetinger: "Warum uns Alles in der heil. Schrift so grob und massiv vorkommt, kommt von dem platon. Begriff von den Körpern als blossen Erscheinungen her . . . Alles lebt in jener Welt leiblich, auch sogar der Altar Apoc. 17, 7 und die sieben Donner, denn sie führen eine Rede. Es giebt aber Leiber, die zwar eine Substanz haben, aber doch durchdringlich sind, wie Alles in dem Raum des Himmels ist" (quoted in ibid., 701).

[169]"Dass die meisten derselben ihrer rechten, buchstäblichen Erfüllung noch harren, dass vor allem den endlich bekehrten Juden die Herbeiführung einer ganz neuer Herrlichkeitsepoche des irdischen Gottesreiches beschieden sei, ist eines ihrer Hauptaxiome, und deshalb hadert sie mit der Orthodoxie um das dogmatische Recht des Chiliasmus" (ibid., 702).

numbers in the book of Revelation as a veiled chronology, predicted the establishment of the millennial kingdom in the year 1836. That interpretation had a far-reaching effect on popular views of the events that followed the Napoleonic wars. Napoleon was taken as the beast of Revelation 13 who had put an end to the kingdom of Rome— one thousand years after the Holy Roman Empire was established in A.D. 800. For his part, Vitringa devoted considerable attention to the question of whether Isaiah 33:7 refers to the death of Gustavus Adolphus in 1612 and to which Europeans king the "destroyer" in that passage referred. The biblical prophetic books were, in the minds of these scholars, little more than "proleptic histories."[170]

The outcome of such a realistic reading of Scripture was that formal categories of thought, so familiar in orthodox theologies, were largely replaced by broadly cast eschatological images such as "the kingdom of God" and "the day of the Lord."[171] All in all, the Bible ceased to be a system of doctrine, as it had been in classical orthodoxy, and came to be understood rather as a realistic vision of the apocalyptic future. The overall structure of that vision was determined primarily by the imagery of the book of Revelation, and the time frame of the events was shaped by Daniel's apocalyptic imagery. The whole of the scriptural material was taken over as a realistic and literal depiction of actual events.[172] It is important to note that such an appropriation of the Scriptures as a whole, in fact, represented a late, but logical, development of the early apocalyptic writers themselves: "The entire contents of the Scriptures were contained in an 'eschatological physiognomy.' The whole of the past was understood only as a moment and a type of the future. The past was not the ripe fruit, but only a germ in the process of growing to full maturity."[173] To this extent, the biblical realists were faithful to a part, at least, of the biblical texts, namely the apocalyptic books. A case can also be made that their overriding interest in reading the whole of Scripture in light of the apocalyptic visions may even reflect a similar concern on the part of those who shaped the OT canon.

The Scriptures that we have been describing had the effect of encouraging even further the tendency of biblical realists to view the Bible as a coherent and meaningful whole. Each and every prophecy or apocalyptic image, indeed every narrative detail, had its place and was to be related or linked in some way to the whole. The whole was, in turn, understood as a complete and single vision of the kingdom of God. All of the parts were connected into the one final, grand, but yet incomplete, picture.[174] The very incompleteness of the final picture fueled an even more intense search for new and missing pieces among the details of the scriptural text.

---

[170]This type of interpretation can be found already in Coccejus and Gürtler: Johannes Coccejus, *Summa Doctrinae de Foedere et Testamento Dei*, Opera Omnia, VII, 39; Nicolai Gürtler, *Systema Theologiae Propheticae*, 1724.

[171]Diestel, *Geschichte*, 701.

[172]"Was bisher also Bild galt, soll nun Realität. Thatsache werden oder dafür gelten" (ibid., 702).

[173]Ibid.

[174]"Jene Gedanken motiviren sein Verfahren, die gesammte Bibel unterschiedslos in sich zu kombiniren, vor allem die allgemeinen Weissagungen durch die späteren speciellen zu erläuten: denn Alles ist

The strongly "realistic" cast of this approach nurtured a view of the present and future as a time of literal fulfillment of the biblical apocalyptic imagery. Current events provided textual clues to the meaning of obscure biblical passages. Moreover, the biblical thrust of the approach meant that current and historical events were linked to and aligned with the events of the biblical narratives in such a way that both the past and the present were strewn with fulfilled prophecy; and the consummation of all history, the kingdom of God, lay within the foreseeable and predictable future. In such a view of Scripture, in fact, there was an almost inexhaustible source of "fulfillments" awaiting only the appropriate current event to bring them to life. Passages that had lain dormant for centuries breathed new life and shed new meaning on the whole of Scripture. Because the meaning of these texts lay in the composite final picture, the immediate literary context usually contributed little to the sense of a text. What mattered was the contribution that the text made to the global picture of the final events of history. At the same time, such confirmations of prophetic interpretations had the additional effect of validating the biblical-realistic reading of Scripture itself. Increasingly the Scriptures came to be understood as a mine to be quarried, not only for signs of the times, but for nuggets of truth fit for equipping the saints to live a life of faith while waiting for the return of the Lord. Eschatology was thus brought into the service of Christian ethics, much as it had originally been intended by the biblical writers.

The heavy debt biblical realism owed to classical orthodoxy's view of Scripture (verbal plenary inspiration), rendered it outside the pale of academic theology after the close of the eighteenth century. It continued unabated, however, in popular religious movements, particularly in those spawned by evangelical revivals.[175] Only those biblical realists who were willing to hedge on the question of the verbal inspiration of Scripture, such as Hofmann and Delitzsch, were able to achieve academic recognition, although they, and a few others like them, might well be classed as "historical realists" because their ultimate focus lay on the "holy history" (*Heilsgeschichte*) behind the texts and not on the texts themselves. Nevertheless, and in spite of their ostensive concern for historical events, Hofmann, Delitzsch, and others, remained faithful to the Scriptures as such, viewing them, in most cases, as a part of the holy history itself. So strongly did Hofmann believe that the Scriptures presented real and sacred "inspired" historical events, that he saw no fundamental difference between the inspiration of those events and the inspired recording of those events in Scripture itself. The message of the Bible was, in fact, the message of history: the fulfillment of the kingdom of God. Jesus and his kingdom is not only the key to the Scripture, but also the key to the whole of human history. Like the Scriptures, history itself is prophetic. History displays an increasingly clear picture of the future kingdom in which God will restore

---

Eine Reichsgeschichte, Alles Offenbarung desselben Geistes und desselben Gottes, dessen consilia et molimina aber nur gradatim zu Tage treten" (Diestel, 703). Here lie the roots of the "prophecy chart" so essential to the later generation. The chart, in my opinion, replaced the verbal imagery of the Bible with a graphic substitute for a generation not so well-versed in the biblical literature.

[175]For an excellent and near exhaustive survey of these "biblical-realists," which are there called "fundamentalists," see Stephan Holthaus, *Fundamentalismus in Deutschland* (Bonn: Verlag für Kultur und Wissenschaft, 1993), 373–448.

his relationship with humanity. "The link between history and prophecy is so close that both lose something of their own uniqueness. The origin of both does not lie in something external, but rather in a 'dynamic inner working of the living God present in both the world and in humanity.'"[176] So close was this link for Hofmann, that he saw the whole of the composition of the Scriptures, as well as the collection and shaping of the Canon, as a revelatory work of God within the human processes of history. The OT Scriptures themselves were thus assigned to the position of merely witnessing to the work of God in history.[177] As such they participated in the same revelatory "holistic mass" as history itself, history, that is, conceived of as holy history (*Heilsgeschichte*). Revelation lay in the historical facts witnessed to by the details of written Scripture. There was, thus, an unexamined link between the inexhaustible written details of Scripture and the myriad of revelatory facts of history to which they witness.[178]

In the following two centuries, the nineteenth and twentieth, this "scriptural" access to the "facts of history" would play itself out in two quite different directions. On the one hand, the apocalyptic search of current events would run its course by further identifying the events of history as links to the textual world of Scripture. In the United States, the Civil War, and in the twentieth century, the world wars, provided more than enough historical facts to fill in the biblical picture of the "last days." Zionism and the eventual establishment of the modern state of Israel provided an unanticipated source of reference points.

The other direction taken by the biblical realists was the focus given to biblical archaeology and ancient Near Eastern history in the late nineteenth and twentieth centuries. With the establishment of the "Albright School" of biblical archaeology, nonapocalyptic biblical realists found a new and nearly inexhaustible source of historical facts with which to link the scriptural texts. Some biblical realists focused on historical facts drawn from archaeology and ancient history as well as on apocalyptic current events in their attempt to identify the meaning of Scripture in revelatory facts. Characteristic of all the biblical realists, however, is the belief that not only is biblical revelation historical, but also history, as such, is revelational. Underlying such a view of revelation lies a chiefly uncritical attitude toward the nature of historical events and the writing of history itself.

2.4.1.3. Essential Factors in the Rise and Development of Biblical and Old Testament Theology

Our survey of the various histories of biblical and OT theology has attempted to bring to light several prominent features of the movement as a whole. It may be helpful here to summarize them since they inevitably play an important role in shaping our understanding of the nature and task of OT theology.

---

[176]Diestel, *Geschichte*, 704.

[177]Ibid., 705.

[178]"Ferner fasst Hofmann die Geschichte fast ausschliesslich als Gottesthat und das A.T. als heilige Geschichte. Unerwiesen bleiben diese Sätze, während sie allein die Brücken bilden von der Behauptung, dass das Wesen der Offb. Thatsache sei, zu der andern, dass auch jede im A.T. berichtete Geschichte eine Heilsthatsache, mithin Vorausdarstellung Christi sei; denn die Auswahl wird nicht kritisch gerechtfertigt" (ibid., 705).

(1) VERBAL INSPIRATION

It is widely recognized that the notion of an inspired text of Scripture has played an important, indeed central, role in the growth and development of OT theology. The prominence of the Protestant doctrine of verbal inspiration has been traced to the writings of John Calvin.[179] With Flacius we see the full development of the identification of Scripture and God's Word.[180] In both Lutheran and Reformed orthodoxy, God's Word, as the basis of Christian theology, has been defined in purely textual categories. Scripture, the written canon of the Old and New Testaments, is identified as God's Word. At certain points through its history, the notion of verbal inspiration was extended even to include the vowel points of the Hebrew text.[181] Although in the second half of the eighteenth century the notion of verbal inspiration was completely abandoned by most biblical theologians, even in this abandonment, the concept of an inspired text continued to have a powerful influence, if only as a foil for the new forms of biblical theology being shaped. As we have attempted to show in the previous discussions, many concepts related to the orthodox view of Scripture (e.g., infallibility) were merely transformed to the new sources of revelation, namely, reason and history. Where orthodoxy had sought certitude and infallibility in the inspired text, many biblical theologians found it in human reason and historiography. The orthodox notion of an inspired text, however, survived intact, though with some modification, among the biblical realists.

(2) BIBLICISM AND DOGMATIC BIBLICISM

The term *biblicism* came into use in the mid-nineteenth century, originally used negatively to characterize approaches to the Bible that were, to one degree or another, uncritical or unhistorical. Today the term refers to any approach to theology in which the Bible itself is understood as divine revelation and the sole source in matters of faith and practice, not merely in its general concepts and teaching but in the very details of its words and letters.[182] Biblicism is obviously of great importance to the concept of biblical theology.

Dogmatic biblicism is a particular kind of biblicism—one that has aligned itself to a specific dogmatic system by arguing that the Bible, in its entirety, teaches precisely

---

[179]Hans Emil Weber, *Reformation, Orthodoxie und Rationalismus* [Darmstadt: Wissenschaftliche Buchgesellschaft, I, i, 1966], 307.

[180]"die Heilige Schrifft wie im anfang / da sie Gott geredt hat / also auch jtzt Gottis wort wey" (*Von der h. Schrifft und jrer wirckung / wider Caspar Schwenckfeld* [1554], quoted by Weber, I, i, 308).

[181]Flacius, for example, believed that "God spoke through the mouth of his instruments, human beings, which are represented as ἔνθεοι, pleni Deo; the axiom that the Spirit of God could not reveal something unclearly, demanded that even the vowels of the Hebrew text were original" (Weber, I.i. 308). That this understanding of the Scriptures continued even into the eighteenth century is evident in Carpzov's *Critica Sacra* (1728): . . . . iisdem quoque animetur vocalibus et punctis, ac in αὐτογράφοις (93).

[182]"Biblizismus selber soll die Denkrichtung bezeichnen, die in allen Fragen des Glaubens, der Lehre, des Handelns und der persönlichen Frömmigkeit, oft bis in die Sprache hinein, die Bibel als das geschichtlich offenbarte Wort Gottes in ihrer Ganzheit oder im einzelnen möglichst nachdrücklich, ausschliesslich und unmittelbar als Norm oder Quelle zur Geltung bringen will" (*TRE*, 6, 478).

that specific system. Though early traces of such a biblicism can be seen in Luther's insistence on both *sola fide* and *sola scriptura*,[183] Calvin's *Institutes*,[184] and Melanchthon's *loci*, Weber has traced the actual formulation of dogmatic biblicism to Flacius' *Clavis Sacrae Scripturae*. Not only did Flacius fully identify the written Scriptures with the Word of God, but he also identified the Scriptures with the *loci* of Malanchthon by carefully selecting and restructuring the Bible's content to fit that system.[185]

In our opinion, it was biblicism rather than dogmatic biblicism that made the most lasting impression on biblical theology. Dogmatic biblicism was by and large rejected after the rise of Pietism and historicism. Dogmatic biblicism was even rejected by the biblical realists. The only traces of dogmatic biblicism in later OT theologies are in the strongly confessional approaches of Hengstenberg and Vos. Biblicism, on the other hand, has played a central role in shaping OT theology. The Scriptures as such have always been the primary focus of OT theology—even at those moments when the text had been virtually abandoned by historicist approaches. The modern resurgence of biblicism in canonical OT theologies and literary studies of Scripture is a witness to the continuing vitality of biblicism.

(3) *SENSUS LITERALIS*

A focus on the text of Scripture leads naturally to the question of the literal meaning of that text. Thus a central issue in the early development of OT theology was the identification and explication of the *sensus literalis* of the Hebrew Bible. This involved two assumptions. We saw, first, that Protestant theologians uncritically assumed that the literal meaning of Scripture (*sensus literalis*) was identical with that of the simple (*peshat*) meaning given the text in medieval Judaism. The problem embedded in that assumption was that the Jewish *peshat* meaning had been designed specifically to counter the Christian, messianic interpretation of the OT (*sensus spiritualis* or *mysticus*). Thus for the Reformers as a group, the literal or simple meaning of the OT could not point to Christ. It was rather necessary to take recourse to a deeper, allegorical (*sensus mysticus*) meaning of the text. In this, the Jewish concept of *kabbalah* played an important role.

It is not difficult to see the consequences of such an uncritical identification of the literal meaning of Scripture with the *peshat* interpretation. Once the literal mean-

---

[183]Luther's "dogma" of justification by faith alone was to find its source in Scripture alone.

[184]"Und wenn er den Glauben gewiss auch als Vertrauen versteht, so ist er doch für ihn vor allem Überzeugung, die Gewissheit zum Kennzeichen hat. Woher kommt solche gewisse Überzeugung? Sie gründet sich auf die heilige Schrift. . . . Die Schrift wird mit aller Grundsätzlichkeit als kritisches Prinzip für Theologie und Kirche gehandhabt. . . . Aus der Schrift ist das theologische System zu erheben" (Hans Emil Weber, *Reformation, Orthodoxie und Rationalismus* [Darmstadt: Wissenschaftliche Buchgesellschaft, I,i, 1966], 230–31).

[185]"Nun ist freilich bei ihm gewiss so gut wie bei Osiander die Auswahl und die Umgestaltung der biblischen Wahrheit zu beobachten. Aber das kennzeichnet ja gerade den dogmatischen, rationalen, orthodoxen Biblizismus, der die Schrift, die ganze Schrift mit aller rationalen Folgerichtigkeit als das Prinzip verkundet, um in der Schrift doch eben nur das orthodoxe Dogma zu finden" (Weber, I,i, 309). Flacius, in fact, prefaced his major work on church history with the summary of church dogma by Wigand-Judex, *Syntagma*.

ing (*sensus literalis*) was identified with the historical meaning (*sensus historicus*), the question of the historical author's intent was diverted away from a spiritual or messianic reading of Scripture and onto a quest for the mere historical referent. The historical meaning of the text could not be identified as messianic.

As part of the overall proposal for an approach to OT theology offered in this book, we strongly urge the consideration of a return to the notion that the literal meaning of the OT may, in fact, be linked to the messianic hope of the pre-Christian, Israelite prophets. By paying careful attention to the compositional strategies of the biblical books themselves, we believe in them can be found many essential clues to the meaning intended by their authors—clues that point beyond their immediate historical referent to a future, messianic age. By looking at the works of the scriptural authors, rather than at the events that lie behind their accounts of them, we can find appropriate textual clues to the meaning of these biblical books. Those clues, we also suggest, point to an essentially messianic and eschatological focus of the biblical texts. In other words, the literal meaning of Scripture (*sensus literalis*) may, in fact, be the spiritual sense (*sensus spiritualis*) intended by the author, namely, the messianic sense picked up in the NT books. Such a view of the meaning of the OT is quite similar to that of the apostle Paul in Romans 16:25–27. There Paul speaks of the Gospel of Jesus Christ, which, though hidden in ages past, "has now been revealed and made known through the prophetic writings." Paul notes three things about the Gospel in these verses: (1) it was formerly a hidden "mystery" in "long ages past" (v. 25); (2) it has now been revealed (v. 26); and (3) it is "made known through the prophetic writings" (v. 26).

Paul's view of the OT text is remarkably sensitive to the details of that text. He understands the OT text as latent in undiscovered "mysteries." But he also acknowledges that many of those "mysteries" have come to light in his own day and that they can be shown in the "prophetic writings" themselves. Paul is not suggesting that these revealed mysteries come from outside the text or must be read into the text, as for example was the understanding of prophetic Scripture at Qumran.[186] For Paul, the "mysteries" about Christ and the Gospel were there all along in the OT text. They merely had to be discovered.

In OT theology, then, the goal of interpretation continues to be the literal meaning (*sensus literalis*) of Scripture, which should be defined as the intent of the historical author of the biblical books. Again we must stress the fact that we are looking at the authorship and composition of the biblical *books*, not the meaning or sense of the events that lie behind these texts. Moreover, we must be open to the possibility that the literal meaning (*sensus literalis*) may, in fact, be that very spiritual meaning (*sensus spiritualis*) which the NT writers saw in the OT. Paul's assessment of the OT Scriptures as latent with hidden meanings, may in fact, be a quite accurate view of these particular texts.

---

[186]In the Habbakuk Commentary, for example, the "mysteries" that were spoken by the OT prophets were unknown both to the prophets themselves and later generations. Only the "correct teacher," to whom God revealed the "mysteries," could decipher their meaning (*The Dead Sea Scrolls of St. Mark's Monastery*, ed. Millar Burrows [New Haven: American Schools of Oriental Research, 1950], pl. LVIII, col. vii).

(4) RELATIONSHIP OF OLD AND NEW TESTAMENTS

We have seen in our survey of the history of biblical theology that the basic issues and tasks of OT theology have been at work in the history of theology since the time of the NT. A central question raised by that history may be formulated in this way: How do we relate, or integrate, the message of the Old Testament with that of the New? Or, How do we relate the specifically Israelite religion of the Sinai Covenant with the universal proclamation of the Gospel in the New Testament?

To begin with, this is not merely a problem of the message of the OT and its relationship to the NT. Already within the OT itself this very question arises and is, in fact, settled by the later OT writers. We will attempt to show this at two levels. The first is the level of the composition of the OT books themselves (inner-textuality). We have argued elsewhere that the final shape of the OT books, in fact, represents an essentially New Testament interpretation of the events and characters of Israel's history. The way in which, for example, the poetic texts in Numbers 24 allude to and interpret those of the preceding chapter, shows that an inner typology of events of the past and future was already operative within the level of composition of the OT books. The author of the Pentateuch already uses the Exodus theme as an eschatological image. The Pentateuch, at the level of its compositional strategy, typologizes the events of Israel's past, like the Exodus, as a picture of Israel's future, the establishment of the messianic Kingdom.

Furthermore, at the second level, the level of the inter-relationship of texts within the OT (inter-textuality), we also find a New Testament viewpoint. At the point of the composition of the book of Hosea, for example, we can see that, following the lead of the Pentateuch, the events of the historical Exodus were cast as prototypes of Israel's future redemption (cf. Hos 11:1 and Num 24:8). Moreover, in Nehemiah 9:20, God's gift of the manna in the wilderness (Ex 16) is seen as a picture of the new covenant concept of the work of the Spirit (Eze 36:26). All of those texts fit well into the broad scheme laid out in the book of Jeremiah when, for example, in 31:31–34, the new covenant which God will make with Israel in the future is contrasted with the covenant made with them at Mount Sinai. If one looks closely at the shapes and contours of the OT books, it is not hard to see a level of composition that is remarkably homogeneous both in its form and content. It is a level of composition that lays great stress on the future (eschatology) and that portrays that future in messianic terms drawn from God's promise to David in 2 Samuel 7, the Davidic covenant.

(5) HISTORICAL AUTHOR'S INTENT

The history of theology provides several viable models for defining the nature and task of OT theology. On the whole, these models can be classified as either confessional (making a faith commitment) or descriptive (objective history). It is important to note, however, that neither of these two basic approaches necessarily excludes the goal of seeking the original intent of the author. It seems, in fact, always to be the goal of each approach to start with the historical author's intent, even when, as in some confessional approaches, that may be understood in terms of the divine author alone.

In our view, the surest way to uncover the intent of the "original author," whether divine or human, is to make a conscious attempt to approach the Scriptures from the perspective of the individual human author. In other words, we must read those texts historically, asking what the authors of the biblical books intended to say to their readers. We will suggest in the final chapter that the means for doing this lie in an approach to these texts that is sensitive to the inner relationships of the book's own textual composition (inner-textuality); the interrelationships between the various books of the OT (inter-textuality); and the final shape of the OT canon (con-textuality). Such an approach, we will argue, provides a helpful model for a historical approach that can be either confessional or descriptive.

(6) OPPOSITION TO TRADITIONAL DOCTRINE

A marked characteristic of biblical theology and OT theology has been its pronounced opposition to ecclesiastical creeds and church doctrine. Nitzsch and König have particularly pointed to this characteristic though it is also recognized by others. Whether such opposition was realized in opposition to classical Christological formulations of the early church, reactions to medieval Scholasticism, or polemical revisions of Protestant dogmaticism, a recurring theme of biblical theology has been its attempt to restate the message of the Scriptures themselves, apart from traditional and orthodox systems. We suggest that this is a feature of biblical theology that must be carefully maintained. We also want to add, however, that such an opposition does not imply a negation of the truth of tradition and classical orthodox creeds. Tradition and orthodoxy should be understood as recasting and restating the meaning of the Bible. To the extent that they fail to do this, biblical theology and OT theology act as their judge and norm. What must always be guarded against is the viewpoint of dogmatic biblicism that the Bible teaches only and always the specific *loci* of a particular church creed or orthodox system. The Westminster Confession shows remarkable sensitivity to this issue within the creeds themselves: "The whole counsel of God, concerning all things necessary for his own glory, man's salvation, faith, and life, is either expressly set down in Scripture, or by good and necessary consequence may be deduced from Scripture. . . ."[187] A creed or a system of doctrine can be expected to be more than a biblical theology in that it draws "necessary consequences" from the teaching of Scripture; but it should never be less than a biblical theology. It must present the "whole counsel of God."

2.4.1.4. Nonessential Factors in the Rise and Development of Biblical Theology and Old Testament Theology

In the histories we have reviewed, certain elements have been taken to be essential by some which have not proved essential in others. The link of biblical theology's origin to proof texts, for example, so often found in modern accounts of the history of biblical theology, does not appear to be an essential feature in all accounts. Moreover, an emphasis on historical development (*ordo temporum*) is not a pervasive feature.

---

[187]"The Westminster Confession of Faith, 1647," Chapter I, paragraph VI, quoted from Philip Schaff, *The Creeds of Christendom* (Grand Rapids: Baker, 1985), 3.

Though such features may have dominated the study of OT theology at certain periods, they are not characteristic of OT theology as such. They may be "distinguishing characteristics" of some forms of OT theology, but they are not defining characteristics of OT theology itself.

2.4.2. The Descriptive Approach

2.4.2.1. Definition

According to the descriptive approach, the task of OT theology is merely to describe the content of what the OT meant to its original readers. It leaves to the systematic theologian the question of what the OT means today.[188]

2.4.2.2. Early History of the Descriptive Approach[189]

2.4.2.2.1. Johannes Clericus (1637–1736)

Johannes Clericus, a biblical scholar of great repute throughout Europe, did not produce a complete and systematic work on hermeneutics, much less one on biblical hermeneutics. He did, however, formulate several basic principles for interpreting ancient texts which became foundational for subsequent biblical studies.[190] Though he was by no means the first to do so, Clericus stressed the importance of reading ancient texts in their original languages and devoted considerable attention to the specific task of understanding words and expressions in such texts.[191] His primary contribution to hermeneutics and biblical theology lay in two areas. First, Clericus argued that the time-honored notion of looking for the "emphasis" (*de eruendis styli sacri emphasibus*) of a biblical text or passage was not valid for ancient documents. Orthodox and pietist biblical scholars had argued that because the Bible was the inspired Word of God, much importance could and should be attached to the sense of each particular word in the text. Accordingly the rule was followed that "there is no word in Scripture upon which does not depend great mountains of material."[192] Since, as many believed, each word was placed in the text by the author at the specific bequest of the Holy Spirit, the sense of each word and its contribution to the sense of the whole text was of fundamental importance to the inspired meaning of the text.[193] Against this view, Clericus

---

[188]Stendahl, *IDB*, 1:418–32.

[189]See Gottlob Wilhelm Meyer, *Geschichte der Künste und Wissenschaften* (Göttingen: Johann Friedrich Röwer, 1805), IV:333–41; Hans-Joachim Kraus, *Die biblische Theologie, Ihre Geschichte und Problematik* (Neukirchener Verlag, 1970), 31ff.

[190]Clericus's major work on the subject of hermeneutics was *Ars critica, in qua ad studia linguarum latinae, graecae et hebraicae via munitur; veterumque emendandorum, spuriorum scriptorum a genuinis dignoscendorum, et judicandi de eorum libris ratio traditur* (Amsterdam, 1969). Of particular importance is the first volume in which he deals with "de interpretatione veterum scriptorum." In the first section he treats "de ordine in lectione veterum observando" and in the second section, "de vocum et locutionum significatione." See Meyer, IV:334.

[191]Meyer, *Geschichte*, IV:334.

[192]"Nullum in scriptura sacra est verbum, a quo non pendeant magni rerum montes" (Augustus Pfeifferus, *Thesaur. hermen.*, cap. VI:283).

insisted that when read in the original languages, and not in the versions, the words of the Bible lost most of what appeared to be their emphatic sense. "Many things which appear to be emphatic in the versions," argued Clericus, "have no emphasis in the actual original texts."[194]

Clericus's second major contribution lay in his insistence on the use of the historical background of the biblical authors for an understanding of the meaning of the biblical text.[195] If one is to understand the meaning of the words in a biblical text, one must know the customs and opinions of the time in which it was written.[196] Kraus argues that such a notion was already active in the exegetical method of Calvin, and that both Melanchthon and Calvin believed that in order to find the historical sense (*sensus historicus*), it was necessary to have a fundamental understanding of the contemporary events and geographical situation of the biblical authors.[197] Kraus, however, does not clearly distinguish between the knowledge of the "life and times" of the biblical authors obtained from the biblical texts themselves and that obtained independently from historical sources. Calvin, and the Reformers generally, of course, relied heavily on the former. As such their approach is best described as "inter-textual," and not, strictly speaking, "historical." They were linking the events of one text with those of another.

Clericus, on the other hand, represents quite another kind of approach. His is an interest in the historical context that goes beyond that supplied by the biblical narratives. It is historical background in the true meaning of the term. Through his development and elaboration of these basic principles, Clericus's work had a lasting effect on the interpretation of the Bible. His was the first major effort to approach the Bible, and specifically the OT, as an ancient document from the past, and hence, to approach the OT as any other book.[198]

---

[193]The concept of "emphasis" is directly tied to that of verbal inspiration by Johnnes Rambach, the most influential hermeneutician of the early eighteenth century. He wrote, for example, that "the real basis of the emphasis of sacred scripture lies in the fact that not only the things which are comprehended in the sacred page are inspired by the most wise God but also the words themselves are inspired and suggested to the most holy authors. Thus, quite rightly, so much magnitude and weight of signification is to be assigned to the words as is able to be sustained by the nature of the underlying sense of that which is being described" ("*Fundamentum* emphasium sacrarum in eo positum est, quod non solum res, sacris paginis comprehensae, sed ipsa etiam *verba* a sapientissimo numine inspirata fuerint, sanctisque scriptoribus suggesta; unde merito vocibus tanta significationis amplitudo, tantumque pondus adsignatur, quantum per rei substratae naturam sustinere possunt") (*Institutiones Hermeneuticae Sacrae* [Jena, 1725], 319).

[194]"Multa videri in versionibus emphatica, quae in ipsis fontibus nullam emphasin habent" (Cap. IV:170).

[195]Meyer, *Geschichte*, IV:335.

[196]"Ut probe intelligatur scriptor quivis, consuetudines et opiniones popularium esse tenendas" (Cap. IV:275).

[197]Hans-Joachim Kraus, *Geschichte der historisch-kritischen Erforschung des Alten Testaments* (Neukirchener Verlag, 1969), 10.

[198]". . . erwarb sich Clericus das wichtige Verdienst, nicht bloss einzelne Puncte der Hermeneutik überhaupt und der biblischen insbesondre in ein helleres Licht zu setzen, sondern auch aufs überzeugend-

2.4.2.2.2. Johann Alphons Turretini (d. 1737)

Turretini's major work, *De sacrae scripturae interpretandae methodo tractatus*,[199] was directed principally against what he considered to be the four central hermeneutical fallacies of his day: (1) the Roman Catholic view that church tradition was to have the final word over against the sacred Scriptures; (2) the view of Christian mystics that the "inner word of God" was to guide the believer in understanding Scripture; (3) the orthodox and pietistic view that the meaning of each and every word of Scripture consisted of all and every meaning that could be drawn out of that word; and (4) the view that the meaning of the Hebrew words in the OT could be sufficiently understood from the language of the OT itself, and that no other sources for its meaning (e.g., early versions, Semitic dialects, or rabbinical commentary) were necessary.[200]

Central to all these approaches was the view that the interpretation of Scripture was to be governed by a prior faith commitment to a confessional statement of some kind. Turretini argued to the contrary that exegesis and biblical interpretation should not proceed from such a prior understanding of the meaning of the text. The mind of the interpreter should be a "blank tablet" (*instar tabulae rasae*). The modern interpreter should read the text by putting himself into the world of the original author and reading the text from that perspective.

"Judgments about the meaning of the sacred authors should not be made on the basis of opinions and systems derived from today's standards, but rather one's mind is to be transferred to those times and places in which [the biblical authors] wrote and is to be viewed in terms of whatever ideas were capable of arising in those who lived at that time."[201] A clear mind intent on reading Scripture, needs to be like an blank tablet, so that it might understand the true and genuine sense of Scripture.[202] Turretini can thus be credited with introducing into biblical studies an approach to the Scriptures that was, or at least attempted to be, completely cut off from the faith or beliefs of the contemporary reader.[203]

Turretini's contribution to biblical hermeneutics[204] was nothing short of "revolutionary," according to Kraus. Turretini laid down seven basic principles of biblical interpretation:[205]

---

ste zu lehren, dass die Bibel wie jedes andre menschliche Buch auszulegen sey; und daduch eben sowohl eine freiere Ausicht von derselben zu eröffnen, als eine liberalere Behandlung derselben einzuleiten" (Meyer, *Geschichte*, IV:335–36).

[199]*De sacrae scripturae interpretandae methodo tractatus bipartitus, in quo falsae multorum interpretum hypotheses refelluntur, veraeque interpretandae scr. s. methodus adstruitur,* Traajecti Thuriorum, 1728.

[200]Such a view had been argued by Jacob Gousset [d. 1704], in his *Commentarii linguae hebraicae* (Amsterdam, 1702). Turretini's work is primarily directed against Gousset's thesis.

[201]"De mente sacrorum scriptorum non judicandum est ex hodiernis placitis ac systematibus, sed est animus in ea, quibus scribebant, tempora et loca transferendus, et quaenam in eorum, qui tum vivebant, animo oriri potuerunt ideae, videndum" (372).

[202]"Animus vacuus, ut ita dicam, ad scripturam legendam afferendus, debet esse instar tabulae rasae, ut verum et geniunum sensum scripturae percipiat."

[203]Meyer, *Geschichte*, IV:338.

[204]See note 199.

[205]Hans-Joachim Kraus, *Die biblische Theologie* (Neukirchener Verlag, 1970), 31.

(1) Scripture is to be interpreted according to the same procedures as any other book.

(2) Scripture is to be interpreted according to the grammatical rules of Greek and Hebrew.

(3) The text of Scripture is to be read within its context.

(4) The text of Scripture is to be interpreted in terms of its "scopus," that is, its focus or central topic.

(5) The interpreter of Scripture is to follow the dictates of natural reason.

(6) The biblical authors are to be understood in terms of their own historical background, and not according to modern standards.

(7) The OT is to be compared with ancient documents other than the NT.

In these principles, Turretini was followed by Ernesti.[206] According to Kraus, "this book [Turretini's] opened the way for the strict use of the philological method of research. It continually called for the *sensus literalis et grammaticus*; gave much thought to the relationship of *res et ratio* [the world of things and the mind or ideas]; shed much light on the nature of biblical imagery and rhetoric; and stated quite clearly that there was only one sense to Holy Scripture."[207]

2.4.2.3. Siegmund Jakob Baumgarten (d. 1757)[208]

In many respects, Baumgarten stands outside of the developing descriptive approach in biblical interpretation. He held to many features of biblical interpretation shared by both the classical orthodox scholars and the pietists, including the concept of the inspiration of Scripture,[209] the importance of the *analogia fidei* and "emphasis" (*de eruendis styli sacri emphasibus*) for understanding the meaning of a biblical text, and the belief that some parts of the Scriptures contain more meaning than that of the mere historical sense of the words and should thus be read as types and allegories.[210] In spite of this close affinity between Baumgarten and orthodoxy, however, Baumgarten also held and helped foster hermeneutical views that played an important role in developing a purely descriptive approach. Principle among Baumgarten's views is the insistence on the need to interpret the biblical text in light of its historical circumstances.[211] This idea was not new to Baumgarten; however, what was new was Baumgarten's identification of a historical approach in exegesis with that of the traditional grammatical approach. For those who followed in the path of Baumgarten, the

---

[206] *Institution interpretis Novi Testamenti*, 1765.

[207] Kraus, *Die biblische Theologie*, 32.

[208] Siegmund Jakob Baumgarten, *Unterricht von Auslegung der heiligen Schrift* (Halle, 1742).

[209] "Dass die ganze heilige Schrift von Gott eingegeben ist; das nämlich nicht nur die Sachen, welche darin vorkommen, göttlichen Ursprungs, sondern auch die Ausdrücke, mit welchen diese Sachen vorgetragen werden, von der göttlichen Eingebung herzuleiten seyn, und dass diese Eingebung der Schrift auf die Grundsprachen gehe, wie wir sie jetzt haben" (quoted in Meyer, *Geschichte*, IV:344).

[210] Meyer, *Geschichte*, IV:344–45.

[211] "... und vorzüglich, was dieser Baumgartenschen Theorie zu einem ganz eigenthümlichen Lobe gereicht, ist hier viel bestimmter, ausführlicher und treffender, als bey irgend einem frühern Hermeneutiker, ins Licht gesetzt, wie man auf die historischen Umstände auszulegender Schriftstellen zu achten habe" (ibid., IV:346).

"grammatical sense" of the biblical text was increasingly identified with the "historical sense." Up to that time the identification had been conceived the other way around. The "historical sense" was the "grammatical sense" (*sensus literalis*). In the widely read introduction to the OT by Andreas Rivetus, for example, the goal of biblical interpretation was the "historical sense, that is, the literal sense of Scripture" (*sensum historicum seu literalem sacrae scripturae*).[212] As Rivetus expressed it, the "historical sense" *was* the "grammatical sense." After Baumgarten, however, the goal of biblical interpretation was the "historical *and* grammatical sense" or the "grammatical-historical sense." Once the meaning of the Bible had become synonymous with its historical sense, any dogmatic prior understanding of the biblical text was automatically excluded.

In the further development of biblical hermeneutics, two scholars marked the actual transition to the descriptive approach, Johann August Ernesti (1707–1781) and Jean Alphonse Turretini (1671–1739) (see above, pp. 159–60).

2.4.2.4. Johann Philipp Gabler

The origin of the descriptive approach to biblical theology has commonly been identified with Johann Philipp Gabler's lecture at the University of Altdorf in 1787.[213] In actual fact it was only later in the nineteenth century that Gabler was credited with having initiated a new approach to biblical theology.[214] Thus it appears that his lecture was more a product of a changing attitude toward biblical theology than an actual cause of that change. In any event, Gabler's lecture gives expression to all the fundamental characteristics of the descriptive approach.

Gabler began his lecture with a problem and then offered a solution. The problem, simply put, was the variety of biblical interpretations that he saw around him in the theology and church doctrine of his day. The solution, seen from a modern perspective, is somewhat naive. His hope lay in the new techniques in philology (the study of ancient languages and texts) and exegesis which he thought would lead the way to a more sound and scientific interpretation of the Bible.[215] Optimistically, Gabler believed that the application of these new scientific studies would result in conclusions with which every intelligent person would agree. The optimism of Gabler regarding the objective results he expected from the new historical methods should not be overlooked. Such optimism has been a hallmark of the historical method from its inception and is largely, and correctly I think, regarded today as unmerited.

Gabler offered his "historical" (descriptive) solution in opposition to three other solutions: (1) the orthodox Lutherans, who, he argued, were bent on making the bib-

---

[212] *Isagoge seu Introductio generalis, ad Scripturam Sacram Veteris et Novi Testamenti* (Batvia, 1627), 257.

[213] Gabler's lecture, *De justo discrimine theologiae biblicae et dogmaticae regundisque recte utriusque finibus* ("On the proper distinction between biblical and dogmatic theology and the specific objectives of each"), has been translated and aptly discussed in John Sandys-Wunsch and Laurence Eldredge, "J. P. Gabler and the Distinction Between Biblical and Dogmatic Theology: Translation, Commentary, and Discussion of his Originality," *SJT*, 33 (1980): 133–58. Sandys-Wunsch's article has been excerpted in *The Flowering of OT Theology*, eds. Ben C. Ollenburger, Elmer A. Martens, Gerhard F. Hasel (Winona Lake: Eisenbrauns, 1992), 492–502.

[214] Sandys-Wunsch, "J. P. Gabler," 149.

[215] Ibid., 145.

lical texts fit their own creedal statements; (2) the pietists, who believed that all they had to do to have a biblical theology was merely to use biblical words; and (3) the rationalists, who attempted to make the biblical texts fit their own convictions about the truths of reason.[216]

To apply his solution rightly, Gabler insisted on drawing a clear distinction between the concepts of *religion* and *theology*. Religion, according to Gabler, consisted of simple beliefs needed for living in this world and attaining salvation. Theology, on the other hand, consisted of the elaborate statements of historically conditioned beliefs of particular individuals and peoples.[217] For Gabler the goal of biblical theology was the study of religion, not theology (dogmatics). The task of biblical theology was to separate the religion of the Bible, which is its core truth, from the theology of the writers, which is always historically conditioned. Since the biblical writers used the language and thoughts of their own day to give expression to their religion, the exegete must use the tools of philology and historical criticism to separate the religion of the Bible from the theology of the biblical writers. Having arrived at the writers' pure religion, biblical theology then must organize these basic concepts (propositions) into a coherent system, which can then become the basis for doing theology (dogmatics) in the modern world. The task of the systematic theologian was to take the work of the biblical theologian and represent it within the new historical conditions of contemporary life.

The result of Gabler's lecture can be seen in at least three areas. First, biblical theology and dogmatics (systematic theology) were separated as distinct subjects. Secondly, biblical theology was either made the basis or foundation of church dogmatics, or the two went their own separate ways. Finally, biblical theology, as such, became a historical study using the tools of historical research. Dogmatics, however, remained a task of the church and tradition.

The purely descriptive approach advocated by Gabler in his now famous lecture took on quite different forms in the course of the next two centuries. Its application to the OT fluctuated with the changing attitudes toward the study of history itself and with changes in attitudes toward theology. It may be helpful to look at a representative sample of the application of Gabler's method in the course it took through the next two centuries.

2.4.2.4.1. Gabler's Method Applied in the Eighteenth Century

Gabler himself did not write a biblical theology, and the direct result of his program is not clearly evident in the eighteenth century. However, two important works in the late eighteenth century that attempted to carry out a distinction between biblical theology and dogmatics, and that saw the task of biblical theology as primarily descriptive are the theologies of Gotthelf Traugott Zachariä,[218] and Christoph Friedrich Ammon.[219]

---

[216]Ibid., 145–46.

[217]Ibid., 146.

[218]Gotthilf Traugott Zachariä, *Biblische Theologie oder Untersuchung des biblischen Grunde der vornehmsten theologischen Lehren*, I (1771), II (1772), III (1774), and IV (1775).

[219]Christoph Friedrich Ammon, *Biblische Theologie* (1792), 3 vols.

For Gabler, as for the eighteenth century in general, the religious truths of eternal value found in the OT were virtually identical to the universal truths of reason celebrated in the Enlightenment: freedom, God, and the immortality of the soul.[220] Thus their "description" of the religion of the OT was little more than a mirror image of the views of the Enlightenment. This can be clearly seen in the biblical theology of C. F. Ammon. Ammon's identification of the religion of the Bible with the "truths" of the Enlightenment can be seen with particular clarity in his section on biblical anthropology.[221] After a brief introduction, Ammon begins this section with a paraphrase of Genesis 3 in which he sets forth his basic thesis. Here he argues that the so-called *fall* of man in Genesis 3 is, in reality, an account of the *rise* of humanity to the status of being fully human. It is the story of humanity's animal origins as well as ultimate achievement of freedom. In this section the Bible recounts humanity's obtaining autonomy—one of the cardinal doctrines of the Enlightenment.[222] Ammon traces the history of the interpretation of this passage to show the difficulties this passage has presented to many interpreters in the past (eighteenth century). Responsible biblical scholarship has not taken Genesis 3 in a strictly literal sense, but has rather sought to find essential divine truths embodied in it. According to Ammon, neither the literal nor the allegorical interpretation is, in fact, possible,[223] so he sets out to find the "true sense of the document." Having ruled out a literal and allegorical interpretation, he concludes that only one approach remains, that is, to put himself in the mind (*in die Seele*) of the ancient writer with the help of the insights from psychology and ancient literature, and to study the original context to determine what the writer was, in fact, saying.[224] For his summation of the meaning of Genesis 3, Ammon quotes (at length) a study of this passage by the Enlightenment philosopher, Immanuel Kant. Kant:

Early man (Urmensch) needed no other direction or guidance for his physical needs than the voice of God, which, like all the other animals, he followed from his own natural instincts. As long as he followed these instincts and avoided what God had forbidden, all went well for him and he, like the other animals, ate from the tree of life. Soon, however, his reason (Vernunft) dared to enlarge the boundaries of his instinct, and finding a fruit to be beautiful (3:6), which only the snake had eaten of, he went against the warning of the instincts, which would have led him into a long life (3:19), and ate of the fruit itself. This brave step opened the eyes of early man (3:7). As the juices of this delicate fruit shot through his body, the instincts became more vigorous and the power of thinking was stirred up so that these were now able to improve and raise themselves to even new heights. The satisfaction of mere animal desires was now subordinated to the rising power of reason. They learned to evade the object of their senses by the use of fig leaves;

---

[220]Sandys-Wunsch, "J. P. Gabler," 147.

[221]Ammon, *Biblische Theologie*, Vol. 1, 278–339.

[222]Ibid., 292–93.

[223]Ibid., 299–310.

[224]. . .bleibt dem Forscher kein anderer Ausweg übrig, als dieser: so viel es möglich ist, sich in die Seele des Verfassers hinein zu denken, durch Hülfe der Psychologie und Erfahrung ächte Bruchstüke der ältesten Geschichte des urmenschen aufzusuchen; und in ihrer Vergleichung mit der Denkart des muthmasslichen Verfassers und seines Zeitalters, den Schlüssel zu dieser ehrwürdigen Urkunde selbst zu find" (ibid., 310).

they learned to give duration and strength to their instincts by moderation; they learned to direct the senses away from extraneous attractions to lasting beauty; and thus they learned gradually to instill in their hearts a feeling for modesty, love and virtue. At the same time, however, such a development of human reason was not free from the many sorrows and anxious feelings which are inseparable from the limits of human nature: the wife of the early man became a mother; she felt unavoidable pain in giving birth; and she saw herself subjected to the care of her coarse husband (3:16). Early man found himself with the sorrow of having to care for his weaker wife and his growing family; he had to farm the land with all his might in order to produce enough to live on; and when in moments of rest he looked fearfully into the future, all he saw was the prospect of returning to the womb of the earth, his mother, like all other animals around about him (17–19). . . . With so many sorrows accompanying man's rise from the womb of nature, it is natural that he would want to return, at first, to his earlier life where he lived like the animals and ate of the tree of life (which was not immortality, but longevity). But, alas, the irresistible voice of reason prohibited him from returning to this state of imaginary joy and spurred him on, in the face of all these difficulties, indefatigably, to the way of life he had set for himself and to its end in the grave (22–24).[225]

Having thus quoted Kant's exposition of Genesis 3, which was the sense which he thought best represented the original meaning of the biblical text, Ammon then added several conclusions of his own to those of Kant. The fundamental idea of this Mosaic document, he argued, was that the origin of all evil on this earth is to be found in the "individuality" of man's existence, which, by its nature, cannot partake of any higher level of completeness. It follows from this that moral evil (incompleteness of human virtue) is an unavoidable result of the limits of the human spirit. When all is said and done, for Ammon evil was a metaphysical problem.

It then becomes clear, says Ammon, that early humanity (*Urmenschen*) could find consolation in his fate only because in the maturity of his reason he had become more prudent and more reasonable (rational). It is also now clear how in the history of humanity, personal freedom has led to great evils; but also this new stage of reason has led to a greater destiny. It is finally clear, argued Ammon, that the formation of pure and religiously ennobled reason is of vital concern to all humanitarians because reason is the only source of virtue and well-being.[226]

Such was Ammon's view of the meaning of Genesis 3. It is not hard to see how Gabler's call for a historical, non-confessional approach to biblical theology had come to play itself out in his own day, the age of the Enlightenment. All too quickly, "enlightened" biblical scholars found their own views of "reason" and "freedom" to be the actual "historical sense" of the Bible. Ammon's theology leaves little room for doubt that the ideals of the Enlightenment were simply read into the text of Scripture. It is clear that by means of the descriptive, historical approach, enormous room was opened up for human subjectivity. Just as much room remained for human subjectivity in the descriptive approach in the late eighteenth century as had been the case in the earlier orthodox confessional approaches.

---

[225]Immanuel Kant, "Ueber den muthmasslichen Anfang der Menschengeschichte," *Berlin Monatschrift* (Jan. 1786): 5–13 (quoted in ibid., 311–14).
[226]Ibid., 318.

2.4.2.4.2. Gabler's Method Applied in the Nineteenth Century

Two developments in the intellectual history of the nineteenth century greatly influenced the nature of the use of Gabler's descriptive method. The first was the rise of Romanticism as a reaction to the Enlightenment. Romanticism was characterized by an emphasis on (1) irrationality and feeling, over against reason; (2) history as the central category of thought, over against logical propositions; and (3) organic developmentalism, that is, a model of intellectual development that stressed growth and development of ideas, over against artificial systems.

The second development in the nineteenth century was an evolutionary viewpoint which stressed the pattern of progress of ideas ranging from simple to complex. Within such a perspective of the development of ideas, biblical theology, as a descriptive discipline, came to view the religion of the OT no longer as a mirror image of the Enlightenment, but rather as an authentic example of the true spirit of Romanticism, that is, the development of a primitive religious nationalism.

A typical example of the influence of Romanticism and primitive nationalism on the understanding of the OT is the description of Israelite religion and life by Johann Gottfried Herder (1744–1803). With Herder, those aspects of the OT that were an embarrassment to the eighteenth century (e.g., the coarse, simple narratives of everyday life) became the irreplaceable essence of biblical religion. The OT was now quarried for its witness to the primitive way of life of the early Hebrews. Herder argued that to understand the religion of the OT, and hence the religion of primeval humanity, the purest form of religion, one must read the biblical narratives by reliving them and rethinking one's own self-identity in terms of them. Only then can one escape the sterility and empty rationalism of the modern era and experience again the simplicity of the biblical religion.[227] The biblical narratives and poetry were understood as the clearest examples of true religion because they were the earliest, most primitive expression of human beliefs.[228]

If the orthodox theologians had made the biblical writers "Protestant dogmaticians," and the eighteenth-century theologians had made them "Enlightenment rationalists," Herder, and those in the nineteenth century, made the biblical writers into idyllic shepherds who understood God and the world in pre-reflective pastoral imagery.

The result of the combination of Gabler, Herder, and Romanticism in biblical theology came to be known as the "history of religions" school. The objective of this approach was to describe the origin and development of the religion of the OT in its simplest, most primitive terms. According to that approach, the origin of Israel's religion was twofold. First, there was an internal development of religious ideas in the direction of simple to complex. This was often seen in the results of literary analysis and form criticism of the biblical text. From within a simple biblical narrative, for example, several earlier sources were discovered and arranged in what was thought to be a chronological sequence. One source was then viewed as a recasting or reinterpre-

---

[227]Kraus, *Die biblische Theologie*, 207.
[228]Cf. Johann Gottfried Herder, *Spirit of Hebrew Poetry*.

tation of a previous document. These documents were then identified as expressions of various stages of Israel's religion. Second, there was external importation of religious ideas from the world of the ancient Near East (Egypt, Babylon, Canaan). Israel's religion was often viewed as little more than a unique offshoot of the religions of the ancient world. Though the uniqueness of biblical religion was faithfully maintained, it often got lost in the numerous comparisons between Israel and the ancient world.

The result of such a historical approach was that the Scriptures came to be viewed in terms of a linear development of the religion of the OT from the earliest (primitive) ideas held in common with all ancient Near Eastern cultures, to the latest reinterpretation and transformation of those ideas in the postexilic Jewish community.[229]

In such an approach, the theological task came to be understood primarily as isolating and demonstrating the unique stamp put on the general ideas of the ancient Near East by the final shaping of the OT material. This "uniqueness" of the religion of Israel was seen as the theological and religious contribution of the OT. The legacy of Romanticism in biblical theology can be seen in its emphasis on the earliest stages with little or no concern for the final stages of Israel's thought.

2.4.2.4.3. Gabler's Method Applied in the Twentieth Century

Stendahl's article on biblical theology in the *Interpreter's Dictionary of the Bible* has come to represent the descriptive approach of Gabler in the twentieth century.[230] According to Stendahl, the task of contemporary biblical theology is descriptive. Stendahl contrasts biblical theology with old liberalism and orthodoxy. Old liberalism had read the OT with the presuppositions of the Enlightenment in mind. The OT was understood as a witness to the evolutionary development of Israel's religion into an increasingly more ethical monotheism. Protestant orthodox theology, on the other hand, had read the OT in light of the NT. Where both the Enlightenment and classical orthodoxy had failed, was in reading the OT in sympathy with their own culture and ways of thinking. The descriptive task had begun to be carried out by the studies of the history-of-religions school, which formed the basis of the new "biblical theology." What emerged was a purely descriptive study of biblical thought. It was characterized by three new elements: (1) it did not superimpose such nineteenth-century ideas as evolutionary development on the text; (2) it did not concern itself with the question of "truth" in discussing historical events; and (3) it did not address the question of the relevance of the text to the modern day. The primary focus of such a descriptive approach was merely on what the meaning of the OT had been to its original readers—what it meant to them, rather than what it means today. A wide gulf was thus put between "what it meant" and "what it means." The OT was described as any other ancient religious text, without raising the question of contemporary relevance and meaning.

A further contrast that made its way into the descriptive approach to biblical theology was the contrast between Semitic and Greek thought. The quest for "what it

---

[229]Gustav Hölscher, *Geschichte der israelitischen und jüdischen Religion*, 1922.
[230]K. Stendahl, "Biblical Theology, Contemporary," *IDB*, 1: 418–32.

meant" was usually formulated in categories supposed to represent Semitic thinking.[231] "What it means" today, on the other hand, would have relevance only in categories of Western, that is, Greek, thought.[232]

The task of OT theology, then, is merely to describe what the theology of the OT text meant to its original readers, and to describe it in terms of its own distinct way of thinking. To ask if it is true or if it is relevant, is to go beyond the limits of OT theology. The step beyond OT theology is to be taken via the task of hermeneutics, that is contextualization or demythologization.

What, asks Stendahl, have been the hermeneutical responses to this kind of OT theology? His answer consists of a catalogue of various twentieth-century responses. Some have simply substituted biblical categories for those of Western theology. According to Stendahl, "The achievements of the descriptive biblical theology (what ancient Israel believed) were dumped right into the twentieth century."[233] It was argued that to understand the Bible "we need to think like the Hebrews, not Greeks (Western thought patterns)." The effect of this, says Stendahl, was to identify revelation with biblical patterns of thought and culture. Biblical revelation, it was believed, was not only linked to ancient patterns of thought, but also locked into those patterns. The Bible, as such, really could not speak to people today.

On the other hand, systematic theologians such as Paul Tillich and Rudolph Bultmann attempted to transform the biblical theological sense of "what it meant" into what it might mean today if understood in modern, twentieth-century concepts. E. Bloch, in his *Theology of Hope*, linked the message of the Bible to modern revolutionary dogmas.[234] However, in each of these modern attempts to "transplant" ancient biblical patterns of thought into the modern world, an appreciable loss was suffered on the part of the biblical text. In the end, the biblical authors were made to sound suspiciously like modern existentialist thinkers and social activists.

2.4.2.5. Assessment of the Descriptive Approach

It must be said on the positive side that the descriptive approach freed the biblical theologian from the pressure of having to view the OT in systematic and dogmatic categories. The OT was allowed to speak for itself. Moreover, the descriptive

---

[231]The questionable issue of a distinctive form of "Hebrew thought," introduced by Thorleif Boman (*Das hebräische Denken im Vergleich mit dem griechischen* [Göttingen, 1952]) should be kept distinct from the more plausible concept of language as a means of shaping reality: ". . .eine jede Sprache eine spezifische 'Einteilung von Welt' und damit eine (mit-) Konstitution von Wirklichkeit bedeutet, die nicht von dieser als 'ontologie' oder 'metaphysik' ablösbar ist" (Heinzpeter Hempelmann, "Veritas Hebraica als Grundlage christlicher Theologie," *Hebraica Veritas,* eds. Klaus Haacker and Heinzpeter Hempelmann [Wuppertal: R. Brockhaus Verlag, 1989], 40–41).

[232]Though the thesis that "Hebrew thinking" was fundamentally different than "Greek thought" introduced by Thorleif Boman (*Das hebräische Denken im Vergleich mit dem griechischen* [Göttingen, 1952]) has been challenged by James Barr (*The Semantics of Biblical Language* [Oxford, 1961]) and others, the notion continues to persist, e.g., Klaus Bockmühl, "Die systematische Theologie muss von dem hebräischen Denk- und Sprachformen lernen, statt von den griechischen" ("Aufgaben der systematischen Theologie heute," *Theologie und Lebensführung* [Band II, Giessen, 1982]: quoted in Haacker and Hempelmann, 41).

[233]Stendahl, "Biblical Theology," 427.

[234]Hans-Joachim Kraus, *Biblisch-theologische Aufsätze* (Neukirchener-Vluys: Neukirchener Verlag, 1972), 102.

approach also freed the biblical theologian from the pressure of relevancy. The OT was allowed to determine the important agenda. The biblical theologian did not have to respond to a set of prearranged questions.

2.4.2.6. Weaknesses of the Descriptive Approach

As we have already suggested, however, the descriptive approach often assumes an unrealistic objectivity in reconstructing the "original" meaning of the text. In reality, such objectivity is rare or nonexistent. It is inevitable that when reading the biblical text we bring something of ourselves to the text and that this will influence how we understand the text. We cannot read the text from a neutral corner. Furthermore, understanding the biblical text, like understanding any other text, involves what E. D. Hirsch called a "genre-guess"[235] along with its validation. In reading a text one makes an educated guess about what the text is saying. The guess must then be validated by the text itself. Does the normative strategy of a text, for example, support the guess or suggest that some other guess should be made? The capacity for making good genre-guesses is dependent on a certain kind of affinity between the author and the reader. The reader must have some initial idea of what the writer is talking about before understanding can take place. Since it can reasonably be argued that "faith" understands "faith" better than "unbelief" understands "faith," it stands to reason that the believer, not the disinterested observer, is in a better position to understand the biblical text. There is an affinity between the subject (reader) and the object (biblical text). We should also hasten to add that such an involved, "interested" reader, is all the more susceptible to misunderstanding the text as well. Reading and understanding a religious text like the Bible is a highly charged and volatile process. The very elements that serve as catalysts for understanding such texts (e.g., faith) also can be explosive and counterproductive to genuine understanding. Without such catalysts, however, the biblical text remains inert to the modern reader.

Thus the nature of much of the OT, which is a book of faith, makes the descriptive approach largely inadequate. With few exceptions, the texts are written, not to neutral observers, but to believers—of one sort or another (obedient/disobedient). The meaning of these texts includes not simply the ostensive meaning of the words and clauses but, as well, the meaningfulness of the words and clauses (significance). The descriptive approach, even if it could get objectively to the "original" sense of the text, would still not be capable of getting at the "original" meaning because that would include an intended response of the reader to the message proclaimed in the text. The meaning of the biblical text is ongoing, not static. The meaning lies between what the text says and the reader's response.[236] What, for example, is the meaning of Psalm 105:1 (NIV): "Give thanks to the LORD, call on his name; make known among the nations what he has done"? The meaning is more than merely the description of what is said (i.e., the psalmist calls on his hearers to give thanks). The meaning is also "give thanks,"

---

[235]E. D. Hirsch, *Validity in Interpretation* (New Haven: Yale University Press, 1967).

[236]These statements are not meant to be understood in light of the current discussions about "Reader Response" in OT hermeneutics. The reader's response does not affect or determine the author's intent. On the contrary, the author's intent includes a specific response on the part of the reader to what is said in the text.

that is, "do it." When the psalmist says, "We are his people, the sheep of his pasture," he is speaking not only for himself, but also for the reader. The text, in other words, implies participation in the author's meaning on the part of the reader or hearer.

There is another sense in which the nature of much of the OT makes the descriptive approach inadequate. The historical narratives owe their meaning to the truthfulness and factuality of their content. In Deuteronomy 6:20–21 (NIV) the Scripture states, "In the future, when your son asks you, 'What is the meaning of the stipulations, decrees and laws the LORD our God has commanded you?' tell him: 'We were slaves of Pharaoh in Egypt, but the LORD brought us out of Egypt with a mighty hand.'" According to this text, the meaning of the whole of Exodus 1–12 is that the events recorded there did, in fact, happen and that they happened as described (with "miraculous signs and wonders"), not merely that Israel said or believed these events happened. According to Nehemiah 9:1–38, the meaning of Genesis through Kings is *that God did these things* in Israel's history and with Israel's forefathers. To bracket the question of the truthfulness of the texts is to fail to treat them on their own terms.

Another major weakness of the descriptive approach as it has been practiced is its starting point. As has often been pointed out, the descriptive approach too readily distinguishes between "what Scripture meant" and "what it now means." Why should these two meanings differ so radically? Is Semitic thought really different from Western ways of viewing the world? Though this issue is by no means finally resolved, it seems most likely that human thought patterns are essentially similar in all cultures and time periods. Although languages and cultures differ, and some correlations likely exist between ways of thinking and specific languages, the idea that the meaning of the Israelite literature is essentially irretrievable and incomprehensible to the modern mind has yet to be demonstrated on purely linguistic grounds.[237] Such an idea cannot be merely assumed, or even less proven, merely on the basis of differences in the various languages used to write and translate the Bible.

One further set of questions deserves to be raised against the descriptive approach. Does the close relationship between language and culture make Semitic thought and culture normative in biblical theology? This in turn raises the question of the extent to which biblical thought is, in fact, Semitic thought. Is the OT itself possibly at odds with its own ancient Near Eastern culture? May there not be a polemic as well as an assimilative relationship between the OT and its culture? May not the OT narratives themselves present a world, a "cosmic map" that transcends or, at least, transforms the view of the world found in other ancient Near Eastern literature? Though we are not in a position to give a final answer to these questions, the problems themselves are enough to call a purely descriptive approach into serious question.

2.4.3. The Confessional Approach

2.4.3.1. Definition

According to the *confessional approach*, the task of OT theology is to define the message of the OT within the context of one's own personal faith. The task of OT the-

---

[237]Benjamin Kedar, *Biblische Semantic* (Stuttgart: Verlag W. Kohlhammer, 1981), 49.

ology is thus not merely to describe the meaning of the text but also to stand under its authority. There was a saying among the early Protestant theologians that expresses the confessional approach quite succinctly: "One should read the Scriptures as if they were written with the blood of Christ."[238] Though extreme, this gets at the heart of the matter and provides a vivid contrast to the descriptive approach discussed above.

In principle, the confessional approach consists only of describing the message of the OT under the assumption that this message is to be understood as the Word of God. In practice, since most OT theologians are Christian (Catholic or Protestant), the confessional approach means that the OT message is described as part of the message of the whole Bible (OT and NT) as the Word of God. This means that the problem of the relationship of OT and NT is of fundamental importance for OT theology. Do the OT and NT have the same message? If not, which is to be given priority and final authority? Is there an inescapable tension between the OT and NT?

2.4.3.2. History of the Confessional Approach

We have already surveyed the early history of biblical and OT theology and have shown that in this early period, biblical theologians were all, in fact, "confessional." Even the early "prooftext" theologies were confessional in nature since their purpose was to show that the theology of the OT and NT was identical to that of the church dogmas.[239] It was the rise of the descriptive method at the time of Gabler that eclipsed the confessional approach and led to such historical approaches as the history of religions school. There have been, however, notable examples of confessional OT theologies during the last two centuries: Ernst Wilhelm Hengstenberg (1802–1869),[240] Johann Christian Konrad von Hofmann (1810–1877),[241] Heinrich Andreas Christoph Hävernick (1811–1845),[242] and Gustav Friedrich Oehler (1812–1872).[243] Each of these works has the common assumption that only the believer, who is led by the Spirit, can truly understand the message of the OT.

After Oehler's theology, OT theology in the late nineteenth and early twentieth centuries was virtually synonymous with the study of the history of Israel's religion. However, there were two important works in the twentieth century that helped reestablish a new basis for the confessional approach. These works attempted to show that a confessional approach does have a place in the scholarly study of the OT. The first of these was an article by Otto Eissfeldt, entitled "Israelite-Jewish History of Religion and Old Testament Theology"[244] and the second was Walther Eichrodt's article

---

[238]"Scripturam ita legendam esse, ac si sanguine Christi scripta foret." Credited to "Theologus quidam" by Abraham Calovius (1612–86), *Biblia illustrata*, 1672–76, *Prolegomena ad Pentateuchum*, 210.

[239]It has too rarely been pointed out that these early "proof text" theologies were largely written by Lutherans against Catholics and Reformed theology.

[240]The confessional approach of Hengstenberg is evident in the title of his major work, *Christology of the Old Testament* (reprint, Grand Rapids: Kregel, 1973).

[241]*Weissagung und Erfüllung im alten und im neuen Testamente* (Nördlingen: C. H. Beck'schen Buchhandlung, 1841); *Der Schriftbeweis* (Nördlingen: C. H. Beck'schen Buchhandlung, 1857).

[242]*Vorlesungen über die Theologie des Alten Testaments* (Erlangen: Verlag Carl Heyder, 1848).

[243]*Theology of the Old Testament* (reprint, Minneapolis: Klock & Klock, 1978).

[244]"Israelitisch-jüdische Religionsgeschichte und alttestamentliche Theologie," *ZAW*, 38 (1926):1–12.

"Does the Study of Old Testament Theology Still Have Meaning Within the Context of the Scientific Study of the Old Testament?"[245]

Eissfeldt began by setting the problem of OT theology within the larger theological problem of the absolute and the relative, that is, divine revelation and human history. Out of this distinction he posed the question: Should we study the religion of the OT as any other historical entity, or should we approach the OT under the assumption that it is the true religion, the revelation of God?

Eissfeldt maintained that two distinct viewpoints regarding that question had emerged in biblical theology. One view held that the OT religion as a factor of history should be studied in the same way as any historical entity, that is, the sources should be studied sympathetically but objectively, and the results should be presented accordingly. No attention should be given to the worth or truth of the religion (the descriptive approach). On the other hand, Eissfeldt said, there was the view that OT religion should be studied as an object of personal faith. Since, for the Christian, personal faith means faith in the Christ of the NT, one's theological understanding of the OT is necessarily guided by the NT (the confessional approach).

It is unfortunate, Eissfeldt argued, that one has to choose between these two quite distinct approaches. It would be far better if one could hold both approaches at one and the same time. Human psychology itself has a similar dual aspect which corresponds to these two approaches. Human experience, said Eissfeldt, draws on both faith and knowledge for its understanding of the world. This basic makeup of human nature corresponds to the two approaches to OT theology. Faith is the means whereby we come before God and seek his self-revelation. Knowledge is the way we approach the history of Israel and the events from the past in which that revelation occurred.

$$\frac{\text{Knowledge / Faith}}{\text{History / Revelation}}$$

Human knowledge is active; that is, it decisively and intentionally seeks to know what happened in the past. Faith, however, is passive. It is obtained from a higher subject. One receives faith. Human beings, according to Eissfeldt, have two options:

(1) One can attempt to combine knowledge and faith, as in the classical orthodox position, which leads to a form of historical positivism. Their faith was based on "salvation history" as real history. Eissfeldt's critical assessment of biblical history leads him to reject this position. Old liberalism, on the other hand, based faith on its critical knowledge of the past. Their faith focused, for example, on the concept of the "historical" Jesus. This was a form of "historicism." Other forms of liberalism attempted to base their faith either on rational knowledge (rationalism), or on the fact of human experience (idealism).

(2) The only other option for Eissfeldt was to hold the two approaches to faith (faith and knowledge) in a sort of dynamic tension. Although it may sound perplexing, Eissfeldt held that this was not an adverse dilemma but a fortunate one, because

---

[245]Walther Eichrodt, "Hat die alttestamentliche Theologie noch selbständige Bedeutung innerhalb der alttestamentlichen Wissenschaft?" *ZAW,* 41 (1929): 83ff.

by radically separating knowledge and faith, both forms of viewing reality can add to the other and thus contribute to a greater source of understanding Scripture. Thus the study of both Israelite-Jewish religious history (knowledge) and OT theology (faith) have their place in OT study. Israelite-Jewish religious history is a historical science. Its task is to describe the religion of the OT in its historical development.

> The question of the absolute worth or the truth of the object, the historian does not claim to answer. He must be content only to affirm that the entity with which he is working makes the claim to be revelation and the Word of God; whether this claim is correct or not, he cannot decide.[246]

The task of writing a history of Israelite religion can be done, and should be done, without any regard for one's own particular religious beliefs. The theological understanding of the OT, on the other hand, is entirely different. Here the theologian describes what he or she takes to be the revelation of God. Thus, OT theology is of the character of a witness to the Word of God, especially as it is understood within a particular circle of faith—it is confessional.

One's theological understanding of the OT (faith) cannot be presented in the form of a historical process. It must, because it has to do with present, timeless truth (revelation), be presented in systematic categories. To hold both approaches in tension is not to say they are irreconcilable. Knowledge and faith belong to two parallel planes that do not meet in this finite sphere. Reconciliation of these two aspects of human experience is not the task of an OT theology. Eissfeldt himself never wrote an OT theology. The theologian who most closely followed his programmatic outline was Theodor Vriesen (see below).

The second twentieth-century OT theologian who contributed much to the revitalization of the confessional approach to OT theology is Walther Eichrodt. In an article entitled "Does the Study of OT Theology Still Have Meaning Within the Context of the Scientific Study of the OT?" Eichrodt responded to the state of OT theology in his day—a state that was characterized by the dichotomy of history and faith reflected in Eissfeldt's article.[247] Eichrodt attempted to show that Eissfeldt's dichotomy of history and faith (science and theology) was not necessary and that it was, in fact, possible to have an OT theology that could claim to be scientific, that is, historical. Eichrodt argued that Eissfeldt's dichotomy was false for two reasons. First, he argued, a purely scientific (historical) study of the religion of Israel was not possible or even desirable because the science of history always contained an important element of subjectivity. The organization of the various historical facts (*facta*) into a meaningful whole, for example, represented a systematization that required working with general ideas and judgments. Moreover, a selection was necessary, and this required a principle outside of the individual events. That is, a judgment of value was necessary in making a selection. For example, in making sense of history, one event is

---

[246]Eissfeldt, "Israelitisch-jüdische Religionsgeschichte," 10.
[247]See note 245.

chosen over another because it is seen as a link in a chain leading to a particular series of events. The historian's own "present" time is always the highest value. The limitations, background, and particular concerns of the historian will determine the range and direction of his perspective on events.

Secondly, Eichrodt argued, a purely scientific (historical) study of the religion of Israel was not only not possible, but not even desirable. The understanding of history is more than a piecing together of mere events and persons into a meaningful whole. Understanding history requires a sympathetic reading on the part of the historian of the events and persons being studied. A congeniality must exist between the historian and his or her object. To truly understand one's historical object, the historian must know, even relive, the very forces that drove those historical events. One must understand this history as those who were part of that history. To write about the religion of Israel one must have some direct source of understanding of the faith of those Israelites; that is, in fact, one must share their very faith.

Eichrodt thus concludes that an OT theology can and should be scientific (historical) in the true sense of the term because it is only by organizing (systematizing) the events and religious ideas of Israel's religion and by being in sympathy (faith) with them that the religion of Israel can be properly understood. All OT theologians must admit their subjective starting points. For Eichrodt this meant one must have faith in Christ to properly understand the faith of Israel. It is only by starting with an understanding of Christ and the NT that a Christian theologian can properly understand the religion of the OT. Eichrodt's approach is therefore confessional. Unlike Eissfeldt, who never wrote an OT theology, Eichrodt put his views to the test by producing a major OT theology.[248]

To summarize Eichrodt's important essay we should recall the following points: (1) History is more than mere recording of facts. (2) History involves the arrangement of facts into a meaningful whole. It thus requires a subjective element of selection and arrangement as well as focus. Since all history has this subjective element, this does not rule out its place in historical science. (3) The OT theologian must recognize his or her own subjective element as the acknowledgment of the NT understanding of Jesus Christ. The arrangement and selection of the material of the OT, then, will be influenced by this subjective element. Such an approach clearly puts Eichrodt in a category that is essentially confessional in nature.

We should briefly note one more contemporary confessional OT theologian, Th. C. Vriezen.[249] Vriezen follows the same basic approach as Eissfeldt, giving us an actual OT theology that reflects Eissfeldt's approach. According to Vriezen, Eissfeldt had made an important distinction between the study of the history of Israelite religion and OT theology. There was a place for the history of religion, but it was not a part of the study of OT theology as such. Theology, Vriezen argued, deals with revelation and thus finds its true place within the context of faith (Christian church). While the study of the history of religions is concerned with the religion of Israel, OT

---

[248]Walther Eichrodt, *Theology of the Old Testament* (Philadelphia: Westminster, 1961).
[249]Th. C. Vriezen, *An Outline of Old Testament Theology*, 143–52.

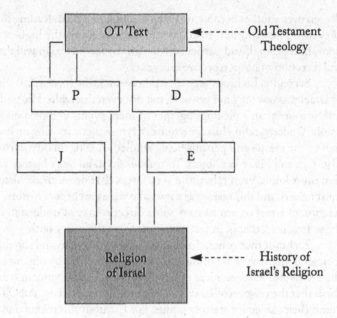

Figure 5.1

theology is concerned with the message of the OT. The chart in Figure 5.1 outlines Vriezen's approach.

The distinction which Vriezen makes above is crucial for understanding the goal of OT theology. There is a real difference, Vriezen maintained, between the faith and practice of Israelite religion during the biblical period, and the faith and practice taught in the texts of the OT. Though one might well take issue with the critical element in Vriezen's approach to OT theology, that is, his dependence on the documentary hypothesis, that should not be allowed to overshadow his important insight on the goal of an OT theology.

If one approaches OT theology from the starting point of faith, then for the Christian faith that means faith in Jesus Christ (NT). Thus, a theological standard is placed over the message of the OT, the standard of Christian theology. OT theology cannot simply be a commitment (faith) to the message of the OT. It must be a commitment to the message of the OT insofar as it corresponds to the message of the NT. In other words, revelation and the OT Canon are not synonymous. For Vriezen, only parts of the message of the OT are revelation. The criterion of what is canonical and of value to the Christian OT theologian is the message of the NT.

2.4.3.3. The Varieties of the Confessional Approach

Those who hold to a confessional approach hold views that range anywhere from Vriezen's radical canon-within-a-canon to the simple acknowledgment of Eichrodt that every attempt to summarize will have its biased viewpoints.

In Figure 5.2 we have attempted to summarize the various options one might take in applying the confessional approach. Taking faith in Christ as a starting point, for example, may be viewed by some as a necessary, but not a positive step in a Christian OT theology. Others may see such a starting point as a positive step even though it may also be a necessary one. The chart also attempts to show that the Christian faith can find its expression within an OT theology in both an external and an internal way. Externally, one may import the Christian faith into the theology of the OT by means of an actual credal statement. Such a statement may be a historic creed, such as the Westminster Confession, or merely a contemporary doctrinal statement. Internally, one may speak of the Christian faith as a personal faith that arises out of the indwelling of the Spirit of God in the life of the believer. The chart shows four basic positions one may take in relating the Christian faith to the theology of the OT.

2.4.3.4. The Value of the Confessional Approach

The chief value of the confessional approach is that it acknowledges and attempts to deal with the problem of the evident tensions that Christians find within the Bible. These tensions include the relationship between the OT and NT; law and grace; cultural particulars and universal principles; Scripture and tradition; religion and theology. Moreover, the confessional approach acknowledges the responsibility of a theology of the OT to go beyond mere description to provide normative conclusions. It acknowledges that the Bible (OT) is God's Word and that God does speak to the reader through his Word.

2.4.3.5. The Weaknesses of the Confessional Approach

The primary weakness of the confessional approach in the eyes of many is its subjectivity. How can one justify the use of an outside standard (confession of faith) to interpret God's Word? Even the use of the NT as a standard over against the OT

	Negative/Neutral	Positive
External (Credal)	My creed affects my understanding of the OT. It is the context from which I read the OT. This bias must be minimized.	My creed enables me to understand the OT in a certain way. This bias is a help.
Internal (Spirit)	Work of the Spirit is to enable me to read what is in the text by neutralizing my own sinful opposition to the text's meaning.	Work of the Spirit is to enable me to understand the text.

Figure 5.2

submits God's Word in the OT to the judgment of God's Word in the NT. This amounts to a "canon-within-the-Canon."

The evident subjectivity of the confessional approach raises the question of whether such an approach can make any claim to objectivity. We can here briefly note four responses to that question: (1) Some have argued that a confessional approach is the only way we can expect, as Christians, to arrive at a genuine objectivity. The work of the Spirit in the heart of the Christian aims at removing the blindfolds of depravity so that an accurate reading of the biblical text can be achieved. The Spirit of God thus makes the believer's mind truly objective. Without the Spirit, the Christian would resist the message of the text and twist it to his or her own liking. The Spirit, however, counters that impulse by overcoming that part of the Christian's nature. (2) Some, on the other hand, have argued that only by the interplay of the subject (historically and theologically conditioned) and the object (actual meaning of the text) can the meaning of texts such as the Scriptures be known. This is what is now called the "hermeneutical circle." The more closely one becomes attuned to the horizons of the text, the more one understands the text as such. Such a view does not usually hold out any final hope in obtaining an absolutely objective reading of the text of Scripture. There is hope, however, for controlling one's misreading of the text, since the more one's personal horizons become meshed with those of the Scriptures, the more clearly one understands its message. From this perspective, the hermeneutical circle is a positive aid to an accurate understanding of the Scriptures. (3) The traditional concept of illumination holds that it is the Spirit of God who inspired the words of the Bible and who leads us and teaches us in our understanding of it. The Spirit of God leads the obedient Christian to a clear understanding of the OT Scriptures. (4) Finally, as we saw above, some have argued that objectivity is not a truly desirable standpoint from which to read an ancient text such as the OT. It is only in our sympathizing with the faith of Israel that we can know it. Our subjectivity (faith) is an aid to understanding Scripture.

2.4.4. The Use of the Historical Method in Old Testament Theology

Early on in this book we sought to draw a distinction between the text of Scripture and the historical events to which the Scriptures refer. In the present context we want to return to that distinction and note that the OT is both a history (text) and about a history (events). The word *history* thus can have two quite different meanings. When we speak of the use of historical methodology in OT theology, we must be sure to include both of these aspects of the OT. Before we focus our discussion on the use of historical methodology in OT theology, we should point briefly to two aspects of the OT that bear upon the question of history. Those aspects are (1) that the OT is a history (Scripture) and (2) that the OT has a history (tradition).

2.4.4.1. The Old Testament Is a History

Since we have discussed this aspect of the OT earlier, we will add here only a brief review of the histories that make up so much of the OT. A survey of the various books in the OT quickly reveals that many of them consist of narratives about past events. The first book of the Bible, the Pentateuch (Torah), begins with an account of Creation and concludes with an account of the death and burial of Moses. Many events and a wide range of topics are covered in this first book (Genesis through Deuteronomy). It is important to note, however, that the biblical narrative does not end with the death of Moses in Deuteronomy 34. The book of Joshua picks up precisely where the Pentateuch leaves off by recounting the continuing history of Israel, "After the death of Moses" (Jos 1:1). The book of Joshua, and thus its history, is linked to Judges, Samuel, and Kings. In actual fact, as the books are now arranged in the OT, the history that begins with Creation does not conclude until after the events of the Exile to Babylon (2 Ki 25:27–30).

In the Hebrew Bible, the books of Ezra, Nehemiah, and Chronicles come at the very end of the Canon. They thus recount the history a second time, beginning with Adam (1 Ch 1:1) and concluding in the postexilic period. Between those two large blocks of historical narratives are placed the prophetic books as well as the Psalms and Wisdom books. What is important to note is that in their present form, the prophetic books, as well as the Psalms and Wisdom books, are for the most part cast as historical accounts. The prophetic books are, in fact, written as historical portraits of the great prophets of Israel. The Psalms and Wisdom books are also cast as accounts of the wisdom of Israel's two great kings, David and Solomon. Within this group we also find historical accounts of the lives of Job, Esther, and Daniel. It is hard to escape the conclusion that the OT is a book of histories.

2.4.4.2. The Old Testament Has a History

To approach the OT historically means to recognize the obvious fact that it is a collection of books written within a definite historical context and concerned about actual historical events. To approach the OT historically in this sense is to acknowledge that it did not drop out of the sky as a complete book, bound in morocco leather. It is to acknowledge that the OT is the work of humans as well as God and that there was a historical process by which it came to be. It has come to us, at least from the human perspective, like any other book. The human dimension of Scripture, like the humanity of Christ, cannot be ignored without great loss to our theology. In this sense then, the historical approach to Scripture is an unmistakable given.

2.4.4.3. The Objective of a Historical Approach

The primary objective of a historical approach is to understand as accurately as possible the content of the theology of the OT as it was understood when it was first written. Its first and fundamental task is to ask what the OT meant to its original readers. What did its individual authors intend and what would the original readers have understood? In the development of this primary goal, the historical approach must pursue a variety of avenues. Always, however, its primary task remains the same: seeking the meaning of the original documents.

2.4.4.4. Historical Distance

If the meaning of the original documents is the fundamental aim of a historical approach, there is another feature of the approach that has given it a distinct character, especially over against theological method. That feature is *the imposition of a historical distance between the present and the past*. This aspect of a historical approach has had a great influence on the theological understanding of what it means to read a historical document like the OT.

A historical document that has been read and preserved within a community over a period of time will necessarily bring with it into the present a "history of interpretation." The OT is certainly no exception. From the beginning, even before its completion, the earlier parts of the OT were being interpreted by the later books of the OT. The relationship that exists between the Law, the Prophets, and the Writings, for example, is one of constant interpretation and application of the written Word of God. After the completion of the OT, it continued to be read and interpreted, first within early Jewish communities, and then by Christians. The New Testament is a thoroughgoing interpretation and application of the Old. The NT writers left little doubt that they understood the OT to be the source book for their teaching about the person and work of the Savior. Their interpretation and application of the OT to Jesus marks a major turning point in the interpretation of the OT. It marks the dividing line between Christianity and Judaism.

But neither Jews nor Christians were content with the interpretations of their predecessors. They continued to interpret and apply these texts in their teaching, in their preaching, and in their daily living. The Christian and the Jewish reader today both stand at the end of a long and rich history of interpreting the Hebrew Bible. Connecting them with the original documents of the OT there lies a vast plain of time intersected by many pathways worn by the interpretations of the past.

It is precisely at this point that a major difference exists between the historical and theological method. The difference can be encapsulated in a simple question: Do the pathways worn by the interpretations of the past lead us to an accurate understanding of the OT (theological method) or do those pathways lead us away from such an understanding (historical method)? Are we *connected* to the text by the distance that lies between it and us or is this distance, this gap of time, the major *barrier* that must be overcome?

Basic to the classical expression of the historical approach is the supposition that the distance between the text and ourselves is a barrier that must be overcome. The goal of classical historical method is the attempt to clear away from the text the pathways of interpretation which, by the historian's reckoning, have marred and obscured its meaning over the years. The historian's aim is to open up the past to the present by clearing away that which lies between it and the past. Such a historical approach sees the OT, as it were, lying buried beneath countless traditions and interpretations—all of which have at one time or another laid claim to being the final word on its meaning. The historical method insists that to understand the original meaning of the documents of the OT, one must clear away the later debris much like an archaeologist clears the mound of a ruined city.[250] The OT in its original form must be allowed to

---

[250]There is an interesting lesson to be found in viewing the OT in terms of an archaeological dig. The lesson can be construed, in fact, as an argument against a strictly historical approach to the OT. Many archaeological digs are conducted on old, abandoned sites. There is nothing that is disturbed by the digging. The OT, however, is like an ancient site in the midst of a modern city. Many important archaeologi-

speak for itself. It cannot be prompted by any creed or dogma no matter how ancient or authoritative. We must hear the Word of God in its original clarity.

This second feature of the historical approach has, then, a necessarily negative component. It means that the historical approach, by nature, has been suspicious of any previous understanding of the OT documents. It must hold even the NT and later church tradition at arm's length. It cannot rest content with a mediated understanding of the OT. Nothing can stand between the original author and the modern reader. Any mediation of meaning would be understood as an attempt to supplant the historical understanding by a later interpretation. Even if the later interpretation itself claims to have the authority of God's Word, as in the case of the New Testament writers, the historical approach holds it to be illegitimate to substitute any other meaning for the meaning of the original documents themselves.

To hold such a historical approach one need not pit the New Testament against the Old or stand against the theological traditions of the church. The distance put between the present and the past need only be methodological, not theological. It need only be a safeguard against arbitrarily reading the New Testament interpretation of the Old back into the theology of the OT. While it is true that in time this methodological distance became, for many, a theological distance, there was and is no inherent reason why the original meaning of the OT must be different than the meaning of the OT for the modern world. The question, What *did* the original authors of the OT mean in their texts? has its natural corollary in the question, What *do* those texts mean today? When, as a result of the historical approach, a methodological gap was placed between these two questions, however, a theological distance was often not long in coming. That, in our opinion, is an unfortunate and unnecessary result of a historical approach.

The task of a historical approach, then, includes the removal of any paths or roadways lying between the past and the present. The distance between the past and the present can only be crossed by moving from the present back into the past. Any movement that relies on already established pathways of interpretation is suspect. This means that the distance between the past and the present can only be bridged by means of the tools of historical research: the grammatical-historical or the historical-critical method.

What then becomes of the lines of interpretations that trail after the OT texts? Of what value are they to a historical approach? Have they a place in historical method? There are good reasons for including the interpretive traditions in a historical approach to OT theology. With new developments in historiography has come a greater appreciation for this "effective history," that is, the stream of interpretation that ancient texts create within communities that preserve them.

---

cal sites in Jerusalem today, for example, lie beneath modern buildings and structures still in everyday use. Many of these sites have been occupied since the biblical period. The foundation of a modern house may rest on the wall of an ancient city. Such structures would be destroyed if they were removed to dig up the past. Thus the past must be explored without disrupting the structures of the present. In the same way, traditions that are still meaningful today have been built on the OT Scriptures. These traditions should not be disturbed in the process of exploring the past.

First, it has become widely recognized that the OT itself consists of a web of inter-biblical interpretations.[251] The composition of the biblical books itself involved the hermeneutical task of interpreting authoritative texts.[252] Thus the historical study of the composition of the OT cannot dispense with a consideration of its effective history.

Second, much attention has been given to the fact that not only do texts such as the books of the OT arise out of communities of faith, as in the case of ancient Israel, but just as importantly, communities of faith arise out of texts. While it is true to say that the OT text is an expression of the community of faith in ancient Israel,[253] it is equally valid to argue that without the OT there would not have been a community of faith in ancient Israel. Without such texts to bolster the faith of God's people there would have been little hope for the survival of the faithful. The same faith that lay behind the formation of the books of the OT was nourished, sustained, and propagated by those very books. The communities that ultimately were responsible for the preservation of the Hebrew Bible, Judaism, and Christianity, were themselves formed by the faith engendered by the Hebrew Bible.

What this means is that not only did the hermeneutical task of interpretation contribute to the formation of the OT itself, but also those communities founded and sustained by the text of the OT were the social and historical matrix out of which much of the interpretation arose. As Geiger once put it, "In the same way as an understand-ing of Jewish history contributes to our knowledge of the history of the Bible, a knowl-edge of the Bible's history cast light on the history of Judaism."[254] There was a close absorption of life between the text and its community. While this does not guarantee that those communities always preserved the original meaning of the texts, it shows that later interpretations of the OT grew out of contexts which, on the face of it, had a great deal of affinity with those texts. Such communities were likely safe havens for preserving the "original" meaning of the Scriptures, especially if this is understood in terms of the final shape of the Canon. What is needed, of course, is more sensitive his-torical tools suited for reconstructing the trajectories of meaning that the biblical texts created and encountered within such faith communities.[255]

Thus a historical approach is not inherently or even finally opposed to later interpretations and traditions that have arisen out of the OT. Its relationship to them, however, is always secondary. It cannot be ruled by them, but it must always learn from them, and at times it must even be willing to exist on equal footing with them. But a historical method cannot concede to tradition and later interpretation any special

---

[251]Two seminal works are Abraham Geiger, *Urschrift und Übersetzungen der Bibel in ihrer Abhängigkeit von der innern Entwicklung des Judenthums* (Frankfurt-on-Main: Verlag Madda, 1928); and I. L. Seelig-mann, "Voraussetzungen der Midrasch-Exegesis," *SVT*, 1 (1953): 150–81. Also Michael Fishbane, *Bibli-cal Interpretation in Ancient Israel* (Oxford: Clarendon Press, 1985).

[252]John H. Sailhamer, "1 Chronicles 21:1—A Study in Inter-Biblical Interpretation," *TrinJ*, 10 (Spring 1989): 33–48 (reprinted as Appendix D in this book).

[253]Walther Eichrodt, *Theology of the Old Testament*, 1:11.

[254]See note 251.

[255]The works of Geiger, Seeligman, Fishbane, and Vermes (cf. n. 251 and n. 24 in ch. 4) are exam-ples of such studies.

right. Its only primary relationship is with the sense of the original text. That text, because it is God's Word or simply because it is the *editio princeps*, is the only text that demands and receives the historian's full attention.

2.4.4.5. The Importance of Historical Background Material

Another feature of a historical approach to the OT is its recognition of the importance of the cultural and historical context in determining the meaning of the original documents. In treating the documents of the OT historically, it is necessary to recognize that like all such documents from the past, they were written at various times and places and that in each case they were written for a specific occasion. Just as a knowledge of the early history of the United States and the Revolutionary War can contribute to an understanding of a historical document like the Constitution, so also a knowledge of the history and culture of ancient Israel and the Near East can be an important factor in understanding the OT documents. The historical approach, then, includes an attempt to understand the OT in light of the knowledge we have of the world of the ancient Near East.

The sources of our knowledge of the world of the Bible can vary greatly. The two major categories of sources are biblical sources and extra-biblical sources.[256] The biblical sources are the OT documents themselves. Since the OT deals in large measure with the history of Israel, they are a primary source for reconstructing the setting and occasion of the OT documents. An example is the superscription to Psalm 51. According to this superscription, the psalm is to be read within the context of David's sin with Bathsheba and Nathan's rebuke (2Sa 11–12). On the strength of such examples, many interpreters of the OT have attempted to place each of the psalms within a particular historical setting marked out by the historical documents of the OT itself.[257] A historical approach not only sees this attempt as helpful, but also considers it necessary if the OT documents are to be rightly understood.

For many, the OT documents can and should be used at face value, as reliable historical records. Others, more critically, argue that since, as we have them today, they were not firsthand eyewitness accounts, though in themselves accurate and trustworthy, the biblical texts must be used only indirectly as witnesses to the historical events in the OT. The history of Israel can be reconstructed from the biblical records, but those records cannot be taken as face-value accounts of the events they depict. Here is where the *critical or canonical* component comes directly into play. Do we accept the historical narratives at face value (canonical) in using them as historical sources? Most conservative biblical theologians would answer in the affirmative. Others would likely treat them as historical only after they have been submitted to close scrutiny and critical analysis (critical). In either case the OT itself is seen as an important source for establishing the setting of the writing of the OT documents.

---

[256] Herbert Donner, *Geschichte des Volks Israel und seiner Nachbarn in Grundzügen* (Göttingen: Vandenhoeck & Ruprecht, 1984), 17–29.

[257] In actual fact, the superscription of Psalm 51 refers not to the historical event of David and Bathsheba as such but to the text of 2 Samuel. It is thus not a true example of using historical background but rather an example of "inter-textuality."

There are many kinds of extra-biblical sources of ancient Near East history. The most common are archaeological remains, inscriptions, and ancient records. To these may be added the human sciences by which we may attempt to reconstruct the past based on observations and analogies from the present: sociology, anthropology, and history. A historical approach is committed to the use of any method that proves capable of casting light on the historical-cultural context of the OT documents.

2.4.4.6. The Historical Approach Is Descriptive

In a historical approach, the task of an OT theology is often understood merely as a description of the theological content of the documents. Thus in approaching the text historically one should maintain the same objectivity that would be expected in writing about any other ancient religious documents. There should be no attempt to evaluate the truthfulness of the contents of the OT theology. All that is required is an honest and fair description of the documents. In other words, one's task is descriptive not prescriptive.

To approach the theology of the OT descriptively does not require that the interpreter be without conviction or have no belief in the truthfulness of the content of the OT. It only requires that the individual personal judgments of the theologian be set aside or postponed until the contents of the OT are actually understood for what they are. It means that we must first ask, What did the OT documents mean? Only then may we ask, What do they mean today? These are not the same question, and only the first question, strictly speaking, is the aim of the historical approach. The question of what the OT means today, no matter how important that may be, can only be answered after the original meaning has been determined. The answers given to both of these questions are not necessarily in opposition to each other, though for many, they may be. The important point for a historical approach is that the two questions are to be treated separately.

2.4.5. Summary: Descriptive or Confessional

We have been discussing throughout this section the place of one's own personal faith in the study of OT theology. Although there are many aspects to this question, ultimately they reduce to the problem one faces in attempting to apply the rigorous tools of history to a document like the Bible. Is it possible or desirable to approach the study of the theology of the OT in an objective, historical manner? Should we treat the OT like we would any other ancient book? To understand Israel's faith, do we also have to have that faith in ourselves? Do we have to read the OT through the eyes of our faith in the NT?

We have suggested in this section that a historical approach is possible, though such an approach need not rule out some element of faith in the process. Strictly speaking, an approach that acknowledges the need for faith is not a purely historical one. But we have attempted also to show that personal faith can find a place of value, if not importance, in a historical approach. By the same token, a confessional approach to OT theology need not be an arbitrary imposition of one's personal faith onto the text or history of the OT. In other words, a confessional approach need not be "ahistorical" even though it may not be "historical" in the true sense of the term. However, a historical approach to OT theology should and does bracket faith issues and attempt to treat the OT descriptively—asking only the question of what the OT meant to its original readers. As the proposal at the conclusion of this book will argue, it is our opinion that an OT theology for the Christian is necessarily confessional.

The tree diagram below expands the options we have discussed so far. The arrows indicate the choices represented in the proposal for a canonical OT theology represented in this book.

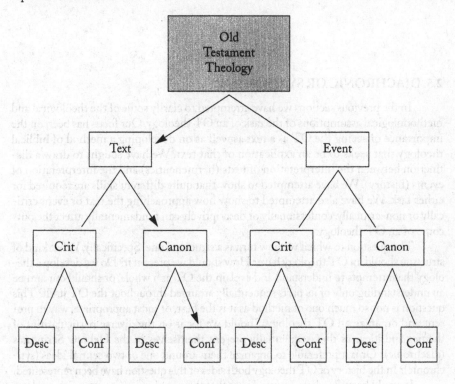

Figure 5.3

SIX

DIACHRONIC OR SYNCHRONIC

2.5. DIACHRONIC OR SYNCHRONIC

In the previous sections we have attempted to clarify some of the theological and methodological assumptions of the task of an OT theology. Our focus has been on the importance of seeing the OT as a text as well as on developing a method of biblical theology that seeks to be an explication of that text. We have sought to draw a distinction between the interpretation of texts (hermeneutics) and the interpretation of events (history). We have attempted to show that quite different skills are required for either task. We have also attempted to show how approaching the text or event critically or non-critically, confessionally or descriptively can fundamentally affect the outcome of an OT theology.

The question to which we now turn is a structural one. Specifically, What kind of structure should an OT theology have? How should we present it? Do we develop a theology that attempts to understand and explain the OT as a whole, or should our aim be an understanding only of its parts sequentially arranged throughout the OT itself? This question is not so much one of method as it is the best, or most appropriate, way to present and organize an OT theology. Should we focus on the diverse particularities of themes and ideas as they sequentially present themselves in the Hebrew Scriptures (diachronic)? Or is it preferable to organize them around one or two central ideas (synchronic)? In the history of OT theology both sides of this question have been represented.

It would be well to keep in mind here that the question we are now raising relates to each of the levels discussed in the previous sections of this book. It relates, for example, to the issue of whether the focus of our theology should be on the text or the event. Should we view the *text* diachronically or synchronically? Should we view the *event* diachronically or synchronically? There are, in other words, several distinct permutations to each of these methodological questions. (See the tree diagram at the conclusions of the previous chapters.) In the discussion that follows we will not take the time to view the question at each of these levels, but it should be kept in mind throughout.

2.5.1. Diachronic Presentation of Old Testament Theology

Literally the term *diachronic* means "through time." Because of that, it is hard not to portray a diachronic approach in a fundamentally temporal mode. This has also been particularly true in light of the overwhelmingly historical focus of the discipline of OT theology in the last two hundred years. Here, however, the term *diachronic* is taken to represent any view that includes the notion that an OT theology should present itself as an unfolding of the central theological message of the OT. In a diachronic approach, each element of the OT's theology is viewed distinctly and discreetly within a sequence rather than within a total system. While it is true that most OT theologies have represented the diachronic unfolding in terms of a *temporal* sequence, that is, as a form of historical progression, we are attempting here to see it also in terms of a *logical* unfolding, as well as a predominately *thematic* unfolding. We will thus approach the question of a diachronic presentation of OT theology as it is construed temporally, logically, and thematically.

2.5.1.1. Temporal Diachronic Presentation of Old Testament Theology

The most common diachronic approach to OT theology is that which attempts to trace the historical development, or progression, of the message of the OT. The structure of the theology itself follows the temporal contours of the revelatory periods represented in the OT. The attempt is made to demonstrate the earliest stage of theology in the OT and, starting from there, to follow its development and progression down to its latest stages. For example, Geerhardus Vos,[1] representative of many conservative theologies in the nineteenth and twentieth centuries, begins with "the content of the preredemptive special revelation" which he takes to be the theology given to Adam before the Fall. From there he treats, consecutively, "the content of the first redemptive special revelation" (Ge 3:15); "the noachin revelation and the development leading up to it" (Ge 4–9); "the revelation in the patriarchal period" (Ge 12–50); and finally, the "revelation in the period of Moses." Vos follows this section with a discussion of "The Prophetic Epoch of Revelation," and then a final section, "Biblical Theology—New Testament." It is quite easy to see that Vos has structured his theology along a historical, temporal sequence. Each stage is treated in its own right.

Such an approach is by no means limited to theologies with a conservative view of history. The classical historical-critical biblical theologies of the Wellhausen era were also structured in a temporally diachronic way. Hölscher, for example, began his *History of Israelite and Jewish Religion* with an exposition of the pre-Israelite religions of Canaan. In the remainder of the book he discussed, in order, the "early Israelite period,"[2] the "Assyrian-Babylonian period," the "Persian period," the "Hellenistic period," and, finally, the "Roman period." His was a diachronic treatment, though the course of events followed a critically reconstructed history of Israel based on the results of the documentary hypothesis.

Among contemporary OT theologies, the classical works of Eichrodt and von Rad can also be considered temporally diachronic. Von Rad's approach is patently diachronic: "The revelation of Jahweh in the OT is divided up over a long series of separate acts of revelation which are very different in content. It seems to be without a

---

[1]Geerhardus Vos, *Biblical Theology Old and New Testaments* (Grand Rapids: Eerdmans, 1948).
[2]Gustav Hölscher, *Geschichte der israelitischen und jüdischen Religion* (Giessen: Alfred Töpelmann, 1922).

centre which determines everything and which could give to the various separate acts both an interpretation and their proper theological connection with one another. We can only describe the Old Testament's revelation of Jahweh as a number of distinct and heterogeneous revelatory acts."[3] Eichrodt, by means of a "cross-sectional"[4] approach, attempts to view the theology of the OT both synchronically and diachronically. Beginning with the Mosaic period, Eichrodt samples the nature of Israel's religion by viewing "cross-sectional" cuts into it at various temporal moments in their history.

2.5.1.2. Logical Diachronic Presentation of Old Testament Theology

Though it is not always easy to distinguish between a temporal sequence and a logical one, it is helpful to attempt to note the difference. An OT theology that is structured along strictly logical lines of progression may or may not follow a temporal sequence. The important point is that underlying the temporal sequence of divine revelation there is often the recognition of a more basic logical one. A logically diachronical approach to OT theology seeks to present its material in such a way that these logical connections become transparent. It is, in fact, this sort of sequence that can be seen in the earliest forms of covenant theology. The structure of Coccejus's biblical theological study of the covenants,[5] for example, appears to follow an historical, that is, temporal sequence of revelatory events. A closer look, however, reveals that Coccejus is concerned primarily with an underlying logical structure that moves from a "pre-Fall" revelatory status, and its nature (a covenant of works), to a "post-Fall" one, and its nature (a covenant of grace). The movement of the structure of Coccejus's theology turns on logical relationships between the covenant of works and the covenant of grace. The differences between the two covenants, as well as those between the two testaments, do not lie in differences in time periods (*ordo temporum*) so much as in different human relationships with God which these distinct covenants reflect. The central issue throughout Coccejus's presentation of the revelatory content of Scripture is that of one's status before God, which changes only when the covenants change, not necessarily in the passage of time (*ordo temporum*).

The theology of Johann Christian Konrad von Hofmann,[6] can also be cited here as an example of a logically diachronic structure. Like most promise-fulfillment theologians, Hofmann structured his theology around the inherently logical relationship between faith in a promise and faith in a fulfillment.[7]

---

[3]Gerhard von Rad, *Old Testament Theology*, vol. 1, *The Theology of Israel's Historical Traditions*, trans. D. M. G. Stalker (New York: Harper & Row, 1962), 115.

[4]By "cross-sectional" Eichrodt means periodic samplings of the nature and structure of Israel's religion at various periods throughout its history. These samplings are then compared and aligned along a sequential, historical axis (Walther Eichrodt, *Theology of the Old Testament*, trans. J. A. Baker [Philadelphia: Westminster, 1961], 27).

[5]Johannes Coccejus, *Summa Doctrinae de Foedere et Testamento Dei*, Opera Omnia, VII, 39–130.

[6]J. Chr. K. von Hofmann, *Weissagung und Erfüllung im Alten und im neuen Testamente* (Nördlingen: C. H. Beck'schen Buchhandlung, 1841).

[7]The "static," that is, essentially non-temporal, nature of "promise" theology can be seen even in Beecher's insistence on the identity of the promise throughout its varied historical realizations: "The more adequate idea is not that of many predictions meeting in one fulfillment, but that of one prediction, repeated and unfolded through successive centuries, with many specifications, and in many forms; always the same

2.5.1.3. Thematic Diachronic Presentation of Old Testament Theology

There are several contemporary diachronic approaches to OT theology that stress a basically thematic structure. Most notable among them is the proposal of Gerhard Hasel.[8] Though not actually worked out in a complete OT theology, Hasel's approach entails, first, a temporally diachronic structure that follows sequentially "the date of origin of the books, groups of writings, or blocks of material within these writings."[9] Hasel, however, builds upon this temporal structure a thematic one. OT theology, according to Hasel, "attempts to draw together and present the major themes of the OT."[10] These various OT themes (e.g., election, promise, covenant, wisdom) are to be traced through the Scriptures, beginning with the first passages that mention them. Again, though Hasel's proposal follows a temporal sequence, its underlying structure is thematic.

2.5.1.4. Accumulative Diachronic Presentation of Old Testament Theology

Kaiser's "epigenetic growth"[11] model for the development and arrangement of an OT theology is diachronic, but with a unique twist. For Kaiser, the proper understanding of the theology of the OT entails not only an appreciation of the progressive focus of the books of the OT on the development of the "promise" theme, but also an openness to the fact that new themes are introduced without real, or at least apparent, antecedents. Not everything in the OT is a natural outgrowth of the earliest, most basic, ideas. New material and themes are added to the OT in the course of time. Thus the theology of the OT is not only being continually rejuvenated, but it is also being added to by new revelation. As Kaiser sees it, an initial promise of redemption and blessing was made in the prepatriarchal era. Over time and throughout the remainder of the theology of the OT, that promise is increasingly developed and clarified, finding its focus and fulfillment in the coming of Jesus Christ. The growth of the promise

---

in essential character, no matter how it may vary in its outward presentation or in the illustrations through which it is presented" (Willis Judson Beecher, *The Prophets and the Promise* [Grand Rapids: Baker, 1963], 176–77). This assessment does not seem to hold for the "promise theology" of Kaiser, which builds on an actual historical (temporal) progression of the promise theme. Kaiser, in fact, allows for the periodic addition of genuinely new material into the promise schema (Walter C. Kaiser, Jr., *Toward an OT Theology* [Grand Rapids: Zondervan, 1978], 51–52).

[8]Gerhard Hasel, *Old Testament Theology: Basic Issues in the Current Debate* (Grand Rapids: Eerdmans, 1991).

[9]Hasel leaves the impression that this temporal structure is to serve only as "a guide for establishing the order of presentation of the various theologies" which run through the OT. Because it is, "admittedly difficult to fix," such literary chronologies would otherwise render an OT theology extremely tentative if relied on too heavily (ibid., 204).

[10]Ibid., 180.

[11]"So there was real progress in revelation. But such progress did not exclude either an organic relatedness or the possibility of realizing every now and again a full maturation of one or more points of revelation along this admitted route of growth. . . . More often than not the growth was slow, delayed, or even dormant, only to burst forth after a long period in a new shoot off the main trunk. But such growth, as the writers of Scripture tell it, was always connected to the main trunk: an epigenetic growth, i.e., there was a growth of the record of events, meanings, and teachings as time went on around a fixed core that contributed life to the whole emerging mass" (Kaiser, *Toward an OT Theology*, 8).

theme is "epigenetic" because it always proceeds from the center to the edges, like the growth of a seed into a tree. At whatever historical stage of development the tree may be, it always has the same center. Such, argues Kaiser, is the development of the theology of the OT. It grows and changes, but always retains the same center, the "promise."

There is, however, in Kaiser's view, an additional element to reckon with in the presentation of an OT theology. At key points along the way, sometimes unexpectedly,[12] new elements are added to the OT which draw new themes and theological moments into the larger message. Such new themes can be seen in the sudden appearance of wisdom literature in the OT canon,[13] and in the addition of the Mosaic law "alongside the Abrahamic-Davidic promise."[14] Though these additional elements are not, in fact, without true antecedents in previous revelation, Kaiser argues, their appearance is so sudden and new that most modern readers cannot help but regard them as total innovations. Each biblical writer added to the theme of the promise, but "the writers of the OT were more than mere parrots. They were participants in a long line of revelation, true, but they were also recipients of additional revelation *par excellence*."[15]

2.5.1.5. Summary of the Diachronic Approach

It is possible to organize an OT theology on a diachronic basis. That may mean the themes and ideas of the OT are studied within the context of their progressive development and are explained as part of that development. Sometimes the development is explained purely in terms of historical processes; that is, ideas and themes change or evolve in the course of changing times and contexts. Others explain the development of OT ideas as a natural, logical consequence of earlier ideas. Still others attempt to organize the OT along a primarily thematic development. Whatever the specific nuance given to the idea of progressive development, these various approaches all share the idea that a diachronic arrangement of the ideas in the OT is the most appropriate means of disclosing its true nature.

2.5.2. Synchronic Presentation

Though diachronic approaches to the structure of OT theology have been numerous, they have by no means represented the only alternative. Many biblical theologians have preferred to argue for the necessity of a systematic arrangement of the Old Testament's theology, which we will call a *synchronic* approach. Even Coccejus, the OT theologian who contributed more than anyone to developing and popularizing the diachronic approach, also represented the message of the OT in a synchronic

---

[12]"While each of these fresh branches of teaching were frequently linked by historical antecedents or by way of response to the accumulated canon up to that point, often they were so startling in their novelty as to threaten later attempts at tracing their continuity with the existing canon" (ibid., 51).

[13]"It was so disparate and diverse from the revelation which claimed to precede it that many to the present day still cannot see any connection at all. Consequently, it can be used as a sure sign of a unique and innovative item if some are willing to conclude that it is a novel, unattached oddity" (ibid., 51).

[14]Ibid.

[15]Ibid., 52.

fashion. The most mature stage of Coccejus's own theological position is represented by a major synchronic study of biblical theology, his *Summa Theologiae ex Scripturis Repetita*.[16] In that work, Coccejus follows an exhaustive series of *loci* (theological topics)[17] in the arrangement of his material. The fact that Coccejus understood himself to be writing a biblical theology, and not a work on dogmatics or systematics, is clear not only from the title, "derived from Scripture alone" (*ex Scripturis Repetita*), and from the work itself,[18] but also from a comparison of his work with other systematic theologians of his day.[19]

What, then, is the synchronic shape of an OT theology? What should determine its structure? The actual nature of any given synchronic approach, as well as its internal structure, is determined by a number of factors—the principle factor being the organizing idea(s) or central concern(s) of the whole. Should the structure of an OT theology center around the general rubrics of systematic theology—God, humanity, and salvation? Should it follow the rubrics (*loci*) of church dogmatics?[20] Or, should one seek to structure an OT theology around central ideas derived from Scripture itself?[21] How one answers these and other similar questions will determine the actual shape an OT theology takes. We will discuss each of these possibilities below.

2.5.2.1. Synchronic-Systematic Presentation

Here the emphasis is on the word *systematic*. A synchronic-systematic[22] approach to the presentation of an OT theology is an attempt to give a comprehensive arrangement of the material of the OT around a single idea, or set of ideas. A *system*, in the technical sense of the word (σύστημα), is a coherent collection of ideas and statements arranged around a single premise.[23] In a broader sense, a system is a collection

---

[16]*Opera Omnia*, VII, 131–403.

[17]For example, Coccejus begins with the *locus* (topic) on Scripture (Locus Primus, De Sacra Scriptura), then follows with *loci* on God and his existence, God's Divinity, the Trinity, and so on. There are some 37 *loci* in all.

[18]The work is, in fact, a massive collection of exegetical discussions of individual scriptural passages and their interrelationships.

[19]The two most notable in Coccejus's own day were Herman Witsius, *De Oeconomia Foederum Dei cum Hominibus* (Basel, 1677), and Gisbertus Voetius, *Selectae disputationes theologicae* (Utrecht, 1648–69).

[20]See Philip Melanchthon's *Loci Communes*: Deus, Unus, Trinus, Creatio, Homo, Peccatum, Fructus peccati, Poenae, Lex, Promissiones, Instauratio per Christum, Gratia, etc. G.L. Plitt, *Die Loci Communes Philipp Melanchthons in ihrer Urgestalt* (Leipzig, 1925), 60.

[21]This was the aim of Gotthilf Traugott Zachariä, *Biblische Theologie oder Untersuchung des biblischen Grund der vornehmsten theologischen Lehren*, 4 vols, 1771–1775, which gave to this work the recognition of having opened OT theology into an entirely new direction (see Kraus, *Die Biblische Theologie*, 31).

[22]According to Weber, "The term and the phenomenon of a systematically constructed dogmatics is first found in Bartholomew Keckermann, *Systema SS. Theologiae*, appended to vol. II of the *Opera* (1614)" (Otto Weber, *Foundations of Dogmatics*, trans. Darrell L. Guder [Grand Rapids: Eerdmans, 1981], 1:51, n. 26).

[23]"Das System steht dem Aggregat, der Menge, wo eins neben dem andern ohne Verbindung und Einheit steht, entgegen, und ist in strengem Sinne des Worts ein Inbegriff von Sätzen, die alle einem obersten Princip (d.i. einem allgemeinen Satze, in dem die andern Sätze als Folgesätze enthalten sind, und der daher der Grundsatz heisst) untergeordnet sind, und aus diesem in einer zusammenhängenden deutlichen Ordnung hergeleitet" (Karl Gottlieb Bretschneider, *Systematische Entwickelung aller in der Dogmatik vorkommenden Begriffe* [Leipzig: Verlag von Johann Ambrosius Barth, 1825], 39).

of ideas or statements so interrelated that they represent a logically or functionally coherent whole. Not only must the single idea or set of ideas be grasped as an expression of the whole, but also the relationship of each of its parts to the whole must be demonstrated.[24] The essential elements of a system, according to Bretschneider, are:

(1) Simplicity: the unity of the goal or purpose of a system with its constituent parts. All its parts contribute to the purpose of the overall system.

(2) Consequence: all the parts are logically related to each other and to the basic premise of the whole.

(3) Completeness: the whole contains all the parts necessary to accomplish its purpose.

(4) Foundation: all the parts of the whole are sufficiently and appropriately grounded. There is, in other words, sufficient reason for each part as an element of the system.[25]

In Christian theology, the concept of Jesus Christ as the eternal *logos* (the Word) has played a central role in the development of theological systems.[26] First initiated by Origen, this "logos systematics" remained "formative for theology for approximately a millennium."[27] By means of the all-embracing concept of God as the eternal and incarnate Word (*logos*), Christian theology found a discreet integration point between divine truth and human reason. "In setting up such a 'principle,' a universal idea, the concept was generated that man is capable of grappling with the whole intellectually, or to put it another way, the whole is so constituted that it can be condensed to one human thought."[28] This type of systematic interest in OT theology forms the structure of the theology of Otto Procksch.[29] For Procksch, "All theology is Christology."[30] The whole of the theology of the OT forms the historical as well as the conceptual background and foundation of the incarnation of the eternal Word (*logos*). "Jesus can as little be understood without the OT as the OT can be understood without him."[31] Just as the whole of Christian theology is united and grounded in Jesus, so also the whole of the theology of the OT is united and grounded in him.

What other kinds of "systems" have found their way into the structures of Christian theology? Essentially there are two, ontological systems and anthropological systems.

(1) Ontology: An ontological system is one that takes its starting point and integrating principle from a philosophical statement about the nature of God and human

---

[24]"We understand by 'system' the totality of an intellectual structure which is based upon a fundamental concept (a 'principle') and which develops it logically and methodically. The presupposition is, accordingly, that the 'principle' contains potentially the one and total content which is then explained in greater detail in the systematic exposition. This means in turn that in its exposition the system cannot contain elements which are not already given in the 'principle.' The 'principle' is, therefore, the intellectual condensation of an all-embracing totality" (Weber, *Foundations*, 1:51).

[25]Bretschneider, *Systematische Entwickelung*, 39–40.

[26]Weber, *Foundations*, 1:52.

[27]Ibid., 1:53.

[28]Ibid., 1:52.

[29]Otto Procksch, *Theologie des Alten Testaments* (Gütersloh: C. Bertelsmann Verlag, 1950).

[30]Ibid., 1.

[31]Ibid., 7, 8.

existence. Philosophical systems attempt to lay bare the nature of reality (metaphysics) and existence (ontology). Theological systems have often grounded their organization and expression of Christian theology in the concepts of reality and existence derived from philosophy. Thomas Aquinas, for example, accepted Aristotle's understanding of God as the "unmoved Mover" (the First Cause), and developed his theology as a logical extension of that first principle. It is a well-known fact that such classical ontologies as Platonism and Aristotelianism greatly influenced Christian theology, though they did not thrive in the philosophical climate that followed Kant's critique of human reason. In the modern era, ontological systematics are not found in great number outside the realm of classical orthodoxy and its descendants. Modern metaphysical systems such as idealism, phenomenology, materialism, and process, often form the bases of Christian theology in the modern world. As such they may also serve as structures for OT theology.

(2) Anthropology: In the wake of Kant's critique of human reason, theologians were quick to turn from their focus on God's being and existence to look more intently at their own "subjective" selves. Human experience thus became the resource from which basic systematic principles were drawn. A typical anthropological "first principle" in the early years of the nineteenth century, for example, was the phenomenon of faith. The use of just such a principle in Schleiermacher's systematic theology, *The Christian Faith*, had a long lasting effect on OT theology.[32]

2.5.2.2. Synchronic-Synthetic Presentation

The most common form of synchronic structure of Christian theology has been the *synthetic* approach. The ultimate aim of a synthetic approach to theological systems is to provide a meaningful framework on which to hang the whole of Christian beliefs. It does not seek to uncover the essential structure of the material itself. It seeks only an appropriate means for presenting the material in a logical and coherent way. Van Imschoot, for example, represents a modern synthetic approach to OT theology. "Without doing violence to Israelite thought, it is permissible to disengage and to group these ideas in order to unite them into a synthesis, which, while respecting the originality of each author and the differences which at times separate them, highlights both the basic unity of the revelation, that was entrusted to the chosen people and set down in their sacred books, and its continuity with the revelation of the New Testament for which it was the preparation."[33] There is also an implicit assumption that the biblical material itself does not have an ostensive structure or inherent arrangement. Moreover, in building a synthetic framework, there need not be a single underlying principle. The parts of the whole need not have an inherent relationship to each other or to the whole. The validity of the framework is measured by its adequacy in clearly representing the various facets of the Christian faith. Moreover, the theological framework in a synthetic model need not necessarily be biblical in its origin. It may be a biblically neutral framework that functions simply by presenting the material in an understandable manner.

---

[32]Weber, *Foundations*, 1:57.
[33]Paul van Imschoot, *Theology of the Old Testament* (New York: Desclee Co., 1965), 4.

The most common "synthetic" approach employed in the structure of OT theology is that of the abbreviated classical model: God, humanity, and salvation. In Peter Lombard's *Sententiarum libri IV* we find the first formal statement of the structures of theological discussion from the Middle Ages. Lombard's *Sentences* consisted primarily of summations of church traditions relating to certain central topics: the Trinity, creation and sin, the incarnation, and the sacraments. Underlying the arrangement of Lombard's *Sentences* is an analytical system that takes its starting point in the ultimate goal of theology, that is, God, and follows with the subject of theology, human beings, and concludes with the means of salvation. Lombard's *schema* gave a definitive shape to Christian theological systems, that is, the "God, man, salvation" structure.[34] Melanchthon's *schema*, on the other hand, began from the "first principle," God, then treated the "means" by which divine blessing was obtained, Christ and the sacraments, and concluded with the final purpose of all theology, eternal blessing. Melanchthon's *Loci communes*, which was the first Protestant systematic theology, relied on the theological topics of the book of Romans for its structure.

In the synthetic approach, the classic shapes of systematic theology are adopted as the structures for OT theology. As a rule these theologies address three primary concerns: What does the OT have to say about God? About humanity? About salvation? Sellin[35] and Ludwig Köhler[36] have adopted just such a synthetic structure in their approaches to OT theology.

2.5.2.3. Synchronic-Scriptural Presentation

There are many biblical theologians who have argued that when viewed as a whole, the OT itself displays an inherent synchronic structure, that there is a biblical integration point around which the material can be shaped. There is more agreement that such an integration point exists, however, than about the exact identification of that point. Numerous attempts have been made to show that the center point of the OT is the concept of the covenant,[37] for example, or the kingdom of God.[38] Still others have argued that the present shape of the OT itself—the Law, the Prophets, and the Writings—is a biblical structure that should be used as the framework for an OT theology.[39]

2.5.3. Summary

The question of how one should structure an OT theology has been frequently discussed. Problems arise primarily when one takes the position that the whole of the OT must be fit into a single idea or concept and then narrows that concept to such an

---

[34]Bretschneider, *Systematische Entwicklung*, 118.

[35]Ernst Sellin, *Theologie des Alten Testaments* (Leipzig: Verlag von Quelle, 1936).

[36]Ludwig Köhler, *Theologie des Alten Testaments* (Tübingen: J. C. B. Mohr [Paul Siebeck], 1966).

[37]Walther Eichrodt, *Theology of the Old Testament* (Philadelphia: Westminster, 1961).

[38]A. B. Davidson, *The Theology of the Old Testament* (Edinburgh: T & T Clark, 1904).

[39]Claus Westermann, *Theologie des Alten Testaments in Grundzügen* (Göttingen: Vandenhoeck & Ruprecht, 1978), 7.

extent that it begins to distort the biblical material. It is possible to arrange the theology of the OT around a single idea or cluster of themes without insisting that everything in the OT conform precisely to that idea or those themes. The purpose of structure is to enhance our understanding of the material, not to distort that material. A heavy dependence on structure often leads to a reductionist misreading of the OT.

The important functional question discussed in this chapter was whether an OT theology is best arranged diachronically or synchronically. The answer to that question perhaps lies in the larger question of *systems analysis*. Systems analysis is an attempt to evaluate systems in the contexts for which those systems were designed. Communication systems exist as parts of larger communication situations and can be assessed more readily within those contexts.[40] It is generally very difficult to judge the value of one system (e.g., diachronic approach) over that of another (e.g., synchronic approach) because by the nature of the case, a system, whether diachronic or synchronic, is valid if it meets all the functional requirements of its system. Systems, in other words, are self-contained by definition. A systems analysis approach to OT theology attempts to raise the broader issue of what purpose the system, in this case, the OT theology, is to have. One could argue, for example, that an OT theology meant as a guide to reading the Bible might best be designed diachronically. Such a system would meet the broader requirements better than a synchronic one. On the other hand, an OT theology meant as a guide to understanding the OT as a whole, perhaps in the role of comparing it to another religion (e.g., Islam) would probably be more appropriately structured as a synchronic system. The validity of a system, therefore, depends not only on how well formed and appropriate the system itself is, but also on how well it meets the requirements of the communication situation for which it is designed. An OT theology that presents the OT in terms of the concept "promise" might well be evaluated along two lines. First, does it meet the minimal requirements of a system; that is, does it adequately describe the total meaning of the OT? And secondly, does it appropriately address its communication situation? That communication situation, of course, may vary with use, and thus such an OT theology might be more appropriate in some contexts than others.

---

[40]See Siegfried J. Schmidt, *Texttheorie* (München: Wilhelm Fink Verlag, 1976), 146.

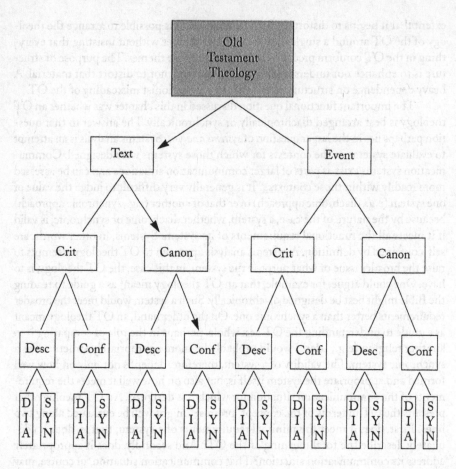

Figure 6.1

PART III

A CANONICAL THEOLOGY
OF THE
OLD TESTAMENT

SEVEN

A PROPOSAL
FOR A
CANONICAL THEOLOGY

3.1. A PROPOSAL FOR A CANONICAL THEOLOGY

The purpose of this final chapter is to offer a proposal for doing OT theology. We do not intend our proposal to be understood as the only possible way of doing OT theology. On the contrary, we intend to illustrate by this proposal the fact that there are many and various ways to go about the task. This proposal is one of them. It will attempt to utilize the components of OT theology developed in this book and to provide an example of how the various approaches can be brought together into a single theology.

We will begin our proposal with a restatement of our understanding of the nature and purpose of an OT theology. That will be followed by a discussion of the various components which we think should constitute it.

3.1.1. What Is Old Testament Theology?

We start with the definition of the term *theology* proposed early on in this book. Theology, being to some extent a science, is an attempt to formulate God's revelation into themes and propositions. It is the scientific explication of revelation. It works on the premise that God has revealed himself in ways that can be observed and restated in more or less precise language. Thus the task of theology is the restatement of God's self-revelation. As we understand it, the Bible is the Word of God. In the Bible God has spoken. Thus the Bible is not merely a record of what God said in the past, but also a record of what God is saying today. By means of the words of Scripture, God has spoken and continues to speak to us today.

If God has spoken in his Word, the Bible, then the task of theology is made considerably more clear. The task of theology is to state God's Word to the church in a clear and precise manner. To that end, we offer, once again, the following definition: Old Testament theology is the study and presentation of what is revealed in the Old Testament.

This is a definition that focuses on the textual nature of the Old Testament as well as on the fact that in it, and along with the New Testament, we find a complete statement of the will of God. For reasons which will become clear in the following discussion, we have also chosen to describe our OT theology as a canonical theology of the Old Testament.

Here a word of warning is in order. Though the word *canonical* has received much attention in recent years, our use of this term is still in need of some qualification when used of an approach to OT theology. For one thing, our use of the word *canonical* should not be understood in light of the particular focus of *canon criticism*. Though there are surface similarities between canon criticism and the canonical theology of the OT that we are proposing here, there are, as well, fundamental differences. Chief among those differences are the understanding of the historicity of the biblical narratives and the nature of the composition of the biblical books.

Canon criticism, as a rule, lays little stress on the historicity of the biblical narratives. As it is usually practiced, it assumes the validity of the conclusions of modern historical criticism and source criticism and hence has a minimalist view of the facticity of the events recorded in the OT Scriptures. Apologetically, therefore, it has little to offer an evangelical approach that is concerned with the truth value of the biblical texts. For canon criticism, the truthfulness of the Bible lies not so much in its historical accuracy, as in its ongoing ability to speak to the human condition. The authority of the biblical texts lies in their ability to embody the identity and aspirations of the community. There are, however, no such underlying assumptions for a canonical theology of the OT. Since the Bible, as such, is God's Word, the question of its truthfulness is directly linked to the question of its historical accuracy.

Since canon criticism usually builds on the results of the other forms of biblical criticism, its view of the composition of the biblical books is often quite different from a canonical theology of the OT. Owing to its premise that Scripture is the authoritative Word of God, a canonical theology of the OT takes as its starting point the representation of the authorship of the biblical books found in the text itself. For example, if within the text itself the authorship of the book of Jeremiah is tied closely to the prophet Jeremiah and his amanuensis (Jer 36), then it is not only legitimate, but also essential, to interpret the book within that historical context. By the same token, if a biblical book is not specific about its authorship, a canonical theology would respect the author's choice of remaining anonymous and not attempt to reconstruct its authorship and setting. To argue, for example, that Jeremiah was the author of the books of Kings goes far beyond the clear statements of Scripture. Those books, along with many other OT books, simply do not identify their author or the time of their composition. On questions of authorship and date of specific books of the OT, a canonical theology would resist going beyond what is actually supplied by the Scriptures themselves. Fortunately, these texts can be understood apart from both critical reconstructions and tradition-laden identifications of authorship.

3.2. COMPONENTS OF AN OLD TESTAMENT THEOLOGY

We turn now to the basic configuration of our OT theology. Looking back over the options we have discussed in this book, we propose the following combination of options:

1. Text or Event	+	1. *Text:* An OT theology based on the text of the OT rather than the event;
2. Criticism or Canon	-	2. *Canon:* It views the text of the OT just as we have it in the OT canon;
3. Descriptive or Confessional	-	3. *Confessional:* It treats the OT with a special hermeneutic—not like any other book.
4. Diachronic or Synchronic	+	4. *Diachronic:* It approaches the OT in terms of each of its parts rather than attempting to view it as a whole

Figure 7.1

PROLEGOMENA

Our justification for these options begins with an acceptance of the notion of an inspired text: "All Scripture is inspired" (2Ti 3:16). If our starting point is verbal inspiration, then the text should be the focus of our biblical theology. Our OT theology will thus be text-centered. It is not necessary, however, to approach this starting point in exactly this way. One could argue, apart from Paul's statement, that an OT theology is by definition a textual enterprise since the OT is, in fact, a text. A theology of a text is then a textually focused theology. It is thus very conceivable that one could construct a text-centered theology quite apart from a belief in inspiration.

3.2.1. A Text-Centered Approach (+ Text)

A canonical theology of the OT focuses on the text of Scripture rather than on the events independently of those texts (see Fig. 7.2).

In the approach to OT theology which we are here proposing, the words of Scripture and the meaning of the biblical authors are the first and primary goal of interpretation. Though there was inevitably revelation of some sort in God's actions in history, our only access to divine revelation now is through the interpretation of the inspired writers in the text of Scripture. It is not as though events are unimportant, but the issue is not the historicity of the biblical events. The issue is that God's revelation for us today consists of the words of Scripture which give an account of the events of the past. The historical narratives of Scripture are, in fact, the means of knowing what God has done in the past. Only by means of those texts are we able to know and understand God's revelation.

Care should be taken to make clear the nature of the distinction between revelation in Scripture and God's saving acts in history. The facticity of historical events

| 1. Text or Event | + | 1. *Text:* An OT theology based on the text of the OT rather than the event |

Figure 7.2

such as the Exodus and, for the NT, the death and resurrection of Jesus, are essential to the truthfulness of biblical theology. These events, however, are meaningful for us only when they are recorded and interpreted for us in the biblical narratives. For an OT theology to focus on the biblical text does not mean it is ambivalent to the truth claims of those texts. It simply means that unless we focus on the scriptural accounts of God's acts in history, those very historical events are open to an uncontrollably wide range of meaning and interpretation. In the last analysis, the central question is what do the Scriptures say about God's acts in history? The chart in Figure 7.3 is intended to clarify this point.

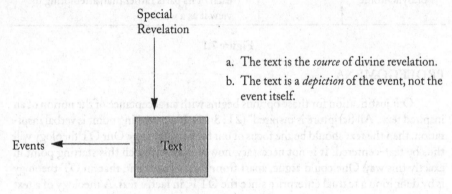

Figure 7.3

When OT theology focuses on the meaning of the text, it must intentionally distinguish that meaning from either the empiricist's focus on events or the idealist's focus on general truths or ideals. In this regard, a canonical theology of the OT is similar to a precritical reading of the text. Though we cannot claim today to read the OT precritically, we can benefit from earlier theologies and commentaries that have read it that way. The locus of revelation for a text-centered OT theology remains that meaning which is derived from the Scriptures themselves (see Fig. 7.4).

A text-centered OT theology raises a number of secondary issues which we must now discuss.

3.2.1.1. Textuality, Text Theory, and Text Linguistics

One troubling result of the "eclipse" of biblical narrative over the last two centuries has been the lack of serious reflection on the nature of the textuality of Scripture.[1] What is a text? How does a text work? Because biblical theologians in the past have focused largely on historical events, much of their attention has been devoted to the study of nontextual entities such as historiography, archaeology, and the nature of historical events as such. With the renewed interest in the biblical text as the locus of

---

[1]There is a growing literature on the nature and study of textuality. Schmidt explains *textuality* as "structural features of socio-communicative (and thus linguistic) actions of or between communication partners." A *text* is a concrete realization of such a socio-communicative, linguistic action. A text is an instance of textuality (Siegfried J. Schmidt, *Texttheorie, Probleme einer Linguistik der sprachlichen Kommunikation* [Muenchen: Wilhelm Fink Verlag, 1976], 144).

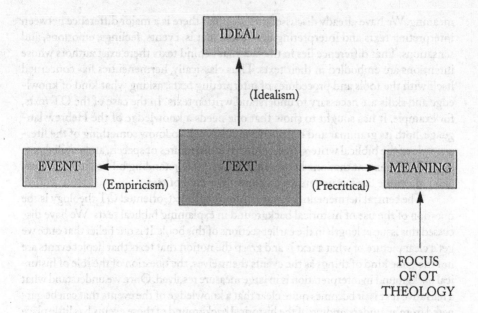

Figure 7.4

revelation and the focus of theology, there is a growing urgency for a better understanding of texts. Such an understanding must begin with a well-formed text theory.[2]

A text theory is a comprehensive description and explanation of communication situations involving written texts.[3] It is not really a "theory" as such, but a "model" of text productions and communication situations involving texts. It attempts to explain what happens when human beings communicate via written texts. By viewing written texts within the larger framework of communication situations, text theory provides a clearer understanding of the unique features of texts. Text linguistics,[4] a related field of study, is the attempt to describe the internal language-related mechanisms that enable texts to function and produce meaning. Both "sciences of texts"[5] are devoted to the task of elucidating the nature of textual communication such as we find in the OT.

3.2.1.2. Hermeneutics

Technically and classically, *hermeneutics* is the science of the interpretation of texts. In a less technical sense, hermeneutics involves any kind of interpretation and

---

[2]Although a large volume of literature has developed around the theme of text theory, text linguistics, and discourse analysis, the standard work on text theory remains Siegfried J. Schmidt's *Texttheorie* (see n1 above).

[3]Ibid., iv.

[4]The standard work on Text linguistics is Robert de Beaugrande and Wolfgang Dressler, *Introduction to Text Linguistics* (London: Longman, 1981).

[5]For the concept of "science of texts" (*Textwissenschaft*) see Heinrich F. Plett, *Textwissenschaft und Textanalyse* (Heidelberg: Quelle & Meyer, 1979).

meaning. We have already discussed the idea that there is a major difference between interpreting texts and interpreting non-texts, that is, events, feelings, emotions, and sensations. That difference lies in the fact that behind texts there exist authors whose intentions are embodied in their texts. Thus classically, hermeneutics has concerned itself with the tools and procedures of interpreting texts, asking what kind of knowledge and skills are necessary to understand written texts. In the case of the OT texts, for example, it has sought to show that one needs a knowledge of the Hebrew language, both its grammar and lexicon. One also needs to know something of the literary style of the biblical writers, their world of ideas, figures of speech, and parallel passages. To the extent that one knows such things, understanding biblical texts follows along the same lines as understanding any other kind of text.

The central hermeneutical issue confronting a text-oriented OT theology is the question of the use of historical background in explaining biblical texts. We have discussed this issue at length in the earlier sections of this book. It is our belief that once we get a clear picture of what a text is and grasp the notion that texts that depict events are not the same kind of things as the events themselves, the question of the role of historical background in interpretation is in large measure resolved. Once we understand what a narrative text is, it becomes quite clear that a knowledge of the events that can be garnered from an understanding of the historical background of those events has little place in our understanding of the text *as a text*. To understand a text, one must read it.

We should also note that in calling into question the hermeneutical role of knowing the historical background of the events, we are not questioning the *apologetic* importance of such knowledge. Historical background material often leads to and provides the basis for the defense of the historicity of Scripture. Nor are we questioning the importance of knowing the historical background of the authorship of the OT. To the extent that we can determine the context within which a text was written, that may shed some light on the author's purpose.

The question often arises at this point about the meaning of words. Don't we need a knowledge of historical background to understand the meaning of the words of the Bible? The answer is that in ordinary, nontechnical language,[6] we know the meanings of words in terms of the world of a particular language, or, in the case of a non-native language, in terms of the world of a translational language. We know what words "mean" by identifying their equivalencies in our own language. We say "this word means such and such in my language," or "this word in language A means that word in language B." We do not say, or at least should not say, "this word means that thing."

Words point to things, but their meaning consists of what they say *about* the things they point to. The meaning of words does not reside in the things they point to. For biblical Hebrew, for example, we may use a Hebrew lexicon with Hebrew definitions,[7] or a Hebrew lexicon *with English definitions* (equivalences).[8] If one uses a

---

[6]In technical language, words and terms are used to point precisely to specific categories of "things." An ornithologist, for example, has a vast inventory of technical terms for every species of birds. Yet in ordinary language, they can all be called "birds."

[7]The standard Hebrew biblical lexicon is Joshua Steinberg, *Milon HaTanak* (Tel Aviv, 1977).

[8]The standard Hebrew-English lexicon is *A Hebrew and English Lexicon of the Old Testament*, eds. Francis Brown, S. R. Driver, and Charles A. Briggs (Oxford: Clarendon, 1907).

Hebrew lexicon that gives definitions of words in Hebrew, then one must know Hebrew to know the meanings of the words. This is exactly what we do in looking up the meaning of an English word in an English dictionary. The definition is given in English and it consists of English words. A lexicon is a book about words. It is not, and should not be, a book filled with photographs or drawings of things. What is important to understand is that historical background information, which is information about "things" (*res*), is not, and should not be, used to define the meaning of words. Historical background information tells us about the things the biblical words refer to. It does not tell us about the meaning of those words that do the referring.

While on the subject of the meaning of words, we should also mention briefly the distinction between the meaning of words and the meaning of texts. Words *refer* to "things" in the external world (see Fig. 7.5). That reference is, of course, an important part of their purpose, but it does not determine their meaning.

Historical narrative texts, however, do not point to "things" in the external world, but rather to "things" in their own narrative world (see Fig. 7.6). They, in effect, represent that world to the reader.

In a text, words are like the paint an artist uses to represent a "world" on canvas. The paint comes in various colors, and the artist chooses the desired color and shade to represent the canvas world. In the same way it is the words which render the "things" meaningful in a text and not the "things" themselves. The meaning of a text is always and only a function of the author's intent and choice of words. An author must use a word within its acceptable semantic field which any accurate lexicon will show. Like the color of the paint an artist uses, the lexical meaning of a word is fixed. The textual meaning of the word, however, is a function of the author's intention as it is realized in the rendering of a particular text. The author uses the lexical meaning of a word as part of the textual meaning.

Some time ago a story was circulated that Christians in the former Soviet Union were without proper printing equipment to produce copies of the Bible. Resourcefully,

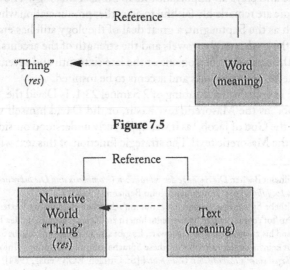

Figure 7.5

Figure 7.6

they collected as much printed Communist literature as they could obtain. Taking those printed texts, they cut out each word and pasted them back together to produce a printed Bible. Originally, these same words, when configured within the Communist documents, had depicted the world of the Communist literature they printed. Once reconfigured as the Bible, these words had quite a different textual meaning. The meaning of each individual word (lexical meaning) did not change, but the meaning of the two texts (textual meaning) was fundamentally different.

3.2.1.3. Language and Translation

A text-oriented approach to OT theology must take seriously the fact that textual meaning, and hence, revelation and theology, is always mediated through language. The meaning of a biblical text consists of the verbal meaning of the language of that text. An OT theology cannot dispense with a thorough grounding in the Hebrew language of the text of Scripture, or, at least, with a good and accurate translation. What gives the task of biblical grammar and lexicography its somewhat unique problems is the fact that biblical Hebrew, as a language, had long died out before concerted attempts were made for its preservation.[9] In other words, since there are no living informants to tell us what the words and sentences mean, the language of the Bible is a dead language.[10]

What are the implications of this situation for a text-centered biblical theology? It means, for one thing, that not only are there no longer any competent speakers of biblical Hebrew, but there are also no longer any competent readers.[11] Biblical philology, which is the study of the ancient biblical languages, must therefore approach the Hebrew text in a way quite differently than its original readers did. The modern reader of the ancient biblical texts, for example, must rely on the vowels and accents supplied the text by the Masoretes.[12] While this point should not be overemphasized, it is not a minor issue and plays an important role in biblical theology. Though the Hebrew texts as a whole are remarkably faithful to an earlier pronunciation when tested against versions such as the Septuagint, a great deal of theology still lies embedded in such minutiae as the quality of the vowels and the strength of the accents. It was for good reason that the orthodox theologians of the late sixteenth and seventeenth centuries held both the Masoretic vowels and accents to be inspired.

A case in point is the meaning of 2 Samuel 23:1. Is David the "Anointed of the God of Jacob," as the Masoretic text has it, or did David himself write about "the Anointed of the God of Jacob," as it was apparently understood outside the group that transmitted the Masoretic text? The strategic function of this text within the book of

---

[9]See Wilhelm Bacher, *Die Anfänge der hebräischen Grammatik and Die hebräische Sprachwissenschaft vom 10. bis zum 16. Jahrhundert* (Amsterdam: John Benjamins, 1975).

[10]"Die althebr. Sprachwissenschaft hat es nur mit schriftlich überlieferten Texten zu tun. Die althebr. Sprache is zudem 'tot'; denn von den Sprachteilnehmern zur Zeit der Abfassung der Texts führt kein kontinuierliches Band bis zu denen in der Gegenwart. Es gibt also keinen kompetenten Sprecher des Althebr. Mehr und somit keinen, der kompetent über diese Sprache informieren könnte ('Informant')" (Wolfgang Richter, *Grundlagen einer althebräischen Grammatik* [St. Ottilien: EOS Verlag, 1984]).

[11]Ibid., v.i, p. 6.

[12]Ibid.

Samuel and its relationship to one's interpretation of the Psalms, makes this a crucial question. The issue at stake is whether the OT texts are to be read eschatologically, that is, messianically, as was the case in the NT, or historically and thus understood only in terms of the anointed David of Israel's past. The question itself, however, turns on little more than the nature of a single vowel and an accent. Is the vowel with the word על a long vowel? (so the MT), or a short vowel (so the LXX and Vulgate)? Is its accent a disjunctive accent? (MT) or a conjunctive accent? (LXX, Vulgate)

Not only is the modern reader of the biblical text dependent on a late system of vocalization, but also the actual everyday language of the Bible, as such, is no longer accessible to us. What we have in its place is the *literary* language of the biblical texts, which itself comes to us in a fragmentary form.[13] This language, moreover, shows very few signs of diachronic development, leading to the conclusion that biblical Hebrew as a whole experienced a leveling towards the final stages of the Old Testament's composition. The language of biblical Hebrew, in other words, is remarkably uniform.[14]

All these linguistic features of the Hebrew Bible have important implications for biblical theology. They mean, first, that a study of the text and the language of the text should focus primarily on the text itself. Careful attention should be given to the Masoretic vowels and accents. The fact that they may be secondary does not diminish their importance. On the contrary, it makes understanding them all the more important. The present consonants, vowels, and accents of the Hebrew Masoretic text, though sometimes secondary, are nevertheless the text of Scripture that we now have. We must understand them, as such, before we can make a judgment about their meaning and originality since for the most part, they represent the original intent of these texts with remarkable accuracy. A text-oriented OT theology cannot dispense with the task of biblical philology.

What we have just said about the Hebrew Masoretic text of the OT throws into striking relief the theological importance of biblical translations. In the Greek Septuagint, for example, we have a version of the OT nearly a thousand years earlier than the Masoretic text. That is not to say that the Masoretic text is always, or even often, a late, or inferior, text. It is rather to suggest that in the early versions of the OT we have a viable alternative witness to the meaning of the text of Scripture, and thus the potential for an alternative biblical theology. For a text-oriented approach to OT theology, such early versions are of inestimable value. When we add to this the fact that the NT writers often used the Septuagint version of the OT in their quotation of the OT, it becomes quite clear that we can scarcely overestimate the importance of these early biblical translations.[15]

Finally, the fact that the language of biblical Hebrew comes to us in the form of literary texts, and not as an independent language per se, makes the study of the literary shape and compositional structure of the OT Scriptures all the more important. When we look at what we actually have of biblical Hebrew in the Bible, it becomes obvious that

---

[13]"Die althebr. Umgangssprache lässt sich hinter der Literatursprache (fast) nicht mehr erreichen. Identität beider kann nicht vorausgesetzt, sondern muss nachgewiesen werden" (ibid., v.i, p. 7).

[14]Ibid.

[15]A definitive discussion of the importance of the Hebrew text and Greek versions is found in Klaus Haacker and Heinzpeter Hempelmann, *Hebraica Veritas, Die Hebräische Grundlage der biblischen Theologie als exegetische und systematische Grundlage* (Wuppertal: R. Brockhaus, 1989).

we are not dealing with purely linguistic raw data. Every word, every phrase, every clause comes to us as part of a larger interconnected whole. It is a whole in which every part has been construed in a specific and particular way. The parts are pieces of meaningful texts, not discreet utterances of a neutral language. OT theology is thus dependent on an understanding of the biblical languages as parts of texts and stages in compositional strategies.

3.2.1.4. Compositional Strategies

Earlier in this book we discussed *composition criticism* as the study of the literary strategy of the biblical books. It attempts to trace the ways the biblical writers organized and fashioned literary units into unified texts and whole books as well as to understand the theological characteristics of their finished works (see Fig. 7.7).[16]

When viewed as a whole, biblical texts can be approached as single literary units composed of many smaller units of texts. In the interweaving of these parts into a whole, a discernible strategy can be traced throughout the entire work. That strategy is the key to the theology of the book. In the Pentateuch, for example, key poetic texts are deliberately placed after large narrative segments in order to provide those segments with a poetic, and often eschatological and messianic interpretation.[17] The various law codes within the Pentateuch are also deliberately placed within a larger nar-

COMPOSITION CRITICISM

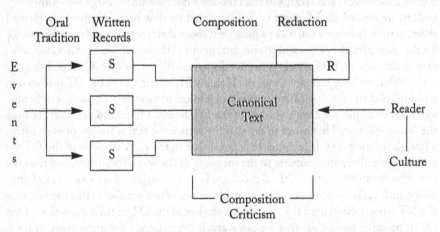

1. Approaches the OT text as a literary unit
2. Describes the literary strategy of the scriptural text

Figure 7.7

---

[16]Georg Fohrer, *Exegese des Alten Testaments, Einführung in die Methodik* (Heidelberg: Quelle and Meyer, 1983), 142; "Dabei liegt das Hauptgewicht auf dem Bemühen, Aufbau, Komposition und Absicht der Endgestalt der einzelnen Bücher zu erfassen. . . . Mit der Frage nach der Komposition der jetzigen Bücher tritt jedoch ein neuer Gesichtspunkt hinzu, der über die bisherigen Fragestellungen hinauszuführen versucht" (Rolf Rendtorff, *Das Alte Testament, Eine Einführung* [Neukirchen- Vluyn: Neukirchener, 1983], ix–x).

[17]John H. Sailhamer, *The Pentateuch as Narrative* (Grand Rapids: Zondervan, 1992), 35–37.

rative framework consistent with a text strategy showing the continual failure of the law to produce obedience to God's will.[18] In the case of the Pentateuch, the theological motivation behind the strategy of the work is twofold. First, the Pentateuch demonstrates both the failure of the Sinai covenant and the hope that lies in the yet-future new covenant. In this respect it is similar in meaning and intent to the rest of the books of the OT, particularly those of the prophetic literature. Secondly, the Pentateuch looks forward to the eschatological future for the coming of a savior-king who will defeat Israel's enemies and restore the blessing God originally intended for all humanity "in the last days."[19] (A study of the compositional strategy of the Pentateuch is found in Appendix A.)

3.2.1.5. In-Textuality

The compositional strategy of a biblical text can be traced at various levels.[20] The cohesive nature of the strategy of the smallest literary unit is called *in-textuality*. Schmidt defines in-textuality as a distinct "illocutionary act" performed by a segment of a text. A text as a total communication act is a coherent network of such discreet utterances. Any one of these discreet segments is an in-text (see Fig. 7.8).[21] This simply means that the various parts of even the smallest literary units can be expected to belong together and to make sense as a whole.[22] In-textuality, then, is the inner coherence of the smallest units of text.

An analysis of the compositional strategy of a biblical book begins with the in-textuality of each biblical passage. The inner cohesion of the smallest passage is as important as the structural unity of the entire book. Finding the in-textuality of a biblical passage involves a close analysis of the smallest literary unit. One may employ various kinds of critical analysis. Form criticism, for example, may be necessary to demonstrate the boundaries of a discreet textual unit. By means of form criticism, a poem or a psalm may be detected by certain formal characteristics. Source criticism can also be of service. The isolation of an earlier source in Isaiah 2:1–4 and Micah 4:1–4, for exam-

---

[18]Ibid., 47–59.

[19]John H. Sailhamer, "The Canonical Approach to the OT: Its Effect on Understanding Prophecy," *JETS*, 30 (September 1987): 307ff; Sailhamer, "The Mosaic Law and the Theology of the Pentateuch," *Westminster Theological Journal*, 53 (1991): 241–61.

[20]For a helpful discussion of the concept of "levels" within a biblical narrative text, see Shimon Bar-Efrat, "Some Observations on the Analysis of Structure in Biblical Narrative," *VT*, 30 (1980).

[21]"Werden in einem Kommunikationsakt mittels verschiedener Aeusserungsmengen verschiedene unterscheidbare Illokutionsakte realisiert, und lassen sich diese Illokutionsakte hierarchisch in ein kohaerentes System einordnen, dann gilt die gesamte Aeusserungsmenge, die die Illokutionshierarchie vollzieht, als Text; die Aeusserungsmengen, die unterscheidbare integrierte Illokutionsakte vollzeihen, heissen Intexte" (Schmidt, *Texttheorie*, 150).

[22]This point was made decisively clear for the OT by Otto Eissfeldt, "Die kleinste literarische Einheit in den Erzählungsbüchern des Alten Testaments" (*Kleine Schriften*, Erster Band eds. Rudolf Sellheim and Fritz Maass [Tübingen: J. C. B. Mohr (Paul Siebeck), 1962], 143–49).

Text

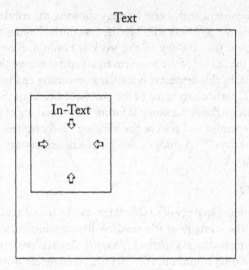

Figure 7.8

ple, is a necessary prelude to an assessment of the compositional strategy of segments of these books.[23]

In a text-oriented approach, one must be careful, in seeking to describe the in-textuality of a passage, not to view the various critical methodologies as ends in themselves. Normally, the aim of using form criticism is to reconstruct the early "life setting" or *Sitz im Leben* of a specific literary unit. When using form critical tools in the analysis of in-textuality, however, the aim is always the *Sitz im Text* or "text setting." Isolating a distinct literary form is of value here only to the extent that it elucidates the present text strategy. In the opening chapter of the book of Nahum, for example, form critical analysis of 1:1–8 reveals a poetic text arranged in an alphabetic acrostic. What is of interest to the in-textuality of the passage, however, is that the acrostic is only partially preserved. In this acrostic, in fact, the last half of the alphabet has been omitted. We can thus see that in the composition of this chapter, an acrostic hymn was used, but it was deliberately shaped and arranged to suit the textual strategy of the first chapter. The form critical analysis of the early acrostic enables us to see better the new contours of the present text. Thus form criticism is not used for its own sake, but to elucidate the present shape of the text.

Much attention has been devoted to the in-textuality of biblical texts in recent years, often in response to the emphasis on literary and source criticism of the previous generations. In the Genesis flood account, for example, source criticism has long held that two distinct flood narratives have been merged into the present narrative. Recent studies of this passage, however, have revealed a distinct compositional strategy which encompasses the entire text:

---

[23]See John H. Sailhamer, "Evidence from Isaiah 2," *A Case for Premillennialism, A New Consensus*, eds. Donald K. Campbell and Jeffrey L. Townsend (Chicago: Moody Press, 1992), 90–101.

Transitional introduction (6:9–10)
1. Violence in creation (6:11–12)
2. First divine speech (6:13–22)
3. Second divine speech (7:1–10)
4. Beginning of flood (7:11–16)
5. The rising flood (7:17–24)
    God remembers Noah
6. The receding flood (8:1–5)
7. Drying of the earth (8:6–14)
8. Third divine speech (8:15–19)
9. God's resolve to preserve order (8:20–22)
10. Fourth divine speech (9:1–17)
Transitional conclusion (9:18–19)[24]

What this analysis of the flood account demonstrates is that there is a distinct in-textuality to the flood narrative. It has a shape and a strategy. The discovery and elucidation of such strategies is vital to a text-oriented OT theology. It is precisely in such structures that one would expect to find the beginnings of a larger compositional strategy and ultimately a biblical theology. (The in-textuality of a section of the Pentateuch is demonstrated at length in Appendix B.)

3.2.1.6. Inner-Textuality

Not only do we find strategies within the smallest units of text, but such strategies, in fact, make up the whole fabric of biblical narrative books. Such inner-linkage binding narratives into a larger whole is called inner-textuality.

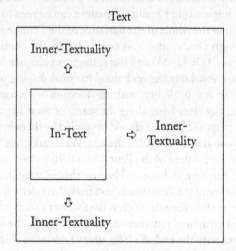

Figure 7.9

---

[24]B. W. Anderson, *JBL*, 97 (1978): 38. Quoted by Gordon Wenham, *Genesis 1–15* (WBC; Waco, Tex.: Word, 1987), 1:156.

By means of such links the biblical authors thematize their basic message. Inner-textuality is thus of central concern to a text-oriented OT theology. As an example of such strategies, we will note here some observations about the shape of the Pentateuch which we have made elsewhere.[25]

Several major poetic texts are found interspersed throughout the narratives of the Pentateuch, most notably in Genesis 49:1–27; Exodus 15:1–17; Numbers 23:7–10, 18–24; 24:3–9, 15–24; and Deuteronomy 32–33. A close study of the author's use of narrative and poetry sheds considerable light on the final shape of the work. The technique of using a poetic speech and a short epilogue to conclude a narrative is well known in biblical literature and occurs frequently within recognizable segments of the Pentateuch itself. The Creation account in Genesis 1 and 2 concludes with the short poetic discourse of Adam in 2:23 which is followed by an epilogue (2:24). The account of the fall in Genesis 3 concludes with the poetic discourse in 3:14–19 and an epilogue in 3:20–24. The account of Cain in Genesis 4 concludes with the poetic discourse in 4:23 and the epilogue (4:24–26). The fact that this same pattern can be found throughout the Pentateuch suggests that it was an important part of the compositional technique of the author of the book. Most notable is the occurrence of this pattern in the Joseph story (Ge 37–48) which concludes with the poetic discourse of Jacob's blessing of Ephraim and Manasseh (48:15–16, 20).

This pattern recurs at a much higher level within the Pentateuch itself, suggesting that the technique was part of the structure embracing the whole of the book. First, the pattern is found in the inclusion of the large poetic text, Genesis 49:1–27, at the close of the patriarchal narratives, along with the epilogue of Genesis 50. Secondly, the two major narrative units which follow that of Genesis, the Exodus narratives and the Wilderness narratives, are both concluded by a similar poetic section, Exodus 15 and Numbers 23–24 respectively. Finally, the pattern can be seen to embrace the whole of the Pentateuch in that the whole of the narrative of the Pentateuch, which stretches from Genesis 1 through Deuteronomy, is concluded by the poetic "Song of Moses" and "Blessing of Moses" (Dt 32–33) and the epilogue of chapter 34.

If such a compositional scheme lies behind the final shaping of the Pentateuch, as it appears, it would be wise to begin here with the question of the compositional purpose of the book. Are there any clues lying along the seams of these large units that point to the author's ultimate purpose? If so, we should be guided by them in any further probing into the author's purpose at a lower level in the text. We should thus begin our investigation of the compositional purpose of the Pentateuch with a closer look along the seams of these large units of narrative and poetry. Here we should attempt to uncover the basic hermeneutic of the author of the Pentateuch, and from there demonstrate the use of that hermeneutic at lower levels in the text. Such is the focus of a study of inner-textuality.

At three macro-structural junctures in the Pentateuch, the author has spliced a major poetic discourse onto the end of a large unit of narrative (Ge 49; Nu 24; Dt 31). A close look at the material lying between and connecting the narrative and poetic sections reveals the presence of a homogeneous compositional stratum. It is most noticeably marked by the recurrence of the same terminology and narrative motifs. In each

---

[25]See John H. Sailhamer, *The Pentateuch as Narrative*, 35–37.

of the three segments (especially Ge 49:1; Nu 24:14; Dt 31:28–29), the central narrative figure (Jacob, Balaam, Moses) calls an audience together (imperative) and proclaims (cohortative) what will happen in the "end of days."

The brief narrative prologue to the poetic text in Genesis 49 tells us that the central figure, Jacob, had called together his sons to announce to them "that which will happen at the end of days" (Ge 49:1b). Thus, however we may want to translate the terminology he has employed,[26] in this seam introducing the poetic discourse of Jacob the author has provided the reader with an indispensable clue to its meaning. Jacob's poetic discourse was about what will happen at the "end of the days."

In an identical macro-structural position within the seam connecting the poetic text of Deuteronomy 32 with the whole preceding narrative of the Pentateuch, we find another narrative prologue with the same terminology and motif. The central figure, Moses, had called together the elders of the tribes (Dt 31:28) to announce to them the trouble that will happen "in the end of days" (Dt 31:29b). Thus in the seams connecting both poetic texts to the preceding narrative segments, and using the same terminology, the author has inserted an identical message to the reader as a clue that the poetic discourses are to be read eschatologically, that is, about "the end of the days."

At one other crucial juncture connecting the large units of poetic and narrative texts in the Pentateuch (Nu 24:14) the same terminology occurs. Here, in the narrative prologue to the last words of Balaam, the author again provides the reader with the necessary hermeneutical clue to the meaning of the poetic texts. Again it has to do with the "last days." As in the other two passages, the events that lie ahead in the future days are revealed in the last words of the central narrative figure, Balaam.

Such convergence of macro-structure, narrative motifs, and terminology among these three strategically important poems of the Pentateuch can hardly be accidental. The fact that the terms occur only one other time in the Pentateuch, and that also within a macro-structural seam (Dt 4), argues strongly for our taking these connecting segments to be the work of the final composer or author of the Pentateuch. As such, they are also a clear indication of the hermeneutic of the author. Not only does the author show throughout his work an intense interest in events of the past, but also the fact that he repeatedly and strategically returns to the notion of the "last days" in giving his work its final shape reveals that his interest lies in the future as well.

The study of the inner-textuality of the poems in the Pentateuch should also raise the question of the internal links between the poems themselves. The poem in Genesis 49:9, for example, speaks of a future king from Judah who "lays down and spreads out like a lion and like a lion, who will arouse him?" In the next major poetic seam (Nu 24:9), the prophetically announced future Israelite king is described in terms identical to those of Genesis 49:9. He is a king who, after defeating the enemy, "lies down and spreads out like a lioness and like a lion who will arouse him?" (Nu 24:9).

Such verbatim use of one text by another through quotation and allusion is the means by which themes and theological ideas are carried along and developed within

---

[26]We believe the phrase should be rendered "in the last days" or "in the end of days," and not merely "in the future." The point we are making here, however, does not depend on how the phrase is translated or, ultimately, what the phrase means. The point here is the role the phrase plays, whatever its meaning, in the final strategy of the book's composition.

the compositional strategy of the book. By means of Numbers 24:17–24, the future king of the tribe of Judah in Genesis 49 is linked to the eschatological king of Israel who, when he comes, will defeat not only the immediate enemies of God's people, the Moabites (Nu 24:17), Edomites (vv. 18–19), and Amalekites (vv. 20–22), but also their future enemies, Assyria and Eber (Babylon?), and their eschatological enemies, the Kittim (vv. 23–24). So striking is the final eschatological victory of this king envisioned in Numbers 24 and so closely are these images paralleled in the later visions of Daniel (e.g., Da 11:30), that classical literary criticism was unanimous in assigning these verses to a later, postexilic, apocalyptic, redactor.[27] The links between these poems in the Pentateuch and later biblical texts such as Daniel point to the importance for OT theology of a consideration of inter-textuality (see below) within the biblical books.

To summarize what appears to be the overall strategy, or inner-textuality, of the Pentateuch in these three segments, we are suggesting that one of the central concerns lying behind the final shape of the Pentateuch is an attempt to uncover an inherent relationship between the past and the future. That which happened to God's people in the past portends of events that lie yet in the future. To say it another way, the past is seen as a lesson of the future and for the future. Because of the terminology used, viz. "the end of the days," we could call it an eschatological reading of the historical narratives. The narrative texts of past events are presented as pointers to foreshadow events that lie yet in the future.

For our purposes these observations lead us to conclude that a consideration of the inner-textuality of the books of the OT is crucial for a text-oriented OT theology.

3.2.1.7. Inter-Textuality

While inner-textuality is the study of links within a text, inter-textuality is the study of links between and among texts. Many written texts, especially biblical ones, were written with the full awareness of other texts in mind. Their authors assumed the

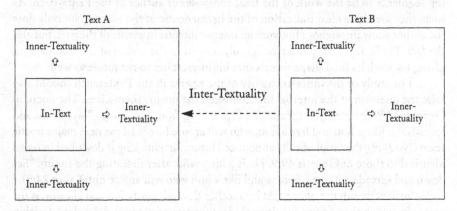

Figure 7.10

[27]H. Holzinger, *Einleitung in dem Hexteuch* (Freiburg: J. C. B. Mohr [Paul Siebeck], 1893), 9 of charts.

readers would be thoroughly knowledgeable of those other texts. The New Testament books, for example, assume a comprehensive understanding of the OT. Many OT texts also assume their readers are aware and knowledgeable of other OT texts.

Inter-textuality can either be *explicit*, as, for example, the verbatim quotation of Micah 3:12 in Jeremiah 26:18, or *implicit* as is shown in Isaiah's question, "Who is this one who comes from Edom?" (Isa 63:1). In this passage, Isaiah's description of the bloodied warrior wreaking revenge upon God's enemies contains many textual clues that link the passage with the poetic texts in the Pentateuch. The reader who is in touch with the themes and images of the Pentateuch will have no trouble answering the question "Who is this one?" The reader who is unaware of the inter-textuality, however, will be lost, or at the most, will fail to appreciate all that the text has to offer. Inter-textuality can also consist of allusions such as Isaiah 1:9, "Unless the Lord of Hosts had spared us a remnant, we would have been like Sodom and like Gomorrah," referring to the story of the destruction of Sodom and Gomorrah in Genesis 19.

It is important to note that, as a rule, the inner-textuality of most biblical texts is sufficient for understanding a biblical book. That is, there are usually enough clues to meaning within a single passage to enable the reader to understand it, at least in general terms. If, however, there is an authorially intended inter-textuality, then it stands to reason that some loss of meaning occurs when one fails to view the text in terms of it. On the other hand, if there has been no intentional inter-textuality, then an attempt to read the text in terms of a supposed linkage with another text will likely distort the meaning of that text. Clear criteria of inter-textuality must therefore be established in biblical exegesis. Although poor or incompetent readers will not "get" everything they read in a text, for there to be a valid inter-textuality there must be some genuine clues for competent readers to follow.

3.2.1.8. Con-Textuality

Con-textuality is the notion of the effect on meaning of the relative position of a biblical book within a prescribed order of reading. What is the semantic effect of a book's relative position within the OT Canon? The book of Ruth, for example, follows the book of Judges in the English Bible, whereas in the Hebrew Bible it follows the book of Proverbs. How does its changing canonical position affect its overall meaning? As is well known, the book of Proverbs closes with an acrostic on the theme of a "virtuous woman" (אֵשֶׁת חַיִל). The acrostic opens with the statement, "*a virtuous woman*, who can find?" (Pr 31:10); and closes with the statement, "her deeds will praise her *in the gates*" (Pr 31:31). In the Hebrew Bible, following directly on these last words of Proverbs, we find the book of Ruth. Climactically within the plot structure (inner-textuality) of the book of Ruth, the defining moment of the book is cast in Boaz's words to Ruth, "All those *in the gate* of my people know that you are a *virtuous woman*" (Ru 3:11). If read within the context of the acrostic at the close of Proverbs, Boaz's words do more than simply acknowledge and thematize what every reader already understands about Ruth from the narrative itself. Viewed con-textually, when Boaz calls Ruth a "virtuous woman," he also links her, as a narrative character, to the wisdom idea in the book of Proverbs. Such a linkage can play a major role in integrating the theme of the book of Ruth with those of the wisdom literature in general.[28]

The concept of con-textuality does not necessitate an intentional linkage of books within the structure of the OT Canon. Con-textuality, as such, merely recognizes the obvious fact that context influences meaning. In this regard, con-textuality is a form of what the cinematographer Sergei Eisenstein called "montage."

According to Eisenstein, montage in cinematography is the effect of meaning which one achieves by juxtaposing two related or unrelated pieces of film. In making a movie, "two film pieces of any kind, placed together, inevitably combine into a new concept, a new quality, arising out of that juxtaposition. This is not in the least a circumstance peculiar to the cinema, but is a phenomenon invariably met with in all cases where we have to deal with juxtaposition of two facts, two phenomena, two objects. We are accustomed to make, almost automatically, a definite and obvious deductive generalization when any separate objects are placed before us side by side."[29]

What makes con-textuality work? And what is its purpose? Again we can approach it as a form of montage. Montage works, says Eisenstein, because competent viewers (or readers) always seek to understand the parts in light of the whole. Juxtaposition of parts implies a whole, so that even where such a whole does not actually exist, a whole is supplied by the viewer (or reader). When the film projector begins to roll the film, there will be montage. The semantic purpose of montage in film (and biblical texts) is to represent themes and images that are larger than the limitation of the medium itself—that is, larger than an individual "shot-piece" (a discreet piece or frame of film). When the materials within two distinct "shot-pieces" are linked by juxtaposing them on the projector reel and thereby onto the screen, the viewer is forced to identify elements of both shots that are characteristic of a single theme or image. A montage thus actually forces the viewer of a film to construct a theme or an image of a theme.[30] The same can be said of the act of reading a canonical sequence such as that found in the OT texts. A canonical order insures that the books of the OT are read in a predetermined context. In the history of the OT Canon there are, in fact, several such canonical contexts, e.g., the order of the English Bible, the Greek Septuagint, or the Hebrew texts, for which, in fact, there are several contending orders.[31] Each of these contexts has its own particular semantic effect (montage) on the meaning of the individual biblical books.

Has con-textuality in the shape of the OT text been intentionally determined? Was Ruth, for example, deliberately placed after Proverbs in the Hebrew Bible because of the link between the "virtuous woman" acrostic at the end of Proverbs and Boaz's use of the same expression in Ruth 3:11? Or, Was the "virtuous woman" acrostic added to the book

---

[28]It should be noted, for example, that each of the five books which follow Proverbs in the Hebrew Canon (Ruth, Song of Songs, Qoheleth, Lamentations, Esther) has a grammatically feminine singular subject: Ruth, the Shulamite, Qoheleth (fem. sing. noun), the daughter of Jerusalem, and Esther. These are the only books in the Hebrew Canon that have a feminine singular subject throughout. This suggests a conscious and intentional grouping of these books after the theme of wisdom as a young woman in the book of Proverbs (cf. Prov 8; 31).

[29]Sergei Eisenstein, *The Film Sense*, trans. Jay Leyda, (New York: Harcourt Brace, 1942), 4.

[30]Ibid., 11.

[31]Christian D. Ginsburg, *Introduction to the Massoretico-critical Edition of the Hebrew Bible* (London: The Trinitarian Bible Society, 1897), 7.

of Proverbs to provide a link for the attachment of the book of Ruth? The concept of con-textuality does not propose to answer such questions. They are important questions, but they go beyond the limits of the concept. Con-textuality only raises the question of the effect of context on meaning, not of the intent that lies behind it. The question of intentionality is addressed by means of the study of OT composition and redaction.

3.2.1.9. Old Testament Introduction

We have already pointed to the fact that a text-oriented OT theology must work closely with and build upon the results of introductory studies of the OT. The study of OT introduction seeks to answer questions about the authorship, date, and circumstances of the biblical books. Did the OT writers use sources in the composition of their books? What was the nature of their work as authors? Introductory questions such as these can bear directly on the meaning of the texts and hence on OT theology.

The study of OT introduction has undergone perhaps more changes and development than any other area of biblical study. In the last century and the early part of this century, OT scholarship was preoccupied with the quest for the earliest versions of the OT books. Both conservative and critical OT scholars sought to locate and describe the first stages of literary and oral composition of the OT. For critical scholars this meant a minimalist approach to the OT since they were often able to find only small fragments of "original" material. But to build a theology on such bits and pieces proved tenuous. Von Rad's famous "old Credo" in Deuteronomy 26:5–9 is a case in point. For von Rad,

> The oldest form of the history of the patriarchs which has come down to us is the opening sentence of the old Credo in Deut. xxvi. 5. Here laconic mention is made of the "wandering Aramean who went down into Egypt and there became a great nation." By this Aramean is meant Jacob. Between this very simple formulation, which is probably also the most concise, and the form in which the history of the patriarchs now appears in Genesis, there lies a very long road in the history of tradition, the main stages of which can, however, be approximately reconstructed. The various units of material with which the history of the patriarchs was slowly enriched derived, of course, from very diverse groups and localities, and also had, initially, only a local and restricted validity. . . . But this building up of the history of the patriarchs from a variety of units of tradition that were originally independent is of great significance for Biblical theology.[32]

One can see in von Rad's approach a desire to find the *earliest expressions* of theology in the OT. Conservative scholarship has also directed its attention to the earliest stages, often going beyond even the textually oriented theology of Moses and the Pentateuch to that of Adam and Eve in the Garden of Eden.[33]

In recent years the interest of OT scholarship has radically shifted. Biblical scholars now find themselves asking questions about the final stages of the biblical traditions. Curiously enough it was von Rad who first sparked that interest. While seeking to trace the development of Israel's faith from its earliest stages, von Rad dramatically brought to light the fact that the final stages of Israel's faith also contained much

---

[32]Gerhard von Rad, *Old Testament Theology* (New York: Harper & Row, 1962), 1:166.
[33]Geerhardus Vos, *Biblical Theology Old and New Testaments* (Grand Rapids: Eerdmans, 1948), 37.

of interest to biblical theology. The principle value of the last stages of Israel's faith lie, von Rad and others began to see, in its proximity to the faith of the New Testament. By focusing on the final shape of the OT, biblical theologians such as Hartmut Gese were able to show that much of the theology of the NT writers, and the early church for that matter, had already been anticipated in the last stages of the composition of the OT.[34]

To my knowledge, little or no attention by conservative or evangelical OT scholarship has focused on this important insight. It has, in fact, always been the chief concern of conservative OT scholarship to find the unity of the OT and NT Scriptures (*unitas scripturae*). In my opinion there is an important and legitimate overlap of interest in some areas of critical OT introduction and Evangelical concerns. Much work remains for conservative biblical scholarship in the area of OT introduction. While the apologetic task of demonstrating the reliability of the OT Scriptures remains a vital issue, attention should also be focused on the final stages of the OT text.

3.2.1.10. Narrativity and Memesis

At several points throughout this book we have alluded to or discussed the concept of the "world making" role of biblical narratives. The fundamental aim of these narratives is to present a world that is to be taken by the reader as a true representation of the real world. But the biblical narratives present more than a worldview. Their primary task is to re-present the "world" itself. That "world" is the one we find described and carefully articulated throughout these narratives.

The ability of the biblical narratives to create such a world lies in its capacity for what Auerbach has called "memesis."[35] The capacity for "memesis" is the biblical narrative's ability to "re-present" its world, a whole world of reality, in such a way that it presents itself to the reader as the real world—the only real world. Moreover, the biblical narratives are also concerned with much more than merely grounding their story in history. They are doing that. But they do it by narrating the very history in which their story is grounded. The biblical narratives are not content to leave the task of representing history to allegedly neutral or independent sources. The only history, the only world that matters, is that which is depicted in their own stories. The reader is invited to become a part of that world and to make its history the framework for his or her own personal life. The reader of the Bible is called upon to submit to the reality represented in Scripture and to worship its Creator.

It is important to see that the biblical narratives are not merely fabricating their world and its history. The Bible is not fiction, but history. The clear intent of the biblical narratives is to establish the fact that this is the only true account of the world. Auerbach has given a telling description of the world that we find depicted in the biblical narratives:

---

[34]Hartmut Gese, "Die Weisheit, der Menschensohn und die Ursprünge der Christologie als konsequente Entfaltung der biblischen Theologie," *Svensk Exegetish Arsbok* (Lund: C. W. K. Gleerup, 1979), 77–114.

[35]Erich Auerbach, *Mimesis, The Representation of Reality in Western Literature,* trans. Willard R. Trask (1946; reprint, Princeton: Princeton University Press, 1953).

The world of the Scripture stories is not satisfied with claiming to be a historically true reality—it insists that it is the only real world, [it] is destined for autocracy. All other scenes, issues, and ordinances have no right to appear independently of it, and it is promised that all of them, the history of all mankind, will be given their due place within its frame, will be subordinated to it. The Scripture stories do not, like Homer's, court our favor, they do not flatter us that they may please us and enchant us—they seek to subject us, and if we refuse to be subjected we are rebels.[36]

As we said earlier, Hans Frei referred to such a reading of the biblical narratives as "precritical." It is precritical because it reflects the attitude of taking the Bible at face value and reading it as a true depiction of reality. Biblical criticism was unwilling or unable to accept such a reading of the Bible. Their view of the world was so markedly different than the Bible's that they eventually rejected the biblical world in favor of their own. Whether they were right in doing so is not the question we are attempting to raise here. We believe they were wrong and that the biblical world can stand the test of modern historical criticism. Nevertheless, the issue at the moment is that biblical criticism, in rejecting the sense of the narrative as "world making," failed to appreciate fully both the true intent of the biblical narratives and the powerful influence these narratives were, and are, capable of exerting on society and the life of the individual. Therefore, one of the chief concerns of a text-oriented approach to OT theology which we are here proposing is the renewal of focus on the world of the biblical narratives. We believe that the Bible and the biblical world continue, and should continue, to play a central role both in the church and in society.

The urgency of this issue lies in the fact that the world depicted in the biblical narratives is crucial for the identity of the Christian Gospel. As Lindbeck has argued, "To become a Christian involves learning the story of Israel and of Jesus well enough to interpret and experience oneself and one's world in its terms."[37] Notions as pervasive as "God" and "the world" are derived in the NT and in our own day from the narratives of the OT. It is an undeniable fact that the whole of the message of the Gospel is grounded in the narratives of Genesis 1–3. Basic NT concepts such as "sin" and "redemption" are meaningful only as they are grounded and developed in these OT narratives. Such concepts are not intuitive or derived from reason or common human experience. They come from reading the biblical narratives. Only the readers of the Bible can know them as part of the real world. The biblical narratives represent the world in such a way that terms such as "sin" and "redemption" have value and make sense only within its frame. The biblical narratives are "a comprehensive scheme or story used to structure all dimensions of existence. . . . [they are] a medium in which one moves, a set of skills that one employs in living one's life."[38] These narratives are, in fact, the very "grammar" and "lexicon" by which we learn the meaning of the Gospel and in which the Gospel makes sense and can be shown to be unique. (See Appendix C for a further discussion of this aspect of biblical narrative.)

---

[36]Auerbach, *Memesis*, 12.

[37]George A. Lindbeck, *The Nature of Doctrine, Religion and Theology in a Postliberal Age* (Philadelphia: Westminster, 1984), 34.

[38]Ibid., 35.

3.2.1.11. Postbiblical Interpretation (Effective History)

A textual approach to biblical theology must recognize and be prepared to deal with the fact that the OT Scriptures have had and continue to have an "effective history,"[39] that is, they continued to be read and studied as Scripture by ongoing communities. The effect of that continued use can be seen within the present text of the OT itself, that is, within what has come to be known as the Masoretic text.

If we think of the Masoretic text as that form of the Hebrew text which was fixed by means of its medieval "tradition" (Masorah), then we should understand it both as the Hebrew text and as an outer shell designed to lock it in place. The thin rigidity of the Masoretic text serves only to mask a delicate state of flux that lies just below its surface. Within that flux, to recall the classic study of Abraham Geiger,[40] there lies a distinct layer of postbiblical exegetical tradition.

In the past, the analytical method of choice in approaching such a text has long been from the "bottom up," that is, the classic diachronic methods of source and tradition criticism. Such methods have rarely resulted in moving beyond their immediate goal, that is, the reconstruction of sources and traditions. To make the step from the sources to the final text and beyond demands a quantum leap. Recent years have seen the flourishing of various synchronic "top down" approaches.[41] Such approaches, however, commonly overlook important historical and theological moments in the postbiblical development of the biblical texts. For that reason, a purely synchronic approach is inadequate.

In place of either a "bottom up" diachronic approach or a "top down" synchronic one, a text-oriented approach should employ an approach that is diachronic and "top down," a text-archaeology, if you will. Starting with the Masoretic text as the last layer of occupation, we should attempt to peel back the postbiblical layers until we uncover the layer of the canonical text (or canonical texts), and from there attempt to isolate both the compositional layer of the individual books and the canonical redaction.[42]

Given the complicated nature of the Masoretic text, a text-archaeology should first attempt to locate the "solid ground" of an individual biblical book (e.g., the Pentateuch) by getting a fix on its beginning and end. We have called this the level of composition, following recent terminology.[43] From there we will have to feel our way out toward the later layers of redaction and canon, eventually reaching the "postbiblical

---

[39]For a further explanation of the concept of "effective history" (*Wirkungsgeschichte*) see Hans-Georg Gadamer, *Wahrheit und Methode* (Tübingen: J. C. B. Mohr [Paul Siebeck], 1960 [4. Auflage 1975]), 284ff.; (*Truth and Method* [New York: Seabury, 1975], pp. 267ff. from the 2d German edition).

[40]*Urschrift und Übersetzungen der Bibel in ihrer Abhängigkeit von der innern Entwickelung des Judenthums* (Breslau: Verlag von Julius Hainauer, 1857).

[41]E.g. structuralism (French, Prague School) and literary analyses of the Bible.

[42]It would be possible to begin at the compositional level and feel one's way back to the sources, as some have advocated recently (Erhard Blum, *Studien zur Komposition des Pentateuch* [Berlin: Walter de Gruyter, 1990]), but that is not the concern of the present study. We are interested here in working in the other direction—from composition to Canon.

[43]Compositional analysis is to be distinguished from redactional analysis. The focus of a compositional analysis is on the features of a text that enable it to be read as a unitary work. The focus of a redactional analysis, on the other hand, is on the features of a text that have resulted from its being included within a larger context (Fohrer, *Exegese*, 140).

crust," that is, the Masoretic or pre-Masoretic text. For an evangelical text-oriented theology, in the process of working with the various layers of postbiblical interpretation, we will have to remain clear in our understanding of the level at which the classical notion of verbal inspiration applies. As we will argue below, that level exists, for the most part, at the point of the composition of each biblical book. We cannot rule out, however, that there are some inspired texts in the OT Scriptures which serve the larger canonical purpose of linking together large units of books.

3.2.1.11.1. Formative Textual Studies of Postbiblical Interpretation

The general concept of *postbiblical interpretation* is not new. The OT has always had its interpreters. What is new, or at least newly appreciated, is the concept that postbiblical interpretation can be found already embedded within the Hebrew biblical texts. This, needless to say, makes it significantly more relevant for biblical theology. Parts of what we might at first have identified as the OT itself, sometimes prove to be postbiblical interpretation—as in the case of textual variants, for example. Moreover, it is also true that parts which have been sometimes taken as postbiblical interpretation, prove to be part and parcel of the OT itself—as in the case of what are sometimes called "harmonistic glosses." Several formative studies of the OT have advanced such a notion:

3.2.1.11.1.1. Abraham Geiger[44] was one of the earliest to argue that the early versions and Hebrew manuscripts of the OT, including the Masoretic text, show discernible traces of postbiblical interpretation. According to Geiger, the final forms of these texts reflect a period of time when local religious groups within postexilic Judaism were actively involved in producing their own versions of the Hebrew Bible. These groups were clearly involved in the process of biblical theology and they left discernible traces of their work in the texts which they handled.

3.2.1.11.1.2. Hans Wilhelm Hertzberg[45] suggested that just as the material in the OT had a "pre-history" (e.g. various literary sources) so also elements in the final Hebrew text continued to have a "post-history" (*Nachgeschichte*). For Hertzberg, these elements show up primarily as "glosses" within the Hebrew texts themselves. Such glosses are heavily laden with theological interpretation. In Isaiah 6:13b, for example, the identification of the remaining "stump" (after the tree has been felled) as an image of "the holy seed" is clearly a gloss, though one that is an integral part of the present text and thus not to be deleted. The same is to be said of the identification of the "many waters" as the royal "seed" in Numbers 24:7. In identifying such texts as glosses, one should not thereby, or at least automatically, delete them from the text. Insofar as they are part of the canonical Hebrew text, that is, were a part of the text at the time of the formation of the Canon, they belong to a text-oriented canonical OT theology.

3.2.1.11.1.3. I. L. Seeligmann[46] demonstrated quite convincingly that the form of biblical exegesis known primarily in later postbiblical commentaries as *derash* had

---

[44]See above note 40.

[45]H. W. Hertzberg, "Die Nachgeschichte alttestamentlicher Texte innerhalb des Alten Testaments," Beiheft 66, *ZAW* (1936): 110–21.

[46]I. K. Seeligmann, "Voraussetzungen der Midraschexegese," *SVT*, 1 (1953): 150–81.

its origin in OT times and in the OT text. There are derashic techniques evident already in the biblical text (*word play*: Isa 5:11; 63:11; *multiple meaning*: Ge 30:23–24; *gematria:* Ge 15:2; Ex 21:1; *atbash:* Jer 51:1, 41; *exegesis:* Ge 15:2) and traces of *derash* no longer extant (Isa 29:22/Ge 15:7, cf. Vulgate, *de igne Chaldeorum*, Ne 9:7).

3.2.1.11.1.4. Michael Fishbane[47] continued the line of thought of the above named scholars, arguing that the received biblical tradition (*traditum*) continued to be carried along by its continual reinterpretation (*traditio*) in subsequent historical contexts. Evidence of such activity can be found in the scribal glossing of texts (Jos 14:14f/21:12) as well as harmonizations that reflect behind-the-scenes discussions of the meaning of these texts.

3.2.1.11.1.5. Moshe Kochavi[48] contributed greatly to the validity of such approaches by publishing an early, 1200–1050 B.C., proto-Canaanite "abecedary" showing that derashic techniques such as *atbash* and *albam* where already known and practiced during the time of the formation of the biblical texts.

3.2.1.11.2. Stages of Postbiblical Interpretation of the Old Testament

Without attempting to establish a strict chronological sequence, the following stages of postbiblical interpretation have been identified by one or more of the above studies. By identifying these stages we are merely saying that some type of postbiblical interpretation can be found, to some extent, at each level. We are not suggesting that the entire level reflects a postbiblical interpretation. In the case of the Masoretic vowels, for example, the fact that some later, postbiblical interpretation can be detected in the vowel patterns of certain individual words does not imply that the Masoretic vowels are late and entirely secondary. These stages are merely ways of identifying the gateways into the Hebrew Bible that were found by later interpretation.

3.2.1.11.2.1. Interpretive Stages in the Formation of the Masoretic Text. The Masoretic text, which developed over a period of nearly a millennium, shows many signs of postbiblical, that is, secondary interpretation.[49] In the consonantal system there are many curious mechanisms for harboring biblical interpretation. The "suspended nun" in Judges 18:30, for example, was introduced into the text to safeguard the honor of Moses. Ginsburg says "that the grandson of the great lawgiver should be the first priest of idolatry was considered both degrading to the memory of Moses and humiliating to the national susceptibilities. Hence . . . the redactors of the text suspended the letter *Nun* (נ) over the name Moses (מֹשֶׁה), thus making it Manasseh [מנשה]."[50] The identification of the prophetically announced future king in Numbers

---

[47]M. Fishbane, *Biblical Interpretation in Ancient Israel* (Oxford: Clarendon Press), 1985.

[48]M. Kochavi, "An Ostracon of the Period of the Judges from 'Izbet Sartah"; and Aaron Demsky, "A Proto-Canaanite Abecedary Dating from the Period of the Judges and Its Implications for the History of the Alphabet," *Aphek-Antipatris 1974–1977* (Tel Aviv: Tel Aviv University, 1978), 34–46.

[49]The most comprehensive study of the textual variants of the MT and their meaning for the postbiblical interpretation of the OT is Friedrich Delitzsch, *Die Lese- und Schreibfehler im Alten Testament* (Berlin: Walter de Gruyter & Co, 1920).

[50]Christian D. Ginsburg, *Introduction to the Massoretico-Critical Edition of the Hebrew Bible* (London: The Trinitarian Bible Society, 1897), 335–36.

24:7b as the victor of Agag (Masoretic text) rather than Gog (Samaritan Pentateuch, Septuagint, Aquila, Symmachus, Theodotion) is clearly intended to link the fulfillment of the prophecy to David's day (e.g., 1Sa 15:8) rather than the Messiah's (Eze 38:3).

Not only do the consonants of the Hebrew Bible reflect postbiblical interpretation, but the vowels do as well. For example, in the Masoretic text, the *qamas* in עַל (2Sa 23:1), which accordingly reads "*on high*," appears to have also been read as with a *pathah* (עַל), meaning "concerning."[51] The effect of the difference in the length of the vowel is such that the title "anointed one" in the MT refers to king David, whereas in other, non-Masoretic versions of the text, David's words are taken as a reference to the Messiah (cf. 2Sa 22:51). Another well-known example of exegesis embedded in the Tiberian Masoretic vocalization system is the revocalization of the names of foreign gods using the vowels of the noun for "shame" (בֹּשֶׁת).[52]

The MT accentuation of a key messianic text, Isaiah 9:5, also reflects the history of the debate that has surrounded this passage. On the face of it, the Davidic king, whose birth is the subject of the verse, is referred to as "Almighty God" in Isaiah 9:5 (EVE 6): "And his name shall be called Wonderful Counselor, Almighty God, Eternal Father, Prince of Peace." The MT accents, however, "insert intermediate points, as though 'eternal Father, Prince of Peace,' were the name of the child, and all that precedes, from 'Wonder' onwards, the name of God, who would call him by these two honorable names."[53] The accents thus represent a fundamentally different reading of this passage than in the NT (Luke 1:32–33).

The Masorah[54] which accompanies the MT reflects a thorough exegesis of the Hebrew Bible that in turn reflects an implicit biblical theology. We have already discussed the effect which the order of the books[55] in the Hebrew Canon has had on the meaning of the Bible. The sectional divisions[56] of the MT also play an important role in assigning meaning to the larger structures of the text. One can see in the open and closed sections, for example, that the MT read the account of the "Sons of God and Daughters of Man" (Ge 6:1–4) as a conclusion to the genealogy of Genesis 5 and not as a prelude to the Flood story. Such a division of the passage can have a profound effect on the interpretation of the pericope.[57] The MT's division of words in Deuteron-

---

[51]Judging both from the external evidence in the Septuagint (ἐπι) and Vulgate (*de*), and the internal, secondary characteristics of the MT's reading. The MT, however, could be original here. In any event, whichever way one decides the case, the passage serves as an example of postbiblical interpretation making its way into the vocalic text.

[52]The pagan diety Melech, "the (divine) king," is called Molech in the MT (2 Kings 23:10) because the vowels of the word "shame" (b-o-sh-e-t) are attached to the consonants (M-l-ch) of Melech, hence, M-o-l-e-ch. Friedrich Delitzsch, *Die Lese- und Schreibfehler*, 69.

[53]Franz Delitzsch, *Biblical Commentary on the Prophecies of Isaiah* (Grand Rapids: Eerdmans, repr. 1969), 1:249.

[54]Christian D. Ginsburg, *Introduction to the Massoretico-critical Edition of the Hebrew Bible* (London: The Trinitarian Bible Society, 1897).

[55]Ibid., 1–8.

[56]Ibid., 9–24.

[57]Cf. John H. Sailhamer, *The Pentateuch as Narrative*, 120–22.

omy 33:2 distinguishes between the concept of "angels,"[58] who brought the law to Moses on Sinai, and the "fiery law"[59] which God himself gave to Moses. Thus, two views of the nature of the Mosaic Law are represented within the MT itself.

3.2.1.11.2.2. The Interpretive Nature of the Early Versions. That early, postbiblical interpretation is to be found throughout the early versions has long been recognized. The account of Creation in the Septuagint of Genesis 1, for example, reflects an attempt to read that account in terms of Hellenistic Greek cosmology.[60] The earliest Targum of Genesis 1 (Neofiti I) read the Genesis account of Creation (Ge 1:1) in light of the "sophia-theology" in Proverbs 8 as well as the "Son of Man" vision in Daniel 7.[61] Neofiti I renders Genesis 1:1, "In the beginning, with Wisdom, the Son of God created the heavens and earth." A rather famous postbiblical interpretation in the Vulgate is its reading of the masculine singular pronoun "he"[62] (Ge 3:15b) as "she," which was taken as a reference to the role of Mary in giving birth to Jesus who would crush the head of the serpent.[63]

3.2.2. A Canonical Approach (- Criticism)

A canonical theology of the OT is based on the canonical text of the OT rather than a critically reconstructed one (see Fig. 7.11).

Because our approach begins with a theological premise, that is, the verbal inspiration of Scripture, we believe the biblical text must be taken as authoritative, that is, as canonical.

---

[58]Reflected in the Septuagint text, reading the Hebrew אשדרת as one word.

[59]Reflected in the MT, reading the Hebrew אשדרת as two words (דת אש).

[60]"The presence of interpretation in the Septuagint of Genesis can be demonstrated from several different angles. In the realm of language Hebrew and Semitic idioms are adapted to the structure of the Greek language and to its feeling for style. . . . It is frequently possible to demonstrate the Egyptian and Alexandrian background from within which the interpretation is made. Particular instances of Greek and hellenistic interpretation are found in the primeval history and in the realm of anthropology. Interpretation can also be seen in a concern to exclude possible misunderstandings. In isolated instances specific religious terms from the Greek and hellenistic world are introduced into the Septuagint. Finally the outlook of this world is manifested in the way the divine name is rendered" (Armin Schmitt, "Interpretation der Genesis aus hellenistischem Geist," *ZAW*, 86 [1974]: 163).

[61]A marginal note in the critical edition of Neofiti I suggests that the translation is a secondary Christian reworking of an original, which read: "In the beginning, with Wisdom, Yahweh created and completed the heavens and earth." The question resolves ultimately into that of the originality of the conjunction "waw" (and) in the translation "and completed" above. It is clear from photographs of the manuscript that the "waw" has been erased by a second hand. In the absence of the "waw" the Aramaic Targum ברא would mean "the son" rather than "he created," hence "The Son of Yahweh created. . . ." The photographs of the manuscripts also show, however, that though the "waw" has been erased, it still appears to have been secondary because there is not enough room between the two words for the "waw" and a space dividing the words. The present text of Neofiti I thus shows a complex history. The earliest text did not have a "waw." The "waw" was written into the text and then subsequently erased.

[62]The originality of the masculine singular pronoun is established with some certainty from the masculine singular form of the verb "(he) shall crush."

[63]"Ergo B. Maria contrivit serpentem; quia ipsa semper plena et gloriosa fuit victrix diaboli. . . ." (Cornelius A. Lapide, *Commentaria in Scripturam Sacram*, Tomos Primus [Paris: Ludovicus Vives, 1868], 106).

2. Criticism or Canon	-	2. *Canon:* It views the text of the OT just as we have it in the OT canon

Figure 7.11

Since the focus of our OT theology is the canonical text, we should seek to ground it in that text rather than in a "critically reconstructed" text or a "traditionally received" text (*textus receptus*). We should emphasize here that in starting with the canonical text, we are not suggesting that we start with the Hebrew Masoretic text, or with any one of the ancient versions. There is, in other words, a text-critical question embedded in the canonical approach: What is the original canonical text of the OT? Choosing the Canon (- Criticism) option, thus, does not mean that one does not engage in biblical criticism. It means rather that the aim or goal of the use of criticism, textual criticism or otherwise, should always be the establishment or exegesis of the canonical text.

What exactly, however, is the canonical text of the OT? This is not an easy question to answer, though we maintain it is answerable. The state of the art in OT textual criticism has left us in a position of some, but not complete uncertainty about the goal of reconstructing the original text of the OT.[64] Where does the process of text formation end and transmission of that text begin? How do we distinguish between the work of an author, a redactor, an editor, and a scribe? Many textual critics today are doubtful that there ever was a point or period of time when an "original" text existed. All we can hope for, they say, is to attempt to reconstruct the earliest form of the text based on the currently available sources. Others allow for an original text, but only as a theoretical goal to aim at, not as something actually obtainable. These are vexing questions indeed.

Fortunately, however, the canonical OT theology which we are proposing, does not have to resolve the question of an original text—even though we hold it to be possible to do so. A canonical approach to OT theology focuses its attention on the shape of the OT text at the time of the formation of the Canon. A canonical approach recognizes as a fundamental axiom of textual studies that the very process of forming the OT Canon has made itself felt in the textual shape of the OT.

A canonical approach to textual criticism is somewhat analogous to a "Flood geologist's" view of Creation. For a Flood geologist, who explains the present shape of the earth by appealing to the catastrophic effect of the biblical Flood, there is little left of the physical appearance of the present earth that sheds light on the original Creation. For a canonical OT textual critic, the present shape of the OT text is explained primarily by an appeal to the catastrophic nature of the formation of the OT Canon. The original text lies buried beneath the present shape of the canonical text. We use the word "catastrophic" only to press the analogy with Flood geology and to stress the global nature of the effect

---

[64]For a helpful discussion see Emanuel Tov, *Textual Criticism of the Hebrew Bible* (Minneapolis: Fortress Press, 1992), 164–80.

of canonization on the text of the OT. To say it another way, and within the same analogy, the effect of the canonization process on the text of the OT was not like the effect of a local flood on the earth's surface. The canonization process was global in that it left its mark over all the surface of the biblical text. We do not intend to imply that the canonization process was "catastrophic" in the extent of its effect on the textual surface of the OT. Most of what remains of the textual surface of the OT is the effect of the composition, or "original creation," of the individual books. Nevertheless, the canonical flood waters have washed over the entire OT text and have shaped that text considerably.

Moreover, because the OT Canon was formed in the pre-Christian era, the subsequent state of the text and its transmission are not the immediate focus of a canonical OT theology. The history of the Masoretic text is of vital importance, however, because it is the starting point of textual criticism, not because it is the final destination.[65] There are thus many questions that are immediately suggested by an appeal to the canonical text as the basis of an OT theology, and we must supply answers for each of them. The point to be made here, however, is that our answers are to be guided and governed by our commitment to the canonical text as the basis of our OT theology. We believe it is precisely such a commitment that gives methodological coherence to the process of doing OT theology.

In Figure 7.12, we have again listed the various methodologies of OT studies. Those on the left aim at the pre-history of the text. Those on the right aim at the canonical form of the OT text.

We should thus recognize that there is an important distinction between the text (canon) and the prehistory of the text (criticism). It is the written text as we have it in its final canonical form that is inspired and useful for instruction (2Ti 3:16). It is the message of this text that is the locus of revelation. Whatever pre-history (criticism) or posthistory (tradition) we may attempt to reconstruct for the text, it should not be considered a source of revelation and hence not the focus of a text-oriented canonical OT theology.

3.2.3. A Confessional Approach (– Descriptive)

A canonical theology of the OT is confessional rather than descriptive (see Fig. 7.13). The recognition of the authoritative nature of the text of Scripture also, we believe, greatly influences our choice of a confessional rather than descriptive approach to the OT's theology. The recognition of the OT as the Word of God entails treating it as a special book. Moreover, if the OT is the Word of God today, our concern cannot be merely with what it once meant to the people of God but must include what it means to us today.

3.2.3.1. Old Testament Theology and the Historical Method

Before turning to the main point of this section, a proposal for a confessional approach to OT theology, we must address a possible misunderstanding about the role and value of the historical method. It should be clear by now that our specific interest

---

[65]Evangelicals, in the desire to stress the verbal inspiration of the OT text, should be careful not to identify the "original" Hebrew text with the MT. This, of course, is what happened during the seventeenth century; but even then, the position actually held was highly nuanced.

CRITICAL AND CANONICAL STAGES IN BIBLICAL NARRATIVE

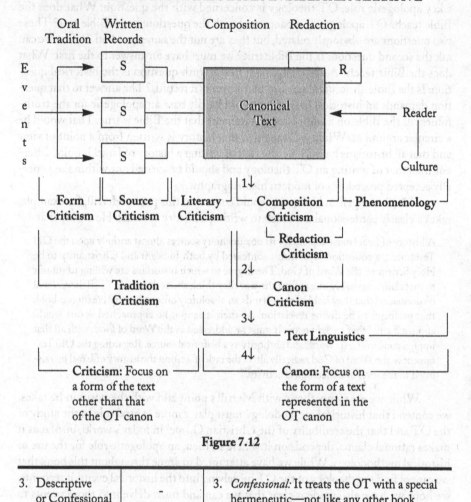

Figure 7.12

| 3. Descriptive or Confessional | - | 3. *Confessional:* It treats the OT with a special hermeneutic—not like any other book |

Figure 7.13

throughout this book in a confessional approach relates specifically to the task of a text-oriented OT theology and not to that of the study of the OT in general. We are thus not suggesting here, or throughout the book, that the historical method has no place in OT studies. On the contrary, we maintain that in many other areas of OT studies, for example, historiography of ancient Israel, archaeology, textual criticism, and philology, the use of historical methodology[66] is essential. For an evangelical

---

[66]We do not intend here to reopen the question of the nature of a genuine historical method and the role of specifically "critical" studies.

approach to the study of the OT in general, for example, historical methodology plays a key apologetic role. OT theology is concerned with the question: What does the Bible teach? OT apologetics is concerned with the question: Is the Bible true? These two questions are obviously related, but they are not the same question. Before we can ask the second question: Is the Bible true? we must have an answer to the first: What does the Bible teach? A key component of the truth question is the historical question: Is the Bible an accurate account of the events it records? The answer to that question demands an historical basis. One could hardly base an apologetic for the truthfulness of the Bible on a confessional statement that the Bible is true. That would be a circular argument. While we recognize that history is written from a point of view and that all historians have a bias, the task of writing a history of Israel is quite different than that of writing an OT theology and should be carried out within the generally accepted procedures of modern historiography.

Not all evangelical historians would concur on this point. Merrill, for example, takes a clearly confessional approach to writing a history of Israel. He argues that

> A history of Israel must depend for its documentary sources almost entirely upon the Old Testament, a collection of writings confessed by both Judaism and Christianity to be Holy Scripture, the Word of God. The degree to which historians are willing to submit to that claim inevitably must affect the way they think about their task. . . . Believers will be persuaded that they hold in their hands an absolutely unique literary creation, a book that professes to be divine revelation. As such it cannot be approached as one would approach any other ancient texts. It must be addressed as the Word of God, with all that implies concerning its worth and authority as a historical source. Regarding the Old Testament as the Word of God radically alters the task of writing the history of Israel by raising it to the level of a theological activity.[67]

While we are sympathetic with Merrill's point and with the position he takes, we contend that historical methodology must play a more central role in the study of the OT and that the credibility of the Christian Gospel in today's world, insofar as it makes rational claims, depends on it. There is, then, an apologetic role for the use of historical methodology. While we have attempted to argue throughout this book that we cannot find the theology of the OT by delving into the historical events it recounts, we hope we have also made it clear that we can and must delve into those events to determine and demonstrate the Bible's trustworthiness as an accurate account of God's actions.[68]

---

[67]Eugene H. Merrill, *Kingdom of Priests, A History of Old Testament Israel* (Grand Rapids: Baker, 1987).

[68]The apologetic use of historical and archaeological method is as old as the sciences of history and archaeology themselves. For a recent discussion of the Old Testament and history see Kenneth A. Kitchen, *The Bible in its World, The Bible & Archaeology Today* (Downers Grove: InterVarsity, 1978). Wenham correctly argues that "although the theology of the biblical writers is not proved by the historicity of their narratives, it would be invalidated if the events or situations it professes to explain could be shown never to have occurred. Thus, modern historians cannot prove the biblical theologies of history, but they can, in principle, disprove them" (Gordon J. Wenham, "History & the Old Testament," in *History, Criticism, & Faith* [Downers Grove: InterVarsity, 1976], 30).

3.2.3.2. Old Testament Theology and Hermeneutics

The heart of the matter in a confessional approach to OT theology is the question of how we should interpret the OT. Does the OT require a special hermeneutic (*hermeneutica sacra*)[69] to properly understand its theological message? We maintain that it does. We also maintain, however, that such a decision does not rule out an essentially historical goal, that is, understanding the original author's intent. We maintain that we can best achieve our historical purpose, the biblical author's intent, by means of a special hermeneutic (*hermeneutica sacra*).

At the start of our discussion we must remind ourselves that our goal here is not the apologetic task of demonstrating or proving the OT to be true. Our task is understanding what the Bible says. Though we cannot separate these two tasks for long, we must separate them long enough to obtain a satisfactory answer to the question: What does the OT teach? The answer to that question depends directly and precisely on what the OT is—not merely what it claims to be, but what it, in fact, is. There is, in other words, a prior question. If the OT is divine revelation, then, as Gerhard Maier has argued, understanding the Bible and interpreting it has to do with the unique, one-time situation, that in this written text God has spoken.[70] If that *datum* is true, then there is a need for a special hermeneutic.

In earlier times, the need for a special hermeneutic for the Bible was universally recognized. The reason for such a recognition was the universal agreement that God had spoken in the biblical texts. Given the understanding of the OT as divine revelation, the idea that it requires a special hermeneutic was self-evident. We may say, then, that while we would maintain the importance of a general apologetic,[71] we would insist on a special hermeneutic. Moreover, it is by means of such a special hermeneutic that we arrive at the historical goal of the biblical author's intent.

What should a *hermeneutica sacra* consist of today? Are there examples from the past or present which we can draw from to sketch the main outlines of such an approach? In what follows we will review the central features of two examples, one from the past and one from the present, taking them as clues for our own development of a confessional approach to OT theology. They serve as particularly apt examples for this proposal because they are both predicated on the notion of the divine inspiration of the OT Scriptures.

In the past, the most influential statement of the principles of *hermeneutica sacra* was Rambach's *Intitutiones Hermeneuticae Sacrae* (1725).[72] In Rambach's textbook, in

---

[69]"*Hermeneutica sacra*, if one looks at the origin of the sense of the word, is that faculty of interpreting the divine Scriptures. It is called *sacra*, however, when it is to be distinguished from profane (hermeneutics), which has to do with the interpretation of human writings" (Johannes J. Rambach, *Institutiones Hermeneuticae Sacrae* [Jena: Ex Officina Hartungiana, 1725]).

[70]"Aber Bibelverständnis und Bibelauslegung haben es mit dem einmaligen Fall zu tun, dass sie einer schriftgewordenen Botschaft begegnen, die mit dem einzigartigen Anspruch auftritt, dass hier, und hier allein Gott zuverlässig redet" (Gerhard Maier, *Biblische Hermeneutik* [Wuppertal: R. Brockhaus Verlag, 1990], 11).

[71]It matters little at this point whether such a "general apologetic" consists of a form of classical foundationalism (evidentialism), voluntarism (belief in God is properly basic), or fideism (faith alone). For a helpful discussion of these alternatives see the essays in *Faith and Rationality, Reason and Belief in God*, ed. Alvin Plantinga and Nicholas Wolterstorff (Notre Dame: University of Notre Dame Press, 1983).

fact, *hermeneutica sacra* reached its definitive form.[73] Gerhard Maier has recently produced an excellent contemporary example of a *hermeneutica sacra* in his *Biblische Hermeneutik* (1990).[74] It would go far beyond the purpose of this book to attempt a full exposition of all that a *hermeneutica sacra* would entail. We will settle here for a general survey both of the classical approach of Rambach and the contemporary approach of Maier.

3.2.3.2.1. Rambach's Hermeneutica Sacra

Most of what is found in Rambach's textbook is directly applicable to the task of OT theology today. Rambach, and most others in his day,[75] believed that the special qualities of Scripture required special qualities, or gifts (*dona*), of the interpreters of Scripture. If the Scriptures were inspired by God (*theopneustia*) then the interpreters of Scriptures must be "born again" (*regenitus*) and led by God's Spirit (*illuminatus*). Given the central premise of the present book, which is similar, if not identical to that of Rambach's, there is much to be gained from a closer look at his hermeneutic. We should also keep in mind that it was against Rambach's hermeneutical principles that Jean Alphonse Turretini[76] and Johann August Ernesti[77] directed their critique of *hermeneutica sacra* and thereby initiated the purely historical approach to the interpretation of Scripture.

For Rambach, biblical hermeneutics could be viewed both in a popular form, which was applicable to virtually all Christians, and a specialized form, which was

---

[72]Rambach was preceeded by Johann Conrad Dannhauer, *Hermeneutica Sacra*; Johannes W. Baier, *Compendio Theologiae Exegeticae*; August Pfeiffer, *Hermeneutica Sacra*; August Hermann Francke, *Praelectioni Hermeneutici*; Johann Henrich Maius, *Introductio ad Studium Philologicum, Criticum et Exegeticum*; Valentine E. Loescher, *Breviario Theologiae Exegeticae, Legitimam Scripturae Sacrae Interpretationem*; Andrew I. Dornmeier, *Philologia Biblica* (Leipzig, 1713).

[73]In Rambach's own day this assessment of his textbook was widely accepted: "Omnibus autem dubiam hic palman reddidit IO. IAC. RAMBACHIUS, in *institutionibus hermeneuticae sacrae.* . ., in quibus plene, perspicue, solide, cuncta, quae sacrarum litterarum interpretem instruere possunt, complexus est" (Johann F. Buddeus, *Isagoge Historico-theologia* [Leipzig, 1730], 1244); It remains the opinion of contemporary historians: "Franckes hermeneutische Grundsätze sind in wissenschaftlich strengere Form gebracht und weiter entfaltet worden durch das ein Menschenalter lang beliebteste hermeneutische Lehrbuch: die Institutiones hermeneuticae sacrae . . . des Joh.Jakob Rambach" (Emanuel Hirsch, *Geschichte der Neuern Evangelischen Theologie* [Gütersloh: C. Bertelsmann Verlag, 1951], 2:178).

[74]"Die genannten Beobachtungen . . . veranlassen uns, eine besondere 'biblische Hermeneutik' zu bejahen. . . . wir müssten unsere Augen vor der Wirklichkeit verschliessen, wenn wir die Besonderheit der göttlichen Offenbarung in der Bibel verleugnen und das Verstehen der biblischen Botschaft zu einem Teilbereich der 'normalen' menschlichen Hermeneutik machen wollten" (Gerhard Maier, *Biblische Hermeneutik* [Wuppertal: R. Brockhaus Verlag, 1990], 16).

[75]Though Rambach was a Pietist, the central themes of his *hermeneutica sacra*, as well as its influence, extended far beyond pietistic circles. As the discussion throughout his work shows, Rambach was doing little more than systematizing the hermeneutical practices of his orthodox predecessors, both Lutheran and Reformed.

[76]*De Sacrae Scripturae interpretandae methodo tractatus bipartitus, In quo Falsae Multorum Interpretum Hypotheses Reflectuntur, Veraque Interpretandae Sacrae Scripturae Methodus adstruitur* (1728).

[77]*Institutio interpretis Novi Testamenti* (1765).

applicable to a select group of learned theologians. In a popular sense, *hermeneutica sacra* was a practical ability (*facultas practica*) of all Christians, instructed by a sound mind and the right tools as well as illumined by the Spirit of God, to find the basic meaning of Scripture as it pertained to their salvation and use in everyday life.[78] In a more developed sense, however, Rambach understood *hermeneutica sacra* as a practical learnedness (*habitus practicus*) by which trained theologians, instructed in the necessary disciplines and led by the Holy Spirit, are rendered fit for investigating the legitimate sense of Scripture, expounding it, and applying it wisely to life in such a way that God's glory and human salvation are promoted. Rambach quotes approvingly Dannhauer's comparison of Scripture to a great work of art which anyone can appreciate to a certain extent, but which the learned observer is able to study in depth and defend against false interpretations.[79]

3.2.3.2.1.1. The Necessary Characteristics of the Interpreter. Rambach begins by focusing on the personal character (*dispositio*) of the interpreter.[80] Though any individual Christian qualifies as an interpreter of Scripture, proper interpretation rests on three types of gifts (*dona*) which the interpreter of Scripture must possess: (1) natural gifts, (2) acquired gifts, and (3) spiritual gifts. Natural gifts, that is, those obtained from birth, consist of simple good sense attributes such as judgment, ingenuity, and a good memory. There is little hope for proper interpretation of Scripture without those personal qualities. Acquired gifts consist of a thorough knowledge of the original languages of Scripture, grammar, rhetoric, logic, doctrine, mathematics, history, chronology, geography, and ancient customs. Neither these acquired gifts nor one's natural gifts are sufficient, however, for an adequate interpretation of Scripture. The interpreter must also possess spiritual gifts which neither nature nor diligence are able to produce. What is required, according to Rambach, is a "soul imbued with a living sense of divine things and joined to God."[81] Such a disposition is necessary because the Bible itself teaches that "divine mysteries are revealed only to those who fear him."[82] Thus one's intellect must be "flooded with that purer heavenly light which dispels the dense night of ignorance in which the minds of mortals, immersed in the vices of nature, have fallen, and without which they are not able to know rightly and wholesomely the mysteries of the Word of God."[83] To

---

[78]Rambach, *Institutiones*, 2.

[79]"Iam quid est universa scriptura sacra, nisi pictura rerum divinarum? Nemo christianorum est, qui non hic videre possit, quantum ad salutem ei sufficit: nec deest illi regula communis, quam quum sequitur, aberrare nequit. At theologus pluribus subsidiis instructus, exercitatioribus sensibus politus, pro gradu talenti et vocationis, plus videre debet; nec videre tantum, sed et vindicare a pseud-hermenia" (quoted in Rambach, *Institutiones*, 3).

[80]"De legitima interpretis sacri dispositone" (Rambach, *Institutiones*, 9).

[81]"Atque hic generatim requiritur, ut. . ., adsit animus vivo rerum divinarum sensu imbutus, ac DEO junctus" (ibid., 16).

[82]"Arcana enim Domini cum timentibus ipsum communicantur" (ibid.).

[83]"Speciatim INTELLECTUS sacri interpretis perfusus sit puriore illa ac caelesti luce, quae spissam ignorantiae noctem, cui mentes mortalium naturae vitio immersae iacent, dispellit, sine qua verbi DEI mysteria recte ac salutariter agnosci non possunt" (ibid.).

this basic need for spiritual illumination is added "divine wisdom," "love for Jesus Christ," "love for Scripture which testifies of Christ," "sincerity of heart," "humility," and "tranquility."

It is important to understand that for Rambach, these qualities, or gifts, do not replace the long and arduous study of the literal sense of the biblical text. On the contrary, the exercise of these gifts comes only through just such attentive and constant focus on Scripture.[84] Moreover, Rambach fully recognized the problems that human frailty and depravity posed to such a view of hermeneutics, and thus warned of the importance of constant prayer and self-criticism. Perhaps because of his dependence on spiritual illumination in understanding Scripture, Rambach has sometimes been described as holding the idea that one must assign to the meaning of a word or passage all that the word or passage is capable of meaning. Hence his view is sometimes credited with leading to pietistic excesses.[85] It is clear from Rambach's *Institutiones*, however, that this is a false characterization of his position. Rambach expressly condemns as an "excess" the view that "the words of Scripture mean all that they are capable of meaning."[86] His express goal is to allow for a spiritual dimension in exegesis, not to replace sober grammatical-textual study with spiritual excesses.

3.2.3.2.1.2. The Necessary Characteristics of the Scriptures. For Rambach, *hermeneutica sacra* not only involved necessary personal qualities in the interpreter of Scripture, but also certain qualities resident in the Scriptures themselves. For the most part, Rambach's list of characteristics parallels that of classical orthodoxy. Basic to those characteristics is the divine origin and authority of the written texts, including the consonants, vowels, and accents.[87] The integrity of the OT text was assured by divine providence so that it has come down to us without corruption.[88] The text we now have is, moreover, characterized by a singular and majestic simplicity. Anyone who reads it will know what is to be believed and how it is to be applied to life. Behind this simplicity also lies a great depth and profundity, as well as a real and effectual power

---

[84]"Hinc porro efflorescet sedulum atque *indefessum studium* in legendis attentissime ac meditandis scripturis, tantaque patientia laboris, quae nullis difficultatibus deterreatur" (ibid., 18–19).

[85]Hirsch says of Rambach, "Er hat die Formel geprägt, man müsse jedem Wort der Bibel soviel Fülle des Sinns und Soviel Schwergewicht beilegen, als die Natur der mit ihm gemeinten Sache überhaupt nur zulasse" (Emanuel Hirsch, *Geschichte der Neuern Evangelischen Theologie* [Gütersloh: C. Bertelsmann Verlag, 1951], 2:178).

[86]"Excessu scilicet peccant . . . COCCEII sectatores, ex quorum hypothesi verba scripturae tantum significant ubique, quantum significare possunt" (Rambach, *Institutiones*, 56–57). Rambach goes on to suggest that Coccejus himself used this principle with moderation.

[87]Ibid., 24. Like many in his day, Rambach mistakenly identified the medieval Masoretic text(s) with the original: "A viris tamen prudentioribus, qui periculosissimas istius theseos consequentias curatius pervident, merito punctis vocalibus Theopneustos auctoritas vindicatur. . . ." (27). His reasons for doing so, however, were not historical, but theological: "quia illis demitis, scriptura neque perfecta esset, neque certa . . ." (27–28).

[88]". . . all those details which consitute the biblical text, divine providence has carefully guarded, lest in any important or meaningful part of them there should be the slightest corruption" (ibid., 29).

in the life of the reader. Behind the natural impact of the human words of Scripture lies a supernatural power which is clearly seen in their ability to produce spiritual effects and resources beyond the merely human.[89] It was certainly this view of the nature of Scripture which lay at the heart of Rambach's confessional approach. The aim of heremeneutics is to understand Scripture in all its spiritual dimensions. That requires an accurate understanding of the nature of the written text itself as well as a receptivity to the work of God accomplished through that text.

Rambach also had an understanding of the unity of Scripture and of its interconnectedness. His discussion of the "coherence" of Scripture is, in fact, remarkably modern in its understanding of the textuality of the meaning of the biblical text. In Rambach we find a full appreciation for the textual nature of divine revelation coming of age. His textbook, in fact, represents a level of textual understanding that was to remain dormant for over two centuries during the "eclipse" of the biblical narrative phase.

3.2.3.2.1.3. The Single Literal and Mystical Sense of Scripture. Rambach is clear that he holds to the *single meaning* of the words of Scripture.[90] Like many before him, however, he distinguished between the meaning of the words (*verba*) of Scripture and the meaning of the things (*res*) which those words portrayed to the mind.[91] Both senses were part of the single meaning of Scripture. This allowed him to establish a linkage between the literal meaning of Scripture and its mystical sense. Both were linked to the single meaning by identifying the literal sense with the meaning of the words (*sensus litterae*)[92] and the mystical sense with the meaning of the things which the words call to mind (*sensus mysticus*).[93] Since, according to Rambach, meaning resided in "words and things," the single meaning of Scripture could entail both a literal and a mystical sense.[94] Note should be taken here not to confuse Rambach's notion of "things" with historical entities in the external world. For Rambach and those who preceded him, the "things" to which words referred were understood simply as the meaning which words render to the mind. A "word," as Rambach understood it, was merely a sign for a meaning of a "thing" (*res*). This was a common usage of the Latin word *res* throughout much of the history of hermeneutics. After Rambach, beginning

---

[89]". . . sed scripturae sacrae, praeter vim illam naturalem, supernaturalis etiam inest, quae in adfectibus spiritualibus, et supra hominum vires positis, producendis luculenter conspicitur" (ibid., 35).

[90]"Equidem unius sermonis unicus tantum esse potest sensus" (ibid., 55).

[91]". . .interim sensus ille, ab auctore intentus, vario respectu varie dividi potest . . ." (ibid., 55). The origin of this view of words and meaning in Christian theology can be traced back to Augustine: "All doctrine concerns either things or signs, but things are learned by signs . . ." (*On Christian Doctrine*, book 1, part 2).

[92]". . . sensus *litterae* dicitur, estque ille conceptus, quem verba ipsa, non nisi grammatice intellecta, in animo legentis gignunt" (Rambach, *Institutiones*, 57).

[93]". . . sensus mysticus, per quem intelligitur ille conceptus, qui non proxime per verba, sed per res, vel personas, verbis designatas, a spiritu sancto intenditur" (ibid., 67).

[94]That Rambach is simply representing the classical orthodox view here is clear from Soloman Glassius' definition of the *sensus mysticus* as that sense "which is signified not in the words (verbis) of Scripture immediately, but in the things themselves (ipsis rebus) denoted literally by the words and intended by the Holy Spirit, the author of Scripture . . ." (*Philologia Sacra* [Leipzig, 1623], 406).

in the late eighteenth century, the Latin word *res* came to mean an historical entity, an object or event in the external world. Rambach does not use the term in that sense.

What is important to see in Rambach's approach to the meaning of the words of Scripture is the commitment he feels toward both the literal sense of OT and its spiritual value. Even in defining the spiritual sense of the OT, Rambach is careful to note that this sense was intended by the Holy Spirit in the words of the original authors.[95] In other words, one cannot find a spiritual meaning in the OT without some warrant from the text itself that this was the intended meaning.[96] Rambach has little new to offer his reader in validating such a spiritual meaning in the OT text. He follows the traditional Christian practice of allowing a "mystical" sense in those texts which attribute a grander, more elevated, sense to persons or things than the ordinary meaning of the words would suggest,[97] or to those texts which elsewhere in Scripture are interpreted with a mystical sense.[98] In seeking the "mystical" sense of Scripture, Rambach seeks to avoid two extremes, (1) that which finds unwarranted hidden mysteries everywhere in the OT and (2) that which does not look for them at all and therefore never discovers the divine wisdom contained in the Word of God.

3.2.3.2.1.4. The Analogy of Faith (*Analogia Fidei*). There is a clear logic to Rambach's description of *hermeneutica sacra*. Having opened the door on discovering hidden mysteries in the Scriptures, he turns immediately to the necessity of the control of such interpretations, namely, the use of the analogy of faith (*analogia fidei*). For Rambach, as for the whole of the confessional church before and after him, the analogy of faith is the consensus of truths (*veritatum consensum*) found in the whole of Scripture.[99] Whatever truths one discovers in Scripture must meet the test of conforming to the teaching of the whole of Scripture. The parts must conform to the whole. The *analogia fidei* is the norm by which all interpretations of Scripture are judged.[100] For Rambach, that such a norm truly exists is based on the concept of divine inspiration. The same Spirit of God revealed his singular will through each and every biblical writer. A basic unity thus underlies the whole of Scripture. Moreover, for Rambach, the *analogia fidei* cannot consist of a system of doctrine (*habitus credentis*) because that would make it an arbitrary human standard and hence capable of error.[101]

---

[95]". . . a spiritu sancto intenditur" (Rambach, 67); ". . . mysticus a spiritu sancto, summo scripturae auctore, non minus intendatur, quam litteralis" (ibid., 68).

[96]". . . minime tamen putandum est, in quolibet scripturae loco illum esse quaerendum: Sed ibi tantum indagandus atque amplectendus est, ubi illum a spiritu sancto intendi, ex certis criteriis constat" (ibid., 73).

[97]"Intra ipsum textum vestigia sensus mystici conspiciuntur, quando rei, vel personae, de qua verba proxime agunt, adeo augusta atque illustria praedicata tribuuntur, quae ei secundum omnem verborum emphasin non conueniunt" (ibid., 74).

[98]"Nonnumquam criteria sensus mystici aliunde accersenda sunt, quando spiritus sanctus in alio loco sive expresse, sive implicite nos de sensu mystico alicuius loci reddit certiores" (ibid., 75).

[99]"ANALOGIAM FIDEI intelligimus . . . nihil aliud designat, quam mutuum perpetuumque veritatum caelestium consensum, e planissimis sacrarum litterarum testimoniis collectum" (ibid., 88).

[100]"Ut adeo *analogia pisteos* sit summa praecipuorum doctrinae sacrae capitum, quae arctissimo inter se vinculo connexa, normam velut ac regulam constituunt, ad quam cuncta sunt exigenda" (ibid., 90).

[101]"Nam . . . habitus fidei per doctrinam fidei demum producitur, adeoque ipsius doctrinae norma esse non potest. Norma enim prior est suo normato"; "Fidei habitus variis infirmitatibus expositus est. Nunc

A norm must be infallible and certain[102] and thus must consist of the actual statements of the Scriptures insofar as they are viewed harmonistically and as a whole. Though human reason is an instrument by which we come to discern the meaning of Scripture,[103] it can never become the norm itself. That would mean excluding from Scripture all that appears to exceed the bounds of human understanding.[104] In the same way, church tradition and the history of interpretation serve as visible standards by which we evaluate our understanding of Scripture, but they can never be the norm.[105] In the final analysis, "the laws of legitimate interpretation demand that we ask what the author wished to say, not that which we ourselves think should be said."[106] Thus the source of the *analogia fidei* is Scripture alone,[107] rightly interpreted according to the sound principles of hermeneutics.[108]

We have looked at some length at the *hermeneutica sacra* of Rambach because we think there is much in his approach that is helpful for an evangelical confessional OT theology today. Rambach's starting point, a divinely inspired text, is identical with current evangelical views of Scripture. Rambach is thoroughly "textual" in his approach and thus stresses the importance of all the linguistic tools of textual study. Moreover, Rambach stresses the need for long and intensive reading of Scripture as the key to its understanding. As we have already noted, his sensitivity to the basic textuality of Scripture and divine revelation make his observations remarkably current and relevant. His notion of the "analogy of faith" is essentially the same as the concepts of con-textuality and canonical redaction discussed earlier in this book. The theologian is not constrained by church doctrines, but by the sense of the whole of Scripture. Moreover, that global sense is textually discernible in the seams and strategies of the final shaping of the Hebrew Canon.

Finally, the linkage that Rambach and others have seen between the meaning of the words of Scripture and its "mystical sense" is not far from the insights of modern studies in inter-biblical interpretation. We have attempted to show throughout this book that the OT text does not come to us without its own interpretation. Some

---

[102]erroribus . . . scrupulis . . . titubationibus . . . laborat: adeoque in scripturae interpretatione normae loco adhiberi non potest" (ibid., 90).

[102]"Norma enim debet esse infallibilis ac certa" (ibid.).

[103]"Nam licet usus eius instrumentalis in negotio exegetico neutiquam repudietur . . ." (ibid., 93).

[104]"Minime igitur audiendi sunt, qui humanam rationem scripturae tamquam iudicem obtrudunt, nihil in divinis tamquam verum admissuri, quod ratio capere non possit" (ibid.).

[105]"Videndum tamen est, ne in alterum extremum ruamus, abdicatoque rationis usu, ecclesiae traditionibus, aut partrum auctoritati eum honorem deferamus, ut hunc demum genuinum putemus dictorum sensum, quem illi nobis summo consensu tradiderunt" (ibid., 100).

[106]"Leges enim legitimae interpretationis poscunt, ut quaeramus, quid auctor dicere voluerit; non quid ex nostra mente dicere debuerit" (ibid., 93).

[107]"Fons, unde analogia fidei haurienda, est ipsa scriptura sacra, eiusque planissima oracula, quae nulla prorsus obscuritate laborant" (ibid., 101).

[108]"Scilicet si adfirmative de sensu alicuius loci pronuntiare velimus, tum non semper inferre licet: hic sensus analogiae fidei est conformis, ergo verus, et ab auctore intentus. . . . Necesse igitur est, ut et reliqua veri sensus criteria in subsidium vocentur, nisi quis falli ac fallere velit; ut adeo is demum genuinus scripturae sensus habeatur, qui secundum regulas hermeneuticas, rite adhibitas, exsurgit, et fidei analogiae est conformis" (ibid., 105).

of that interpretation is postbiblical and some of it is compositional and canonical. In any event, a textual approach to the theology of the OT Scriptures cannot afford to disregard the growing evidence that a significant layer of meaning in the biblical texts gives up its secrets only after much careful observation of the parts and the whole. One aspect of that meaning, the messianic sense of the whole of the OT, will be illustrated in the next section.

3.2.3.2.2. *Gerhard Maier's* Hermeneutica Sacra

Another helpful example of a confessional approach to biblical hermeneutics is the recent work of Gerhard Maier.[109] In this book, Maier calls for an approach to biblical interpretation that is commensurate with the unique nature of the Bible itself and yet does not give up important historical interests. As a description of his approach, Maier has chosen the name "biblical-historical" exegesis[110] to distinguish it from the historical-critical exegesis of modern biblical scholarship and the historical-biblical exegesis of his earlier writings.[111] In suggesting a new name, however, Maier has not changed his original proposal. He contends that putting the word *historical* first in the name, as he had earlier argued for, leaves open the possibility of misunderstanding the central role of the Bible in his approach. The method is specifically biblical rather than strictly historical in nature. Thus the name "biblical-historical," with the word *biblical* placed first, expresses the priority and uniqueness of the Bible and does not overlook the importance of history.

Throughout this book, Maier goes to some lengths to show his acknowledgment of the waning interest in history as such in the modern world and, in the face of it, to plead the case for its continuing importance for biblical Christianity. Maier acknowledges that ethical and environmental concerns have taken center stage in biblical and theological studies and thus "truth" often is cast in categories other than historical fact. Truth, says Maier, is more apt to be conceived in terms of "relevancy" than in terms of "the past."[112] In today's world, says Maier, historical truth is on the defensive. Nevertheless, biblical revelation which testifies to the acts of God in history cannot minimize the importance of history. "Even if the whole world wanted to dispense with the notion of history, the people of the Bible could never permit it for themselves."[113]

In attaching the prefix *biblical* to the word *historical*, however, Maier wishes to make an even more important distinction. In a biblical-historical method of interpretation, the biblical data takes precedence over the historical. It is thus possible to speak of a "biblical-ethical" or "biblical-spiritual" exegesis alongside that of a "biblical-his-

---

[109]Gerhard Maier, *Biblische Hermeneutik* (Wuppertal: R. Brockhaus Verlag, 1990).

[110]"Diese Ueberlegungen haben mich dazu bewegt, hier den Begriff 'biblisch-historisch' zuwählen. Er wird m.E. der Besonderheit der Bibel eher gerecht, die eben eine bibelgemässe Auslegung fordert. Er bewahrt aber zugleich das ernsthafte historische Interesse, das nicht aufgegeben werden darf" (ibid., 332).

[111]Gerhard Maier, *The End the Historical-Critical Method*, trans. Edwin W. Leverenz and Rudolph F. Norden (St. Louis: Concordia, 1977 [orig. 1974]).

[112]"Nicht, was 'war', sondern, was 'wahr' ist, treibt uns um" (Maier, *Biblische Hermeneutik*, 333).

[113]Ibid.

torical" one (p. 333). That is not to depreciate the importance of history, but serves rather to show the central importance of the Bible. In all of these hermeneutical approaches, Maier argues, the Bible must come first and thus serve as the norm by which history, ethics, or even spirituality is handled. There is, thereby, an openness (*Offenheit*) in methodology, because all approaches to the Bible lie under the final authority of the Bible and not that of a predetermined "scientific" (*wissenschaftliche*) method (p. 334).

3.2.3.2.2.1. The Context of *Hermeneutica Sacra*. Along with its openness to method, Maier's approach is also bound by certain controls. Principle among them is its ties to the *ecclesia*, the community of faith. Just as the historical-critical (*hermeneutica profana*) method is linked to the community of *academia* (the university), *hermeneutical sacra* must answer to the church. It is within that context that biblical interpretation must operate. There are, in fact, several contexts within the community of faith to which *hermeneutical sacra* is responsible. The first, and most fundamental, is the individual life of the biblical interpreter: "Our exegesis begins with our own life history" (p. 335). This is not to say that the meaning of the Bible is merely a function of our particular life experience. On the contrary, it is only by placing ourselves under the authority of the biblical text and conforming our lives to it through prayer, repentance, and godliness, that we can come to understand the meaning of the historical authors: "Being rooted in faith means that the interpreter of Scripture does not stand before an isolated text or an abstracted linguistic medium, but rather there, in the text, the interpreter always hears the voice of the living God . . . a voice that demands a response" (p. 335). Biblical interpreters stand before the Scriptures; the Scriptures do not stand before them. Biblical authority means submitting oneself to the teaching of the Bible.

Not only do interpreters stand within their own personal faith when they approach the text of Scripture, but they must also reckon with a wider context, the community of faith. Every generation of biblical interpreters has had to answer to the needs of its own community, and every community of faith has had its own specific needs. "The specific issues of each generation bring specific aspects of the biblical message into clearer light" (p. 335). Biblical interpretation, if it is to meet the needs of its generation, must not operate in an academic vacuum. Interpretation is not the task of a guild or clique. It stands bound and responsible to the church.

Maier casts the relationship of *hermeneutical sacra* to the church in terms of five spiritual dimensions: prayer, interaction, conversation, correction, and praxis. (1) Prayer: The biblical interpreter must, in prayer, ask for divine guidance and help in understanding Scripture. (2) Interaction: The biblical interpreter must recognize his or her need of the gifts of others within the believing community (1Co 12). (3) Conversation: The results of biblical interpretation must be given in such a way that they are understood and appreciated by the whole of the church. "The lack of conversation between theologians and non-theologians in the recent past has much to do with the fact that theologians hardly even strive to be understood anymore, indeed, any attempt to do so hints at superficiality." (4) Correction: The goal of biblical interpretation is a total involvement of the community of faith in a common understanding of Scripture. For biblical theologians that means not only speaking to the community but also listening to the community and being willing to accept its corrective insights. (5) Praxis: As a member of the community of faith, the interpreter, like all other members, is called upon to serve in praxis. The biblical theologian must also visit the sick, help the poor, and win the lost (p. 336).

3.2.3.2.2.2. The Beginning Process of *Hermeneutical Sacra*. Maier lists three initial steps in the process of *hermeneutical sacra*. First, the biblical interpreter comes to the text as a continuation of his or her own situation in life, not as a distant object of study, but as the source for hearing the voice of God. "He does this with prayer. In his prayer he seeks to be filled with the same Holy Spirit to do his work as the biblical authors themselves in their work. He knows that his prayer—one thinks here of Luther's oratio!—will not keep him from error. But he also knows that even with his errors he may serve the community for which he has been called as an interpreter of the Bible. He knows that his prayer is determinative for the fellowship which he has with God, who also speaks to him perhaps in this very text. And he knows that this fellowship is decisive for his interpretation of Scripture and the fruit it will bear" (pp. 337–38).

Second, in interpretation, one comes to the biblical text expecting a struggle between oneself and God who speaks in this text. The interpreter knows his or her own heart and its tendency to distort and change the voice of God which speaks in the text. One knows the limits of one's own willingness and readiness to see what is written there. Moreover one knows the distance that separates one's duty and one's actions. In all of this there lies the temptation to distort God's Word (p. 338).

Third, one comes to the Scripture recognizing the deep dependency of the interpreter on a thorough familiarity with the meaning of the text itself. One strives to know it and expects a revelation, a basic insight, from it. One's position before Scripture must be characterized by prayerful expectation and humble openness (pp. 338–39).

3.2.3.2.2.3. Interpretation Is Grounded in the Text. All interpretation for Maier begins with the scriptural text. There is thus a need to establish correct manuscript witnesses to the text and to determine the meaning of the individual words. These tasks are the aim of textual criticism and classical biblical philology.[114] To these is added the "historical" task of exegesis. The Bible must be understood and interpreted "historically" (p. 343). There is, however, a distinctly biblical dimension to Maier's historical interpretation. "The biblical-historical interpreter must take special note of the fact that also here one does not work as a historian, nor is he merely concerned with the process of reconstructing historical events, but rather as a theologian in service to the church. History therefore is not understood by him as an independent series of actions, but rather it always remains the realm where God acts (*Aktionsraum*)" (p. 343). This is quite different than the usual historical methodology which does not recognize God as a factor in historical events. The biblical historian, however, reckons not only with the events of history but with God himself in history

---

[114] Maier prefers to speak of "establishing the text" (*Textfeststellung*) rather than "textual criticism" because historical criticism has taken this legitimate concept of "criticism" as a justification for its own application of negative criticism to Scripture (ibid., 340–41).

(p. 343). There is thus room for miracles and prophecy in one's understanding of God's acts recorded in Scripture (p. 345).

Not only must the biblical interpreter deal with the events of history as they are portrayed in Scripture, but also with the literary composition of Scripture as it is presented in the biblical Canon. For Maier, the "hypotheses" of modern critical methods are an inadequate basis for a divine revelation for the church. *Hermeneutica sacra* therefore must take its starting point in the biblical Canon,[115] ". . . a biblical-historical exegesis in every case is based on the final form (*Endgestalt*) of the canonical text. 'In,' 'with' and 'under' the developmental history (*Entstehungsgeschichte*) of a biblical text the activity of God is at work. The historical event of inspiration has allowed this text to develop in just such and such a way and thus has brought it to its final form and placed it in a distinct position within the Canon. While the voice of the living God can be heard at best only very indistinctly, it is heard loud and clearly in the final form of text that lies before us" (p. 344).

3.2.4. A Diachronic Approach (+ Diachronic)

A canonical theology of the OT arranges what is revealed in the OT diachronically (see Fig. 7.14). The historical dynamics of the formation of the Hebrew Bible, we believe, are such that a diachronic approach to its theology is the most appropriate method. As we have argued earlier, however, we should not forget that the particular structure we give to our OT theology is more a matter of systems theory than it is any inherent rightness or wrongness. The first question is that of purpose. What do we expect to achieve in giving an OT theology this or that shape? Given a specific purpose, a synchronic approach may well be preferred. We are suggesting here, however, that if our general purpose is to understand the theology of the OT in its own terms, given the nature of the material itself, a diachronic approach is to be preferred.

There are three characteristics of the Hebrew Bible which lend themselves to a diachronic approach: inter-textuality, canonical redaction, and con-textuality.

3.2.4.1. Inter-textuality

It is of the nature of inter-textuality itself to proceed diachronically. Some biblical texts presuppose, on the part of their readers, a rather thorough knowledge of

4. Diachronic or Synchronic	+	4. *Diachronic:* It approaches the OT in terms of each of its parts rather than attempting to view it as a whole

Figure 7.14

---

[115]"Historische Arbeit bleibt verschwistert mit der Bildung von Hypothesen. Offenbarung und Glaube aber zielen auf Gewissheit. Die Exegese wagt sich also mit ihrer historischen Arbeit stets auf eine stürmische, immer wechselnde See. Um im Bild zu bleiben: Diese See ist allerdings nicht uferlos, sondern hat feste Ufer. Aber nicht die Hypothesen sind es, die diese Ufer bilden können, sondern nur der kanonische Text" (ibid., 344).

other, previously written texts. Here the order of reading is important. On a larger scale, it is not hard to see that the NT books presuppose a knowledge of the OT on the part of their readers. Within the OT itself, however, what is the order of priority? Which books are assuming a knowledge of other writings? And of what other writings are they assuming a knowledge?

It is important to make clear that these questions are not being asked within the context of the literary history of the OT. We are not asking, for example, whether the Pentateuch preceded or followed the prophetic literature.[116] We are rather asking, from within the texts themselves, what order of priority of the existing texts is being maintained? The fact, for example, that the opening paragraph of the book of Joshua refers to an authoritative written "Mosaic Torah" (Jos 1:7), is crucial for understanding the meaning of the book of Joshua. The clear conceptuality of the Joshua narratives is that we are to read them in the light of the canonical Pentateuch. Moreover, when the "book of the Torah" was later discovered in the temple during the reign of Josiah (2Ki 22:8), it is highly probably that we are to understand this as the same Torah which Joshua had and which had been subsequently lost. The use of these texts to argue for and against the Mosaic authorship of the Pentateuch has unfortunately obscured the narrative purpose of these inter-textual references. We are not gainsaying the importance of using these texts for such an apologetic purpose. We are rather saying that such a purpose was not a part of the narrative strategy and meaning of the text and thus does not play a direct role in developing the theology of these texts.

It is safe to say provisionally that the underlying assumption of the Hebrew Canon is that the Pentateuch is the fundamental document to which the rest of the Hebrew Bible is related inter-textually. Its mere priority within the Canon is enough to establish the essential correctness of this assumption. This is, moreover, clearly demonstrated in the example of Joshua 1:8, and can be documented as well in later texts such as Nehemiah 9, Daniel 9, and Psalm 78 which build unequivocally on the pentateuchal Scriptures and assume a high level of authority for them. The structure of the book of Chronicles, whose composition was nearest the time period of the formation of the Canon and which assumes the priority of the pentateuchal material by beginning with Adam, also strongly suggests the Pentateuch's fundamental role within the Canon. The evident reflection of these texts on the message of the Pentateuch shows that already within the Hebrew Canon, its first section is considered basic and essential.

A major question, then, is resolved by the structure of the Hebrew Canon itself: How is the theology of the OT to be arranged diachronically? Taking our clues from

---

[116]It seems to me that here lies the principle weakness of Walter Kaiser's otherwise helpful concept of the "analogy of antecedent Scripture" (Walter C. Kaiser, Jr., *Toward an Old Testament Theology* [Grand Rapids: Zondervan, 1978], 16). Kaiser's "analogy" means he must know which texts were antecedent to others. It is not enough, for example, to say that since the events of the book of Judges preceded those of the books of Samuel, that Judges is antecedent to Samuel. The "events" of the narratives were certainly antecedent, but not necessarily the narratives themselves. Kaiser must show that the book of Judges was written before the book of Samuel if he is to have any "antecedent Scripture (written text)." In other words "antecedent events" are not the same as "antecedent Scripture."

the Canon itself, we arrive at the structure: The Law, the Prophets, and the Writings. The Law (Pentateuch) is basic to the rest of the books, which they in turn assume and build inter-textually on the Pentateuch. Internal analogies to the structure of the Canon as a whole come from parallel compositions, such as Genesis–Kings and Chronicles, and parallel segments, such as 2 Samuel 22 and Psalm 18.

3.2.4.2. Canonical Redaction

The recent interest in the "end redaction" of the books of the Hebrew Bible, has alerted biblical scholarship to the possibility that there may be more to lists of canonical books than merely the establishment of authoritative boundaries. There may also have been an accepted shape, or end redaction, to the Hebrew Bible as a whole. The notion that the Hebrew Bible has a meaningful shape is not new.[117] What is new is the focus of scholarship on the hermeneutics and semantics of that shape. Lying behind that interest is the attention given in recent years to text theory, text linguistics, and the semantics of macro-structure, not to mention the obvious impact of canon criticism on OT studies. Though much remains to be worked out in detail, it is possible to say something about the "macro-structure" of the Hebrew Bible.

We will begin with an exploration of the compositional shape of the first book in the Hebrew Bible, the Pentateuch (Ge 1:1–Dt 34:12), which is also the first major segment of the OT Canon. From the "top down," I will seek to locate its beginning and end by assessing its internal shape and something about the semantics of that shape. The beginning of the Pentateuch is Genesis 1:1 and, I will argue, its original conclusion is not Deuteronomy 34:12, but rather Deuteronomy 32:52. Such an assessment of the compositional history of the Pentateuch suggests that the last segment, Deuteronomy 33:1–34:12 has been added secondarily to the original Pentateuch to form the canonical Pentateuch.

Gen.	Dt.	Dt.
1:1	32:52	33:1–34:12

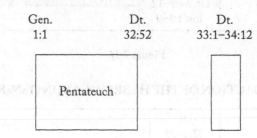

Figure 7.15

---

[117]The discussion that accompanied the lists of canonical books in Baba Bathra 14b, for example, frequently addresses the question of the rationale for the sequence found in those lists. Regarding the order of the major prophets, which put Jeremiah and Ezekiel before Isaiah, the question of sequence is raised, "Isaiah prophecied earlier than Jeremiah and Ezekiel, so shouldn't his book be first?—The book of Kings concludes with desolation, the book of Jeremiah contains all desolation, Ezekiel begins with desolation and ends with consolation, and Isaiah contains only prophecies of consolation; [in the present canonical order, therefore] desolation is thus linked to desolation and consolation is linked to consolation" (*Baba Bathra* 14b).

Second, in what remains of the canonical Pentateuch (Dt 33:1–34:12), we can identify at least two further levels of composition. The first is that which belongs to the composition of the book of Joshua and the remaining historical books (Dt 34:1–8). The second is that which belongs to the canonical shape of the entire Hebrew Canon, the TaNaK (Dt 33:1–29; 34:9–12; Jos 1:1–9) (see Fig. 7.16).

Our goal is not to reconstruct the earlier forms of these various texts, but rather to describe them as the connecting links which give the TaNaK its present shape. Having located the level of composition linking the first two segments of the TaNaK, that is, the Law and the Prophets, we can then compare it with the similar links connecting the Prophets and the Writings (Mal 3:22–24; Ps 1) (see Fig. 7.17).

In our discussion below we will also raise the question of the semantics of the present shape of the canonical TaNaK. Central to the shape of the TaNaK is the attempt to understand the Torah as wisdom and to see it within the context of a futuristic, that is, eschatological hope. When viewed from the "top down," we can discern at least four semantic components underlying the redaction of the canonical TaNaK:

(1) An Ethical Component: Here biblical wisdom is viewed as an "interim ethic." In the viewpoint of the "canonicler," the wise man has replaced the

REDACTION OF THE HEBREW CANON (TaNaK)

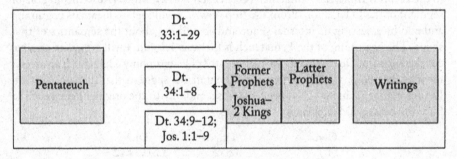

Figure 7.16

REDACTION OF THE HEBREW CANON (TaNaK)

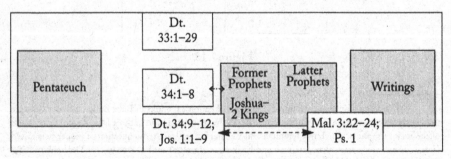

Figure 7.17

prophet as the ideal leader of God's people until the eschaton when the true prophet like Moses will return.

(2) An Apologetical Component: Until the return of the prophet like Moses, the role of prophecy in Israel has ceased. Hence, the Canon, conceived of as prophetic writings, is complete.

(3) A Hermeneutical Component: God's Word is the *written text* of Scripture, rather than the *spoken word* of the prophet. Hence the focus of divine guidance is on reading and interpreting Scripture, rather than on writing it.

(4) An Eschatological Component: With its focus on the return of prophecy, the Canon is open to a new work of God in the future.

3.2.4.2.1. The Final Shape of "the Law"

We turn first to the "Law," that is, the Pentateuch. Over the years, much discussion has gone into the question of where the Pentateuch begins and ends.[118] Does it conclude before or after the account of the death of Moses? Rabbinical and Christian tradition did not speak with one voice on this question. While texts such as Baba Bathra 14a saw the last eight verses (Dt 34:5–12) as a later addition to the Law of Moses, it was not uncommon to refer to the phrase "to the eyes of all Israel" (Dt 34:12) as the last words of the Law. Literary criticism has also not arrived at a consensus on the end of the various documents that lie behind the Pentateuch. We are not here attempting to reopen these discussions, but rather to approach the question from the perspective of a compositional analysis of the present shape of the Pentateuch.

3.2.4.2.2. The Compositional Strategy of the Canonical Pentateuch

From the perspective of its macro-structure, the Pentateuch appears to be composed of four basic kinds of texts: narrative, poetry, genealogy, and laws. When viewed in its totality, only two of these types of texts—narrative and poetry—appear to embrace the whole of the book.

We have noted earlier in this book that at three macro-structural points in the Pentateuch, a major poetic discourse has been spliced onto the end of a large unit of narrative (Ge 49; Nu 24; Dt 32). Moreover, we have suggested that a close look at the material lying between and connecting these narrative and poetic sections reveals the presence of a homogeneous compositional stratum noticeably marked by the recurrence of identical terminology and narrative motifs. In each of the three segments, the central narrative figure (Jacob, Balaam, Moses) calls an audience together and proclaims what will happen at the "end of days." Such convergence of macro-structure, narrative motifs, and terminology among these three strategically important parts of the Pentateuch can hardly be accidental. The fact that this compositional activity

---

[118]See Brevard S. Childs, *Introduction to the Old Testament as Scripture* (Philadelphia: Fortress Press, 1979); Michael Fishbane, *Biblical Interpretation in Ancient Israel* (Oxford: Oxford University Press: 1985); Rolf Rendtorff, *Das Alte Testament: Eine Einführung* (Neukirchen-Vluyn: Neukirchener Verlag, 1983); Wolfgang Richter, *Exegese als Literaturwissenschaft* (Göttingen: Vandenhoech & Ruprecht, 1971); J. A. Sanders, *Torah & Canon* (Philadelphia: Fortress Press, 1972).

encompasses the entire range of the Pentateuch argues strongly for our taking these connecting segments to be the work of the one who gave the Pentateuch its final shape. To state it clearly, they reveal the work of the composer or author of the Pentateuch.

We now raise the question of the boundaries of the Pentateuch. What do the above compositional observations about the shape of the Pentateuch tell us about its "end"? An important clue lies in the observation that each of these poetic texts is followed by a brief narrative epilogue which, in at least two of the three examples, deals with the anticipation of the death and burial of the central figure (Jacob, Ge 49:29–33; Moses, Dt 32:44–52), and in each of the three epilogues the focus is on the identification of a successor (Joseph, Phineas, Joshua). In other words, the central character is still alive, but his successor has been duly chosen in light of his anticipated death. Given such structural clues, it seems probable that the Pentateuch "compositionally" closes with the last of these three epilogues, namely Deuteronomy 32:52.

It is of interest to note that, in terms of the narrative, Moses is still alive at the end of this Pentateuch. I make that point, not for the sake of proving the Mosaic authorship of the Pentateuch, but rather to show why it makes sense that the narrative would cast Moses in the proleptic role of the author of the song in Deuteronomy 32 (31:19, 22) as well as the author of the book itself (Dt 31:24).[119] The history of the question of the Mosaic authorship of the Pentateuch bears ample testimony to the difficulty created by this passage. How can Moses be the author of a book in which he himself dies and is buried?[120] As it now stands in the canonical Pentateuch, the straightforward portrayal of Moses writing out the Torah "completely" and putting it alongside the ark in Deuteronomy 31:24–26, seems oblivious to the narrative fact of his death recounted at the close of the book. At this point in the composition, however, there is no thought of his death and burial having already occurred. It is not without importance that this view of Moses changes significantly in the chapters following Deuteronomy 32, namely, Deuteronomy 33–34.

A curious feature and perhaps an important clue about the compositional closure of the Pentateuch lies in the fact that two poems, not one, are at the end of the Pentateuch (Dt 32, 33). Moreover, the second poem (33) follows the epilogue of Deuteronomy 32:44–52 and thus, if we are correct, appears to lie outside the larger

---

[119]". . . und dann folgt der Schluss des Ganzen 31,24 . . .—es konnte aber nicht der eigentliche Schluss hier eintreten, weil das Lied Mosis zwar angekündigt aber noch nicht mitgetheilt war . . . so sind wir durch diese Schlussformel genöthigt anzuerkennen, dass das Werk als ein dem schriftlichen Ursprunge nach von Moses herrührendes angesehen seyn will . . ." (H.A.Ch. Hävernick, *Handbuch der historisch-kritischen Einleitung in das Alte Testament*, Erster Theil. Zweyte Abtheilung [Erlanger: Carl Heyder, 1837], 161–62).

[120]". . . verse 24 (of Dt 31) is the commencement of an appendix by another hand, whose author distinguishes his work sufficiently from that of Moses . . ." (Carl F. Keil, *Manual of Historico-Critical Introduction to the Canonical Scriptures of the Old Testament* [Edinburgh: T&T Clark, 1881], 1:161); "it follows that his [Moses'] composition ends at ver. 23, and that the remainder, from ver. 24 onwards, forms an appendix by another hand" (Keil, 162); "Eichhorn, (i, 1, p. 223) considers ch. xxxi. 24 to be the subscription by the hand of Moses himself at the end of his work, and vers. 25–30 to be the proper conclusion, necessarily added so as to give, by way of supplement to the history, the song of Moses which had been already announced but not yet communicated" (quoted in Keil, 163).

compositional framework of the Pentateuch. It does not come as a surprise, then, that the poem in Deuteronomy 33 is introduced with a specific and sudden reference to the death of Moses: "and this is the blessing which Moses, the man of God, blessed the sons of Israel before his death" (33:1). All of a sudden, Moses is dead—even though his death has not yet been recorded. It is immediately obvious that this small seam (33:1), which serves to attach Deuteronomy 33 to the rest of the Pentateuch, follows abruptly on Deuteronomy 32:44–52. It does not anticipate, but rather presupposes, the account of the death of Moses in Deuteronomy 34:5.[121] I venture to say, therefore, that viewed from the top down, the most natural closure of the Pentateuch is Deuteronomy 32:52 and that Deuteronomy 33:1–34:12 is an addition to an already completed composition.

When and by whom was the addition made? To answer that question we must look closely at the material in Deuteronomy 33–34 itself, as well as at the larger picture of the formation and shaping of the Hebrew Canon.

3.2.4.2.3. The Canonical Redaction of the Pentateuch

3.2.4.2.3.1. Inner-textual Canonical Redaction. There are a number of further observations that support the conclusion that chapters 33–34 are an addition to an already completed literary composition. These can be grouped under two headings. The first looks at the fact that the various text units which make up Deuteronomy 33–34 intentionally take up and rework earlier texts from the Pentateuch. There are, of course, many places within this Pentateuch where earlier material is taken up and reworked. The difference in Deuteronomy 33–34 is that here the earlier material is not so much retold or restated as it is the object of reflection and exegesis. In other words, these texts reflect a deliberate inter-textuality with the Pentateuch itself. In a word, they are canon-conscious rather than compositional-conscious.[122] They seek to apply or adjust the earlier material in the Pentateuch to a new situation rather than merely attempt to reinterpret aspects of its meaning within the same textual setting.

The second observation about Deuteronomy 33–34 is that the viewpoint or perspective from which the texts were written is noticeably different from the earlier texts. Specifically, their viewpoint reflects what I would call a "Torah-Wisdom eschatology." By that I mean, first, that it represents a view of divine revelation that centers on the written Word as the locus of and source of Wisdom, or divine guidance. God's Word is found by meditating on the written Scriptures. Secondly, within this viewpoint, the dependence on Scripture as a source of Wisdom is viewed as a temporary measure. And thirdly, there is an anticipation of a future return of the role of prophecy as a source of divine revelation. These texts (Dt 33–34) work under the assumption that at the present time prophecy has ceased, but in the future it will be revived. In the meantime Scripture, which was given by the prophets of old, is the source of divine wisdom.

---

[121]Furthermore, Dt 34:1–4 is an explicit *Wiederaufnahmung* of the epilogue in Dt 32:49–52, serving as the introduction to the account of the death of Moses (34:5–8).

[122]The texts I have in mind are Dt 33 (and its relationship to Ge 49); Dt 34:1–8 (and its relationship to Dt 32:48–52/Num 27:12–23); and Dt 34:9–12 (and its relationship to Dt 18:15).

To know the will of God and to become wise, one must meditate day and night on Scripture. It may be helpful at this point to say a word about each of these texts and attempt to show how they reflect the viewpoint just described.

3.2.4.2.3.1.1. Deuteronomy 33:1. As we have said, Deuteronomy 33:1 presents a surprisingly new and quite different perspective on Moses. Up to this point in the narrative, Moses has been treated as a living *persona*, active in the events of the story. In 33:1, however, the narrative character Moses is viewed as a voice out of the past (cf. Ge 50:16). What is particularly striking about this shift in the narrative's perspective on Moses is the fact that there has been no mention of his actual death in the previous narrative. We should note as well that in this text the name Moses occurs with a title, that is, he is a "man of God."[123] It is well known that this title elsewhere in the Hebrew Bible means one who holds the prophetic office.[124] This is the only time the title is used in the Pentateuch. This leads us to the general observation on the sense of 33:1, that here in this part of the book, the words of Moses in 33 are presented as those of an ancient prophet. Moses is thus viewed as a dead prophet.[125]

3.2.4.2.3.1.2. Deuteronomy 33:2–29. The poem itself in 33:2–29 appears to be a deliberate reshuffling of the material found in the poem of Jacob in Genesis 49. As a glance at the textual apparatus will show, this recasting did not stop with the composition of the book itself. It continued in the Hebrew texts which were used by the LXX, the Samaritan Pentateuch, and ultimately was still at work in the formation of the Masoretic text. Though it is far too complicated to deal with adequately here, the following general points can be stressed.

(a) First, the blessing of Moses is preceded by a description of the appearance of God at Sinai "surrounded by angelic hosts."[126] The purpose of this preface is to portray Moses as a prophet who received the Torah from the hand of angels (cf. 1Ki 22:19–23). It is important to note that it is just at this point, with the mention of angels, that the textual history begins to fragment. Not even the Ben Asher text of B19 was able to arrive at a uniform reading of this verse. The Kethib of the MT reads "at his right hand are the mighty ones, viz, the angels [אשׁדת = angel]."[127] The Qeri reads this line as "at his right hand is the fiery law."[128] Thus, in the Kethib, the angels are at the right hand of God to give the Torah to Moses, whereas in the Qeri the flaming Torah itself is at

---

[123]Cf. Jos 14:6; Ps 90:1.

[124]Cf. 1 Ki 13; S. R. Driver, *A Critical and Exegetical Commentary on Deuteronomy* (ICC; Edinburgh: T&T Clark, 1895), 389; Carl Steuernagel, *Das Deuteronomium und Josua* (HAT; Göttingen: Vandenhoeck & Ruprecht, 1900), 123.

[125]Cf. Joseph Blenkinsopp, *Prophecy and Canon* (Notre Dame: University of Notre Dame Press, 1977). In this respect it is similar to the superscription of Ps 90 and the references to the Mosaic Torah in Da 9:10–13 (promise/fulfillment).

[126]Steuernagel: "MT wäre allenfalls zu deuten: von den heiligen Myriaden her, d.h. aus der Versammlung der Engel, die ihn im Himmel dienend umstehen . . ." (127). ". . . apparens cum magna caterva Angelorum, qui per millia sanctorum hic intelliguntur" (S. Münster, *Crit. Sac.*, 266). Aquila: ἀπὸ μυριάδων ἁγιασμοῦ ἀπὸ δεχιᾶς αὐτοῦ = ex myriadibus sanctorum ad dexteram ejus; Cf. 1 Kings 22:19; Psa 89:7; Dan 7:11 (Driver, ICC, 392).

[127]LXX: ἄγγελοι μετ' αὐτοῦ = angeli cum eo; Neofiti 1: "And with him were myriads of holy angels."

[128]Cf. Symmachus: πυρινὸς νόμος; Aquila: πῦρ δόγμα αὐτοῖς = ignis doctrinae eis.

God's right hand and Moses receives it directly from him. According to the traditional interpretation of this passage, it was taken to mean that the Torah was written in fire— black and white fire.[129] In any event, whether by angels or from God himself, written in fire, the Torah is portrayed as divine revelation.

In the next verse, Deuteronomy 33:3, Moses addresses the people, telling them that each one of them has God's holy angels ("His holy ones") in his hand.[130] According- ing to Deuteronomy 33:4, the poetic lines of the preceding verses are to be understood as "the Torah which Moses gave to us." Verse 4 must be explained as an exegetical gloss.[131] This is shown from the fact that it is not Moses who speaks in this verse but rather someone from the congregation (cf. "us") who speaks about Moses. Thus in Deuteronomy 33:4b, the Mosaic Torah is presented as "the possession of the commu- nity of Jacob" just as in Psalm 119:111, "Your statutes are my eternal inheritance." God's people can read the Torah of Moses and meditate on it forever, even after Moses is dead. The fiery words which Moses commanded are now contained in the written words of the Torah. In the Torah are found the words delivered by angels.[132] The angels, as it were, are in their hands.

This view of the Torah contrasts significantly with the viewpoint we have in Deuteronomy 31:24–26 where we find Moses, as an author or scribe, writing out the Torah by hand and giving it to the priest for safekeeping. That seems a far cry from fiery letters or words hand carried by angels. Deuteronomy 33:1–4 appears to add sig- nificant development to the concept of the written Torah. According to Deuteronomy 33, the Torah is clearly presented as divine revelation given by divine inspiration. Moses receives the words of the Torah directly from the angels, the messengers of God (33:3b–4a). The Torah is thereby an oracle of God, written in the tongues of angels. We must immediately note that here we find a view of the written Torah that is remarkably similar to Psalm 1 (cf. 19 and 119). The written Torah is the locus of divine revelation. It is a Torah that has taken the place of the prophet Moses, who gave it to Israel.

(b) A second important feature of the poem in Deuteronomy 33 is the margin- alized role given to the tribe of Judah. In Genesis 49:8–12 Judah is given a central place

---

[129]"i.e. the Law which had been written before Him from olden times in black fire upon white fire" (Rashi).

[130]That the 2ms pronoun ("your hand") refers to each individual Israelite in this passage is clear from Deut. 33:29, "blessed are you [2ms], O Israel." According to 33:3b, "They (the angels) gather at your (Israel) feet," following the sense which Kimchi gives to תכו, viz., "to join together." Each one (of the angels) lifts up a portion of your (Israel) words." The general sense of most interpreters is that this refers to Israel's pos- session of the Law: "they bore upon themselves the yoke of the Law" (Siphre, quoted by Rashi); "they take up your words upon their lips and meditate on them continuously" (Ramban, ad loc.); "Hoc amoris Dei pignus erat, quod ministerium verbi in hoc populo instituisset, ubi licebat ad pedes ejus auditores sedere, et audire verbum ejus in synagogis, et in templo, vel in tabernaculo" (Vatablus, Crit. Sac., 267).

[131]Steuernagel, Das Deuteronomium und Josua, 124.

[132]This is precisely the view expressed by Calvin: "Sed quoniam non quotidiana e coelis redduntur oracula, et scripturae solae exstant quibus visum est Domino suam perpetuae memoriae veritatem conse- crare: non alio iure plenam apud fideles autoritatem obtinent, quam ubi statuunt e coelo fluxisse, ac si vivae epsae Dei voces illic exaudirentur" (Inst. 7:1).

in the leadership of the people. In Deuteronomy 33, however, the leadership of the people is entrusted to the priests whose role it is to teach the Torah (v. 10). Curiously, in Deuteronomy 33:5 Moses the Levite lawgiver is cast in the role of king. Divine guidance is thus a function of the written Torah rather than of a political leader of the house of Judah.

There is only a brief statement about Judah in Deuteronomy 33. It is the cryptic prayer (33:7): "May you bring [בוא] him to his people." The terminology used here suggests that this prayer refers to the illusive phrase in Genesis 49:10, "until Shiloh comes [בוא]." As such, it continues to look to the future for a role for the tribe of Judah. In this poem, then, we find the viewpoint that at the present time the people of God are governed by the priests who teach the written Torah. Yet a prayer remains for the tribe of Judah—a prayer that recalls the central role of that tribe in the future blessing promised in Genesis 49.[133] The inner-textuality with Genesis 49:10 suggests that the poem in Deuteronomy 33 is cast in such a way as to focus the attention given to Judah precisely on the promise of the royal seed and to emphasize the fact that that promise had not yet been fulfilled. It is fitting therefore that the poem in Deuteronomy 33 concludes on a note of future blessing, peace, and prosperity for God's people (vv. 24–29).

3.2.4.2.3.1.3. Deuteronomy 34:1–12.
We turn now to Deuteronomy 34:1–12, the last chapter of the canonical Pentateuch.

3.2.4.2.3.1.4. Deuteronomy 34:1–8 (Dt 3:23–29; 32:48–52/Nu 27:12–13).
The most obvious compositional purpose of Deuteronomy 34:1–8 is to tie together the loose ends in the Pentateuch regarding the death of Moses, which has long been anticipated. But there is more to this passage than that. If Moses has already been told he will die and thus not enter the land with Israel (Nu 27:12–13; Dt 3:23–29; 32:49–50), why repeat it again here?[134] The answer perhaps lies in the additional information supplied in verse 4 where God says, "This is the land which I swore to Abraham, Isaac, and Jacob, saying, 'to your seed I will give it.'" This passage shows that the future possession of the land (Transjordan) is linked to the patriarchal promises. The death of Moses does not mean the end of God's promises. There is, in other words, an important future hope embodied in these words. That hope rests on the promise to the fathers embodied in the Pentateuchal narratives. It transcends the death of Moses.

3.2.4.2.3.1.5. Deuteronomy 34:9 and Numbers 27:23.
In Numbers 27:18–21, it was recounted that Joshua would replace Moses as God's leader. Moreover, in that same passage, Joshua was commissioned by Moses (vv. 22–23). Why then is the commissioning of Joshua recounted a second time in Deuteronomy 34:9? The answer appears to lie in the fact that this verse adds an important feature to the description of Joshua, Israel's new leader. In Numbers 27:18, Joshua is described as a "Spirit-filled" leader, which in that context identifies him as a prophet (cf. Nu 11:25). In Deuteronomy

---

[133]The origin of this interpretation of Genesis 49:10 may lie in the line, "nor the מְחֹקֵק from between his feet" (Gen. 49:10b). מְחֹקֵק is interpreted as "lawgiver."

[134]Literary criticism would attempt to explain such apparent redundancy as evidence of "literary strata" in the text. We are suggesting that it is the intentional result of "literary strategy."

34:9, however, Joshua is described as one who is "filled with the Spirit of wisdom." Joshua the prophet in Numbers 27 has thus become Joshua the wise man in Deuteronomy 34:9. The new leadership represented by Joshua at the close of the canonical Pentateuch is thus characterized by "wisdom" rather than "prophecy." This, it should be noted, is the same view of the narrative character Joshua as we find in Joshua 1:8 where he is instructed to meditate on the Torah day and night—just as was the wise man in Psalm 1. If we have correctly described the perspectives on Moses and Joshua in these last two chapters, we perhaps can then be permitted to say that in the narrative of these chapters, when Joshua replaces Moses, wisdom replaces prophecy. Moses, the inspired prophet, is replaced by a new form of leadership: Joshua, the wise scholar (cf. Isa 2:2–4).

3.2.4.2.3.1.6. Deuteronomy 34:10–12 (Dt 18:15). Deuteronomy 34:10 adds several significant points to the conclusion of the Pentateuch. It is important first to see that this verse looks back to the words of Moses in Deuteronomy 18:15, "the Lord will raise up for you a prophet like me from your brothers."[135] According to Deuteronomy 34:10, however, "a prophet like Moses never arose." In making this statement, this verse sets the record straight on two counts. First, as was observed long ago,[136] it shows that Joshua was not "the prophet like Moses" who was to come. The ideal leader to be emulated at the present time was Joshua, a wise man, not Moses, the prophet. The leader of the future, however, continues to be idealized in the person of the prophet, Moses.

The second point made by 34:10 is that the promise of a future prophet in 18:15 did not find its fulfillment either in the institution of the office of the prophet or with the rise of any one prophet during the biblical period. The all-important question is the syntactical meaning of the clause "no prophet like Moses ever arose in Israel," in 34:10. Such a statement clearly assumes that the end of prophecy had already come.[137] It should be stressed that the text does not say that "no prophet like Moses *has yet* come."[138] That translation, as Blenkinsopp has rightly shown, is not syntactically plausible, though it has received wide circulation in English translations. The passage should be read in a conclusive sense, "no prophet ever came,"[139] and thus removing the possibility of a historical fulfillment sometime in Israel's past.[140] As it stands, Deuteronomy 34:10 assumes that prophecy, or at least the office of prophecy, had already ceased

---

[135]"It seems quite clear, to begin with, that the scholiast who is here extolling Moses over the prophets wished to refer explicitly to the promise of a 'Mosaic' prophet occurring earlier in the book" (Blenkinsopp, *Prophecy and Canon*, 86).

[136]Steuernagel, *Das Deuteronomium und Josua*, 129.

[137]Joseph Blenkinsopp, *Prophecy and Canon*, 86.

[138]As NIV, NASB: "Since then, no prophet has risen in Israel like Moses. . . ." Cf. LXX, Vulg.

[139]". . .in all instances where this particular construction occurs in the Hebrew Bible [עוֹד. . . .לֹא with the past tense] it never means 'not yet' with the implication 'it hasn't happened yet but it will later.' Following attested usage it must on the contrary be translated 'never again,' 'never since,' or 'no longer' with no limitation of time unless expressly stated." (ibid., *Prophecy and Canon*, 86). As in KJV and JPS, "Never again did there arise in Israel a prophet like Moses. . . ."

[140]"The phrase in Deut. 34:10, therefore, implies an all-inclusive retrospective evaluation of the period from the death of Moses to the time of writing" (ibid., 86). It does not, however, remove the possi-

and that a prophet like Moses never arose. It is worthwhile to note here that the concept of the cessation of prophecy was part and parcel with the concept of the closing of the OT Canon.[141] This passage, with its similar focus on the cessation of prophecy, suggests that concept may already have played a key role in shaping the Hebrew Canon.

3.2.4.2.3.2. Inter-textual Canonical Redaction.

3.2.4.2.3.2.1. Deuteronomy 34:5–12 and Joshua 1:1–8. We have suggested that one of the central purposes of Deuteronomy 34:5–12 was to portray Joshua as an ideal wise man and, as such, a model for the kind of piety that was to accompany the reading of the written Scriptures. Joshua, the wise man, is presented in the narrative as the ideal reader of the Torah. Moreover, the written Torah has taken the place of the words of Moses the prophet, or more precisely, the written Torah is the embodiment of the prophetic words of Moses and as such recognizes no rivals from the past.

Joshua 1:1–8 is an expansion of that same picture of Joshua the wise man. God's way is known through meditation on the Torah which Moses commanded: "You shall meditate on it day and night so that you might do all that is written in it. Then you will prosper" (v. 8). The written word has replaced the fiery words which Moses heard and saw.

3.2.4.2.3.2.2. Deuteronomy 34:10–12 and Malachi 3:22–24. Deuteronomy 34:10ff. and Malachi 3:22ff. have much in common. Neither is an integral part of the book to which it is attached. Deuteronomy 34:10ff. centers on the "prophet" Moses who is the one who did great signs and wonders and Malachi 3:22ff. centers on the "prophet" Elijah who did great signs and wonders. Moses is the key prophet in the Torah, Elijah the key prophet in the Prophets. Both stress the central role of Moses and the Law. Both call Moses the "servant" of the Lord. Both are future oriented, projecting into the future an expectation of the return of the great men of the past. Moses' grave was unknown and Elijah had no grave, since he was taken into heaven.

What is the relationship between these two canonical seams and what do they appear to contribute to the overall sense of the final shape of the Canon? In other words, what sense to they make when read together in the Hebrew Canon? When viewed on its own, the statement about the return of Elijah gives the impression that he is the prophet like Moses of Deuteronomy 18: "Remember the Law of Moses, my servant,. . . . Behold, I am sending Elijah the prophet" (Mal 3:22). However, when viewed canonically, that is, in light of Deuteronomy 34:10, the understanding of the

---

bility of a future fulfillment. The precise meaning of Deut. 34:10 and its relationship to Deut. 18:15 is complex. By qualifying the expression "like Moses," Deut 34:10 may be giving Deut. 18:15 an historical interpretation. By saying no prophet exactly like Moses (who did miraculous signs) arose, Deut. 34:10 is taken to mean "similar to Moses." In fulfillment of Deut. 18:15, the Lord raised up prophet(s) similar to Moses but not exactly like Moses whom God knew face to face. It is also possible to say that Deut. 34:10 is giving Deut. 18:15 an eschatological sense. That prophet which the Lord promised to send, never arose, the implication being that God would still send him in the future.

[141]Herbert Edward Ryle, *The Canon of the Old Testament* (London: MacMillan & Co., 1899), 173.

role of Elijah the prophet appears quite different. The statement about the cessation of prophecy in Deuteronomy 34:10, by excluding all historical prophets from the promise in Deuteronomy 18, has anticipated and excluded perhaps the most likely of Israel's prophets, that is, the prophet Elijah. When read as a part of the whole Hebrew Canon, Deuteronomy 34:10, therefore, states that not even the prophet Elijah was to be understood as the fulfillment of Deuteronomy 18.

There is still more that a canonical reading of Deuteronomy 34:10 and Malachi 3:22–24 lends to the meaning of the OT Scriptures. If in fact Deuteronomy 34:10 is taken as a statement about all prophets, including Elijah, then it raises a further question regarding the words in Malachi 3:22f. Why is Elijah to return again to Israel? Though the answer to that question is not explicitly given in Malachi, the only interpretive option given the canonical reader is to see the role of Elijah in Malachi 3:22–24 as merely preparatory to the coming of another prophet. Elijah is coming again, but not as the prophet like Moses. That prophet, however, according to Deuteronomy 34:10, is coming in the future. Elijah's coming must, then, be to prepare the people for the coming of the prophet like Moses (Mal 3:24). Thus we see emerging from the shape of the Hebrew Canon the notion that at the present time prophecy has ceased in Israel, and the authoritative Law of Moses is complete. God's will is known in Scripture—the written Word. Prophecy does not belong to the present but to the future. By reading and meditating day and night on the Torah, one may know the will of God. Just as Joshua 1:1–8 reinforced the conclusion of the Pentateuch by portraying Joshua as an ideal wise man meditating day and night on the Torah, so also Psalm 1, which follows Malachi 3 in the TaNaK, presents the ideal of the wise man who meditates day and night on the Torah (Ps 1:2–3). The verbal and textual links between Joshua 1:1–8 and Psalm 1:2–3 are transparent.

If we pull back and view the TaNaK in terms of its boundary markers, comparing Deuteronomy 34 with Malachi 3 and Joshua 1 with Psalm 1, we can see a remarkably coherent line of thought. Prophecy, or at least the great prophets of old, have ceased to be the means for gaining divine guidance. For the time being, the wise man has taken the role of the prophet as the ideal leader. Scripture is now the locus of divine revelation. There still lies in the future, however, the hope of a return of prophecy. The Scriptures themselves (e.g., Dt 18) point in that direction. In the meantime, one "prospers" by meditating on the written Word of God.

The Hebrew Bible as we now have it comes to us with a particular shape: the TaNaK (the Law, the Prophets, and the Writings). It appears that this shape was not an historical accident, but rather the result of a deliberate attempt to establish certain fundamental notions about the Hebrew Bible. Specifically, it was an attempt to provide an apologetic for the Hebrew Canon itself. That apologetic was necessary, it appears, in light of the decline of the role of prophecy and the growing importance of the written Word as a means for determining the will of God.

3.2.4.2.4. Con-Textuality (Montage)

Of the three approaches to the theological shape of the OT Canon, the notion of con-textuality, or montage, is the most problematic. It is the aspect of the canonical shape that is least traceable to a distinct authorial or compositional intention. It is, nevertheless, an important component of a consideration of the semantics of the shape of the Canon, as anyone familiar with the concept of montage knows. For that reason we cannot dispense with a discussion of it.

The evident rationality behind the major divisions of the OT Canon, as well as that which lies behind the selection of books within each section,[142] strongly suggests that the order of the books within the sections of the Canon is also intentional. If so, then some degree of montage or con-textuality was at work in the process.[143] Perhaps the most obvious example of this is the arrangement of the books in the Former Prophets: Joshua, Judges, Samuel, and Kings. Whatever one might say about the original shape of these books and their relationship to a "deuteronomic history," it cannot be doubted that in their present form they represent four distinct books and that they are arranged in the Hebrew Canon according to the chronological order of the events they record. This is also the case for the Latter Prophets section (Isaiah, Jeremiah, Ezekiel, and the 12 Minor Prophets) in BHS (*Biblia Hebraica Stuttgartensia*).[144] The immediate, albeit obvious, implication of the order of these books is that both the Former Prophets and Latter Prophets sections of the Canon are arranged to be read in chronological sequence. The Hebrew Bible thus encompasses the whole of its contents in a single narrative history that extends from creation to the return from exile.

That there is a global chronological sequence assumed within the arrangement of the Minor Prophets is also likely. It can at least be said that those books in the Minor Prophets that have chronological references are arranged in relative chronological sequence. The fact that those books without chronological references are interspersed among the others, leaves open the possibility that they too were placed where the canonical assumption of their chronological position would have put them. Strongly supporting this notion is the placement of the two clearly postexilic prophets, Haggai and Zechariah, at the end of the Minor Prophets. This, of course, leaves Malachi, which has no chronological references, at its conclusion. The canonical presumption, then, appears to be that Malachi was a postexilic prophet who followed or overlapped with Haggai and Zechariah. The fact that the book of Malachi is almost universally taken as the work of a postexilic prophet, when in fact there is no statement to that effect in the book itself, is strong evidence for the semantic effect of con-textuality.

The theological impact of the con-textuality on the meaning of the various parts of the Canon can be illustrated from the books of Amos and Obadiah. The book of Amos closes with the "salvation oracle" of Israel's restoration. Consistent with the inter-textuality of the Hebrew Bible, the salvation of Israel is made to rest on God's promise to the house of David in 2 Samuel 7. Amos says, "In that day I will restore David's fallen tent . . . so that they may possess the remnant of Edom" (9:11–12 NIV). Not only does this oracle ground the prophetic hope in the Davidic Covenant (2Sa 7), but, by the mention of the "remnant of Edom," it traces that covenant back to the

---

[142]Roger Beckwith, *The Old Testament Canon of the New Testament Church* (Grand Rapids: Eerdmans, 1985), 110–66.

[143]As we have also suggested, con-textuality, like montage, is present with or without intentionality.

[144]The order in Baba Bathra differs slightly, placing Isaiah after Jeremiah and Ezekiel.

eschatology of the poetic seams in the Pentateuch: "A star will come out of Jacob . . . and Edom will be [his] possession" (Nu 24:17–19). The inter-textuality is transparent. The eschatology of Amos is the same as that of the Pentateuch. The future Davidic king will rule victoriously over Israel's enemies and establish his eternal kingdom. Israel's enemies are collectivized here in the form of the nation of Edom, not only because Edom was historically a perennial enemy of Israel, but more importantly because the Hebrew name *Edom* can also be read as "humanity." Thus the imagery of the Davidic king's subjugation of Edom can also be understood in terms of the universal rule of the future King (cf. Da 7:10–14).

At this point we should recall that the book of Amos is followed in the canonical sequence by the book of Obadiah. Ostensively about the destruction of Edom, the book of Obadiah is a composite of a poem about the future divine judgment of Edom (1–18) and a narrative epilogue which briefly recounts the events of the establishment of God's messianic kingdom (19–21). Though the translation of this brief narrative is difficult, the gist of it is clear: Israel's *possession* of Edom is taken as a sign of Edom's (humanity's) membership in God's kingdom. The "survivors" of Edom will be no more (Ob 18b) because the "exiles" of their armies, who are Canaanites(!),[145] will belong to Israel and God's kingdom (Ob 20). The messianic Savior will rule over Edom from Mount Zion in Jerusalem (Ob 21).[146] In the final composition of the book of Obadiah, the writer envisions the inclusion of Edom into God's messianic kingdom as an image of the universal reign of the messianic king. The picture of Edom in the book of Obadiah, then, portrays the inclusion of the gentile nations into God's blessings. The theology found here in the composition of the book is clearly that of the Pentateuch (cf. Ge 12:3).

Viewed con-textually with the book of Amos, the book of Obadiah sheds much light on the imagery of Amos 9:12, Israel's possession of the "remnant of Edom" in the days of the restored Davidic kingdom. By taking up precisely that theme from the close of the book of Amos, and employing the same terminology and imagery, the book of Obadiah provides a theological interpretation of Amos's "remnant." It represents the inclusion of the Gentile nations in God's messianic kingdom. The Septuagint translation of Amos 9:12, "and the rest of mankind and all the nations will seek (the Lord). . . ." shows that such an interpretation was already known at that early period. The fact that the Septuagint's translation is likely also based on a different Hebrew text[147] shows that its interpretation antedates the process and time period of that translation. The hermeneutical and theological interpretation reflected in the con-textual sequence of the Hebrew Canon has played a fundamental role in the interpretation of these crucial texts. The fact that a central issue in the NT, that is, the Gentiles' rela-

---

[145]The NIV translates verse 20, "who are in Canaan," and the NASB, "who are *among* the Canaanites."

[146]The fact that critical scholars such as Marti have deleted the reference to Esau (Edom) in this verse is evidence of the extremely unusual nature of its content. Marti suggests, "Darum is es vorzuziehen, die Bemerkung: 'um Esau zu richten' zu beanstanden" (Karl Marti, *Das Dodekapropheton* [Tübingen: J. C. B. Mohr (Paul Siebeck), 1904], 240).

[147]The LXX read דרשׁ rather than the MT ירשׁ.

tionship to Judaism, turns precisely on this passage (cf. Ac 15:16–21) and, in fact, on the very words of Amos 9:12, shows the important role which this passage played at the time, or at least shortly after the time, of the formation of the Hebrew Canon.

There should be no doubt that con-textuality can, and often has played an important role in understanding the meaning and theology of the OT. We should remind ourselves of what Eisenstein said of montage and its meaning in film: competent viewers (or readers) always seek to understand the parts in light of the whole. Juxtaposition of parts implies a whole. Even where such a whole does not actually exist, a whole is supplied by the viewer (or reader). The semantic purpose of montage in film (and biblical texts) is to represent themes and images that are larger than the limitation of the medium itself—that is, larger than the individual frames of film (or texts). When the materials within two distinct "shot-pieces" are linked by juxtaposing them on the projector reel and thereby onto the screen, the viewer is forced to identify elements of both shots that are characteristic of a single theme or image. A montage thus actually forces the viewer of a film to construct a theme or an image of a theme.[148] The same can be said of the act of reading a canonical sequence such as that found in the OT texts. A canonical order ensures that the books of the OT are read in a predetermined context.

---

[148]Eisenstein, *The Film Sense*, 11.

APPENDIX A:
THE MOSAIC LAW AND
THE THEOLOGY OF THE PENTATEUCH

I. INTRODUCTION*

The purpose of this appendix is to raise the question of the role of the Mosaic Law in the theology of the Pentateuch. By "theology of the Pentateuch," I mean the major themes and purposes that lie behind its final composition.

1. The Final Composition of the Pentateuch

Much has been written in recent years about the final composition of the Pentateuch.[1] In an earlier paper, I attempted to demonstrate the influence of prophetic hope and eschatology in its composition.[2] The Pentateuch, I argued, represents an attempt to point to the same hope as the later prophets, namely, the New Covenant.[3] "The narrative texts of past events are presented as pointers to events that lie yet in the future. Past events foreshadow the future."[4] Along similar lines, though working from quite different assumptions, Hans-Christoph Schmitt has argued that the Pentateuch is the product of a unified compositional strategy that lays great emphasis on faith.[5] According to Schmitt, the same theme is found within the composition of the prophetic books, like Isaiah, and ultimately can be traced into the NT, e.g., the book of Hebrews.

---

*John H. Sailhamer, "The Mosaic Law and the Theology of the Pentateuch," *Westminster Theological Journal*, 53 (1991): 24–61.

[1]Erhard Blum, *Studien zur Komposition des Pentateuch* (Berlin: Walter de Gruyter, 1990); Rolf P. Knierim, "The Composition of the Pentateuch," in *SBLSP* 1985, 395–415; Erhard Blum, *Die Komposition der Vätergeschichte* (Neukirchen-Vluyn: Neukirchener Verlag, 1984); Rolf Rendtorff, *Das Überlieferungsgeschichtliche Problem des Pentateuch* (BZAW 147; Berlin: Walter de Gruyter, 1977).

[2]John H. Sailhamer, "The Canonical Approach to the OT: Its Effect on Understanding Prophecy," *JETS*, 30 (1987): 307–15.

[3]This does not necessarily imply that the final composition of the Pentateuch is later than that of the prophetic books. On the contrary, if the composition of the Pentateuch were dated before that of the prophetic books, it would help explain the origin of the message of those books. In the discussion that follows, the date of the final composition of the Pentateuch as such is taken to be Mosaic.

[4]Sailhamer, "The Canonical Approach," 311.

[5]Hans-Christoph Schmitt, "Redaktion des Pentateuch im Geiste der Prophetie," *VT*, 32 (1982): 170–89.

Schmitt's approach differs from many critical approaches in that he treats the Pentateuch as one would the later historical books, that is, as the product of an intentional theological redaction or composition. One must start from the final form of the book and ask what each part of the whole contributes to its theological intention. Schmitt argues that each major unit[6] of narrative in the Pentateuch shows signs of a homogeneous theological redaction. A characteristic feature of this redaction is the recurrence of the terminology of "faith" (e.g. הֶאֱמִין־בְּ).[7] At crucial compositional seams throughout the Pentateuch, Schmitt is able to find convincing evidence of a "faith theme," that is, a consistent assessment of the narrative events in light of the rule of "faith" הֶאֱמִין־בְּ.[8] According to Schmitt, it does not reflect an emphasis on keeping the priestly law codes (viz., the Mosaic Law) but rather on preserving a sense of trust in God and an expectation of God's future work that the redaction lays great stress on "faith."[9] Schmitt's study goes a long way in demonstrating an important part of the theological intention and orientation of the Pentateuch as a narrative text. Put simply, Schmitt shows that the Pentateuch is intended to teach "faith" in God.[10]

An important question raised by Schmitt's study is whether the concept of "faith" in the Pentateuch is intended to stand in opposition to the Mosaic Law or whether this faith is to be understood simply as "keeping the law."[11] To say it another way, can we find evidence in the composition of the Pentateuch that the author is concerned with the question of "faith versus works for the law"?

---

[6]The largest literary units (grösseren Einheiten) which are linked in the final redaction of the Pentateuch, according to Schmitt, are the Primeval History, the Patriarchal Narratives, the Exodus Narratives, the Sinai Narratives, and the Wilderness Narratives. See Rendtorff, *Das Überlieferungsgeschichtliche Problem*, 19ff.

[7]It is important to note that, according to Schmitt, the terminology of "faith" (הֶאֱמִין־בְּ) occurs only at the redactional seams. See n. 8.

[8]The key texts of that redaction are Gen 15:6, "And Abraham believed in [הֶאֱמִין־בְּ] the Lord and he reckoned it to him for righteousness"; Exod 4:5, "In order that they might believe [יַאֲמִינוּ] that the Lord, the God of their fathers . . . has appeared to you"; Exod 14:31, "And they [the people] believed in [הֶאֱמִין־בְּ] the Lord and in Moses his servant"; Num 14:11, "How long will they [the people] not believe in [הֶאֱמִין־בְּ] me"; Num 20:12, "And the Lord said to Moses and Aaron, 'Because you did not believe in [הֶאֱמַנְתֶּם] me'"; See also Deut 1:32 and 9:23. Schmitt has not discussed Gen 45:26, the only occurrence of the term for "faith" outside of Schmitt's redactional seams, because it does not show other signs of belonging to the "Glaubens-Thematik."

[9]"So steht am Ende der Pentateuchentstehung nicht die Abschliessung in ein Ordnungsdenken theokratischen Charakters. Vielmehr geht es hier darum, in prophetischem Geiste die Offenheit für ein neues Handeln Gottes zu wahren und in diesem Zusammenhang mit dem aus der prophetischen Tradition entnommenen Begriff des "Glaubens" eine Haltung herauszustellen, die später auch das Neue Testament als für das Gottesverhältnis zentral ansieht" (Schmitt, "Redaktion des Pentateuch," 188–89).

[10]It is important to note that such a reading of the Pentateuch, as a lesson on faith, can be found throughout the subsequent canonical literature. Pss 78 and 106, two psalms that look at the meaning of the whole of the Pentateuch, both read the events of the Pentateuch as evidence of the Israelites' faith or faithlessness (cf. Ps 78:22, 32, 37; 106:12, 24). A similar reading is found in Nehemiah 9, which is a rehearsal of the pentateuchal narrative in its present form (cf. Neh 9:8). The example of Hebrews 11 has already been pointed out.

[11]There are indications in Schmitt's study that the notion of faith in the Pentateuch is put in opposition to that of "obedience to the law." Schmitt has argued, for example, that the "faith" seams overlay and reinterpret the narratives which have stressed obedience to the law (cf. comments below on Num 20:12).

It is well known that this issue surfaces a number of times in other OT texts. In Psalm 51:18–19 (English vv. 16–17), for example, David says, "For thou hast no delight in sacrifice. . . . The sacrifice acceptable to God is a broken spirit" and in Micah 6:6–8 it says, "With what shall I come before the Lord . . . Shall I come before him with burnt offerings? He has showed you, O man, what is good. . . . To do justice, and to love kindness, and to walk humbly with your God." Since such texts do, in fact, exist within the OT, we may, with some justification, look for similar ideas within the theological macrostructure of the Pentateuch.

In the present article, we will attempt to show that the issue of "faith versus works of the law" was, indeed, central to the theological purpose of the Pentateuch. Specifically, we will argue that, among other things, the Pentateuch is an attempt to contrast the lives of two individuals, Abraham and Moses. Abraham, who lived before the law (*ante legem*), is portrayed as one who kept the law, whereas Moses, who lived under the law (*sub lege*), is portrayed as one who died in the wilderness because he did not believe. If such a contrast between faith and works is, in fact, a part of the compositional strategy of the Pentateuch, then we may rightfully conclude that part of the purpose of the book was to show not merely the way of faith, but also the weakness of the law.

2. The Genre of the Pentateuch

In a recent article, Rolf Knierim has focused attention on the question of the genre of the Pentateuch as a whole.[12] Knierim has argued that the Pentateuch consists of two major generic sections: Genesis and Exodus–Deuteronomy. According to him, Genesis is to be taken as an introduction to the whole of the Pentateuch. The genre of the central section of the Pentateuch, Exodus–Deuteronomy, is not so much that of a narrative history of Israel, as is commonly supposed in biblical scholarship, but rather its genre is that of a biography, specifically, a biography of Moses.

This is not the place to enter into a full discussion of Knierim's description of the genre of the Pentateuch. It is enough to say that his general observations about the Pentateuch are convincing. The Pentateuch devotes its attention more to the individual Moses than to the nation of Israel. Hence its overall purpose in all likelihood should be understood in relationship more to the life of Moses, per se, than to the history of the nation. As such it is reasonable to conclude that the Pentateuch reads much like, and apparently aims to be, a biography.

Since the purpose of a biography is the presentation or conceptualization of the work or life of an individual person, the Pentateuch can well be viewed generically as a presentation (conceptualization) of the work of Moses. The events of the life of Moses (*Vita Mosis*) are not told entirely for their own sake but are intended as a narrative explication of the nature of a life lived within the context of the call of God and the covenant at Sinai. The Pentateuch seeks to answer the question of how well Moses

---

[12]Knierim, "The Composition of the Pentateuch," 395–415.

carried out his calling, that is, his work under the Sinai covenant. It seeks to tell how well he performed his task.

There is room for doubt, however, whether Knierim's description of the *whole* of the Pentateuch as a biography of Moses is entirely adequate. In the first place, the whole of the collections of laws which make up a major part of the final composition of the Pentateuch do not fit within the narrow limits of a biography. However, according to Knierim's reckoning, these laws, e.g., the Sinai-pericope and Deuteronomy, make up 68.5 percent of the total text of the Pentateuch. Although Knierim treats these legal sections as part of the Moses texts, they clearly are not part of the Moses narratives per se. The course of the narratives is distinctively broken into and suspended until these large collections of laws are exhausted. It appears that in the final stage of the composition, the focus on Moses, the individual lawgiver, has been intentionally expanded to include a substantial portion of the law itself. This state of affairs raises the question of why, in light of the genre of the Pentateuch, these laws were placed in the midst of the biography.

The traditional answer to this question has been that they were put there simply as legislation, that is, as laws which were to be kept—thus the Pentateuch's reputation as a "Book of the law." In this view the Pentateuch is read as if it were a collection of laws intended to guide the daily living of its readers. This view of the purpose of the laws in the Pentateuch is so pervasive that it is often, if not always, merely assumed in works dealing with the problem of the law.

However, it is also possible that the Pentateuch has intentionally included this selection of laws for another purpose, that is, *to give the reader an understanding of the nature of the Mosaic Law and God's purpose in giving it to Israel.* Thus it is possible to argue that the laws in the Pentateuch are not there to tell the *reader* how to live but rather to tell the reader how Moses was to live under the law. To use an example from the Pentateuch itself, it is clear to all that the detailed instructions on the building of the ark in Genesis 6 were not given *to the reader* so he or she could build an ark and load it with animals, but those detailed instructions were given to show what *Noah* was to do in response to God's command. Competent readers of the Pentateuch easily understand that God's instructions to Noah in the narrative is directed only to Noah and not to the readers. These instructions are included as narrative information *for* the reader. The message of the Pentateuch, in other words, is not that its readers should build an ark like Noah.

The same may be true for the legal instructions found in the Mosaic Law. Though the nature of the instructions to Noah and those to Moses (the building of the tabernacle in Exodus 25ff., for example) are similar in form and narrative function, we often read them entirely differently. We read the instructions to Noah as given *for* the reader, and those to Moses as given *to* the reader.[13] It is possible, however, that the

---

[13]"From the earliest days of the church Christians have asked about the commands of the Old Testament: do they apply to us? The question, however, is ambiguous. It may be a question about authority, or it may be a question about prescriptive claim. A prescription, we said, instructs somebody to do, or not to do, something. We may ask in each case who is instructed and who instructs. If, as I walk down the street, somebody in a blue coat says, 'Stop!', I shall have to ask, first, 'Is he speaking to *me*?'—the question of claim— and, then, 'Is he a policeman?'—the question of authority. And so it is with the commands of the Old Testament: we must ask, 'Do they purport to include people like us in their scope?'—the question of claim—

two sets of instructions within the Pentateuch are intended to be read in the same way. In other words, to put it in the terms introduced into OT studies by Mendenhall, the inclusion of the selection of laws (viz., the Mosaic Law) in the Pentateuch was not so much intended to be a source for legal action (technique) as rather a statement of legal policy.[14]

This understanding of the purpose of the laws in the Pentateuch is supported by the observation that the collections of laws in the Pentateuch are incomplete. This suggested by the fact that many aspects of ordinary community life are not covered in these laws. Moreover, there is at least one example in the Pentateuch where a "statute given to Moses by the Lord" is mentioned but not actually recorded in the Pentateuch.[15] The selective nature of the laws included in the Pentateuch is further illustrated both by the fact that the number of laws (611) is the same as the numerical equivalent of the Hebrew title of the Pentateuch, "Torah" (תורה),[16] and by the fact that within the structure of the collections of laws the number seven and multiples of seven predominate. The listing of 42 (7 x 6) laws in the Covenant Code (Exod 21:1–23:12), for example, equals the numerical value of the title of that section "And these (are the judgments)." This is not to suggest that secret numerical codes were intended to conceal mysteries within these texts. The use of the numerical values of titles and catch phrases was a common literary device at the time of the composition of Scripture. The same principle of numerical selectivity may also be seen within the Book of Proverbs, where the total number of proverbs in chapters 10:1–22:16 (375) equals the numerical value of the name "Solomon."[17] This suggests that, just as in the publication of law in the ancient Near Eastern world in general,[18] the laws in the Pentateuch were not

---

and, 'If so, ought we to heed them?'—the question of authority. In the patristic church, after the rejection of the Gnostic temptation, especially in its Marcionite form, the question of authority was not really open for discussion; Old Testament commands were evaluated entirely in terms of their claim. Our own age, conversely, has been so dominated by the question of authority that the question of claim has been obscured and forgotten" (O. M. T. O'Donovan, "Towards an Interpretation of Biblical Ethics," *TynBul,* 27 [1976]: 58–59).

[14]"That common body of what might be called the sense of justice in a community we shall call 'policy.' What happens in a law court, however, is usually much more directly related to the technical corpus of specialized legal acts and tradition. These are 'techniques'" (George E. Mendenhall, "Ancient Oriental and Biblical Law," *The Biblical Archaeologist Reader 3* [ed. E. F. Campbell and D. N. Freedman; New York: Anchor, 1958], 3).

[15]The "statute of the law that the Lord gave Moses," referred to by Eleazar in Num 31:21, is not found elsewhere in the Pentateuch, though a part of what Eleazar commands (the water of cleansing) was given in Numbers 19. This shows either that the laws included in the Pentateuch are selective, that is, not every law given to Moses was included, or that any law given by a priest could have been called a "statute of the law that the Lord gave Moses" (cf. Deut 33:10). The former alternative appears more likely because the text expressly says "the Lord gave [it] to Moses." The omission of "to Moses" in the Samaritan Pentateuch is evidence that at an early period there was already a tendency to read the laws of the Pentateuch as complete.

[16]The traditional number of laws in the Pentateuch (613) is obtained by treating both Deut 6:4 (the "Shema") and Exod 20:2 ("I am the Lord your God") as "laws."

[17]Barry J. Beitzel, "Exodus 3:14 and the Divine Name: A Case of Biblical Paronomasia," *TrinJ,* 1 NS (1980): 6. See also J. M. Sasson, "Wordplay in the OT," *IDBS,* 968–70.

[18]"Das grosse Gesetzgebungswerk des Königs nur Representation geblieben und niemals Rechtswirklichkeit geworden sei" (W. Eilers, *Rechtsvergleichende Studien zur Gesetzgebung Hammurapis*

intended to be used in the administration of justice as a collection of laws to be enforced.

In his study of law codes in the ancient world, F. R. Kraus[19] has provided a helpful analogy to the nature and purpose of the laws included in the final composition of the Pentateuch. According to Kraus, literary works such as the Code of Hammurapi were not intended to be used in the actual administration of law. They were not, in fact, associated with the systems of justice in the ancient world. According to Kraus, they were rather intended to tell us something about the lawgiver, viz., important people like Hammurapi himself.[20] For example, when the whole of the present shape of the document, including the important but often overlooked prologue of Hammurapi's Code, is taken into consideration, it becomes clear that a text such as Hammurapi's was not to be used to administer justice, but was rather intended to promote the image of Hammurapi as a wise and just king.[21] What Kraus has argued for the Code of Hammurapi suits the phenomenon of law in the Pentateuch remarkably well. It explains the existence of the relatively large collections of laws strategically placed throughout the pentateuchal narratives dealing with the *life* of Moses. Applying the analogy of the Code of Hammurapi helps confirm the judgment that the selection of laws in the Pentateuch is not there as a corpus of laws as such (*qua lex*), but was intended as a description of the nature of divine wisdom and justice revealed through Moses (*qua institutio*).

An inter-biblical example of this is found in the book of Proverbs, with its prologue and selection of wise sayings of Solomon. The book of Proverbs was not intended to be read as an exhaustive book of right actions but as a selective example of godly wisdom.

In the narratives of Exodus–Deuteronomy, then, we are to see not only a picture of Moses, but we are also to catch a glimpse of the nature of the law under which he lived and God's purpose for giving it. Along with the narrative portrait of Moses we see a selected sample of his laws. Returning to Knierim's thesis of the genre of the Pentateuch, what emerges from a genre analysis of the Pentateuch in its present shape is that it is a biography of Moses, albeit a modified one. It is a biography of Moses, which portrays him as a man *who lived under the law* given at Sinai. It is a biography of Moses *sub lege*.

[1917], 8, quoted in R. F. Kraus, "Ein zentrales Problem des altmesopotamischen Rechtes: Was Ist der Codex Hammu-rabi?" *Genava*, 8 [1960]: 283–96).

[19]Kraus, "Ein zentrales Problem."

[20]"In seiner Selbstdarstellung sind Gerechtigkeit und Klugheit die Eigenschaften, die er sich, von den üblichen Cliches abweichend, immer wieder zuschreibt. . . . *emqum*, 'klug', ist ein typisches Prädikat des Schreibers. . . . nur Hammu-rabi, gleichzeitig gerechter Richter und gelehrter Autor, hat seine Rechtssprüche aufgezeichnet und der Welt zur Verfügung gestellt genauso, wie die Autoren der Eingeweideschaukompendien ihre Erfahrungen und Erkenntnisse zu Nutz und Frommen der Welt in ihren Werken niederlegen. Zu Nutz und Frommen der Welt hat auch Hammu-rabi seinen Codex verfasst und öffentlich aufstellen lassen" (Kraus, "Ein zentrales Problem," 290–91).

[21]"Eine Welt trennt diese sehr deutlich formulierte Denkweise von der unserer heutigen Gesetzgeber und unserer modernen Konzeption von der Geltung der Gesetze. Die Gültigkeit, welche Hammu-rabi für sein Werk erhofft, ist grundsätzlich anderer Natur als die unserer Gesetze, und seine Hoffnung ruht auf anderen Voraussetzungen als der Geltungsanspruch moderner Gesetzbücher. Seine sogenannten Gesetze sind Musterentscheidungen, Vorbilder guter Rechtsprechung" (ibid., 291).

A second difficulty in Knierim's assessment of the genre of the Pentateuch is the fact that although Knierim treats Genesis as an introduction to the life of Moses, there are significant problems in accounting for this section of the Pentateuch within the genre of Biography of Moses. According to Knierim, Genesis adds the dimension of "all of human history" to the biography of Moses. But it is self-evidently clear that not all of Genesis is about "all of human history." It is only the first eleven chapters of the book which have all of humanity specifically in view. Though the rest of Genesis is, in fact, drawn into the scope of "all humanity" by means of the reiterated promise that in the seed of Abraham "all the families of the land will be blessed," the narratives in chapters 12–50 focus specifically on the family of Abraham. In fact, the three major sections of Genesis 12–50 appear to consist of *genres* nearly identical to that of Knierim's view of the whole Pentateuch, namely, biographies of Abraham (chaps. 12–26), Jacob (chaps. 27–36), and Joseph (chaps. 37–50).

Knierim rightly makes much of the fact that the whole of Genesis, covering some 2000 years, takes up only about 25 percent of the total text of the Pentateuch, whereas Exodus–Deuteronomy, which covers only the span of the life of Moses, takes up the other 75 percent. "The extent of material allotted to each of the two times spans is extremely disproportionate, a factor that must be considered programmatic."[22] However, when the Moses-narratives (Exod 1–18 and Num 10:11–36:13) are counted alone, without the laws (Deuteronomy and the Sinai-pericope), they make up only about 20 percent of the whole of the Pentateuch. The material in Genesis devoted to the Patriarchs (Genesis 12–50) is also about 20 percent, making the narratives about Moses and those about the Patriarchs appear of equal importance within the final text.

It thus is not satisfactory to group the patriarchal narratives together with Genesis 1–11 and consider them both as the introduction to Moses' biography. It appears more probable within the framework of the whole of the Pentateuch that the patriarchal material in Genesis is intended on its own to balance off the material in the Moses narratives. The biographies of the patriarchs are set over against the biography of Moses.

The early chapters of Genesis (1–11) play their own part in providing an introduction to the whole of the Pentateuch, stressing the context of "all humanity" for both the patriarchal narratives and those of Moses. The Moses material, for its part, has been expanded with voluminous selections from the Sinai laws in order to show the reader the nature of the law under which Moses lived.

If this is an adequate description of the Pentateuch, then its genre is not simply that of a biography of Moses but rather it is a series of biographies similar perhaps to those in Kings or Samuel where the life of Saul, for example, is counterbalanced to that of David. Within this series of biographies in the Pentateuch a further textual strategy appears evident.

The chronological framework of Genesis (periodization) and the virtual freezing of time in Exodus–Deuteronomy (a single period for time only, viz., the lifespan of Moses) suggests that there has been a conscious effort to contrast the time before

---

[22]Knierim, "The Composition of the Pentateuch," 395.

and leading up to the giving of the law (*ante legem*) with the time of Moses under the law (*sub lege*).[23] Abraham lived *before* the giving of the law and Moses lived *after* it was given.

With this background to the compositional strategy for the final shape of the Pentateuch, we can now turn to its treatment of Abraham and Moses. Specifically, we wish to raise the question of what the Pentateuch intends to say about the lives of these two great men that contributes to our understanding of faith and keeping the Mosaic Law.

A complete answer to this question cannot be given within the scope of this appendix. We will limit ourselves to two strategically important pentateuchal texts from the standpoint of its final composition, Genesis 26:5 and Numbers 20:12. Both texts are similar in that they offer reflective looks at the lives of Abraham and Moses respectively and give an evaluation that stems from the final stages of the composition of the Pentateuch. Furthermore, both texts evaluate the lives of these two great men from the perspective of the theology of Deuteronomy. We will see that in Genesis 26:5 Abraham is portrayed as one who "kept the law," whereas in Numbers 20:12 Moses is portrayed as one who "did not believe."

II. ABRAHAM AND THE MOSAIC LAW (GEN 26:5)

In Gen 26:5, God says, "Abraham obeyed my voice [שמע . . . קלי] and kept my charge [וישמר משמרתי], my commandments [מצותי], my statutes [חקותי], and my laws [תורתי]." Though on the face of it, the meaning of this verse is clear enough, it raises questions when viewed within the larger context of the book. How was it possible for Abraham to obey the commandments, statutes, and laws before they were given? Why is Abraham here credited with keeping the law when in the previous narratives great pains were taken to show him as one who lived by faith (e.g., Gen 15:6)? There has been no mention of Abraham's having the law or keeping the law previous to this passage. Why, now suddenly, does the text say Abraham had kept the law?

The verse is recognized as "deuteronomic" by most biblical scholars, both critical[24] and conservative.[25] Earlier biblical scholars went to great lengths to explain the

---

[23]Though it is not part of our immediate concern, one could also note indications within the final shape of the Pentateuch of a time "after the law" (*post legem*). Deuteronomy 30, for example, looks to a future time quite distinct from that of Moses' own day. There are close affinities between this chapter and passages in the prophetic literature that look to the time of the New Covenant, e.g., Jer 31:31ff.; Ezek 36:22ff.

[24]See Erhard Blum, *Die Komposition der Vätergeschichte* (Neukirchen-Vluyn: Neukirchener Verlag, 1984), 363, for a discussion of the critical views.

[25]F. Delitzsch says of the verse, for example, "Undoubtedly verse 5 in this passage is from the hand of the Deuteronomist" (*A New Commentary on Genesis* [Edinburgh: T. & T. Clark, 1888], 137ff.). C. F. Keil also recognized that these same terms were later used to describe the Mosaic Law: "The piety of Abraham is described in words that indicate a perfect obedience to all the commands of God and therefore frequently recur among the legal expressions of a later date [in der späteren Gesetzessprache]" (*Biblical Commentary on the Old Testament* [Grand Rapids: Eerdmans, 1971], 270). Cf. Benno Jacob, "Aber diese Ausdrücke besagen, dass er auf den verschiedensten Gebieten sein Leben ähnlich den späteren Ordnungen des Gesetzes nach den speziellen Weisungen Gottes, wie sie ihm erteilt wurden oder er sie sich selbst erschliessen mochte, eingerichtet hat" (*Das erste Buch der Tora Genesis* [Berlin: Schocken, 1934], 548). Since, throughout the Pentateuch and especially in Deuteronomy, these terms denote the Mosaic Law (e.g., Deut 11:1; 26:17) this passage says, in no uncertain terms, that Abraham kept the Mosaic Law.

verse in view of its inherent historical and theological difficulties. For those who saw the verse as a description of Abraham's legal adherence to the law, the major problem was how Abraham could have had access to the Mosaic Law. Early rabbinical approaches, for example, attempted by word associations to identify each of the terms used here with a specific act of obedience of Abraham within the patriarchal narratives. in that way it could be demonstrated that Abraham knew the Mosaic Law and thus kept it.[26] This approach, however, did not gain wide acceptance because, apart from a remote link to circumcision, none of the terms in Genesis 26:5 could be associated with events or actions of Abraham within the biblical narratives.[27]

Another, and more common, rabbinical explanation of 26:5 made use of the Talmudic teaching of the "Noahic laws."[28] This approach was also accepted among the early Protestant scholars.[29] Thus the deuteronomic terms for the law in Gen 26:5 were identified by some as those general laws given to all men since the time of Noah.[30] However, because these specific terms are, in fact, used later in the Pentateuch to represent the whole of the Mosaic Law, it proved difficult to limit them only to the concept of the Noahic laws. Thus for this particular passage (Gen 26:5) the Talmud itself rejected the notion of Noahic laws and took the position that, in his own lifetime, Abraham was given the whole of the Mosaic Law.[31]

As to how Abraham would have known the law, the assumption was that God had revealed it to him.[32] It was also held by many that Abraham derived the laws of

---

[26]The terms משרתי and מצותי, for example, were related to Abraham's obedience in circumcision since, according to Gen 17:9, Abraham was to "keep" (תשמר) God's covenant in circumcision and 21:4 records that Abraham circumcised Isaac "as God had commanded [צוה] him."

[27]The terms חקות and תורתי, for example, could not otherwise be associated with Abraman's piety in the patriarchal narratives and no amount of midrashic attempts to do so proved successful. Another, but similar, attempt to demonstrate that Abraham had the law of Moses is that of Walter Kaiser: "In spite of its marvelous succinctness, economy of words, and comprehensive vision, it must not be thought that the Decalogue was inaugurated and promulgated at Sinai for the first time. All Ten Commandments had been part of the law of God previously written on hearts instead of stone, for all ten appear, in one way or another, in Gen. They are: The first, Gen 35:2: 'Get rid of the forbidden gods.' The second, Gen 31:39: Laban to Jacob: 'But why did you steal my gods?' The third, Gen 24:3: 'I want you to swear by the Lord'" (*Toward Old Testament Ethics* [Grand Rapids: Zondervan, 1983], 81–82).

[28]The Talmud teaches that all descendants of Noah who did not follow the practices of idolatry were given seven divine laws. See *Der babylonische Talmud* (ed. L. Goldschmidt; Berlin: Jüdischer Verlag, 1930), 2.373.

[29]". . . observantia Sabbati et Circumcisionis, esus Sanguinis, cultus unius Dei, et multa hujusmodi" (Sebastian Münster [1489–1552], *Critici sacri: annotata doctissimorum virorum in Vetus ac Novum Testamentum* [ed. J. Pearson et al.; Amsterdam, 1698], 1.616. Münster explicitly cites Ibn Ezra's commentary on this passage).

[30]E.g., Seforno, בני נח (*Torat Chaim Chumash* [Jerusalem: Mossad Harav Kook, 1987], 13).

[31]*Yoma* 28b (*Die babylonische Talmud*, 3.75). See Str-B 3.204–5 for further examples. Jacob suggested that this Talmudic interpretation was an attempt to counter the argument of Paul in Gal 3:17ff. ("polemisch gegen Paulus," *Das erste Buch*, 549). Andreas Rivetus specifically rejects this view as "false" (*Opera theologica* [Rotterdam, 1651], 1.457). According to the Kabbalah, the laws mentioned in this verse are those of the Decalogue because the verse contains 10 words and the Decalogue has 172 words, the same number as the Hebrew word עקב in Gen 26:5. See Baal Hatturim, *Chumash* (New York: Philipp Feldheim, 1967), 81.

[32]"God disclosed to him the new teachings which He expounded daily in the heavenly academy" (Louis Ginzberg, *The Legends of The Jews* [Philadelphia: Jewish Publication Society of America, 1968], 1.292). Rivetus held that "praeter naturae legem, habuisse patres multas observationes, praesertim circa div-

Moses from his own observations,[33] or even from written tradition, which could be traced back to Enoch.[34] In *Jub.* 21:10, for example, when explaining the various laws for sacrifice, Abraham says, "for thus I have found it written in the books of my fore-fathers, and in the words of Enoch, and in the words of Noah."[35] The tractate *Nedarim* 32a states that Abraham was three years old when he first began to obey the law. By means of *gematria*, the rule that permits deriving significance from the numerical value of the consonants of a word, the first word, עקב, is read as the number 172 (years).[36] Thus 26:5 was read as if it said "For 172 [עקב] years Abraham obeyed me." Since Abraham lived for 175 years, it would have been at the age of three years that he first began to obey God's law.[37]

It is difficult to see in these early rabbinical attempts a convincing explanation of the Genesis passage. They are rather attempts at harmonization. If, in fact, to keep the "commandments, statutes and laws" meant to keep the Mosaic Law as the rabbis had understood these terms in Deuteronomy, then what other explanation remained? Abraham must have known the Mosaic Law.

As is always the case in the reading of a text, their understanding of the sense of the whole determined their interpretation of this part. What was clearly not open to these commentators was the possibility that this verse was intended as an interpreta-tion of the life of Abraham from another perspective than that of the law.[38]

The view of the later medieval Jewish commentaries, on the other hand was that these "laws" were merely a form of general revelation of moral and ethical precepts.[39]

---

inum cultum ex speciali Dei revelatione, et majorum qui ea acceperant imitatione, ut de mundis animalibus offerendis et talia, praeter circumcisionem, et alios mandatos ritus" (*Opera theologica,* 1.457). According to rabbinic teaching God himself was guided by the Torah in creating the world, but he hid the Torah from mankind until the time of Abraham: שלא נברא העולם צפן הקב"ה את התורה עד שעמד אברהם שנאמר עקב אשר שמע אברהם בקולי (*Yalkut Shemoni* [Jerusalem, 1960], 972).

[33]Str-B, 3.205.

[34]Ibid., 205-6.

[35]*APOT,* 2.44.

[36]The number 172 is derived from ע = 70; ק = 100; and ב = 2. See Wilhelm Bacher, *Die exegetische Terminologie der jüdischen Traditionsliteratur* (Hildesheim: Georg Olms, 1965), 127.

[37]*Midrash Rabbah* (New York: KTAV, n.d.), 135. The purpose of this explanation was apparently to deal with the problem of idolatry in Terah's household (Josh 24:2). If Abraham had received the Mosaic Law already at age three, he could not have been influenced by his father's idolatry.

[38]Although Calvin is not clear in his comments on this passage, he appears to follow the same line of interpretation as that reflected in the rabbis. He writes, "And although laws, statutes, rites, precepts and ceremonies, had not yet been written [nondum erant scriptae], Moses used these terms, that he might the more clearly show how sedulously Abraham regulated his life according to the will of God alone—how care-fully he abstained from all the impurities of the heathen" (*Commentaries on the First Book of Moses Called Genesis* [trans. John King; Grand Rapids: Baker, 1979], 60). Henry Ainsworth also appears to follow this line of interpretation, ". . . under these three particulars, the whole *charge* or *custody* forespoken of, is com-prehended; as afterward by *Moses* God gave the ten *Commandments,* or morall preceps, Exod 20. *Judgements,* or judiciall lawes for punishing transgressors, Exod. 21, & c. *and statutes, or rules ordinances* and *decrees* for the service of God, Lev. 3.17. and 6.18.22. Exod. 12.24 & 27.31. & 29.9 & 30.21. All which *Abraham* observed, and is commended of God therefore" (*Annotations upon the Five Bookes of Moses, The Booke of the Psalmes, and the Song of Songs, or, Canticles* [London: M. Parsons, 1639], 99).

[39]Jacob, *Das erste Buch,* 549. Rashi, for example, says, "'my commandments' are those things which even if they had not been written [in the Law] it is evident [ראוין] that they are commanded [להצטוות],

A similar interpretation is found in many Christian commentaries.[40] The difficulty with such an interpretation is not merely the fact that elsewhere in the Pentateuch each of these terms is used specifically to describe an aspect of the Mosaic Law, but, more importantly, elsewhere in the Pentateuch the same list of terms denotes the *whole* of the Mosaic Law.[41]

Literary critics, on the other hand, are virtually unanimous in assigning the verses to a "deuteronomic redaction."[42] Gunkel assigned it to a later (more legalistic) period, though he agreed that the terms are *deuteronomistisch*.[43] Westermann associated the verse with the "post-deuteronomic" interpretation of Israel's relationship to God in terms of obedience to the law (*Gesetzesgehorsam*).[44]

Though such responses are predictable of critical methodology, they serve better as illustrations of the nature of the problem than they do its solution. What criti-

---

such as stealing and murder" (*Torat Chaim Chumash*, 13). Regarding the last two terms, however, "my statutes" and "my laws," Rashi held that they were unobtainable by reason alone but were given as a command from God.

[40]The Belgic Confession (1561), for example, takes the מצוה here to be the moral law (*praecepta*), the תורות as doctrine (*leges*) necessary to be believed, and the משפטים as political law (*judicia*). Thomas Cartwright (1535–1603) follows Nicholas of Lyra (1270–1340), who follows Rashi, "Lyra ait, *ea esse, quae sunt de dictamine rationis rectae, et servanda etiamsi nulla lex esset posita*" (*Critici sacri*, 632). Lyra, however, did not follow Rashi on the last two terms, much to Cartwright's surprise, ". . . a quo mirum est Lyram dissentire." Lyra understood these terms as follows: "חקות cerimonias, seu statuta, ea esse, quae pertinent ad modum colendi Dei; תורת leges esse ista, quae non obligant, nisi quia sunt a Deo, vel homine instituta, vel praecepta" (ibid.). Ultimately the dependency on Rashi and innovations (see previous note) go back to Lyra, "cerimonias meas, seu statuta mea, et leges meas," and the Vulgate, "praecepta et mandata mea et caerimonias legesque." Johannes Drusius (1550–1616) defined these terms thus: "[משמרתי] quaecunque mandavi ut custodiret . . . [מצותי] praecepta moralia quae post decalogo comprehensa sunt. [תורתי] forenses, sive quae ad judicia pertinent" (*Critici sacri*, 622). Johannes Mercerus distinguishes sharply between each of the five terms: (1) the first term refers generally to Abraham's obedience in such cases as the command to leave Ur of the Chaldeans and the binding of Isaac; (2) the second term refers to general religious practice which Abraham carried out diligently as God had prescribed; (3) the third term refers to general moral principles, such as the Decalogue, and are posited in the natural mind; (4) the fourth term refers to rituals by which God is worshiped as well as statutes whose rationale is not immediately obvious, such as the Decalogue, and are posited in the natural mind; (4) the fourth term refers to rituals by which God is worshiped as well as statutes whose rationale is not immediately obvious, such as the red heifer; and (5) the fifth term refers to documents by which one is instructed in doctrine. "Sic Dei voluntatem partitur Moses hoc loco, ut postea in Lege tradenda divisa est [but the Jewish view that Abraham had the whole of the Mosaic Law is to be rejected]. . . . Sed nondum haec in legem certam abierant, ut postea sub Mose, ubi sacerdotium certa familia, et certis ritibus est institutum, etc. Cum ergo hic Moses in Abrahamo, hac legis in suas partes distributione utitur, significat eum absolutissime Dei voluntati paruisse, et per omnia, morigerum fuisse, ut nihil omiserit eorum quae tunc praescripserat Dominus agenda aut seruanda" (in *Genesin Primum Mosis Librum, sic a Graecis Appellatum, Commentarius* [Genevae, 1598], 458).

[41]E.g., Deut. 11:1.

[42]H. Holzinger, *Einleitung in den Hexateuch* (Freiburg: J. C. B. Mohr [Paul Siebeck], 1893), 3, Tabellen über die Quellenscheidung; Otto Procksch, *Die Genesis übersetzt und erklärt* (Leipzig: A. Deichert, 1913), 151.

[43]"The thought that Abraham had fulfilled so many commandments does not suit the spirit of the ancient narratives [*Sage*], but betrays that of a later (legalistic) piety" (Hermann Gunkel, *Genesis* [Göttingen: Vandenhoeck & Ruprecht, 1977], 300).

[44]Claus Westermann, *Genesis* (BKAT 2; Neukirchen-Vluyn: Neukirchener Verlag, 1981), 518.

cal scholarship is unanimous in affirming is that at some point in the composition of the Pentateuch, this statement about Abraham's piety was inserted to show that he kept the Mosaic Law. Critical scholarship has also affirmed that the verse stems from the same process of composition that resulted in the addition of Deuteronomy to the Pentateuch.[45]

Ultimately, we should attempt to find the meaning of this verse in the larger strategy and purpose of the Pentateuch.[46] Did the author of the Pentateuch intend to depict Abraham as a model of faith or as a model of obedience to the law? Curiously enough, the overwhelming majority of biblical scholars have read this passage as if the verse intended to show Abraham's life as an example of obedience to the law (*Gesetzesgehorsam*).

However, several considerations make this assumption unlikely. The first is the fact that the final shape of the Abrahamic narratives is closely aligned with the faith theme that forms the larger structure of the Pentateuch. This same faith theme is also part and parcel with the "deuteronomic composition" of Gen 26:5. That being the case, it is unlikely that the same author would want to stress "faith" at the expense of law at one point in the composition of the Pentateuch and law at the expense of "faith" at another.

The chronological setting of the patriarchal narratives offers further evidence that this text (Gen 26:5) intends to teach Abraham's faith and not his obedience to the law as such. It is well known that the early chapters of the Pentateuch are governed by an all-embracing chronological scheme. This scheme runs throughout the patriarchal narratives up to the time of the giving of the law at Sinai. At that point, the linear chronology broadens out into a literary present. Thus the events of the Pentateuch are divided between those events before and those events during the giving of the law. Within this scheme, then, the patriarchs are necessarily portrayed as those who lived *before* the law (*ante legem*). They are chronologically separated[47] from those who lived *under* the law" (*sub lege*). Thus any statement about Abraham would likely be intended as a contrast to life *under* the law. Furthermore, the very existence of such a wide range of "explanations" of Abraham's "living under the law" (*sub lege*), so common in rabbinical and Christian exegesis, testifies to the difficulties of reading Genesis 26:5 as a statement about Abraham's obedience to the Mosaic Law.[48]

---

[45]On the "deuteronomic redaction of the Pentateuch," see Rolf Rendtorff, *Das überlieferungsgeschichtliche Problem*, 164; Erhard Blum, *Die Komposition der Vätergeschichte*, 362ff.; C. Brekelmans, "Die sogenannten deuteronomischen Elemente in Gen.-Num. Ein Beitrag zur Vorgeschichte des Deuteronomiums," in *Volume du Congrès. Genève 1965* (VTSupp 15; Leiden: Brill, 1966), 90–96.

[46]Such an approach follows from the observation that, on most reckonings, the verse belongs to the work of the author in shaping the final form of the Pentateuch.

[47]For "change of time" as a segmentation marker in narrative, see Elisabeth Gülich and Wolfgang Raible, "Überlegungen zu einer makrostrukturellen Textanalyse: J. Thurber, The Lover and His Lass," in *Untersuchungen in Texttheorie* (Göttingen: Vandenhoeck & Ruprecht, 1977), 132–75.

[48]Moreover, the "Glaubens-Thematik," which is central to the Abrahamic narratives, is also related to the assessment of the life of Moses. The Pentateuch tells us that at the end of his life, Moses died in the wilderness, not entering into the good land, because he "did not believe" God (Num 20:12). At that point the author of the Pentateuch labeled the action of Moses as "faithlessness." Within such a scheme it would follow that the Pentateuch would also view Abrahams's "faith" as obedience to the law.

It appears reasonable to conclude, therefore, that the importance of Genesis 26:5 lies in what it tells us about the meaning of the deuteronomic terms it uses. It is as if the author of the Pentateuch has seized on the Abrahamic narratives as a way to explain his concept of "keeping the law." The author uses the life of Abraham, *not Moses,* to illustrate that one *can* fulfill the righteous requirement of the law. In choosing Abraham and not Moses, the author shows that "keeping the law" means "believing in God," just as Abraham believed God and was counted righteous (Gen 15:6). In effect the author of the Pentateuch says, "Be like Abraham. Live a life of faith and it can be said that you are keeping the law."

We turn now to a consideration of the Pentateuch's portrayal of Moses. We will not attempt a survey of the whole of the life of Moses, but rather, we will look only at the assessment of Moses that lies within the compositional seams.

III. MOSES AND THE FAITH OF ABRAHAM (NUM 20:1–13)

According to Schmitt, Numbers 20 contains an original account of the rebellion of Moses and Aaron that has been secondarily reworked into the faith theme. He argues that the narrative of Numbers 20:1–13 was originally a self-contained unit which, apart from v. 12, formed a coherent whole. Verse 12, however, intrudes into this original narrative and gives it a specific theological interpretation ("Glaubens-Thematic"). The original theme of the passage was the rebellion of the people. This theme, however, was replaced in v. 12 by a focus on faith—an idea that had not hitherto played a part in the narrative.[49] As chapter 20 opens, the Israelites were encamped at Kadesh (20:1) but had begun to contend (וירב) with Moses on account of the lack of food and water. When the Lord told Moses to take a rod and speak to the rock to bring forth water, he did "as [the Lord] commanded him" (20:9). This statement gives an initial impression that Moses and Aaron were obediently following the Lord's commands. At least so far. Then Moses, saying to Israel, "You rebellious ones" (המרים, 20:10), struck the rock twice and water came out for both the people and their animals (20:11).

Though in popular exposition the nature of Moses' sin is emphasized, it is not, in fact, immediately clear from the text why the Lord says Moses (and Aaron) "did not believe" (20:12). Only the bare outline[50] of the events are retained in the narrative.[51]

---

[49]In Deut 1:37; 3:26; and 4:21, Moses says he could not enter the land because of the rebellion of the people—an idea consistent with Num 20:10–11, 13. The presence of the theme of rebellion underlying the present text is betrayed by several wordplays throughout the narrative between the people's rebellion (e.g., רבו, המרים,וירב) and the place name Meribah (מריבה). Also, the fact that later allusions to the Meribah incident (Num 20:24; 27:14; Deut 32:51) speak of the people's rebellion there and not the "unfaithfulness of Moses and Aaron," further supports Schmitt's argument that originally that was the central theme of the story. See below.

[50]The difficulty of determining the nature of Moses' sin because of the brevity of the narrative was already acknowledged by early biblical scholars. Regarding this problem Münster said, "Et quidem verba Mose sunt tam succincta ut nemo facile ex illis advertere possit in quo peccaverit" (*Critici sacri,* 2.323).

[51]At the conclusion of the story the place of the waters is called Meribah (מריבה), which is linked by means of a wordplay to the Israelite's rebellion (רבו) in 20:3. The last statement, 20:13b, "and he was sanctified [ויקדש] among them," links the narrative to the location of the people at the beginning of the story, Kadesh (קדש), and to the next section (20:14) where the location is again Kadesh.

Nevertheless, attempts to find the error of Moses and Aaron and relate it to their lack of faith are numerous.[52] Moses' sin has generally been related to three aspects of the narrative, (1) his striking the rock with the rod (20:11), (2) his (harsh) words to the people (20:10), and (3) the *lacunae* within the narrative itself.

(1) There are those who argue that Moses' lack of faith is exhibited in his striking the rock rather than merely speaking to it. However, as the narrative presents it, the Lord certainly intended Moses to use the rod in some way since it was the Lord who told Moses to get the rod and, according to the narrative, Moses is commended for doing "as he commanded" (20:9). The narrative, however, does not recount the Lord's instructions concerning how or why Moses was to use the rod. Keil, like many, thus supposed that the Lord's instructions to "speak to the rock" meant that Moses was merely to hold the rod in his hand while he spoke to the rock.[53] In this way it is inferred from the narrative that Moses erred in striking the rock.[54]

That such a meaning is not likely a part of the author's intention is clear from other narratives where Moses was explicitly commanded to strike (הכה) an object with his rod to work a sign demonstrating God's power. In Exodus 17:6, for example, the Lord told Moses, "I will stand before you there on the rock at Horeb; and you shall strike [והכית] the rock, and water shall come out of it, that the people may drink." Moreover this explanation has frequently met with the additional argument that if God told them to take the rod, what else would have been expected but to use it to strike the stone?[55] In response, some have argued that the rod was the budding rod of Aaron and hence should not have been used for striking.[56] This, for example, was the position of Jamieson who argued that the error of Moses consisted of his striking the rock "*twice* in his impetuosity, thus endangering the blossoms of the rod."[57] Some have laid stress merely on the fact that Moses struck the rock twice.[58]

---

[52]Drusius, "De peccato Mosis variae sunt interpretum opiniones, quas omnes recensere longum esset" (*Critici sacri*, 2.328).

[53]Keil, *Biblical Commentary*, 3.130.

[54]This, for example, is the interpretation of the passage given by Rashi. Rashi states, "God did not command him to strike the rock but to speak to it."

[55]"Quorsum virga sumenda erat, nisi ut percuterent" (T. Malvenda, *Commentaria in sacram Scripturam una cum nova de verbo ad verbum ex hebraeo translatione, variisque lectionibus*, 1650, quoted in M. Pol, *Synopsis criticorum* [Utrecht: Leusden, 1684], 1.689).

[56]Franziscus Junius, 1587, quoted in Pol, *Synopsis* 1.689, "At florida illa virga Aaronis non erat ad percutiendum vel imperata, vel commoda." Also Johannes Drusius (1550–1616), "Sed si verbo educenda erat aqua, cur jussus est accipere virgam? Nam ea nihil opus, si sermone res transigi debebat" (*Critici sacri*, 2.328).

[57]Robert Jamieson, A. R. Fausset, and David Brown, *A Commentary Critical, Experimental and Practical on the Old and New Testaments* (Grand Rapids: Eerdmans, 1945), 564.

[58]Also Ainsworth, "the doubling of his stroke shewed also the heat of his anger" (*Annotations*, 127). Jamieson writes, "Hence some writers consider that his hasty smiting of the rock twice was an act of distrust—that such a rebellious rabble would be relieved by a miracle; and that as the water did not gush out immediately, his distrust rose into unbelief, a confirmed persuasion that they would get none" (*Commentary*, 564). Keil turns Moses' striking the rock into an evidence of lack of faith by suggesting that striking the rock was an exercise of human works rather than trust in God: "He then struck the rock twice with the rod, 'as if it depended upon human exertion, and not upon the power of God alone,' or as if the promise of God 'would not have been fulfilled without all the smiting on his part'" (*Biblical Commentary*, 131). Rashi

(2) Another line of explanation of Moses' faithlessness in Numbers 20:7–13 focuses on *what he said* when he struck the rock. The Septuagint translators apparently attempted to resolve the problem by translating Moses' words to the people (v. 10) by "Hear me, you faithless ones [οἱ ἀπειθεῖς]."[59] This was a convenient solution to the passage in Greek because it took advantage of the semantic range of the Greek word ἀπειθεῖν, used elsewhere in the Pentateuch to render the Hebrew word "to rebel" (מרה).[60] The Greek ἀπειθής can mean either "disobedient" or "unbelieving."[61]

For some the sin of Moses consisted simply of his speaking *to the people* rather than *to the rock*.[62] Some have argued that the source of Moses' error lay rather in the harsh words he spoke to the people. Rather than speaking *to the rock*, as the Lord had commanded, Moses spoke *harshly to the people*.[63] Some have read the Hebrew מורה (Num 20:10) as the Greek word μωρός,[64] and thus said Moses sinned in calling God's people *fools*.[65] According to Jamieson, "his speech conveyed the impression that it was by some power or virtue inherent in him or in the rod that the miracle was wrought."[66] Jamieson is apparently dependent on Sebastian Castellio (1515–1563) who understood the sin of Moses and Aaron to consist of their saying "shall we draw water?" Such words, according to Castellio, showed that they were taking credit for doing that which only God could do.[67] Others have argued that when Moses struck the rock the first time no water came out and at that point the people began to murmur and doubt that God would give them water. Thus Moses called the people "you rebellious ones" and struck the rock a second time.[68] Several early biblical scholars[69] have read the interrogative in המן הסלע in the sense of "whether" (*num*)[70] and hence rendered Moses' words as "Are we really able to bring water out for you?" In so doing, they are able to show Moses' words to be an expression of doubt. An equally ingenious solution noted

---

suggested that the first time Moses struck the rock only a few drops (שפין) came out because God had told him to speak to it.

[59]The Vulgate follows the Septuagint with the conflated *rebelles et increduli*.

[60]Deuteronomy 1:26; 9:7, 23, 24.

[61]LSJ, 182. It is also possible that an attempt has been made to associate the word מרה with סרה, which was translated with ἀπειθής in Deut 21:18. It may also be an unintended variant in the *Vorlage* of the Septuagint, but that is less likely in this case. The history of the difficulty in interpretation in this passage argues against an unintended variant.

[62]Paul Fagius, *Critici sacri*, 2.324. According to Fagius, this was a view known *inter Hebraeos*.

[63]"Instead of speaking to the rock with the rod of God in his hand, as God directed him, he spoke to the congregation, and in these inconsiderate words. . . . which, if they did not express any doubt in the help of the Lord, were certainly fitted to strengthen the people in their unbelief, and are therefore described in Ps. cvi. 33 as prating (speaking unadvisedly) with the lips" (Keil, *Biblical Commentary*, 130–31).

[64]"Matching the Hebrew consonants מורה to their Greek equivalents, מ = μ, ו = ω, and ר = ρ, with the nominative ending ος.

[65]*Critici sacri*, 2.323.

[66]Jamieson, *Commentary*, 564.

[67]"In eo peccatum est quod dixerunt, *Eliciamus*, quod Dei erat, sibi tribuentes" (*Critici sacri*, 2.326).

[68]See Drusius, *Critici sacri*, 2.3.2.8. Drusius was probably referring to Rashi when he attributed this view to the *antiquissimi Ebraei*.

[69]Fagius, Vatablus, Drusius, Grotius (*Critici sacri*, 2.324ff.), and Cornelius à Lapide (1567–1637). See Pol, *Synopsis*, 1.689.

[70]Following the Vulgate.

by Drusius, though hardly possible, was that the verb דברתם (דבר) in v. 8, "you shall speak [to the rock]," was to be derived from the noun דבר, "pestilence, plague," and hence should be translated "you shall destroy [the rock]."[71]

(3) Finally, the sparsity of the narrative itself, that is the *lacunae*, has provided the occasion for various explanations of Moses' error. Jamieson, for example, suggested that there were perhaps circumstances "unrecorded which led to so severe a chastisement as exclusion from the promised land."[72] Münster suggested that the people wanted to receive water from one particular rock and Moses wanted to give them water from a different rock, saying, "We are not able to give water from that rock are we?" Thus, Münster argued, Moses caused the people to think that God could give them water from some rocks but not others.[73] Lightfoot argued that the miracle of the water from the rock, having been given already at the beginning of the wilderness wanderings, implied to Moses that a still longer time of waiting in the desert was to follow. The sin of Moses, then, lay in "discrediting God's promise to lead the people into Canaan."[74]

Another major element of uncertainty in the story is the nature of the sin of Aaron. Because the story itself is silent about the actions of Aaron, the common, but implausible, explanation is that he sinned in remaining silent and not correcting Moses.[75]

These many and varied attempts at explaining verse 12 illustrate that which is already obvious from the text itself, that is, the passage does not explicitly tell us the nature of Moses' (or Aaron's) lack of faith.[76] Judging from the passage alone, the faithlessness of Moses does not appear to have consisted in his striking the rock or in his harsh words but rather lies just out of reach somewhere in the numerous "gaps"[77] of the story. We should stress that this is not a result of a deficiency in the story.[78] It rather

---

[71] *Critici sacr,* 2.328. Drusius rejected the view because the verb did not have a direct object with את but rather an object with אל.

[72] Jamieson, *Commentary,* 565.

[73] *Critici sacri,* 2.323.

[74] See Jamieson, *Commentary,* 565.

[75] Pol, *Synopsis,* 1.689.

[76] Gray's comment has merit, "The sin which excluded Moses and Aaron from Canaan is described in v.[12] as unbelief, in v.[24] [and] 27[14] as rebellion. But in v.[8-11], as they now stand, neither unbelief nor rebellion on the part of Moses and Aaron is recorded; either the one or the other has often been read into the verses, but neither is there" (George Buchanan Gray, *A Critical and Exegetical Commentary on Numbers* [ICC; Edinburgh: T. & T. Clark, 1903], 261).

[77] "From the viewpoint of what is directly given in the language, the literary work consists of bits and fragments to be linked and pieced together in the process of reading: it establishes a system of gaps that must be filled in. This gap-filling ranges from simple linkages of elements, which the reader performs automatically, to intricate networks that are figured out consciously, laboriously, hesitantly, and with constant modifications in the light of additional information disclosed in later stages of the reading" (Meir Sternberg, *The Poetics of Biblical Narrative* [Bloomington: Indiana University Press, 1985], 186).

[78] Critical scholarship shows little patience with the story as it now stands. "The truth is, the story is mutilated" (Gray, *Numbers,* 262). The classic critical study of Num 20:1–13 is that of Hugo Gressmann in *Mose und seine Zeit. Ein Kommentar zu den Mose-Sagen* (Göttingen: Vandendoech & Ruprecht, 1913), 150–54. Gressmann divided the account into two separate stories. One, the Elohist, is an "Ortssage" explaining the abundant oasis at Kadesh. The other, the later Priesterkodex, is only partially preserved and attempts

appears to be part of the story's design. It is just at the point of recounting the nature of their sin that the author abbreviates the narrative and moves on to the divine speech (Num 20:12). Moreover, it is just this divine speech that "fills the gap" with the word about faith, giving the story a sense far larger than that of its own immediate concerns. Thus Schmitt concludes, the reason the exact nature of the error of Moses is not immediately clear from the passage is because the author *has deliberately suppressed it in order to stress the divine pronouncement of Moses' lack of faith.*[79] Though we may not want to follow Schmitt's line of argument fully,[80] we believe his analysis points the way to the central message of the narrative. The rebellion of Moses and Aaron (מריתם, 20:24), which appears at some point to have been an important feature of the narrative, has been replaced with the focus on their faithlessness (לא האמנתם, 20:12). Such an interpretation has raised the actions of Moses and Aaron in the narrative to a higher level of theological reflection—the issue of faith versus obedience to the law.[81] Their

---

to explain why Moses and Aaron did not go into the land. Cornill treated Numbers 20:1–13 as an original unity but saw it largely "mutilated" (*verstummelt*) by a later redactor (see H. Holzinger, *Einleitung in den Hexateuch* [Freiburg: J. C. B. Mohr, 1893], app. 1, Quellenscheidung von Genesis bis Josua, 9).

[79]The importance of the divine word about Moses' lack of faith in Numbers 20:12 can be seen all the more in the fact that it abruptly breaks into a narrative that appears to be primarily concerned with Israel's rebellion. The centrality of the idea of rebellion in the narrative can be seen in the fact that at the close of the chapter (20:24), when the death of Aaron is recounted, there is a back-reference to the earlier failure of Moses and Aaron. Surprisingly, according to the narrative of 20:24, it was not their lack of faith that disqualified them from entering into the land, as in 20:12, but rather their rebellion (מריתם). Furthermore, the reference to their rebellion (מריתם) in 20:24 provides the basis for a wordplay on the name of the waters, "Waters of Meribah" (מריבה). Then again, later in the book, as the death of Moses approached and he was reminded that he could not enter the land with the people (Num 27:14), there is another back-reference to Numbers 20:1–13. It is recalled that Moses could not enter the land because, the Lord said, "You rebelled [מריתם] to sanctify me [להקדישני] . . . at the waters of Meribah [מריבה]." Similarly, in Deuteronomy 32:51 the Lord states that Moses (and Aaron) "acted treacherously [מעלתם] with me not sanctifying me [לא קדשתם] in the midst of the Israelites at the waters of Meribah [מריבה]." *In each case the Numbers 20 passage is read without reference to the lack of faith of Moses and Aaron* (20:12). Mention should also be made here of the reading in Psalm 95 which also does not make reference to their "lack of faith" at Meribah. This, however, is probably due to the fact that the primary text for Psalm 95 was the similar passage in Exodus 17 rather than Numbers 20. When the allusions to the Meribah passage in Numbers 20 are compared with the text in its present state, one can see quite easily, Schmitt argues, that the terms for rebellion (e.g., מריתם, 27:14; מעלתם, Deut 32:51) have been interpreted by the term "faith" (לא האמנתם) in Num 20:12. Since, according to Schmitt, the theme of faith forms the motif of the completed version of the Pentateuch, the account of the rebellion of Moses and Aaron at the waters of Meribah has become an example of the theme of faith found throughout the Pentateuch. A similar type of interpretation can be seen in the reading of Psalm 95 in Hebrews 3:7–18. After an extensive quotation of the psalm, which does not make reference to the faithlessness of Moses, the writer of Hebrews proceeds to interpret the psalm in light of the theme of faith. The crucial statement in Psalm 95 is verse 10, "They always go astray in their hearts" (תעי לבב הם). It is just this statement that the writer of Hebrews then interprets as, "Take care, brethren, lest there be in any of you an evil, unbelieving [ἀπιστίας] heart, leading you to fall away from the living God."

[80]We need not, however, work from Schmitt's premise regarding the priestly material or draw the same conclusion regarding the time of this redaction. Verse 12, in fact, is linked to the rest of the narrative by means of the repetition of the notion of "sanctifying God," להקדישני (20:12) and ויקדש (20:13). Cf. D. A. Carson, "Redaction Criticism: On the Legitimacy and Illegitimacy of a Literary Tool," in *Scripture and Truth*, ed. D. A. Carson and J. D. Woodbridge (Grand Rapids: Zondervan, 1983), 119–42.

[81]Schmitt has argued that this "Glaubens-Thematik" can be traced to the influence of Deuteronomy. This is not without significance for those who hold to a Mosaic authorship of the Pentateuch. Given the

actions epitomize the negative side of the message of faith. Moses and Aaron, who held high positions under the law, did not enjoy God's gift of the land. They died in the wilderness because they did not believe.[82]

IV. CONCLUSION

The narrative strategy of the Pentateuch contrasts Abraham, who kept the law, and Moses, whose faith was weakened under the law. This suggests a conscious effort on the part of the author of the Pentateuch to distinguish between a life of faith before the law (*ante legem*) and a lack of faith under the law (*sub lege*). This is accomplished by showing that the life of God's people before the giving of the law was characterized by faith and trust in God, but after the giving of the law their lives were characterized by faithlessness and failure. Abraham lived by faith (Gen 15:6), in Egypt the Israelites lived by faith (Exod 4), they came out of Egypt by faith (Exod 14:31), and they approached Mount Sinai by faith (Exod 19:9). However after the giving of the law, no longer was the life of God's people marked by faith.[83] Even their leaders, Moses and Aaron, failed to believe in God after the coming of the law.

If we have accurately described this aspect of the compositional strategy of the Pentateuch, then we have uncovered an initial and clear indication of the Pentateuch's view of the Mosaic Law. The view is, in fact, remarkably similar to that of Jeremiah 31:31ff. Just as Jeremiah looked back at the failure of the Sinai covenant and the Mosaic Law which the Israelites had failed to keep, so the author of the Pentateuch already held little hope for blessing *sub lege*. Jeremiah looked forward to a time when the Torah would be internalized, not written on tablets of stone (cf. Ezek 36:26), but written on their heart (Jer 31:33). In the same way the Pentateuch holds up the example of Abraham, a model of faith, one who did not have the tablets of stone but who

---

[82]fact that in Deuteronomy it is Moses who is the speaker, Schmitt's "Glaubens-Thematik" is, narrtively at least, Mosaic in origin. In Deuteronomy 9:23, for example, Moses tells the Israelites, "And when the LORD sent you from Kadesh-barnea, . . . you rebelled [ותמרו] against the commandment of the LORD your God and did not believe [לא האמנתם] him or obey [ולא שמעתם] his voice." The view which Moses expresses here in Deuteronomy is precisely that of the "Glaubens-Thematik."

[82]An identical interpretation can be found in Numbers 14:11, where the Lord says of the rebellion (מרר, v. 9) of the people of Israel, "how long will this people despise me? And how long will they not believe [לא יאמינו] me?"

[83]This strategy of the author of the Pentateuch can be seen clearly in the vocabulary of faith (האמין) which he employs in the Pentateuch. For example, throughout the Pentateuch, each use of the word "faith" as part of the "Glaubens-Thematik" before the giving of the law at Sinai is positive: Abraham believed, Israel believed, and so on. After the giving of the law, however, the positive statements of faith disappear. The statements about Israel's faith are all negative, that is, after Sinai, Israel (Num 14:11) and Moses and Aaron (Num 20:12) "did not believe." Thus, standing between the narratives that stress the faith of God's people and those that stress their faithlessness is the account of the giving of the law at Sinai. The last positive statement of faith in the Pentateuch is Exodus 19:9a, the prelude to the giving of the law. It is significant that in Hebrews 11:29, as the writer rehearses the examples of faith in the Pentateuch, he ends his examples from the Pentateuch with the crossing of the Red Sea and moves immediately to the book of Joshua. He is clearly following here the line of argument of the "Glaubens-Thematik" in the Pentateuch.

nevertheless kept the law by living a life of faith. At the same time it offers the warning of the life of Moses, who died in the wilderness because of his lack of faith. In this respect it seems fair to conclude that the view of the Mosaic Law found in the Pentateuch is essentially that of the New Covenant passages in the prophets.[84]

---

[84]This view of the nature of the Pentateuch and its view of the law is similar to that of Walther Eichrodt who argued that in the Pentateuch the law is presented in such a way that it is "impressed on the heart and conscience. Application to individual concrete instances is then left in many cases to a healthy feeling for justice" (*Theology of the Old Testament* [2 vols.; Philadelphia: Westminster, 1961], 1.77).

APPENDIX B:
COMPOSITIONAL STRATEGIES
IN THE PENTATEUCH

1. INTRODUCTION

In recent years the attention of biblical scholarship has focused as much on textual strategies in the Pentateuch as on textual strata. While source criticism has long been practiced in Pentateuchal studies, more recently increasing attention is being given to compositional criticism—the attempt to describe the semantics of the arrangement of source material in the biblical texts.[1] Its goal is to describe the compositional strategy of an entire book or text. One of the advantages of compositional criticism is that its holistic approach allows the biblical exegete to view the Bible much the same way as it was viewed before the rise of historical criticism and thus to address anew and afresh many classical problems in dogmatics and systematic theology. As an example of such a use of composition criticism, we intend to apply it to the classical problem of the role of the law in the Sinai Covenant.

There are many ways to formulate the question, but we will put it as follows: When God entered into a covenant with Israel at Sinai and gave them his laws, were these laws to be understood as part of the Sinai covenant itself or were they merely to be seen as a secondary addition to the covenant? Present-day covenant theologians and dispensationalists, although they come to vastly different conclusions on this question, are in general agreement on at least the nature of the law. As a rule, both groups today maintain that the Mosaic laws are an essential part of the Sinai covenant.[2]

---

[1]Georg Fohrer, Hans Werner Hoffmann, Friedrich Huber, Ludwig Markert, and Gunther Wanke, *Exegese des Alten Testaments, Einführung in die Methodik* (Heidelberg: Quelle & Meyer, 1983), 141ff.

[2]For covenant theology the essentially legal aspects of the covenant are seen as the basis for their emphasis on the role of the law in the life of the Christian. For dispensationalists, however, the essentially legal aspects of the covenant are seen as the basis for their separation of the Sinai covenant, with its laws, from the life of the Christian.

Historically, however, the question of the place of the law in the Sinai covenant has been the source of much debate, particularly among covenant theologians.[3] The problem is not new to post-Reformation theology, however. Beginning with Justin Martyr, a recurring theme can be found in the theology of the church and in Judaism that suggests that the bulk of the laws given to Israel at Sinai were not originally intended for the Sinai covenant. The covenant, it has been argued, was originally intended as a covenant of grace and the laws were only secondarily added to it.[4] Since the time of the Reformation, the chief representative of this view has been Johann Coccejus, the father of covenant theology. Berkhof summarized Coccejus's view as follows: "Coccejus saw in the decalogue a summary expression of the covenant of grace, particularly applicable to Israel. When the people, after the establishment of this national covenant of grace, became unfaithful and made a golden calf, the legal covenant of the ceremonial service was instituted as a stricter and harsher dispensation of the covenant of grace. Thus the revelation of grace is found particularly in the decalogue, and that of servitude in the ceremonial law."[5] Although not mentioned by Berkhof, we should note that Coccejus found his primary exegetical support in Galatians 3:19 where Paul says, the law "was added because of the transgressions, till the offspring should come to whom the promise had been made." Berkhof's primary critique of Coccejus lies in his judgment that Coccejus's view could not find support from Scripture itself.[6] This is interesting because not only did Coccejus make extensive use of Scripture in his argument,[7] but also on his part, Berkhof offered no evidence from Scripture to refute him.

In the remainder of this paper we will attempt to show that Coccejus's view of the law does indeed find support in the Scriptures. When viewed in light of its final composition, the overall literary strategy of the Pentateuch suggests a view of the role

---

[3]Gottlob Schrenk, *Gottesreich und Bund im Aelteren Protestantismus Vornehmlich bei Johannes Coccejus* (Darmstadt: Wissenschaftliche Buchgesellschaft, 1967), 116–23; Hans Heinrich Wolf, Die Einheit des Bundes, *Das Verhältnis von Altem und Neuem Testament bei Calvin* (Neukirchen: Verlag der Buchhandlung des Erziehungsvereins, 1958), 38–54; Mark W. Karlberg, "Moses and Christ—The Place of Law in Seventeenth-Century Puritanism," *TrinJ*, 10 NS (1989):11–32.

[4]Justin Martyr, *Dialogue with Trypho*: "Thus also God by the mouth of Moses commanded you to abstain from unclean and improper and violent animals: when, moreover, though you were eating manna in the desert, and were seeing all those wondrous acts wrought for you by God, you made and worshipped the golden calf" (*The Ante-Nicene Fathers*, 1:204). Irenaeus, *Against Heresies*: "And He did Himself furnish guidance to those who beheld Him not in Egypt, while to those who became unruly in the desert He promulgated a law very suitable [to their condition]. . . . when they turned themselves to make a calf, and had gone back in their minds to Egypt, desiring to be slaves instead of free men, they were placed for the future in a state of servitude suited to their wish,—[a slavery] which did not indeed cut them off from God, but subjected them to the yoke of bondage . . ." (*The Ante-Nicene Fathers*, 1:479).

[5]Louis Berkhof, *Systematic Theology* (Grand Rapids: Eerdmans, 1941), 299.

[6]"These views are all objectionable for more than one reason: (1) They are contrary to Scripture in their multiplication of the covenants. It is un-Scriptural to assume that more than one covenant was established at Sinai, though it was a covenant with various aspects. (2) They are mistaken in that they seek to impose undue limitations on the decalogue and on the ceremonial law" (Berkhof, *Systematic Theology*, 299).

[7]Johann Coccejus, *Summa Theologiae ex Scripturis Repetita, Opera Omnia*, 7:281–90.

of the law very similar to that of Coccejus's. The Pentateuch teaches that God's original plan for Israel at Sinai had not included the vast collections of law found in the Pentateuch. Rather, the Pentateuch suggests the law had been added to the Sinai Covenant because of Israel's many transgressions in the wilderness.

1.1. Textual Strata in the Pentateuch

There still is little agreement in OT studies today regarding the hypothetical shape and extent of the pentateuchal material before its use in the Pentateuch.[8] On the other hand there appears to be a growing consensus regarding the nature of the material in its present shape as part of the Pentateuch. There are many OT scholars today, who in rejecting the documentary hypothesis, hold that the present Pentateuch consists of a mosaic or collage of written sources, much like the later historical books, e.g., Judges, Samuel and Kings, and the Gospels.[9] Indeed, among the older conservative and orthodox scholars it was widely acknowledged that the Pentateuch was composed of a broad range of ancient documents[10] some even describing them as "differing in style, and distinguishable by the primitive formality of their introductions."[11]

---

[8]Rolf Rendtorff, *Das überlieferungsgeschichtliche Problem des Pentateuch* (BZAW 147; Berlin: Walter de Gruyter, 1977); Hans Heinrich Schmid, *Der sogenannte Jahwist. Beobachtungen und Fragen zur Pentateuchforschung* (Zürich, 1976); R. N. Whybray, *The Making of the Pentateuch. A Methodological Study*, JSOTS 53 (Sheffield: JSOT Press, 1987).

[9]Erhard Blum, *Studien zur Komposition des Pentateuch* (Berlin: Walter de Gruyter, 1990), 1–5.

[10]**Heidegger**, "quanquam ex traditione Majorum, utpote quartus a Jacobo, neque adeo remotus ab iis temporibus, quibus Adamus ipse superstes fuit, plurima haurire potuit . . ." (Iohann Henrich Heidegger, *Enchiridion Biblicum* [1st ed. 1681] [Jena: Io. Felicum Bielckium, 1723], 18; **Vitringa**, "schedas et scrinia patrum, apud Israelitas conservata, Mosem collegisse, digessisse, ornasse et ubi deficiebant, complesse et ex iis priorem librorum suorum confecisse" (Campegius Vitringa, *Observationum Sacrarum Libri VI* [1683–1708]); **Rivet**, "multa enim scripserunt, quae aut ipsi viderunt, aut etiam ab alijs hominibus acceperunt" (Andrew Rivet, *Isagoge, seu Introductio generalis* [1627], 10); **Carpzov**, the leading Lutheran orthodox OT scholar of the early eighteenth century, held to the possibility of sources in the Pentateuch, but his view of the nature of inspiration, viz., dictation, precluded his attaching any importance to them. "Quamvis enim nonnulla de his, quae tradidit in Genesi, habere potuerit ab Amramo patre suo. . . . rectius tamen soli θεοπνευστίαι omnia tribuimus" (Johann Gottlob Carpzov, *Introductio ad Libros Canonicos Bibliorum Verteris Testamenti Omnes* [Leipzig, 1757], 62–63); **Gaussen**, "Whether they describe their own emotions, or relate what they remember, or repeat contemporary narratives, or copy over genealogies, or make extracts from uninspired documents—their writing is inspired, their narratives are directed from above . . ." (L. Gaussen, *The Divine Inspiration of the Bible* [Grand Rapids: Kregel Publications, 1971], 25).

[11]Robert Jamieson, A. R. Fausset, and David Brown, *A Commentary Critical, Experimental and Practical on the Old and New Testaments* (Grand Rapids: Eerdmans, 1945): "Independently of any hypothesis, it may be conceded that, in the composition of those parts of the Pentateuch relating to matters which were not within the sphere of his personal knowledge, Moses would and did avail himself of existing records which were of reliable authority; and while this admission can neither diminish the value nor affect the credibility of his history as an inspired composition, it is evident that, in making use of such literary materials as were generally known in his time, or had been preserved in the repositories of Hebrew families, he interwove them into his narrative conformably with that unity of design which so manifestly pervades the entire Pentateuch" (xxxii).

In the Pentateuch as a whole there are three major types of literary sources: collections of laws (legal corpora), narratives, and poetry. We will briefly discuss these types of sources and then present some ideas on their arrangement (compositional strategy) in the final shape of the Mosaic Pentateuch.

1.1.1. Collections of Laws (Legal Corpora) in the Pentateuch

The legal codes make up the largest portion of the center section of the Pentateuch. Clearly recognizable collections of laws in the Pentateuch are the **Decalogue** (Ex 20:1–17), the **Covenant Code** (Ex 20:22–23:33), the **Holiness Code** (Lev 17–26), and the **Code of the Priests** (Ex 25 – Lev 16).[12] Belonging to this last corpus are the instructions concerning the pattern of the tabernacle (Ex 25–31) and its construction (Ex 35–40). Although in classical source criticism, questions regarding the setting and date of such strata predominate, when viewed from the point of view of compositional strategy, one is confronted with quite a different set of problems. Primarily one seeks to discover the purpose these various collections have in the final arrangement of the text. What does each contribute to the sense of the whole? How and why has the author of the Pentateuch put them where they are in the present shape of the text?

It has long been recognized that certain basic differences exist between these collections of laws. The requirements for the building of an altar in the Covenant Code (Ex 20:24–25), for example, are quite different than those in the Code of the Priests (Ex 27:1ff). According to the Covenant Code, the altar was to be made of earth or stones and could be set up "in every place" where God caused his name to be remembered (Ex 20:24f). This was a very simple form of altar reminiscent of the altars in the patriarchal period. According to the Code of the Priests, however, the altar was to be made of acacia wood overlaid with bronze (Ex 27:1ff) and was to be placed in the tabernacle where only the priests would have access to it. This appears to be an entirely different sort of altar.

There have been numerous attempts to harmonize these two laws. According to one traditional harmonization, there were in fact to be two altars, an earthen one for the burnt offering and a wooden one for burning incense.[13] Another common harmonization is that the bronze altar of Exodus 27 was to be hollow (Ex 27:8) and was therefore to be filled with dirt or stones to make the earthen altar of Exodus 20.[14] Thus what appears to be a description of two distinct altars is, in fact, only two aspects of the description of one. Such attempts, however, serve better to demonstrate the literary problem than to provide a solution. Among modern conservative biblical scholars the

---

[12]The "Code of the Priests" is not to be confused with the so-called "Priestly Document" denoted in the documentary hypothesis by the signum "P."

[13]Michael Walter, *Harmonia Totius S. Scripturae* (Argentorate: Eberhard Zetzner, 1627), 176. Walter, however, rejected this harmonization because in Exodus 38:1 the altar used for the burnt offering was to be made of wood.

[14]"מזבח נחשת מלא אדמה תעשה ליה", *Mechilta D'Rabbi Ismael*, ed. H. S. Horovitz (Jerusalem: Wahrmann Books, 1970), 242; "alij melius sic conciliant, internam altaris partem fuisse de terra solida et compacta, externam autem de lignis dictis" (Walter, *Harmonia Totius*, 176); "The enclosing copper case served merely to keep the earth together" (Jamieson, Fausset, and Brown, *A Commentary*, 391).

two passages are allowed to coexist without a harmonization, the earthen altar being taken merely as a temporary measure.[15] Though this explanation may provide a solution to the historical problem of the purpose of the two altars, it completely misses the literary question of why the two types of altars are prescribed in the Pentateuch without an attempt to harmonize or explain their differences.

Critical scholarship has been unanimous in seeing the two laws as arising out of different historical settings.[16] It is commonly argued, for example, that along with the other laws in the Covenant Code, the instructions for building an earthen altar come from a more primitive period in Israel's religion, a time when their forms of worship were much like those of the Patriarchs in the Genesis narratives. Individuals and groups could provide local centers of worship by building an altar and giving gifts to God.[17] Critics have argued that in the early stages of their religion, Israel, like Abraham in the Genesis narratives, built a new altar at each place they settled. The laws dealing with the bronze altar, on the other hand, are taken to represent the final stages of Israel's religion when a single official worship site was recognized.

The major weakness of the critical view, however, is its lack of a convincing explanation of why such an obvious dissonance would have been tolerated in the final canonical text. Eissfeldt, clearly sensing the need for an explanation, argued that in the process of redaction, after the Covenant Code had been replaced by the laws of Deuteronomy, the law regarding the primitive altar could not be removed from the text because it was "already so rooted in the popular mind that such a transformation of it would not be possible." Such a "neutralizing" of the Book of the Covenant, Eissfeldt argued, "seems to us not merely remarkable, but also impracticable. But we must bear in mind that the attempt has been successful not only in this case but also in many others. . . . Older precepts which are allowed to remain, are now quite naturally understood in the light of the newer, or, where that is not possible or necessary, they simply remain unheeded."[18]

To my mind, Eissfeldt's explanation is quite remarkable. While it must be admitted as possible that the biblical writer intended his readers to ignore the Covenant Code in their reading of the Pentateuch, it is by no means likely. On the contrary, its position alongside the Decalogue and within the Sinai narrative itself suggests the author intended to call attention to it in the overall structure of his work. Unlike literary criticism, it is the task of compositional criticism to explain its placement in the final shape of the Pentateuch rather than try to explain it away. We will attempt to do this below.

1.1.2. Narratives in the Pentateuch

Numerous narrative texts of varying lengths are also found in the central portion of the Pentateuch. These texts not only provide the general framework for the

---

[15]Walter C. Kaiser, Jr., "Exodus," *Expositor's Bible Commentary* (Grand Rapids: Zondervan, 1990), 2:428.

[16]Otto Eissfeldt, *Introduction to the Old Testament*, trans. Peter R. Ackroyd (New York: Harper & Row, 1965), 218.

[17]F. Horst, *RGG* 3, 1:1523ff.

[18]Eissfeldt, *Introduction*, 222f.

legal collections, but they are also found embedded within the various collections of laws. The general framework of this center section is formed by three complex narratives—the Exodus narrative (Ex 1–18), the Sinai narrative (Ex 19–34), and the wilderness narrative (Nu 10:11ff). There are several smaller, but strategically important narratives within this section that are also related to the larger framework, e.g., the oppression narrative (Ex 1); the call of Moses (Ex 3 and 6) and the call of Joshua (Nu 27:12–23); the accounts of the faith of Moses, Aaron, and the people (Ex 4 and 19), and the accounts of their lack of faith (Nu 13–14, 20); the narrative of Aaron's calf idol (Ex 32) and the narrative of Israel's goat idols[19] (Lev 17:1–9); the narrative of Moses and Pharaoh (Ex 7–12) and the narrative of Balaam and Balak (Nu 22–24). Though each of these units of narrative has a discernible internal structure, our interest in them at the present time is in their relationship with each other and with the collections of laws discussed above.[20]

1.1.3. Poetry in the Pentateuch

Several poetic texts are found interspersed in the center of the Pentateuch—most notably in Exodus 15:1–17 and Numbers 23:7–10, 18–24; 24:3–9, 15–24. Elsewhere I have attempted to show the role of poetic texts such as Genesis 49:1–27, Numbers 24:15–24, and Deuteronomy 32–33 in the compositional strategy of the Pentateuch as a whole.[21] It seems warranted to seek the role of similar texts at a lower level in this center section of the Pentateuch; however, this will not be the aim of the present appendix.

1.2. Textual Strategy in the Pentateuch: The Collections of Laws (Legal Corpora) and the Sinai Narratives

The chart in Figure B.1 shows the general relationship between the narrative sections[22] of the central part of the Pentateuch and the collections of laws.

A curious feature of the Sinai narratives is the way in which they envelop and thus serve to link the Decalogue, the Covenant Code, and the Code of the Priests, just those collections of laws that, at least according to critical theory, differ most markedly from each other.[23] The Decalogue follows the account of the covenant ceremony in Exodus 19:1–25. This narrative is quite complex and includes two major segments.

---

[19]The Hebrew word שְׂעִירִם usually means simply "goats," but it can also mean "goat idols" since in 2 Chronicles 11:15 these שְׂעִירִם are said to have been "made" by Jeroboam along with his "calf idols." (Ludwig Koehler and Walter Baumgartner, *Hebräisches und Aramäisches Lexikon* [Leiden: Brill, 1990], IV:1250).

[20]"It is one of the tasks of Pentateuchal criticism to explain how this interruption of the narrative by large blocks of law took place" (Eissfeldt, *Introduction*, 157).

[21]John Sailhamer, *The Pentateuch as Narrative: A Biblical–Theological Commentary* (Grand Rapids: Zondervan, 1992).

[22]"This section, more precisely its actual narrative kernel . . . is exceptionally difficult to analyze" (Eissfeldt, 193).

[23]In most critical assessments of these two corpora, the Covenant Code is taken as the earliest of the legal codes and the Code of the Priests is assigned the latest date.

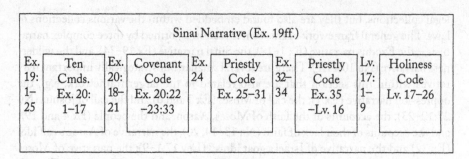

Figure B.1

The first is an account of the establishment of an initial covenant on Mount Sinai (19:1–16a), and the second is an account of Israel's fearful retreat from God (19:16b–25). The Decalogue (20:1–17), in turn, is followed by a short narrative, again recounting the fear of the people at Sinai (Ex 20:18–21). The Covenant Code is then embedded in the Sinai narrative between Exodus 20:21 and 24:1ff, and this narrative is followed by the Code of the Priests (Ex 25 – Lev 16). Furthermore, the account of the making of the golden calf (Ex 32) and the reestablishment of the Sinai Covenant (Ex 33–34), both parts of the Sinai narrative, break into the Code of the Priests just after the instructions for making the tabernacle (Ex 25–31) and before the account of its completion (Ex 35–40). Consequently, the instructions for building the tabernacle are separated from the remainder of the Code of the Priests by the account of the failure of the house of Aaron in the incident of the golden calf (Ex 32) as well as by the account of the renewal of the Sinai covenant (Ex 33–34). These observations raise an important literary question. What is the effect of the arrangement of the laws and the narrative in the present shape of the text? Is there a sense to be gained from the pattern of events and laws reflected in the text as we now have it? Is the shape of the text semantically relevant? In the remainder of this appendix, we will address this question by attempting to unravel and retrace the literary strategy lying behind the present shape of the Sinai narrative.

By means of the arrangement of the narrative, the Sinai Covenant *before the incident of the golden calf* is characterized by the laws of the Decalogue, the Covenant Code, and the instructions for building the tabernacle. However, the Sinai Covenant *after the golden calf* is characterized by the fundamentally different and more extensive Code of the Priests (Ex 35–Lev 16). In other words, after the golden calf incident, the bulk of the priestly laws (Ex 35–Lev 16) take the place earlier occupied in the original Sinai narratives by the Decalogue, the Covenant Code, and the Tabernacle (Ex 19–24). It thus appears that the incident of the golden calf has signaled a change in the nature of Israel's covenant relationship.

The following chart shows the relationship of the Decalogue, the Covenant Code, and the Tabernacle to the narrative of the original covenant at Sinai, and the relationship of the Priestly Code to the covenant renewal narrative after the incident of the golden calf.

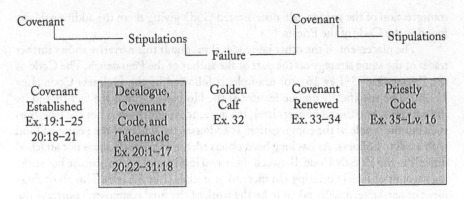

Figure B.2

When viewed within the context of the striking differences between the laws of the Covenant Code and those of the Code of the Priests, which we have alluded to above, the arrangement of this material appears to reflect a definite strategy.

On the face of it the association of the original covenant at Sinai with the Covenant Code, and the association of the renewal of that covenant with the Code of the Priests suggests a differing narrative assessment of the two codes. It is also clear that the incident of the golden calf, which has been strategically positioned between these two codes of law, is the underlying cause of the changes in law codes. In positioning the texts this way, the changes perceived between the laws in the two codes are now narratively presented as part of a larger change in the nature of the Sinai covenant itself—a change that has come as a result of the incident of the golden calf. Rather than attempting to render the differences between the two law codes invisible, as modern critical studies suggest, the author appears to be using these very differences as part of a larger strategy. In their present textual position, it is these very differences that show that a change had come over Israel's covenant with God owing to the sin of the golden calf. Israel's initial relationship with God at Sinai, characterized by the patriarchal simplicity of the Covenant Code, was now represented by the complex and restrictive laws of the Code of the Priests.

What begins to emerge in this assessment of the narrative strategy is the notion that the biblical portrayal of Israel's relationship with God in the covenant at Sinai was not intended to be read in a static way. The author apparently wants to show that Israel's relationship with God, established at Sinai, underwent important changes due to Israel's repeated failure to obey God's will.[24] What began as a covenant between God and Israel, fashioned after that of the patriarchs (the Covenant Code), had become increasingly more complex (the Code of the Priests) as Israel failed to obey God. Israel's propensity to follow "other gods," demonstrated in these narratives by the

---

[24]Not only is there an *ordo temporum* between the covenants, but there is an *ordo temporum* within the covenants as well.

transgression of the golden calf, necessitated God's giving them the additional laws found in the Code of the Priests.[25]

The placement of the other law codes throughout this narrative shows further traces of the same strategy on the part of the author of the Pentateuch. The Code of the Priests (Ex 25–Lev 16), for example, is followed by the Holiness Code (Lev 17–26). The specifically unique feature of the Holiness Code is the fact that in its introduction, and throughout its laws, the audience it addresses is not the priests as such but the whole of the congregation. It addresses the whole of the people of God with a call to holiness. As has long been observed, the Holiness Code is not attached directly to the Priestly Code. Between these two legal codes lies an obscure but striking account of Israel's offering sacrifices to goat idols (Lev 17:1–9). This short fragment of narrative, usually taken to be the work of the final composer,[26] portrays the Israelite people as forsaking the tabernacle and sacrificing "outside the camp."[27] Though brief, the content of the narrative is, in fact, quite similar to the incident of the golden calf.[28] The people have forsaken the Lord and his provisions to worship and follow after other gods, in this case, the "goat idols." Unlike the narrative of the golden calf which places the blame on the priesthood, in this narrative it is the people, not the priests, who are responsible for the idolatry. Thus within the logic of the text, the incident of the people's sacrificing to the goat idols plays a similar role to that of the priests' involvement in the golden calf. Just as the narrative of the golden calf marked a tran-

---

[25]Eissfeldt's argument that the Covenant Code was shaped as a polemic against a more complex form for worship suits the role the code has assumed within the strategy of the Pentateuch. It is, in fact, a polemic of sorts against the more complex requirements of the Priestly Code. In this light the view of Welch, *Deuteronomy, The Framework to the Code* (1932); Caspari, "Heimat und Soziale Wirkung des at. Bundesbuches," *ZDMG*, 83 (1929): 97–120; and Cazelles, "L'auteur du code de l'alliance," *RB*, 52 (1945): 173–91, that the Covenant Code was compiled in Kadesh or the east Jordan, by Moses or during the time of Moses, is of considerable importance.

[26]Literary critics of the old school of Wellhausen took this composer to be a late redactor, usually associated with the priestly circles (Alfred Bertholet, *Leviticus* [Tübingen: J. C. B. Mohr (Paul Siebeck), 1901], 58). Composition criticism, however, should remain neutral on the question of the historical time period of the final composition of the Pentateuch. As an evangelical, of course, I would view the work of the final composition of the Pentateuch in light of the role of Moses as its author.

[27]Wenham, along with Keil, suggests that these verses are a prohibition not just of sacrifices, but of any kind of animal slaughter, and that the prohibition was limited only to the time Israel was in the wilderness. However, the fact that what is prohibited is not every kind of slaughter but, specifically, slaughter for sacrifice, is shown in the relationship of Leviticus 17:3–4 to 17:5. According to 17:5, the slaughter of 17:3–4 was specifically and only for sacrifice, that is, it was not a general slaughter for food. It should be noted as well that later in this same chapter (Lev 17:13ff.), provision is made for animals slain in hunting. This would also suggests that slaying animals for food was permissible and hence only slaughtering for sacrifice was expressly prohibited. Moreover, in 17:7 the prohibition is called an "eternal ordinance," which would rule out its limitation to the time of the wilderness sojourn. Furthermore, Deuteronomy 12:15, which appears to be a clarification of this law, restates the provision that mere slaughtering of animals could be done anywhere. What was specifically prohibited in Deuteronomy was sacrificing anywhere except the central altar.

[28]There are also literary parallels between this text and the opening sections of the other law codes, e.g., the establishment of the proper place of worship in Exodus 20:24–26, Exodus 25ff., Deuteronomy 12, and Ezekiel 40ff. (Bertholet, 58).

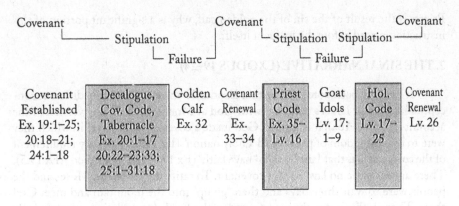

Figure B.3

sition in the nature of the covenant and additions to its laws, so here also the incident of the goat idols marks the transition from the Code of the Priests to the additional laws in the Holiness Code. The chart in Figure B.3 shows this relationship.

We can see from the chart that the three major law collections, the Covenant Code, the Code of the Priests, and the Holiness Code, are not only embedded in the whole of the Sinai narratives, but they are arranged around two quite similar narratives. Both narratives focus on the Lord's displeasure with Israel's fall into idolatry, the first involving idolatry in the form of calf worship and the second that of goats.[29] Such a structure betrays a strategy at a very high level in the constitution of the Pentateuch. In this arrangement, the laws of the Covenant Code are intentionally linked to the original covenant at Sinai (Ex 19–24). The laws of the Code of the Priests, on the other hand, are associated with the covenant renewal after the sin of the golden calf (Ex 32–34). Finally, the laws of the Holiness Code are placed in the context of the incident of the people's offering sacrifices to the goat idols outside the camp (Lev 17) and the covenant renewal in Leviticus 26.

It will not be possible here to continue to trace the strategy apparent in the detail of the arrangement of the laws and the narrative texts of the Pentateuch.[30] We will limit ourselves here to a brief discussion of two central questions raised by our observations. The first is the internal shape of Exodus 19–24. How does the structure of the initial Sinai narrative (Ex 19–24) fit into the larger scheme of the Pentateuch and its view of the law which we have traced above? The second question has to do with the location of the instructions for the tabernacle (Ex 25–31). Why are they placed before the incident of the golden calf (Ex 32) rather than after it? If the addition of the Code of the

---

[29]There appear to be intentional compositional links between the golden calf erected by the priests (עֵגֶל, Ex 32:4) and the young bull (עֵגֶל, Lev 9:1ff.) required as sin offering for the priests as well as the goat idols worshiped by the people (שְׂעִיר, Lev 17:7) and goats (שְׂעִיר, Lev 4:23) required as a sin offering for the people. For a discussion of the literary connections see the author's *Pentateuch as Narrative*.

[30]I have attempted to do this in *The Pentateuch as Narrative*.

Priests is the result of the sin of the golden calf, why is a significant portion of this instruction placed before the incident itself?

2. THE SINAI NARRATIVE (EXODUS 19–24)

It has long been noted that within Exodus 19 there are two quite different conceptualizations of Israel's covenant with God at Mount Sinai. In one version of the account (Ex 19:1–16a), it is argued, God made a covenant with Israel in which they were to be a "kingdom of priests and a holy nation" (Ex 19:6). The only requirement of the covenant was that Israel was to "have faith" (Ex 19:9) and "obey God" (Ex 19:5). There appear to be no laws in this covenant. To ratify the covenant, Moses and the people were to wait three days and then "go up" into the mountain and meet God there. Though this is not always reflected in the English translations, there is little doubt that it is the view of the Hebrew text.[31] This same view of the Sinai covenant can also be found earlier in Exodus 3:12[32] and in later biblical texts that refer back to this chapter. In Jeremiah 7:22–23, for example, the Lord says, "For in the day that I brought them out of the land of Egypt I did not speak to your fathers or command them concerning burnt offerings and sacrifices. But this command I gave them, 'Obey my voice, and I will be your God, and you will be my people; and you will walk in the way I will command you so that it would be well to you.'"[33]

In the other version of the Sinai Covenant in Exodus 19 (16b–25), however, there is a quite different view of things. Instead of the notion of a "kingdom of priests," now there is a distinction between the people and the priests—it is not a kingdom *of* priests but a kingdom *with* priests (Ex 19:22–24). Moreover, instead of the people being called up before God in the mountain, the people were to "be kept from going up" the mountain and only Moses and Aaron were allowed up the mountain to be with God (19:12, 13a, 21–23). Finally, instead of simple faith and obedience, the Decalogue and the Covenant Code have become the basis of Israel's keeping their covenant with God. Curiously enough, this is the view of the Sinai Covenant found in Ezekiel 20:18–26, ". . . 'I am the Lord your God, walk in my statutes and keep my judgments and do them; keep my sabbaths holy and it will be a sign between you and me to know that I am the Lord your God.' But they rebelled against me. . . . And I gave them statutes which did not result in good [for them] and judgments in which they could not have life."[34]

---

[31] The (N)JPS has correctly rendered 19:13b, "they may go up on בָהָר) the mountain." See the discussion of this verse below.

[32] "When you (sing.) bring the people out of Egypt, you (plur.) shall worship God on this mountain (עַל הָהָר הַזֶּה)." According to the viewpoint of this verse, the anticipation clearly was that Moses and the people were to worship God on the mountain. Cf. Exodus 4:27b and 5:3.

[33] The translation above follows the RSV, NASB, KJV, and (N)JPS. The NIV translation, "I did not just give them commands about burnt offerings and sacrifices," appears to be a harmonistic attempt of the translators to remove an obvious problem.

[34] The NIV and New Scofield Reference Bible's translation of נתתי להם חקים as "I also gave them *over to* statutes" is an unfortunate harmonization of this difficult passage (cf. RSV, NASB, (N)JPS, and KJV, which render it as above). The same is to be said of the addition of "in fire" (Ez 20:26) in some English ver-

According to literary critical theory, these two versions of the Sinai covenant are a reflection of the composite nature of the present text. It was the view of the "Elohist" that both Moses and the people were to "go up" to the mountain to meet with God (Ex 19:13b). As conceived by the "Elohist," the nature of the covenant was that which we find in 19:2b–8, namely, a simple renewal of the patriarchal covenant of faith and obedience. Owing to their fear of God's presence (Ex 19:16b), however, the people appointed Moses to speak with God on their behalf and they remained behind at the foot of the mountain (Ex 19:17, 19b).[35] In the "Jahwist" account, however, the people were forbidden to go up the mountain from the start (Ex 19:12–13a). They were to watch the whole of the display of God's presence at a safe distance (Ex 19:18, 20–25).[36]

Long before the rise of literary criticism, the tensions within this narrative were already apparent and various harmonizations had been offered. As to the question of the relationship of the covenant made in Exodus 19:3–8 and that of Exodus 24, Rashi argued that we should not read the narrative in chronological order. Thus, the covenant made in chapter 19, is the same as the one later established in chapter 24. Rashi's explanation of this difficulty has had little influence Christian interpretation.[37] The common explanation among Christians was that in Exodus 19:3–8, God had only begun to expound to Israel the nature of the Sinai covenant. Before he had fully explained it, Israel quickly agreed to the terms. According to Calvin, for example, the people "were carried away by a kind of headlong zeal, and deceived themselves."[38]

The question of who was to go up into the mountain has been the most difficult to solve. According to Rashi, the key to the solution is the mention of the "blast"

---

sions, making it appear that the "statutes" in 20:25 relate to offering their firstborn "in the fire." The words "in fire" do not occur in the Hebrew text and are not implied. The passage is rendered correctly by (N)JPS: "When they set aside every first issue of the womb." As the identical phraseology shows, the statement, "when they set aside every first issue of the womb" (בהעביר כל פטר רחם) is a reference to God's claim of the firstborn in Exodus 13:12, "You are to give over to the LORD the first offspring of every womb" (העברת כל פטר רחם), not to child sacrifice (cf 34:19; Num 3:12–13). Moreover, "causing one's children to pass through the fire" (העברה בנו ובתו באש) is expressly forbidden in Deuteronomy 18:10. The collocation העביר פטר רחם does not occur in the OT with באש but, as in Exodus 13:12, with reference to the first born. When העביר occurs with באש, the object is not פטר רחם but rather בן (Deut 18:10; 2 Kings 17:17; 21:6; 23:10; 2 Chron 33:6; Ez 20:31 [omitted in LXX]).

[35]Otto Eissfeldt, Hexateuch-Synopse, Die Erzählung der fünf Bücher Mose und des Buches Josua mit dem Anfange des Richterbuches (Darmstadt: Wissenschaftliche Buchgesellschaft, 1973), 146–47.

[36]Ibid., 146–48.

[37]Keil may depend on Rashi when he suggests that Exodus 19:3–8 is associated with the proclamation of the "fundamental law of the covenant in the presence of the whole nation (chap. xix. 16- xx. 18)." C. F. Keil and F. Delitzsch, Biblical Commentary on the Old Testament (Grand Rapids: Eerdmans, 1971), 2:101. Recently, Rashi's view has apparently been adopted by G. C. Chirichigno, "The Narrative Structure of Ex 19–24," Biblica, 68 (1987): "We have argued that the awkward surface structure of the narrative, which results in the non-linear temporal ordering of events, can be explained when one takes into account the sequence structure of the narrative, particularly the use of the literary device called resumptive repetition" (479).

[38]John Calvin, Commentaries on the Four Last Books of Moses Arranged in the Form of a Harmony, trans. Charles William Bingham (Grand Rapids: Baker, 1979), 320; Ainsworth: "The people not yet knowing the unpossibility of the Law, which is weak through the flesh, Rom 8:3. make promise of more than they were able to performe. After, when the Law was pronounced, they feare and flee away, Exod. 20. 18, 19" (Henry Ainsworth, Annotations upon the Five Bookes of Moses [London: M. Parsons, 1639], 68).

(במשך) of the horn that signaled Israel's move up the mountain (Ex 19:13b). Rashi reasoned that a long blast (קול אריך) of the ram's horn signified that God was departing from the mountain and hence, when God had departed, the people were permitted to go up the mountain.[39] Thus, though the people were warned not to go up into the mountain in verse 12, they were allowed to go up into the mountain when the horn was sounded. Rashi's interpretation has found its way into several early scholarly versions[40] and it is as old as the Septuagint.[41]

Nicholas von Lyra, however, departed from Rashi's explanation by suggesting that "to go up the mountain" meant the people could go only so far as the limits that had been established by Moses (Ex 19:12).[42] This appears to be the sense taken by many modern English versions, "When the horn blasts, they shall come up to the mountain."[43] The obvious problem with this view is that the text does not say "up *to* the mountain" but "up *in* the mountain" just as in Exodus 19:12.[44]

Still another problem within the narrative is the statement in 19:12, "Beware of going up the mountain. . ." (JPS). This statement is often taken by literary critics as an absolute prohibition of the people's going up the mountain, but it does not necessarily have this sense. The warning could just as well be "Watch yourselves going up"

---

[39]Rashi's interpretation is represented in several Christian commentaries, e.g., **Münster**: "*Cum prolixius buccina sonuerit*; prolixior enim sonus signum erat Dominum majestatis montem deseruisse." **Fagius**: "Sensus est, Dum satis protractus adeoque finitus est sonitus tubarum, tum ascendere potest populus; at praesente Domino nequaquam. Neque enim veto ut in perpetuum non ascendatis. Dum ergo sonitus cornu cessaverit, potestis ascendere. Prolixior sonus signum erat, Dominum majestatis montem deseruisse." According to **Eben Ezra**, Rashi's explanation was inadequate because the Lord's glory was always on the mountain until the completion of the tabernacle.

[40]**Calvin**, *Commentary* (1563): "quum protraxerit buccina, ipsi ascendent in montem"; **Münster**, *Biblia sacra* (1534): "cum prolixius buccina insonuerit, tunc poterunt ascendere montem"; **Tyndale**, *The Seconde Boke of Moses* (1530): "when the horne bloweth: than let them come up in to the mounten'" **Geneva Bible** (1599): "When the horne bloweth long, they shall come up into the mountaine"; **Junius and Tremellius**, *Biblia Sacra* (1575): "cum tractim sonabit cornu, ea ascendere poterunt in ipsum montem"; **NJPS**: "When the ram's horn sounds a long blast, they may go up on the mountain."

[41]The LXX translated the sense of the phrase, not the words: "Whenever the sounds and the trumpets and the cloud departs from the mountain, they may go up the mountain." (ἐπὶ τὸ ὄρος. Cf. the Vulgate: *cum coeperit clangere bucina tunc ascendant in montem*; and Targum Onkelos, "When the horn blast is protracted, they may go up into the mountain" (במיגד שופרא אנון מרשן למסק בטורא).

[42]*In montem hic est versus montem, usque ad terminos a Mose Dei jussu praefixos* (*Synopsis Criticorum* 1:398). Lyra apparently followed Eben Ezra on Exodus 19:17, "[under the mountain] means outside the borders set by Moses" (מחוץ לגבול שחגבילם משה). A similar interpretation may already be present in the Samaritan Pentateuch's reading ההר in Exodus 19:12a rather than העם as in the MT.

[43]This translation is represented in the NIV, NASB, and KJV. That it is a harmonistic attempt to avoid the problem of the Hebrew text is suggested by the fact that these same versions render the identical expression (עָלָה בָהָר) in the preceding verse not by "go *up to* the mountain" but rather "go *up* (or *into*) the mountain" (Ex 19:12). Only the (N)JPS renders עָלָה בָהָר in 19:12 and 13b, as to "go up (on) the mountain."

[44]A third explanation was offered by Drusius (*Critici Sacri*). Following Eben Ezra, Drusius identified the pronoun "they" (Ex 19:13b) with Moses, Aaron, Abihu, and the elders and thus avoided the suggestion that the people were allowed to go up the mountain. This is also the position of Targum Neofiti 1, "when the trumpet is sounded, Moses and Aaron are authorised to come up into the mountain." That it was the people rather than Moses and the elders, however, is seen from 19:17 and 19:12 where "the people" are expressly in view.

(עֲלוֹת) as "Beware not to go up" (מֵעֲלוֹת).[45] In either case, however, if read in the context of Israel's waiting three days (19:11) until "the horn is blown" (19:13b), the warning in 19:12 is merely a warning not to enter the mountain *until* the appropriate time.

According to the narrative, then, there is an expectation that the people are to go up the mountain with Moses to meet with God. In other words God's intention to meet the people on the mountain itself is not merely the viewpoint of a hypothetical document, such as the Elohist, but is, in fact, the consistent viewpoint of the entire narrative. It is also clear from the narrative that subsequently the people were barred from going up the mountain (19:21, 23). However, as 19:23f makes clear, the people are first barred from the mountain in 19:21, not in 19:12.[46] In 19:12 the people cannot go up the mountain until the horn blast. In 19:21, the people cannot go up the mountain at all. Before 19:21, the expectation of the narrative is that when all the people heard the blast of the horn, they were to go up into the mountain.

The above consideration of the strategy of the composition of this passage raises several important questions. Why, for example, does the viewpoint of the narrative change so radically with respect to the people's going up into the mountain? Is it merely that two conflicting accounts have been preserved intact in this chapter, as critical theory suggests? Or are there clues of a changing situation within the narrative that account for such a shift in God's purpose? Furthermore, does the change in the people's right to go up the mountain reflect the intention of the author of the Pentateuch? In other words, are the tensions which are so transparent in the Hebrew narrative merely the result of conflicting sources, or are these tensions semantically and theologically relevant? Are they part of the author's intent?

Fortunately, the narrative does not leave us without an answer to these questions. According to 19:16, on the third day, when the people were to be ready to "go up the mountain," the horn was blown. Curiously enough, however, the text says that when the people saw the great display of God's power on the mountain they "were afraid in the camp." Moreover, the text goes on to recount that "Moses brought the people out from the camp to meet with God and they stood at the base of (בְּתַחְתִּית) the mountain" (19:17). When they saw the Lord's appearance on the mountain, "they were afraid in the camp," and thus they remained standing at the foot of the mountain (19:17b). Moses ascended to meet with God alone.

Important from the standpoint of narrative strategy is the fact that it is just at this point in the narrative that the people are warned not to "break through to look upon the Lord" (19:21). As we have seen, this is not a repeat of the warning in 19:12, but is a new warning. According to Moses' own words in 19:23, God had "testified against the people" (19:21) that they were not to go up the mountain. What the whole of Exodus

---

[45]The variant suggested in the BHS apparatus (מֵעֲלוֹת) shows precisely what would be expected for an unequivocal negative sense.

[46]The similarity of terms, e.g., הָעֵד in 19:21 and 19:23, as well as identical meaning, shows that 19:23 is explanatory of 19:21 and not 19:12. The use of הַגְבֵּל in 19:12 and 19:23 is sometimes taken as the grounds for seeing 19:23 as a harmonization of 19:12 and 19:13b. However, the phrase "set limits for the people" (19:12) is not the same as "set limits for the mountain" (19:23). The reading of the Samaritan Pentateuch in 19:12, הַהַר rather than הָעָם, points precisely to the difficulty of making 19:23f refer back to 19:12.

19 then shows is that God's original intention to meet with the people on the mountain (19:13b) was fundamentally altered because of the people's fear of God (19:16b).

At this point it may be important to note that in Exodus 20:18–21, a later reflection on this same incident,[47] we find precisely the same point of view about the failure of the people to draw near to God. We will thus turn to a brief discussion of that narrative.

There are marked similarities as well as differences between the two narratives on either side of the Decalogue (Ex 19:16–24 and 20:18–21). Both narratives explain why Moses went up to the mountain alone and not with the people (19:16b; 20:19). In 19:21, the Lord instructed Moses to keep the people from the mountain "lest they break through to see the Lord and many of them fall (dead)." In 20:18f, however, the people flee "a great distance" from the presence of the Lord on the mountain, telling Moses, "You speak to us and we will hearken so that the Lord not speak to us lest we die." Furthermore, according to 19:19, the Lord spoke only to Moses, whereas in 20:19 the narrative infers that God intended to speak with the people as well as Moses.

Without raising the question of whether such variations can be related to hypothetical literary documents,[48] we will turn directly to the question of the role these variations play in the composition of the Pentateuch. Do the similarities and differences in the two narratives advance the author's purpose or intention?

It can be argued that in the present shape of the Pentateuch, the Decalogue (Ex 20:1–17) is intended to be read as the content of what Moses spoke to the people *upon his return* from the mountain in 19:25.[49] After the Decalogue (20:1–17) the narrative

---

[47]This similarity of viewpoint raises the question of the relationship of the narrative in chapter 19 with that of chapter 20. It is frequently argued that the narrative about Israel's retreat from the mountain and fear of God in Exodus 20:18–21 most naturally follows Exodus 19:25 rather than the Decalogue (Ex 10:1–17), (Eissfeldt, *Synopse*, 45f.). Moreover, the Decalogue begins with God speaking ("And God said all the words, saying . . ." [Ex 20:1]) rather than with Moses as is suggested by its current position after 19:25, ("And Moses said to them . . ."). Therefore, according to literary critical theory, the narrative in its present state has been rearranged, with the Decalogue now coming before Exodus 20:18–21 rather than after it where it more naturally belongs (cf. Dt 5:5–6). The purpose of this rearrangement, it is held, was redactional. It was to include the Covenant Code along with the Decalogue as part of the "word" which God spoke to Israel in the Sinai covenant. Whereas originally the Decalogue was the only "word" which God spoke at Sinai, in its present shape that word also includes the Covenant Code. Hence Exodus 24:3a, "and all the judgments" is taken as a harmonistic gloss. Though there is little grounds for this hypothetical reconstruction, the basic structural observation on which it rests is sound. As the narrative now stands, the Decalogue (Ex 20:1–17) is presented not as the word which God spoke to the people, but rather the word that Moses spoke to the people in 19:25. To be sure, Moses' words to the people in 19:25 recounted what God had spoken to him earlier on the mountain (19:19). However, these words are in fact presented in the narratives as first given to Moses' by God (19:19) and then given to the people by Moses (19:25ff.). In other words, the narratives show that there is now a growing distance between God and the people—one that was not intended at the outset of the Sinai narrative (19:12f.).

[48]Eissfeldt identified Exodus 19:19a, 20–25 with the Jahwist and 20:18–21 with the Elohist (*Synopse*, 147–50).

[49]By the time Moses speaks the words of the Decalogue to the people in 19:25–20:17, however, the narrative suggests he had already received both the Decalogue and the Covenant Code. It thus makes sense that when Moses spoke the Decalogue (Ex 20:1–17) to the people in 19:25, it is introduced as "and God said . . ." (Ex 20:1). Rather than betraying the presence of a mislocated text, the clause structure of Exodus 20:1 follows precisely that sense of the whole. Moreover, as can be seen from the syntax of Exodus 20:22 and 24:1, the narrative of the events at Sinai, which began in Exodus 19, continues further (24:1) on the

in 20:18–21 looks back once again to the people's fear in 19:16ff.[50] In retelling this incident, the second narrative fills in important gaps in our understanding of the first. Whereas Exodus 19:16–24 looks at the people's fear from a divine perspective, 20:18–21 views it from the viewpoint of the people themselves.[51] What we learn from both narratives is that there was a growing need for a mediator and a priesthood in the Sinai covenant. Because of their fear of God's presence, the people are now standing "afar off" (20:21). Already, then, we can see the basis being laid within the narrative for the need of the tabernacle (Ex 25–31). The people who are "afar off" must be brought near to God. This is the purpose of the instructions for the tabernacle which follow.

The chart in Figure B.4 shows the dynamic state of the Sinai covenant throughout Exodus 19–25.

3. THE PLACE OF THE TABERNACLE INSTRUCTIONS (EX 25–31)

We can now turn briefly to our second question, which was, Why are the instructions for the Tabernacle given before the sin of the golden calf? If it was the golden calf that led to the priestly laws, why does the tabernacle precede the golden calf? Rashi maintained that the sequential arrangement in the Pentateuch does not reflect the chronological order of the events. In actual fact, says Rashi, "the incident of the golden calf happened much earlier than the instructions for the building of the Tabernacle."[52] For Rashi, then, the giving of all the priestly laws, including those for the tabernacle, came after the sin of the golden calf.

However, the sense of the narrative strategy of Exodus 19–24, as outlined above, suggests another reason for the position of the tabernacle instructions in the present narrative. We have seen above in the depiction of the Sinai covenant an emphasis was placed on the need for a mediator as well as a priesthood. The people, in their fear of

---

other side of the Covenant Code. The narrative link that is established syntactically in Exodus 24:1 by means of a chiastic coordination from Exodus 20:22—וַיֹּאמֶר יהוה אֶל מֹשֶׁה ... (20:22) is continued by וְאֶל מֹשֶׁה אָמַר .... (see Francis I. Andersen, The Sentence in Biblical Hebrew [The Hague: Mouton Publishers, 1980], pp. 122–26.) Thus, in Exodus 24, we find Moses still on the mountain receiving God's word. In 24:3, when God had finished speaking, Moses went down the mountain to bring God's words to the people. The expression "All the words of the Lord and all of the judgments" (24:3) shows an intentional linking of the Decalogue and the Covenant Code to the final ceremony of 24:3–8. The mention of Moses, Aaron, and the priests in Exodus 24:1, then, anticipates the role of Moses, Aaron, and the priests in 24:9 and is a carryover from 20:21 where the people's "fear" necessitated a mediator and priesthood.

[50]The syntax of 20:18, which begins with a circumstantial clause (W + NC), suggests that the narrative in Exodus 20:18–21 is not to be read sequentially as a new narrative event but rather as a return to the previous events of chapter 19, or more specifically, 19:16ff.

[51]The position taken here, though arrived at independently, is in some respects similar to the view of Chirichigno ("The Narrative Structure . . .," Biblica, 68 [1987]) that the two passages reflect two different perspectives on the covenant—19:16ff represents the Lord's perspective and 20:18–21 represents the perspective of the people. Also for Chirichigno, 20:18–21, "elaborates in detail the fear of the people" (p. 479). I also agree with Chirichigno that 20:18–21 "acts as a causal link between the fear of the people and their sinful acts below the mountain in Exod. 32" (p. 479).

[52]Rashi's Commentry on the Torah (Hebrew), ed. Chaim Dov Shual (Jerusalem: Mosad Harav Kook, 1988), 303.

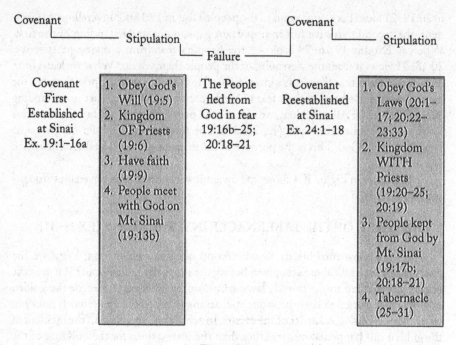

Figure B.4

God, stood "afar off." Just as the people could no longer go up into the mountain to meet with God (Ex 19:21–23), they could also not go into the tabernacle to meet with him. Thus according to the logic of the narrative it was Israel's fear that had created the need for a safe approach to God. It was precisely for this reason that the tabernacle was given to Israel.

4. CONCLUSION

When viewed from the perspective of the strategy of its composition and its treatment of the various collections of laws, the pentateuchal narratives present themselves as an extended treatise on the nature of the Sinai covenant. The author of the Pentateuch seems intent on showing that Israel's immediate fall into idolatry with the golden calf brought with it a fundamental shift in the nature of the Sinai covenant. At the outset of the covenant, the text portrays the nature of the covenant in much the same light as that of the religion of the patriarchs. Like Abraham, Israel was to obey God (Ex 19:5; cf Ge 26:5), keep his covenant (Ex 19:5; cf Ge 17:1–14), and exercise faith (Ex 19:9; cf Ge 15:6). Though they immediately agreed to the terms of this covenant (Ex 19:8), Israel quickly proved unable to keep it (Ex 19:16–17). In fear, they chose Moses to stand before God while they themselves stood "afar off" (Ex 19:18–20; 20:18–21). In response to the people's fear, God gave Israel the Decalogue, the Covenant Code, and the Tabernacle. As depicted in the Covenant Code, Israel's relationship with God was based on the absolute prohibition of idolatry and the simple offering of praise and sacrifice. The covenant was still very much like that of the patriarchal period.

The people of Israel, however, led by the priests of the house of Aaron, fell quickly into idolatry. Even while the laws were being given to Moses, Aaron, the priest, was making the golden calf. Hence, the covenant was broken almost before it was begun (Ex 32). The incident of the golden calf, then, marks a decisive moment in the course of the narrative. In his grace and great compassion (Ex 33), however, God did not cast Israel off, and so the covenant was renewed (Ex 34). In the renewal of the covenant additional laws were given. These are represented in the remainder of the code of Priestly laws (Ex 35–Lev 16). Though these laws appeared to keep the priests in check, it became apparent in the people's later sacrifices to goat idols that more laws were needed. Thus God gave them the Holiness Code (Lev 17–25) and again renewed the covenant (Lev 26).

It should now be clear that the narrative strategy which we have outlined above is quite similar to that which has been read from these texts since the time of Justin Martyr and particularly that developed by Johann Coccejus in his treatment of the place of law in the covenant of grace. It also appears to reflect the argument of the apostle Paul in Galatians 3:19, that the law was added to the covenant because of the transgressions of the people. It seems reasonable to conclude, therefore, that if the view of Coccejus is to be rejected by modern theologians, such as Berkhof, it cannot be done simply with the judgment that Coccejus's view cannot find support from Scripture. A compositional approach to the meaning of the pentateuchal narratives suggests that Coccejus' view finds a great deal of support from the biblical text.

APPENDIX C:
THE NARRATIVE WORLD
OF GENESIS*

An essential feature of biblical narrative is its ability to "mimic" the real world, that is, to reproduce a real world in linguistic form. It is easy to overlook this characteristic by simply taking it for granted. Although the biblical authors were clearly interested in the "lessons" embodied in the stories they wrote, their first, more fundamental, concern was the depiction of a world in which those lessons made consummate sense. They were not merely depicting a view of the world. They were at one and the same time creating the world they were depicting. By representing reality in their narratives, they were defining its essential characteristics. This is surely not to say they were making it up. There is every reason to maintain that the world we find depicted in these narratives was, in fact, intended by them to be identified as the real world.

A biblical narrative text takes the raw material of language and shapes it into a version of the world of empirical reality. Its essentially linguistic structures are adapted to conform to events in everyday life—e.g., the limitations of time, space, and perspective—in order to present events and characters before the reader as happening *just as they happen in everyday life*. Readers thus look at the events in the narrative in much the same way as they would look on events in real life. Events happen in the text before one's eyes. As Emile Benveniste has put it, "The events are chronologically recorded as they appear on the horizon of the story. . . . The events seem to tell themselves."[1]

Most traditional Christians and Jews will be quite familiar with the world we find depicted in the Bible. Indeed it can be argued that until very recently the biblical world was the sole contender for the Western world's conceptualization of reality, at least in the popular mind. This very familiarity with the world presented in the Bible, however, can also be an obstacle to our appreciation of the role that the Bible has had, and indeed should have, in our world today. A fuller understanding of the literary

---

*Adapted from John D. Sailhamer, "Genesis," in *A Complete Literary Guide to the Bible*, ed. Leland Ryken and Tremper Longman III (Grand Rapids: Zondervan, 1993), 110–19.

[1]Quoted in Hayden White, "The Value of Narrativity in the Representation of Reality," *Critical Inquiry* 7, (1980): 7.

strategies of biblical narrative can be of great service in this venture. It helps us to see not simply this or that lesson taught by the Bible; it also provides the means for appreciating and applying the basic structure of the biblical world to contemporary life. My interest in this chapter is not the lessons about God and people taught in the Bible. My concern is rather directed to aspects of the world depicted for us in the Bible.

Although there are many aspects of the narrative world presented to us in the book of Genesis that merit our attention, I will focus on two: divine causality and divine retribution. Not only do these two notions pervade the Genesis narratives; they are also the two aspects of these narratives that seem most out of place in the modern world.

Why does the Pentateuch begin the way it does? Why not begin with the list of laws given at Mount Sinai? Why begin with a narrative of God's creating the world? Rabbinical commentaries were particularly concerned with this question, in large measure because they saw the Sinai laws as central to the purpose of the Pentateuch. If the Torah was about law, why did it not begin with a discussion of the law? The answer given by Rashi shows remarkable appreciation for the role that these narratives play in the purpose of the writer: "If the nations of the world should say to Israel, 'You are thieves because you have stolen the land of the Canaanites,' they may reply, 'All the earth belongs to God. He made it and gives it to whomever he pleases.'"[2] The purpose of the Creation narrative is not only to teach religious truth, though it allows for that, but also to establish a claim about the nature of the world and God's relationship to it. He made the world. It is thus his world, and he can do with it what he pleases.

Thus from the very beginning the narrative defines the nature of the real world it depicts. It is a world in which God is an active agent. It is his world, and one who lives in that world must reckon with him. Of course there is the possibility that people will fail to acknowledge the divine presence, and thus throughout the book of Genesis the reader is continually reminded of the consequence of failing to reckon with the presence of God in the world. A number of the stories in the book seem specifically directed toward establishing this fact: the fall of humankind (Ge 3), the Flood account (Ge 6–9), the confusion of languages in the city of Babylon (Ge 11), and the destruction of the cities of Sodom and Gomorrah (Ge 19).

We find in these narratives a virtual chain of events depicting a world governed by a God who holds the people of his world responsible for their actions. In this world, "chance" is just another way to speak of divine causality, as in the story of Abraham's servant seeking a bride for Isaac (Ge 24:12). Literally the servant prays, "O Lord, cause a chance to happen today," and "before he had finished speaking" it happened (24:15). This is a world very different from the world of modern thought, but it is a world that the biblical narratives present to us and challenge us to accept as our own.

---

[2] Chaim Dov Shual, *The Commentary of Rashi on the Torah* (in Hebrew) (Jerusalem: Mossad Harav Kook, 1988), 1–2.

NARRATIVE TECHNIQUE AND THE CONSTRUCTION OF "REALITY"

Of many narrative techniques present in Genesis, I will concentrate on three: recursion, contemporization, and foreshadowing.

The narrative technique of "recursion" is the author's deliberate shaping of narrative events so that key elements of one narrative are repeated in others. The cumulative effect of such stories is the sense that the whole of the real world has a shape and order that is reflected in the shape and order of the biblical narratives. An example of recursion in the Genesis narratives can be seen in the way in which the story of the restoration of the land after the great Flood (Ge 7:24–9:17) follows the same pattern and order as the earlier account of Creation in Genesis 1:

Creation Account	*Flood Account*
1. And darkness was over the face of the deep (1:2)	And the sources of the great deep were broken up (7:11)
2. "And let the dry land appear" (1:9)	And the tops of the mountains appeared (8:5)
3. "Let the land bring forth vegetation" (1:11–12)	There in its beak was a freshly plucked olive leaf (8:11)
4. "They shall be for signs and seasons, days and years"	On the first day of the first month . . . (8:13f.)
5. And God said, "Let the land bring out the living creatures" (1:24)	And God said, . . . "And bring out the creatures" (8:17)
6. And God blessed them saying, "Be fruitful and multiply and and fill the land" (1:22)	And God said, "Be fruitful and multiply upon the land" (8:17)
7. "Let us make man" (1:26)	And Noah came out (8:18)
8. And God blessed them and said to them, "Be fruitful and multiply and fill the land" (1:28)	And God blessed Noah . . . and said to them, "Be fruitful and multiply and fill the land" (9:1)
9. "And rule over the fish of the sea" (1:28b)	". . . and among all the fish of the sea, they are given into your hands" (9:2)
10. And God sasid, "Behold, I give to you . . . for food" (1:29)	"To you it shall be for food" (9:3)

The implication of such similarities and recursions in narrative structure is that the world depicted by these narratives also has this same design and purpose. Furthermore, the fact that the author of the Pentateuch has appended to the Flood account the short narrative of Noah's drunkenness (9:18–27) further suggests a divine designated plan to the events recounted in the narrative. It does so because the narrative of Noah's drunkenness closely emulates the earlier account of the Fall (Ge 2–3), thereby becoming an example of recursion.

The Fall (Genesis 2–3)	Noah's Drunkenness (Genesis 9:20ff.)
1. And the Lord God planted a garden . . . and put the man there (2:8)	And Noah planted an orchard (9:20)
2. And she took from the tree and ate (3:6)	And he drank from the wine and became drunk (9:21)
3. And they knew that they were naked (3:7)	And he uncovered himself in the midst of the tent (9:21)
4. And they made clothing for themselves (3:7)	And they covered the nakedness of their father (9:23)
5. And their eyes were open and they were naked (3:7)	And Noah woke up from his sleep and he knew what his young son had done (9:24)
6. "Cursed are you" (3:14)	"Cursed is Canaan" ((:25)
7. Cain, Abel, and Seth (4:1–2, 25)	Shem, Ham, and Japheth (9:25–27)

These examples show that a major aspect of the meaning of the biblical narratives lies fundamentally in the patterns of divine purpose that they infuse into our understanding of the world. According to Hans Frei, the effect of these narratives on the readers of Scripture has been appreciated by countless generations of readers:

> Christian preachers and theological commentators, Augustine the most notable among them, had envisioned the real world as formed by the sequence told by the biblical stories. That temporal world covered the span of ages from creation to the final consummation to come, and included the governance both of man's natural environment and of that secondary environment which we often think of as provided for man by himself and call "history" or "culture."[3]

A second narrative trait of Genesis is contemporization, meaning that the past is often portrayed in light of events and institutions of the present. For example, the narrative of Cain and Abel (Ge 4:1–24), the first case of manslaughter in the Bible, is cast along the same lines as the last case, that is, the provisions for the cities of refuge at the end of the Pentateuch (Nu 35:9–34; Dt 19:11–13). In each of these narratives God gives the same provision for protection against the "avenger of blood," that is, a city in which there is the rule of law. The writer would have us see that the same God is at work throughout all of history.

This same technique is surely at work in the portrayal of Abraham's battle with the four kings from the East in Genesis 14. As the details of the narrative show, when Abraham battles the kings of the East, he follows the provisions later laid down in

---

[3]Hans W. Frei, *The Eclipse of Biblical Narrative: A Study in Eighteenth and Nineteenth Century Hermeneutics* (New Haven: Yale University Press, 1974), 1, 13.

Deuteronomy 20 for the conduct of war with nations afar off. Moreover, his response to the king of Sodom in the same chapter matches what would be expected of one from Deuteronomy 20.[4] The pattern of the narrative thus reinforces the reader's understanding of the world as itself in conformity with the plan and purpose of God. People who are like Abraham in walking with God find themselves at home in God's world.

Third, the narratives in Genesis recount events in such a way as to foreshadow and anticipate later events. This technique differs from recursion noted above in that foreshadowing anticipates fulfillment and not mere repetition of the past. By means of foreshadowing, central themes are developed and continually drawn to the reader's attention, with the result that a further sense of purpose is added to the reader's understanding of events. The sense of the biblical narratives is not only that God and his plan are at work in the history recounted in them but also that this history has a goal. The "first things" anticipate the fulfillment of the "last things."

For example, the account of Abraham's entry into the land of Canaan is notably selective. Only three sites in the land are mentioned, and at these sites Abraham built an altar—at Shechem (12:6), between Bethel and Ai (12:8), and in the Negev (12:9). As Cassuto has pointed out,[5] it can hardly be accidental that these are the same three locations visited by Jacob when he returns to Canaan from Haran (Ge 34–35), as well as the sites occupied in the conquest of the land under Joshua (Jos 1–11). Jacob and Joshua built altars at these very same sites.

A small narrative segment that has attracted an extraordinary amount of attention over the years is the account of Abraham's visit to Egypt in Genesis 12:10–20. The similarities between this narrative and those of Genesis 20 and 26 are well known. Such similarities are best seen as part of the larger typological scheme of these narratives, intended to show that future events in God's world are often foreshadowed by events from the past. This can also be seen from a comparison between Genesis 12:10–20 and the large narrative unit that deals with the Israelites' sojourn in Egypt (Ge 41–Ex 12). The following chart suggests that the composition of Genesis 12:10–20 has been intentionally structured to prefigure or foreshadow the events of Israel's sojourn in Egypt:

12:10 There was a famine in the land	41:54 There was a famine in all the lands
12:11 When he drew near to go into Egypt	46:28 When they came toward the land of Goshen ...
12:11 He said to Sarai his wife	46:31 Joseph said to his brothers
12:11 "I know that ...	46:31 "I will go up and say to Pharaoh ..."
12:12 "And it shall come to pass when the Egyptians see you, they will say ..."	46:33 "And it shall come to pass when Pharaoh calls you, he will say ..."

[4]John Sailhamer, "Genesis," *EBC*, vol. 2 (Grand Rapids: Zondervan, 1990), 122ff.
[5]Umberto Cassuto, *Encyclopedia Biblica*, vol. 1 (Jerusalem: Bialik Institute, 1955).

12:13	"Say…"	46:34	"Say…"
12:13	"That it may be well with me on account of you"	46:34	"That you may dwell in the land of Goshen"
12:13	And the officers of Pharaoh saw her and declaired to to Pharaoh	47:1	And Joseph came and declared to Pharaoh…
12:15	And the wife was taken into the house of Pharaoh	47:5	And Pharaoh said, … "Settle your father and brothers in the best part of the land"
12:15	And Abraham acquired sheep and cattle	47:6	"Put them in charge of my livestock"
		47:27	They acquired property and were fruitful and increased greatly
12:17	And the Lord struck Pharaoh with great diseases	Ex. 11:1	"One more plague I will bring against Pharaoh"
12:18	And Pharaoh called to Abram and said…	12:31	And Pharaoh called to Moses and Aaron and said…
12:19	"Take… and go"	12:32	"Take… and go"
12:20	and sent them away	12:33	to send them away
13:1	And Abram went up from Egypt toward the Negev	12:37	And the sons of Israel traveled from Rameses toward Succoth
13:1	And Lot went with him	12:38	And also a great mixed multitude went with him
13:2	And Abraham was very rich with livestock, silver, and gold	12:38 12:35	And they had very much livestock, silver, and gold
13:4	(Returned to the altar and worshipped God)	12:11	(The Passover)

It seems clear that a "narrative typology" lies behind the composition of these texts. The author wants to show that the events of the past are pointers to those of the future.

THE JOSEPH NARRATIVE

There is no story in the Pentateuch better suited to show the work of God in the world than that of the Joseph narrative. Not only in the narration of the story itself, but also in the dialogue and conversation of the characters, the work of God in the world is the central topic. It is not that the story itself is intent on "teaching" this lesson as an item of dogma or religious knowledge. The purpose is rather to portray the world as the kind of place in which God's will is accomplished regardless of human efforts to the contrary.

As with our discussion of the Genesis narratives generally, two aspects of the narrative world of the Joseph story deserve special attention—divine causality and divine retribution. It is impossible to read the story without seeing that God is actively at work in the world he is depicting. This is brought out by four primary techniques of dialogue—thematization in dialogue, motivation in dialogue, summary in dialogue, and scripted dialogue.

Throughout the narrative, the dialogue of key characters gives expression to the notion of divine causality. This is thematization in dialogue. For example, Joseph says to Pharaoh, "The reason the dream was given to Pharaoh in two forms is that the matter has been firmly decided by God, and God will do it soon" (41:32). Joseph's steward says to the brothers, "The God of your father has given you treasure" (43:23). The reader knows that the steward's words cannot be taken seriously. There has been no mention of money given to the steward. Nevertheless, his words echo the thrust of the narrative and the major themes of the book.

Dialogue is also used to exhibit motivation, which sets the events of the story in motion and provides a guide to its plot and resolution. When key characters speak in the Joseph narratives, their words become programmatic of the events that follow. Jacob, sending his sons to Egypt, declares, "Go down there . . . so that we may live and not die" (42:2). Jacob surely has in view only their survival through the famine. But the narrator has a much larger end in view. He sees God's overall purpose of sustaining the house of Jacob and the people of Israel throughout their earthly sojourns. God's faithfulness to his covenant promise is in view. As the story unfolds, the words of 42:2 prove definitive for the outcome of the narrative, as the lives of the sons of Jacob are spared in Egypt. The echo of Jacob's words can be seen in those of Joseph: "It was to save lives that God sent me" (45:5). Through such dialogue that attributes motivation to events the work of God is shown to be an essential part of the course of events recounted in the narrative.

Similarly, Joseph's brothers say to him in a fit of jealousy, "Do you intend to reign over us?" (37:8). Their words anticipate the central events of the narrative that follows. At the conclusion of the story we are brought back to the picture of Joseph's brothers bowing down to him (42:6), as we are told that at that moment Joseph "remembered his dreams about them" (v. 9).

Summary in dialogue occurs when key characters summarize the central thesis of the story. At the close of the story, Joseph says to his brothers, "It was to save lives that God sent me ahead of you" (45:5). Thus, though the brothers were responsible for Joseph's being sold into Egypt, and though they intended to do him harm, Joseph's words show us that God was ultimately behind it all and had worked it out for good (cf. 50:20).

We can also speak of scripted dialogue in the story. Throughout the story of Joseph, lesser characters speak lines that prove far more important than their sense in the immediate context. Their "off the cuff" remarks appear as if scripted for the larger occasion of the story. In the words of the cupbearer, for example, the reader's attention is redirected to the earlier event of Joseph's interpretation of dreams in prison. The cupbearer says of him, "Things turned out exactly as he interpreted them to us"

(41:13). As it turns out, even the cupbearer's forgetfulness worked in Joseph's favor since, just at the opportune moment, he remembered Joseph and recounted his wisdom before the king. By drawing the reader's attention to the events of the previous passage, both the wisdom of Joseph and the divine causality of the events are expressed.

When we turn from the motif of divine causality to that of divine retribution, we find some of the same uses of dialogue, beginning with thematization in dialogue. The Joseph story shows that through Joseph's own schemes his brothers came to an awareness of their guilt and they were ready to acknowledge it. Toward the end of the story their utter frustration finds expression in their question, "What can we say?" (44:16). Then comes the expression of their guilt: "How can we show ourselves to be right?" Within the logic of the narrative, the rhetorical answer to these questions is an implied negative: "We have nothing to say, we cannot show ourselves to be right." Thus the conclusion that the brothers are forced to draw is, "God has found the iniquity of your servants" (v. 16).

Although we can clearly see that the brothers have only the immediate issue of the lost cup in mind, within the compass of the whole of the Joseph narrative their words take on the scope of the much broader confession of their former guilt as well. As readers we know that the brothers have not taken the cup and are thus innocent here. Joseph had it put into Benjamin's sack. We also know that the brothers know they did not take the cup. Thus when they speak of God's "finding out their guilt" (44:16), we are forced to generalize their sense of guilt within the context of the narrative as a whole. The author leads us to read their words with a broader significance than they might have intended on that occasion. We see the narrative interconnections that were not a part of their own understanding within the situation itself.

Divine retribution also emerges through scripted dialogue. The words of the brothers when they discover that their money has been returned to them in their grain sacks almost inadvertently expresses the notion of divine causality. When each saw his own money returned, he asked, "What is this that God has done to us?" (42:28). Whatever the brothers might have meant by it, in the logic of the narrative their words have an ironic ring of truth. Though we know it was Joseph who had the money put back into their sacks, their words point us to the work of God, serving to confirm the direction the narrative as a whole appears to be taking. God is at work in the schemes of Joseph, and we are allowed to see in this narrative a preliminary reminder of the ultimate theme: "God meant it for good" (50:20).

APPENDIX D:
1 CHRONICLES 21:1—A STUDY IN
INTER-BIBLICAL INTERPRETATION*

The composition of the OT was a long and hermeneutically rich process. Books were written (e.g., the Pentateuch), supplemented (e.g., Dt 34:10ff.), exegeted (e.g., Nehemiah 9; Psalm 8; Hosea 12:5), applied (e.g., the prophetic books), borrowed (Chronicles), and developed (Daniel 9). Each one of these tasks involved a full set of principles and procedures for understanding and interpreting texts. The whole of the growing context as well as each of the specific contexts for the individual books played a decisive role in the shaping and final articulation of the message of the OT. This process of interpretation and adaptation of Scripture did not stop with the completion of the OT. For Christians, at least, it continued into the first century. Such a situation presses on us the responsibility of looking far beyond first-century Judaism for our context of understanding the NT's use of the Old. The NT's reading of the Old is not the beginning of a way of reading the Hebrew Scriptures, but the end (τέλος). That is, it is the end of a long process of exegesis and interpretation of Scripture. Thus before we can answer the question of the NT's use of the Old, we must address the question of the OT's use of the Old.

The book of Chronicles offers an interesting opportunity to address the question of inter-biblical interpretation in the OT. In large measure its sources are available to us today much the same as they were to its original author. We can, thus, follow the Chronicler in his task of composition, comparing his sources before and after they entered his work. It is relatively certain that the primary sources of the book of Chronicles were the Pentateuch and the historical books, Joshua–Kings.[1] There may also have been other non-canonical texts from which he drew. It is well-known, for example, that he alludes to other sources such as "the words of Samuel the seer," the "words of Nathan the prophet," and the "words of Gad the visionary" (1 Chr 29:29).[2]

---

*John D. Sailhamer, "1 Chronicles 21—A Study in Inter-Biblical Interpretation," *Trinity Journal*, vol. 10 (Spring 1989): 33–48.

[1]Wilhelm Rudolph, *Chronikbücher* (Tübingen: Mohr, 1955), x; H. G. M. Williamson, *1 and 2 Chronicles* (Grand Rapids: Eerdmans, 1982), 19.

[2]There is also the mention of the "midrash of the prophet Iddo" (בְּמִדְרַשׁ הַנָּבִיא עִדּוֹ, 2 Chr 13:22) and the "midrash of the Book of Kings" (בְּמִדְרַשׁ סֵפֶר הַמְּלָכִים, 2 Chr 24:27). See Williamson, *1 and 2 Chronicles*, 18, for a discussion of whether these were, in fact, his sources or, which appears more likely, merely references already included in the sources he used.

It can be said that in comparing the book of Chronicles with its earlier canonical sources, the Chronicler did not attempt to create a totally new literary piece. He often seems content merely with reproducing major sections of the earlier biblical texts. But, as von Rad has observed, "he regularly interfered (*eingegriffen*) with his originals and sources, sometimes by omissions or slight insertions, sometimes by revisions or rearranging the sequence of events. . . ."[3]

1 Chronicles 21:1, David's sin of numbering his army, offers a challenging example of the Chronicler's use of earlier biblical texts. There are few, if any, more difficult passages in Scripture. It is reasonably certain that the Chronicler had before him the current text of 2 Samuel 24:1ff.,[4] yet there are significant differences between the two accounts. In the Samuel text, it states:

> Again the anger of the Lord was kindled against Israel (וַיֹּסֶף אַף יְהוָה לַחֲרוֹת בְּיִשְׂרָאֵל) and he incited David against them (וַיָּסֶת אֶת דָּוִד בָּהֶם) saying, "Go, number Israel and Judah. . . ."

The Chronicler, however, writes:

> Satan stood up against Israel (וַיַּעֲמֹד שָׂטָן עַל יִשְׂרָאֵל), and incited (וַיָּסֶת) David to number Israel (לִמְנוֹת אֶת יִשְׂרָאֵל).

Attempts to explain the relationship of these two passages are varied but can be arranged under three headings: harmonistic, redactional, and exegetical (*Auslegung*).

HARMONISTIC APPROACHES

The older approaches are generally harmonistic. The Talmud, for example, appears to read the statement in 1 Chronicles 21:1a, "Satan stood up against Israel (וַיַּעֲמֹד שָׂטָן עַל יִשְׂרָאֵל)," as the parallel to 2 Samuel 24:1b, "and he incited David against them (וַיָּסֶת אֶת דָּוִד בָּהֶם)," rather than 24:1a, "Again the anger of the Lord was kindled against Israel (וַיֹּסֶף אַף יְהוָה לַחֲרוֹת בְּיִשְׂרָאֵל)," thus understanding שָׂטָן as the subject of וַיָּסֶת in 2 Samuel 24:1b.[5] Many Christian exegetes have followed a similar

---

[3]Gerhard Von Rad, *Old Testament Theology*, 2 vols. (New York: Harper & Row, 1962), 1:348.

[4]"Die Abweichungen von der alten Quelle sind in diesem Kap. stärker als wir es seither erlebt haben. Aber trotzdem liegt kein Grund vor, dem Chr. die Aufnahme einer von 2 Sm 24 verschiedenen Quelle zu unterstellen. . . . Denn nicht bloss der Gesamtaufriss, sondern auch viele Einzelheiten stimmen in beiden Texten völlig überein . . ., und die Abweichungen sind theologisch oder sonstwie sachlich begründet und setzen stets den vorhandenen Text von 2 Sm 24 voraus . . ." (Rudolph, *Chronikbücher*, 141).

[5]See Ber., 62 .

[6]Tremellius translated 2 Sam 24:1b as "Quum incitasset adversarius Davidem" (Junius, Francis, and Immanuel Tremellius, *Testamenti Veteris Biblia Sacra* [Geneva, 1587]); Conrad Dannhauer (1603–1666), "τὸ וַיָּסֶת monet capi posse impersonaliter, cum concitasset quis (sc. qvi solet, Satan) & sic ו esse causale" (*Hodomoria spiritus calviniani*, 1015, quoted in Augusti Pfeifferi, *Dubia Vexata Scripturae Sacrae* [Dresden, 1685], 405). Thus Dannhauer understood 2 Sam 24:1 as "The anger of the Lord again arose against Israel because he (that is Satan) incited David against them . . ."; Hugo Grotius, "In eis nempe diebus commovit David, activum pro passivo, ut saepe, id est, commotus est, nempe à diabolo, ut expressè habemus 1 Paralip. II.I. [sic] Diablo autem locum facit incuria ac negligentia circa mandationem Legis ac preces"; Sixtinus Amana (1593–1639), ". . . si id non placet, interseri nomen *Satanae*. Primò novum non est personalia per impersonalia, quando agens non exprimitur."

line of harmonization.[6] Kimchi, on the other hand, explained the word שָׂטָן as the "(evil) inclination in man's heart from his youth" (הוא הנטוע בלב האדם מנעוריו) and was followed,[7] for example, by the Christian exegetes Franz Vatablus (1545), and Sebastian Munsterus (1539), as well as many others.[8]

The Targum to Chronicles[9] offers yet another harmonization: ואקים יהוה סטנא על ישראל ואתגרי בדויד לממני ית ישראל ("And the Lord raised up the adversary against Israel and he was aroused[10] against David to number Israel" [1 Chr 21:1]). The Targum is similar to a common theme in Christian harmonizations of these texts, namely, the appeal to the notion of *concursus divinus* or *permissio Dei*.[11] For example, *permissio Dei* can be seen in the Geneva Bible notes to 2 Sam 24:1b[12] comments, "in both passages the matter is presented simply from two different sides."[13] Jamieson combines all three types of harmonizations to the problem.

---

[7]The later מצודה דוד follows Kimchi הוא היצר הרע.

[8]Vatablus, "Hîc dicitur Deus concitasse cor Davidis ut numeraret populum, at I Par. 21.1. dicitur *Satan incitasse ipsum Davidem:* unde intelligimus Satanam irae Dei flabellum esse, ut corda hominum, quocunque voluerit Deus, impellat"; Munsterus, "Secundum Hebraeos Deus non incitavit David contra populum, sed cor David incitavit ipsum, ut diceret intra se, *Vade et numera Israel . . .*" (*Critici Sacri*, 3:1057). See also *Synopsis Criticorum aliorumque Sacrae Scripturae Interpretum et Commentatorum* (Matthaeus Pol; London: Johannis Leusden, 1684), 403.

[9]Alexander Sperber, *The Bible in Aramaic*, Vol. IV A, *The Hagiographa* (Leiden: Brill, 1968), 23.

[10]אִתְגָּרִי, "gereizt, aufgeregt werden gegen Jem., auch sich erregen . . ." (Jacob Levy, *Chaldäisches Wörterbuch Über die Targumim und einen Grossen Theil des Rabbinischen Schriftthums* [Leipzig: Baumgärtner's Buchhandlung, 1881], 154).

[11]The idea of *concursus divinus* was a central theme in Lutheran orthodoxy. It was an attempt to explain the relationship between divine acts (*causa prima*) and free will (*causae secundae*) as one of "concurrence." See *RGG 1*, 1716f. Reform orthodoxy rejected the Lutheran understanding of *concursus* as irreconcilable with divine causality. In Reformed theology *concursus divinus* was ultimately based on the immediate and predetermined work of God. In this sense it was the result of *permissio Dei*. See Heinrich Heppe, *Die Dogmatik der evangelisch-reformierten Kirche* (Neukirchen: Kreis Moers, 1935), 200ff. and L. Berkhof, *Systematic Theology* (Grand Rapids: Eerdmans, 1949), 171ff. For a sense of the difference between the Lutheran and Reformed view note the summarization of the Reformed interpretation of 2 Sam 24:1 by the Lutheran Pfeiffer, "Calviniani hinc inferunt, DEUM instigare s. impellere hominem occulte ad peccata" (Augusti Pfeifferi, *Dubia Vexata Scripturae Sacrae* [Dresden, 1685], 405).

[12]"The Lord permitted Satan, as 1.Chron.21,2 [sic]" (*The Bible, That is, The holy Scriptures conteined in the Olde and Newe Testament* [London, 1599]). Also, Cornellius a Lapide (1568–1637), "'Commovit' Deus Davidem, non per se suggerendo ei, et dicendo: 'Vade et numera populum' (sic enim incitasset eum ad peccatum, quod facere nequit), se permittendo diabolo ad id parato, et anhelanti, ut Davidem ad superbam hanc populi numerationem incitaret. Deus ergo indirecte, diabolus vero directe excitavit Davidem ad hanc numerationem, uti expresse dicitur 1 Paral. XXI, 1" (*Commentaria in Scripturam Sacram* [Paris, 1889]).

[13]Otto Von Gerlach, *Das Alte Testament nach Dr. Martin Luthers Uebersetzung mit Einleitungen und erklärenden Anmerkungen* (Berlin: Gustav Schlawitz, 1858), 190. Keil remarks simply "In the parallel text of Chronicles, Satan is mentioned as the tempter to evil, through whom Jehovah led David to number the people" (*Biblical Commentary on the Books of Samuel* [Grand Rapids: Eerdmans, 1950], 503). Curiously, the original Scofield Bible has no comment on either verse. *The New Scofield Reference Bible* contains the following comment, "It is stated in 1 Chr.21:1 that Satan moved David to do this. Evidently God permitted the devil to influence His servant in order that His own purposes might be carried out."

God, though He cannot tempt any man (Jas. i. 13), is frequently described in Scripture as doing what He merely permits to be done; and so in this instance He permitted David to fall into temptation, by withholding His supporting and restraining grace.[14] It will be observed that "he" before "moved" is improperly introduced. [יָסֶת has no nominative; and as this verb signifies *stimulated, incited,* often in a bad sense, the meaning seems to be that David had been stirred up to the adoption of this measure either by the urgency of some minister, whose evil influence predominated in the privy council,[15] or by the suggestion of some worldly and unhallowed passion,[16] which had acquired the ascendancy in his own breast.[17]

Each of these harmonistic approaches is inadequate for much the same reason. Though they all express important theological and biblical insights into the nature of the problem, none of the approaches finds support within the immediate text itself. They are, in fact, not so much attempts to explain the difficulty of the text as attempts to explain it away. Perhaps for this reason, modern biblical scholarship has generally abandoned any serious effort to see a unity between the two texts.[18]

REDACTIONAL APPROACHES

Critical scholarship has generally explained the differences between the two passages in terms of literary development. For most modern scholars, the Chronicler's text represents a second redaction or correction of 2 Samuel 24.[19] According to Smith, ". . . the Chronicler could not conceive of Yahweh's inciting David to sin, and he therefore begins the account (1 Chr 21:1) ויעמד שטן על ישראל ויסת.[20] In Smith's view, the Chronicler did not intend to give another perspective on the same event, but rather a new account of the event itself. He has rewritten the history from a different theological position.

---

[14]*Concursus divinus.*

[15]Targum.

[16]Kimchi.

[17]Robert Jamieson, A. R. Fausset, and David Brown, *A Commentary Critical, Experimental and Practical on the Old and New Testaments,* 6 vols. (Grand Rapids: Eerdmans, 1945), 3:287.

[18]Gleason Archer has recently offered an original harmonistic explanation of the two passages. According to him, both statements ("He [God] incited David" and "He [Satan] incited David") are true. The Lord encouraged David to number Israel as a means of bringing David "to his knees once more." Satan, seizing the opportunity for his own interest, "moved in to encourage the desire on David's part and in the hearts of his leaders to carry through this egotistical undertaking . . ." (*The Encyclopedia of Bible Difficulties* [Grand Rapids: Zondervan, 1982], 186–88, 221–22.)

[19]"Die Stelle 1 Ch 21,1 ist aber insofern nicht ohne weiteres ausdeutbar, als der Zusammenhang gar nicht ursprünglich vom *satan* gehandelt hat, sondern erst sekundär dieser Begriff aus religiösen Bedenken als Korrektur in den Text gekommen ist" (*TWNT* 2 [1035]: 73).

[20]Henry Preserved Smith, *A Critical and Exegetical Commentary on the Books of Samuel* (Edinburgh: T. &T. Clark, 1899), 389f. See also Edward Lewis Curtis, *A Critical and Exegetical Commentary on the Books of Chronicles* (Edinburgh: T. &T. Clark, 1910), 246; and Rudolph, *Chronikbücher,* 142.

EXEGETICAL (*AUSLEGUNG*) APPROACHES

A view, which we can call the "exegetical" view, has recently gained wide acceptance and differs considerably from that of the previous literary critical position. In this view the Chronicler *did not intend* his text to be read as an alternative view to that of the earlier text in Samuel. Although he had found the Samuel text difficult, what we read in the Chronicler's version of Samuel was an attempt on his part to explain it, not to replace it. To use the language of the day, the Chronicler had attempted to give a דרש,[21] or commentary, to the difficult text of 2 Samuel.

In a recent monograph, Thomas Willi has developed this position at great length.[22] For Willi the Chronicler is to be viewed as an interpreter or "exegete" of the earlier canonical books, the Pentateuch and the deuteronomic history. Though he is careful not to call the book of Chronicles itself a "midrash," Willi argues that the method of interpretation that the Chronicler follows was similar to that of later midrashic exegesis.[23] The Chronicler thus saw his own work as an explication of these earlier works and assumed throughout that his reader was aware of the content of these books (e.g. Samuel and Kings). For Willi, then, the Chronicler's version of the cause of David's census does not represent a new meaning later given to the event recorded in Samuel but is, in fact, the meaning which the Chronicler actually saw in the scriptural account in 2 Sam 24:1f. The Chronicler's version was not an alternative view intended to rival or replace the view of 2 Samuel 24—as the literary critic sees it—but was intended as an *explanation* of 2 Samuel 24 itself.

Important for our discussion of inter-biblical interpretation is the question which Willi raises about the origin of the Chronicler's interpretation of 2 Sam 24:1. Willi argues that like many of the later *midrashim*, the Chronicler's interpretation was imported into the account from the outside by means of established exegetical rules. Although the sense which the Chronicler saw in 2 Samuel 24 was not immediately obvious in the Samuel passage, by using the exegetical rule of word analogy[24] the Chronicler was able to supply the difficult text of 2 Samuel 24 with an appropriate interpretation grounded both in the text of 2 Samuel 24 itself and in two related bib-

---

[21]Wilhelm Bacher gives the following explanation of דרש: "Aus der Bedeutung suchen, forschen (Deut. 13, 5; 17, 4.9) entwickelte sich mit Beziehung des Verbums auf die heilige Schrift die Bedeutung: Den Sinn, den Inhalt des Schrifttextes erforschen, zu verstehen suchen; den Schrifttext auslegen, erklären" (*Die Exegetische Terminologie der jüdischen Traditionsliteratur* [Hildescheim: Georg Olms, 1965], 25); see also I. L. Seeligmann, "Voraussetzungen der Midraschexegese" (*VTSupp* 1; Leiden: Brill, 1953), 150–81.

[22]*Die Chronik als Auslegung, Untersuchungen zur literarischen Gestaltung der historischen Überlieferung Israels* (Göttingen: Vandenhoeck & Ruprecht, 1972). See also Brevard Childs, *Introduction to the Old Testament as Scripture* (Philadelphia: Fortress, 1979), 645ff.

[23]By this term Willi means the same as Geza Vermes, "Bible and Midrash: Early Old Testament Exegesis" (*The Cambridge History of the Bible*, Vol. 1 [Cambridge: Cambridge University Press, 1970], 199–231): *midrash* is the early attempt to explain difficult biblical texts (*pure exegesis*) and to apply the message of Scripture to new situations (*applied exegesis*).

[24]Usually referred to as גְּזֵרָה שָׁוָה. "Die Anwendung desselben Wortes gilt als Beweis für die gleiche Geltung einer Bestimmung für beide Gebote" (Bacher, *Exegetische Terminologie*, 14).

[25]"Der Begriff *analogia fidei* ist aber von den Protestanten selbst verschieden gefasst worden, zunächst mehr formal, dass der Sinn jeder einzelnen Stelle mit dem Sinne aller der andern Stellen, die auf denselben

lical texts, Zechariah and Job. Thus the goal of the kind of "exegesis" that Willi has in mind for the Chronicler is not the original meaning (*mens auctoris*) of 2 Samuel 24. He rather sees the Chronicler as giving the passage a meaning within the larger context of the Old Testament Scriptures. In that regard the type of exegesis Willi finds in the Chronicles is analogous to the Christian notion of *sensus plenior* or *analogia fidei*.[25]

According to Willi, the starting point of the Chronicler's interpretation was the difficult statement at the beginning of chapter 24, וַיֹּסֶף אַף־יְהוָה לַחֲרוֹת בְּיִשְׂרָאֵל ("and the anger of the Lord was again against Israel . . ."). The Chronicler first replaced this difficult clause with the simple paraphrase וַיַּעֲמֹד עַל־יִשְׂרָאֵל ("and he stood against Israel"). This use of עָמַד עַל in the text of Samuel led further to the association of the passage with Zechariah 3:1b, a passage which also contained the words, עֹמֵד עַל ("and the adversary [הַשָּׂטָן] was standing [עֹמֵד עַל] upon his right hand to oppose him"). Willi argues that a reader familiar with the prophetic literature would not likely have missed the links between these passages.[26] By means of a word association (גְּזֵרָה שָׁוָה), then, the 2 Samuel 24 passage was brought by the Chronicler into the corpus of proof texts dealing with the adversary (שָׂטָן), and "the anger of the Lord" was thereby given an effective agent, the "adversary" (שָׂטָן), the real cause of David's census.

But is such a link enough to explain the Chronicler's interpretation of 2 Samuel 24? Willi further argues that there was an additional factor leading to the Chronicler's identification of the "adversary" as the agent of God's anger, namely, the presence of the two verbs סוּת[27] and שׁוּט in 2 Sam 24:1–4.[28] Willi points out that just as in the Chronicles text, Job 2:3 identifies הַשָּׂטָן as the Lord's agent who "moved Him (וַתְּסִיתֵנִי) against (Job)."[29] So also the verb שׁוּט in 2 Sam 24:2 is found in Job 2:2 (מִשֻּׁט) and, just as in Job 2:2, שׁוּט is rendered by הָלַךְ in the Chronicles text (לְכוּ). Thus, the use of these two verbs in his source text provided the Chronicler with an associative link between the 2 Samuel 24 passage and the scene in Job 2:3 where the adversary (שָׂטָן) was the effective agent of the will of God. In his interpretation of the difficult text of 2 Samuel 24, then, the Chronicler followed the accepted procedures of early exegetical technique[30] and rendered explicit the sense that he saw in 2 Samuel 24.

Willi's procedure in developing the Chronicler's method is appealing for a number of reasons. It shows a willingness to focus on what the Chronicler may have in *com-*

Gegenstand sich beziehen, übereinstimmen muss, wie Gerhard . . . oder noch allgemeiner: die Harmonie und der Zusammenhang der Bibelstellen, wie *Hollaz* . . ." (*RE* 5 [1956], 783).

[26]Willi notes, for example, the close association of these passages (2 Sam 24, 1 Ch 21, and Zec 3) by means of the priestly representation of Israel in Zechariah and the "removal" (עבר Hiphil) of their iniquity (עון). Compare 2 Sam 24:10, הַעֲבֶר־נָא אֶת־עֲוֹן עַבְדְּךָ; 1 Chr 21:8, הַעֲבֶר־נָא עֲוֹן עַבְדְּךָ; and Zech 3:4, הֶעֱבַרְתִּי מֵעָלֶיךָ עֲוֹנֶךָ.

[27]סוּת is also a key word in 2 Chr 18:2, 31. See Willi, *Chronik*, 144.

[28]Williamson follows Willi on this point, ". . . it was reflection on Job in particular which held him to introduce the figure of Satan where 2 Sam 24:1 has the 'anger of the Lord'" (*1 and 2 Chronicles*, 143).

[29]Compare 2 Sam 24:1b, וַיָּסֶת אֶת־דָּוִד; Job 2:3, וַתְּסִיתֵנִי בוֹ; and 1 Chr 21:1b, וַיָּסֶת אֶת־דָּוִיד בָּהֶם.

[30]There is need for discussion on the terminology to describe the nature of this exegetical technique. Based on the analogy of Ezra 7:10, "For Ezra had set his heart to study (לִדְרוֹשׁ) the law," I would prefer the term דרשׁ. Others, on the evidence of 2 Chr 13:22 (בְּמִדְרַשׁ הַנָּבִיא עִדּוֹ), would prefer the term מִדְרָשׁ. The later connotations of מִדְרָשׁ, however, would lead many to avoid its use in describing biblical writers. Willi appears to accept the term "Ur-midrasch" (proposed by Martin Buber) for the earliest stages of inter-biblical interpretation.

mon with his sources (2 Samuel 24) rather than their *differences*. Second, it provides an alternative to the conclusion that the differences between these two texts simply reflect a conflict in their theological point of view. Finally it provides an explanation from a perspective that has gained considerable acceptance within biblical and historical scholarship, namely, inter-biblical interpretation. A further, and important, implication of Willi's study is that it suggests there may yet be opportunities for a *harmonistic* reading of Scripture that is at the same time true to the historical author's original intention.

Some may object to Willi's supposition that the biblical writers relied on exegetical rules commonly employed in post-biblical books, such as גְּזֵרָה שָׁוָה. There is, however, ample evidence that the practice of such rules was already in place during the biblical period and can be found in the biblical sources themselves.[31] For example, the rule of אתבש[32] has long been recognized[33] by Christian exegetes in the use of the name שֵׁשַׁךְ for Babylon (בָּבֶל)[34] in Jeremiah 25:26b and 51:41a[35] and לֵב קָמָי for the Chaldeans (כַּשְׂדִּים)[36] in Jeremiah 51:1a.[37]

There are, however, important problems in Willi's specific links between 1 Chronicles 21, Zechariah and Job. As Schenker has pointed out, the role of "the adversary" (הַשָּׂטָן) in the Zechariah and Job passages is fundamentally different than in 1 Chronicles. In Zechariah, הַשָּׂטָן is the accuser of Joshua the High Priest but Joshua is protected from him by the Lord. Unlike his role in 1 Chronicles, Satan does not stir up Joshua against Israel in order to bring punishment upon the people.[38] The same is

---

[31]See René Bloch, "Midrash," *DBSup,* 5:1263-81; I. L. Seeligmann, "Voraussetzungen der Midrasch-Exegese," *VTSup 1* (Leiden: Brill, 1953), 150–81; Barry J. Beitzel, "Exodus 3:14 and the Divine Name: A Case of Biblical Paronomasia," *TrinJ* 1 (1980): 5–20, for a survey of types and examples of word plays in the Old Testament. Many of the illustrations listed by Beitzel are examples of exegetical rules known from the post-biblical period.

[32]"Atbash, a method of interchanging the first letter of the Alphabet (א) with the last (ת), the second (ב) with the last but one (ש) . . ." (Marcus Jastrow, *A Dictionary of the Targumim, The Talmud Babli and Yerushalmi, and the Midrashic Literature* [New York: The Judaica Press, 1971], 131.

[33]Johann Buxtorf, *Lexicon Chaldaicum, Talmudicum et Rabbinicum* (Basel: Ludovic König, 1640), 249.

[34]שׁ = ב; כ = ל. "*Sheshach* is a cryptogram for Babylon," marginal note in *The New International Version of the Holy Bible* (Grand Rapids: Zondervan, 1978).

[35]The fact that in both texts שֵׁשַׁךְ is omitted in the Septuagint suggests that the use of the rule in this case is a part of the complicated textual history of the book of Jeremiah. See J. Gerald Janzen, *Studies in the Text of Jeremiah* (Cambridge: Harvard University Press, 1973), 127; Wilhelm Rudolph, *Jeremia* (HAT; Tübingen: Mohr, 1968), XXII–XXIII.

[36]ל = כ, ב = ש, ק = ד, מ = י, ' = מ.

[37]". . . nam לֵב קָמָי, per literarum transmigrationem illam frequentem Chaldaeis, quae dicitur אתבש, facit כַּשְׂדִּים (sic), quod *Chaldaeos* sign." (Grotius); "Literae לֵב קָמָי, si Alphabetum praepostere numeres, in eodem sunt numero in quo כַּשְׂדִּים (sic)" (Sebastian Castalio, 1551). See also C. F. Keil, *Biblical Commentary on the Old Testament, The Prophecies of Jeremiah* (Grand Rapids: Eerdmans, 1968 [repr.], 1:383), "The name is formed acc(ording) to the Canon *Atbash*. . . . The assertion of Gesen(ius) that this way of playing with words was not then in use, is groundless, as is also Hitz(ig)'s, when he says it appeared first during the exile, and is consequently none of Jeremiah's work." Note that the Septuagint renders לֵב קָמָי as Χαλδαίους.

[38]Adrien Schenker, *Der Mächtige im Schmelzofen des Mitleids* (Göttingen: Vandenhoeck & Ruprecht, 1982), 72.

true, says Schenker, of the role of Satan in Job. In Job, Satan is not the instrument of God's anger. On the contrary, it is Satan who instigates Job's trial, not God.[39] God says, for example, in Job 2:3, "You (Satan) have provoked me (וַתְּסִיתֵנִי) to destroy him without cause." Though I agree with Schenker's points against Willi, I would argue there is an even more basic problem in Willi's approach. That is, it fails to take seriously enough the context of the Chronicler's own sources in explaining the origin of the Chronicler's interpretation.

A close look at the Chronicler's text of Samuel suggests he may well have had ample means for developing his interpretation from the context of his own "sources," namely those of Joshua–Kings. If such is the case, the nature of the Chronicler's exegetical method would be markedly different than that described by Willi. Rather than imposing his themes and interpretations from the outside, it would appear that the Chronicler's exegesis was based on a close reading of his own biblical sources. This may also suggest that the links that the Chronicler saw in his biblical sources were, in fact, an original element in those texts. With such questions in mind, the remainder of this appendix will attempt to describe how the Chronicler may have read his biblical sources and what support can be found in those texts for his interpretation.

The equivalencies between 2 Samuel 24 and 1 Chronicles 21 in the first verse are:

	2 Samuel 24:1	1 Chronicles 21:1
1.	וַיֹּסֶף אַף יְהוָה לַחֲרוֹת בְּ	וַיַּעֲמֹד שָׂטָן עַל
2.	יִשְׂרָאֵל	יִשְׂרָאֵל
3.	וַיָּסֶת אֶת דָּוִד	וַיָּסֶת אֶת דָּוִיד
4.	בָּהֶם לֵאמֹר לֵךְ מְנֵה	לִמְנוֹת
5.	אֶת יִשְׂרָאֵל וְאֶת יְהוּדָה	אֶת יִשְׂרָאֵל

As Willi has noted, the key difference between the two texts lies in the Chronicler's treatment of וַיֹּסֶף אַף יְהוָה לַחֲרוֹת. We should first note that this phrase is common in the historical books (Joshua–Kings) and that it plays an important role in the thematic development of those narratives. For example, the expression occurs in Judges 2:14:

> So the anger of the Lord was kindled against Israel (וַיִּחַר אַף יְהוָה בְּיִשְׂרָאֵל), and he gave them over to plunderers (שֹׁסִים), who plundered them; and he sold them into the power of their enemies round about, so that they could no longer withstand (לַעֲמֹד) their enemies.

Further examples of the similar uses of the expression (חָרָה אַף יְהוָה עַל) are numerous, e.g., Judges 2:20; 3:8; 10:7; 2 Kings 13:3; 23:26. As these passages show, when the anger of Yahweh was kindled against Israel, it resulted in the Lord's giving them over to their enemies. If the Chronicler were seeking an interpretive equivalency for the phrase וַיֹּסֶף אַף יְהוָה לַחֲרוֹת (2 Sam 24:1) from within the "larger context" of his own biblical sources, the sense he would have found was just that seen in the above texts, the threat of invasion by foreign powers. Thus, using the context of the whole of

---

[39]Ibid.

[40]The exegetical rule is קְצָרָה דֶרֶךְ: "Abgekürzte oder elliptische Ausdrucksweise" (H. L. Strack and G. Stemberger, *Einleitung in Talmud und Midrasch*, 7th ed. [Munich: Beck, 1982], 34).

his sources as his "lexicon," the Chronicler could have read 2 Samuel 24:1a as an abbreviated[40] statement that God had again (וַיֹּסֶף) raised up the enemy against them. It follows, from this, that the Chronicler would have had good grounds for paraphrasing the Samuel passage with the simple statement וַיַּעֲמֹד שָׂטָן עַל.

We turn now to the question of why in his paraphrase of Samuel's text the Chronicler would have used the term "adversary" (שָׂטָן) for the enemies of Israel? An answer to this question is also evident within the sources themselves.[41] Within the historical books (Joshua–Kings), the term שָׂטָן, "adversary" (without the article[42]) plays a prominent role in the application of the deuteronomic lesson to the failure of Solomon as king. The deuteronomic lesson that if the king is not faithful his kingdom would fall into the hands of his enemies is applied to Solomon in 1 Kings. First, in a positive sense, as Solomon prepared to build the Temple, he told Hiram, king of Tyre, "But now the Lord my God has given me rest on every side; there is neither adversary (שָׂטָן) nor misfortune" (1 Kgs 5:18 [RSV, 5:4]). Here it is clear that "to have rest" is "to have no adversary" (שָׂטָן). Second, in the negative lesson, at the very point when Solomon's unfaithfulness is fully demonstrated, the biblical writer draws out the consequences, in 1 Kings 11:9–14, "And the Lord was angry (וַיִּתְאַנַּף יְהוָה בִּשְׁלֹמֹה) with Solomon, because his heart had turned away from the Lord, the God of Israel . . . (14) and the Lord raised up (וַיָּקֶם יְהוָה) an adversary (שָׂטָן) against Solomon, Hadad the Edomite. . . ." And again in 1 Kings 11:23, "God also raised up (וַיָּקֶם אֱלֹהִים לוֹ) against him an adversary (שָׂטָן), Rezon the son of Eliada" and 11:25 "and he was an adversary (שָׂטָן) against Israel all the days of Solomon." A similar use of the term "adversary" (שָׂטָן) is found also with David in 1 Samuel 29:4 and 2 Samuel 10:23. The point to be made from these passages is this—if the Chronicler were looking for a term from the deuteronomic history itself to express his understanding that the anger of Yahweh against Israel meant the threat of foreign invasion, the term "adversary" (שָׂטָן) was one of the most readily available. In using this term, the Chronicler not only would have interpreted his sources in their own language and with their own ideas, but he also would have linked the failure of David with the notorious failure of King Solomon in the book of Kings.[43]

---

[41]The following explanation illustrates the exegetical rule בִּנְיַן אָב (creation of a class): similarities among a group of texts form a family in such a way that what is true about their central text is true of each member of the group. See Bacher, Exegetische Terminologie, 9.

[42]It is commonly held that the reason שָׂטָן does not have an article (הַשָּׂטָן), as all other uses with the sense of "Satan," is that by the time of the writing of the book of Chronicles, the term had become a proper noun (Ernst Jenni and Clause Westermann, Theologisches Handwörterbuch zum Alten Testament [Munich: Kaiser, 1976], 2:823). It is more likely, however, that the lack of an article was intended to show that the "adversary" (שָׂטָן) in 1 Chronicles 21 was to be distinguished from the being Satan (always written with an article [הַשָּׂטָן]) and associated with Israel's historical enemies, who are always referred to without the article (שָׂטָן).

[43]It might be asked that if the texts from the book of Kings were in view in the Chronicler's interpretation, why did he use עָמַד rather than קוּם, the word found in those earlier texts? The answer lies in the fact that the Chronicler and other later writers characteristically used עָמַד rather than קוּם in contexts depicting foreign invastion (cf. 2 Chr 20:23). See BDB, 64; and Edward L. Curtis, A Critical and Exegetical Commentary on the Books of Chronicles (ICC; Edinburgh: T. & T. Clark, 1910), 249.

There is yet another feature of the 2 Samuel 24 text that may have contributed to the Chronicler's use of the term שָׂטָן. When David told Joab to go out through all the tribes of Israel, his words are שׁוּט נָא. We have already seen that Willi has argued from this term that the Chronicler associated this verb with the same verb in Job 2 which describes Satan's moving throughout (מִשֻּׁט בָּאָרֶץ) all the earth. There is, however, another possibility if we look at these two words from the point of view of early post-biblical exegesis. The practice of reading pairs of words as if they were one word is well known already in the Masoretic Text[44] and is as old as the Qumran Scrolls and the Septuagint.[45] It is also generally held that behind such readings often lies an explicit interpretation.[46] With this in mind, it may be significant that the consonants of David's command to Joab, at an early stage in the orthography of the text, would have appeared as שׁט נא. If read as one word rather than two, that is, שׁטנא, the word would appear the same as the Aramaic[47] noun "adversary," שָׂטָנָא/שָׂטְנָא.[48] This veiled presence of the term already in the text, then, may have contributed[49] to an interpretation that associated 2 Samuel 24 with the adversaries (שָׂטָן) of Solomon.[50] An example of this technique in

---

[44]Gerard E. Weil, *Massorah Gedolah Iuxta Codicem Leningradensem B19a* (Rome: Pontificium Institutum Biblicum, 1971), 26.

[45]1Q Isa 9:6, למרבה, shows that the pair was read as one word. The αὐτῷ μεγάλη LXX, however, presupposes לם רבה as in B19a *Kethib* (Bernhart Duhm, *Das Buch Jesaia* [HKAT; Göttingen: Vandenhoeck & Ruprecht, 1892], 68).

[46]For example, כְּטוֹב (*Qere*), in Judges 16:25 appears to be an attempt to avoid the *Kethib*, כִּי טוֹב, which could be read as saying that the heart of the Philistines was good; or the tradition merely failed to recognize that טוֹב was a Perfect (George F. Moore, *A Critical and Exegetical Commentary on Judges* [ICC; Edinburgh; T. & T. Clark, 1895, 360). That the latter is not likely is evident from the fact that the same verbal form in 1 Samuel 16:16, 23 is not altered.

[47]There are other indications that the knowledge of Aramaic played a role in the composition of later biblical books, eg., Ps 2:12, נַשְּׁקוּ בַר; Dan 2:4ff, אֲרָמִית; Hab 3:19, לַמְנַצֵּחַ / τοῦ νικῆσαι (LXX = לִמְנַצֵּחַ Aramaic—see Gustaf Dalman, *Grammatik des Jüdisch-Palästinischen Aramäisch* [Darmstadt: Wissenschaftliche Buchgesellschaft, 1960], 291–94); cf. Gen 31:47 and Jer 10:11.

[48]Unlike the later Aramaic סָטָנָא the שׂ would have been distinguished from ס at this time. See Carl Brockelmann, *Grundriss der vergleichenden Grammatik der semitischen Sprachen* (Hildesheim: Georg Olms, 1982) 1:135; also, Gotthelf Bergsträsser, *Einführung in die Semitischen Sprachen* (Munich: Max Hueber, 1928), 61.

[49]This was perhaps by way of a *homiletical* rather than an *exegetical* midrash.

[50]The interpretation introduced into the Targum to Chronicles, "and the Lord set up the adversary against Israel" (ואקים יהוה סטנא על ישראל) offers an indirect confirmation that the Chronicler based his reading of 2 Samuel 24 on analogies from 1 Kings 11:14. Whatever may be said about the meaning of סטנא in the Chronicles Targum, it seems clear the translation is patterned after the Targum to 1 Kings 11:14, ואקים יוי סטן לשלמה, which is a literal equivalent of the Hebrew of 1 Kings, וַיָּקֶם יְהוָה שָׂטָן לִשְׁלֹמֹה. The Chronicles Targum, then, demonstrates that 1 Kings 11 did influence the reading of 1 Chronicles 21 at one point in its history.

[51]The Hebrew word בָּרָא, "he created," is read as an Aramaic emphatic noun "the son," בְּרָא. This would be analogous to Matthew 2:23 where the title Ναζωραῖος appears to come from נֵצֶר in Isaiah 11:1b (Hermann L. Strack, *Das Evangelium nach Matthäus erläutert aus Talmud und Midrasch* [Munich: C. H. Beck'sche, 1969], 93).

early post-biblical interpretation is Genesis 1:1 in Targum Neophyti 1. The targum reads the Hebrew text of Genesis 1:1, בָּרָא אֱלֹהִים ("God created . . ."), as if it were an Aramaic phrase, בְּרָא דייי ("The Son of God . . .").[51] The interpretation of the Targum, then, is homiletically related to the Hebrew text.

The Chronicler's version of 2 Samuel 24:1 appears, then, as an attempt to bring an interpretation to that passage that draws both on the terminology and themes of the biblical sources themselves. The sense, as the Chronicler saw it, was that David had sinned[52] and, as in the days of old and Solomon's kingdom after him, Israel was threatened by invasion from their enemies because of the disobedience of their leaders.[53]

These brief observations appear to me to support the following generalizations about inter-biblical interpretation.

(1) As has long been acknowledged in biblical scholarship, it appears likely that the techniques and practices of biblical exegesis known from the post-biblical literature already played a role in the OT's own interpretation of itself. If this is true, there is no reason to doubt such practices were already operative in the earliest biblical texts.

(2) The application of these techniques and practices by the biblical writer was different in some important aspects from that of later post-biblical exegesis. First, the exegesis of the biblical writer appears to be controlled by the principle that Scripture is its own interpreter (*sui ipsius interpres*). Secondly, the scriptural texts that most influenced his exegesis (*Auslegung*) were the biblical sources on which he was dependent.

(3) If using such exegetical rules as גְּזֵרָה שָׁוָה was the practice of the early biblical authors, then in pursuing the goal of historical grammatical interpretation, it may

---

[52]In the deuteronomic history, Yahweh's giving his people over into the hand of the enemy is preceded by the sin of the people and their leaders. Thus the threat of foreign invasion is seen as a result of divine anger and justice. R. A. Carlson has argued that the arrangement of 2 Samuel 24:1, following the list of David's heroes, is intended to connect this "punishment" with David's sin with Bathsheba by "an important associative link, 'Uriah the Hittite,'" a phrase placed immediately before 2 Samuel 24:1 (*David the Chosen King* [Stockholm: Almquist & Wiksell, 1964], 203). A similar argument is found in the recent commentary on Samuel by Jehuda Qayl, חקן 1981, p.] [הוצאת מוסד הרב קוק:ירושלים] ספר שמואל מפורש. If Carlson is correct, then the clue to the reason for the new outbreak of Yahweh's anger in 2 Samuel 24 is given within the compositional strategy of the text of Samuel and is given in a way that is virtually identical to the exegetical techniques of גְּזֵרָה שָׁוָה and סמך ("Das Nebeneinander zweier Abschnitte kann dazu benützt werden, den einen mit Hilfe des andern zu erklären: der eine der beiden Abschnitte 'lernt' von dem andern" [Bacher: *Exegetische Terminologie*, 133]). It is quite possible that the Chronicler would have taken notice of this clue.

[53]The fact that one of the three punishments proposed to David after he repented is oppression by his enemies (אֹיְבִים, צָרִים) may also have played a part in the Chronicler's interpretation.

[54]The following statement by Milton Terry shows clearly the low esteem in which such rules have been held: "It is easy to see how such hermeneutical principles must necessarily involve the exposition of the Scriptures in utter confusion. The study of the ancient Jewish exegesis is, therefore, of little practical value to one who seeks the true meaning of the oracls of God" (*Biblical Hermeneutics* [Grand Rapids: Zondervan, n.d.], 609).

[55]"Das stück (chapter 14) gehört nach allgemeiner Annahme zu keiner unserer Quellenschriften" (Hermann Gunkel, *Genesis* [Göttingen: Vandenhoeck & Ruprecht, 1964], 288).

[56]These are terms that occur in these texts but are not common or do not occur elsewhere in the Pentateuchal narratives.

be necessary to include approaches to the text which heretofore have generally not been regarded as important or even legitimate.[54] In other words, historical grammatical exegesis, in being true to the original author's intention, may have to pay closer attention to such exegetical techniques in the texts of Scripture.

Genesis 14:14–15:2 offers a specific example. Although modern literary criticism has emphasized the elements of discontinuity between chapters 14 and 15 of Genesis,[55] there are numerous verbal links[56] between the two passages:

4:13	הָאֱמֹרִי	15:16, 21	הָאֱמֹרִי
14:13b	בְּרִית	15:18a	בְּרִית
14:14b	דָּן	15:14a	דָּן
14:15 1	דַּמֶּשֶׂק	15:2b 1	דַּמֶּשֶׂק
14:14b	318 men	15:2b	אֱלִיעֶזֶר =318 318 =ר=200, ז=7, ע=70, י=10, ל=30, א=1 (1
14:16a	הָרְכֻשׁ	15:14b	בִּרְכֻשׁ
14:18a	צֶדֶק	15:6b	צְדָקָה
14:18a	שָׁלֵם	15:15a,	בְּשָׁלוֹם
14:19b, 22b	שָׁמַיִם	15:5a	הַשָּׁמַיְמָה
			שָׁלֵם 16b-
14:20a	מִגֵּן	15:1b	מָגֵן
14:21	הָרְכֻשׁ	15:1b	שְׂכָרְךָ reverses רכש שכר)

It appears evident from this list alone that a carefully constructed plan binds the two passages together. Not only is the plan itself based on the technique of Hebrew word association (גְּזֵרָה שָׁוָה) but in two of the examples a far more subtle linkage is evident. Both involve techniques known in later post-biblical literature. In the first instance, 14:14b, the mention of the 318 men of Abraham's household is linked to chapter 15 by means of חֶשְׁבּוֹן גִּימַטְרִיָּא (γραμματεία / *gematria*).[57] The mention of the number of men with Abraham was no doubt intended to stress how few in number his forces were against the kings from the East (cf Judg 7:6). Since the passage has apparently been influenced by Deuteronomy 20, the legislation for carrying out wars with those afar off,[58] the purpose of stressing the small number was to show that Abraham faced the same situation spoken of in Deuteronomy 20:1. He faced a people greater than he (רַב מִמְּךָ, Deut 20:1a) in number and strength, and God was with him (יְהוָה אֱלֹהֶיךָ עִמָּךְ, Deut 20:1b). Thus it was God and not Abraham who was responsible for the defeat of the eastern kings at Damascus (דַּמֶּשֶׂק). But why link this passage to chapter 15? By means of the gematrial link between the number of men (318) in 14:14 and the name of Abraham's servant (אֱלִיעֶזֶר = 318), along with the note, הוּא דַמֶּשֶׂק, before the servant's name in 15:2, the two texts are brought together in support of the central theme of the passage—God alone will care for the well-being of his chosen ones. It is just this theme that is, in fact, explicitly drawn out in the servant's name, which means "My God is a helper" (אֵלִי עֶזֶר).[59]

---

[57]"Deutung nach dem Zahlenwerth der Buchstaben" (Bacher, *Exegetische Terminologie*, 127). When the sum of the numerical value of a word equals the sum of the numerical value of another, the two words are associated. The existence of *gematria* in the name אֱלִיעֶזֶר has long been recognized (ibid.).

[58]See the author's commentary, "Genesis," *EBC*, vol. 2 (Grand Rapids: Zondervan, 1990).

[59]The importance of the meaning of names in the Genesis narratives is well-documented, e.g., Genesis 16:14; 29:32–30:24; 49:2–27. The meaning of מֶשֶׁק (Gen 15:2) is unknown (see KB, 616). The fact that the LXX has merely transliterated it (Μασεκ), suggests that already at an early date the meaning of the

The second instance of a midrashic link between chapters 14 and 15 involves the reversal of רכש (14:21) in שכר (15:1b).[60] By means of this reversal a link is made between Abraham's refusal to be made wealthy with the Canaanite spoils (רְכֻשׁ) and God's promise that Abraham's reward (שָׂכָר) would be great.[61] The practice of reversing consonants is also found elsewhere in Scripture as a means linking passages together.[62]

(4) In approaching the question of the NT's use of the Old, we may have to modify our understanding of those exegetical practices of the NT writers which appear to be merely a reflection of the interpretations and exegesis of first-century Judaism. It may rather be the case that the NT writers, and the first-century Jews for that matter, stand in an ancient exegetical tradition that finds its origins in the hermeneutics of the composition of the OT itself.

An example from the New Testament is the Melchizedek passage in Hebrews 7. In 7:2 the writer identifies Melchizedek by translating his name מַלְכִּי צֶדֶק, "He first, by translation of his name (ἑρμηνευόμενος), king of righteousness." He then identifies him by reading "king of Salem (שָׁלֵם) as "king of peace (שָׁלוֹם)." Could such a meaning have been the intention of the original writer of the Genesis narratives? Part of the difficulty with this reading of Genesis lies in the uncertainty about the meaning of the term צֶדֶק in Melchizedek's name, as well as the semantic relationship between שָׁלֵם and שָׁלוֹם. According to most lexical authorities, צֶדֶק in the name מַלְכִּי צֶדֶק not only does not mean "righteousness"[63] but also it is a predicate in a nom-

---

[60]term was unknown. The phrase הוּא דַמֶּשֶׂק appears as an explanation of the obscure phrase בֶּן מֶשֶׁק בֵּיתִי. The motive of the explanation is to further link Abraham's words to the events of the preceding chapter by means of the word play of מֶשֶׁק with דַמֶּשֶׂק, in 14:15b. By the same token נָתַתָּה זֶרַע appears to explain the obscure עֲרִירִי... מַה תִּתֶּן לִי in the preceding verse. This can be seen from the repetition of key elements of verse 2 in verse 3: 15:2 מַה תִּתֶּן לִי... עֲרִירִי 15:3 וַיֹּאמֶר אַבְרָם... לֹא נָחַתָּה זֶרַע... וַיֹּאמֶר אַבְרָם הֵן לִי. The key term זֶרַע (15:3, 5, 13) explains the rare עֲרִירִי by reversing the two consonants רע > ער (see הפך Bacher, Exegetische Terminologie, 44). Note that in Jeremiah 22:30 עֲרִירִי is again explained by זֶרַע. In the only other occurrence of the term, עֲרִירִי is explained by עֶרְוָה, that is, by a word link: ער = זֶרַע. ער. may also be linked to the name זרע אֱלִיעֶזֶר reverses עוזר.

[60]The technical term is הֲפֹךְ אֶת הַתֵּיבָה וְדָרְשָׁה, "Reverse the letter(s) and interpret it" (Bacher, Exegetische Terminologie, 44).

[61]It is significant that the noun רְכֻשׁ occurs in this form (defective scriptum) only in Genesis (except for 21:18, רְכֻשׁ occurs only in Genesis 14 and 15), where it also occurs as רְכוּשׁ (Gen 12:5; 13:6; 36:7; 46:6). Elsewhere in Scripture the form is רְכוּשׁ. The importance of this is that רְכוּשׁ would not have been a reversal of שכר. This suggests that these exegetical considerations have been preserved throughout the history of the Hebrew Bible.

[62]Cf. Isaiah 10:11, where the poetic passage is linked to a narrative text by reversing (עצב) וְלַעֲצַבֶּיהָ into (10:12) יָבֹצַע (בצע). The difficult עֻפְּלָה (עפל) in Habakkuk 2:4a may be an intended link with the phrase פָּעַל פֹּעַל (פעל) in 1:5b and פָּעָלְךָ (פעל) in 3:2a.

[63]Sedek is usually taken as a divine name: "'K(önig) ist Z(edek)' od(er) 'M(ilki) ist gerecht'" (KB 2:561); "my king is Sedek" (BDB, 575). Cf. Ras Shamra Parallels (ed. Stan Rummel; Rome: Pontificium Institutum Biblicum, 1981), 409: "In these theophorous PN's מלכי צדק and אדני צדק, Josh 10:1, 3), the divine element is apparently צדק."

inal clause ("My king is . . .") rather than a genitive ("King of . . .").[64] Furthermore, in the Genesis narrative, שָׁלֵם is a place name, "king of Salem," and not related to the noun שָׁלוֹם. Moreover, שָׁלֵם is later identified as the name of the city of Jerusalem (Psalm 76:3). Also, in the Greek Septuagint, the word εἰρήνη is not an equivalent of the Hebrew stative verb שָׁלֵם. Thus it is generally held that the writer of Hebrews has borrowed this interpretation from earlier Jewish sources[65] since it is found in Josephus,[66] Philo,[67] and the Palestinian Targum.[68] Though there are significant differences,[69] the Hebrews passage does show the same basic approach to the OT narrative. Does this mean that the writer of Hebrews has used or borrowed a later exegetical method to derive a deeper meaning out of the Genesis narrative?

The observations made about Genesis 14 and 15 above have shown that in the Genesis narrative the צֶדֶק in Melchizedek's name (14:18a) has, in fact, been linked to the term צְדָקָה, "righteousness" in 15:6b and the term שָׁלֵם (14:18a) has been linked to שָׁלוֹם, "peace" (15:15a). The interpretation found in the book of Hebrews, then, can already be seen in the narrative strategy of Genesis. Whatever may be said of the nature of the book of Hebrews' exegesis, it does not appear to be out of line with that of the Genesis narratives themselves. Along with this, it is important to note that by linking the term צֶדֶק in Melchizedek's name with צְדָקָה which was reckoned to Abraham by faith (15:6), the Genesis narrative had anticipated the kind of "righteousness" which the writer of Hebrews reads out of this text, namely, that which is "by faith" (Heb 11:8). Also, by linking שָׁלֵם in Genesis 14 with the שָׁלוֹם of Abraham's death (Gen 15:15, "And you shall go to your fathers in peace [בְּשָׁלוֹם]"), the Genesis narrative anticipated the very sense which the writer of Hebrews has given to the notion of peace (εἰρήνη), that is, the hope of eternal rest: "Now may the God of peace [ὁ δὲ θεὸς εἰρήνης] who brings forth from the dead [ὁ ἀναγαγὼν ἐκ νεκρῶν] . . . our Lord Jesus . . . equip you with everything good . . ." (Heb 13:20).

---

[64]Martin Noth, *Die israelitischen Personennamen im Rahmen der gemeinsemitischen Namengebung* (Hildesheim: Georg Olms, 1966), 161. This is confirmed by the fact that מַלְכִּי צֶדֶק is most likely theophorus (e.g., אֲבִיגַיִל, "my father is joyful," the name of a woman, obviously cannot be read as a construct, ibid., 15, 161) and the vowel in the last syllable, כִּי-, is best described as the first person pronoun, "my king." See Hans Bauer and Pontus Leander, *Historische Grammatik der Hebräischen Sprache des Alten Testamentes* (Hildesheim: Georg Olms, 1962), 524; and Rudolf Meyer, *Hebräische Grammatik*, II Formenlehre (Berlin: ~~Walter de Gruyter &~~ Co., 1969), 49.

[65]Otto Michel, *Der Brief an die Hebräer* (KEK; Göttingen: Vandenhoeck & Ruprecht, 1966), 260f.

[66]"Melchisedek; this name means 'righteous king' (βασιλεὺς δίκαιος)" (*Ant.* 1.180).

[67]"Melchisedek, too, has God made both king of peace (βασιλέα τε τῆς εἰρήνης), for that is the meaning of 'Salem'. . . . For he is entitled 'the righteous king (βασιλεὺς δίκαιος)' . . ." (*Allegorical Interpretation*, 3.79).

[68]*Tg Yer. I* has "The righteous king," מַלְכָּא צַדִּיקָא.

[69]James Moffatt, *A Critical and Exegetical Commentary on the Epistle to the Hebrews*, ICC (Edinburgh: T. &T. Clark, 1924), 91; F. F. Bruce, *The Epistle to the Hebrews*, NICOT (Grand Rapids: Eerdmans, 1964), 135.

AUTHOR INDEX

Ainsworth, H., 80, 262, 266, 283
Alter, R, 95
Amana, S., 299
Ammon, C. F., 120, 129, 130, 162, 163, 164
Andersen, F. I., 287
Anderson, B. W., 209
Anselm, 117
Aquinas, T., 45, 52, 73, 74, 191
Archer, G., 301
Arminius, J., 133
Auerbach, E., 54, 73, 74, 216, 217
Augustine, 45, 123, 231, 293

Baal Hatturim, 261
Bacher, W. 204, 262, 302, 306, 308, 309, 310
Bacon, R., 132
Bahrdt, K. F., 130
Baier, J. W., 12, 228
Bar-Efrat, S., 207
Barr, J., 167
Barth, K., 40, 41
Barton, G. A., 131
Barton, J., 98
Barthes, R., 44, 51
Baskin, W., 44
Baumgarten, S. J., 14, 57, 160, 161
Baumgarten-Crusius, D. K. W., 131
Baumgartner, W., 277
de Beaugrande, R-A., 43, 47, 101, 201
Bauer, B., 131
Bauer, G. L., 130
Bauer, H., 311
Beck, J. T., 131
Beckwith, R., 250
Beecher, W. J., 186, 187
Beitzel, B. J., 257, 304
Bengel, J. A., 122, 125, 131, 146, 147, 148
Benveniste, E., 50, 290
Bergstraesser, G., 307
Berkhof, L., 273, 289, 300
Bertholet, A., 131, 280
Bertram, B. C., 138, 139

Beza, T., 136, 137, 138
Biest, H. A., 120
Blenkinsopp, J., 244, 247
Bloch, E., 79, 167
Bloch, R., 94, 304
Blum, E., 218, 253, 260, 264, 274
Bockmuehl, K., 167
Boman, T., 167
Brekelmans, C., 264
Brenz, J., 133
Bretschneider, K. G., 120, 189, 190, 192
Briggs, C. A., 202
Bright, J., 55, 104
Brockelman, C., 307
Brown, C., 40, 53
Brown, G., 101
Brown, F., 202
Bruce, A. B., 64
Bruce, F. F., 311
Budde, K., 131
Buddeus, F., 124, 228
Buechner, G., 122
Buesching, A. F., 130
Bultmann, R., 40, 41, 167
Burgen, P., 132
Burrows, M., 154
Burk, P. D., 125
Buxtorf, J., 132, 304

Carpzov, J. G., 46, 152, 274
Calixt, G., 121, 124
Calov, A., 42, 170
Calvin, J., 119, 121, 124, 128, 133, 136, 137,
    138, 140, 141, 152, 153, 158, 245, 262,
    273, 283, 284
Campbell, D. K., 207
Campbell, E. F., 257
Capellus, 136
Carlson, R. A., 308
Carpzov, J. G., 46, 152, 274
Carson, D. A., 269
Cartwright, T., 263

Cassuto, U., 294
Castalio, S., 304
Champollion, J-F., 78
Childs, B., 83, 97, 98, 113, 241, 302
Chirichigno, G. C., 283, 287
Christian, P., 132
Clericus, J., 125, 157, 158
Coccejus, J., 23, 24, 52, 68, 74, 121, 122,
    124, 129, 131, 134, 149, 186, 188, 189,
    230, 273, 274, 289
Coelln, D. G. K. von, 131
Collingwood, R. G., 54, 55
Crusius, C. A., 125, 131, 148
Cunaeus, P., 133, 134, 139, 140, 142, 143,
    144, 145
Curtis, E. L., 301, 306
Cyprian, 127

Dalman, G., 307
Dannhauer, C., 228, 229, 299
Davenantius, J., 136
Davidson, A. B., 192
Dawson, R. W., 78
Delitzsch, Friedrich, 220, 221
Delitzsch, Franz, 62, 150, 221, 260, 283
Demsky, A., 220
de Wette, W. M. L., 131
Diestel, L., 34, 102, 120, 146, 148, 149,
    150, 151
Dillmann, A., 131
Donner, H., 55, 103, 104, 148, 181
Dornmeier, A. I., 228
Dressler, W. U., 43, 47, 101, 201
Driver, S. R., 202, 244
Drusius, J., 263, 266, 267, 268, 284
Duhm, B., 131, 307

Edsman, C. M., 12
Eichrodt, W., 20, 22, 107, 108, 170, 171,
    172, 173, 174, 180, 185, 186, 192, 271
Eilers, W., 257
Eisenstein, S., 214, 252
Eissfeldt, O., 170, 171, 172, 173, 207, 276,
    277, 280, 283, 286
Eldredge, L., 161
Engel, H., 78, 79
Erasmus, D., 128
Ernesti, J. A., 160, 161
Estius, W., 136
Every, G., 56
Ewald, H., 82, 131
Ezra, 261, 284

Fagius, P. 133, 267, 284

Feuerbach, L., 12
Fishbane, M., 94, 143, 180, 241
Flacius, M., 119, 152, 153
Fohrer, G., 89, 91, 98, 100, 206, 218, 272
Francke, A. H., 228
Freedman, D. N., 257
Frei, H. W., 36, 37, 51, 54, 72, 73, 74, 78,
    79, 121, 122, 217, 293
Fries, J. F., 131
Frye, N., 95

Gabler, J. P., 34, 125, 126, 130, 139, 161,
    162, 163, 164, 165, 166, 170
Gadamer, H. G., 12, 93, 94, 218
Gaussen, L., 274
Geiger, A., 18, 143, 180, 218, 219
Gerhard, J., 42, 136
Gerlach, O. von, 300
Gese, H., 83, 216
Ginsburg, C. D., 214, 220, 221
Ginzberg, L., 261
Glassius, S., 133, 144, 231
Goethe, J. W., 89
Goldschmidt, 261
Gomarus, F., 133
Gousset, J., 159
Gray, G. B., 268
Grotius, H., 267, 299, 304
Gressmann, H., 88, 89, 268
Guelich, E., 264
Guertler, N., 149
Gunkel, H., 54, 263, 308

Haacker, K., 17, 83, 167, 205
Haevernick, H. A. C., 63, 119, 120, 126,
    131, 170, 242
Hardmeier, C., 88, 101
Harrisville, R., 52
Hasel, G., 21, 29, 105, 106, 161, 187
Hayes, J. H., 34
Heath, S., 51
Hegel, G. F. W., 131
Heidegger, J. H., 47, 274
Hempelmann, H., 17, 167, 205
Hengstenberg, E., 64, 126, 153, 170
Henry, C. F. H., 63
Heppe, H., 300
Herder, J. G., 165
Hertzberg, H. W., 219
Hess, J., 126
Hesse, F., 105, 106, 107
Hiller, P. H., 125
Hirsch, E. D., 168
Hirsch, Emanuel, 14, 57, 228, 230

Hitzig, F., 131
Hoelscher, G., 20, 82, 166, 185
Hoffmann, H. W., 272
Hofmann, J. C. K. von, 58, 61, 62, 63, 64,
    65, 66, 67, 68, 71, 72, 126, 127, 131,
    146, 150, 151, 170, 186
Hollaz, D., 13, 122, 303
Holthaus, S., 35, 126, 150
Holzinger, H., 90, 212, 263, 269
Hornig, G., 35, 42, 43, 45, 102
Horovitz, H. S., 275
Horst, F., 276
Huber, F., 272
Hufnagel, W. F., 129, 130
Hume, D., 12

Imschoot, P. van, 191
Irenaeus, 127, 273
Iser, W., 39

Jacob, B, 260, 262
Jamieson, 266, 267, 268, 274, 275, 300, 301
Janzen, J. G., 304
Jastrow, M., 304
Jenni, E., 306
Josephus, 137, 311
Judex, M., 119, 153
Junilius, 127, 128
Junius, F., 132, 266, 284, 299
Justin Martyr, 123, 273, 289

Kaehler, M., 119
Kahnis, W. F. A., 65, 66
Kaiser, W. C., 63, 74, 81, 88, 101, 102, 113,
    187, 188, 238, 261, 276
Kant, I., 131, 163, 164, 191
Karlberg, M., 273
Katchen, A. L., 132, 133, 134, 137, 139
Kautzsch, E., 82, 91, 131
Keckermann, B., 189
Kedar, K., 30, 169
Keil, C. F., 81, 242, 260, 266, 267, 280,
    283, 304
Kelly, H., 56
Kierkegaard, S., 40
Kimchi, D., 245, 300, 301
Kitchen, K. A., 55, 104, 226
Kittel, R., 20, 82, 90, 131
Klieforth, T., 65
Knierim, R., 253, 255, 256, 258, 259
Knox, D. B., 57
Knudson, C., 131
Koch, K., 136
Kochavi, M., 220

Koehler, L., 19, 192, 277
Koenig, E., 20, 77, 82, 108, 129, 130, 131,
    156
Kraus, H-J., 21, 23, 34, 35, 58, 60, 61, 62,
    79, 83, 91, 102, 108, 118, 119, 120,
    121, 122, 133, 140, 141, 157, 158, 159,
    160, 165, 167, 189,
Kraus R. F., 258
Kuenen, A., 131

Lane, M. 96
à Lapide, C., 80, 222, 267, 300
Lavers, A., 44
Leander, P., 311
L'Empereur, 139
Lepsius, K. R., 78, 79
Leverenz, E. W., 234
Levy, J., 300
Lindbeck, G. A., 217
Loescher, V. E., 228
Loewith, K., 52
Lombard, P., 192
Lonergan, B., 55
Luthardt, E. E., 65
Luther, M., 119, 120, 124, 128, 132, 133,
    140, 141, 153, 236
Lyons, J., 30
Lyra, N. de, 132, 140, 263, 284

Magritte, R., 46
Maier, G., 17, 52, 53, 63, 87, 109, 227, 228,
    234, 235, 236, 237
Maimonides, 123, 132, 137, 138, 139
Malvenda, T., 266
Majus, J. H., 122, 129, 130, 228
Markert, L., 272
Marti, K., 131, 251
Martin, R., 132
Martins, E., 161
Marx, K., 52
Melanchthon, P., 119, 133, 153, 158,
    189, 192
Mendenhall, G. E., 257
Menken, G., 126
Menochius, J., 136
Mercerus, J., 263
Merrill, E., 113, 226
Meyer, G. W., 102, 157, 158, 160
Meyer, R., 311
Michel, O., 311
Michaelis, J. D., 35, 125
Mirandola, P., 142
Moeller, W., 20, 82, 110, 111
Moffatt, J., 311

Montanus, Arias 76, 77
Moore, G. F., 307
Mueller, J., 131
Muenster, S., 132, 133, 141, 244, 261, 265, 268, 284, 300
Murrho, S., 132

Nahmanides, 132
Nitzsch, A. B., 12, 127, 128, 129, 156
Norder, R. F., 234
Noth, M., 311

Oberforcher, R., 48, 101
O'Donovan, O. M. T., 257
Oecolampadius, J., 133
Oehler, G. F., 62, 110, 123, 124, 125, 126, 127, 131, 170
Oetinger, F. C., 125, 148
Oeming, M., 54
Ollenburger, B., 161
Origen, 123, 127, 132, 190

Packer, J. I., 56, 57
Pagnini, S., 132
Pannenberg, W., 40
Payne, J. B., 23, 24
Pellican, C., 132
Pesch, C., 59, 60, 61, 67
Pfeiffer, A., 157, 228, 300
Philippi, F. A., 60, 64, 65
Philo, 137, 311
Pick, R., 132
Pictet, B., 42
Piscator, J., 136
Plantinga, A., 227
Plett, H. F., 101, 201
Pol, M., 136, 266, 267, 268, 300
Procksch, O., 23, 190, 263
Prussner, F. C., 34

Qimchi, D., 135, 136

von Rad, G., 21, 40, 82, 83, 92, 185, 186, 215, 216, 299
Raible, W., 264
Rambach, J. J., 19, 158, 227, 228, 229, 230, 231, 232, 233
Rashi, 132, 134, 135, 141, 245, 262, 263, 266, 267, 283, 284, 287, 291
Raymond, W., 132
Ratschow, C. H., 12
Raven, J. H., 70, 71
Rendtorff, R., 83, 98, 206, 241, 253, 254, 264, 274
Reuchlin, J., 123, 132, 133, 142

Reventlow, H. G., 84, 95, 96
Richter, W., 87, 88, 89, 92, 204, 205, 241
Ricoeur, P., 95
Riehm, E., 131
Rivetus, A., 13, 133, 144, 161, 261, 274
Rilke, R. M., 12, 13
Rohnert, W., 65
Roos, M. F., 125
Rosenbaum, M., 141
Rosenthal, E. I. J., 134, 135, 136
Rothe, R., 58, 59, 60, 61, 62, 63, 64, 66, 67, 69, 146
Rudolph, W., 298, 299, 301, 304
Rummel, S., 310
Ryle, H. E., 248

Saadia Gaon 134, 135
Sailhamer, J. H., 18, 39, 50, 54, 99, 180, 206, 207, 209, 221, 253, 277, 290, 294, 298
Sanders, J. A., 241
Sandys-Wunsch, J., 161
Sasson, J. M., 143, 257
de Saussure, F., 44
Schaff, P., 156
Schedel, H., 76, 77
Schenker, A., 304, 305
Shereshevsky, E., 134
Schicklberger, F., 101
Schleiermacher, F. D. E, 59, 191
Schlottmann, K., 132
Schmid, H. H., 274
Schmidt, M., 64, 126
Schmidt, S., 120, 129
Schmidt, S. J., 43, 47, 54, 193, 200, 201, 207
Schmitt, A., 18, 222
Schmitt, H-C., 253, 254, 265, 269, 270
Scholder, K., 74, 75, 102
Schrenk, G., 121, 273
Schultz, H. 131
Schultz, F. W., 132
Schrenk, G., 121, 273
Seeligmann, I. L., 94, 143, 180, 219, 302, 304
Seforno, 261
Sekine, M., 45
Sellin, E., 20, 192
Semler, J. S., 35, 42, 125
Shual, C. D., 287, 291
Silbermann, M., 141
Smalley, B., 1140
Smend, R., 82, 131
Smith, C., 44
Spener, J., 130

Sperber, A., 300
Stade, B., 82, 131
Stadelmann, H., 40, 58, 63
Steinberg, J., 202
Stemberger, G., 305
Stendahl, K., 157, 166, 167
Stephan, H., 64, 126
Sternberg, M., 44, 54, 57, 58, 72, 73, 95, 268
Steudel, J. C. F., 126, 131
Steuernagel, C., 244, 245, 247
Strack, H., 305, 307
Stuhlmacher, P., 52, 53, 54
Summerhart, C., 132

Teller, W. A., 130
Temple, W., 66, 67
Terry, M., 308
Tertullian, 123, 127
Tholuck, F. A. G., 65
Tillich, P., 167
Tirinus, J., 136
Torczyner, H., 46
Tov, E., 223
Townsend, J. L., 207
Trask, W. R., 73, 216
Tremellius, I., 284, 299
Troeltsch, E., 52, 54
Turrettini (Turretini), F., 68
Turretini, J. A., 159, 160, 161
Tyndale, W., 284

Uphill, E. P., 78

Vatablus, 245, 267, 300
Vatke, W., 131
Vermes, G., 94, 180, 302
Vitringa, C., 47, 122, 123, 142, 143, 144,
    145, 146, 147, 148, 149, 274
Vogel, M., 128
Vos, G., 67, 68, 69, 70, 111, 112, 153,
    185, 215
Voetius, G., 189
Vriezen, Th. C., 21, 23, 173, 174

Walther, F., 65
Walter, Michael, 275
Wanke, G., 272
Warfield, B. B., 63, 64
Weber, H. E., 120, 147, 152, 153
Weber, O., 189, 190, 191
Weil, G. E., 307
Wegscheider, J. A. L., 131
Wellhausen, J., 82, 131, 185, 280
Wenham, G. J., 209, 226, 280
Wessel, J., 132
Westcott, B. F., 133
Westermann, C., 192, 263, 306
White, H., 50, 54, 290
White, M., 71
Wigand, J., 119, 120, 153
Willi, T., 94, 302, 303, 304, 305, 307
Williamson, H. G. M., 298, 303
Witsius, H., 189
Wolf, H. H., 273
Wolff, C., 37, 148
Wolterstorff, N., 227
Woodbridge, J. D., 269
Wright, G. E., 36
Whybray, R. N., 274

Yule, G., 101

Zachariae, G. T., 125, 129, 130, 162, 189

SUBJECT INDEX

Acts of God, 36, 50, 234
"Albright School" (the), 151
Allegorical, 133, 144, 145, 153, 163, 311
Allegory, 123, 145
Amanuensis, 198
Ancient Near East, 24, 25, 69, 166, 181, 182
Analogy, historical, 52, 53, 58, 81
Analogy of faith, 232, 233
Analogia fidei, 160, 232, 233, 302, 303
Analogy of antecedent Scripture, 238
Anthropology, 18, 116, 163, 182, 191, 222
Apologetics, 46, 132, 226
Aquila, 221, 244
Archaeology, 20, 51, 53, 69, 72, 82, 116,
    151, 200, 225, 226
Aristeas, Letter of, 137
Atbash, 220, 304
Author, 16, 20, 39, 43, 44, 46, 47, 48, 51, 54,
    57, 69, 71, 72, 73, 74, 84, 85, 93, 94, 98,
    154, 155, 156, 157, 159, 168, 169, 179,
    191, 198, 202, 203, 210, 211, 223, 227,
    231, 233, 242, 245, 254, 264, 265, 266,
    269, 270, 275, 276, 279, 280, 281, 285,
    286, 288, 292, 295, 297, 298, 304, 309
Authority, 13, 15, 16, 25, 42, 63, 112, 132,
    170, 179, 198, 226, 230, 235, 238, 256,
    257, 274
Authority, biblical 235
Authorship, 18, 101, 154, 198, 202, 215,
    238, 242, 269

Bible, 2, 4, 11, 12, 14, 15, 16, 17, 18, 19, 20,
    22, 23, 24, 25, 29, 34, 35, 36, 39, 41, 42,
    43, 45, 49, 53, 54, 55, 56, 57, 58, 59, 61,
    66, 68, 70, 72, 73, 74, 75, 76, 77, 79, 82,
    83, 84, 88, 91, 93, 94, 95, 97, 100, 104,
    109, 110, 113, 115, 117, 119, 120, 121,
    122, 123, 124, 125, 126, 127, 128, 131,
    132, 133, 135, 138, 139, 140, 144, 147,
    148, 149, 150, 152, 153, 156, 157, 158,
    161, 162, 163, 164, 166, 167, 168, 169,
    170, 175, 176, 177, 178, 180, 181, 182,
193, 197, 198, 202, 203, 204, 205, 213,
    214, 216, 217, 218, 219, 220, 221, 223,
    226, 227, 229, 234, 235, 236, 237, 238,
    239, 244, 247, 249, 250, 272, 274, 276,
    282, 284, 290, 291, 293, 294, 300, 301,
    302, 304, 309, 310
Biblical hermeneutics, 45, 79, 87, 157, 161,
    228, 234, 308
Biblical-historical exegesis, 234, 236, 237
Biblical realism, 73, 146, 150
Biblical text, 17, 36, 38, 44, 45, 48, 57, 68, 73,
    76, 77, 79, 80, 82, 83, 88, 93, 95, 98, 113,
    133, 135, 157, 158, 160, 161, 164, 165,
    167, 168, 176, 200, 204, 205, 207, 220,
    222, 224, 230, 231, 235, 236, 237, 289
Biblical texts, 19, 20, 40, 44, 46, 49, 55, 71,
    76, 83, 91, 92, 97, 106, 128, 129, 147,
    149, 154, 158, 162, 180, 181, 198, 202,
    204, 205, 206, 208, 212, 213, 214, 218,
    219, 220, 227, 234, 237, 252, 272, 282,
    299, 302
Biblical theology, 15, 18, 23, 34, 36, 39, 43,
    56, 58, 62, 67, 68, 69, 70, 72, 82, 90, 91,
    97, 111, 112, 113, 115, 116, 117, 118,
    119, 120, 121, 122, 123, 124, 125, 126,
    127, 128, 129, 130, 131, 132, 133, 135,
    136, 139, 142, 143, 145, 146, 147, 152,
    153, 155, 156, 157, 161, 162, 163, 164,
    165, 166, 167, 169, 171, 184, 185, 189,
    199, 200, 204, 205, 209, 215, 216,
    218, 219
Biblicism, 64, 120, 122, 133, 147, 152,
    153, 156
Binary opposition, 31
Blessing, 99, 101, 141, 187, 192, 207, 210,
    243, 244, 246, 270

Canaanite, 310
Canon, 18, 24, 31, 67, 83, 86, 87, 92, 97,
    103, 109, 111, 112, 143, 149, 151, 152,
    156, 174, 177, 180, 188, 198, 213, 214,
    218, 219, 221, 223, 224, 233, 237, 238,

239, 240, 241, 243, 244, 247, 248, 249,
  250, 251, 252, 304
Canon, OT, 31, 83, 87, 92, 97, 103, 109,
  149, 174, 188, 213, 214, 223, 224, 239,
  248, 249, 250
Canonical approach, 3, 4, 83, 97, 98, 99,
  109, 207, 222, 223, 253
Canonical theology, 5, 195, 197, 198, 199,
  200, 222, 224, 237
Causality (historical), 52, 53, 59, 291, 296,
  297, 300
Christ, 4, 20, 22, 37, 58, 60, 63, 65, 68, 106,
  113, 135, 136, 138, 139, 140, 141, 142,
  144, 145, 148, 153, 154, 170, 171, 173,
  174, 175, 177, 187, 190, 192, 230
Christian, 4, 14, 16, 22, 23, 37, 40, 41, 42,
  45, 52, 59, 73, 75, 76, 77, 95, 113, 117,
  118, 120, 122, 123, 124, 125, 126, 127,
  129, 130, 131, 132, 133, 134, 135, 136,
  137, 138, 139, 140, 141, 142, 144, 145,
  146, 147, 150, 152, 153, 159, 170, 171,
  173, 174, 175, 176, 178, 183, 186, 190,
  191, 192, 214, 217, 220, 221, 222, 226,
  229, 231, 232, 241, 263, 264, 272, 283,
  284, 293, 299, 300, 303, 304
Christian hebraism, 132, 133, 137
Christian hebraists, 123, 132, 133, 134, 136,
  137, 138, 139, 140, 141, 142
Christianity, 77, 141, 178, 180, 226, 234
Church, 15, 16, 37, 42, 61, 68, 76, 113, 117,
  119, 120, 121, 122, 123, 124, 125, 126,
  127, 128, 129, 130, 132, 135, 136, 137,
  138, 144, 147, 148, 153, 156, 159, 161,
  162, 170, 173, 179, 189, 192, 197, 216,
  217, 232, 233, 235, 236, 237, 250, 256,
  257, 273
Code of the Priests, 275, 277, 278, 279,
  280, 281
Coherency (of a text), 43, 47, 88, 147,
  207, 231
Commandments, 260, 261, 262, 263
Communication situation, 47, 83, 193
Componential analysis, 30, 33
Composition, 97, 98, 99, 101, 143, 151, 154,
  155, 156, 180, 198, 205, 206, 208, 211,
  215, 216, 218, 219, 224, 237, 238, 240,
  242, 243, 244, 251, 253, 254, 255, 256,
  257, 258, 259, 260, 264, 272, 273, 274,
  280, 285, 286, 288, 294, 295, 298,
  307, 310
Compositional strategies, 5, 154, 155, 206,
  207, 208, 209, 212, 241, 253, 255, 260,

270, 272, 275, 277, 308
Confession, 113, 156, 175, 263, 297
Confessional, 31, 36, 41, 113, 115, 117, 118,
  153, 155, 156, 159, 164, 169, 170, 171,
  172, 173, 174, 175, 176, 182, 183, 224,
  225, 226, 227, 231, 232, 233, 234
Conquest, 108, 111, 294
Con-textuality, 156, 213, 214, 215, 233,
  237, 249, 250, 252
Correlation (historical), 52, 53, 63, 75, 76
"Cosmic map," 169
Covenant, 21, 24, 65, 99, 107, 108, 121,
  146, 155, 186, 187, 192, 207, 250, 253,
  255, 256, 257, 260, 261, 270, 271, 272,
  273, 274, 275, 276, 277, 278, 279, 280,
  281, 282, 283, 286, 287, 288, 289
Covenants, 65, 121, 129, 186, 273, 279
Covenant Code, 257, 275, 276, 277, 278,
  279, 280, 281, 282, 286, 287, 288
Creation, 20, 48, 54, 58, 75, 76, 110, 111,
  176, 177, 192, 209, 210, 222, 223, 224,
  226, 250, 291, 292, 293, 306
Criteria of disunity , 88
Criteria of originality, 88
Critica sacra, 152
Criticism, 5, 34, 35, 37, 40, 52, 53, 61, 73,
  75, 77, 78, 79, 82, 86, 87, 88, 89, 90, 91,
  92, 97, 98, 99, 100, 103, 104, 105, 106,
  108, 110, 112, 125, 131, 162, 165, 198,
  206, 207, 208, 212, 217, 218, 222, 223,
  224, 225, 226, 236, 239, 241, 246, 269,
  272, 275, 276, 277, 280, 283, 309
Criticism, composition, 97, 98, 99, 206,
  272, 276, 280
Criticism, canon, 97, 198, 239
Criticism, form, 86, 88, 91, 92, 165, 207, 208
Criticism, historical, 34, 35, 37, 52, 61, 73,
  75, 77, 78, 79, 82, 86, 102, 104, 106,
  108, 110, 162, 198, 217, 236, 272
Criticism, literature, 87, 88
Criticism, literary, 88, 89, 131, 212, 241,
  276, 283, 309
Criticism, redaction, 97, 99, 100, 269
Criticism, source, 86, 88, 89, 90, 91, 131,
  198, 207, 208, 272, 275
Criticism, textual, 86, 223, 224, 225, 236
Criticism, tradition, 88, 92, 218
Criticism or canon, 86, 87, 103, 112

Decalogue, 261, 263, 273, 275, 276, 277,
  278, 282, 286, 287, 288
Deism, 74, 77, 78, 79, 125, 126
Derash, 133, 219, 220

Descriptive, 5, 115, 116, 117, 118, 155, 156, 157, 160, 161, 162, 164, 165, 166, 167, 168, 169, 170, 171, 182, 224

Deuteronomic, 250, 260, 261, 263, 264, 265, 302, 306, 308

Deuteronomic history, 250, 302, 306, 308

Deuteronomist, 90, 260

Diachronic, 5, 121, 184, 185, 186, 187, 188, 193, 205, 218, 237

Dicta probantia, 118, 128, 131

Divine revelation, 12, 13, 14, 15, 21, 37, 39, 41, 43, 57, 59, 60, 61, 63, 65, 68, 70, 78, 83, 84, 85, 112, 113, 125, 126, 127, 147, 152, 171, 186, 199, 226, 227, 231, 233, 237, 243, 245, 249

Dogmatic biblicism, 120, 122, 147, 152, 153, 156

Early church, 123, 129, 156, 216

Election, 187

Eclecticism, 30

Eclipse (of biblical narrative), 36, 37, 51, 54, 72, 73, 74, 122, 200, 231, 293

Effective history, 93, 179, 180, 218

Eighteenth century, 35, 73, 74, 78, 116, 121, 122, 123, 128, 150, 152, 158, 162, 163, 164, 165, 232, 274

Elohist, 90, 268, 283, 285, 286

"Emphasis" (in Scripture), 157, 158, 160

Empiricism, 37, 131

Enlightenment, 60, 61, 113, 130, 163, 164, 165, 166

"Epigenetic growth," 63, 187, 188

Eschatological, 99, 146, 148, 149, 154, 155, 206, 207, 211, 212, 240, 241, 248

Eschatology, 146, 150, 155, 243, 251, 253

Evangelical, 37, 39, 40, 42, 45, 53, 56, 57, 58, 63, 64, 65, 67, 69, 70, 72, 82, 113, 119, 146, 150, 198, 216, 219, 225, 226, 233, 280

Evangelical theology, 39, 58

Evangelical view of Scripture, 42, 57, 63

Evangelicalism, 37, 62, 63, 67

Evangelicals, 39, 40, 41, 42, 57, 63, 67

Event, 31, 36, 37, 39, 41, 45, 51, 52, 53, 54, 56, 57, 60, 62, 63, 66, 67, 70, 71, 72, 74, 75, 80, 82, 83, 86, 101, 102, 104, 105, 107, 110, 112, 136, 150, 161, 172, 184, 221, 232, 234, 237, 245, 287, 296, 301, 302

Event-centered, 109

Event-oriented, 41, 55, 86, 105

Events, 20, 31, 36, 37, 39, 40, 41, 42, 45, 46, 48, 50, 51, 52, 53, 54, 55, 56, 57, 58, 60, 61, 62, 63, 64, 66, 67, 68, 69, 71, 72, 73, 74, 75, 76, 77, 78, 79, 80, 82, 83, 84, 85, 91, 92, 98, 101, 102, 103, 104, 106, 108, 109, 110, 112, 113, 121, 125, 127, 136, 145, 146, 148, 149, 150, 151, 154, 155, 158, 166, 169, 171, 172, 173, 176, 177, 181, 184, 185, 186, 187, 198, 199, 200, 202, 211, 212, 226, 236, 237, 238, 244, 250, 251, 253, 254, 255, 261, 264, 265, 278, 283, 286, 287, 290, 291, 292, 293, 294, 295, 296, 299

Events "behind the text," 37, 39, 56, 83, 98

Exegesis, 18, 43, 49, 53, 58, 72, 75, 87, 88, 90, 91, 94, 120, 123, 124, 128, 132, 133, 134, 135, 136, 137, 139, 140, 141, 142, 145, 159, 160, 161, 213, 219, 220, 221, 223, 230, 234, 235, 236, 237, 243, 264, 298, 302, 303, 305, 307, 308, 309, 310, 311

Exodus, 41, 56, 75, 77, 78, 79, 80, 82, 108, 111, 155, 169, 200, 210, 256, 266, 275, 276, 277, 278, 280, 281, 282, 283, 284, 285, 286, 287

Extra-biblical sources, 181, 182

Facta probantia, 146

Faith, 14, 15, 16, 40, 42, 53, 63, 69, 75, 83, 87, 92, 93, 96, 107, 108, 109, 110, 113, 115, 117, 119, 120, 122, 128, 129, 135, 138, 145, 150, 152, 153, 155, 156, 159, 168, 169, 171, 172, 173, 174, 175, 176, 180, 182, 183, 186, 191, 215, 216, 226, 227, 232, 233, 235, 236, 253, 254, 255, 260, 264, 265, 266, 268, 269, 270, 271, 277, 282, 283, 288, 311

Faith and science, 96

Fall, the, 68, 185, 210, 291, 292

Feature analysis, 30, 31

Federal theology, 121

Fiction, 54, 55, 216

Fictionality, 54

Gematria, 20, 262, 309

God's Word, 16, 22, 35, 42, 43, 115, 116, 152, 175, 176, 179, 181, 197, 198, 236, 241, 243, 287

Geneva Bible, 284, 300

Golden calf, 273, 278, 279, 280, 281, 282, 287, 288, 289

Gospel, 57, 69, 113, 123, 142, 144, 154, 155, 217, 226

Grammatical-historical sense, 161, 179

Grammatical sense, 161
Gustavus Adolphus, 149

Habitus, 13, 229, 232
Haggadah, 134
Halakah, 134
Hebraism, 132, 133, 137, 139
Hebrew, 18, 22, 44, 45, 49, 50, 82, 83, 86,
    97, 100, 123, 132, 133, 135, 137, 138,
    140, 141, 142, 144, 152, 153, 159, 160,
    177, 178, 180, 184, 202, 203, 204, 205,
    213, 214, 218, 219, 220, 221, 222, 223,
    224, 233, 237, 238, 239, 240, 243, 244,
    247, 248, 249, 250, 251, 252, 257, 267,
    274, 277, 282, 283, 284, 285, 287, 291,
    298, 308, 311
Hebrew Bible, 45, 49, 97, 100, 123, 132,
    133, 135, 140, 144, 153, 177, 178, 180,
    205, 213, 214, 219, 220, 221, 223, 237,
    238, 239, 244, 247, 249, 250
Hebrew grammar, 44, 45, 50, 57, 132, 202,
    204, 217, 229
Hebrew Scriptures, 83, 97, 133, 140, 141,
    142, 184, 298
Hebrew syntax, 44, 45, 50, 286, 287
Hebrew lexicography, 45, 204
Heilsgeschichte, 39, 40, 45, 58, 64, 65, 106,
    150, 151
Heilstatsachen, 105, 106
Hermeneutica profana, 235
Hermeneutica sacra, 227, 228, 229, 230, 232,
    233, 237
Hermeneutics, 17, 45, 47, 54, 72, 79, 82, 87,
    95, 139, 144, 157, 161, 167, 184, 201,
    202, 227, 228, 230, 231, 233, 234, 239,
    293, 310
Hidden mystery, 145, 147, 154
Historical background, 158, 160, 181,
    202, 203
Historical-biblical, 109, 234
Historical-critical, 35, 74, 82, 103, 105, 106,
    109, 179, 185, 234, 235
Historical criticism, 34, 35, 37, 52, 61, 73,
    75, 77, 78, 79, 82, 86, 103, 104, 106,
    108, 110, 162, 198, 217, 236, 272
Historical distance, 118, 178
Historical methodology, 35, 106, 176,
    226, 236
Historical narrative, 49, 50, 51, 54
Historicism, 69, 153, 171
History, 15, 18, 20, 31, 34, 36, 37, 39, 40,
    41, 42, 43, 46, 48, 50, 51, 52, 53, 54, 55,
    56, 57, 58, 60, 61, 62, 63, 64, 65, 67, 68,

69, 70, 71, 72, 73, 74, 75, 76, 77, 78, 79,
    80, 82, 83, 84, 93, 94, 102, 103, 104,
    105, 106, 107, 108, 109, 110, 111, 112,
    113, 117, 118, 121, 122, 123, 125, 126,
    127, 129, 130, 131, 132, 133, 136, 142,
    143, 145, 146, 147, 148, 150, 151, 152,
    155, 156, 157, 162, 163, 164, 165, 169,
    170, 171, 172, 173, 176, 177, 178, 179,
    180, 181, 182, 183, 184, 185, 186, 199,
    200, 214, 215, 216, 217, 218, 220, 221,
    222, 224, 226, 229, 231, 233, 234, 235,
    236, 237, 238, 239, 242, 244, 250, 255,
    259, 274, 293, 294, 301, 302, 306
History of Israel, 20, 31, 37, 48, 55, 57, 67,
    78, 103, 104, 105, 106, 110, 112, 170,
    171, 181, 185, 226, 255
History of religion, 108, 170, 173
History of religions, 130, 165, 170, 173
History, real, 37, 67, 71, 73, 75, 105, 171
Holy nation, 282
Holy Roman Empire, 149
Holiness, 275, 280, 281, 289
Holiness Code, 275, 280, 281, 289
Horizon of the reader, 94
Horizon of the text, 94
Humanity, 12, 15, 19, 37, 53, 59, 64, 76,
    111, 116, 151, 163, 164, 165, 177, 189,
    192, 207, 251, 259

Idealism, 37, 148, 171, 191
Idolatry, 220, 280, 281, 288, 289
Inerrancy of Scripture, 113
Infallibility of Scripture, 152
Inner-textuality, 155, 156, 209, 210, 211,
    212, 213, 246
Inspired events, 146
Inspired text, 40, 56, 57, 58, 66, 152, 199
Inspiration, 14, 35, 42, 43, 45, 46, 59, 60, 61,
    62, 63, 64, 65, 66, 71, 72, 73, 112, 113,
    115, 144, 150, 152, 160, 199, 219, 222,
    224, 227, 232, 237, 245, 274
Inspiration (verbal plenary), 150
Inspiration of Scripture, 35, 42, 61, 150,
    160, 222
Inter-biblical interpretation, 5, 84, 94, 95,
    143, 180, 233, 258, 298, 302, 304, 308
Inter-textuality, 43, 95, 155, 156, 212, 213,
    237, 243, 250, 251
In-textuality, 207, 208, 209
Israel, 20, 21, 31, 37, 42, 48, 55, 56, 57, 67,
    68, 69, 70, 72, 75, 76, 78, 79, 80, 82, 83,
    90, 91, 92, 93, 94, 97, 98, 99, 102, 103,
    104, 105, 106, 107, 108, 109, 110, 112,

113, 124, 126, 131, 135, 136, 137, 138,
143, 148, 151, 155, 165, 166, 167, 169,
170, 171, 172, 173, 176, 177, 180, 181,
182, 185, 186, 205, 207, 211, 215, 216,
217, 220, 225, 226, 241, 243, 245, 246,
247, 249, 250, 251, 255, 256, 263, 265,
272, 273, 274, 276, 277, 278, 279, 280,
281, 282, 283, 284, 285, 286, 288, 289,
291, 294, 299, 300, 303, 304, 305, 306,
307, 308
Israelite religion, 57, 108, 131, 155, 165,
172, 173, 174

Jahwist, 88, 90, 274, 283, 286
Jesus Christ, 113, 154, 173, 174, 187,
190, 230
Jewish, 123, 132, 133, 134, 135, 136, 137,
138, 139, 140, 141, 142, 143, 144, 145,
153, 166, 178, 180, 185, 262, 311
Jewish Bible exegesis, 133
Judaism, 22, 75, 127, 133, 134, 135, 137,
144, 153, 178, 180, 219, 226, 252, 273,
298, 310

Kabbalah, 123, 133, 134, 139, 140, 142,
143, 144, 145, 153
Karaism, 134
Karaites, 134
Kethib, 244, 307
Kingdom, 21, 77, 113, 125, 148, 149, 150,
155, 192, 226, 251, 282, 306, 308
Kingdom of God, 21, 148, 149, 150, 192
Kingdom of priests, 113, 226, 282
Kingship, 104
Knowledge of God, 21

Land of Canaan, 69, 294
Land (promised), 268
Language, 13, 17, 18, 24, 31, 40, 43, 44, 45,
47, 49, 50, 54, 55, 57, 58, 96, 132, 138,
159, 162, 169, 197, 202, 204, 205, 206,
222, 290, 302, 306
Last days, 58, 99, 151, 207, 211
Law, 5, 43, 99, 121, 123, 128, 136, 137, 138,
139, 140, 143, 144, 145, 175, 178, 188,
192, 206, 207, 222, 239, 240, 241, 244,
245, 248, 249, 253, 254, 255, 256, 257,
258, 259, 260, 261, 262, 263, 264, 265,
269, 270, 271, 272, 273, 274, 276, 277,
279, 280, 281, 283, 289, 291, 293
Law, biblical, 128, 137, 138, 139, 143
Law codes, 99, 206, 254, 279, 280
Law, Mosaic, 5, 99, 123, 136, 137, 138, 139,
140, 143, 188, 207, 222, 253, 254, 256,

257, 260, 261, 262, 263, 264, 270, 271
Lexical meaning, 203, 204
Liberalism, 166, 171
Literary type, 49
Literate readers, 49
Locus of revelation, 31, 37, 56, 66, 84, 146,
200, 224
Logic, 121, 141, 229, 232, 280, 288, 297
LXX, 17, 18, 136, 137, 204, 205, 214, 221,
222, 244, 247, 251, 267, 283, 284,
307, 311

Masorah, 218, 221
Masoretic Text, 204, 205, 218, 219, 220,
221, 222, 223, 224, 244
Medieval Jewish exegesis, 134, 135, 142
Melchisedek, 311
Messiah, 135, 140, 141, 221
Messianic, 88, 99, 135, 136, 140, 141, 143,
145, 153, 154, 155, 206, 221, 234, 251
Messianic hope, 88, 135, 145, 154
Methodology, 5, 27, 29, 30, 33, 35, 84, 87,
102, 103, 106, 112, 113, 176, 226, 235,
236, 263
Middle Ages, 123, 128, 129, 132, 135, 192
Midrash, 94, 134, 298, 302
Millennial kingdom, 149
Millennialism, 148
Millennium, 55, 69, 104, 190, 220
Mishneh Torah, 132, 137, 138, 139
Missouri Synod Lutheran, 65
Montage, 214, 249, 250, 252
Mosaic law, 5, 99, 123, 136, 137, 138, 139,
140, 143, 188, 207, 222, 253, 254, 256,
257, 260, 261, 262, 263, 264, 270, 271
Muslim rationalism, 134
Mystical, 34, 123, 133, 134, 137, 140, 141,
142, 231, 232, 233
Mystery, 142, 143, 144, 145, 147, 154

Napoleon, 149
Narrative, 2, 5, 36, 37, 39, 43, 44, 45, 49, 50,
51, 54, 57, 67, 69, 70, 71, 72, 73, 74, 75,
76, 77, 79, 80, 81, 82, 95, 99, 112, 121,
122, 140, 144, 149, 165, 177, 200, 202,
203, 206, 207, 208, 209, 210, 211, 212,
213, 217, 221, 231, 238, 241, 242, 244,
247, 248, 250, 251, 253, 254, 255, 256,
258, 265, 266, 268, 269, 270, 274, 276,
277, 278, 279, 280, 281, 282, 283, 284,
285, 286, 287, 288, 289, 290, 291, 292,
293, 294, 295, 296, 297, 311
Narrative, biblical 36, 37, 39, 43, 44, 45, 50,
54, 69, 72, 73, 74, 77, 80, 95, 122, 165,

177, 200, 207, 209, 217, 231, 290, 291, 293

Natural revelation, 41

Near East, 24, 25, 69, 166, 181, 182

Near Eastern religions, 24

Neofiti I, 222, 244, 284

New covenant, 65, 99, 207

Nineteenth century, 54, 58, 72, 90, 130, 131, 146, 161, 165, 191, 293

"Nontextual," 68, 200

Normative, 13, 14, 15, 16, 22, 24, 59, 116, 168, 169, 175

Normativity, 15

NT theology, 11, 21, 23, 118, 119

Oeconomia, 121, 122, 189

Offenbarung, 12, 14, 40, 43, 58, 59, 60, 63, 65, 66, 87, 110, 120, 150, 228, 237

Offenbarungen, 63, 126

Offenbarungsgeschichte, 58, 64, 129

OT introduction, 18, 215, 216

OT Scriptures, 34, 36, 37, 108, 110, 126, 129, 140, 143, 145, 147, 151, 154, 176, 198, 205, 216, 218, 219, 227, 234, 249

OT theology, 4, 11, 13, 14, 15, 16, 17, 18, 19, 20, 21, 22, 23, 24, 25, 29, 31, 34, 35, 37, 62, 63, 70, 82, 83, 84, 85, 86, 87, 88, 90, 91, 92, 97, 98, 101, 105, 106, 107, 108, 110, 113, 115, 117, 123, 126, 151, 153, 156, 167, 170, 171, 172, 173, 174, 175, 182, 183, 184, 186, 187, 188, 189, 191, 192, 193, 197, 198, 199, 200, 202, 205, 206, 209, 212, 215, 219, 223, 224, 225, 226, 227, 233, 237, 238, 299

Onkelos (Targum), 284

Ordo temporum, 120, 121, 124, 156, 186, 279

Original author, 84, 93, 94, 156, 159, 179, 227, 298, 309

Orthodox, 13, 34, 37, 43, 45, 58, 65, 66, 67, 68, 117, 119, 120, 121, 122, 124, 126, 133, 137, 146, 147, 149, 152, 156, 157, 159, 160, 161, 164, 165, 166, 171, 204, 228, 231, 274

Orthodoxy, 53, 68, 118, 122, 124, 128, 129, 133, 147, 148, 149, 152, 156, 160, 166, 191, 230

Ostensive reference, 37, 75, 77, 80, 82, 98, 112

"Outside the text," 39, 51, 154

Patriarchal narratives, 55, 104, 210, 259, 261, 264

Pentateuch, 2, 39, 44, 49, 54, 68, 71, 76, 88, 89, 90, 91, 99, 100, 101, 109, 134, 136,

137, 141, 155, 176, 177, 206, 207, 209, 210, 211, 212, 213, 215, 218, 221, 238, 239, 240, 241, 242, 243, 244, 246, 247, 249, 251, 253, 254, 255, 256, 257, 258, 259, 260, 261, 263, 264, 265, 267, 270, 271, 272, 273, 274, 275, 276, 277, 280, 281, 284, 285, 286, 287, 288, 291, 292, 293, 295, 298, 302

Peshat, 133, 134, 135, 136, 137, 138, 140, 141, 142, 143, 144, 145, 153

Phenomenology, 93, 108, 191

Philology, 161, 162, 204, 205, 225, 236

Pietism, 120, 122, 124, 130, 146, 147, 153

Poetic, 24, 49, 99, 155, 206, 208, 210, 211, 213, 241, 242, 245, 251, 277

Poetry, 49, 99, 165, 210, 241, 275, 277

Postbiblical interpretation, 218, 219, 220, 221, 222

Precritical, 36, 37, 113

Presupposition, 17, 190

Presuppositions, 16, 53, 105, 166

Priestly source, 88, 90, 91, 275

Progressive revelation, 125

Prolegomena, 16, 139

Proleptic history, 149

Proof text(s), 117, 118, 119, 120, 124, 127, 128, 156, 170

Promise, the, 186, 187, 188, 246, 247, 249, 273

Prophets, 49, 60, 63, 65, 66, 131, 134, 140, 143, 144, 145, 154, 177, 178, 187, 192, 239, 240, 243, 247, 248, 249, 250, 253, 271

Protestant, 14, 34, 36, 42, 46, 47, 57, 68, 72, 117, 119, 122, 124, 126, 128, 133, 135, 136, 137, 139, 140, 141, 142, 152, 153, 156, 165, 166, 170, 192, 261

Providence (divine), 52, 53, 73, 74, 76, 77, 230

Principle, 13, 17, 20, 34, 41, 53, 81, 88, 111, 119, 138, 160, 170, 172, 189, 190, 191, 192, 216, 226, 230, 235, 238, 257, 308

Qeri, 244

Rabbinical writings, 123, 134, 137, 139, 140, 141, 143, 159, 241, 261, 262, 264, 291

Ratio, 13, 160, 233

Rationalism, 126, 165, 171

Reader, 11, 34, 37, 39, 44, 45, 46, 47, 48, 49, 50, 51, 57, 60, 67, 72, 75, 77, 80, 94, 143, 147, 159, 168, 169, 175, 178, 179, 203, 204, 205, 211, 213, 214, 216, 231,

232, 248, 249, 252, 256, 259, 290, 291, 294, 296, 302, 303

Readers, 24, 39, 44, 46, 48, 49, 50, 67, 72, 94, 156, 157, 167, 177, 183, 188, 204, 212, 213, 214, 217, 237, 238, 252, 256, 276, 290, 293, 297

Real events, 40, 46, 60, 69, 71, 73, 77, 112

Real history, 37, 67, 71, 73, 75, 105, 171

Real world, 45, 46, 49, 50, 51, 54, 55, 69, 70, 73, 74, 216, 217, 290, 291, 292, 293

Realism, 73, 146, 150

Realistic (narrative), 45, 46, 48, 49, 50, 54, 67, 70, 73, 148, 149, 150

Reason, 13, 19, 21, 40, 41, 43, 53, 55, 56, 84, 134, 136, 152, 160, 162, 163, 164, 165, 168, 179, 190, 191, 204, 213, 217, 218, 227, 233, 250, 269, 273, 287, 288, 290, 296, 301, 308

Redemption, 63, 106, 112, 136, 155, 187, 217

Religion, 11, 12, 14, 15, 20, 22, 41, 57, 69, 70, 82, 90, 91, 107, 108, 109, 110, 122, 126, 130, 131, 134, 146, 155, 162, 163, 165, 166, 170, 171, 172, 173, 174, 175, 185, 186, 193, 217, 276, 288

Religions, 24, 126, 130, 165, 166, 170, 173, 185

Religious, 14, 15, 18, 24, 25, 37, 59, 62, 73, 90, 92, 94, 108, 126, 129, 131, 136, 137, 150, 163, 165, 166, 168, 172, 173, 182, 219, 222, 291, 295

Remez, 133

Representation, 45, 46, 50, 54, 67, 73, 198, 216, 290

Repristination, 64, 126

Res, 45, 47, 52, 53, 54, 55, 67, 68, 72, 74, 79, 124, 125, 160, 203, 231, 232

Res gestae, 45, 53, 54, 55, 67, 68, 72, 79, 203

Revealed theology, 13

Revelation, 11, 12, 13, 14, 15, 16, 20, 21, 22, 31, 34, 36, 37, 39, 40, 41, 42, 43, 46, 54, 55, 56, 57, 58, 59, 60, 61, 62, 63, 64, 65, 66, 67, 68, 69, 70, 72, 74, 75, 78, 82, 83, 84, 85, 87, 110, 111, 112, 113, 115, 116, 117, 125, 126, 127, 131, 146, 147, 148, 149, 151, 152, 167, 171, 172, 173, 174, 185, 186, 187, 188, 191, 197, 199, 200, 201, 204, 224, 226, 227, 231, 233, 234, 236, 237, 243, 245, 249, 262, 273

Revelation in history, 39, 40, 41, 55, 56, 64, 68, 69, 72

Revelation in the events, 40

Revelation in Scripture, 40, 41, 42, 54, 67, 147, 199

Revelation in the text, 83

Revelation, general, 262

Revelation, natural, 41

Revelation, progressive, 125, 188

Revelation, special 11, 37, 42, 56, 67, 68, 74, 75, 111, 126, 185

Roman Catholic, 124, 141, 145, 159

Roman Catholicism, 137

Romanticism, 165, 166

Salvation history, 56, 58, 60, 61, 62, 63, 64, 65, 67, 68, 82, 83, 106, 121, 131, 171

Samaritan Pentateuch, 221, 244, 257, 284, 285

Scholastic, 122, 129

Science, 13, 17, 23, 44, 53, 54, 55, 75, 78, 84, 87, 88, 96, 110, 116, 126, 172, 173, 197, 201

Scientific, 13, 54, 75, 87, 88, 115, 116, 161, 171, 172, 173, 197, 235

Scopus scripturae, 160

Scripture, 4, 14, 16, 21, 22, 29, 31, 35, 36, 37, 39, 40, 41, 42, 43, 44, 46, 52, 54, 55, 56, 57, 58, 59, 61, 62, 63, 64, 65, 66, 67, 68, 69, 72, 73, 74, 75, 79, 82, 83, 84, 85, 86, 87, 88, 95, 101, 102, 104, 108, 109, 110, 115, 117, 119, 121, 122, 126, 127, 128, 130, 132, 133, 134, 139, 140, 141, 143, 144, 145, 146, 147, 148, 149, 150, 151, 152, 153, 154, 156, 157, 159, 160, 161, 164, 169, 172, 175, 176, 177, 186, 187, 189, 197, 198, 199, 200, 202, 204, 205, 216, 217, 218, 222, 224, 226, 228, 229, 230, 231, 232, 233, 235, 236, 237, 238, 241, 243, 244, 249, 257, 273, 289, 293, 298, 299, 301, 304, 308, 309, 310

Scriptures, 11, 15, 16, 34, 35, 36, 37, 42, 45, 56, 58, 59, 60, 61, 62, 66, 68, 75, 83, 84, 86, 96, 97, 108, 110, 112, 113, 119, 122, 124, 125, 126, 129, 130, 133, 137, 140, 141, 142, 143, 145, 147, 148, 149, 150, 151, 152, 153, 154, 156, 159, 160, 166, 170, 176, 180, 184, 187, 198, 200, 205, 216, 218, 219, 227, 228, 230, 232, 233, 234, 235, 238, 242, 243, 248, 249, 273, 298, 303

Sensus historicus, 134, 145, 154, 158

Sensus literalis, 133, 141, 143, 153, 154, 160, 161, 231

Sensus mysticus, 153, 231

Sensus spiritualis, 153, 154

Sensus plenior, 84, 303

Septuagint, 17, 18, 136, 137, 204, 205, 214, 221, 222, 244, 247, 251, 267, 283, 284, 307, 311

Seventeenth century, 74, 121, 124, 132, 133, 224

Sinai covenant, 99, 155, 207, 256, 270, 272, 273, 274, 278, 279, 282, 283, 286, 287, 288

Signs of the times, 150

Sitz im Leben, 91, 208

Sitz im Text, 208

Sixteenth century, 129, 132, 133

Sociology, 51, 116, 182

Sod (interpretation), 133

Sola fide, 153

Sola scriptura, 34, 119, 120, 128, 153

Special revelation, 11, 37, 42, 56, 67, 68, 74, 75, 111, 126, 185

Spiritual sense, 142, 145, 154, 232

Spiritualization, 123

Story, 20, 43, 48, 49, 50, 74, 76, 77, 83, 117, 118, 142, 163, 203, 210, 213, 216, 217, 221, 244, 268, 269, 290, 291, 292, 295, 296, 297

Structuralism, 88, 95, 96, 98, 218

Supernaturalists, 125, 126, 147

Symmachus, 221, 244

Synchronic, 31, 184, 188, 189, 191, 192, 193, 218, 237

Synod of Dort, 133, 137, 139

Systematic theology, 19, 20, 162, 191, 192, 272, 273

Systems analysis, 193

Talmud, 143, 144, 261, 299

TaNaK, 240, 249

Targum, 135, 222, 284, 300, 301, 304, 307, 308, 311

Task of theology, 12, 13, 14, 16, 197

Text, 5, 17, 19, 20, 21, 22, 31, 35, 36, 37, 39, 40, 43, 44, 45, 46, 47, 48, 49, 50, 51, 52, 54, 55, 56, 57, 58, 62, 63, 64, 66, 67, 68, 69, 70, 71, 72, 73, 74, 75, 76, 77, 79, 80, 81, 82, 83, 84, 85, 86, 87, 88, 89, 90, 91, 92, 93, 94, 95, 96, 97, 98, 99, 100, 101, 107, 108, 112, 113, 116, 133, 134, 135, 137, 140, 141, 142, 143, 145, 146, 147, 148, 149, 150, 152, 153, 154, 157, 158, 159, 160, 161, 164, 165, 166, 167, 168, 169, 170, 176, 178, 180, 181, 182, 184, 198, 199, 200, 201, 202, 203, 204, 205, 207, 208, 209, 210, 211, 212, 213, 214,

216, 218, 219, 220, 221, 222, 223, 224, 227, 230, 231, 232, 233, 235, 236, 237, 238, 239, 241, 243, 244, 246, 247, 254, 256, 258, 259, 260, 262, 264, 265, 268, 272, 275, 276, 278, 280, 282, 283, 284, 285, 286, 288, 289, 290, 299, 301, 302, 303, 305, 306, 307, 308, 309, 311

Texts, 17, 18, 19, 20, 24, 39, 40, 43, 44, 45, 46, 47, 48, 49, 50, 51, 54, 55, 67, 69, 71, 72, 76, 83, 85, 86, 89, 91, 92, 93, 97, 99, 104, 106, 112, 113, 127, 128, 129, 135, 140, 141, 143, 144, 145, 146, 147, 149, 150, 151, 154, 155, 156, 157, 158, 161, 162, 168, 169, 174, 176, 178, 179, 180, 181, 184, 198, 199, 200, 201, 202, 203, 204, 205, 206, 208, 210, 211, 212, 213, 214, 215, 218, 219, 220, 226, 227, 230, 232, 234, 237, 238, 240, 241, 242, 243, 244, 251, 252, 253, 255, 256, 257, 260, 272, 276, 277, 279, 281, 282, 289, 295, 298, 299, 300, 301, 303, 304, 305, 308, 309, 310

Text-centered, 37, 199, 200, 204

Text linguistics, 43, 47, 97, 101, 201, 239

Text of Scripture, 21, 22, 31, 36, 37, 39, 40, 56, 57, 58, 67, 68, 69, 72, 83, 84, 85, 86, 87, 88, 147, 152, 153, 160, 164, 176, 199, 204, 205, 224, 235

Text or event, 31, 36, 184

Text-oriented, 55, 56, 72, 84, 85, 86, 100, 202, 204, 205, 208, 209, 212, 215, 217, 218, 219, 224, 225

Text theory, 43, 47, 200, 201, 239

Textual meaning, 84, 203, 204

Textual world, 45, 46, 151

Textuality, 43, 47, 200, 231, 233

Theodotion, 221

Theology, 4, 5, 11, 12, 13, 14, 15, 16, 17, 18, 19, 20, 21, 22, 23, 24, 25, 29, 30, 31, 33, 34, 35, 36, 37, 39, 40, 41, 42, 43, 55, 56, 57, 58, 60, 62, 63, 67, 68, 69, 70, 72, 74, 75, 79, 82, 83, 84, 85, 86, 87, 88, 90, 91, 92, 93, 96, 97, 98, 99, 100, 101, 105, 106, 107, 108, 109, 110, 111, 112, 113, 115, 116, 117, 118, 119, 120, 121, 122, 123, 124, 125, 126, 127, 128, 129, 130, 131, 132, 133, 134, 135, 136, 138, 139, 142, 143, 145, 146, 147, 148, 150, 151, 152, 153, 154, 155, 156, 157, 161, 162, 163, 164, 165, 166, 167, 169, 170, 171, 172, 173, 174, 175, 176, 177, 179, 182, 183, 184, 185, 186, 187, 188, 189, 190,

191, 192, 193, 195, 197, 198, 199, 200, 201, 202, 204, 205, 206, 207, 209, 212, 215, 216, 217, 218, 219, 221, 222, 223, 224, 225, 226, 227, 228, 231, 233, 234, 237, 238, 251, 252, 253, 260, 272, 273, 299

Theosophists, 146

Torah, 132, 134, 135, 137, 138, 139, 176, 238, 240, 241, 242, 244, 245, 246, 247, 248, 249, 257, 270, 287, 291

Tradition, 52, 66, 68, 83, 84, 86, 88, 92, 102, 119, 127, 128, 129, 132, 134, 135, 137, 140, 141, 142, 143, 144, 145, 156, 159, 162, 175, 176, 179, 180, 215, 218, 220, 224, 233, 241, 262, 310

Traditions, 55, 77, 83, 92, 93, 97, 104, 123, 128, 143, 178, 179, 180, 186, 192, 215, 218

Traditionsgeschichte, 83

Translation, 17, 18, 43, 45, 71, 87, 128, 132, 134, 136, 204, 222, 247, 251, 282, 284, 310

Tree-diagram, 85, 113

Twentieth century, 151, 166, 167, 170

Typological, 133, 140, 294

Typology, 34, 84, 155, 295

Unity of Scripture, 231, 232

Ur-Offenbarung, 68

Verbal inspiration, 59, 150, 152, 199, 219, 222, 224

Verbal meaning, 204

Verbal plenary inspiration, 150

Verus Israel, 135

Vowels (Hebrew), 152, 204, 205, 220, 221, 230

Vulgate, 132, 205, 220, 221, 222, 263, 267, 284

Westminster Confession, 156, 175

Wisdom, 13, 177, 187, 188, 213, 214, 222, 230, 232, 240, 243, 247, 258, 296

Word of God, 13, 15, 16, 20, 34, 36, 39, 40, 42, 58, 72, 113, 117, 127, 147, 153, 157, 159, 170, 172, 179, 197, 198, 224, 226, 229, 232

World, 5, 13, 17, 18, 24, 36, 37, 39, 45, 46, 49, 50, 51, 52, 54, 55, 57, 69, 70, 72, 73, 74, 75, 76, 77, 78, 92, 104, 106, 109, 112, 113, 130, 134, 146, 147, 148, 151, 159, 160, 162, 165, 166, 167, 169, 171, 179, 181, 191, 202, 203, 204, 216, 217, 222, 226, 231, 232, 234, 257, 258, 290, 291, 292, 293, 294, 295, 296

"World making," 216, 217

World history, 76, 77

Written word, 40, 42, 44, 56, 58, 178, 243, 248, 249

Zionism, 151

CPSIA information can be obtained
at www.ICGtesting.com
Printed in the USA
LVHW032328060520
655150LV00005B/13